D1552094

63rd ART DIRECTORS ANNUAL

ART DIRECTORS CLUB OF NEW YORK

THE SIXTY-THIRD EXHIBITION

CREDITS

Book Division President,
ERNEST SCARFONE

Book Division V.P.'s,
BLANCHE FIORENZA
DAVID DAVIDIAN

Executive Administrator,
DIANE MOORE

Designer,
CHRIS HILL

Production Coordinator,
FRANK DELUCA

Managing Editor,
MIRIAM L. SOLOMON

News and Hall of Fame Editor,
JO YANOW

Associate,
EMMETT MURPHY

Show Supervisor,
PAULA RADDING

Club Photographer,
DEBORAH WEATHERS THOMAS

Awards Show Photographer,
ROBERTO SANDOVAL

Assistant Show Supervisor,
MICHAEL CHIN

Show Assistants,
DANIEL FORTE
GLENN KUBOTA

Mechanicals,
ARP GRAPHICS
RALPH SMITH
PADRAIC SMITH

Index,
ANGELA CHIARAMONTE DELUCA
JENNIFER DELUCA

Book Packaging,
Supermart Graphics, Inc.
22 East 31st Street
New York, New York 10016

Manufacturing,
Toppan Printing Company
Tokyo, Japan

Distribution:
Book trade in
the United States
Robert Silver Associates
307 East 37th Street
New York, New York 10016

in Canada,
General Publishing Co. Ltd.
30 Lesmill Road
Don Mills, Ont. M3B2T6

in Europe and the U.K.,
Graphic Press Corp.
Dufourstrasse 107
Zurich, Switzerland

Other countries,
Fleetbooks, S.A.
c/o Feffer and Simons, Inc.
100 Park Avenue
New York, N.Y. 10017 U.S.A.

The 63rd Annual of Advertising,
Editorial and Television Art
and Design
Copyright © 1984 by the
Art Directors Club, Inc.
Published by A.D.C. Publications
ISBN 0-937414-04-2

DESIGNER

The designer of this 63rd New York Art Directors Club Annual is Chris Hill of Houston, Texas. His firm, Hill/A Design Marketing Studio, has won numerous awards in art director shows in cities around the country and the clients it serves are national and international in scope.

Before starting his company almost four years ago, the designer worked at the Loucks Atelier. Today Hill also instructs classes in advanced design at Southwest Texas State University and is often asked to speak at other schools. He is a graduate of East Texas State University.

Hill has chosen the Statue of Liberty as the book's graphic theme because he feels "The Lady is the most visible symbol of New York City and the program to refurbish her makes the symbol especially timely."

Hill's divider pages utilize an especially ingenious treatment of the theme. The collages and cut-outs of each piece of art showing portions of the Lady have all been created with actual pieces that appear in the art or photography category.

The Statue of Liberty theme was also used on the Call for Entries for the 63rd Show, on the Awards program and myriads of statues made up the graphic for the exhibition poster.

CONTENTS

NEWSPAPER ADVERTISING

Less than half page, b/w
Half page, b/w
More than half, up to full page, b/w
Campaign, b/w
Full page, color
Campaign, color
Public Service
Public Service Campaign
Section, Insert, Supplement

MAGAZINE ADVERTISING

Consumer, one page, b/w
Consumer, spread, b/w
Consumer, one page, color
Consumer, spread, color
Consumer, less than full page, b/w
Consumer, less than full page, color
Consumer, Campaign, b/w
Consumer Campaign, color
Public Service
Public Service Campaign
Business or Trade, one page, b/w
Business or Trade, more than one page, b/w
Business or Trade, one page, color
Business or Trade, more than one page, color
Business or Trade, less than full page, b/w
Business or Trade Campaign, b/w
Business or Trade Campaign, color
Section, Insert, Supplement

NEWSPAPER EDITORIAL

Full page, color
Full page, b/w
Multi-page, Section

MAGAZINE EDITORIAL

Sunday Magazine Supplement
Consumer, one page, b/w
Consumer, spread, b/w
Consumer, one page, color
Consumer, spread, color
Consumer, multiple pages, single story, b/w
Consumer, multiple pages, single story, color
Consumer, Section or Insert
Consumer Cover
Business, Trade or House Organ, spread, b/w
Business, Trade or House Organ, spread, color
Business, Trade or House Organ, multiple pages, single story, b/w
Business, Trade or House Organ, multiple pages, single story, color
Business, Trade or House Organ Cover
Consumer or Business Magazine Full Issue
House Organ Full Issue

PROMOTION AND GRAPHIC DESIGN

Single Entries
  Annual Report
  Booklet, Folder, Brochure
  Sales Kit
  Direct Mail Piece
  Record Album
  Package, Bottle, Carton, Can
  Calendar
  Menu, Card, Announcement

Letterhead
Trademark, Logo
P.O.P. design, Display
Campaign Entries
Booklets, Folders, Brochures
Sales Kits
Direct Mail
Packages, Cartons, Bottles, Cans, etc.
Cards, Menus, Announcements
Trademarks, Logos
P.O.P. designs, Displays
Corporate Identity Programs

BOOKS AND JACKETS

General Trade Book (primarily text)
Special Trade Book (primarily art/photography)
Paperback Book
Text or Reference Book
Book Jacket; Trade, Text or Reference
Paperback Book Cover

POSTERS

Single Entries
Outdoor
Transit (bus, subway or shelter)
Public Service or Political
In-store, Promotional, etc.
Campaign Entries
Outdoor Campaign
Transit Campaign
Public Service or Political Campaign
In-store, Promotional Campaign

ART CATEGORIES

ART AND ILLUSTRATION

Editorial, b/w
Advertising, color
Promotion, color
Editorial, color
Books and Book Jackets
Section, Insert, Supplement
Television News Graphics

PHOTOGRAPHY

Advertising, b/w
Advertising, color
Promotion, color
Editorial, color
Books and Book Jackets
Section, Insert, Supplement

TELEVISION

Commercial, 10 seconds
Commercial, 30 seconds
Commercial, 60 seconds or over
Commercial campaign, 10 seconds each spot
Commercial campaign, 30 seconds each spot
Commercial campaign, 60 seconds each spot
Public Service
Public Service Campaign
Film; Industrial, Educational or Promotional
Animation

HALL OF FAME

For the past 13 years, we have gathered one evening each year to honor those exceptional talents whose driving force of excellence has set the high standards for, and left a profound influence on, our profession.

This year, selected by a Committee dedicated to documenting the great heritage of our profession, we honor four laureates whose impressive credentials have earned them a permanent place in this illustrious galaxy: Wallace Elton, Sam Scali, Lou Silverstein and the late Charles Eames.

For their inspiration, their courage and their vision—we honor them.

Eileen Hedy Schultz
Hall of Fame Chairman, 1984

HALL OF FAME SELECTION COMMITTEE

EILEEN HEDY SCHULTZ, CHAIRMAN
BOB CIANO
WILLIAM DUFFY
JACK JAMISON
WALTER KAPRIELIAN
ANDREW KNER
GEORGE LOIS
PAUL RAND
BOB SMITH
BILL TAUBIN
JACK TAUSS
BRADBURY THOMPSON

PATRON CHAIRMAN
GENE FEDERICO

PRESENTATION
ARTHUR HAWKINS, CHAIRMAN

MANAGING AND PLANNING
WILLIAM H. BUCKLEY, CHAIRMAN
JACK G. TAUSS

MEMBERS, ADC HALL OF FAME

1972
M.F. AGHA
LESTER BEALL
ALEXEY BRODOVITCH
A.M. CASSANDRE
RENÉ CLARKE
ROBERT GAGE
WILLIAM GOLDEN
PAUL RAND

1973
CHARLES COINER
PAUL SMITH
JACK TINKER

1974
WILL BURTIN
LEO LIONNI

1975
GORDON AYMAR
HERBERT BAYER
CIPE PINELES BURTIN
HEYWORTH CAMPBELL
ALEXANDER LIBERMAN
L. MOHOLY-NAGY

1976
E. McKNIGHT KAUFFER
HERBERT MATTER

1977
SAUL BASS
HERB LUBALIN
BRADBURY THOMPSON

1978
THOMAS M. CLELAND
LOU DORFSMAN
ALLEN HURLBURT
GEORGE LOIS

1979
W.A. DWIGGINS
GEORGE GIUSTI
MILTON GLASER
HELMUT KRONE
WILLEM SANDBERG
LADISLAV SUTNAR
JAN TSCHICHOLD

1980
GENE FEDERICO
OTTO STORCH
HENRY WOLF

1981
LUCIAN BERNHARD
IVAN CHERMAYEFF
GYORGY KEPES
GEORGE KRIKORIAN
WILLIAM TAUBIN

1982
RICHARD AVEDON
AMIL GARGANO
JEROME SNYDER
MASSIMO VIGNELLI

1983
AARON BURNS
SEYMOUR CHWAST
STEVE FRANKFURT

1984
CHARLES EAMES
WALLACE ELTON
SAM SCALI
LOUIS SILVERSTEIN

LOUIS SILVERSTEIN

Louis Silverstein is probably the only art director ever to be nominated for a Pulitzer Prize, a nomination that was put forward by A.M. Rosenthal, executive editor of the *New York Times*. In Rosenthal's opinion, "Everybody who knows anything about American newspapers knows that Lou Silverstein ranks as the outstanding newspaper designer in the country." Silverstein did not win the award; there is no Pulitzer category for simply designing newspapers. In fact, until Silverstein effected the transformation of the *Times* such a job description would never have been found in the classifieds.

While artists have not been unknown to newspapers, the idea that they would join in taking creative responsibility was unthinkable for most newspaper managements. In reshaping the 'gray face' of the *Times*, Silverstein and his editorial colleagues achieved a new journalistic look full of character, style and liveliness, and so brilliantly formatted its detail that it has the ability to bring graphic surprises in each new issue. As well as increasing circulation and gathering countless awards, the redesign has also had a widespread effect on newspapers throughout the world whose managements have sought out designers to change and enliven their own journals.

Today, Silverstein is Corporate Art Director of the *Times*, a position he has held since 1969 which embraces the daily and Sunday editions, the 28 other newspapers in the Times Company, many of which he has also redesigned, and in all 45 communication companies, including *Family Circle* and *Golf Digest* magazines. In addition, as assistant managing editor of the *Times* he is also deeply involved in editorial, managerial and policy decisions.

A native New Yorker, Silverstein found his way to the *Times* by a rather round-about route. With a Bachelor of Fine Arts degree from Pratt Institute, like so many art directors, he started his working life in the advertising industry in New York, then spent three years designing graphics for the U.S. Air Corps. Out of the service, he went back to school for his Master's degree at the Chicago Institute of Design (the new Bauhaus) where his thesis concerned individual responses to tactile experiences. Here in Chicago he began painting in earnest and soon was exhibiting with the American Abstract Artists, a group that at times included Mondrian, George L.K. Morris and Louise Nevelson. Later, in 1964, he was represented in the U.S. Information Agency's major exhibit of drawings and graphics in the Soviet Union.

In Chicago, he was influenced by a variety of experiences. A speech made by Gyorgy Kepes on design as a bridge between man and society made an enormous impact on him. He had business cards printed up, "Designs for People". Assignments came from the Cooperative League of America and after a meeting with A. Philip Randolph,

from the American Federation of Labor and then the U.S. Department of State and for corporations for whom he produced graphic, colorful and fast-moving film-strips. This led him to the State Department's publications branch where he served as art director of *Amerika*, the Russian-language magazine distributed in the USSR and satellite nations.

Silverstein was ready for the *Times* in 1952 where he joined the promotion department under George Krikorian, Irvin Taubkin and Ivan Veit. "These were enormously creative people. I felt privileged to work with them," Silverstein recalls today. A year later, having inherited Krikorian's mantle as art director, his promotion designs captured 18 awards in the AIGA design show and he was put in charge of promotion both for the newspaper and the company's radio station, WQXR.

Soon *Graphis* magazine was commenting that his posters, mailing pieces, educational booklets and ads promoting the *Times* "had raised current graphic standards." Moreover, his "I got my job through the New York Times" promotion campaign, one of the most memorable in recent history, may also prove to be one of the longest-running and it may be said with some degree of truth that Silverstein got his present job *through* that campaign. Not content with his *Times* duties alone, he continued his painting and yet found time to co-author *America's Taste* (Simon & Schuster), a book that reviewed the cultural events of the past century as observed through the feature stories in the *Times*. In another role, he chaired events for the Society of Publication Designers and the American Institute of Graphic Arts and in 1967 helped to run a four-day "Design-In" for the Institute of Ecological Studies in

Central Park.

Louis Silverstein is an affable, self-possessed individual who does not at first glance seem to be the type to lead a revolution, but that is precisely what happened when the *Times* went through a period of great expansion, acquiring a variety of subsidiary firms, newspapers and magazines. With this broadening scope came the demand for a new look for the flagship publication. First, Silverstein was assigned to the book review section. Instead of giving it the expected typographic restyling, he changed everything from column widths to artwork. The concept for the new op-ed page, under the direction of John Oakes, editorial page editor and launched with Harrison Salisbury as editor, set editorial illustration in a new direction because the art commissioned from fine artists and illustrators throughout the world did not depict the articles but suggested emotions and ideas. Although there was no master plan for the paper, Silverstein, with editors A.M. Rosenthal, Seymour Topping and Arthur Gelb succeeded in producing innovations one after another. Out of their efforts came their pace-setting new sections—Sports Monday, Weekend, Style, Home, Science, plus a largely new Sunday paper. Always a national standard for editorial content, the *Times*, with a full measure of Silverstein's creativity, became a hallmark for journalistic design.

Massimo Vignelli sees far greater import: "We are affected by all the factors in the environment around us," says the designer, "and nothing is more ubiquitous than the newspaper. By changing the *Times* and influencing so many newspapers in other cities, we are indebted to him for improving the quality of our lives."

LOUIS SILVERSTEIN

Promotional series using various artists, 1953
Ad series started in early 50s
Travel promotions with art by Silverstein, late 50s
Ad, Times promotion department, 1952
Times ad and promotion series with Robert Frank photos, late 50's
WQXR radio station ad, early 60s

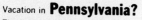

Books are not men and yet
they are alive,

ACTION IN AGATE

New York is

Vacation in **Pennsylvania?**
That's a wonderful spot for a holiday. And for a large choice of accommodations in Pennsylvania, see the Resort and Travel Section of the Sunday New York Times. That's America's biggest vacation guide.

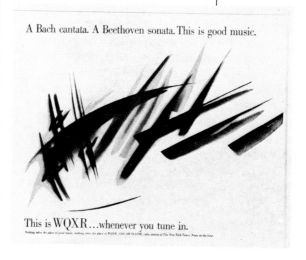

A Bach cantata. A Beethoven sonata. This is good music.

This is WQXR...whenever you tune in.

HALL OF FAME

Promotion brochure, 1964
From "America's Taste" book, 1964
Subway poster series, 1962
Logo for A.M. Ledger, Lakeland, Fla.
Times-owned newspaper
New design for newspaper, 1979
Op-ed page started in 1971

LOUIS SILVERSTEIN

Latest re-design, Book Review, 1984
Design new Home section, 1977
Design, Science Times section, 1978
Sports Monday design, 1978
Travel design, 1981
Living Section 1976
Weekend 1976
Special news page

SAM SCALI

I n 1968, a year after Scali, McCabe was founded, Sam Scali was asked what his goals were. His answer was unequivocal: "To be the best ad agency in the world." Millions of dollars in billings later and with much acclaim for creativity bestowed on the agency from all sides of the communications industry, if asked of his goals today he still says he "wants to have the best ad agency in the world. We work at it every day."

When other people view the agency's reel, more often than not they cheer, nod agreement, laugh or applaud, while Scali is likely to remain pensive and expressionless. "The work is good, but it can always get better," says Scali, a severe self-critic. Scali is the complete advertising professional; there is

nothing in life that pleases him so much as poring over the type books he has studied a dozen times before to uncover the gem of a type for a new campaign. Small details delight him. The face selected for Perdue Chickens was "picked for a specific reason. If you look closely at the inside of the O's, they look like eggs." His attention to every detail—layouts, handling of photography as well as judgements on the big idea—is legendary in the agency that bears his name.

One of the campaigns of which he is proudest was created for Sperry Corporation. Sperry had been spending money for years without a great deal of success with its image. One of their salesmen revealed off-handedly that their people had to listen harder when trying to land a

client because they were cast in the underdog's role. The concept of listening became Sperry's corporate charge and Scali was instrumental in planning a program which involved having the client's employees trained in becoming better listeners. Scali's moving and dramatic ads revealed the unresolved issues that confront people who do not listen. What made it meaningful to him is that the ad effort did not merely confront company problems but human problems as well, and positioned to alter Sperry's image, they then sold hardware.

Says writer-partner Ed McCabe of Scali's sensibilities: "He has a soundness of judgement about concepts that is almost infallible. We call it the 'Sam Test'. If you are pursuing a direction

SAM SCALI

and he agrees with it, you know you're on very solid ground."

When Scali was a teenager, "all he ever wanted out of life was $100 a week and to enjoy what he was doing." He attended the School of Industrial Arts, now the High School of Art and Design, and then went to work at PhotoLettering, spacing type and headlines, but since he "didn't know anything about type", he decided to learn. Scali was always more resourceful and more full of ideas than the pack. Aaron Burns taught Scali in his Advanced and Experimental Typographic Design class at Pratt. "Sam would bring in solutions to design problems," recalls Burns, "that made us all, teacher and fellow students, stop and look with admiration at his exceptional creativity. Sam didn't stop with just one solution to a problem. He would do several and each seemed to be better than the other."

In his next job, with a direct response agency, Scali was engaged in doing mechanicals and small drawings, always with an eye to bettering his lot. As a result, today he is responsive to young people who are impatient to get ahead and sees every portfolio that is dropped off for him because he remembers vividly "how impatient I was when I had so much to learn."

His status improved at his third post, working with Ben Rosen and Herb Koons. They became two mentors who allowed him to freelance as a designer with anything he could get his hands on. This marked the one occasion when he was fired. Rosen said he was getting "too comfortable." That very day he was hired by the Harry Zelinko Studio where he worked for two years and next joined Sudler & Hennessey where he says he was "lucky enough to get a job as a junior art director in the bullpen". The creative department

then included Herb Lubalin, George Lois and writer, Fred Papert. When Lois went to Doyle Dane Bernbach and a spot opened up in the sales promotion department there, Scali didn't hesitate. He liked his sales promotion job well enough but greatly wanted to work on consumer accounts at DDB and would drop off his ads every day in the office of Bob Gage who eventually broke down under the weight of the indisputable evidence of Scali's meritorious creative performances.

Up to now in the agency business, design ingenuity rather than concept was the hallmark of the best advertising. Scali had managed to be employed by two agencies that would change this, Sudler and DDB. Now in the late 50s, Lois, Papert and Julian Koenig started their trend-setting Papert, Koenig and Lois agency and Scali came on board. An industry reporter called the agency "the Stillman's East of the advertising agencies" and it was an exciting place to work. Scali's break came with the Xerox account and the concept of taking office equipment out of the office and dealing with it on personal terms. Who else but Scali would have conceived, when copying machines were a novelty, of having a three-year old child demonstrate the miracles of Xerox? Scali's ideas about advertising took root here. Design wasn't enough. Big ideas weren't the whole story. Research was necessary. And equally important to the equation was the right media. They ran TV for the *Herald Tribune* on the nightly news breaking with their own news headlines for the following day. It was a first time a newspaper had sponsored a television news program. They heralded the fact that "a great newspaper didn't have to be dull."

Scali, McCabe, Sloves, Inc.

was founded by five partners, four of whom came from PKL in 1967. They wanted to create an agency where marketing, media, research and creative shared the spotlight in a full-service no-nonsense ad agency. Alan Pesky, Marvin Sloves and Len Hultgren asked Scali to recommend an art director. He recommended himself. Soon after, Scali called Carl Ally, Inc. to ask Ed McCabe to recommend a writer. McCabe recommended himself. They started out with no billings but quickly picked up Volvo and a host of accounts. Perhaps their most famous campaign has been for Perdue Chickens, for whom they developed an entire new category. Scali's direct, no-frills visuals and innate humor with McCabe's copy have made Perdue a household word in America and have brought presidents from companies all over asking for stardom, all of whom have been refused because it made no marketing sense for them.

Scali believes in creating hard-hitting ads that directly pursue the competition at its weakest point. In spite of his many awards, he refuses to glorify advertising's contribution to society or his own out of proportion—or to put it in any other frame of reference other than a business he loves. "We shouldn't overreact or put what we do out of perspective," says Scali. It is this balanced judgement combined with unwavering standards that has made him one of the best advertising teachers in the field.

It has been observed many times by his peers that Scali is a very nice, quiet guy who is almost unflappable. Inside that quiet exterior, however, resides a raging fire of creativity that catches people off guard with its simplicity, directness and brilliance.

HALL OF FAME

Which is the $2,800 Picasso? Which is the 5¢ Xerox 914 copy?

We bought a famous Picasso picture. We took it out of the frame. Made a copy of it on our Xerox 914. Then we put the original back in its frame and also framed the copy. We photographed both of them. And here they are. Can you tell which is which? Are you sure?

Remember the Xerox 914 makes copies that look as good as the original. Remember the Xerox 914 makes copies on ordinary paper. (It is possible to make copies on the same kind of paper Picasso used.) Remember the Xerox 914 can copy almost everything perfectly. Objects, Pages from books, Colors, Etc. And as you can see, it copies line drawings and signatures flawlessly. Remember the Xerox 914 is easy to operate. Turn a knob, push a button and you get perfect copies like the one above on the right. Or is it the left? Remember you don't have to buy the 914. You can borrow it. You pay only for the copies you make. Including all charges, it costs you about 5¢ a copy based on a minimum number of copies made per month. 5¢ is certainly no more and probably a lot less than you're paying for copies now.

Now—which is the $2,800 original? Which is the 5¢ copy? Why don't you tell us. If you're right we'll reward you with a genuine xerocopy suitable for framing (and dazzling your friends).

Write Xerox Corporation, Midtown Tower, Rochester 4, N.Y. Other offices in principal U.S. and Canadian cities. Overseas: Rank Xerox Ltd., London; Fuji Xerox Co., Ltd., Tokyo.

XEROX

This is an actual photograph of a memorandum copied on the side of a brown paper bag that was hand-fed through the Xerox 914 machine. It proves a point: the Xerox 914 Copier makes copies on ordinary paper.

Xerox ad, PKL, 1963
New York Herald Tribune *campaign, PKL, 1962*
Ad for Xerox, 1961
Ad for WNEW, PKL, 1963

SAM SCALI

Volvo TV spot, Scali, McCabe, Sloves,
1969
Volvo ad, 1968
Ad for Fresh'n, 1975
Volvo, 1967
Perdue, 1973
Perdue, 1971
Sam Scali and Frank Perdue at TV
shoot, early 70s

**Your car has five numbers
on the speedometer. Volvo has six.**

**One could get the impression
that the people who made your car
lack a little confidence.**

The inside of a Volvo is good enough to be an outside.

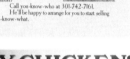

QUICK.
NAME A
CHICKEN.

MY CHICKENS
EAT BETTER
THAN YOU DO.

IT TAKES A
TOUGH MAN TO MAKE
A TENDER CHICKEN.

HALL OF FAME

Northern Tissue, 1982
From Omega Watch campaign, 1983
Ad for Village Voice, 1974
Olivetti campaign, 1978
Sperry Corp. campaign, 1980
Remington ad, 1967

THE MUSEUM OF MODERN ART RECENTLY ACQUIRED AN OLIVETTI LEXIKON 82 TO PUT ON DISPLAY.

WHAT A PITY.

WALLACE ELTON

Shortly before graduating from Brown University, Wallace Elton was interviewed by N.W. Ayer's legendary art director Vaughn Flannery. The youthful Elton was responding to a headline asking, "Have you ever thought of art directing as a profession?" In 1929 few people had, including Elton, who announced his desire to be a copywriter. "You can be a copywriter anytime," Flannery informed him succinctly. "What I need right now is a layout artist."

Thus was launched a 40-year career which saw Elton alternately and sometimes simultaneously as art director and cartoonist, copy chief and painter, ad-agency executive and photographer before his retirement in 1966 as a member of the board of J. Walter Thompson and a senior officer of the American Association of Advertising Agencies. Not content with this remarkably multi-faceted career, Elton immediately developed another as a leading figure in the International Exec-

utive Service Corps, an organization of experienced executives who take their knowledge and talent to the needful nations of the third world in an effort to broaden their job markets and to enrich their economies, a task he sees as an extension of advertising and its aim of raising living standards. Today, at age seventy-six, he approaches his global ventures with the same tireless enthusiasm displayed in his youth.

It was then apparent in his

work on the university humour magazine, the *Brown Jug,* where Elton succeeded S.J. Perlman as editor, writer and illustrator, the combination which so impressed Vaughn Flannery initially. At a time when college magazines had greater stature than in today's glutted market-place, Elton recognized his need for art instruction and became a regular 'unregistered' student at the Rhode Island School of Design. From Providence the road led to Philadelphia and the memorable "Three Little Men" campaign for Atlantic Refining, with a slight detour then to Hollywood, of all places, to design imaginative sets for radio shows, of all things, and for beautiful publicity backgrounds for such stars as Rosalind Russell and Jane Wyman. Back in Philadelphia, still with Ayer, while also working as a freelance copywriter, he created 'the boy in your street' for the Boys' Club of Philadelphia which gained national attention. Such activities led to invitations from the University of Pennsylvania where he gave talks on marketing from the creative man's viewpoint. It was at this time that art director Jack Jamison first met him and was struck even then by Elton's professionalism: "He garnered respect from everyone he met. It was because Elton had such respect for others."

Says Elton in response: "If you're aware of the skill with which media people, account people, typesetters and all the rest do their work, you don't think yours is the only important job." This philosophy, in part, accounts for the ease in which he moved from art director through the corporate life.

Under Charles Coiner at Ayer he soon found himself supervising such accounts as A.T. & T., W.K. Kellogg, the Container Corporation and Ford, the last of which prepared him for the Ford

creative leadership which came later at J. Walter Thompson. It was Coiner, too, who directed him toward New York, but his career there, like that of so many of his generation, was interrupted by three years of military service during which he saw sea duty in the Atlantic and Caribbean aboard aircraft carriers, rising to Lt. Commander, and at the same time he authored two books, "Navy in the Sky", and "A Guide to Naval Aviation."

Returning to Thompson, he found himself in many roles: art director and copywriter, TV pioneer and creative supervisor, account manager and leader in corporate management. One of his most admired talents, that of dealing with people on every level, proved invaluable working with major clients like Pan Am, Lever Brothers, Scott Paper and Cheséborough-Ponds.

Meanwhile, his sense of the incongruous, first on view in the *Brown Jug,* began to reappear in a series of animal cartoons which resulted in the present syndicated newspaper strip, "Zoologic". In his foreword to an annual collection of cartoons, Elton speaks of "the zoo to which we all belong" and pursues his logic with the postulate that animals may say things which we humans at large often let go unsaid. Elton's animals, however, have not been confined to the comics but have also found their way into eminently successful post-war campaigns such as "There's A Ford In Your Future," or his 1950s-vintage bear poster which won the Kerwin Fulton Medal.

These were exuberant and imaginative times at Thompson under the leadership of Stanley Resor and his wife. This was a time for experimentation when artists and copywriters were put together as teams and Elton as creative supervisor pioneered this idea in this golden age. Many

of the various Ford campaign innovations were Elton's: siting Fords in different exotic parts of the world, entering the Falcon in the Monte Carlo rally for TV commercials, and signing the first exclusive contract with Chas Schultz for "Peanuts" in national advertising. For the introduction of the Thunderbird he put his photographic talents to work and spent months of research to achieve just the right angles and lighting.

His photographic efforts continued when he and Norman Rockwell traveled the world for Pan American, the one painting, the other shooting fascinating people and places. Adventure, romance and human interest have always been Elton hallmarks. "In everyman's heart there's a secret place he would like to go," read the headline for Pan Am. Elton's castle became a symbol and a lure for the airline. Today he has traded his vice presidency at Thompson for a vice presidency with the International Executive Service organization where he is in charge of all communications worldwide and is director of the Mediterranean and Near East sectors. The catholicity of his interests have led to the authorship of two recent books, "Responsibilities of Advertising People" based on his experiences in the Far East, and "The First Hundred Years of the American Yacht Club", which evolved from his long association with that group.

Wallace Elton has sailed a long, exciting and fruitful course. Frank Pace, Jr., chairman of the IESC, and former Secretary of the Army and chairman of General Dynamics, hails Elton's introduction to the Hall of Fame: "His selection is a proper recognition of not only his particular genius but of the fact that he has been intelligently and effectively dedicated to the benefit of mankind."

WALLACE ELTON

Ford poster, JWT, 1950
Cartoon for Brown Jug cover, 1929
Atlantic Refining campaign, N.W. Ayer,
1930
Ford magazine campaign, JWT, 1947

HALL OF FAME

Ford, JWT, 1958
Ford posters and ads, 50s
Ford Falcon with "Peanuts" endorsement, 50s
Thunderbird introduction, 50s
Ford "Around the World" campaign, 50s

WALLACE ELTON

"Zoologic", from cartoon strip
Norman Rockwell Pan Am campaign, 50s
International Executive Services Corp
commercial, 1983
"Secret Castle" campaign, Pan Am, 50s
Book, "100 Years of the American Yacht
Club," 1982

says "Pan American was my magic carpet around the world"

"The thing to do with life is *Live it!*"

WORLD'S MOST EXPERIENCED AIRLINE
PAN AMERICAN

IESC's First TV Commercial Presents 9 Men With Something In Common

In every man's heart there's a **S**ecret place he would like to go

More people fly overseas by **PAN AMERICAN**
WORLD'S MOST EXPERIENCED AIRLINE

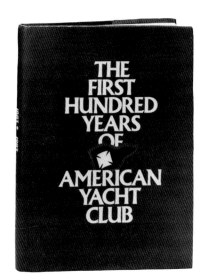

THE FIRST HUNDRED YEARS OF AMERICAN YACHT CLUB

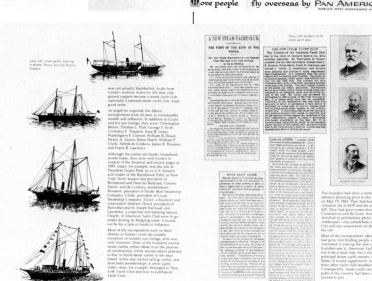

CHARLES EAMES

66 "Let a man get knowledge or buy a rope," Diogenes Laertius advised. It is questionable whether or not Charles Eames knew of this biographer of the Greek philosophers, but his words are doubly appropriate here in this posthumous celebration of the American architect and designer, for Eames was a diligent practitioner of the Greek's credo. In this Age of Communication facts and information of all kinds are instantly and almost miraculously available to us all, true knowledge to only a few, because to acquire it one must pursue the linkages between the plethora of individual items—bits, if you will—of

information.

With good cause the last major exhibition of Eames's work at the University of California, Los Angeles, 1976 was called "Connections: The Work of Charles and Ray Eames". In the narration of a film on the Eames contract storage system (ECS), Eames wrote: "The details are not details. They make the product. The connections, the connections, the connections." Connections between what? Between such disparate materials as rubber and steel, between such apparently unlike disciplines as physics and painting, between people of different callings: mathematicians and poets, philosophers and business execu-

tives. A close student of Eames's work states: "The Eames design practice might be defined as the art of solving problems by making connections."

What were the connections in Eames's personal life? Born in St. Louis, Missouri, in 1907, he left Washington University there at the end of his second year and opened an architectural office. The Great Depression sent him to Mexico for a while and when he returned to St. Louis he opened a second office, with Robert Walsh, supplementing residential architecture commissions with the design and production of furniture and objects, mostly religious, with his friend, Emil Frei. In 1936, Eliel Saarinen

CHARLES EAMES

offered him a fellowship at Michigan's Cranbrook Academy of Art, and later a teaching post. His fellow instructors included Saarinen's son Eero, who, with Charles and the young sculptor-painter, Ray Kaiser, helping out on presentation drawings, submitted designs to the Museum of Modern Art's "Organic Furniture Competition" in 1940.

Their designs won the two first prizes, but it was not possible to manufacture them under the known conditions. Charles and Ray Kaiser married and moved to Los Angeles. As husband and wife they were full collaborators from then on. In California, at the start, Charles worked as a set designer at MGM studios; by night he and Ray experimented with wood-molding techniques. In 1942 early in World War II they were commissioned by the Navy Department to produce molded plywood splints they had developed—later making aircraft parts including parts for special gliders. In those light, closely thought-out products one can easily see the beginnings of the plywood chair groups, the first of which appeared in prototypes in 1946 when the Museum of Modern Art held an unprecedented one-man show of Eames furniture.

That exhibition caused the Herman Miller Furniture Company to seek out Eames as a consultant, a move urged on them by their design director, George Nelson. By that time Charles and Ray had moved out of the small apartment in West Los Angeles where they had carried out their pioneering research and set up shop in a huge garage in Venice which remained Eames's headquarters until his death in 1978. He died in his native St. Louis while there to consult with an architectural firm.

Today, of course, the whole world is familiar with the term "Eames chair" and the revolutionary concepts it represents, but is less aware of Eames's designs and accomplishments in a score of other fields. Eames early on turned his attention to the making of films. "A Communications Primer", begun in 1951 and completed in 1953, was one of the first and is still one of the most successful popular interpretations of communications theory. It grew out of Eames's conviction that computer technology and related game theory were about to become indispensable and inevitable in architectural planning. There was nothing unusual about believing that, but it was very unusual for a designer to believe it in 1951 when Norbert Weiner's cybernetics were just becoming known and the IBM company was just starting to flex its electronic muscles.

Parallel to the motion picture work—movies being a series of connected still pictures, basically—was Eames's exhibition work, typified in 1961 by "Mathematica: A World of Numbers . . . and Beyond", an IBM-sponsored exhibition at the Museum of Science and Industry in Los Angeles. "Mathematica" brought together a large number of features that had come to characterize Eames's work generally: it was loaded with detail, including a massive "history wall" that related significant mathematical developments to each other and to developments in other fields. The "history wall" became a kind of Eames trademark for exhibits and again illustrates his fundamental belief in the over-riding importance of providing linkages. The "Scholar's Walk" at the New York World's Fair in 1964 followed in this tradition.

Always an innovator, when consulted by MIT as to the best way to infuse their technologically-heavy curriculum with art, Eames rejected the idea of additional art courses or fine arts programs. Instead he designed an alternative situation, a program for the enrichment of the students—and the University—by exploring communications capabilities to the point where they could experience the aesthetic possibilities of their own discipline, a program design which has been adopted by many other schools of technology.

The MIT proposal, although difficult to exhibit, is no less a design product than the chairs, the tables, the stretchers, the houses, the toys, the films and the exhibitions which came from the laboratory-studio of Charles and Ray Eames. In his later years, much of Charles Eames's activity was devoted to designing situations rather than products, dealing with social issues in India, the economy in Puerto Rico, the public responsibility of the Metropolitan Museum of Art, the structure of "Headstart" programs.

Of his total career and talent, Eames has been described as "irreplaceable" by Paul Rand and, at greater length, by George Lois in these words: "Every young designer in the fifties and sixties worth his salt worked sitting in an Eames chair, including me.

"Beyond that close contact with Eames, his (and her) analytical approach to putting complicated ideas on film in a communicative but joyful way was an inspiration whenever I approached any job that truly needed *homework*. Their solution was always put down in a way that looked entirely undesigned. *That's* art direction!"

Charles Eames never wrote a book detailing his ideas. A man of his times, he preferred to express himself on film. So here, paradoxically, we honor his memory with this posthumous tribute in print, a last 'connection' with one of the most influential designers of the age.

Moulded plywood chair, 1950s
Eames house interior, 1950
House exterior, 1949
Wire chairs, 1951
Herman Miller ad, 1947 Art Directors
Club gold medal winner
The Toy with child's furniture, 1951
House of cards, 1952

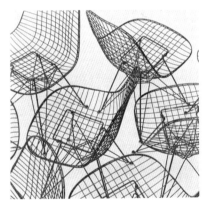

CHARLES EAMES

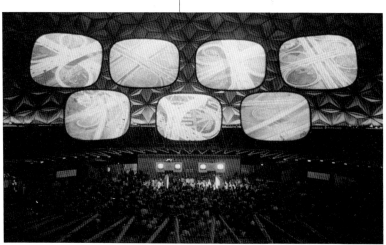

*Ray and Charles Eames with portion
of "Mathematica" exhibit, IBM, 1961
Multi-screen film, "Think" exhibit, IBM,
World's Fair, 1964-65
Eames and solar machine
Lounge chair and ottoman, 1956
Nehru memorial exhibit, government of
India, 1965
Herman Miller ad
U.S. exhibit in Moscow, seven
screen film, "Glimpses of the U.S.A."*

*Furniture details
Work for Herman Miller used in
"Qu'est-Ce Que C'est Le Design?",
Louvre, Paris, 1969*

HALL OF FAME

Multi-screen film "Introduction to Science," U.S. government exhibition, Seattle, 1962
Nicolas Copernicus exhibit, IBM, 1972
"Power of 10" film, IBM, 1967
Eames moulded arm chair with Steinberg drawing

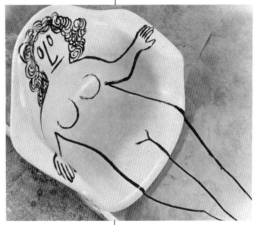

ADVERTISING

Mark Shap

Malcolm End
Tony Gill
Jean Govoni
Brian Harrod
Thom Higgins
Lawrence Miller
Seymon Ostilly
Elissa Querze
Richard Radke
Bob Reitzfeld
Marion Sackett
Bob Wilvers
Tom Wolsey

Whose birthday is it, anyway?

The Episcopal Church believes the important news at Christmas is not
who comes down the chimney, but who came down from heaven. We invite you to come and join
us as we celebrate the birth of Jesus Christ.
The Episcopal Church

GOLD AWARD

1

Art Director	**Nancy Rice**
Designer	**Nancy Rice**
Artists	**unknown, Hoffman RIP, Art Simons**
Writer	**Tom McElligott**
Client	**The Episcopal Ad Project**
Agency	**Fallon McElligott Rice, Minneapolis**
Publication	**Minneapolis Star & Tribune**

If you think being a Christian is inconvenient today, just look back 1500 years.

If you're ready to make the time and commitment that being a Christian sometimes requires,
the Episcopal Church invites you to come and join us in the worship and fellowship of Jesus Christ.
The Episcopal Church

GOLD AWARD

2

Art Director **Nancy Rice**
Designer **Nancy Rice**
Photographer **Andrea Mantegna, RIP**
Artist **Art Simons**
Writer **Tom McElligott**
Client **The Episcopal Ad Project**
Agency **Fallon McElligott Rice, Minneapolis**
Publication **Minneapolis Star & Tribune**

Since 1975 we changed a few things on the Rabbit.

Nothing else is a Volkswagen.

Scoop 43¢ off the price of Oak Farms Luxury Ice Cream.

✦ 43¢ off Oak Farms ✦

✦ Luxury Ice Cream ✦

3

Art Director	**Roy Grace**
Designer	**Roy Grace**
Photographer	**Ken Goldberg**
Writer	**Irwin Warren**
Client	**Volkswagen of America**
Agency	**Doyle Dane Bernbach Inc., New York**

4

Art Director	**David Carlson**
Designer	**David Carlson**
Artist	**Glen Dady**
Writer	**David Carlson**
Client	**The Southland Dairies Group**
Agency	**The Richards Group, Dallas**
Production Manager	**Donna Eddins**

MIND OVER CHATTER.

"Morning Edition"
news and information Monday-Friday, 5-11:30 a.m.
KSJN/1330 AM

HANDEL WITH CARE.

Our music leaves you inspired, our news
leaves you informed and our sponsors leave you alone.
KSJN/91.1 FM

TAKE DEBUSSY TO WORK.

Our music leaves you inspired, our news
leaves you informed and our sponsors leave you alone.
KSJN/91.1 FM

	5		**6**		**7**
Art Director	**Pat Burnham**	Art Director	**Nancy Rice**	Art Director	**Nancy Rice**
Designer	**Pat Burnham**	Designer	**Nancy Rice**	Designer	**Nancy Rice**
Writer	**Jarl Olsen**	Writer	**Dick Thomas**	Writer	**Dick Thomas**
Client	**Minnesota Public Radio**	Client	**Minnesota Public Radio**	Client	**Minnesota Public Radio**
Agency	**Fallon McElligott Rice, Minneapolis**	Agency	**Fallon McElligott Rice, Minneapolis**	Agency	**Fallon McElligott Rice, Minneapolis**
Publication	**St. Paul Dispatch/ Pioneer Press**	Publication	**St. Paul Dispatch/ Pioneer Press**	Publication	**St. Paul Dispatch/ Pioneer Press**

Senior members of the Oshogbo Secret Society, Nigeria. Photo by William Fagg.

If you think all of the world's great textile designers work here in New York's garment district, then you haven't been to see the "African Textiles" exhibition at the American Museum of Natural History. Just one visit and you'll learn all about Africa's most

WHO SAYS ALL EXCITING TEXTILE DESIGNS ARE FOUND ON SEVENTH AVENUE.

brilliant traditional fabrics. What's more, you'll learn all about the brilliant people who helped create them. You'll see Malagasy shawls from Madagascar, quilts from Khartoum, and tapestries from Timbuktu. This is a special exhibition from the British

Museum (Museum of Mankind) and will only be in New York until December 4. So slip into your shawl (it doesn't have to be from Madagascar) and visit "African Textiles."

Better yet, why not make a day of it. Then you'll have time to enjoy a good meal and a good movie.

The American Museum Restaurant is open every day for lunch and Wednes-

day, Friday and Saturday for dinner.

And the Naturemax Theater is showing the superscreen movie "To Fly."

Come see "African Textiles" plus a whole lot more, at the American Museum of Natural History.

AMERICAN MUSEUM OF NATURAL HISTORY

For more Museum information: 873-4225.

The Museum receives substantial support for its facilities and programs from a number of major sources. We are particularly grateful to the City of New York which provides budgetary funds and owns the Museum buildings, and to the New York State Council on the Arts, National Science Foundation, National Endowment for the Arts, National Endowment for the Humanities, Institute for Museum Services, 300 corporations, 60 private foundations, 480,000 members, and numerous individual contributors. Partial support for this ad from Triad Petroleum Corp. This advertisement prepared as a public service by Ogilvy & Mather Advertising.

SILVER AWARD

8

Art Director	**Glenn Gill**
Writer	**Tony Gomes**
Client	**American Museum of Natural History**
Agency	**Ogilvy & Mather Advertising, New York**

It has come to our attention
that many fine spirits merchants
in New York are currently selling
the 750 ml of Johnnie Walker Black Label
at a reduced price.
It might be to your advantage to
investigate this rumor.

MONEY FOR YOUR DRIVING AMBITION.

If your old car is driving you to distraction, come into Minnesota Federal.
And in no time, you could be singing the song of the open road again.
With the do re mi you need to buy a new or used car. We have a pile of
money to loan. So you can get rid of your old heap. And get back into the fast lane.
There's a Minnesota Federal office near you. It's listed in the telephone white
pages. Call us today about a car loan.
Whether you want an economy model or something more ambitious.

Minnesota Federal

USE YOUR BRAINS FOR COLLATERAL.

Getting an education is usually a sound idea.

Getting the money for it is usually pretty hard these days. Unless you have a rich uncle.

If you haven't, we have an alternative to recommend: An education loan from Minnesota Federal.

It's an especially smart thing to consider right now because we have plenty of money available for education loans. At reasonable rates.

Look at it this way. Taking out an education loan at today's interest rates is a good investment in your future (or your children's future).

For another thing, higher income often results from having a higher education.

Which of course can make it even easier to repay the loan.

And what makes it even easier for you to get the loan is the fact that you don't need collateral for it.

For a quick cram course in how to apply, call your local Minnesota Federal office today. We're in the telephone white pages.

Minnesota Federal

12 YEAR OLD BLENDED SCOTCH WHISKY, 86.8 PROOF. BOTTLED IN SCOTLAND. IMPORTED BY SOMERSET IMPORTERS, LTD., N.Y. © 1983

Johnnie Walker Black Label Scotch
YEARS 12 OLD

	9		10		11
Art Director	**Richard Ferrante**	Art Director	**Dean Hanson**	Art Director	**Dean Hanson**
Writer	**Murray L. Klein**	Designer	**Dean Hanson**	Designer	**Dean Hanson**
Client	**Johnnie Walker Black Label**	Writers	**Tom McElligott, Mike Lescarbeau**	Writers	**Tom McElligott, Mike Lescarbeau**
Agency	**Smith/Greenland Inc., New York**	Client	**Minnesota Federal Savings and Loan**	Client	**Minnesota Federal Savings and Loan**
		Agency	**Fallon McElligott Rice, Minneapolis**	Agency	**Fallon McElligott Rice, Minneapolis**
		Publication	**St. Paul Dispatch/ Pioneer Press**	Publication	**St. Paul Dispatch/ Pioneer Press**

AFTER OUR NEW YEAR'S EVE PARTY YOU CAN HIT THE RACK. INSTEAD OF THE ROAD.

Before you make your New Year's resolutions, make your reservations. At the Holiday Inn Airport.

Our New Year's Eve Party comes complete with dinner, party horns and hats, cash bar and 5½ hours of dancing to the live music of Gerber-Ryan. Dinner lasts from 6 until 11:30 p.m.,1983. Dancing from 9:30 p.m. until 4:00 a.m., 1984. There's a $3.00 cover for the lounge. And a room is only $50 per couple for the night. So why not stay? When the party's over you don't have to go home. You can go to sleep. At the Holiday Inn Airport.

✻ Holiday Inn
AIRPORT

How did he lose that eye, anyhow?

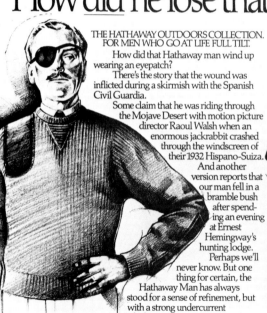

THE HATHAWAY OUTDOORS COLLECTION. FOR MEN WHO GO AT LIFE FULL TILT.

How did that Hathaway man wind up wearing an eyepatch?

There's the story that the wound was inflicted during a skirmish with the Spanish Civil Guardia.

Some claim that he was riding through the Mojave Desert with motion picture director Raoul Walsh when an enormous jackrabbit crashed through the windscreen of their 1932 Hispano-Suiza.

And another version reports that our man fell in a bramble bush after spending an evening at Ernest Hemingway's hunting lodge.

Perhaps we'll never know. But one thing for certain, the Hathaway Man has always stood for a sense of refinement, but with a strong undercurrent of adventure.

With the new Hathaway Outdoors Collection, the sense of adventure is downright palpable.

This collection, *exclusive* in the city with Juster's, is absolutely authentic in spirit and detailing.

There's a solid twill shirt with corduroy gunpatch and a plaid-lined neckband at $35.

We have the same shirt in plaid versions at 32.50, which look especially fine when coordinated with the pure wool Shaker stitch sweaters (with twill gunpatch and elbow patches) at $65.

And there's a brawny cotton print shirt, also at 32.50, that coordinates wonderfully with our deer-pattern sweaters at $60.

We invite you to come in and examine the Hathaway Outdoors Collection at your first opportunity.

Just because you might not already have some legendary stories in your background doesn't mean it's too late to experience them.

Juster's
Nicollet Mall • Southdale
Brookdale • Ridgedale • Maplewood
• Rosedale • Highland Village

<table>
<tr><td colspan="2">12</td><td colspan="2">13</td></tr>
<tr><td>Art Director</td><td>Wayne Gibson</td><td>Art Director</td><td>Joseph P. Duffy III</td></tr>
<tr><td>Writers</td><td>Bill Westbrook, Kerry Feuerman</td><td>Writer</td><td>Gary H. Knutson</td></tr>
<tr><td>Client</td><td>The B.F. Saul Company</td><td>Client</td><td>Juster's</td></tr>
<tr><td>Agency</td><td>Westbrook, Inc., Richmond, VA</td><td>Agency</td><td>DBK&O Advertising, Minneapolis</td></tr>
</table>

Nobody has improved on whole life, either.

"ASK ME."

NEW YORK LIFE

THE 1983 SCHOELLKOPF BARGAIN HUNTERS' SALE AT MARKET HALL

THURSDAY, FRIDAY & SATURDAY ONLY AT MARKET HALL

Here's a picture of someone doing the dishes and reducing the electric bill at the same time.

Vepco

	14		**15**		**16**
Art Director	**Chris Williams**	Art Director	**Tony Diamond**	Art Director	**Tom Layman**
Photographer	**Stock photo, Editorial Photo Archives**	Designer	**Gary Gibson**	Designer	**Tom Layman**
		Artists	**Richards, Brock, Mitchell, Miller, & Assoc. Staff**	Writer	**Mike Hughes**
Writer	**John Frost**			Client	**Vepco**
Client	**New York Life - Nate Kelne**	Writer	**David Fowler**	Agency	**The Martin Agency, Richmond, VA**
Agency	**Compton Advertising, Inc., New York**	Client	**Buddy Schoellkopf Products**	Publication	**Richmond Times Dispatch**
Publication	**Wall Street Journal**	Agency	**The Richards Group/ RBMM & A, Dallas**		
Retoucher	**Frank Pinto, Inc.**				

THERE ARE 9,000 KINDS OF BIRDS IN THE WORLD.
MOST NEW YORKERS ONLY STUMBLE ACROSS ONE OF THEM.

	17		18
Art Directors	**Debbie Peretz, Lila Sternglass**	Art Director	**Glenn Gill**
Artist	**John Alcorn**	Writer	**Tony Gomes**
Writer	**Art Winters**	Client	**American Museum of Natural History**
Client	**New York City Opera**	Agency	**Ogilvy & Mather Advertising, New York**
Agency	**Rumrill Hoyt Advertising, New York**		
Publication	**New York Times**		

BY 1984, SALT LAKE CITY WILL BE UNDER WATER.

WHILE SOME CARS MIGHT MAKE IT TO THE NEXT DECADE, STATISTICS SHOW VOLVOS COULD MAKE IT TO THE NEXT CENTURY.

Today people are trying to hold on to their cars longer than ever.

And while statistics show the average life expectancy of today's cars is eleven years, that figure pales in comparison to the life expectancy of today's Volvo.

Because statistics show the average life expectancy of a Volvo is over sixteen years.

Which could mean over sixteen years of comfortable driving in seats equipped with adjustable lumbar supports that relieve tension and road fatigue.

Years of effortlessly maneuvering through parking lots due to power assisted rack and pinion steering that cuts one of the smallest turning circles of any car.

Years of clean air made possible by a Fresh Air Ventilation System that exhausts stale air from the passenger compartment, and helps prevent odors and fumes from ever getting inside. If all this sounds like a sensible way to transport yourself to the next century, buy a Volvo.

Who knows?

By the year 2000 we may have a car that'll get you through that century, as well.

VOLVO A car you can believe in.

	19		20
Art Director	**Wayne Gibson**	Art Director	**Simon Bowden**
Writers	**Kerry Feuerman, Bill Westbrook**	Writer	**Rodney Underwood**
Client	**Newport News Shipbuilding**	Client	**Volvo of America Corporation**
Agency	**Westbrook, Inc., Richmond, VA**	Agency	**Scali, McCabe, Sloves, New York**

DISTINCTIVE MERIT

	21		**22**		**23**
Art Director	Nancy Rice	Art Director	Nancy Rice	Art Director	Pat Burnham
Designer	Nancy Rice	Designer	Nancy Rice	Designer	Pat Burnham
Photographer	Larry Robins	Photographer	Ibid, Inc.	Photographer	Craig Perman
Writer	Tom McElligott	Writer	Tom McElligott	Writer	Bill Miller
Client	ITT Life Insurance Corporation	Client	ITT Life Insurance	Client	WTCN-TV
Agency	Fallon McElligott Rice, Minneapolis	Agency	Fallon McElligott Rice, Minneapolis	Agency	Fallon McElligott Rice, Minneapolis
Publication	Madison Lake Times	Publication	Wall Street Journal	Publication	Minneapolis Star & Tribune

MANAGING A LAW FIRM ISN'T MUCH EASIER.

"It's a zoo!"
That's the most common complaint among managers of law firms.

Because when it comes to running a business, even the very best legal minds often turn to mush.

After all, lawyers go to law school. Not business school.

But we've developed a way for lawyers to practice law without the pressures of business.

It's really quite simple.

You or your group rent an office or suite from us in the Bar Building. With it comes access to all of our facilities. We can do your billing, your payroll, your taxes. We provide word processing, data processing, copying, a library, administrative and paralegal personnel.

And because you only pay for what you need when you need it, your overhead doesn't get over your head.

Of course, if you already have offices, you can take advantage of many of our services without taking any of our space.

To find out more, call or write Richard Lewis, President, or Joseph Renaghan, Executive Vice President, Legal Facilities Management, The Bar Building, 36 West 44th Street, New York, N.Y. 10036. (212) 382-1466.

You'll see how much better it is to spend your weekdays in a well-run office.

And your Sundays at the zoo.

LFM The law office that doesn't practice law.

Some Of The Greatest Problems In History Have Been Caused Because People Didn't Understand What They Were Signing.

Minnesota Federal

24

Art Director	**Allen Kay**
Photographer	**Steve Steigman**
Writers	**Lois Korey, Allen Kay**
Client	**Richard Lewis/Legal Facilities Management**
Agency	**Korey, Kay & Partners, New York**
Publication	**New York Law Journal**

25

Art Director	**Dean Hanson**
Designer	**Dean Hanson**
Writer	**Tom McElligott**
Client	**Minnesota Federal Savings & Loan**
Agency	**Fallon McElligott Rice, Minneapolis**
Publication	**Minneapolis Star & Tribune**

What Exactly Does "Penalty For Early Withdrawal" Mean?

The language of banking can be very intimidating.

That's because, rather than speak in plain English, bankers tend to talk in bankerese. "Penalty for early withdrawal," for example.

Simply stated, it means that we can't pay you as much interest as we promised if you don't leave your money with us as long as you promised.

This kind of explanation is rare in the financial world. Which is unfortunate, because today, with new banking laws and a changing economy, you need a banker who offers more than industry clichés and buzzwords.

You need someone who'll explain things clearly. Like the people at Minnesota Federal.

We have a program called Plain Talk that puts our employees through special training to make sure they talk the way real people talk.

And Minnesota Federal's Plain Talk also means that our forms are written in the same plain English we speak.

So whether you're talking to a Minnesota Federal employee or filling out a Minnesota Federal loan application, you won't have to bring along a translator to feel comfortable.

Stop in at your nearby Minnesota Federal office soon.

You'll find that Plain Talk is just one example of the things we're doing to make Minnesota Federal your choice when it comes to banking.

Because while other banks may seem preoccupied with what they'll do if you withdraw your money, Minnesota Federal is obsessed with giving you every reason not to.

Minnesota Federal
The Plain Talk Bankers

GOLD AWARD

26

Art Director	**Dean Hanson**
Designer	**Dean Hanson**
Writer	**Tom McElligott**
Client	**Minnesota Federal Savings and Loan**
Agency	**Fallon McElligott Rice, Minneapolis**
Publication	**Minneapolis Star & Tribune**

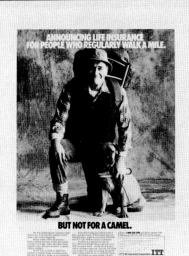

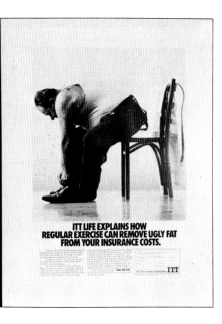

SILVER AWARD

27

Art Directors **Nancy Rice, Dean Hanson**
Designer **Nancy Rice**
Photographer **Larry Robins, Ibid, Inc.**
Writer **Tom McElligott**
Client **ITT Life Insurance**
Agency **Fallon McElligott Rice, Minneapolis**
Publication **Wall Street Journal**

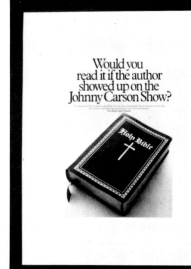

Would you
read it if the author
showed up on the
Johnny Carson Show?

Whose birthday
is it, anyway?

If you think
being a Christian is
inconvenient today,
just look back 1500 years.

"For the price of your last supper, you could
join the art museum."

I

Milwaukee Art Museum

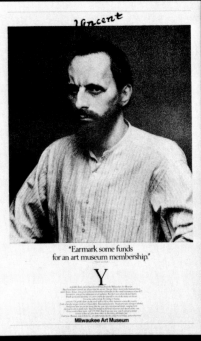

"Earmark some funds
for an art museum membership."

Y

Milwaukee Art Museum

"Art appreciation can make you a bigger person.
Join the Milwaukee Art Museum."

I

Milwaukee Art Museum

DISTINCTIVE MERIT

28

Art Director	Nancy Rice
Designer	Nancy Rice
Photographers	Tom Bach/Marvy Photography, Jim Arndt
Artist	Art Simons
Writer	Tom McElligott
Client	The Episcopal Ad Project
Agency	Fallon McElligott Rice, Minneapolis
Publication	Minneapolis Star & Tribune

29

Art Director	Rachel Stephens
Photographers	Peter Amft, Don Wilson
Writers	Robin Reynolds, Kirk Ruhnke
Client	Milwaukee Art Museum
Agency	Frankenberry, Laughlin & Constable, Milwaukee

To see the finest traditions in British fashion, you can wander from shop to shop on Savile Row, or you can stroll through one shop in Chelsea. Barneys New York.

Aquascutum

Burberrys

Chester Barrie

Christy's

Church's of England

Daks

Fortnum & Mason

Harrison's

Herbert Johnson

Hugh Parsons

Invertère

J&D McGeorge

Kilgour, French & Stanbury

Liberty of London

Rodex

Smedley

Smythson of Bond Street

B A R N E Y S
N E W Y O R K

Your heart doesn't know what a big shot you are.

Your heart's got news for you. It would be more impressed if you worked in the mailroom.

At least there, you'd be giving it some exercise. Exercise it needs.

Of course, if postal skills aren't your strong point, we have an even better suggestion.

Come to Cardio-Fitness.

We'll set up a safe, individualized exercise program to strengthen both your heart and lungs. And lower your pulse rate and blood pressure.

To assure your success, we'll review your progress daily. And we'll keep setting new goals for you.

This all takes place in an atmosphere that's modern, attractive and very civilized.

You'll get through the day with a lot more vim and vigor, as your physical and mental endurance grow stronger.

If you're like most of our members, you'll even strengthen your lower back, tone up your body and lose some of that excess weight.

It's no wonder corporations like American Express, Bankers Trust, Time Inc., Revlon and Seagram send us their people. And why our membership includes over 100 chief executive officers. Some might be even bigger shots than you are.

Another reason why over 90% of our members renew is that we make fitness so easy. There are no classes. No schedules. No appointments.

You come at your own convenience. Never have to wait. And you're in and out in less than an hour. There's not even a gym bag to lug around. We supply fresh shorts, shirts and socks daily.

Come in and see our facilities for yourself.

After all, right now you may be a real big shot. But neglected hearts do have a way of humbling people.

For more information call:

Cardio-Fitness Center

Wall Street Area: 79 Maiden Lane, (212) 943-4510.
Midtown: 345 Park Avenue, entrance on 52nd Street, (212) 838-4570.
1221 Avenue of the Americas, (212) 840-8240.

These people don't have time to exercise either.

That's why they come to Cardio-Fitness.

Cardio-Fitness Center

Midtown: 345 Park Avenue, entrance on 52nd Street, (212) 838-4570.
1221 Avenue of the Americas, McGraw-Hill Bldg, at Rockefeller Center, (212) 840-8240.
Wall Street Area: 79 Maiden Lane, (212) 943-1510.

DISTINCTIVE MERIT

	30	31	32
Art Director	Alex Tsao	Neil Leinwohl	Allen Kay
Photographer	Rudy Molacek	Steve Steigman	
Writer	Erica Ress	Kevin McKeon	Lois Korey
Client	Barneys, New York	Cardio-Fitness Systems/Victor Barnett	Dr. Jerome Zuckerman/ Cardio-Fitness Center
Agency	Epstein Raboy Advertising Inc., New York	Korey, Kay & Partners, New York	Korey, Kay & Partners, Inc., New York
Publication		New York Times	New York Times

How to turn your exercise cycle into something useful.

You told everyone it was the muggers. And the lousy weather. And all that traffic. Of course you wanted to exercise, but New York is not the place to run. Or even to ride.

So you went out and bought an exercise bike and set it up at home. That was the most exercise you ever got from it.

The excuses range from: "I have no time." "It's too much trouble." "I keep forgetting."

The only thing you can't blame are the muggers.

The trouble is you know muscles should be exercised. And the most important muscle to exercise is your heart.

That's where we come in.

We knew what we were doing when we called ourselves Cardio-Fitness. We offer individualized programs for men and women designed to strengthen your heart and lungs.

To reduce your weight and lower your pulse rate and blood pressure. To increase your physical and mental endurance.

A program of safe exercises done under professional guidance. We review your progress constantly, always setting new goals for you. All this takes place in a modern, attractive environment.

Which may be why we boast over 100 chief executive officers. Corporate memberships which include, American Express, Equitable Life, First Boston Corporation, Time Inc., J. Walter Thompson, and Sperry. And many individual members as well.

One reason why over 90% of our members renew is that we make it so easy.

No gym bag to lug around. We supply the fresh shorts, shirts and socks daily. You come at your convenience. There's never a wait. You're in and out in less than an hour.

As for your bike, you could always turn it into a nifty lamp table. A chrome spinning wheel. Or a sculpture labeled simply, "Unused Bicycle, circa 1983."

For more information call:

Cardio-Fitness Center

Midtown: 345 Park Avenue, entrance on 52nd Street, (212) 838-4570.
1221 Avenue of the Americas, McGraw-Hill Bldg. at Rockefeller Center, (212) 840-8240.
Wall Street Area: 79 Maiden Lane, (212) 943-1510.

SILVER AWARD

33

Art Director	**Allen Kay**
Photographer	**Steve Steigman**
Writer	**Lois Korey**
Client	**Dr. Jerome Zuckerman/ Cardio-Fitness Systems**
Agency	**Korey, Kay & Partners, New York**
Publication	**New York Times**

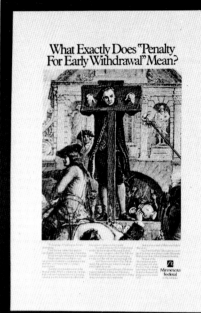

GOLD AWARD

34

Art Director **Dean Hanson**
Designer **Dean Hanson**
Photographers **Craig Perman, Stock,
Jim Arndt**
Writer **Tom McElligott**
Client **Minnesota Federal**
Agency **Fallon McElligott Rice,
Minneapolis**
Publication **Minneapolis Star &
Tribune**

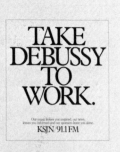

_____ 35 _____

Art Director   **Nancy Rice**
Designer   **Nancy Rice**
Writer   **Dick Thomas**
Client   **Minnesota Public Radio**
Agency   **Fallon McElligott Rice,**
   Minneapolis
Publication   **St. Paul Dispatch/**
   Pioneer Press

_____ 36 _____

Art Director   **Robert Manley**
Artist   **Steven Guarnaccia**
Writer   **Dan Altman**
Client   **MultiGroup Health**
   Plan
Agency   **Altman & Manley, Inc.,**
   Cambridge, MA

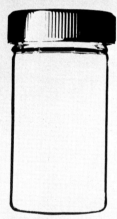

37		38	
Art Director	**Don Harbor**	Art Director	**Ron Anderson**
Designer	**Don Harbor**	Photographer	**Rick Dublin**
Artist	**Don Harbor**	Writer	**Phil Hanft**
Writer	**Sue Fay**	Client	**Med Center Health Plan**
Client	**Virginia National Bank**	Agency	**Bozell & Jacobs, Inc.,**
Agency	**Lawler Ballard**		**Minneapolis**
	Advertising, Norfolk, VA	Publication	**Minneapolis Star &**
			Tribune

IF YOU LITTER,
CUT IT OUT!

LITTER. IT MAKES US ALL LOOK LIKE PIGS.
A Public Service Message from Greater Boston's Advertising Club and Chamber of Commerce

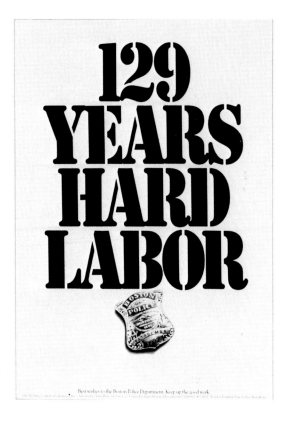

39		40		41	
Art Director	Ralph Moxcey	Art Director	Patrick Flaherty	Art Director	Rex Peteet
Designer	Ralph Moxcey	Writer	Peter Nichols	Designer	Rex Peteet
Artist	Frank Wagner	Client	Hill, Holliday, Connors,	Artists	Rex Peteet, Don Sibley,
Writers	Ron Lawner, Bill Heater		Cosmopulos, Inc.		Waleo Horton
Client	Chamber of Commerce	Agency	Hill, Holliday, Connors,	Writer	Rex Peteet
Agency	Humphrey Browning		Cosmopulos, Inc.,	Client	La Salle Partners/Valley
	MacDougall, Inc.,		Boston		View Shopping Center
	Boston			Agency	Underline, Inc.
Publication	Boston Globe			Design Firm	Sibley/Peteet Design,
					Inc., Dallas

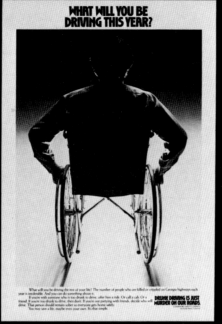

SILVER AWARD

42

Art Director	**Dan Scarlotto**
Photographer	**Mike Granberry**
Writer	**Daniel Clay Russ**
Client	**Governor's Safety Council**
Agency	**Pringle Dixon Pringle, Atlanta**

THERE IS A DIFFERENCE BETWEEN JOHNNY CARSON AND ALAN THICKE.

TURN ON *THICKE OF THE NIGHT* WEEKNIGHTS AT 10:30.

	43		44
Art Director	**Don Harbor**	Art Director	**Pat Burnham**
Designer	**Jeff France**	Designer	**Pat Burnham**
Photographer	**John Olson**	Writer	**Bill Miller**
Writers	**Ken Hines, Bruce Mansfield**	Client	**WFLD-TV**
Client	**Sovran Bank**	Agency	**Fallon McElligott Rice, Minneapolis**
Agency	**Lawler Ballard Advertising, Norfolk, VA**	Publication	**TV Guide**

45

Art Director	**Gary Johns**
Designer	**Gary Johns**
Photographer	**Greg Gorman**
Writer	**Jeff Gorman**
Client	**L.A. Eyeworks**
Agency	**Epiphany, Inc., Los Angeles**

46

Art Director	**Gary Johns**
Designer	**Gary Johns**
Photographer	**Greg Gorman**
Writer	**Jeff Gorman**
Client	**L.A. Eyeworks**
Agency	**Epiphany, Inc., Los Angeles**

47

Art Director	**Dean Hanson**
Designer	**Dean Hanson**
Photographer	**Tom Berthiaume**
Writer	**Rod Kilpatrick**
Client	**ITT Life Insurance Corporation**
Agency	**Fallon McElligott Rice, Minneapolis**
Publication	**Runner's World**

SOMETHING IS WRONG WHEN A SIZE 34 WAIST PAYS THE SAME INSURANCE AS A SIZE 48 WAIST.

It's a sad fact of life. After about age 30, it gets harder and harder to keep your stomach from dominating your body. Most people can't do it without regular exercise.

But studies show that people who do exercise regularly and who *don't* smoke are better life insurance risks. Ironically, however, few insurance companies give genuine rewards to physically fit non-smokers. And while some companies offer non-smoker's

discounts, ITT Life offers a Good Health Bonus® that rewards both non-smokers and regular exercisers with bonus insurance coverage. With the ITT Life plan, if you don't smoke you could earn a 65% life insurance bonus.

For example, your $50,000 policy could be increased to $82,500. *With no increase in premiums.*

If you exercise regularly and don't smoke, you could receive a 100% life insurance bonus.

Over half of the non-smokers applying meet the special underwriting criteria for the ITT Life Good Health Bonus. So if you've been able to defy cigarettes and gravity, why not collect the reward you deserve on your life insurance? For details call free: **1-800-328-2193.** Ask for operator 981. In Minnesota call 612-545-2100. Or mail this coupon.

ITT Life Insurance Corporation **ITT**

OUR NEW METEOROLOGIST HAS HIS HEAD IN THE CLOUDS.

To get a clear picture of the weather and our new meteorologist, tune in 11 NEWS weeknights at 6 and 10.

NEWS

	48		49
Art Director	Dean Hanson	Art Director	Pat Burnham
Designer	Dean Hanson	Designer	Pat Burnham
Photographer	Larry Robins, Ibid, Inc.	Photographer	Craig Perman
Writer	Tom McElligott	Artist	Art Simons
Client	ITT Life Insurance Corporation	Writer	Bill Miller
Agency	Fallon McElligott Rice, Minneapolis	Client	WTCN-TV
Publication	The Ace	Agency	Fallon McElligott Rice, Minneapolis
		Publication	TV Guide

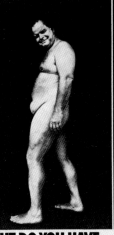

HOW MUCH WEIGHT DO YOU HAVE TO LOSE BEFORE YOUR INSURANCE COMPANY NOTICES IT?

Anyone who's ever tried knows that losing weight can be a real struggle. You go to bed hungry. You wake up hungry. You learn to despise lettuce. You exercise until you ache.

The good news is that according to recent studies, people who stay trim and exercise regularly live longer and are better life insurance risks. So now, ITT Life has come up with a Good Health Bonus® for non-smokers and people who are trim and

fit. Which means that if you don't smoke, you could earn a 65% insurance bonus. *With no increase in your insurance premiums.*

If you stay trim and don't smoke, you could get a 100% life insurance bonus. And over half of the non-smokers who apply meet the special underwriting criteria for the Good Health Bonus.

Look. You work very hard to keep your body trim. Isn't it about time you got the trimmer life insurance premiums you deserve?

For more details call free: **1-800-328-2193** and ask for operator 901. In Minnesota call us at 612-545-2100. Or mail the coupon to us today.

ITT *ITT Life Insurance Corporation*

ITT LIFE BELIEVES A BEAUTIFUL BODY SHOULD BE WORTH MORE THAN A FEW WHISTLES AT THE BEACH.

When you're young, a beautiful body may be something you take for granted. As you grow older, however, keeping your body beautiful takes work.

For those of you who haven't given in to rich foods, cigarettes, and gravity, however, ITT Life has good news: the ITT Life Good Health Bonus.® This is a life insurance plan which truly recognizes that people who exercise regularly and don't smoke live longer on the average and, therefore, are better life insurance risks.

ITT Life rewards them for those good habits.

If you don't smoke, the Good Health Bonus could be worth a 65% insurance bonus to you. For example, your $50,000 policy would be increased to $82,500. *With no increase in premiums.*

If you don't smoke and you also exercise regularly, you could earn a 100% life insurance bonus — *double the protection without any increase in premiums.* And over half of the non-smokers who apply are meeting the special underwriting criteria for the Good Health Bonus.

Isn't it time you began getting the beautiful insurance rates your beautiful body deserves?

For details call free **1-800-328-2193** and ask for operator 599. In Minnesota: 612-545-2100. Or mail the coupon.

ITT *ITT Life Insurance Corporation*

	50		51
Art Director	**Dean Hanson**	Art Director	**Nancy Rice**
Designer	**Dean Hanson**	Designer	**Nancy Rice**
Photographer	**Bob Adelman**	Photographer	**Dick Jones**
Writer	**Tom McElligott**	Writer	**Tom McElligott**
Client	**ITT Life Insurance Corporation**	Client	**ITT Life Insurance Corporation**
Agency	**Fallon McElligott Rice, Minneapolis**	Agency	**Fallon McElligott Rice, Minneapolis**
Publication	**American Health**	Publication	**Minneapolis Athletic Club Gopher**

ITT LIFE
OFFERS YOU ANOTHER
INCENTIVE TO RUN:
MONEY.

Is your life insurance company penalizing you because you're healthy? It probably is if you're running regularly or don't smoke.

Because most life insurance companies don't give non-smoking runners a genuine break on premium rates, even though recent studies indicate that runners live longer.

ITT Life believes you should have a chance to save money on your life insurance if you're staying fit and not smoking.

So we're offering our ITT Life Good Health Bonus® plan for people who qualify.

If you don't smoke, you're already worth a 65% insurance bonus. That means a $100,000 policy would be increased to $165,000 —*with no increase in your premiums.*

What's more, that 65% bonus becomes 100% if you don't smoke *and* you stay fit. *That's double the protection with no increase in premium.*

And over half of the non-smokers who apply are meeting the special underwriting criteria for the bonus.

So take a healthy look at your life insurance now. For more details call free: **1-800-328-2193** and ask for operator 921. In Minnesota call: 612-545-2100. Or mail the coupon.

ITT
ITT Life Insurance Corporation

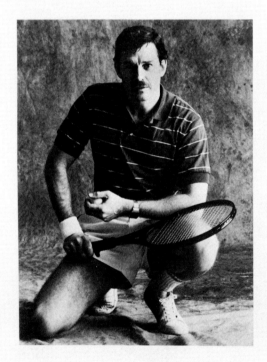

IT'S ABOUT TIME
INSURANCE COMPANIES
GAVE TENNIS PLAYERS THE NET
ADVANTAGE THEY DESERVE.

Playing tennis keeps you in good shape.

Which is a fact your life insurance company should be interested in. But probably isn't.

Because few life insurance companies give genuine rewards to physically fit people — like tennis players — who don't smoke.

Even though statistics indicate that such people live longer. And make better insurance risks.

So now, ITT Life offers a Good Health Bonus® that rewards both non-smokers and regular exercisers.

If you don't smoke, you could earn a 65% insurance bonus from ITT Life. That means a $100,000 policy would be increased to $165,000 — *with no increase in premiums.*

If you don't smoke *and you* exercise regularly, you could earn a 100% life insurance bonus — twice the protection, *with no increase in premiums.*

And over half of the non-smokers who apply for the Good Health Bonus are meeting the special underwriting criteria. Bonus, anyone?

For details, call free **1-800-328-2193** and ask for operator 951. In Minnesota call: 612-545-2100. Or mail the coupon.

ITT
ITT Life Insurance Corporation

52	
Art Director	**Nancy Rice**
Designer	**Nancy Rice**
Photographer	**Larry Robins**
Writer	**Dick Thomas**
Client	**ITT Life Insurance Corporation**
Agency	**Fallon McElligott Rice, Minneapolis**
Publication	**Runners Magazine**

53	
Art Director	**Nancy Rice**
Designer	**Nancy Rice**
Photographer	**Larry Robins**
Writer	**Tom McElligott**
Client	**ITT Life Insurance Corporation**
Agency	**Fallon McElligott Rice, Minneapolis**
Publication	**Tennis**

FINALLY,
AN INSURANCE COMPANY WITH BRAINS ENOUGH TO RECOGNIZE THE IMPORTANCE OF MUSCLE.

If you've been building up your body through regular exercise, there's a good chance you can also start building up your savings.

Because statistics show that people who keep trim by regular exercise and who don't smoke are better insurance risks.

And now ITT Life Insurance Corporation offers a Good Health Bonus™ that rewards both non-smokers and regular exercisers with bonus insurance coverage.

If you don't smoke, you could earn a 65% insurance bonus with the ITT Life plan. Your $50,000 policy, for example, could be increased to $82,500. *With no increase in your premium payments.*

You could earn a 100% bonus if you don't smoke *and* you exercise regularly, *doubling your protection with no increase in premiums.*

And over half of the non-smokers applying are meeting the special underwriting criteria for this bonus.

So if you're a combination of brains and muscle, the smart thing to do is call free right now for details. **1-800-328-2193**. Ask for operator 599. In Minnesota call: 612-545-2100. Or mail the coupon.

ITT
ITT Life Insurance Corporation

More pictures in this magazine were taken with Nikon lenses than all other lenses combined.

This magazine isn't endorsing Nikon lenses, it just looks that way. Because most of the editorial photographs you'll see here were taken with Nikon lenses.

That isn't surprising when you realize that more professional photographers shoot with Nikon lenses than with all other 35mm lenses combined.

Why do professionals choose Nikon in such overwhelming numbers? Because Nikon has always been as dedicated to taking great pictures as they are.

Take this 70-210mm f4 lens, for instance. It's one of Nikon's most versatile lenses, with a 70mm macro function that lets you focus as close as two feet.

Like all 67 zoom and fixed focal length Nikon lenses, it's manufactured without mechanical or material shortcuts.

Every multi-coated optical element is in precise alignment to ensure sharp pictures at every focal length. Nikon even makes its own glass for total quality control.

Of course, we're not claiming that if you buy Nikon equipment, you'll take pictures like the ones in this magazine.

But we're not saying you won't either.

Nikon
We take the world's greatest pictures.™

<table>
<tr><td colspan="2" align="center">__54__</td></tr>
<tr><td>Art Director</td><td>**Nancy Rice**</td></tr>
<tr><td>Designer</td><td>**Nancy Rice**</td></tr>
<tr><td>Photographer</td><td>**Larry Robins**</td></tr>
<tr><td>Writer</td><td>**Tom McElligott**</td></tr>
<tr><td>Client</td><td>**ITT Life Insurance Corporation**</td></tr>
<tr><td>Agency</td><td>**Fallon McElligott Rice, Minneapolis**</td></tr>
<tr><td>Publication</td><td>**The Discus**</td></tr>
</table>

<table>
<tr><td colspan="2" align="center">__55__</td></tr>
<tr><td>Art Director</td><td>**Simon Bowden**</td></tr>
<tr><td>Writer</td><td>**Mary Ann Zeman**</td></tr>
<tr><td>Client</td><td>**Nikon, Inc.**</td></tr>
<tr><td>Agency</td><td>**Scali, McCabe, Sloves, New York**</td></tr>
</table>

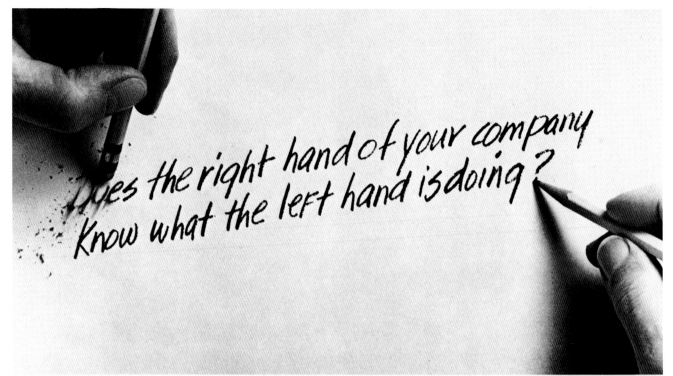

As CEO, just ask yourself a few simple questions.

Does it sometimes seem that there's a diabolic plan to make your company's best efforts cancel each other out?

Do your people seem to work at cross-purposes, instead of in concert?

Does the right information never seem to get to the right place at the right time?

If so, your company isn't alone.

When it comes to white-collar productivity, slow growth (we might more accurately say no-growth) has become a national scandal.

Which isn't to say today's office workers are lazy. They're not. They're working harder than ever, just as you are.

But they're bedeviled by too many meetings. Overwhelmed by too much information. They're asked to spend too much time pushing paper, rather than using their brains.

There is an answer—and AIS/American Bell has it.

We have the products, the know-how, and the systems to help your company manage time and move information.

So you and your people can think smarter, act faster, work happier.

Call 800-AIS-1212. We'll help you work in harmony.

 AT&T

SILVER AWARD

56

Art Directors	**Thom Higgins, Jim Good**
Designer	**Carole Dulak**
Photographer	**Gary Feinstein**
Writers	**John Gruen, Kirk Citron**
Client	**AT&T Information Systems**
Agency	**Oglilvy & Mather Advertising, New York**

No two businesses are alike either.

Your business is unique.
And your problems are unique.
So, if you want to buy a small computer, where can you go to get some understanding and help?
IBM.
We have a range of small computers starting at under $4,000. There's one that can be tailored to fit your unique needs and grow as your business grows.
Thousands of software programs are written for IBM. So whether your business is agriculture or zoology, you can find the right software, right away.
If you ever need help, IBM has the most experienced and widely skilled service organization in the business.
If you didn't think IBM offered so much to solve your unique problems, think of it this way:
We're unique too.
For a free brochure or demonstration of IBM's small computers call your local IBM sales office or our toll-free number below.

IBM

Call *IBM Direct* 1 800 631-5582 Ext. 4. In Hawaii/Alaska 1 800 526-2484 Ext. 4.
(Or write IBM, Dept. lK34, 400 Parson's Pond Drive, Franklin Lakes, N.J. 07417)

Since 1975 we changed a few things on the Rabbit.

Back in 1975 when we introduced the VW Rabbit, *Popular Mechanics* hailed it as a "mechanical masterpiece."
And so it was.
But you didn't expect us to rest on our laurels, did you?
Our habit of starting with a revolutionary design and slowly modifying it towards perfection is a Volkswagen tradition dating back to the Beetle.
So eight years after we sold the first Rabbit in America, we astonished the automotive press when we introduced the 1983 Rabbit GTI.
In November, *Car and Driver* called it, "the car we've all been waiting for."
It has a new 1.8 liter 90 horsepower fuel-injected engine.
It has a new five-speed close ratio manual transmission.
It has new self-adjusting ventilated front disc brakes.
In fact, it's a culmination of over 15,000 things that are new.
If you doesn't look it.
But this too is a Volkswagen tradition.
The more things change, the more they stay the same.

Nothing else is a Volkswagen.

57		58	
Art Director	**Gary Goldsmith**	Art Director	**Roy Grace**
Designer	**Gary Goldsmith**	Designer	**Roy Grace**
Artists	**Gary Goldsmith, Steve Landsberg**	Photographer	**Ken Goldberg**
Writer	**Steve Landsberg**	Writer	**Irwin Warren**
Client	**IBM**	Client	**Volkswagen of America**
Agency	**Doyle Dane Bernbach Inc., New York**	Agency	**Doyle Dane Bernbach Inc., New York**
Publication	**Time Magazine**		

Two major events in the history of locomotion.

In the beginning we all walked. And for centuries, foot-power was basically it. Then some clever person invented the wheel. So we really started to get around. But oxen-power and horse-power had their limitations. After all, oxen and horses had to eat. And had to sleep.

So somebody invented the automobile. Which was a pretty neat idea. Except you had to be rich to buy one. And rich to operate one. Then along came Volkswagen, the "people wagon". Finally, a car people could afford to buy. And afford to run.

Who will ever forget the VW Beetle. It was revolutionary in design and durability. And just about everybody could afford one.

And how about Rabbit. Finally, sophisticated engineering came to a sub-compact car. The front-wheel drive Rabbit was destined to become the most copied car in its class. However, copies are just that. Copies.

Then the Jetta appears. A car in a class by itself. A German engineered sports sedan, yes. Expensive to buy, no. In summary, along came Volkswagen. And the rest is history.

VOLKSWAGEN

True Blue.

The classic "blue label" Keds Sneaker.
Generations of Americans have known and trusted their quality.
Of course, today the original Champion Oxford comes in white,
navy, red, chino, light blue, turquoise, lavender, pink and sweatshirt.
But that classic style hasn't changed.
It hasn't had to. That's what makes it a classic.
Keds. The shoes America grew up in.

Keds

The classic
"blue label" sneaker.

	59		60
Art Directors	Paul Cade, Ann Hollingworth	Art Director	Dick Gage
Photographer	Bruce Horn	Designer	Dick Gage
Writer	Allan Kazmer	Photographer	Carol Kaplan
Client	Volkswagen Canada Inc.	Writer	Ron Lawner
Agency	Doyle Dane Bernbach Advertising Ltd., Toronto	Client	Keds Corporation
Publication	Time Magazine	Agency	Humphrey Browning MacDougall, Inc., Boston
		Publication	Vogue

PUT AN END TO WOMEN'S SUFFERAGE.

There is no such thing as the gentle sex.

When it comes to battering the body, women runners are every bit men's equal. With each step, they send a shock wave roaring through the bones of their foot, up the skeleton to the brain—at over 200 miles per hour.

And you wonder why proper cushioning is so important? Without it, runners are flirting with stress fractures, tendinitis, lower back pain and migraine headaches.

If you're the female of the species, the best place to cool your heels may well be in our new Aurora.

It is the only woman's shoe that features the full-length NIKE-Air™ midsole.

In tests at our Sport Research Lab, we found the simple addition of the NIKE-Air midsole will automatically increase a shoe's cushioning ability a full 12 percent.

And the Aurora will take all the abuse you can dish out. Whereas most EVA midsoles can lose a good fourth of their cushioning after just 500 miles, the NIKE-Air midsole shows no loss

whatsoever. Even after 10,000 miles.

NIKE-Air™ midsole

We should point out, however, that this shoe discriminates on the basis of sex. It is strictly for women. Made on our new woman's curved last. Compared to its male counterpart, the Columbia, the new Aurora is more narrow in the forefoot, more trim at the instep and more snug at the heel.

Of course, that doesn't mean the Aurora is functionally superior to the men's Columbia. We don't think women want those sort of special favors. We just want to make sure they're on equal footing.

NIKE

Banjet/w/ Origen

Imagine having to pass 53 tests just to earn $2.98 after graduation.

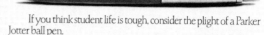

If you think student life is tough, consider the plight of a Parker Jotter ball pen.

Before graduating from the factory, every Jotter undergoes 53 intensive examinations. And even a single skip, blob, or smear is grounds for instant expulsion.

But that's not the worst of it. Each week, hundreds of ball pens are selected at random and held over for post-graduate work.

We bake them in ovens at 140°, then freeze them at -20°, to be certain they don't leak. We make them write 40,000 figure-eights, to confirm they can write up to five miles without a refill. We click their buttons 50,000 times just to check their springs.

Then, when all is said and done, we sell them for $2.98.

Perhaps we're too harsh on them. But it's the only way we know to keep them from ever returning to their old alma mater.

⚕ PARKER

© 1983 TPPC

61	
Art Director	**David Kennedy**
Photographers	**Aaron Jones, Lis Demarco**
Writer	**Dan Wieden**
Client	**Nike, Inc.**
Agency	**Wieden & Kennedy, Portland**

62	
Art Director	**John D'Asto**
Photographer	**David Deahl**
Writer	**Tom Nelson**
Client	**The Parker Pen Company**
Agency	**Ogilvy & Mather, Chicago**
Creative Director	**Tom McConnaughy**

Most heroes are anonymous.

NIKE
Beaverton, Oregon

GOLD AWARD

63

Art Director	**David Kennedy**
Designer	**Peter Moore**
Photographer	**John Turner**
Writer	**Dan Wieden**
Client	**Nike, Inc.**
Agency	**Wieden & Kennedy, Portland**

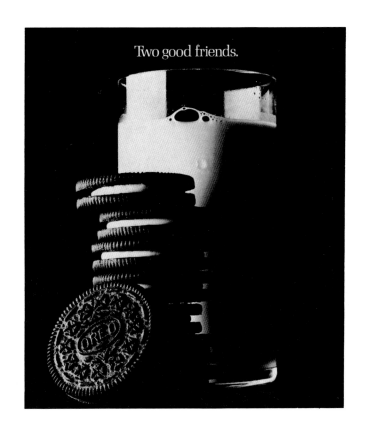

Two good friends.

65

Art Director **Brian Harrod**
Photographer **Phil Marco**
Writer **Ian Mirlin**
Client **Christie Brown**
Agency **McCann - Erickson, Toronto**
Studio **"Mechanical Man"**

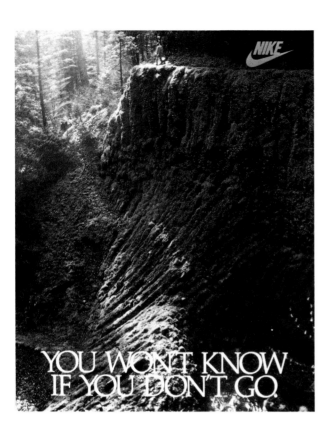

YOU WON'T KNOW
IF YOU DON'T GO.

YOUR EYES ADJUST TO LIGHT. SHOULDN'T YOUR EYEGLASSES?

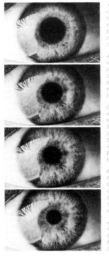

CORNING

DISTINCTIVE MERIT

__66__

Art Director	David Kennedy
Photographer	Alan Kearney
Writer	Dan Wieden
Client	Nike, Inc.
Agency	Wieden & Kennedy, Portland

__67__

Art Director	Peter Hirsch
Designer	Peter Hirsch
Photographer	George M. Cochran
Writer	Ken Majka
Client	Corning Glass Works, Optical Division
Agency	Calet, Hirsch & Spector, Inc., New York
Publication	People
Creative Director	Peter Hirsch

The Christmas bonus fit for
those who give out the Christmas bonus.

Johnnie Walker
Black Label Scotch
YEARS 12 OLD

Send a gift of Johnnie Walker® Black Label anywhere in the U.S.A. Call 1-800-528-6148 Void where prohibited.
12 YEAR OLD BLENDED SCOTCH WHISKY, 86.8 PROOF, BOTTLED IN SCOTLAND. IMPORTED BY SOMERSET IMPORTERS, LTD. N.Y. © 1983

BORN SALT-FREE.

Prehistoric cuisine was salt-free, of course. If you could manage to
make a fire, you were ahead of the game. And if the game was well-
done, you were a four-star chef. Because stone-age man didn't know
there was such a thing as salt. Or high-blood pressure, either.

And his favorite libation came from a pure, sparkling,
naturally salt-free spring. The spring we now call Perrier.®
Earth's first soft drink.

Today, modern man is over-salted. He salts his peas, his porterhouse,
his peanuts. Most of his soft drinks, even the diet drinks, are salted, too.

Not Perrier. Perrier has been salt-free since the day it was born.
And while other beverages have had to change their contents, the
only thing we've had to change is our label. Just to let you know.

Perrier. Earth's First Soft Drink.®

© 1983 Great Waters of France, Inc.

68		69	
Art Director	**Mary Anne Christopher**	Art Director	**Joe LaRosa**
Photographer	**Andrew Unangst**	Artist	**R.O. Blechman**
Writer	**Craig Demeter**	Writer	**Francesca Blumenthal**
Client	**Johnnie Walker Black Label**	Client	**Great Waters of France Inc.**
Agency	**Smith/Greenland Inc., New York**	Agency	**Waring & LaRosa, Inc., New York**
		Publication	**New York Magazine**

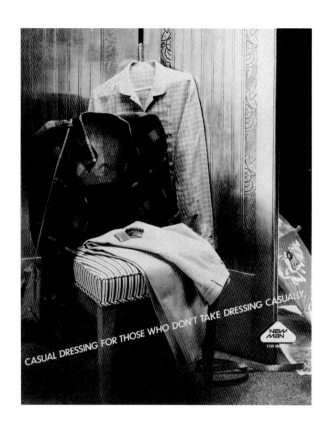

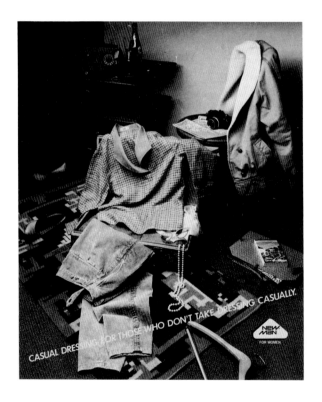

DISTINCTIVE MERIT

	70		71		72
Art Director	**Barbara Schubeck**	Art Director	**Barbara Schubeck**	Art Director	**Barbara Schubeck**
Designer	**Barbara Schubeck**	Designer	**Barbara Schubeck**	Designer	**Barbara Schubeck**
Photographer	**Henry Wolf**	Photographer	**Henry Wolf**	Photographer	**Robert Ammirati**
Writer	**Betsy Mansfield**	Writer	**Betsy Mansfield**	Writer	**Betsy Mansfield**
Client	**New Man**	Client	**New Man**	Client	**New Man**
Agency	**Altschiller Reitzfeld Solin, Inc., New York**	Agency	**Altschiller Reitzfeld Solin, Inc., New York**	Agency	**Altschiller Reitzfeld Solin, Inc., New York**
Publication	**Vanity Fair**	Publication	**Vanity Fair**	Publication	**Vanity Fair**

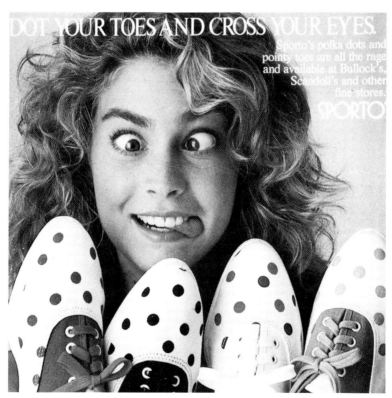

73

Art Director   **John Martinez**
Writer   **Palmer Davis**
Client   **Baccarat, Inc.**
Agency   **Cato Johnson/Y&R Inc., New York**

74

Art Director   **John Martinez**
Writer   **Palmer Davis**
Client   **Baccarat, Inc.**
Agency   **Cato Johnson/Y&R Inc., New York**

75

Art Director   **Barbara Simon**
Photographer   **Alen MacWeeney**
Writer   **Gail Schoenbrunn**
Client   **Gold Seal Rubber Co. Sporto Shoes**
Agency   **Ingalls Associates, Boston**
Publication   **LA Times**

Not many people have seen a bottle of Cruzan Rum.
Most of it disappears in the Virgin Islands.

Not many people have seen a bottle of Cruzan Rum.
Most of it disappears in the Virgin Islands.

76		77	
Art Director	**Bob Taylor**	Art Director	**Bob Taylor**
Writer	**Ted Bell**	Writer	**Ted Bell**
Client	**Schenley**	Client	**Schenley**
Agency	**Leo Burnett Co., Inc., Chicago**	Agency	**Leo Burnett Co., Inc., Chicago**

Home gardening has just stepped out of the Stone Age with new Burpee Garden Tools. These tools, with their unique design, let you do everything from seeding to weeding standing up and make gardening much easier.

Now we understand your attachment to traditional tools. The ones that

that gives your back a break. So you garden standing up in a natural position—more comfortably, faster, easier, better. And as any good gardener knows, it's not how hard you work, but how *well* you prepare and

than ever before. So you can stand tall in your garden knowing you're doing the best you can do. There's a

Finally, man can work upright in his garden.

you've had for years. But we also know how attached you are to your back muscles—the ones that can ache with all the bending, stooping, lifting and chopping you do with traditional tools. That's where Burpee Garden Tools come in. They're designed to be used with a simple *push-pull* motion

maintain your soil that's key to successful gardening.

The secret to these five tools is the angle at which they enter the soil. This angle enables the tool head to *grip* the soil so you don't have to bear down hard. You guide the tool and let *it* do the work. Everything from breaking up the soil, to seedbed preparation, to seeding, cultivating, and weeding is accomplished more easily

garden retailer near you who will be more than happy to show you the complete line of these new Burpee Garden Tools. He'll be standing tall too. After all, it's not every day that such a revolution in the evolution of gardening happens to come along.

Burpee
GARDEN TOOLS

Why you should buy Kiron.

Lock.

Stock.

And barrel.

KIRON

WIMPY RODS CATCH WIMPY FISH.

Do you own a rod that lets trophy fish flick water in your face?

When you hook into a rod-bending, boat-swamping, leaping-lunker of a fish, do you secretly pray that your line will break so that your rod won't?

Fishing scared is something you'll never do with an Ugly Stik rod by Shakespeare. This is a rod of Herculean strength.

It'll flat-out-fish any other rod, thanks to our exclusive Double-Bilt™ process that literally builds the rod *twice*.

First, ribbons of graphite fibers are wound around and around the circumference of the rod for tough "east to west" radial integrity. Then the rod is covered *again*, this time with fiberglass fibers running "north to south" to provide additional strength.

That's why we can make this extraordinary guarantee*: if your Ugly Stik rod should ever break under normal fishing conditions, within 5 years of purchase, we'll replace it. Free.

In the end, fishing with an ordinary rod can yield only one result: ordinary fish. So next time you come face to face with a rod-busting, wrist-cracking, record-breaking fish, do it with an Ugly Stik rod by Shakespeare.

And show the sucker who's boss.

Shakespeare

UGLY STIK RODS

	78		79		80
Art Director	**Rick Elkins**	Art Director	**Greg Clancey**	Art Director	**Paul Debes**
Photographer	**Larry Robins**	Writer	**Dave Butler**	Artist	**Paul Debes**
Writer	**Jane Talcott**	Client	**Kiron**	Writer	**Michael Perri**
Client	**W. Atlee Burpee**	Agency	**Chiat/Day, Los Angeles**	Client	**Shakespeare Fishing Tackle**
Agency	**Doyle Dane Bernbach Inc., New York**			Agency	**Perri Debes Looney & Crane Advertising, Inc., Rochester, NY**

Worth its weight in Chivas Regal.

Mint Summer Night's Dream.

The magic of mint.
It casts a spell upon those who indulge in these creations from Godiva.
They're charming. Enchanting. From their bewitching shapes
to their intriguing fillings. They're enticing. With a cool, minty nuance
that rouses the palate from its deepest sleep. Indeed, to those who revel in delicious
flights of fancy, Godiva® mints are a dream come true.

GODIVA
Chocolatier
BRUXELLES · NEW YORK
PARIS · COLOGNE

Godiva Chocolatier, 701 Fifth Avenue, New York, New York 10022.

81		82		83	
Art Director	Geoff Hayes	Art Director	Mark Hughes	Art Director	Barbara DiLorenzo
Writer	Graham Turner	Designer	Mark Hughes	Photographer	Martin Mistretta
Client	Carillon Importers, Ltd.	Photographer	Larry Robins	Writer	Leticia Hernandez
Agency	TBWA Advertising, New York	Writer	Steven Landsberg	Client	Godiva Chocolatier
		Client	General Wines & Spirits	Agency	Margeotes/Fertitta & Weiss, Inc., New York
		Agency	Doyle Dane Bernbach Inc., New York		

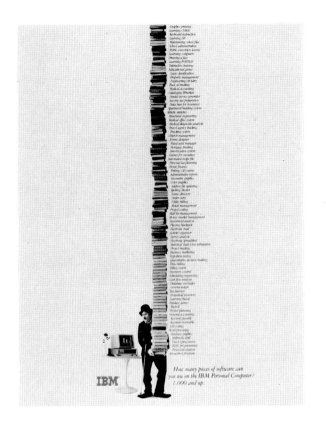

Helping engineers change gears.

The relentless ingenuity of America's engineers has made technological revolution commonplace.

But today, manufacturing engineers face a relentless challenge: to produce goods of ever-higher quality at ever-lower cost. The marketplace, domestic and foreign, demands it.

To meet that challenge, engineers need state-of-the-art training and state-of-the-art tools. This, of course, is a job best done by America's universities. But universities can't do it alone. All sectors of society must help.

That's why IBM is giving $50 million in money and equipment to 22 universities for the creation and expansion of engineering programs in manufacturing systems. The curricula, in part, will include computer-aided design and manufacturing, robotics and lasers, quality control, systems management, and automation.

We expect this investment in education to pay off by helping to keep America's manufacturing in high gear.

And that will pay off for all of us. IBM

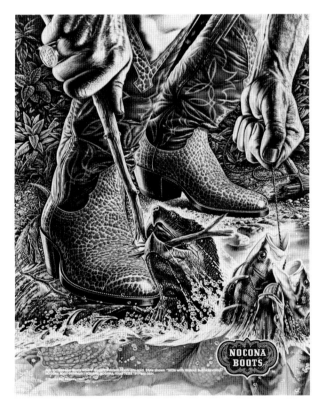

84		85		86	
Art Director	**Bob Tore**	Art Director	**Seymon Ostilly**	Art Director	**Mark Keller**
Designer	**Bob Tore**	Designer	**Seymon Ostilly**	Designer	**Gail Daniels**
Photographer	**Bodi**	Photographer	**Michael O'Neill**	Artist	**Alex Ebel**
Writer	**Arlene Jaffe**	Writer	**Kevin O'Neill**	Writer	**Angus McQueen**
Client	**IBM Corp. (PC)**	Client	**IBM Corp.**	Client	**The Nocona Boot**
Agency	**Lord, Geller, Federico, Einstein, New York**	Agency	**Lord, Geller, Federico, Einstein, New York**		**Company**
Publication	**New Yorker**	Publication	**Time Magazine**	Agency	**Ackerman & McQueen, Oklahoma City, OK**

Why it's smart to make babies work for their meals.

When an infant takes milk from a mother's breast there's a lot that goes on beyond just satisfying a little hunger.

There's the natural sucking action. The contraction and release of certain muscles. The movement of the bottom jaw. The strategic positioning of the tongue.

Milk doesn't simply pour out of the breast. It has to be systematically, almost mechanically pumped away. An instinctive routine that enables a baby to feed while exercising and developing the important muscles.

And if mothers were to tell us that a well-fed, well-exercised baby has a better temperament and sleeps better, we wouldn't be surprised.

The NUK® Orthodontic Nipple was designed to perform like a mother's breast.

This unusual shape is designed to simulate the configuration of a breast during feeding. Every contour has a purpose. In fact, the NUK Nipple is the original orthodontic shape. And the American Academy of Pedodontics suggests the use of a nipple closely resembling a mother's breast.

When the NUK Nipple is positioned for feeding, the hole is on the top so milk hits the roof of the mouth mixing with saliva for easy digestion.

Plus, the hole is smaller than most conventional rubber nipples so your baby gets a work out similar to breast feeding.

And the simple flat tongue rest provides the solid foundation for good, hard sucking.

As you can see, NUK Nipples are available to fit all major brands of disposable and reusable nursers. So you only have to change nipples to give your baby all the NUK advantages.

The NUK Nipple is part of a complete family of NUK® products all designed to help your baby's oral development. We also supply pacifier-teethers, pacifier-exercisers, nursers, teething gel and other fine products.

NUK

Reliance Products Corp.

Stands head and antlers above the rest.

IMPORTED MOOSEHEAD. BREWED BY CANADA'S OLDEST INDEPENDENT FAMILY BREWERY

87

Art Director	**Bryan McPeak**
Artist	**John Burgoyne**
Writer	**Tom Monahan**
Client	**Reliance Products Corp.**
Agency	**Leonard Monahan Saabye, Providence, RI**

88

Art Director	**Jim Clarke**
Artist	**Birney Lettick**
Writer	**Richard Wagman**
Client	**All Brand Importers**
Agency	**The Bloom Agency, New York**
Creative Director	**Stuart Bresner**

MOVING UP An Otis escalator is framed by a bright red Calder mobile at the National Gallery in Washington. Otis, the world's largest manufacturer of elevators and escalators, is part of United

Technologies. So are Pratt & Whitney, Carrier and Sikorsky. We're on the move as the seventh largest manufacturing company in the U.S. United Technologies, Hartford, Connecticut 06101.

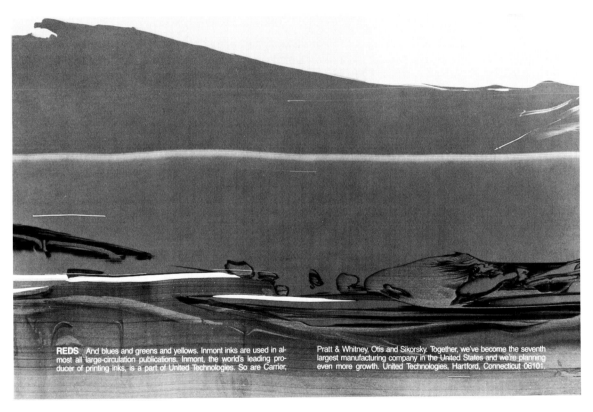

REDS And blues and greens and yellows. Inmont inks are used in almost all large-circulation publications. Inmont, the world's leading producer of printing inks, is a part of United Technologies. So are Carrier,

Pratt & Whitney, Otis and Sikorsky. Together, we've become the seventh largest manufacturing company in the United States and we're planning even more growth. United Technologies, Hartford, Connecticut 06101.

89		90	
Art Director	Gordon Bowman	Art Director	Gordon Bowman
Designer	William Wondriska	Designer	William Wondriska
Photographer	Jay Maisel, Jay Maisel Photography, New York	Photographer	Jay Maisel, Jay Maisel Photography, New York
Writer	Christine Rothenberg	Writer	Christine Rothenberg
Client	United Technologies	Client	United Technologies
Agency	In house—United Technologies	Agency	Inhouse—United Technologies
Publications	N Y Times Sunday Magazine/New Yorker Mag.	Publications	NY Times Sunday Magazine/New Yorker Magazine

WHEN IN DOUBT, WAFFLE.

It's a complicated, confusing world out there.

Just about the time you have it all figured out, everything turns to dust. Or gravel. Or sand. Or a two mile stretch of concrete. Followed by a rain-soaked field.

If you're a runner, there just aren't many simple answers in life. Save one.

The Waffle.

As familiar as this shape has become, nothing is better qualified to see you through the worst the world has to offer.

Because regardless of changes in terrain, each Waffle will continue to act as an independent shock absorber—penetrating softer surfaces, pushing into the midsole on harder ones.

Acting as an independent shock absorber, the Waffle tends to push into the midsole on harder surfaces while penetrating softer ones.

At our research lab in Exeter, New Hampshire, we found the addition of Waffles can increase the cushioning of a running shoe a full 10 percent.

The addition of Waffles to the same shoe significantly reduces impact shock.

Granted, it is possible to achieve somewhat the same thing by going to a flat outsole made of a much thicker, much softer rubber. Unfortunately, that means giving up both traction and wear.

We also suspect the Waffle's

a circle, for example, the Waffle appears to require less torque to rotate, and should lessen both strain and fatigue.

That's not to say we haven't tried to make improvements. We've come out with variations of that famous square ever since we introduced it, way back in 1972.

Via high speed film and computer analysis, we discovered that most runners tend to toe-out when they land. As a result, on some models, we have slightly altered the position of the Waffles.

But that's about it.

As far as discovering some revolutionary new shape or system better able to carry you through a changing world, we simply haven't. And neither has anyone else.

Elite Classic

Internationalist

That's why for racing, we strongly recommend our new Elite Classic. And for training, the Internationalist.

The Waffle is featured on both. True, it isn't exactly new. But it also isn't equaled.

So the next time you're tempted to go with an outsole that looks more radical, remember.

Sometimes there's a definite advantage to being square. **NIKE**

Beaverton, Oregon

GOLD AWARD

91

Art Director	**David Kennedy**
Artist	**David Davis**
Writer	**Dan Wieden**
Client	**Nike, Inc.**
Agency	**Wieden & Kennedy, Portland**

WE HAVEN'T FORGOTTEN WHY THEY'RE CALLED SWEATS.

Call us narrow-minded, but at Nike we like to think that sportswear should be just what it implies. Clothing you play sports in.

A perfect example is the old standby, gray fleece sweats. The kind that get heavier the more you work out. The kind that get better the longer you own them. The kind you wash in a washing machine. And not in Woolite.*

That attitude isn't exclusive to our sweats. Everything we make, from running shorts and warm-ups to singlets and jerseys, is designed first for performance.

The very same philosophy we've used in our shoes for over ten years.

Of course, we can spot a trend as fast as the next guy. And as long as clothes like this are popular among the fashion conscious, we'll make them in colors like turquoise and plum. We might even add some stylish piping here or a few extra pockets there.

But when the trend is gone and forgotten, you'll still be able to wear them to sweat in.

And we'll still be making them in our favorite shade of gray. NIKE

GOLD AWARD

92

Art Director   Houman Pirdavari
Writer   Brent Bouchez
Client   Nike, Inc.
Agency   Chiat/Day, Los Angeles

SUSAN**BENNIS**WARREN**EDWARDS**

SUSAN**BENNIS**WARREN**EDWARDS**

<table>
<tr><td>Art Director</td><td>Stanley Eisenman</td></tr>
<tr><td>Photographer</td><td>John Pilgreen</td></tr>
<tr><td>Client</td><td>Susan Bennis/Warren Edwards</td></tr>
<tr><td>Agency</td><td>Eisenman & Enock Inc., New York</td></tr>
</table>

93	
Art Director	Stanley Eisenman
Photographer	John Pilgreen
Client	Susan Bennis/Warren Edwards
Agency	Eisenman & Enock Inc., New York

94	
Art Director	Stanley Eisenman
Photographer	John Pilgreen
Client	Susan Bennis/Warren Edwards
Agency	Eisenman & Enock Inc., New York

How we came back with the world's finest charcoal from a place where you're lucky to come back at all.

Get a bigger bite with Daiwa.

65 million people fish. There's no limit to how many you can catch with Daiwa.

And there's no limit to your profits.

Daiwa rods and reels are the world's best-selling tackle. And this year, there are even more reasons to keep your store well stocked. Like our new series of Magforce, anti-backlash reels. Autocast reels that take the snags out of one-handed casting. And a complete line of Boron and Graphite rods.

Product is only half the story for 1984. We're also going to help you sell, with the most aggressive sales promotion program in Daiwa history.

Visit the Daiwa booth #203 at AFTMA. You'll see all the new ways Daiwa can help you get a bigger bite.

Daiwa
Rods and reels. Made for each other.

95		96	
Art Director	**Dean Hanson**	Art Director	**Bob Kwait**
Designer	**Dean Hanson**	Designer	**Bob Kwait**
Artist	**Leland Klanderman/ Oasis Art Co.**	Photographer	**Chris Wimpey**
		Artist	**Ron VanBuskirk**
Writer	**Mike Lescarbeau**	Writer	**Tony Durket**
Client	**Winfield Potter's**	Client	**Daiwa Corporation**
Agency	**Fallon McElligott Rice, Minneapolis**	Agency	**Phillips-Ramsey, San Diego**
Publication	**Twin Cities Magazine**		

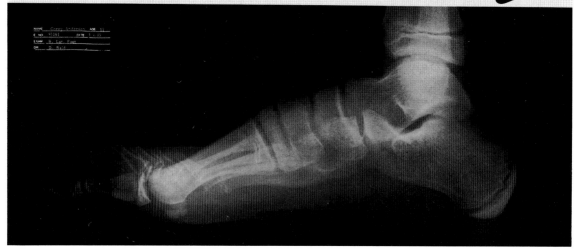

DISTINCTIVE MERIT

97

Art Director	**David Kennedy**
Writer	**Dan Wieden**
Client	**Nike, Inc.**
Agency	**Wieden & Kennedy, Portland**

DISTINCTIVE MERIT

98

Art Director	**David Kennedy**
Photographer	**Dennis Manarchy**
Writer	**Dan Wieden**
Client	**Nike, Inc.**
Agency	**Wieden & Kennedy, Portland**

And so we bid a fond farewell to the Diors. It was a far, far better place they went to than they had ever been and far, far better things they did there than they had ever done.

Christian Dior: Swimwear

Go Bass or go barefoot.

Bass

	99		100
Art Director	Richard Avedon	Art Director	Susan Casey
Photographer	Richard Avedon	Designer	Susan Casey
Writer	Doon Arbus	Photographer	Barry Lategan
Client	Mary Lee Fletcher, Christian Dior - New York, Inc.	Writer	Lynn Stiles
		Client	G.H. Bass
Agency	J. Walter Thompson, New York	Agency	Lord, Geller, Federico, Einstein, New York
		Publication	Seventeen

Paint your nails blue as Blue Moon. Brush them with Mean Green or Black Shimmer or Chrome.

Or cover them with Diamond Dust.

It's the Pop look for nails, new and nervy as the Next Wave, and the way you get it is with Pop Polish from the Cutex Perfect Color collection.

So c'mon. Be a star!

Who needs to show up wearing ho-hum nails when you can knock them out with flash, dazzle & Pop!

Cutex Perfect Color

Hot Dots.

The hottest lacquering idea from Paris is polka-dotted nails. And nobody does dots so daringly as Cutex — with white polish on black, for instance. Or vice versa.

Besides dots, what's hot? Black Shimmer, Purple Passion, Diamond Dust, Slinky Black, Torrid Red and Snow White.

Not for the timid, these are go-the-limit nailcolors with nothing on their mind but having fun and looking lethally beautiful. Are you game?

Cutex Perfect Color

	101		**102**
Art Director	**Jon Parkinson**	Art Director	**Jon Parkinson**
Artist	**Lou Brooks**	Photographer	**Bill King**
Writer	**Alice Moroz**	Writer	**Alice Moroz**
Client	**Cutex Perfect Color for Nails**	Client	**Cutex Perfect Color for Nails**
Agency	**Waring & LaRosa, Inc., New York**	Agency	**Waring & LaRosa, Inc., New York**
Publication	**Mademoiselle**	Publication	**Cosmopolitan**

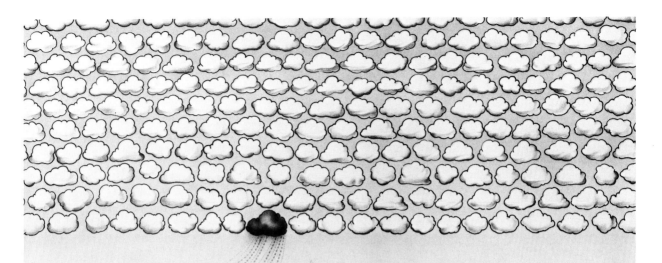

If your failure rate is one in a million, what do you tell your millionth customer?

Millions of parts go into the thousands of machines we build every year. At IBM, we work hard to make sure that everything we make is defect-free, from the smallest circuit to the finished product.

But if an IBM computer or office system ever needs service, we provide our customers with the most experienced and widely skilled service organization in the industry.

IBM customer service people are on call every day of the year for large companies that have many of our machines and small businesses that may have only one.

Our service people can call on computerized data banks where solutions to thousands of hardware and software problems are stored and instantly available to them.

They also work directly with IBM engineers at our laboratories to help design products that need less service and are easier to maintain.

It's all part of our commitment to deliver fast and reliable service to every customer, every time.

Because when it comes to service, we treat every customer as if he or she is one in a million. **IBM**

How you can tell which is which.

The IBM Personal Computer

The IBM Personal Computer XT

103		104	
Art Director	**Seymon Ostilly**	Art Director	**Bob Tore**
Designer	**Seymon Ostilly**	Designer	**Bob Tore**
Illustrator	**Isadore Seltzer**	Photographer	**Bodi**
Writer	**Kevin O'Neill**	Writer	**Arlene Jaffe**
Client	**IBM Corp.**	Client	**IBM Corp. (PC)**
Agency	**Lord, Geller, Federico, Einstein, New York**	Agency	**Lord, Geller, Federico, Einstein, New York**
Publication	**Atlantic Magazine**	Publication	**Forbes**

In choosing a superior professional camera you have to start at the bottom.

Once you buy a camera that's intended for professional use, you can only use the motor drive that's made for it.

Which can be unfortunate if the motor drive isn't engineered to meet the demands of professional photography.

For the pro, of course, that could be devastating. After all, most pictures taken professionally are done with a motor drive. And most pros depend on the motor drive for fast handling and rewinding.

In short, to have a superior professional camera, you have to have a superior motor drive.

Which leads us to the Nikon F3 with motor drive: the most advanced camera/motor drive.

Motor drive and camera designed as one unit.

The balance between the Nikon F3 and its motor drive is so remarkable you can actually place most lenses up to 200mm on the camera, set it down, and it won't tip over.

Try doing that with any other camera/motor drive.

The hand grip on the motor drive is also contoured so you can shoot with one hand if you have to. And to take the bumps and jolts of daily professional use, the motor drive is constructed of the same exterior metal used in the camera body.

Up to 5,000 exposures with one set of batteries.

As soon as you attach the motor drive to the Nikon F3, the camera disconnects its internal camera batteries and gets all its power from the motor drive's batteries.

Remarkably, with only one set of eight alkaline-manganese penlight batteries, the F3 with motor drive gives up to 5,000 exposures. Which amounts to 140 rolls of 36-exposure film. All other camera/motor drive combinations give you about half that number. Yet use more batteries.

Up to six frames-per-second with NiCad battery pack.

The F3's incredibly efficient film-advance mechanism and extensive use of ball bearings enables the F3 to fire mirror up at the amazing rate of six frames-per-second with the optional MN-2 NiCad battery pack.

That's one frame-per-second faster than anyone else.

You can also rewind a 36-exposure roll in less than five seconds with the NiCad battery pack.

The most exciting camera a motor drive can get attached to.

The F3 is the camera that only Nikon's decades of experience could have produced. *Modern Photography* wrote, "...for the Nikon enthusiast the F3 represents a perfection in design, construction, enjoyment, and handling never before achieved."

The following are just some of its incredible features.

Full manual control with quartz timing.

With any of its 15 manual shutter speeds, the F3 offers you precision timing so accurate it's actually measurable to the fourth decimal place.

This accuracy would be impossible to achieve by mechanical means alone.

And just as important. The quartz oscillator is impervious to temperature extremes and fluctuations in voltage.

True automatic bracketing.

Now you can bracket in automatic just as easily as you would in manual. The F3's memory lock button allows you to freeze the automatic shutter speed which lets you vary apertures to bracket your exposures.

No other top-of-the-line camera has this feature.

Exclusive center-weighted pattern for more accurate metering.

Nikon has developed an advanced center-weighted metering pattern for the F3 that gives you approximately 80% sensitivity in the 12mm circle found on most Nikon focusing screens.

With this exclusive pattern, you're able to achieve superior selective metering in both the manual and automatic modes. It is ideal for severe lighting conditions such as sidelight, backlight, and spotlight.

100% viewfinder accuracy.

Nikon's camera assembly techniques are so exacting, the F3 is the only 35mm SLR manufactured today with virtually 100% viewfinder accuracy. And that includes every combination of viewfinder and focusing screen designed for the F3.

Accepts the most comprehensive system of lenses in 35mm photography.

Unlike other brands, the F3 accepts the lenses used by the majority of 35mm professional photographers—Nikkor. There are over 60 lenses to choose from. With focal lengths ranging from 6mm to 2000mm.

Accessories for the F3 include a bulk film back, data back, and Speedlight flash units which provide automatic through-the-lens flash exposure.

So ask your favorite Nikon dealer to hand you a Nikon F3 with motor drive. And find out what's turning the world of photography upside down.

Nikon
We take the world's greatest pictures.

225 MILLION AMERICANS UNDERSTAND HIM PERFECTLY.

He's got awful diction. A terrible temper. And a fanatical following.

Because to the millions upon millions of people who've hugged him at Disneyland and Walt Disney World, chuckled at his antics in cartoons, and made platinum records out of what has to be one of the worst singing voices in history, Donald Duck is saying something loud and clear.

Simply that basic human emotions speak to everyone.

And now, Donald is ready to get his message across in a new medium.

On The Disney Channel. Where the same magical Disney presence will be translated into 16 hours per day of the highest quality family entertainment.

Entertainment unlike anything cable subscribers will be able to find in theaters or anywhere else on television. Programming to engage the mind and the heart. New series like Contraption, Dreamfinders and Wish Upon A Star to get families laughing and talking with each other.

Films and cartoons from the vast Disney library that communicate in the universal language of imagination. Dramatic series. True Life Adventures. Wonder and science. The nostalgia of Zorro and the futureworld of Epcot Center.

It's a programming concept that reflects sixty years of experience in understanding what audiences want. Which may be why The Disney Channel could turn out to be one of the few things in this country 225 million people agree on.

For more information on The Disney Channel, call our toll free number: 1-800-832-4636.

THE DISNEY CHANNEL

	105		106
Art Director	**Simon Bowden**	Art Director	**Yvonne Smith**
Writer	**Earl Carter**	Writer	**Jocelyn Weisdorf**
Client	**Nikon, Inc.**	Client	**The Disney Channel**
Agency	**Scali, McCabe, Sloves, New York**	Agency	**Chiat/Day, Los Angeles**

60 MILLION AMERICANS WANT A MOUSE IN THEIR HOUSE.

In a recent survey,* 71% of the households with children under 18 told us they'd welcome The Disney Channel into their home.

Sight unseen.

Because there's a whole generation of former kids out there who grew up with Disney magic and now want to share it with their children.

Millions of subscribers who knew The Mickey Mouse Club March by heart, who never missed an installment of Spin and Marty, who ran around carving the "Z" for Zorro into the air, can now recapture those moments on The Disney Channel.

And their children can discover the wonder and excitement of Disney for themselves with such films as Mary Poppins, Dumbo and Tron, as well as with made just for them series such as Welcome To Pooh Corner and Wish Upon A Star.

For the whole family, there will be brand new programming to share. New dramatic series, science wizardry in action, voyages through a dream factory, plus a weekly series from the spectacular future world of Epcot Center. There's even the Disney version of aerobics, named, naturally, Mousercise.

It's 16 hours of programming with the exclusive Disney touch, unlike anything else your viewers will be able to see in theatrical release or anywhere else on television.

Of course, programming is just a foot in the door, even for someone as well known as Mickey Mouse. The question is, will he still be a welcome guest six months down the line?

We think so.

Because every time a member of the family visits Disneyland or Walt Disney World, purchases a Disney product, listens to a Disney record or tape or sees a Disney movie, another positive reinforcement for the value of the channel has just been added.

What all of this means to you is really quite simple.

When it comes to talking to subscribers about The Disney Channel, they're already all ears.

For more information, please call The Disney Channel's toll free number: 1-800-832-4636.

THE DISNEY CHANNEL

WHAT FAMILY PROGRAMMING NEEDS IS A GOOD WATCHDOG.

To the rescue.

The answer to endless hours of cat chases and car crashes in the corridors of network kid vid.

The answer to critics of the cable industry who are giving pay T.V. an increasingly "R" rating.

The Disney Channel.

The Disney Channel is a whole new concept in pay T.V.

Sixteen hours a day of the Disney magic formula of fun and learning, unlike anything viewers will be able to find in theatrical release or anywhere else on television.

The watchword is involvement. Interactive shows like You and Me, Kid and Mousercise that encourage family participation. Fresh new series such as Welcome To Pooh Corner and Wish Upon A Star. Specials from Disneyland and Walt Disney World. Programming of the future from Epcot Center. Flights of fantasy, daring quests, soaring adventures that engage the heart and involve the mind at the same time. A library of more than 50 years of unforgettable films, from Dumbo and Mary Poppins to Tron.

There's even a high degree of involvement in The Disney Channel Magazine, a cut out, fill in, put together adventure all of its own.

But in addition to our innovative programming, there's something else. A trust from the public that associates the name Disney with nothing but the highest quality family entertainment. A trust we take quite seriously.

Maybe that's why being a watchdog could become Pluto's finest role.

To become part of The Disney Channel, call our toll free number: 1-800-832-4636.

THE DISNEY CHANNEL

107

Art Director	**Yvonne Smith**
Writer	**Jocelyn Weisdorf**
Client	**The Disney Channel**
Agency	**Chiat/Day, Los Angeles**

108

Art Director	**Yvonne Smith**
Writer	**Jocelyn Weisdorf**
Client	**The Disney Channel**
Agency	**Chiat/Day, Los Angeles**

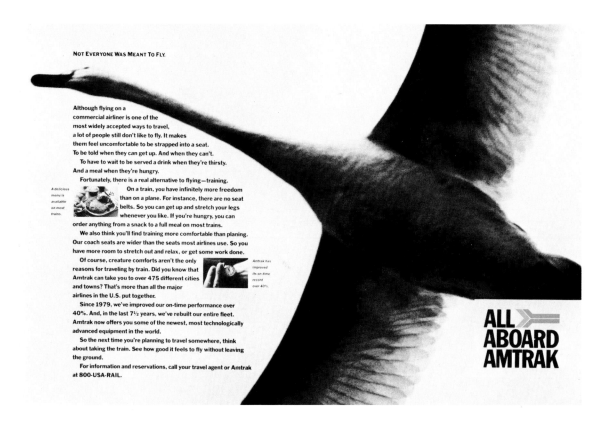

NOT EVERYONE WAS MEANT TO FLY.

Although flying on a commercial airliner is one of the most widely accepted ways to travel, a lot of people still don't like to fly. It makes them feel uncomfortable to be strapped into a seat. To be told when they can get up. And when they can't. To have to wait to be served a drink when they're thirsty. And a meal when they're hungry.

Fortunately, there is a real alternative to flying—training.

A delicious menu is available on most trains.

On a train, you have infinitely more freedom than on a plane. For instance, there are no seat belts. So you can get up and stretch your legs whenever you like. If you're hungry, you can order anything from a snack to a full meal on most trains.

We also think you'll find training more comfortable than planing. Our coach seats are wider than the seats most airlines use. So you have more room to stretch out and relax, or get some work done.

Of course, creature comforts aren't the only reasons for traveling by train. Did you know that Amtrak can take you to over 475 different cities and towns? That's more than all the major airlines in the U.S. put together.

Amtrak has improved its on-time record over 40%.

Since 1979, we've improved our on-time performance over 40%. And, in the last 7½ years, we've rebuilt our entire fleet. Amtrak now offers you some of the newest, most technologically advanced equipment in the world.

So the next time you're planning to travel somewhere, think about taking the train. See how good it feels to fly without leaving the ground.

For information and reservations, call your travel agent or Amtrak at 800-USA-RAIL.

ALL ABOARD AMTRAK

WE GO TO MORE PLACES THAN ALL THE MAJOR AIRLINES COMBINED.

Amtrak can take you to over 475 different places. That's about 390 more than Delta Airlines. 416 more than TWA. And 346 more than United and American.

Amtrak is your ticket to over 475 different cities.

In fact, Amtrak can take you to more places than all the major airlines in the U.S. put together. To big cities, like Chicago, New York, Los Angeles, Dallas and Miami. And not so big cities, like Hastings, Nebraska and New Brunswick, New Jersey.

In short, Amtrak goes where you want to go. And we take you there in style. During the last 6½ years, our entire fleet has been rebuilt. We've added some of the newest and most technologically advanced equipment in the world. Amtrak trains are also more comfortable. For example, our coach seats are wider than the seats most airlines use. So you have more room to stretch out and relax, or get some work done.

And our on-time record has improved dramatically. Since 1979, it has gone up nearly 40%.

If you haven't ridden on a train lately, you're in for a surprise.

The average locomotive is younger than the average airliner.

Amtrak has created a new, nationwide passenger rail system. Literally from the ground up. A system that represents a viable alternative for people who fly. For business or pleasure.

So whether you're planning on traveling 100 miles or 1,000 miles, consider this. Maybe your next flight should be on a train. For information or reservations call Amtrak or your travel agent.

ALL ABOARD AMTRAK

109

Art Director	**Paul Frahm**
Writer	**Michael Robertson**
Client	**National Railroad Passenger Corporation**
Agency	**Needham, Harper & Steers, New York**

110

Art Director	**Paul Frahm**
Photographer	**Bill Troy**
Writer	**Michael Robertson**
Client	**National Railroad Passenger Corporation**
Agency	**Needham, Harper & Steers, New York**

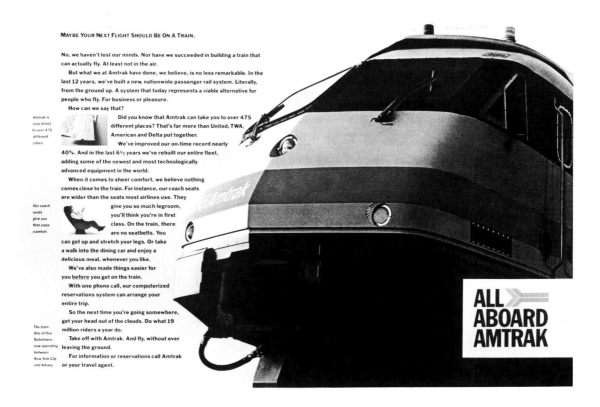

MAYBE YOUR NEXT FLIGHT SHOULD BE ON A TRAIN.

No, we haven't lost our minds. Nor have we succeeded in building a train that can actually fly. At least not in the air.

But what we at Amtrak have done, we believe, is no less remarkable. In the last 12 years, we've built a new, nationwide passenger rail system. Literally, from the ground up. A system that today represents a viable alternative for people who fly. For business or pleasure.

How can we say that?

Amtrak is your ticket to over 475 different cities.

Did you know that Amtrak can take you to over 475 different places? That's far more than United, TWA, American and Delta put together.

We've improved our on-time record nearly 40%. And in the last 6½ years we've rebuilt our entire fleet, adding some of the newest and most technologically advanced equipment in the world.

When it comes to sheer comfort, we believe nothing comes close to the train. For instance, our coach seats are wider than the seats most airlines use. They

Our coach seats give you first class comfort.

give you so much legroom, you'll think you're in first class. On the train, there are no seatbelts. You can get up and stretch your legs. Or take a walk into the dining car and enjoy a delicious meal, whenever you like.

We've also made things easier for you before you get on the train.

With one phone call, our computerized reservations system can arrange your entire trip.

So the next time you're going somewhere, get your head out of the clouds. Do what 19 million riders a year do.

The train: One of five Turboliners now operating between New York City and Albany.

Take off with Amtrak. And fly, without ever leaving the ground.

For information or reservations call Amtrak or your travel agent.

ALL ABOARD AMTRAK

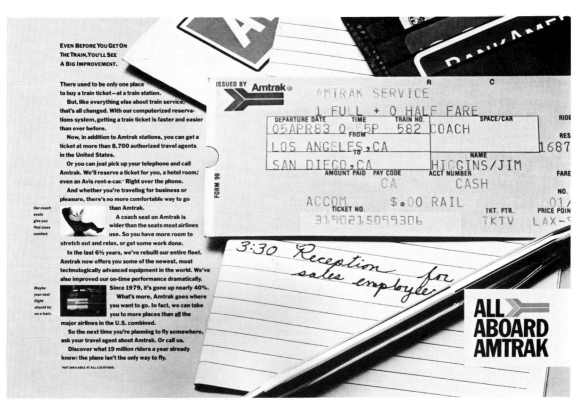

EVEN BEFORE YOU GET ON THE TRAIN, YOU'LL SEE A BIG IMPROVEMENT.

There used to be only one place to buy a train ticket—at a train station.

But, like everything else about train service, that's all changed. With our computerized reservations system, getting a train ticket is faster and easier than ever before.

Now, in addition to Amtrak stations, you can get a ticket at more than 8,700 authorized travel agents in the United States.

Or you can just pick up your telephone and call Amtrak. We'll reserve a ticket for you, a hotel room,* even an Avis rent-a-car.* Right over the phone.

And whether you're traveling for business or pleasure, there's no more comfortable way to go

Our coach seats give you first class comfort.

than Amtrak.

A coach seat on Amtrak is wider than the seats most airlines use. So you have more room to stretch out and relax, or get some work done.

In the last 6½ years, we've rebuilt our entire fleet. Amtrak now offers you some of the newest, most technologically advanced equipment in the world. We've also improved our on-time performance dramatically.

Maybe your next flight should be on a train.

Since 1979, it's gone up nearly 40%. What's more, Amtrak goes where you want to go. In fact, we can take you to more places than all the major airlines in the U.S. combined.

So the next time you're planning to fly somewhere, ask your travel agent about Amtrak. Or call us.

Discover what 19 million riders a year already know: the plane isn't the only way to fly.

*NOT AVAILABLE AT ALL LOCATIONS.

ALL ABOARD AMTRAK

111	112
Art Director **Paul Frahm**	Art Director **Paul Frahm**
Writer **Michael Robertson**	Writer **Michael Robertson**
Client **National Railroad Passenger Corporation**	Client **National Railroad Passenger Corporation**
Agency **Needham, Harper & Steers, New York**	Agency **Needham, Harper & Steers, New York**

THE ADVANTAGES OF GETTING THE SHAFT.

Shaft drive.

Smooth, reliable, maintenance-free.

It's available only on the new Yamaha three-wheelers, the Yamahauler and the Tri-Moto 225DX.

And it's an addition to the sport of three-wheeling that eliminates a few traditions of the sport.

Chain lube for one. Masterlinks for another. And of course, chain adjusting tools. Three items that should take you all of about three seconds to learn to live without.

But while shaft drive is definitely the most innovative feature of these new Tri-Motos, it's definitely not the only feature of these new Tri-Motos.

The Yamahauler, for example, offers a 200cc, four-stroke single with a gear driven balancer and all the mid-range power and stump-pulling low-end torque needed for a utility oriented three-wheeler.

What's more, there's an electric starter instead of a rope. An easy-shifting five speed transmission. Telescopic front forks that offer 100mm of front wheel travel. An enclosed, fade-resistant rear disc brake. An extra-long, extra-comfortable seat. Water-proof electronic ignition. Wide-profile tires for improved handling and greater stability. And front and rear utility racks with a rear trailer hitch. Not to mention a full 90-day warranty that covers both parts and labor.

All standard equipment. Which makes the Yamahauler one of the two best four-stroke three-wheelers money can buy.

The other being the Tri-Moto 225DX. Because the 225DX combines all the features of the Yamahauler (except the utility items) with a few goodies of its very own.

25cc's more engine — making it one of the most powerful four-stroke three-wheelers you can buy. A twist throttle instead of a thumb lever. And something you won't appreciate until the going gets rough.

Monoshock rear suspension. Greatly improving the ride, the handling and the look on your face when you hit a sharp bump.

So whether your needs tend toward the new Yamahauler or the Tri-Moto 225DX, it's plain to see you're getting everything you deserve.

Including the shaft.

YAMAHA TRI-MOTOS

Warranty terms are limited. See your Yamaha dealer for complete details.

Sony Tape. The Perfect Blank.

Color it country.

Color it butterfly.

Color it polka-dot.

Color it pigskin.

Color it shocking punk.

Color it hard rock.

Color it platinum.

Color it bloodcurdling.

Color it blues.

Color it love.

Color it scarlet.

Color it wild west.

SONY L-750 HG HIGH GRADE VIDEO CASSETTE

SONY UCX 90

Bring home a Sony Audio or Video Tape and what do you get? The perfect blank. Electronically designed to capture more sound than you can hear, more color than you can see.

113

Art Director   **Houman Pirdavari**
Writer   **Brent Bouchez**
Client   **Yamaha Motor Corporation**
Agency   **Chiat/Day, Los Angeles**

114

Art Director   **Roberta LaRosa**
Artist   **Elwood Smith**
Writer   **Joe LaRosa**
Client   **Sony Corporation of America**
Agency   **Waring & LaRosa, Inc., New York**
Publication   **Newsweek**

It's wrought from pure silver and writes like pure silk.

You will find writing with the Parker sterling silver Premier fountain pen anything but drudgery.

In fact, it's entirely possible you will find it something of an inspiration.

We can't promise it will give you the wisdom of an Oscar Wilde, although holding the solid silver body does lend itself to contemplation. (It's 92.5% pure, as pure as sterling silver comes.)

MAN IS THE ONLY ANIMAL THAT BLUSHES. OR NEEDS TO.
Mark Twain

When you do finally write, the words will flow with such uninhibited smoothness there will be nothing to block the way should a profound thought happen to wander along.

A cynic is a man who knows the price of everything and the value of nothing.
Oscar Wilde

Thank the nib for that. And the extremes we go to making it. The nib takes three weeks to manufacture, because we do it almost entirely by hand.

We fashion it from 18K gold to make it flexible to the touch. Then at the tip we mount a tiny pellet of ruthenium, a metal four times harder than steel and ten times smoother.

He is a self-made man and worships his creator.
Disraeli on a fellow politician

The ruthenium tip is sculptured under a microscope—a deft operation any surgeon could envy. But an even more delicate task follows.

The nib must be split with a cutting disc only .004" wide. Literally fine enough to split hairs.

Finally, the nib is tumbled in walnut shells for eighteen hours to leave the gold incomparably smooth.

Only after all this, not to mention 131 inspections along the way, will the craftsman who made the nib sign the certificate allowing us to sell you this pen.

Be civil to all; sociable to many; familiar with few.
Benjamin Franklin

Buy the Parker Premier and even if you never write anything magnificent, at least you will never write anything but magnificently.

◆ PARKER

Available from The Parker Pen Company, Airport Corporate Center, 7200 Corporate Center Drive, Suite 336, Miami, Florida 33126. Phone 592-4035.

115

Art Directors	**Richard Kimmel, Garry Horner**
Photographers	**Dave Jordano, Stak**
Writers	**Ron Hawkins, Indra Sinha**
Client	**The Parker Pen Co.**
Agency	**Ogilvy & Mather, Chicago and Ogilvy & Mather, London**
Executive Creative Directors	**Curvin O'Rielly, Don Arlett**

116		117	
Art Director	George D'Amato	Art Director	George D'Amato
Photographer	Irving Penn	Photographer	Irving Penn
Writer	Herb Green	Writer	Herb Green
Client	Beatrice Dautresme/ L'Oreal/COSMAIR	Client	Beatrice Dautresme/ L'Oreal/COSMAIR
Agency	McCann-Erickson, New York	Agency	McCann-Erickson, New York

	118
Art Director	**George D'Amato**
Photographer	**Irving Penn**
Writer	**Herb Green**
Client	**Beatrice Dautresme/ L'Oreal/COSMAIR**
Agency	**McCann-Erickson, New York**

	119
Art Director	**George D'Amato**
Photographer	**Irving Penn**
Writer	**Herb Green**
Client	**Beatrice Dautresme/ L'Oreal/COSMAIR**
Agency	**McCann-Erickson, New York**

These people had the guts to be successful.

There are more OEMs in more places doing more things with Apples' than with any other personal computer in the world.

Because Apples have more available software. More configuration versatility. And an OEM support program that will provide you with everything from our most basic computer products to complete, ready-to-roll systems.

All backed by technical documentation, software assistance, even hands-on training. And all part of a lasting commitment to this important marketplace.

So if you have the courage to succeed, but lack the guts, contact an Apple OEM Representative.

The most personal computer. ⌘ apple

	120
Art Director	George D'Amato
Photographer	Irving Penn
Writer	Herb Green
Client	Beatrice Dautresme/ L'Oreal/COSMAIR
Agency	McCann-Erickson, New York

	121
Art Director	Mike Moser
Writer	Brian O'Neill
Client	Apple Computer
Agency	Chiat/Day, Los Angeles

How to turn a sea of data into data you can see.

There are more people in more places doing more things with Apples than with any other personal computer in the world.

Which is saying a lot.

But we'd like to take the time to explain just one of the things that can make an Apple' Personal Computer

more meaningful to you, personally.

It's called business graphics.

An important business tool that demonstrates, quite graphically, how one picture is worth a few thousand numbers.

More ways to see what you're doing.

That's the beauty of Apple Business Graphics.

The software package that gives your Apple II or Apple III personal computer the power to convert rows and rows of numbers—

or pounds of printout—into one simple, colorful, comprehensible illustration.

And that gives you the power, for example, to thoroughly understand relationships and comparisons in a complex market analysis. Without having to spend hours sitting through

dull data—armed with little more than a ruler, a compass and a few not-so-magic markers.

With Apple Business Graphics, all you do is enter the data or transfer it directly from your VisiCalc' model or a number of other computer files. Your Apple will take it from there.

Helping you to get the big picture in a variety of ways. Line or area graphs, bar graphs, pie charts or scattergrams.

Whichever configuration best suits your application.

When you're through charting market shares you can do the same with forecasts, budgets, stock trends, business plans or customer demographics.

Show your stuff.

In addition to helping you better visualize results, Apple

Business Graphics can make presentations more presentable.

Because whatever you've produced can be rapidly, easily and colorfully reproduced, on virtually any printer or plotter on the market.

Moreover, sophisticated Apple features like exploded views,

unlimited overlays and floating titles allow your displays to be remarkably flexible.

By combining Apple Business Graphics with various slide-show packages, charts and graphs on your monitor can easily be converted into impressive slides and transparencies.

Getting started in pictures.

Start by seeing any of the over 1300 authorized Apple dealers.

They'll show you Apple Business Graphics software can generate more types of pictures, in more colors, using more data

than any other graphics package.

More important, they'll show you what all that can mean to you, your accounting firm, your import business, or your chain of quiche-on-a-bun family restaurants.

They'll even help you produce your first picture.

But business graphics is just one of the things an Apple can help you do. One of thousands. Which is not terribly surprising, when you consider there's more software available for Apples than for any other personal computer.

So consider a trip to your Apple dealer. And draw your own conclusions.

apple

The most personal computer.

Call (800) 538-9696 for the location of the authorized Apple dealer nearest you, or for information regarding corporate purchases through a National Account Program. In Calif. (800) 662-9238. Or write Apple Computer Inc., Advertising and Promotion Dept., 20525 Mariani Ave., Cupertino, CA 95014. VisiCalc is a registered trademark of VisiCorp. © 1983 Apple Computer Inc.

Art Director   **Mike Moser**
Writers   **Brian O'Neill, Steve Hayden**
Client   **Apple Computer**
Agency   **Chiat/Day, Los Angeles**

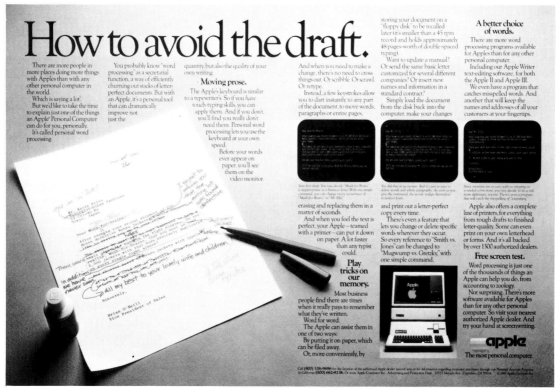

123		124	
Art Director	**Mike Moser**	Art Director	**Mike Moser**
Writers	**Brian O'Neill, Steve Hayden**	Writers	**Brian O'Neill, Steve Hayden**
Client	**Apple Computer**	Client	**Apple Computer**
Agency	**Chiat/Day, Los Angeles**	Agency	**Chiat/Day, Los Angeles**

It took 200 years to draw this picture.

This cheery little doodle represents 432,000 hours of work by some of the brightest minds in computer design.

And yes, they actually got paid for it.

Because it also represents a whole new way for humans to interact with computers on more human terms:

Lisa™ from Apple.

With its unique 32-bit design and 1 million characters of internal memory, it's the most powerful personal office computer ever developed, capable of a lot more than doodling. Each system gives you a whole workbench of powerful business tools, from word processing to electronic project management.

But the real story is the way we used that power — not to make electrons go faster, but to help you go faster.

Because Lisa is the first (and only) computer that works in a visual way. It replaces complex computer commands with pictures familiar to anyone who's ever worked at a desk.

File folders look like file folders. Memos like memos. There's a clipboard, a calculator, even a wastebasket.

To tell Lisa what to do, you simply point to the appropriate symbol.

So you can actually learn to use Lisa in minutes. Instead of days.

And that's the bigger picture.

Soon there'll be just two kinds of people. Those who use computers and those who use Apples.

If you can find the trash can, you can run a computer.

You don't have to know it's the world's most powerful personal computer.

You don't have to appreciate its unique 32-bit architecture. Or get weak in the knees when we tell you it has a million bytes of internal memory.

All you really have to know is that it's the only computer you can learn to use in under 30 minutes.

Because it's Lisa.™ From Apple.

Lisa replaces complex computer commands with simple "icons," pictures of objects familiar to anyone who's ever worked at a desk.

File folders look like file folders. Memos like memos.

There's even a calculator and a clipboard.

To tell Lisa what you want, just point to the appropriate icon using a palm-sized device called a "mouse." As you move the mouse on your desk, the pointer moves on Lisa's screen.

So you work intuitively, right from the start.

And every Lisa program works the same way. Once you've learned one, you'll learn the next even faster.

That's the difference between Lisa and every other computer in the world.

It lets you concentrate on what you want done.

Not on how to get a computer to do it.

Soon there'll be just two kinds of people. Those who use computers and those who use Apples.

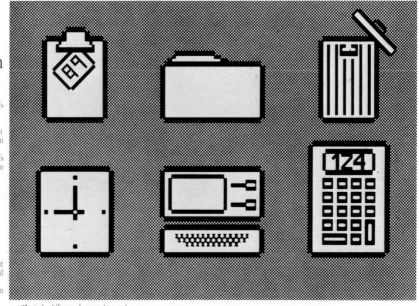

DISTINCTIVE MERIT

125

Art Directors	**Lee Clow, Mike Moser**
Writer	**Steve Hayden**
Client	**Apple Computer**
Agency	**Chiat/Day, Los Angeles**

126

Art Directors	**Mike Moser, Jim Cox**
Writer	**Brian O'Neill**
Client	**Apple Computer**
Agency	**Chiat/Day, Los Angeles**

How to quickly regain your balance.

If you'd like to turn the agony of small business bookkeeping into the ecstasy of total control, you've come to the right place.

Because even if you're starting with a shoe box full of invoices or a pile of checks hiding under a pile of deposit slips, we can tell you how to centralize, organize and monitor all that information, and manipulate it in ways that will make your business a pleasure—all with an Apple III Personal Computer.

Attain instant financial status.

An Apple III, teamed with the BPI General Accounting Package, can put every basic accounting function right at your fingertips. Technically, that means General Ledger, Accounts Payable, Accounts Receivable and Payroll—all in one package. Meaningfully, that means you can turn numbers into answers. With BPI, your Apple III can give you a snapshot of your company's financial condition, an up-to-the-instant balance sheet. It can also generate instant and detailed reports on your customers and vendors. So you know who owes whom, how much, and how come. And just how well your cash flow is flowing.

And where to give credit where credit is due (a customer inquiry feature allows you to make credit decisions based on the most current information).

You can also list your purchases by discount dates. And take advantage of them in no uncertain net terms. You can even keep payroll records without paying more, because it's part of the same package.

Profit from history.

In business as in life, experience is the best teacher. And the Apple/BPI system can provide you with instant comparisons of this-month-this-year vs. this-month-last-year, or this-year-to-date vs. last-year-to-date.

So you can quickly spot changing expense ratios and make decisions with 20/20 foresight.

Make a timely statement.

Add an Apple Dot Matrix or Daisywheel printer to your Apple III, and you can print out your entire balance sheet in minutes. Or any number of reports, from cash receipts to payroll ledger to income. You can even print checks and customer statements. The impressively professional

The BPI General Accounting Package also lets your income statements be coded by location, department or product line. So you know where your money's coming from. And where it's not.

results will make an important statement to everyone you deal with—including your banker.

More ways Apples pay.

There are more people in more places doing more things with Apples than with any other personal computer in the world.

Because for one thing, there's more software for Apples than for any other personal computer in the world. So the same Apple that handles all your accounting needs can also handle financial spreadsheets, word processing and electronic filing.

You'll also find programs that are designed specifically for your kind of business. Be it dentistry, architecture or swine herding.

Of course, the best way to learn all the ways Apples can help you make better business decisions is to visit any one of over 1500 authorized Apple dealers.

So drop in. For a full account.

apple

The most personal computer.

Call (800) 538-9696 for the location of the authorized Apple dealer nearest you, or for information regarding our National Account Program. Or write Apple Computer Inc., Advertising Department, 20525 Mariani Avenue, Cupertino, CA 95014 © 1983 Apple Computer Inc.

127

Art Director	**Mike Moser**
Writer	**Brian O'Neill**
Client	**Apple Computer**
Agency	**Chiat/Day, Los Angeles**

ANTENNA. AUSTIN, TEXAS 288-3717 AMAZING HAIR

SILVER AWARD

128

Art Director **Steven Sessions**
Designer **Steven Sessions**
Artist **Jerry Scott**
Client **Antenna Hair Salon**
Agency **Steven Sessions, Inc.,
Houston**

Portrait of a president in a Ron Chereskin.

Here, "The Perfect Suit" to start off your permanent collection of clothes by Ron Chereskin.
Macy's, San Francisco

Where would
you be without
The Boston Globe?

	129		130
Art Directors	Bruce Bloch, Susan Lloyd	Art Director	John Cooney
Photographer	Ulf Skogsbergh	Writer	Maryann Barone
Writers	Sara Chereskin, Patty Rockmore	Client	The Boston Globe
Client	Ron Chereskin	Agency	Hill, Holliday, Connors, Cosmopulos, Inc., Boston
Agency	AC&R Advertising, New York	Typographer	Rand Typographers
Publication	Town/Country		

How to become a brilliant golfer.

After our Etonic Spectrum™ golf shirts were washed

eight times, three out of five golfers preferred the

Spectrum to such fancy names as Izod, Pickering and Hogan.

The Etonic Spectrum. Beautiful, durable and available

in a spectrum of 31 colors. Truly a stroke of genius.

Spectrum

◉Etonic®

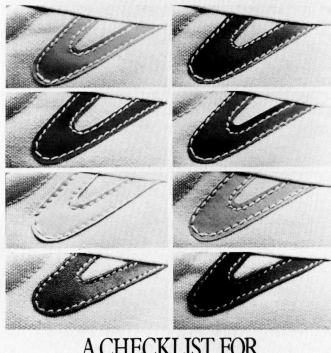

A CHECKLIST FOR GOING BACK TO COLLEGE.

TRETORN®
THE ULTIMATE TENNIS SHOE.

131		132	
Art Director	John Doyle, Rockport, MA	Art Director	John Doyle, Rockport, MA
Designer	John Doyle	Designers	John Doyle, Sue Snitzer
Photographer	Bob Olivera	Photographer	Bob Olivera
Writers	Phillipa Ewing, Ted Charron	Writer	Ted Charron
Client	Etonic	Client	Tretorn
Agency	Creamer, Inc.	Publisher	Seventeen Magazine
Publication	Golf Digest	Agency	Creamer Inc.

DANSKIN FOR THOSE WHO LIVE TO DANCE

GOLD AWARD

134

Art Director	**Michael Wolf**
Photographer	**Richard Avedon**
Writer	**Anita Madeira**
Client	**Danskin, Inc.**
Agency	**Grey Advertising, Inc.,**
	New York
Publication	**Dance Magazine**

DANSKIN ✗ FOR THOSE WHO LIVE TO DANCE™

GOLD AWARD

134

Art Director	**Michael Wolf**
Photographer	**Richard Avedon**
Writer	**Anita Madeira**
Client	**Danskin, Inc.**
Agency	**Grey Advertising, Inc., New York**
Publication	**Dance Magazine**

An ingredient not found in most other frozen onion rings.

Mrs. Paul's® is the only major brand of onion rings that uses real, whole sliced onions. The others are made from onions that have been ground up, extruded and molded to look like onion rings.

And unlike these other brands, Mrs. Paul's contains no artificial additives.

So every time you bite into a Mrs. Paul's onion ring, you get nothing but real, delicious onion taste.

And Mrs. Paul's onion rings go great with anything from hamburgers and hot dogs, to steak and chicken. Or just as a snack.

So use the coupon and pick up a box. You'll see for yourself how good the real thing tastes.

Mrs. Paul's®
It tastes good because it is good.

Save 15¢ on Mrs. Paul's Onion Rings.

15¢   11162 970310   15¢

How to turn your exercise cycle into something useful.

You told everyone it was the muggers. And the lousy weather. And all that traffic. Of course you wanted to exercise, but New York is not the place to run. Or even to ride.

So you went out and bought an exercise bike and set it up at home. That was the most exercise you ever got from it.

The excuses range from: "I have no time." "It's too much trouble." "I keep forgetting."

The only thing you can't blame are the muggers.

The trouble is you know muscles should be exercised. And the most important muscle to exercise is your heart.

That's where we come in. Cardio-Fitness Systems.

We offer individualized programs for men and women designed to strengthen your heart and lungs.

To reduce your weight and lower your pulse rate and blood pressure. To increase your physical and mental endurance.

A program of safe exercises done under professional guidance. We review your progress constantly, always setting new goals for you. All this takes place in a modern, attractive environment.

It's no wonder corporations like American Express, Bankers Trust, Time, Inc., Revlon and Seagram send us their

people. And why our membership includes over 100 chief executive officers.

Another reason why over 90% of our members renew is that we make it so easy.

No gym bag to lug around. We supply fresh shorts, shirts and socks daily. You come at your convenience. There's never a wait. You're in and out in less than an hour.

As for your bike, you could always turn it into a nifty lamp table. A chrome spinning wheel. Or a sculpture labeled simply, "Unused Bicycle, circa 1983."

For more information call or come in.

Cardio-Fitness Center

Wall Street Area: 79 Maiden Lane. (212) 943-1510.
Midtown: 1221 Avenue of the Americas, McGraw-Hill Bldg. at Rockefeller Center. (212) 840-8240.
345 Park Ave. (Entrance on 52nd Street). (212) 838-4570.

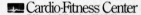

DISTINCTIVE MERIT

	135		136
Art Director	Cathi Mooney	Art Director	Allen Kay
Writer	Jamie Shevell	Photographer	Steve Steigman
Client	Mrs. Paul's Kitchens, Inc.	Writer	Lois Korey
Agency	Scali, McCabe, Sloves, New York	Client	Dr. Jerome Zuckerman/ Cardio-Fitness Systems
		Agency	Korey, Kay & Partners, New York
		Publication	Avenue Magazine

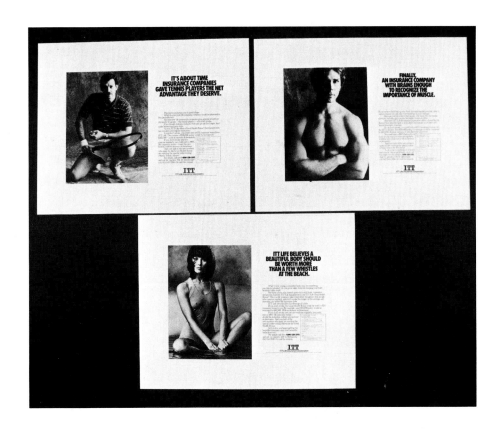

DISTINCTIVE MERIT

	137		138

Art Director   Nancy Rice

Designer   Nancy Rice

Photographers   Dick Jones, Larry Robins

Writer   Tom McElligott

Client   ITT Life Insurance Corporation

Agency   Fallon McElligott Rice, Minneapolis

Publication   The Discus

Art Director   Carlos Torres

Artists   Paul Giovanopoulos, Christine Middleton

Writers   Neal Martineau, Karen Mallia

Client   General Foods Nutrition

Agency   Ogilvy & Mather Advertising, New York

Creative Director   Malcolm End

SOMETHING IS WRONG WHEN A SIZE 34 WAIST PAYS THE SAME INSURANCE AS A SIZE 48 WAIST.

HOW MUCH WEIGHT DO YOU HAVE TO LOSE BEFORE YOUR INSURANCE COMPANY NOTICES IT?

ITT LIFE OFFERS YOU ANOTHER INCENTIVE TO RUN: MONEY.

SILVER AWARD

139

Art Directors	**Dean Hanson, Nancy Rice**
Designer	**Nancy Rice**
Photographers	**Bob Adelman, Larry Robins, Ibid, Inc.**
Writer	**Tom McElligott**
Client	**ITT Life Insurance**
Agency	**Fallon McElligott Rice, Minneapolis**
Publication	**American Health**

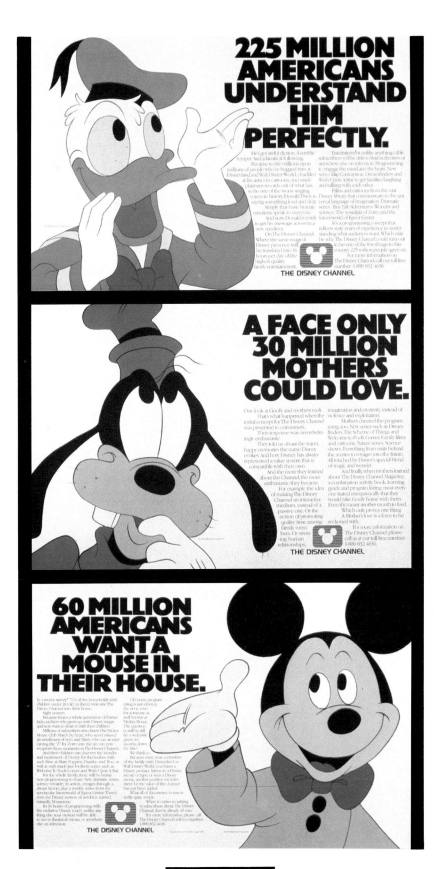

SILVER AWARD

140

Art Director **Yvonne Smith**
Writer **Jocelyn Weisdorf**
Client **The Disney Channel**
Agency **Chiat/Day, Los Angeles**

IMAGINE YOUR TOWN LIVING HAPPILY IN SPACE.

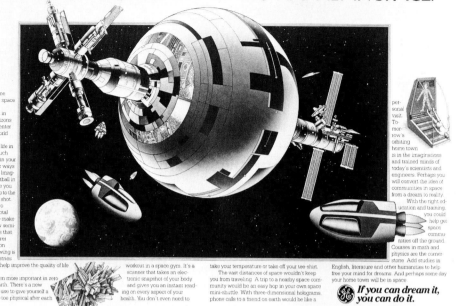

There's a home town like yours in space orbit right now.

You can see it in Florida at the Horizons Pavilion, Epcot Center in Walt Disney World Resort.

In some ways life in that town isn't much different from life in your town. But in other ways it's very different. Imagine playing basketball in zero gravity where you can literally float up to the basket for a layup shot.

That same zero gravity—and the total vacuum of space—make it possible to grow semi-conductor crystals that are bigger and purer than those made on earth. Crystal growing is one of many industries in space that can help improve the quality of life on our planet.

Exercise is even more important in zero gravity than on earth. There's a new system you could use to give yourself a complete head-to-toe physical after each workout in a space gym. It's a scanner that takes an electronic snapshot of your body and gives you an instant reading on every aspect of your health. You don't even need to take your temperature or take off your tee-shirt.

The vast distances of space wouldn't keep you from traveling. A trip to a nearby space community would be an easy hop in your own space mini-shuttle. With three-dimensional holograms, phone calls to a friend on earth would be like a personal visit.

Tomorrow's orbiting home town is in the imaginations and trained minds of today's scientists and engineers. Perhaps you will convert the idea of communities in space from a dream to reality.

With the right education and training, you could help get space communities off the ground. Courses in math and physics are the cornerstone. Add studies in English, literature and other humanities to help free your mind for dreams. And perhaps some day your home town will be in space.

GE ***If you can dream it, you can do it.***

It's a marvel of German engineering.

Starting at the top:
The top of a Volkswagen Rabbit Convertible is a symphony of old fashioned hand fitting and space age weather resistant padding, virtually eliminating wind noise and moisture.

It even has a proper glass rear window that's electrically heated.

The body is made at the Karmann Coachworks in Osnabrück, West Germany where human hands still outnumber machines.

Examine it closely: body panels fit. Doors close flush. And you can see your face in the bright enamel finish. Its engine? A temple of efficiency: 1.7 liters. Fuel injected.

Steering: Rack-and-pinion. Front suspension: MacPherson strut.

So as you can see, the Volkswagen is really the most technologically sophisticated 4 passenger German convertible you can buy.

But then again....

Nothing else is a Volkswagen

Who cares?

141	
Art Director	**George Zipparo**
Artist	**Ed Lindlof**
Writer	**Paul Lippman**
Client	**General Electric**
Agency	**Marsteller Inc., New York**
Creative Director	**Joseph A. Mackenna**

142	
Art Directors	**Gary Goldsmith, Joe DeMare, Ken Amaral**
Designers	**Gary Goldsmith, Joe DeMare, Ken Amaral**
Photographers	**Carl Furuta, Guy Morrison**
Writers	**Irwin Warren, D.J. Webster, Jim McKennan**
Client	**Volkswagen**
Agency	**Doyle Dane Bernbach Inc., New York**
Publication	**Time Magazine**

143

Art Director	**Robert Manley**
Designer	**Robert Manley**
Photographer	**Rob Van Petten**
Artist	**Mark Fisher**
Writer	**Dan Altman**
Client	**Sweet Micro Systems**
Agency	**Altman & Manley, Inc., Cambridge, MA**
Publication	**Softalk**

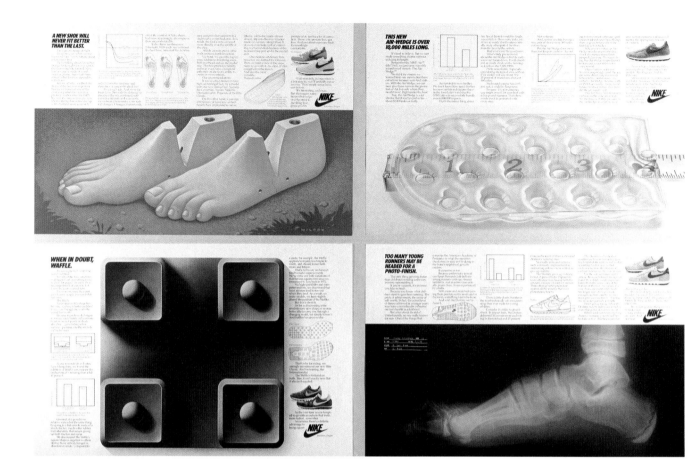

GOLD AWARD

144

Art Director **David Kennedy**
Writer **Dan Wieden**
Client **Nike, Inc.**
Agency **Wieden & Kennedy,
Portland**

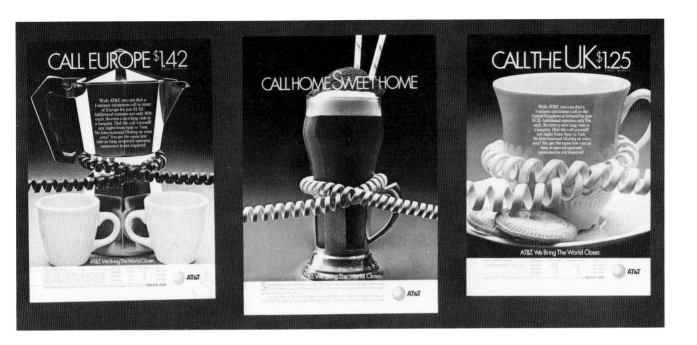

145		146	
Art Director	Rene Kuypers	Art Director	Bruce Bennett Kramer
Photographer	Andre Unangst	Designer	Bruce Bennett Kramer
Writer	Dolores Hanan	Photographer	Harry DeZitter
Client	AT&T Communications	Writer	Bruce McCall
	Intl./Kim Armstrong,	Client	Robert Owens/
	Phil Shyposh		Mercedes-Benz of
Agency	NW Ayer Incorporated,		North America, Inc.
	New York	Agency	McCaffrey and McCall,
Creative			Inc., New York
Director	Ron Salzberg		

DISTINCTIVE MERIT

	147		148
Art Director	George D'Amato	Art Directors	Pat Burnham, Nick Rice
Photographer	Irving Penn	Photographers	William Albert Allard, David Muench
Writer	Herb Green	Writer	Bill Miller
Client	Beatrice Dautresme/ L'Oreal/COSMAIR	Client	U S West
Agency	McCann-Erickson, New York	Agency	Fallon McElligott Rice, Minneapolis

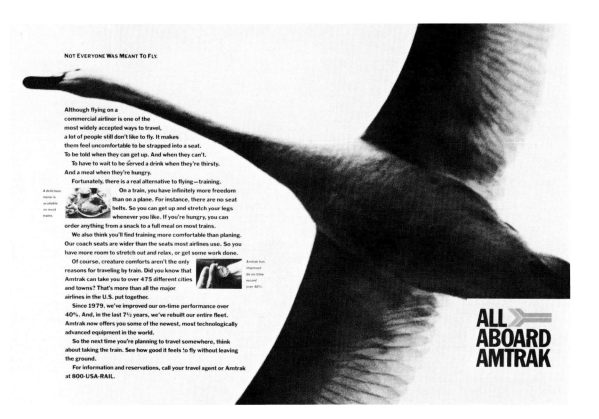

NOT EVERYONE WAS MEANT TO FLY.

Although flying on a commercial airliner is one of the most widely accepted ways to travel, a lot of people still don't like to fly. It makes them feel uncomfortable to be strapped into a seat. To be told when they can get up. And when they can't.

To have to wait to be served a drink when they're thirsty. And a meal when they're hungry.

Fortunately, there is a real alternative to flying—training.

A delicious menu is available on most trains.

On a train, you have infinitely more freedom than on a plane. For instance, there are no seat belts. So you can get up and stretch your legs whenever you like. If you're hungry, you can order anything from a snack to a full meal on most trains.

We also think you'll find training more comfortable than planing. Our coach seats are wider than the seats most airlines use. So you have more room to stretch out and relax, or get some work done.

Of course, creature comforts aren't the only reasons for traveling by train. Did you know that Amtrak can take you to over 475 different cities and towns? That's more than all the major airlines in the U.S. put together.

Amtrak has improved its on-time record over 40%.

Since 1979, we've improved our on-time performance over 40%. And, in the last 7½ years, we've rebuilt our entire fleet. Amtrak now offers you some of the newest, most technologically advanced equipment in the world.

So the next time you're planning to travel somewhere, think about taking the train. See how good it feels to fly without leaving the ground.

For information and reservations, call your travel agent or Amtrak at 800-USA-RAIL.

ALL ABOARD AMTRAK

149	
Art Director	**Paul Frahm**
Writer	**Michael Robertson**
Client	**National Railroad Passenger Corporation**
Agency	**Needham, Harper & Steers, New York**

150	
Art Director	**Gail Daniels**
Designer	**Gail Daniels**
Photographer	**Michael Ives**
Writers	**Angus McQueen, Jeff Nauser**
Client	**Food & Wines from France**
Agency	**Ackerman & McQueen, Oklahoma City, OK**

All work and no play, let's face it, can be hazardous to your peace of mind.

All those responsibilities. And decisions. And deadlines.

All those things that a Royal Caribbean cruise isn't.

What a Royal Caribbean cruise is, is a vacation in the real sense of the word.

You'll spend sunny days in a floating luxury resort. Where you'll be fed, entertained, and unabashedly pampered.

And you'll visit places so far removed from the workaday world, you'll barely remember what it was like to worry.

It's no wonder we've taken more people on 14-day Caribbean cruises than all the other cruise lines, combined.

And we can take you, too. Just ask your travel agent about our air/sea cruise vacations for seven, eight, ten or fourteen days, year-round from Miami.

After all, you've been working long and hard. It's time to reap a few of the rewards.

ROYAL ✠ CARIBBEAN
Song of Norway, Song of America, Nordic Prince, Sun Viking
Ships of Norwegian Registry

Sign Up For Two Weeks Of Workmen's Compensation.

DISTINCTIVE MERIT

151

Art Director	**Larry Bennett**
Photographers	**Randy Miller, Tom McCarthy**
Writers	**Michael Malone, Harriet Frye**
Client	**Royal Caribbean Cruise Lines**
Agency	**McKinney, Silver & Rockett, Raleigh, NC**

DISTINCTIVE MERIT

152

Art Director	**Mike Moser**
Writers	**Steve Hayden, Gary Gusick**
Client	**Apple Computer**
Agency	**Chiat/Day, Los Angeles**

WHY A TENNIS PLAYER AND A GOLFER NEED DIFFERENT VITAMINS TO KEEP IN THE SWING.

About the only similarity between tennis and golf is the shape of the ball.

What is the reason for two new very specially formulated Wilson sports vitamin programs.

Each packet contains what your sport demands most.

As no single vitamin could ever do.

FOR TENNIS PLAYERS, bursts of energy, resistance to joint and tendon injury, increased endurance and hand-eye coordination and replenishment of valuable electrolytes lost through perspiration.

FOR GOLFERS, steady nerves, sustained endurance, concentration and resistance to back injury, allergies and sun exposure.

You'll find these 2 new vitamin programs in 14 and 30-day supplies right next to our new pre-game energy diet and protein powders.

So whether you exercise on the court or off the tee, depend on us. We know what a body needs.

Call or write for free brochure.

Wilson
Sports Vitamins

Sports Nutrition Company

WHY A SWIMMER AND A RUNNER NEED DIFFERENT VITAMINS TO GO THE DISTANCE.

About the only similarity between swimming and running is they occur on the same planet.

Which is the reason for 2 new, specially formulated Wilson sports vitamin programs.

Each packet provides what your sport demands most.

As no single vitamin could ever do.

FOR SWIMMERS, increasing stamina, neutralizing chemical effects on body tissue and resisting cramping and fatigue.

FOR RUNNERS, resisting ligament and tendon injury, increasing aerobic metabolism and preventing dehydration.

You'll find these 2 new vitamin programs in 14 and 30-day supplies right next to our

new pre-game energy diet and protein powders.

So whether you exercise in the water or on the road, depend on us. We know what a body needs.

Call or write for free brochure.

Wilson
Sports Vitamins

WHY A BODY BUILDER AND AN AEROBICISER NEED DIFFERENT VITAMINS TO KEEP IN SHAPE.

About the only similarity between body building and aerobics is perspiration.

Which is the reason for 2 new, specially formulated Wilson sports vitamin programs.

Each packet provides what your sport demands most.

As no single vitamin could ever do.

FOR BODY BUILDERS, optimum muscular development,

an equally strong bone, ligament and tendon framework and the conversion of cramp-producing lactic acid into an energy source.

FOR AEROBICS, a strong heart and lung capacity, active aerobic metabolism and resistance to fatigue and joint, tendon and ligament problems.

You'll find these 2 new vitamin programs in 14 and 30-day supplies

right next to our new pre-game energy diet and protein powders.

So whether your exercise builds up or trims down, depend on us. We know what a body needs.

Call or write for free brochure.

Wilson
Sports Vitamins

Sports Nutrition Company

153

Art Directors	**Ken Sakoda, Randy Papke**
Designer	**Reyes Art Works**
Photographer	**Lamb & Hall, Greg Fulton**
Writer	**Scott Montgomery**
Client	**Vita Fresh Vitamin Co.**
Agency	**Salvati Montgomery Sakoda, Santa Ana, CA**

154		155	
Art Director/ Creative Spvsr.	**Rudolph Valentini**	Art Director	**Robert Manley**
Photographers	**Jerry Friedman, Andrew Unangst, Roy Coggin**	Photographers	**Clint Clemens, Jim Matusik, John Pfahl**
Writer	**Winkie Donovan**	Writer	**Dan Altman**
Client	**Candy McNamara, Nes Cockburn**	Client	**Nielson Moulding Design**
Agency	**Benton & Bowles, New York**	Agency	**Altman & Manley, Inc., Cambridge, MA**
Group Head/ Copywriter	**Ritch Kassof**	Publication	**Decor Magazine**

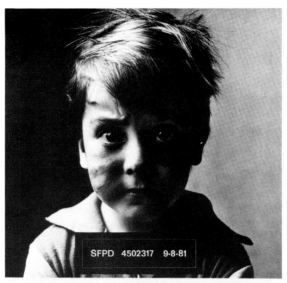

4 out of 5 convicts were abused children.

In the United States, an average of 80% of our prisoners were abused children. That is why we are working so hard to help these children today, before they develop into a threat to others tomorrow.

With your support, we can have a full staff of trained people available 24 hours a day. Abused children desperately need us. Please let us be there to help. Write for our free brochure, or send in your tax-deductible donation today.

San Francisco Child Abuse Council, Inc.
4093 24th Street, San Francisco, CA 94114

DISTINCTIVE MERIT

156		157	
Art Director	Richard Avedon	Art Director	Diane R. Lozito
Photographer	Richard Avedon	Designer	Diane R. Lozito
Writer	Doon Arbus	Photographer	Walter Swarthout
Client	Mary Lee Fletcher, Christian Dior - New York, Inc.	Writer	Diane R. Lozito
Agency	J. Walter Thompson, New York	Agency	Diane R. Lozito Advertising, New York

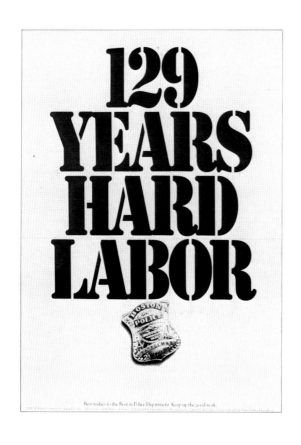

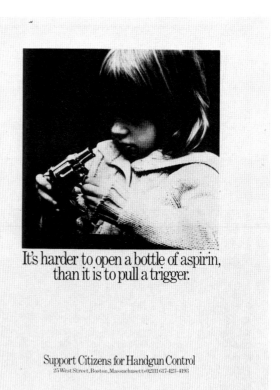

It's harder to open a bottle of aspirin,
than it is to pull a trigger.

Support Citizens for Handgun Control
25 West Street, Boston, Massachusetts 02111 617-423-4190

Now that the Sylvania Superset
has been voted best color picture for the 7th year in a row,
we realize there's nothing more impressive we could say.

158	159	160
Art Director **Patrick Flaherty**	Art Director **Timothy Ryan**	Art Director **Ernie Cox**
Writer **Peter Nichols**	Designer **Timothy Ryan**	Designer **Ernie Cox**
Client **Hill, Holliday, Connors,**	Photographer **Carrie Cook**	Artist **Tamara Lee Cox**
Cosmopulos, Inc.	Writer **Carrie Cook**	Writer **Jeff Linder**
Agency **Hill, Holliday, Connors,**	Client **Citizens for Handgun**	Client **GTE/Sylvania**
Cosmopulos, Inc.,	**Control**	Agency **Doyle Dane Bernbach**
Boston	Agency **Timothy Ryan Art**	**Inc., New York**
	Direction, Brighton, MA	
	Publication **Cambridge Advocate**	

NETWORK TELEVISION HAS BEEN BITTEN.

Ouch! Cable has slithered into the picture and taken a big bite out of the networks' audience.

In 1979, the networks' share of prime-time viewers was 92%. A recent survey shows it has been nibbled down to 77%. At that rate, only 60% will remain by 1990.

The most painful part is that your advertising feels the bite, too.

Fortunately, there's a sure way to ease the pain. You can advertise more in magazines.

Magazine readership is stronger than ever in cable homes.

In fact, a new national survey points out that readership is strongest in homes with 36-channel cable. The biggest magazine readers are the people who watch network the least.

Put more teeth in your media schedule. Advertise more in magazines.

MPA Magazine Publishers Association

MAGAZINES REACH PEOPLE YOU CAN'T GET THROUGH ORDINARY CHANNELS.

Presenting the Nikon line.

One of Nikon's greatest years.

This has been an unprecedented year for Nikon cameras, lenses, accessories, and binoculars.

Obviously, there's more than one reason for our success in the marketplace, but none more important, we believe, than product innovation.

The world's most innovative line of cameras.

No group of cameras in the history of photography has offered so many significant contributions to more types of photographers than Nikon's current line of cameras.

For example, the Nikon FA. The first and only camera in the world with Automatic Multi-Pattern metering. Or the FE2. The world's first automatic camera with a 1/4000 shutter speed. Or the FM2. The world's fastest manual SLR.

Or consider the Nikon One-Touch. Which is the first compact autofocus camera that allows your customer to take flash pictures spontaneously. Or the F3. The most advanced camera/motor drive combination in the history of photography. Or the Nikonos IV-A. The first automatic underwater/all weather 35mm.

Each of these breakthroughs is made possible because of Nikon's dedication to not only making a product that functions, but one that inspires.

The line that keeps on getting better.

The Nikon line on our graph keeps improving, because we never stop improving the Nikon line. No matter what segment of your market there's a Nikon camera engineered to go beyond the restrictions imposed by lesser cameras.

Which is why Nikon is not only the choice of professionals, but the choice of many beginners and serious amateurs as well.

The Nikon line. It looks good no matter how you look at it.

Nikon
We take the world's greatest pictures.

161		162	
Art Directors	Gus Pitsikoulis, Peter Bemis	Art Director	Mark Erwin
Writers	Joey Reiman, Jonathan Cranin	Writer	Earl Carter
Agency	D'Arcy MacManus & Masius, New York	Client	Nikon, Inc.
		Agency	Scali, McCabe, Sloves, New York

To sell a superior professional camera you have to start at the bottom.

When Nikon first introduced the F3 we didn't say very much about the motor drive. Frankly, we didn't have enough of them to go around.

In a way, that was a shame. Because to truly understand how extraordinary the F3 really is, you have to know about its motor drive.

So we've listed a few facts about the motor drive that you probably didn't know about. As well as a few facts about the F3 that you may not have been aware of.

After reading these facts, we're sure you'll have an even better understanding of why the F3 and its motor drive is the most advanced camera/motor drive combination in the history of 35mm photography.

Motor drive and camera designed as one unit.

The balance between the Nikon F3 and its motor drive is so remarkable, you can actually place most lenses up to 200mm on the camera, set it down, and it won't tip over. Try doing that with any other camera/motor drive.

The hand grip on the motor drive is also contoured so the pro can shoot with one hand if necessary. And to take the bumps and jolts of daily professional use, the motor drive is constructed of the same exterior metal used in the camera body.

Up to 5,000 exposures with one set of batteries.

As soon as you attach the motor drive to the Nikon F3, the camera disconnects its internal camera batteries and gets all its power from the motor drive's batteries.

Remarkably, with only one set of eight penlight alkaline-manganese batteries, the F3 with motor drive will give your customer up to 5,000 exposures. Which amounts to 140 rolls of 36-exposure film.

All other camera/motor drive combinations give about half that number. Yet use more batteries.

Up to six frames-per-second with NiCad battery pack.

The F3's incredibly efficient film-advance mechanism and extensive use of ball bearings enables the F3 to fire (mirror up) at the amazing rate of six frames-per-second

with the optional MN-2 NiCad battery pack.

That's one frame-per-second faster than anyone else.

Your customer will also be able to rewind a 36-exposure roll in less than five seconds with the NiCad battery pack.

The most exciting camera a motor drive can get attached to.

The F3 is the camera that only Nikon's decades of experience could have produced. Modern Photography wrote, "...for the Nikon enthusiast the F3 represents a perfection in design, construction, enjoyment, and handling never before achieved." The following are just some of its incredible features.

Full manual control with quartz timing.

With any of its 15 manual shutter speeds, the F3 offers the pro precision timing so accurate it's actually measurable to the fourth decimal place.

This accuracy would be impossible to achieve by mechanical means alone.

And just as important. The quartz oscillator is impervious to temperature extremes and fluctuations in voltage.

True automatic bracketing.

Now the pro can bracket in automatic just as easily as he or she would in manual. The F3's memory lock button allows your customer to freeze the automatic shutter speed and then vary apertures to bracket exposures.

No other top-of-the-line camera has this feature.

Exclusive center-weighted pattern for more accurate metering.

Nikon has developed an advanced center-weighted metering pattern for the F3 that gives the professional approximately 80% sensitivity in the 12mm circle found on most Nikon focusing screens.

With this exclusive pattern, the pro is able to achieve superior selective metering in both the manual and automatic modes. It is ideal for severe lighting conditions such as sidelight, backlight, and spotlight.

100% viewfinder accuracy.

Nikon's camera assembly techniques are so exacting, the F3 is the only 35mm SLR manufactured today with virtually 100% viewfinder accuracy. And that includes every combination of viewfinder and focusing screen designed for the F3.

Accepts the most comprehensive system of lenses in 35mm photography.

Unlike other brands, the F3 accepts the lenses used by the majority of 35mm professional photographers—Nikkor. There are over 60 lenses for your customer to choose from. With focal lengths ranging from 6mm to 2000mm.

Accessories for the F3 include a bulk film back, data back, and Speedlight flash units which provide automatic through-the-lens flash exposure.

So the next time a customer asks to see a superior professional camera, hand them the camera and motor drive that's turning the world of photography upside down.

The Nikon F3 with motor drive.

Nikon
We take the world's greatest pictures.

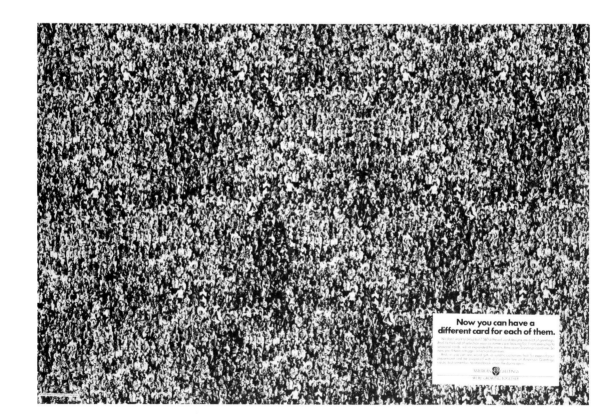

Now you can have a different card for each of them.

<table>
<tr><td colspan="2" align="center">163</td></tr>
<tr><td align="right">Art Director</td><td>Simon Bowden</td></tr>
<tr><td align="right">Writer</td><td>Earl Carter</td></tr>
<tr><td align="right">Client</td><td>Nikon, Inc.</td></tr>
<tr><td align="right">Agency</td><td>Scali, McCabe, Sloves,
New York</td></tr>
</table>

<table>
<tr><td colspan="2" align="center">164</td></tr>
<tr><td align="right">Art Director</td><td>Garrett Jewett</td></tr>
<tr><td align="right">Designer</td><td>Garrett Jewett</td></tr>
<tr><td align="right">Photographer</td><td>Stock</td></tr>
<tr><td align="right">Writer</td><td>Diane Sinnott</td></tr>
<tr><td align="right">Client</td><td>American Greetings</td></tr>
<tr><td align="right">Agency</td><td>Doyle Dane Bernbach
Inc., New York</td></tr>
</table>

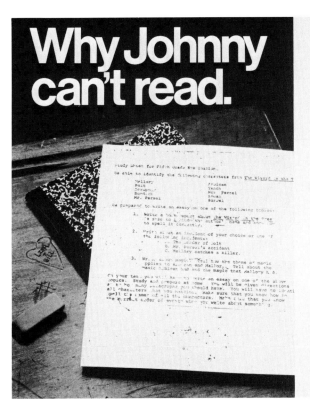

Why Johnny can't read.

 XEROX

As you can see, the illegible can make anyone feel like a slow reader.

And copies that can't be read practically guarantee an assignment that won't make the grade.

So we'd like to suggest a clear alternative to these blurred images. The Xerox Instructional System.

It's based on copiers, of course. Like our 9200, 8200, 7000 and 2400 models that set the standard for clear, crisp copies. With blacker blacks than you'll ever get from those traditional duplicating methods. Which means even children handicapped with "blue vision" read easier.

The 8200

And our Xerox 8200 can run off 70 collated copies a minute. But the Xerox Instructional System goes beyond copying someone else's work.

With it, teachers have the flexibility to create a range of truly original study aids. From overhead transparencies to automatic test correctors.

And no matter how tight your budget is, you'll be pleased by the new math developed by Xerox especially for K-12 schools. We'll not only show how affordable our system is. We'll demonstrate the total costs in the system you're using now.

The Xerox Instructional System even includes our Memory-writer Typewriter. With the latest in electronic features that make it ideal for classroom training.  **Memorywriter**

Backing it all up are our education specialists. They go beyond just making sales by conducting free In-Service Training sessions for teachers. And they can keep you well-stocked with the Xerox paper products and supplies that keep our machines running at their best.

To give your school or district the Xerox Edge in education, give us a call. Or mail in this coupon.

It may be just the edge Johnny needs to catch up on his reading. Call 800-648-5888, operator 614.

The 9200, 8200, 7000 and 2400 model copiers are remanufactured. Other Xerox copiers are either newly manufactured or remanufactured.

Who says you can't find an outfit that stretches without Fortrel?

You can. But when you want durability, fabric versatility, and performance too, E.S.P® yarn of Celanese Fortrel® polyester is man's best friend.

CELANESE FORTREL

165		**166**	
Art Director	**Joanne Pateman**	Art Director	**Paul Guayante**
Writer	**Sharon Lewis**	Designer	**Paul Guayante**
Client	**Xerox Corporation**	Artist	**Jozef Sumichrast**
Agency	**Needham, Harper & Steers, New York**	Writer	**Dan Brooks**
		Client	**Celanese**
		Agency	**Doyle Dane Bernbach Inc., New York**
		Publication	**Daily News Record**

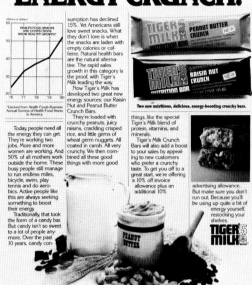

HOW TO PROFIT FROM THE COMING ENERGY CRUNCH.

Today, people need all the energy they can get. They're working two jobs. More and more women are working. And 50% of all mothers work outside the home. These busy people still manage to run endless miles, bicycle, swim, play tennis and do aerobics. Active people like this are always seeking something to boost their energy.

Traditionally, that took the form of a candy bar. But candy isn't so sweet to a lot of people anymore. Over the past 10 years, candy con-

sumption has declined 15%. Yet Americans still love sweet snacks. What they don't love is when the snacks are laden with empty calories or caffeine. Natural health bars are the natural alternative. The rapid sales growth in this category is the proof, with Tiger's Milk leading the way.

Now Tiger's Milk has developed two great new energy sources: our Raisin Nut and Peanut Butter Crunch Bars.

They're loaded with crunchy peanuts, juicy raisins, crackling crisped rice, and little gems of wheat germ nuggets. All coated in carob. All very crunchy. We then combined all these good things with more good

things, like the special Tiger's Milk blend of protein, vitamins, and minerals.

Tiger's Milk Crunch Bars will also add a boost to your sales by appealing to new customers who prefer a crunchy taste. To get you off to a great start, we're offering a 10% off invoice allowance plus an additional 10%

advertising allowance. But make sure you don't run out. Because you'll be using up quite a bit of energy yourself, restocking your shelves.

Two new nutritious, delicious, energy-boosting crunchy bars.

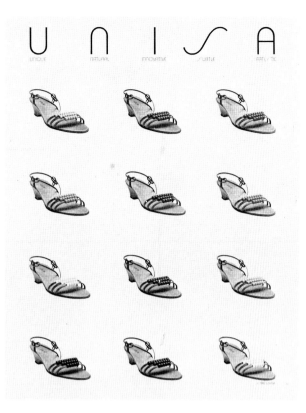

IT TAKES MORE THAN BIG CHESTS AND NICE JUGS TO ATTRACT CUSTOMERS.

We're doing everything imaginable to make Thermos® chests and jugs more appealing and noticeable than ever.

On television, we're showing them off in a commercial that's going to be an unqualified hit. You'll see it during everything from The Today Show to Family Feud.

In People Magazine our consumer advertising will reach millions of people.

New 4-sided self-sell packaging will more effectively display one of our best features: The Thermos name.

Our products have been redesigned and given a new look.

Rebates of up to $5 will also be offered on selected coolers. In short, Thermos is going to keep things hot for you all summer.

® Thermos is a registered trademark of the King-Seeley Thermos Co. Thermos Division King-Seeley Thermos Co., Norwalk, CT 06360 (203) 887-1671.

THERMOS.
We're putting the heat on.

167

Art Director	**Sal DeVito**
Designer	**Sal DeVito**
Photographer	**Cailor/Resnick**
Writer	**Morleen Novitt**
Client	**Plus Products**
Agency	**Slater Hanft Martin, Inc., New York**

168

Art Director	**Leslie Silvas**
Photographer	**Dave Haggerty**
Writer	**Charles Dragonette**
Client	**UNISA**
Agency	**Rumrill-Hoyt, New York**
Publication	**Harper's Bazaar**

169

Art Director	**Bill Puckett**
Designer	**Bill Puckett**
Photographer	**Stuart Heir**
Writer	**John Schmidt**
Client	**King-Seeley Thermos Company**
Agency	**Calet, Hirsch & Spector, Inc., New York**
Publication	**Discount News**
Creative Director	**Neil Calet**

YOU CAN TELL A RESTAURANT IS A SUCCESS WHEN THERE'S A FAMOUS NAME AT EVERY TABLE.

When you put Heinz Ketchup on your tables it's a sure sign that you know how to run your business properly, because Heinz is renowned for quality. Customers will assume that if your restaurant offers the best in ketchup, then everything that you serve will meet that same standard. We've already made a name for ourselves, now let us help you make yours.

Heinz

In choosing a superior professional camera you have to start at the bottom.

Once you buy a camera that's intended for professional use, you can only use the motor drive that's made for it.

Which can be unfortunate if the motor drive isn't engineered to meet the demands of professional photographers.

In short, to have a superior professional camera you have to have a superior motor drive. Which leads us to the Nikon F3HP (High-Eye-point) with motor drive: the most advanced camera/motor drive combination in the history of photography.

Up to 5,000 exposures with one set of batteries.

As soon as you attach the motor drive to the F3HP, the camera disconnects its internal camera batteries and gets all its power from the motor drive's batteries.

Remarkably, with only one set of eight alkaline-manganese penlight batteries, the F3HP with motor drive gives you up to 5,000 exposures.

Up to six frames-per-second.

The F3HP allows you to fire (mirror up) at the amazing rate of six frames-per-second with the optional MX-2 NiCad battery pack. That's one frame-per-second faster than anyone else.

Full manual control with quartz timing.

With any of its 15 manual shutter speeds, the F3HP offers you precision timing so accurate it's actually measurable to the fourth decimal place.

When in automatic, however, you don't have to switch back to manual to bracket. The F3HP's memory lock button allows you to freeze the automatic shutter speed which lets you vary apertures to bracket your exposures.

Exclusive center-weighted pattern.

Nikon has developed an advanced center-weighted metering pattern for the F3HP that gives you approximately 80% sensitivity in the 12mm circle found on most Nikon focusing screens.

100% viewfinder accuracy.

The F3HP is the only 35mm SLR made today with virtually 100% viewfinder accuracy. And for more comfortable viewing, the F3HP allows you to see the entire image area and exposure display with your eye as much as an inch away from the eyepiece. Which makes the F3HP ideal for photographers who wear eyeglasses. Or who like to shoot with their sunglasses on.

So ask your favorite Nikon dealer to hand you a Nikon F3HP with motor drive. And find out what's turning the world of photography upside down.

Nikon
We take the world's greatest pictures.

Objection.

Can we make a case for using the IBM Displaywriter? After all, it is the best-selling stand-alone text processor.

Examine the facts.

With the new Legal Dictionary, the Displaywriter can check and provide the correct spelling for up to 16,000 legal terms.

With software like Reportpack, it can help track time and expense items. And produce final client bills.

What's more, it can exchange information with other IBM office systems. As well as with IBM host computers.

Overruled.

But best of all, the Displaywriter can help revise, edit, reformat, file, footnote, and even process data in minutes. So things won't pile up for days.

Why not try an IBM Displaywriter in your office? It can help speed up the legal process.

To witness a free demonstration of the Displaywriter (the basic model costs just $4990), call your local IBM representative, or IBM toll-free at 1-800-IBM-2468 Ext. 77. Or write to the address below.

IBM

IBM, Dept. 813, DRM, 400 Parson's Pond Drive, Franklin Lakes, NJ 07417.

170		171		172	
Art Director	Michael McLaughlin	Art Director	Simon Bowden	Art Director	Amy Levitan
Designer	Michael McLaughlin	Writer	Earl Carter	Designer	Amy Levitan
Artist	John Martin	Client	Nikon, Inc.	Photographer	Cosimo
Writer	Stephen Creet	Agency	Scali, McCabe, Sloves, New York	Writer	Dean Hacohen
Client	H.J. Heinz Company of Canada Ltd.			Client	IBM
Agency	Carder Gray Advertising Inc., Toronto			Agency	Doyle Dane Bernbach Inc., New York
				Publication	National Law Journal

Our new six pack has more joy for everybody.
It's more of a joy to sell. Because it increases your sales by a third every time you sell one in place of the old four pack.
And more of a joy to drink. Because your customers get an extra swallow of Guinness at no extra cost from our larger (12 full ounces) bottle with new more attractive labeling.

Now that might not seem like earthshaking news to you. But when you've been producing the same excellent all natural brew from the same strain of yeast for 224 years like we have, any change at all is noteworthy.

GUINNESS

THE JOY OF SIX.

Not many people have seen a bottle of Cruzan Rum.
Most of it disappears in the Virgin Islands.

The rest will disappear from your shelves.

This is the new advertising campaign for Cruzan Rum. Beginning in June, it will be appearing in such places as Newsweek, the New York Times Sunday Magazine, Food and Wine, People, Vogue, the America's Cup Program and others. In fact, between June and December, the new Cruzan advertising will make 73 appearances in these and other magazines. But for the ultimate appearance, ask your distributor/salesman to show you the new Cruzan motion display. You'll see the results on your shelves. So stock up now. And watch what happens.

NOT JUST ANOTHER PRETTY FACE.

Mr. T? Pretty?
In the next couple of months, you may think so.
Because action figures of Mr. T and The A-Team® are going on sale in stores across the country right now. We sold our customers these figures as non-televised items, and our customers bought in big quantities.
Now all we have to do is sit back, count our money, and hope. Right?
Well, that's not what we're going to do.
What we're going to do is advertise our A-Team® and Mr. T Action Figures on television.
We'll have an exciting

new commercial for The A-Team® Action Figures which will start running October 31 in 78 markets.
Not only that, but the Mr. T 12-inch Action Figure is going to have a separate commercial and a separate television campaign. It will be advertised in 78 markets, also starting October 31.
Mr. T may not be pretty to look at.
But when our advertising hits, he's going to start looking beautiful.
Lewis Galoob Incorporated, 400 Forbes Boulevard, South San Francisco, California 94080.
Phone (415) 952-1678.

galoob

© 1983 Stephen J. Cannell Productions. All Rights Reserved. ®A Trademark of Stephen J. Cannell Productions. Licensed by Merchandising Corporation of America, Inc.

173	**174**	**175**
Art Director **Joe Petruccio**	Art Directors **Bob Taylor, Paul Boley**	Art Director **Eric Hanson**
Writer **Tony Isidore**	Writers **Ted Bell, Richard Rand**	Photographer **Stan Caplan**
Client **Jim Mullahy, Guinness-Harp Corporation**	Client **Schenley**	Writer **Bob Finley**
Agency **Isidore & Paulson Inc., New York**	Agency **Leo Burnett Co., Inc., Chicago**	Client **David Galoob**
		Agency **Sachs, Finley & Co., Los Angeles**
		Publication **Toy & Hobby World**

They've always been easy to sell. Now they're easy to pour.

Look. No oil spout. Now, with our new, easy-pour, resealable one-quart container, your customer simply unscrews the cap, tips the plastic bottle with the familiar label and pours any of our complete line of five great Mobil products: Mobil 1®, Mobil Super, Mobil Special, Mobil Heavy Duty or Mobil ATF 220.

So now our high-profit line will sell even faster. Because do-it-yourselfers not only can get the products they recognize and trust. They can get them in either the can or the easy-pour container.

For more information about the products, the containers or the co-op program that helps you sell them and reimburses you at national line rates, just write E. D. Bryant, Manager, Resale Lubricants, Mobil Oil Corporation, 3225 Gallows Road, Fairfax, Virginia 22037, or simply call him collect at (703) 849-4949. Then give your customers a choice of the choicest

Mobil

Eyes This Good Need A System This Good.

These are some of the best eyes in Twin Cities advertising. Which means they're among the best in the entire country.

They're sharp eyes. Demanding eyes. Eyes that constantly look for ways to make the job look better.

At Colorhouse, we have such a way. It's the Hell Chromacom Digital Page Composition System. Like the eyes you see here, it can make any job look better.

So what's a digital page composition system? It's a way for an art director to cheat electronically. It's the salvation of the so-so shot. It's a computer that can make a good image great.

The computer scans your photo or art and makes an electronic picture of it. You work with this electronic picture, not a transparency on a lightbox. You can retouch, enhance color or dial color back. You can airbrush. You can get in and tinker with the size, position and proportion of any element in the picture.

And when the entire image is exactly right, the computer pulls color separations. No more loupe over the lightbox. No more grease pencil corrections. Just high quality color separations the first time around.

If you count your eyes among the best in town, you'd better lay your eyes on this new system. Just call Colorhouse at 612-929-1321 for a demonstration. Or just ask your Colorhouse rep about the Hell Chromacom Digital Page Composition System.

 Colorhouse

176		177	
Art Director	Hal Tench	Art Director	Kurt Tausche
Designer	Hal Tench	Designer	Kurt Tausche
Photographer	Cailor Resnick	Photographer	Rick Dublin
Writer	Barbara Ford	Writer	Pete Smith
Client	Mobil	Client	Colorhouse, Inc.
Agency	The Martin Agency, Richmond, VA	Agency	One Man Band, Inc., Minneapolis
Publication	Home & Auto		

Our Coffee is Going Places.

We're proud to announce that 100% Colombian Coffee is spilling all over the United States. Now if you think we're referring to the big cities of New York, Los Angeles, and Houston, you're absolutely right. But even more delicious is the fact that our coffee has poured into lots of tiny towns and villages.

Take Chugwater, Wyoming for instance. (Maybe they should change it to Chugcoffee?)

Then there's a whole slew of other places like Opa-Locka, Florida, Bath, New York,

and East Liverpool, Ohio. It seems that our coffee is spreading like wildfire on the stoves of America. (Juan Valdez® and his partner couldn't be happier.)

It's time for you to join this successful program too. By offering a 100% Colombian Coffee brand you can capitalize on the growing demand. And you can make use of our trademark to help you sell even more. Why not? We're even getting requests from Mars. (Mars, Pennsylvania that is.)

National Federation of Coffee Growers of Colombia, 140 East 57th Street, New York, NY 10022

100% Colombian Coffee

Colombian Coffee, tea, or milk.

A number of major airlines are now serving 100% Colombian Coffee on board. And we'd like to congratulate them on their good business sense. Think about it for a moment.

By serving potfuls of 100% Colombian Coffee, the stewardesses will actually seem like angels. And ordinary airplane meals could become heavenly delights. All of this is bound to sit well with the passengers (especially if the passengers are Juan Valdez® and his partner).

Naturally, airlines aren't the only ones who are interested in our delicious coffee. Over the past months, restaurants and supermarkets from all over the country have been pouring in requests for our coffee.

It's time you did something about it. By offering 100% Colombian Coffee, you can capitalize on this demand. And increase your profitability with our premium coffee. In no time at all your business will be soaring like ours.

National Federation of Coffee Growers of Colombia, 140 East 57th Street, New York, New York 10022

100% Colombian Coffee

	178		179
Art Director	**Mark Hughes**	Art Director	**Mark Hughes**
Designer	**Mark Hughes**	Designer	**Mark Hughes**
Photographer	**Larry Robins**	Photographer	**Larry Robins**
Writer	**D.J. Webster**	Writer	**D.J. Webster**
Client	**National Federation of Coffee Growers of Colombia**	Client	**National Federation of Coffee Growers of Colombia**
Agency	**Doyle Dane Bernbach Inc., New York**	Agency	**Doyle Dane Bernbach Inc., New York**

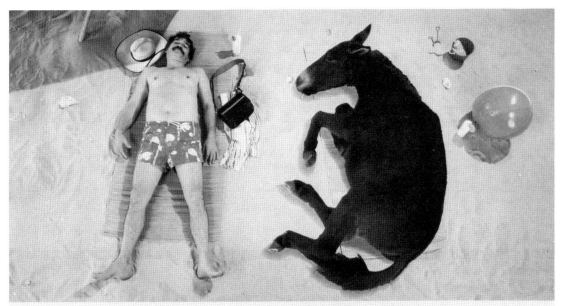

They've earned it.

"My life can't be all coffee. Sometimes there have to be Piña Coladas too," says Juan Valdez." Then he takes off his sombrero, wipes suntan lotion on his face and drifts off to sleep. The Cartagena sun beats down on him and his partner as they enjoy their first real siesta in two years.

They've earned it.

After all, thanks to Juan and his mule, the public awareness of 100% Colombian Coffee has shot up to an incredible 91%.

Furthermore, the statistics show that over half the population believes that Colombian Coffee is the best in the world.

Now's the time for you to act. By offering a 100% Colombian Coffee brand, you can capitalize on the demand for our product. Most of the current brands are already experiencing huge sales increases; one as high as 296%. Carramba! At that rate you'll be able to afford a nice long vacation yourself.

100% Colombian Coffee

180
Art Director   **Mark Hughes**
Designer   **Mark Hughes**
Photographer   **Larry Robins**
Writer   **D.J. Webster**
Client   **National Federation of Coffee Growers of Colombia**
Agency   **Doyle Dane Bernbach Inc., New York**

Please Read This Ad With A Loupe.

Colorhouse

WILL IT COME TO THIS?

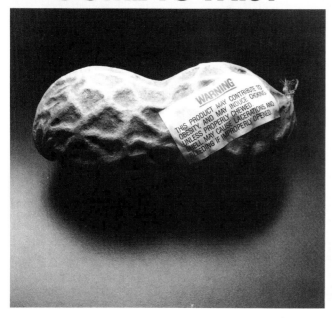

WARNING
THIS PRODUCT MAY CONTRIBUTE TO
OBESITY, AND MAY INDUCE CHOKING
UNLESS PROPERLY CHEWED.
SHELL MAY CAUSE LACERATIONS AND
BLEEDING IF IMPROPERLY OPENED.

Warnings have come a long way since someone had the good sense to put a ☠ on an iodine bottle.

Courts now require warning labels on a whole range of products.

From paint thinner to pajamas.

There have also been rulings on exactly how large such labels should be.

And where they should be.

And what they should say.

And it hasn't stopped at labeling, either.

Requirements relating to all aspects of product safety have mushroomed in recent years.

And while these have been a benefit to consumers, they've often been a problem for manufacturers.

Because even a responsible corporation can face liability by unintentionally overlooking a new regulation or an obscure ruling.

That's why at INA, a CIGNA company, we're prepared to do more than just insure our clients against product liability.

We do everything we can to keep them out of court.

To start with, we have a staff of product liability specialists who can examine every step in the manu-

facturing and marketing process.

From design to advertising.

And we're not only likely to spot weaknesses people within a company may overlook, we're also more likely to spot weaknesses general and less specialized loss control examiners might overlook, as well.

We even look for problems before they occur.

We'll help design a product recall program, for example, to have in place, ready to quickly implement if the need for it ever arises.

And, needless to say, on an ongoing basis, we monitor legislation, court rulings, and agency regulations that can affect our client's liability.

If you'd like more information on this topic, please write to INA at 1600 Arch St., Dept. RA, Philadelphia, Pennsylvania 19101.

Or, if you'd like to know how we can help protect you against product liability exposures, call your agent or broker.

After all, in an area as complex as this one it's entirely possible a consumer isn't the only one who can benefit from a warning. **CIGNA**

181

Art Director	**Kurt Tausche**
Designer	**Kurt Tausche**
Writer	**Pete Smith**
Client	**Colorhouse, Inc.**
Agency	**One Man Band, Inc., Minneapolis**

182

Art Director	**Harvey Baron**
Designer	**Harvey Baron**
Photographer	**Phil Marco**
Writer	**Diane Rothschild**
Client	**CIGNA**
Agency	**Doyle Dane Bernbach Inc., New York**

IN AMERICA THE ARCHITECTS COULD STILL BE LIABLE FOR IT.

They might be hard to find.

But they could be liable.

Because in most states architects can be sued for the work they did no matter how long ago they did it.

And so can engineers.

So if a roof falls in or a floor gives out, they, or their firms, or even their estates, can be brought to court over something built 50 years ago.

Or 150 years ago.

In fact, even if a roof doesn't fall in, architects and engineers can still be involved in a suit.

After a crime in a suburban mall, for example, an architectural firm was actually sued for designing a shopping center that was "conducive to kidnapping."

And if that seems absurd, consider this: an engineer was called in as a consultant on a problem limited to the roof at the Hyatt Hotel in Kansas City. He was later sued for failing to notice structural weakness in the skywalk that collapsed there.

The point of all this is that the threat of professional liability is not only real, but growing.

Which is why, at INA, a CIGNA company, we have a special division dealing exclusively with this risk.

And we'll not only insure architects and engineers for claims made against them while they're our clients, we can even cover their liability for work they did before coming to us.

We'll also provide protection after they retire.

And, maybe most important, we'll do everything we can to help them reduce their likelihood of being sued in the first place.

With seminars and manuals specifically on that topic.

And with a highly specialized in-house claim staff that may well know more about the fine points of design liability than any other group in the business.

If you're interested in this subject and would like more information, please write to Insurance Company of North America at 1600 Arch Street, Dept. RC, Philadelphia, Pa. 19101.

Or if you're an architect or engineer and would like to discuss your specific situation, please call your agent or broker.

After all, you never know when something might go wrong.

CIGNA

FOR SOME RETIRED PEOPLE, STAMP COLLECTING ISN'T A HOBBY.

Not all senior citizens are living in the sun belt worrying about their golf scores.

Too many of them are living on the edge of poverty worrying about making ends meet.

Because today, a Social Security check doesn't go very far.

And even pensions don't always provide enough to sustain people.

Not surprisingly, more and more employees are now taking a hard look at their retirement plans.

And so are their employers.

And the days when people left a company with just a gold watch and a fixed income are farther behind us than ever.

Employers today are not only providing their employees with pensions, they're also offering a range of savings options to give people additional security after retirement.

And at Connecticut General, a CIGNA company, we're particularly well equipped to help in that.

For one thing, we offer all the major tax-advantaged savings plans that are currently available. From plans everybody's heard of like IRA's, to more exotic ones like 401(k)'s.

On top of that, with one of the largest, most experienced staffs in the industry, our Group Pension people can offer a customized program for each of their clients.

They can also offer administrative support, help with employee communications, and exceptional experience in enrollment.

In fact, they're already providing these services to over 5,000 companies with combined pension assets of $12.7 billion.

So if you'd like more information on this topic, please write to Connecticut General, Dept. A-141-B, Hartford, Connecticut 06152.

Or, if you'd like to know what we can offer your corporation, call your broker or local Connecticut General representative.

Because after a lifetime of hard work, people deserve more than years of hard times.

CIGNA

	183		184
Art Director	**Harvey Baron**	Art Director	**Harvey Baron**
Designer	**Harvey Baron**	Designer	**Harvey Baron**
Photographer	**Stock**	Photographer	**Mike O'Neill**
Writer	**Diane Rothschild**	Writer	**Diane Rothschild**
Client	**CIGNA**	Client	**CIGNA**
Agency	**Doyle Dane Bernbach Inc., New York**	Agency	**Doyle Dane Bernbach Inc., New York**

You also won't see no bollworm, no pink bollworm, no tobacco budworm, no leaf perforator, no lygus bugs, no beet armyworm or no cabbage looper.

SEE NO WEEVIL.

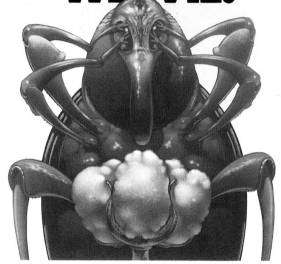

And you won't hear them little buggers, either. **FMC**

HEAR NO WEEVIL.

GOLD AWARD

185

Art Director **Harry Kerker**
Artist **Bob Krogel**
Writers **Bob Ross, Richard D'Andrea**
Agency **Marsteller, Inc., Los Angeles**

Once upon a time there was a cable operator who didn't offer any programming just for kids.

Such a naughty thing to do, his own Fairy Godmother turned him into a frog!

"What shall I do?" he cried.

"To break the spell, you must offer Nickelodeon," she replied.

Call your Nickelodeon® Fairy Godmother today.
New York: Leslye Schaefer 212/944-4770. Chicago: E.A. Buzz' Hassett 312/565-2300.

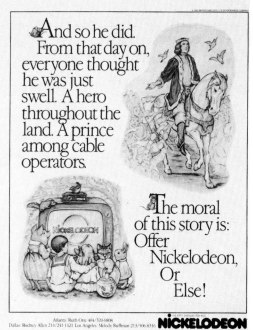

And so he did. From that day on, everyone thought he was just swell. A hero throughout the land. A prince among cable operators.

The moral of this story is: Offer Nickelodeon, Or Else!

Atlanta: Ruth Otte 404/320-6808
Dallas: Rodney Allen 214/241-1421. Los Angeles: Melody Ruffman 213/506-8316.

NICKELODEON

The Pied Piper of Cable Television

Offer the leader in children's cable television. Call your Nickelodeon® Fairy Godmother today. New York: Leslye Schaefer 212/944-4770.
Chicago: E.A. 'Buzz' Hassett 312/565-2300. Atlanta: Ruth Otte 404/320-6808. Dallas: Rodney Allen 214/241-1421. Los Angeles: Melody Ruffman 213/506-8316.

NICKELODEON

186	**187**
Art Director **Mark Moffett**	Art Director **Mark Moffett**
Writer **David Metcalf**	Writer **David Metcalf**
Client **Warner Amex Satellite Entertainment Co.**	Client **Warner Amex Satellite Entertainment Co.**
Agency **Scali, McCabe, Sloves, New York**	Agency **Scali, McCabe, Sloves, New York**

National Bickford
Foremost

GOLD AWARD

188

Art Director	**Tyler Smith**
Designer	**Tyler Smith**
Photographers	**John Goodman, Myron Taplin, Graeme Outerbridge**
Writers	**Geoff Currier, Gail Welch**
Client	**National Bickford Foremost, Providence, RI**

Some folks put things off. Not me. Like the filters
on my tractors. I even change them before I have to.
Then I know it's done.
    And I'm the same way with my beans.
I treat them early with 'Sencor, so I prevent my weed
problem before it gets so bad I have to worry about it.
    I just like to take care of things, because when
I do, I'm doing it on my terms.

SENCOR. Some things just shouldn't be put off.

Grandpa didn't like alarm clocks. He always said,
"You never have to wind a rooster." But I still count
on my clock to sing out at 5 a.m. every morning.
    That's early, but being an early riser is part of
being a farmer.
    It's part of being a weed, too. So I'm out there
in my beans, putting down my 'Sencor early. Earlier
than the weeds. Stayin' ahead. Stayin' in control.
    I don't let the sun come up before I do.
I'm not about to let the weeds do it.

SENCOR. Start early, and come out ahead.

I'm a farmer, not a gambler. I'm not one to take
chances with my livelihood.
    So I'm out there early every year with my
'Sencor, taking care of my weed problem, improving
the odds for my beans.
    You know, when you look at it that way,
maybe I am a gambler.
    Maybe every farmer is.

SENCOR. Keeping the odds in my favor.

SILVER AWARD

189

Art Director	**Bob Jensen**
Designer	**Bob Jensen**
Photographers	**Dick Kruger, Stock**
Writer	**Tom Hansen**
Client	**Mobay Chemical**
Agency	**Valentine-Redford Adv., Kansas City, MO**
Publications	**Farm Journal, Progressive Farmer**

REMEMBER WHEN A NICKEL GOT YOU A LOAF OF BREAD, A QUARTER GOT YOU A HAIRCUT AND $10 MILLION GOT YOU A DECENT NETWORK BUY?

When it comes to buying TV these days, it seems like all you see for $10 Million is spots before your eyes.

So if you think spot TV coverage is spotty at best, now you can cover the USA with USA. The cable network that runs like a broadcast network.

And that means every hour of the day is programmed to the largest available audience. Unlike 24 hour cable programming that programs to one audience whether it's available or not.

Instead, at USA we have a daytime schedule for women. An afternoon schedule for kids. Prime sports for men and late nights for teens. Plus we're adding prime time movies and specials as well as bringing back such classics as "Hitchcock" and "Dragnet."

It's just what's making the USA Network the one to watch. And now the one to buy.

So talk to us soon. We can't help you get a haircut for under $10 and a good loaf of French bread still has its price. But we'll get you a decent network buy for one tenth of $10 Million.

USA
CABLE NETWORK
WE FEATURE A 24 HOUR AUDIENCE

LAURIE JAGLOIS IS HAVING A BABY. JOE SOSA IS HAVING A FIT.

Laurie Jaglois is tops in all areas of print production.

She communicates with art directors, gets the most out of printers and keeps her head under the most ridiculous deadlines.

Unfortunately, Laurie also seems to be good at reproduction.

Which means we need a print production manager.

If you're interested, don't call. Send art director references and your best samples to Joe Sosa, Chiat/Day Advertising, 517 South Olive St., Los Angeles, CA 90013.

But only if you have three to five years experience and all of Laurie's qualities.

Except the craving for pickles and ice cream.

CHIAT/DAY

190

Art Director	**Mark Yustein**
Writer	**Rita Senders**
Client	**U.S.A. Cable Network**
Agency	**Della Femina, Travisano & Ptnrs., New York**

191

Art Director	**Houman Pirdavari**
Writer	**Brent Bouchez**
Client	**Chiat/Day Inc., Advertising**
Agency	**Chiat/Day, Los Angeles**

192	193
Art Director **Mark Moffett**	Art Directors **Anne Occi, Brett Shevack**
Writer **David Metcalf**	Writer **Marc Erickson**
Client **Warner Amex Satellite Entertainment Co.**	Client **Adidas, U.S.A.**
Agency **Scali, McCabe, Sloves, New York**	Agency **LCF&S, New York**

WILL IT COME TO THIS?

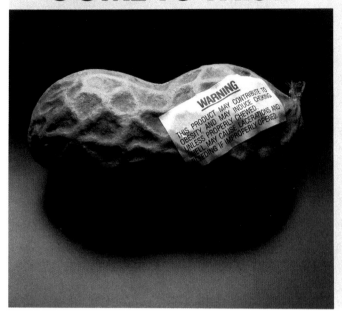

WARNING
THIS PRODUCT MAY CONTRIBUTE TO OBESITY. AND MAY INDUCE CHOKING UNLESS PROPERLY CHEWED. SHELL MAY CAUSE LACERATIONS AND BLEEDING IF IMPROPERLY OPENED.

Warnings have come a long way since someone had the good sense to put a ☠ on an iodine bottle.

Courts now require warning labels on a whole range of products.

From paint thinner to pajamas.

There have also been rulings on exactly how large such labels should be.

And where they should be.

And what they should say.

And it hasn't stopped at labeling, either.

Requirements relating to all aspects of product safety have mushroomed in recent years.

And while these have been a benefit to consumers, they've often been a problem for manufacturers.

Because even a responsible corporation can face liability by unintentionally overlooking a new regulation or an obscure ruling.

That's why at INA, a CIGNA company, we're prepared to do more than just insure our clients against product liability.

We do everything we can to keep them out of court.

To start with, we have a staff of product liability specialists who can examine every step in the manu-facturing and marketing process.

From design to advertising.

And we're not only likely to spot weaknesses people within a company may overlook, we're also more likely to spot weaknesses general and less specialized loss control examiners might overlook, as well.

We even look for problems before they occur.

We'll help design a product recall program, for example, to have in place, ready to quickly implement if the need for it ever arises.

And, needless to say, on an ongoing basis, we monitor legislation, court rulings, and agency regulations that can affect our client's liability.

If you'd like more information on this topic, please write to INA at 1600 Arch St., Dept. RA, Philadelphia, Pennsylvania 19101.

Or, if you'd like to know how we can help protect you against product liability exposures, call your agent or broker.

After all, in an area as complex as this one it's entirely possible a consumer isn't the only one who can benefit from a warning.

CIGNA

GOLD AWARD

194

Art Director	**Harvey Baron**
Designer	**Harvey Baron**
Photographers	**Phil Marco, Stock, Mike O'Neill, Carl Fischer**
Writer	**Diane Rothschild**
Client	**CIGNA**
Agency	**Doyle Dane Bernbach Inc., New York**

EVERY ART DIRECTOR HAS HIS BREAKI- NG POINT.

It's bad enough having to deal with outrageous deadlines and whining account guys. Must you be asked to put up with insensitive typography as well? At Typesetting, we say there's simply no excuse for it. Type isn't just words. It's art. And it should be treated as such. Call Jay Higgins, 421-2264. Because it's time the breaks started going your way.

TYPESETTING

211 Eddy Street, Providence, Rhode Island 02903

SILVER AWARD

195

Art Director	**Bob Saabye**
Writer	**Ernie Schenck**
Client	**Typesetting**
Agency	**Leonard Monahan Saabye, Providence, RI**

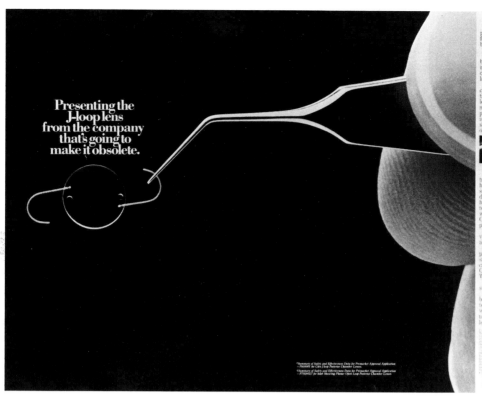

Presenting the
J-loop lens
from the company
that's going to
make it obsolete.

It's official: the Cilco® J-loop posterior chamber lens has been found safe and effective for use by all ophthalmologists.

Now we're out to replace it.

After all, it's our responsibility as the nation's number one intraocular lens manufacturer to continue to lead the way with the latest technology.

For example, our major competitor still relies on injection molding. We lathe cut our lenses from Perspex® CQ polymethylmethacrylate. And our proprietary polishing technique is unmatched for eliminating sharp edges, seams, burrs and other imperfections.

Ours.   Theirs.

In fact, the two scanning electron microscopy views shown here demonstrate just how much smoother our lenses are. No wonder 95.9%* of Cilco J-loop patients had visual acuity of 20-40 or better in the Core Study of patients without preoperative pathology. Only 88.7%† of our competitor's patients did as well.

What's more, other SEM views show that the loop tips are as smooth as the lenses.

We'd like to tell you more, particularly about our work with single-piece, flexible lenses. Just call us toll free at 800-624-3418. Or write Box 1680, Huntington, West Virginia 25717.

And be sure to read the brief summary on the next page.

We think you'll find that nobody anywhere makes a lens better than Cilco. And that's because we're constantly out to make the other lenses obsolete.

CILCO®

*Summary of Safety and Effectiveness Data for Premarket Approval Application – P810009 for Cilco J-loop Posterior Chamber Lenses.
†Summary of Safety and Effectiveness Data for Premarket Approval Application – P770300127 for Iolab Slevering Planar Open Loop Posterior Chamber Lenses.

WE'RE LOOKING FOR A BIKER WHO WEARS WING TIPS.

A suit and tie would be nice too, but we're not that picky.

All we want is a top-notch Account Executive with at least two years experience to join our motorcycle gang.

So, if you're a quick thinker and have a penchant for details, you should send off a resume with salary requirements to David Luhr.

But, whatever you do, don't call.

Motorcycle gangs don't like to be bothered.

CHIAT/DAY

517 South Olive Street, Los Angeles, California 90013

194-A

Art Directors **Harry Jacobs, Tom Layman**
Designer **Harry Jacobs**
Photographer **Jamie Cook**
Writer **Mike Hughes**
Client **Cilco**
Agency **The Martin Agency, Richmond, VA**
Publication **Ophthalmology Times**

195-A

Art Director **Houman Pirdavari**
Writer **Brent Bouchez**
Client **Chiat/Day Inc., Advertising**
Agency **Chiat/Day, Los Angeles**

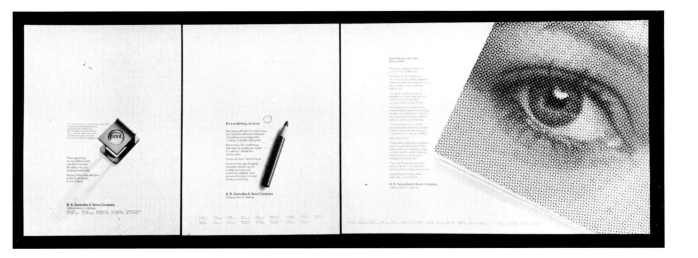

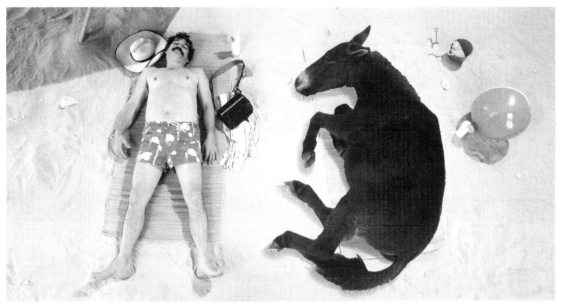

They've earned it.

"My life can't be all coffee. Sometimes there have to be Piña Coladas too, says Juan Valdez." Then he takes off his sombrero, wipes suntan lotion on his face and drifts off to sleep. The Cartagena sun beats down on him and his partner as they enjoy their first real siesta in two years.

They've earned it.

After all, thanks to Juan and his mule, the public awareness of 100% Colombian Coffee has shot up to an incredible 91%.

Furthermore, the statistics show that over half the population believes that Colombian Coffee is the best in the world.

Now's the time for you to act. By offering a 100% Colombian Coffee brand, you can capitalize on the demand for our product. Most of the current brands are already experiencing huge sales increases: one as high as 296%. Carramba! At that rate you'll be able to afford a nice long vacation yourself.

100% Colombian Coffee

196		197	
Art Director	**Gordon Hochhalter**	Art Director	**Mark Hughes**
Designer	**Bob Meyer**	Designer	**Mark Hughes**
Photographer	**Brian Nightengale**	Photographer	**Larry Robins**
Writer	**Gordon Hochhalter**	Writer	**D.J. Webster**
Client	**R.R. Donnelley & Sons Company**	Client	**National Federation of Coffee Growers of Colombia**
Agency	**O'Grady Advertising Arts, Chicago**	Agency	**Doyle Dane Bernbach Inc., New York**

GOLD AWARD

198

Art Director   **Hal Tench**
Designer   **Hal Tench**
Photographers   **Burton McNeely, Dean Hawthorne**
Artist   **Spanno Roccanova retouching**
Writer   **Mike Hughes**
Client   **General Motors, Electro-Motive Division**
Agency   **The Martin Agency, Richmond, VA**
Publication   **Railway Age**

Until We Plug In A Pair Of These, Our New Computer Is Just A Pile Of Junk.

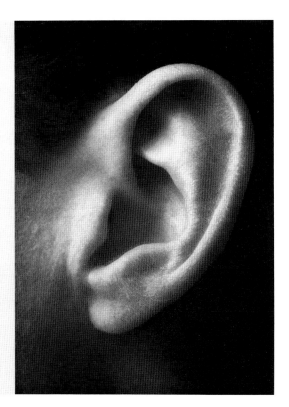

Our new Hell Chromacom System can do quite a bit. It's one of the most advanced digital page composition systems in the world.

It does hard and soft airbrushing.

It produces round or elliptical dots.

It gives you total size, color and position control of every element on the page.

It does all this before any film is exposed. Yet, as precise and advanced and complex as this system is, it requires something more to perform at its peak.

It needs the ears and eyes of a Colorhouse representative.

By listening, observing and understanding as you explain your project, a Colorhouse rep can suggest ways to save time and money and get better results with our Chromacom System.

At Colorhouse, we think even the world's most advanced technology still requires basic human understanding.

Just call Colorhouse at 612-929-1321 and we'll show you how well they work together.

 Colorhouse

chatelaine She opens Chatelaine.

SILVER AWARD

	199		200
Art Director	**Kurt Tausche**	Art Director	**Brian Harrod**
Designer	**Kurt Tausche**	Photographer	**Tim Saunders**
Photographer	**Rick Dublin**	Writer	**Ian Mirlin**
Writer	**Pete Smith**	Client	**Maclean Hunter**
Client	**Colorhouse, Inc.**	Agency	**McCann-Erickson**
Agency	**One Man Band, Inc.,**		**Toronto**
	Minneapolis	Studio	**"Mechanical Man"**

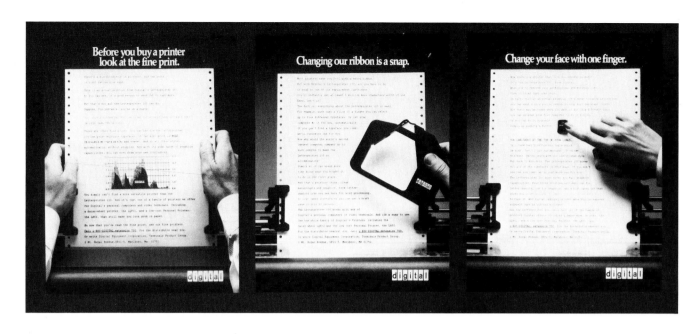

	201		202
Art Directors	**Dean Noble, Don McCormick**	Art Director	**Alan H. Zwiebel**
		Designer	**Bruce Newman**
Photographer	**Walter Bibikow**	Photographer	**Daniel Rubin**
Artist	**Christine Amisano**	Writer	**Alan H. Zwiebel**
Writer	**Steven West**	Client	**Newel Art Galleries, Inc.**
Client	**Digital Equipment Corporation**	Agency	**Kaufmann Advertising, New York**
Agency	**Schneider Parker Jakuc, Inc., Boston**	Publications	**Architectural Digest, Connoisseur, Avenue, Town & Country**

WHAT GOOD IS A PRODUCT OF THE FUTURE FROM A COMPANY WITHOUT ONE?

Dealing with a company you've never heard of can often lead to an experience you'll never forget.

A missed delivery here. Some critical down-time there. And all of a sudden, that breakthrough product you were so high on at last year's trade show is breaking your back when it comes down to actual application.

At ITT Courier, we can get as excited about new technology as anyone. In fact, last year alone, ITT spent over $1 billion on R&D. And millions more preparing each new product for the real world.

What's more, because the real world is filled with uncertainty, we back up every product with 150 ITT Service Centers in North America alone.

That's how you build a company that's installed over 325,000 terminals worldwide.

And that's why instead of gambling on the company that makes a new product first, you're a lot better off waiting for the company that knows how to make it last.

Contact your nearest ITT Courier Representative. Or call the ITT Courier Sales Support Department at 1-800-528-1400, toll free.

ITT COURIER

YOU KNOW WE'LL BE AROUND.

EVERY COMPUTER COMPANY TALKS SERVICE UP FRONT. BUT HOW MANY OF THEM CAN BACK IT UP?

These days, you've got to be real careful that the service a company promises you is more than just lip service.

Because if something goes wrong with your new equipment, and their service isn't right, you've just bought yourself a real headache.

At ITT Courier, we've been around long enough to know you can't sell customers short when it comes to service.

So we back up every ITT product with 150 service centers in North America alone.

We staff every one of those ITT Service Centers with field engineers who get their training at our state-of-the-art service school, not on your equipment.

And we give every ITT customer the security of a 24-hour service hotline, seven days a week.

Of course, no company can promise you a fail-safe product. But at ITT Courier, we're very proud of how quickly we can rise to the occasion should your system ever go down.

ITT Courier Service. It's one important reason we'll be around long after a lot of those other companies are long gone.

Contact your nearest ITT Courier Representative. Or call the ITT Courier Sales Support Department at 1-800-528-1400, toll free.

ITT COURIER

YOU KNOW WE'LL BE AROUND.

NOW THAT EVERYBODY AND HIS BROTHER ARE GETTING INTO THE DATA BUSINESS, HOW DO YOU DECIDE WHO GETS YOURS?

Suddenly, companies that make everything from motor oil to wrapping tape are trying to make big money in the data business.

And so are hundreds of upstarts that never made a thing. They all want a piece of your "office of the future." But how can you be sure they have a future?

Of course, that's no problem if your decision is ITT Courier. With 325,000 terminals installed worldwide, we're neither a Johnnie-come-lately nor an upstart. Plus, we have the financial strength and the product pathway to give your office of the future a real future.

For instance, we can provide ASYNC terminals small in price. Or SNA terminals big on communications.

We can give your people personal computing power. Or a telephone system that lets them talk to computers and other people.

And, unlike everybody and his brother, you know you can count on us to be here from generation to generation.

Contact your nearest ITT Courier Representative. Or call the ITT Courier Sales Support Department at 1-800-528-1400, toll free.

ITT COURIER

YOU KNOW WE'LL BE AROUND.

203

Art Directors	**Gil Franceschi, Floyd Yost**
Designer	**Gil Franceschi**
Photographer	**Reid Miles**
Writers	**Charlie Thomas, Pete Chasar**
Client	**ITT Courier**
Agency	**WFC Advertising, Phoenix**

GOLD AWARD

204

Art Directors/ Designers	**David Edelstein, Nancy Edelstein, Lanny French**
Photographer	**Jim Cummins**
Writers	**Ron Koliha, David Edelstein, Doug Edelstein**
Client	**Generra Sportswear**
Agency	**Edelstein Associates, Inc., Seattle**
Publication	**Sportswear Intl.**
Production Co.	**Wilkins & Peterson**

205

Art Director **John C. Jay, New York**
Photographer **Dan Kozan**
Writers **Owen Edwards, Betty Cornfeld**
Editor **Pam Thomas**

206

Art Director **David Deutsch**
Photographer **Frank Cowan**
Writer **Gil Ziff**
Client **Scholastic, Inc.**
Agency **David Deutsch Associates, Inc., New York**

QUINTESSENCE
THE QUALITY OF HAVING *IT*

BY BETTY CORNFELD AND OWEN EDWARDS
DESIGN BY JOHN C JAY

	207		208
Art Directors	David Edelstein, Nancy Edelstein, Lanny French	Art Director	John C. Jay, New York
Designers	David Edelstein, Nancy Edelstein, Lanny French	Photographer	Dan Kozan
		Writers	Owen Edwards, Betty Cornfeld
Photographer	Jim Cummins	Editor	Pam Thomas
Writer	David Edelstein		
Client	Generra Sportswear		
Agency	Edelstein Associates, Inc., Seattle		
Publication	Menswear Magazine		
Production Co.	Wilkins & Peterson		

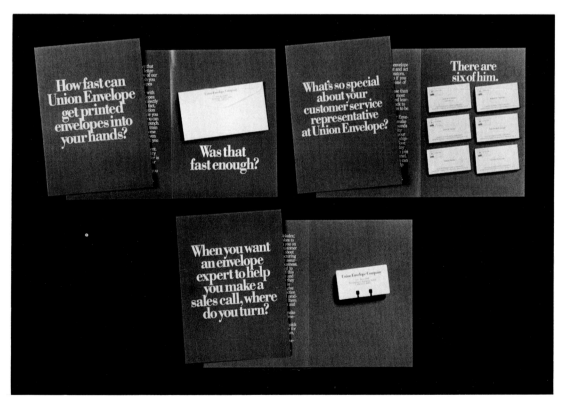

DISTINCTIVE MERIT	DISTINCTIVE MERIT
209	**210**

Art Director **Ann Phares**
Photographer **Beth Galton**
Writer **Veronica Nash**
Client **Avon Products**
Agency **Ogilvy & Mather
Advertising, New York**
Creative
Director **Malcolm End**

Art Director **Hal Tench**
Designer **Hal Tench**
Photographers **West/Edwards**
Writer **Barbara Ford**
Client **Union Envelope**
Agency **The Martin Agency,
Richmond, VA**
Publication **Paper Sales**

EDITORIAL

Will Hopkins

Mary Baumann
Robert Best
Mike Brock
Bill Cadge
Frank DeVino
Paul Hardy
Kristina Jorgensen
David Levy
Frank Rothmann
Neil Shakery
Lou Silverstein
Melissa Tardiff
Adrian Taylor
Pete Turner
Rodney Williams

DISTINCTIVE MERIT

211		212		213	
Art Director	Michelle Chu	Art Director	Michelle Chu	Art Director	Michael Keegan
Designer	Michelle Chu	Designer	Michelle Chu	Designer	Michael Keegan
Photographer	Rob Brown	Writer	John Sherwood	Writer	Camille Hamilton
Writer	Johannes Tesselaar	Client	Los Angeles Herald	Client	Los Angeles Herald
Client	Los Angeles Herald		Examiner		Examiner
	Examiner	Editor	Fred Heldman	Editor	Woody Hochswender
Editor	Fred Heldman	Publisher	Los Angeles Herald	Publisher	Los Angeles Herald
Publisher	Los Angeles Herald		Examiner, Los Angeles		Examiner, Los Angeles
	Examiner, Los Angeles	Graphics &		Graphics &	
Graphics &		Production		Production	
Production		Editor	Saul Daniels	Editor	Saul Daniels
Editor	Saul Daniels				

214		215		216	
Art Director	Nanette Mary Bisher	Art Director	David Hadley	Art Director	David Hadley
Writer	Robert Ferrigno	Artist	Elwood H. Smith	Artist	Robin Moline
Publisher	Dave Threshie	Editor	Terrie Blair	Editor	Terrie Blair
Publication	The Register, Santa Ana, CA	Publisher	Minneapolis Star and Tribune	Publisher	Minneapolis Star and Tribune
Assistant Managing Editor	Richard Cheverton	Publication	Minnesota Guide, Minneapolis	Publication	Minnesota Guide, Minneapolis

SILVER AWARD

217

Art Director **David Hadley**
Artist **Seymour Chwast**
Editor **Terrie Blair**
Publisher **Minneapolis Star and Tribune**
Publication **Minnesota Guide, Minneapolis**

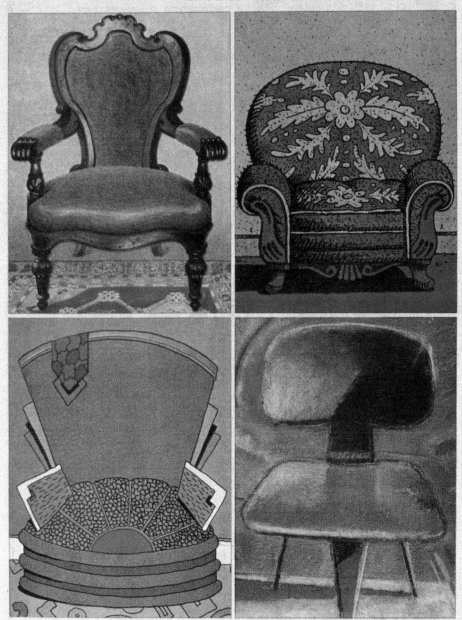

SILVER AWARD

218

Art Director	**David Hadley**
Artists	**Christopher Blumerich, Elwood Smith, Vivienne Flesher, Seymour Chwast**
Editor	**Terrie Blair**
Publisher	**Minneapolis Star and Tribune**
Publication	**Minnesota Guide, Minneapolis**

THE LAWN & THE SPORT OF IT
(OR, LETTING THE GRASS GROW UNDER YOUR FEET)

219	220	221
Art Director **David Hadley**	Art Director **David Hadley**	Art Director **David Hadley**
Artist **David Hadley**	Photographer **Judy Olausen**	Artist **David Hadley**
Editor **Terrie Blair**	Editor **Terrie Blair**	Editor **Terrie Blair**
Publisher **Minneapolis Star and Tribune**	Publisher **Minneapolis Star and Tribune**	Publisher **Minneapolis Star and Tribune**
Publication **Minnesota Guide, Minneapolis**	Publication **Minnesota Guide, Minneapolis**	Publication **Minnesota Guide, Minneapolis**

	222		**223**		**224**
Art Director	Michael Keegan	Art Director	Michael Keegan	Art Director	Tom Bodkin
Designer	Michael Keegan	Designer	Michael Keegan	Designer	Tom Bodkin
Photographer	Chad Slattery	Photographers	Paul Chinn, Stuart Franklin	Artist	Paul Meisel
Writer	Janet Nairn			Client	The New York Times
Client	Los Angeles Herald Examiner	Client	Los Angeles Herald Examiner	Editor	Mike Leahy
Editor	Sheena Paterson	Editor	Fred Heldman	Publisher	The New York Times, New York
Publisher	Los Angeles Herald Examiner, Los Angeles	Publisher	Los Angeles Herald Examiner, Los Angeles	Publication	The New York Times Travel Section
Graphics & Production Editor	Saul Daniels	Graphics & Prduction Editor	Saul Daniels		

SHOP HOP

Photographer • Gary Green   Design • Christina de Lancie   Fashions • Roman, designed and handcrafted by Sylvain, Sylvain   Models • Billy DeArsitis, Christina di Lancie and Roxy

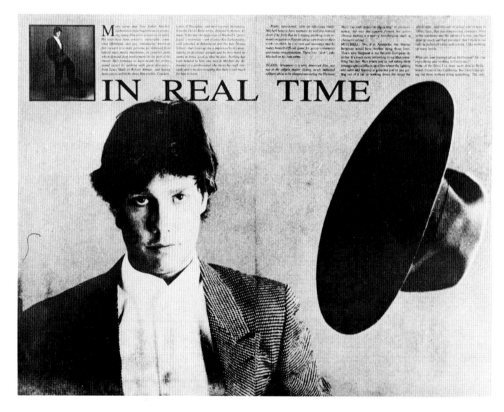

IN REAL TIME

225

Art Director	**Christina de Lancie**
Designer	**Christina de Lancie**
Photographer	**Gary Green**
Writer	**RAGS**
Editors	**Arnold Barkus, Steve Neumann**
Publisher	**Arnold Barkus, Steve Neumann**
Publication	**Island**, New York

226

Art Director	**Christina de Lancie**
Designer	**Christina de Lancie**
Photographer	**George DuBose**
Editors	**Arnold Barkus, Steve Neumann**
Publisher	**Arnold Barkus, Steve Neumann**
Publication	**Island**, New York

CRUISES
FOR RENT
BY AUDREY CLINTON

Scudding along in a cooling breeze under sail or power on bay, sound or ocean is not only one of the finer escapes, it's one you don't have to own a boat to enjoy. For as little as $5 or as much as $500, you can embark for an afternoon, a day or longer on craft ranging from luxury yachts, with brass and brightwork, to roomy but graceful copies of 19th Century coasting schooners. Cruises operate from the East River to Long Island's East End. Among the excursions are a day trip across Long Island Sound aboard a sailing cargo schooner out of Port Jefferson, four-hour day sails aboard a gaff-rigged schooner in Montauk waters, an after-dinner trip with cocktails aboard a large power excursion boat in Long Beach waters, harbor hopping aboard a smaller open power boat along the North Shore. Add to these Cross-Sound ferry excursions and sightseeing power and sail trips in New York Harbor. Excursions can be combined with other activities. For example, a day-long power boat trip from

—Continued on Page 9

	227
Art Director	**Warren Weilbacher**
Designer	**Jeff Massaro**
Writer	**Audrey Clinton**
Client	**New York Newsday, Part II**
Editor	**Stuart Troup**
Publisher	**Newsday Inc., Melville, NY**

	228
Art Director	**Lucy Bartholomay**
Designer	**Lucy Bartholomay**
Artist	**Dave Calver**
Publisher	**The Boston Globe, Boston**
Publication	**The Boston Sunday Globe**

	229
Art Director	**Nancy Kent**
Designer	**Nancy Kent**
Artist	**Kimble Mead**
Client	**The New York Times**
Editor	**Alex Ward**
Publisher	**The New York Times, New York**
Publication	**The New York Times Living Section**

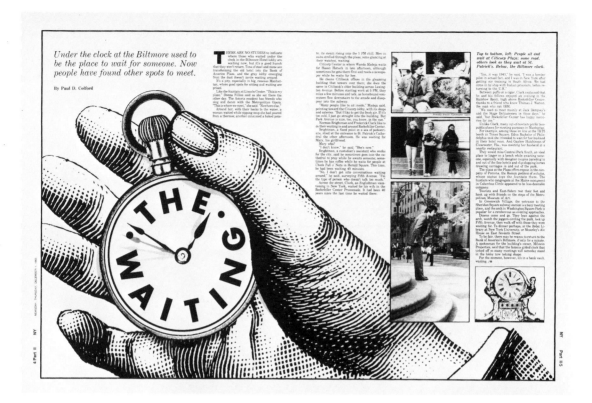

230		231	
Art Director	Warren Weilbacher	Art Director	Richard Aloisio
Designer	Gary Rogers	Designer	Richard Aloisio
Artist	Gary Rogers	Client	The New York Times
Writer	Paul Colford	Editor	Mike Leahy
Client	New York Newsday, Part II	Publisher	The New York Times, New York
Editor	Stuart Troup	Publication	The New York Times Travel Section
Publisher	Newsday, Inc., Melville, New York		

THE DOOM SELLERS

BY ALEXANDER THEROUX

Our great fear today is of utter annihilation, a threat perhaps related to the current nuclear buildup, economic insecurity, and even the immensity of space above us, which, while a new frontier, also engulfs and somehow diminishes us. This anxiety is reflected everywhere, from Jules Feiffer's cartoons to Tom Lehrer's songs to bumper stickers (for instance, "Where Will You Be When the Lights Go Out?"). The term "ground zero" is understood by most school-children. Handguns proliferate. We're afraid to turn on the news.

There is nevertheless an entire business, amazingly enough, being built around these same fears and apprehensions — and it's going (so to speak) great guns. I call it the Doomsday Industry.

Remember God's anger? "I will blot out man whom I have created from the face of the ground, man and beast and creeping things and birds of the air." And then, sure enough, it was glub, glub, glub, the watergates opened, and we had the Flood. The world — at least according to prophecy — is going to end again. And it would be disingenuous, I think, seeing as this time we're even helping out, to feign surprise. The warnings have long been posted. We're due back somewhere, it appears, and soon, for if signs of the times aren't wrong — and we seem hell-bent to prove them right — the skies above are now as dark as homemade thunder.

Are you in the mood for doom? Unless statistics lie, my friend, it's one of your favorite subjects. You positively adore it! And nowadays, thanks to the far-reaching magic of film, television, and the printed word, it's been made possible for all of us to be scared to death not only quite frequently but in some rather marvelous ways. For so real, so multifarious — *so chic!* — is the prospect of total annihilation that the interest in *Continued on page 40*

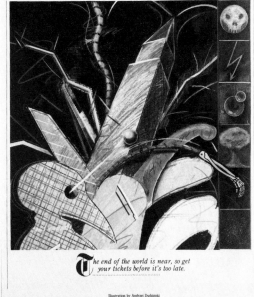

The end of the world is near, so get your tickets before it's too late.

Illustration by Andrzej Dudzinski

232

Art Director	**Ronn Campisi**
Designer	**Ronn Campisi**
Artist	**Andrzej Dudzinski**
Editor	**Michael Larkin**
Publisher	**The Boston Globe, Boston**
Publication	**The Boston Globe Magazine**

233

Art Director	**Steven Heller**
Designer	**Steven Heller**
Artist	**Arnold Roth**
Client	**The New York Times**
Editor	**Mike Levitas**
Publisher	**The New York Times, New York**
Publication	**The New York Times Book Review**

CHRISTMAS IN LOSTVILLE

TALES OF
NEW YORK · BY PETE HAMILL

I. AT TWO MINUTES PAST NOON on the day before Christmas, snow began falling on Lostville. The name was Spencer's invention, used by him to describe the endless ruined acres of the place where he had once been young and was now old. Lostville, he said one morning, walking through the rubble. Welcome to Lostville. And now Spencer stood alone in the apartment on the top floor right of 211 Marley St., watching fat white flakes melt into the broken brick and gashed streets that stretched away to the snow-blurred horizon, and he thought: I could play today. I haven't played in 13 years, but if I had a horn I could play today. A blues for Lostville. A Christmas blues.

"Don't anybody remember?" he said out loud. But there was no other human to answer him. His cat Dakota, curled on the threadbare couch, purred in sleep. "Don't anybody know we're here?"

He watched the snow and remembered the rows of white wooden houses in the black part of the neighborhood, and how after a while they looked like houses in the South, with hanging vines and plump trees and garden in the backyards. He remembered the summer streets, noisy with stickball and argument and women scolding children; and the time Jackie Robinson came to these streets, a year after he joined the Dodgers, and how all the kids came to him in a rush, and the adults, too, some of them crying, and how everybody knew that some things would never be the same. His friend Charlie Koenig was with Spencer that day, smart and quick and tough, a great stickball player, and looking at Robinson he said to Spencer, "Now this is a great man."

In the fall that year, Spencer joined the Navy and Charlie Koenig went off to college. There was a party for them at 211 Marley St. with Spencer's mother and Charlie's mother making all the food, and a great mob of black

and Jewish kids shouting on the stairs and dancing in the parlor, right here in this parlor, Spencer thought: right here. He and Charlie saw each other once more, at Christmas, and then they never saw each other again. The Koenigs moved. Spencer played alto in the Navy band in San Diego, and then stayed on the Coast after discharge. By the time he got back to New York, he had the problem. That problem. And it was the problem that got him into real trouble, the problem that sent him away and ruined his life. When he came home from jail, the trees were gone, and the white frame houses, and only his mother was left. When she died, Spencer inherited the top floor right at 211 Marley St. And 211 Marley was alone on the block.

That was the wonder. This building stood alone, the last tenement in Lostville. Sometimes the cops came around to see if everything was all right. And once in a while, somebody would show up from Welfare, counting heads or checking names. Just a week ago, a guy in a suit was around while Spencer was out. Knocking on doors. Asking questions. Wondering why people still lived in this wasteland. A reporter, maybe. Or a real-estate guy.

"Don't anybody remember nothin', cat?" Spencer said out loud. The kettle began to whistle. "People used to live here, cat. A lot of 'em."

The cat purred.

II. IN THE SECOND FLOOR LEFT, Fran Bernstein raised the window shade to see the falling snow. On TV, a reporter was saying that the mayor had declared a snow emergency, and the reporter said this sounds like another snow job, ho ho. It all sounded like fun. But Fran watched the swirling flakes and was afraid. They don't even know Marley Street exists. So the would have a terrible time, walking those 11 blocks to the Key Food. Snow was not good for the old. And now there was nobody around here who was young, some small boy who would run to the store to buy a few things. I used to

do that for people when I was young. Now I'm alone and old.

The snow was sticking. She remembered as a girl hurrying home from school in the snow, and the boys all yelling in the muffled streets. "Good packing" is what they called this kind of snow. And good packing meant snowballs and snow men and giant snow forts, the smell of wet wool in the apartment, and newspapers on the linoleum floors. She was always excited on those days. Sometimes the school was closed by the snow, and she would have the long dazzling snowy day in which to play, and then at night she would listen to her father talk in the kitchen in his great deep gravelly voice, slamming the table for emphasis, warning all of them about The Boss Class, and the need for solidarity.

"There were farms out here then," she said out loud. But she had no husband to answer her anymore, and her daughter was living with her children in Florida. "Farms," she said. Her father would walk past the farms when they went to the subway; those small fields of tomatoes and lettuce, and tell her they were doomed. The small farmers were doomed, the real-estate speculators were coming, they were all doomed. And then they would ride on the El until it went underground at Sutter Avenue, and he would take her to New York to listen to the speakers in Union Square. All the way home, he'd tell her about the revolution and the need to support the Soviet Union, and sometimes, if it was summer, he would take her to listen to the Communists on Pitkin Avenue, always talking outside a bank, or to the party headquarters on Thatford Avenue. They were all loud and intense, but Frank never knew what they were saying, or why her father was so angry.

At Christmas time, he was even angrier than usual. Not at the goyim for their religious faith. He dismissed all religion. He was angry, as always, at the capitalists.

"You see what they did?" he shouted one Christmas Eve. "They invented Santa Claus! You see how clever they are! How ruthless! They knew they couldn't get Jews to buy

Christmas presents if there was pictures of Jesus everywhere in the stores. So they invent this fat guy in a red suit! That's what galls me! A red suit! Red! The color of revolution! And they took it and made it the color of this orgy of capitalist swindling!"

Thinking of her father, Fran suddenly wondered about her daughter. She went to the phone and dialed the 305 area code and the number, listened to it ring seven times, sighed and hung up. Then for a long time she sat at the window. This was some storm. And she imagined the snow falling on Loew's Pitkin and Herman's Cafeteria, on the Little Oriental and the Labor Lyceum, and she remembered being 20, going into a deli for warmth, and the mixed odors of pickles and herring and men. On the way home, the snow blue at dusk, she'd pass the women in Belmont Avenue, shawls over their heads, shouting from behind pushcarts, offering a snow sale. How full were those streets: with carpenters and stonecutters, shoemakers and butchers.

And now all of them were gone. Husbands and fathers, daughters and mothers, friends and enemies; the weak and the strong. All gone. Like some village in Poland erased by the Holocaust. Gone.

III. BY LATE AFTERNOON, THREE inches had fallen on the city. In the first floor left, behind the barred windows of his apartment, Bobby Crews prepared a stew. Beef went into the pot, onions and carrots, celery and potatoes. On the wall behind him was the old red and yellow poster from the Torres fight. It showed him when he was young, with the name "Bobby (Bad News) Crews" underneath. Now when he looked at the poster, all he could remember was the cab ride to the Garden. He didn't remember knocking out Torres, or Teddy Brenner coming to the dressing room later to offer him a shot at Marvin Stamps. Those things happened, but Bobby Crews didn't remember them. That fight was now just a ride to the Garden and a poster

continued on next page

PETE HAMILL'S 'TALES OF NEW YORK' WILL NOW APPEAR EVERY WEEK IN THE MAGAZINE.

ILLUSTRATION BY HOVIK DILAKIAN

SUNDAY NEWS MAGAZINE • NEW YORK • DECEMBER 25, 1983

Famous Roosters:
Rudyard Kipling
Enrico Caruso
Groucho Marx
Peter Ustinov

1909
1921
1933
1945
1957
1969
1981
1993

ROOSTER

Contrary to the common association of a Rooster with dawn, in the Chinese zodiac the Rooster is consigned to the hours of "Sunset," from 5 to 7 P.M. and faces West in the zodiac circle. If you are a Rooster you have a reputation for being a hard worker, a talented, deep thinker who is happier working alone than with others. You are also extravagant in dress with a tendency to be flashy. Nevertheless, you are shrewd, persevering and definitive. You should be happy as a restaurant owner, a publicist, a soldier or a world traveler. You get along best with the Ox, the Snake and the Dragon.

THIS PAGE WAS SET IN ITC SERIF GOTHIC AND ITC ISBELL.®

Famous Dogs:
Socrates
George Gershwin
Benjamin Franklin
Herbert Hoover
David Niven

1910
1922
1934
1946
1958
1970
1982
1994

DOG

The time of day assigned to the Dog is "Twilight," from 7 to 9 P.M. Born under the sign of the Dog, you are a person of strong principles. You are loyal, faithful, trusted. You are able to keep secrets but you are plagued by a sharp tongue. You must curb your tendency to be a faultfinder and a worrier. You should make an excellent businessman, activist, teacher or secret agent. You ought to get along best with the Horse, the Tiger and the Rabbit.

Famous Boars: 1911
Ernest Hemingway 1923
Albert Schweitzer 1935
1947
1959
1971
1983
1995

Boar

Happy New Year. This is the Year of the Boar. It is also the beginning of the end of the twelve-year cycle of the Chinese zodiac. According to the Chinese calendar, we are in the year 4681 and the Boar will return to reign again in 4693 or 1995 by the Western calendar. When we read the Chinese zodiac as a clock, counting the day in double hours, the Boar dominates the hours at the close of day—9 to 11 P.M.—which is known as the "Hour of Rest." If you were born in the year of the Boar, you are

quiet, sincere, studious and thorough. You set difficult goals for yourself and carry them out, expending much energy and time in the pursuit of knowledge. Although you do not care about nor make many friends, your relationships are very deep, devoted and honest. Your quest for material possessions may be a source of trouble. You are likely to do well in the arts as an entertainer, but you might also consider the field of law. You get along very well with the Hare and the Goat.

THIS PAGE WAS SET IN ITC BENGUIAT® CONDENSED AND ITC GORILLA.™

234

Art Directors **Janet Froelich, Thomas, P. Ruis**
Artist **Hovik Dilakian**
Client **New York Sunday News Magazine**
Publication **New York Sunday News Magazine, New York**

235

Art Directors **Bob Farber, Mike Quon**
Designers **Bob Farber, Mike Quon**
Artist **Mike Quon**
Writer **Marion Muller**
Client **Upper & Lower Case**
Publisher **International Typeface Corp.**
Agency **Mike Quon Design Office, Inc., New York**

SILVER AWARD

236

Art Director	**Michael Keegan**
Designers	**Michelle Chu, Dave Bhang**
Client	**Los Angeles Herald Examiner**
Editors	**Mary Anne Dolan, John Lindsay, Sheena Paterson, Stan Cloud**
Publisher	**Los Angeles Herald Examiner, Los Angeles**
Graphics & Prod. Editor	**Saul Daniels**
Consultant	**Jackie Young**

'ALL IN ITC AMERICAN TYPEWRITER'

237		238	
Art Director	**Bob Farber**	Art Director	**Michael Keegan**
Writer	**Edward Gottschall**	Designers	**Michelle Chu, Dave Bhang**
Editor	**Edward Gottschall**		
Publication	**U&lc, New York**	Client	**Los Angeles Herald Examiner**
Ass't Art			
Director	**Ilene Mehl**	Editors	**Mary Anne Dolan, John Lindsay, Sheena Paterson, Stan Cloud**
		Publisher	**Los Angeles Herald Examiner, Los Angeles**
		Graphics & Prod. Editor	**Saul Daniels**
		Consultant	**Jackie Young**

DISTINCTIVE MERIT

239		240	
Art Director	**Bob Farber**	Art Directors	**Louis Silverstein,**
Writer	**Marion Muller**		**Walter Bernard**
Publication	**U&lc, New York**	Designer	**Walter Bernard**
		Photographer	**various**
		Artist Cover	**Seymour Chwast**
		Writer	**Various**
		Client	**The New York Times**
		Editor	**Mike Leahy**
		Publisher	**The New York Times,**
			New York
		Publication	**The New York Times**
			Sophisticated Traveler

A poet without a country

BY PAUL D. BUSH

As he pauses during our walk, Dennis Brutus, the South African poet, talks to himself, as he often does in the evening. It helps him order the day's events, he says, and helps clear his head. From a hill on Amherst College's campus, the view of the red and gold sunset is clear, and for the second time today Brutus has lost himself in his surroundings. Earlier, ice crystals on the snow prompted a few appreciative words. Absentmindedly, he hoists an armload of books, papers, and court documents and composes a sunset haiku. He doesn't make a big deal of his poetry, he later says; if he did, the poetry wouldn't be any good.

At 58, Dennis Brutus is considered by many the poet laureate of Africa. He has gained attention and respect since his first serious attempt at poetry won the Mbari Prize for Poetry in Africa in 1961.

Brutus' hair, combed back from his forehead, outlines his face like a tightly groomed lion's mane. He is of moderate build, and his bearing is dignified. He projects gentleness, yet he is not meek. Caught up in creating a poem, he is passionate and intense.

Brutus has survived forced labor, beatings, even gunshot wounds, and he has stood up under the terror of South Africa's worst prisons. Brutus has never been simply a poet; he has also been a teacher, a sportsman, and an implacable, creative opponent of apartheid. South Africa's official policy of racial segregation.

Since his first visit to the United States in 1966 on behalf of the South African Non-Racial Olympic Committee (SAN-ROC), a group dedicated to desegregating South African sports teams, the United States Immigration and Naturalization Service (INS) has labeled Brutus a "subversive." The INS, however, recognizing his stature as a poet, allowed him to take up temporary residence here in 1970. Until 1980 his visas were routinely renewed, but the Reagan administration has used his "subversive" classification to justify denying him a visa and issuing a deportation order. Brutus and his supporters fear that if the deportation hearing, scheduled for July, leads to his expulsion from the United States and he returns to Africa, his life will be in danger.

BORN IN THE BRITISH COLONY OF RHODESIA IN 1924, Brutus moved with his parents, both schoolteachers, to South Africa when he was an infant. He grew up in the ghettos of Port Elizabeth and considers himself a South African. To the South African government, he is "coloured," of mixed African and European descent. Brutus was slow, almost retarded, he says, until late in childhood, when he blossomed, intellectually overtaking his classmates. In college on a merit scholarship ("Without it I would have ended up in a shoe factory or working on the shop floor at Ford"), he took his first

PAUL D. BUSH, THE FORMER MANAGING EDITOR OF NEW ROOTS MAGAZINE, IS A FREELANCE WRITER WHO LIVES IN NEW SALEM, MASSACHUSETTS.

tentative steps in protesting apartheid.

At Fort Hare University, the only university in South Africa for blacks, Brutus earned degrees in psychology and teaching. There, his interest in sports brought him in contact with black athletes, who had been excluded from national teams, despite the fact that their records proved they were better qualified than whites. His letter writing on behalf of two weight lifters, whose strength should have qualified them for the whites-only Olympic team, led to his election as secretary of the local sports association.

After Brutus graduated and returned to Port Elizabeth to teach high school, his protests intensified. Remembering the 1950s, he said recently, "I saw the inequalities between black and white education, and I attacked them. And that was enough to get me in trouble but I also lived in a ghetto and saw the differences in housing, white housing and black housing, and I attacked that. I worked with parent-teacher associations, where you were dealing not only with the problems of the kids but the problems of the parents: discriminated against, unemployed, beaten up, jailed. There was no way you could escape that reality.

"One of the most fortunate days of my life," he continued, "was stumbling upon a copy of the constitution of the Olympic Games — the Charter of the International Olympic Committee — and discovering that Clause One said that any country that discriminates on the grounds of race, religion, or politics cannot be included in the Olympics. And that was the kind of stick I could use to beat the racists with."

Brutus soon found how effective that stick was. After a decade of efforts in local and regional sports groups, he suddenly jumped to the international level. At first, his efforts met with responses such as "You're not supposed to do this," or "But this is South Africa," but eventually the reaction from international sports bodies took its toll in sports-mad South Africa. Teams around the world refused to play in South Africa or to compete with its teams in other countries, and sports federations began to prohibit South Africa from participating in international contests. (In 1964 South Africa was excluded from the Olympic Games, but it was later temporarily reinstated, after it agreed to allow nonwhites on teams *Continued on page 28*

Continued on page 28

Dennis Brutus, a South African foe of apartheid, may be facing his toughest battle yet.

Photograph by John Goodman

241		242	
Art Director	Bob Ciano	Art Director	Ronn Campisi
Designer	Lou Valentino	Designer	Ronn Campisi
Photographer	Michael O'Neill	Photographer	John Goodman
Writer	Peter Kaplan	Editor	Michael Larkin
Editors	Richard B. Stolley, Mark Mulvoy	Publisher	The Boston Globe, Boston
Publisher	Time Inc.	Publication	The Boston Globe Magazine
Publication	LIFE Magazine, New York		

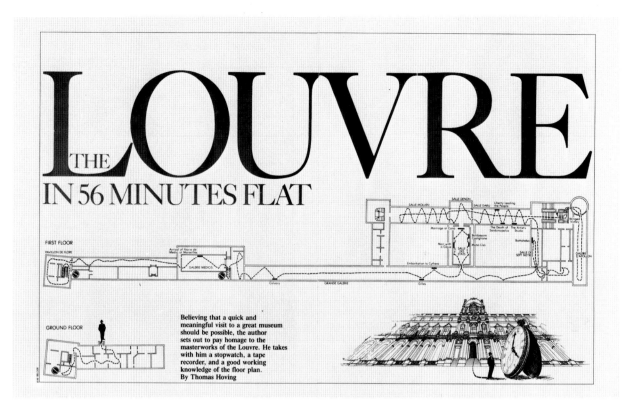

THE LOUVRE
IN 56 MINUTES FLAT

Believing that a quick and meaningful visit to a great museum should be possible, the author sets out to pay homage to the masterworks of the Louvre. He takes with him a stopwatch, a tape recorder, and a good working knowledge of the floor plan.
By Thomas Hoving

HOW TWO GAY FATHERS DEAL WITH THEIR CHILDREN AND EX-WIVES **THE DOUBLE CLOSET**

by Anne Fadiman

	243
Art Director	**Mary Shapiro**
Designer	**Mary Shapiro**
Artist	**Kim Belger**
Writer	**Thomas Hoving**
Client	**Connoisseur Magazine**
Publisher	**Connoisseur Magazine/ Hearst Corp., New York**

	244
Art Director	**Bob Ciano**
Designer	**Charles W. Pates**
Photographer	**Ross Baughman**
Writer	**Anne Fadiman**
Editors	**Richard B. Stolley, Mark Mulvoy**
Publisher	**Time Inc.**
Publication	**LIFE Magazine, New York**

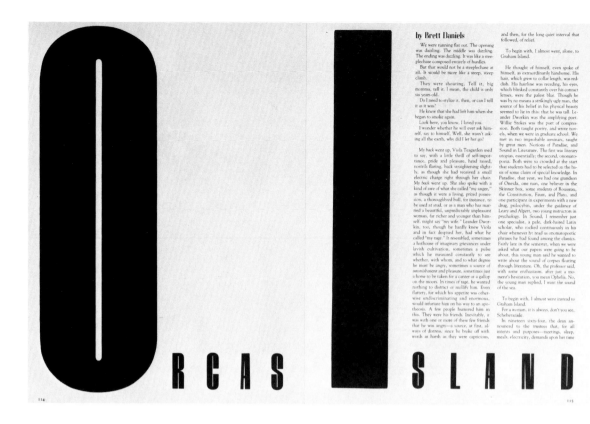

by Brett Daniels

We were running flat out. The opening was dazzling. The middle was dazzling. The ending was dazzling. It was like a steeplechase composed entirely of hurdles.

But that would not be a steeplechase at all. It would be more like a steep, steep climb.

They were shouting. Tell it, big momma, tell it. I mean, the child is only six years old.

Do I need to stylize it, then, or can I tell it as it was?

He knew that she had left him when she began to smoke again.

Look here, you know, I loved you.

I wonder whether he will ever ask himself, say to himself, Well, she wasn't asking all the earth, why did I let her go?

My back went up, Viola Teagarden used to say, with a little thrill of self-importance, pride and pleasure, head raised, nostrils flaring, back straightening slightly, as though she had received a small electric charge right through her chair. My back went up. She also spoke with a kind of awe of what she called "my anger," as though it were a living, prized possession, a thoroughbred bull, for instance, to be used at stud, or as a man who has married a beautiful, unpredictably unpleasant woman, far richer and younger than himself, might say "my wife." Leander Dworkin, too, though he hardly knew Viola and in fact despised her, had what he called "my rage." It resembled, sometimes a hothouse of imaginary grievances under lavish cultivation, sometimes a pulse which he measured constantly to see whether, with whom, and to what degree he must be angry, sometimes a source of astonishment and pleasure, sometimes just a horse to be taken for a canter or a gallop on the moors. In times of rage, he wanted nothing to distract or mollify him. Even flattery, for which his appetite was otherwise undiscriminating and enormous, would infuriate him on his way to an apotheosis. A few people humored him in this. They were his friends. Inevitably, it was with one or more of these few friends that he was angry—a source, at first, always of distress, since he broke off with words as harsh as they were capricious,

and then, for the long quiet interval that followed, of relief.

To begin with, I almost went, alone, to Graham Island.

He thought of himself, even spoke of himself, as extraordinarily handsome. His hair, which grew to collar length, was reddish. His hairline was receding, his eyes, which blinked constantly over his contact lenses, were the palest blue. Though he was by no means a strikingly ugly man, the source of his belief in his physical beauty seemed to lie in this: that he was tall. Leander Dworkin was the amplifying poet. Willie Stokes was the poet of compression. Both taught poetry, and wrote novels, when we were in graduate school. We met in two improbable seminars, taught by great men. Notions of Paradise, and Sound in Literature. The first was literary utopias, essentially; the second, onomatopoeia. Both were so crowded at the start that students had to be selected on the basis of some claim of special knowledge. In Paradise, that year, we had one grandson of Oneida, one man, one believer in the Skinner box, some students of Rousseau, the Constitution, Faust, and Plato, and one participant in experiments with a new drug, psilocybin, under the guidance of Leary and Alpert, two young instructors in psychology. In Sound, I remember just one specialist, a pale, dark-haired Latin scholar, who rocked continuously in his chair whenever he read us onomatopoeic phrases he had found among the classics. Fairly late in the semester, when we were asked what our papers were going to be about, this young man said he wanted to write about the sound of corpses floating through literature. Oh, the professor said, with some enthusiasm, after just a moment's hesitation, you mean Ophelia. No, the young man replied, I want the sound of the sea.

To begin with, I almost went instead to Graham Island.

For a woman, it is always, don't you see, Scheherazade.

In nineteen sixty-four, the dean announced to the trustees that, for all intents and purposes—meetings, sleep, meals, electricity, demands upon her time

Discipline in the Church

Issues: Everyone gets hurt when the church fails to discipline a member who is guilty of glaring disobedience to the Scriptures. Discipline that leads to brokenness and repentance—and then to forgiveness from the church—is the right way and the loving way to respond to open sin.

by LUIS PALAU

WHAT SHOULD the church do when a member turns to alcohol to avoid a personal problem—turn the other way and hope nobody smells his breath?

What should the church do when a member is an incessant gossip, continually sowing discord? Do we retaliate and start gossiping about that person?

What should the church do when a member commits sexual immorality? Do we say, "It's complicated and

Illustration by TOM CURRY

DISCIPLESHIP JOURNAL 17

245

Art Director	Lloyd Ziff
Designer	Lloyd Ziff
Writer	Brett Daniels
Editor	Richard Locke
Publisher	Conde Nast Publications, Inc., New York
Publication	Vanity Fair

246

Art Director	Hilber Nelson
Designer	Hilber Nelson
Artist	Tom Curry
Writer	Luis Palau
Client	NavPress
Editor	Tom Womack
Publisher	NavPress
Publication	Discipleship Journal, Colorado Springs, CO

He's Arthur Reed, and he's 123
MEET THE OLDEST MAN

By Dick Schaap

Born in 1860, he's lived under 25 Presidents and says that FDR was best

continued

Arthur Reed celebrates his 123rd birthday at the Phoenix Iron Works in Oakland. Among the well-wishers are his friend, Weldon Russell (r.), head of Phoenix, and Russell's daughter Mary, who was born when Reed was 100.

PAGE 6 - NOVEMBER 20, 1983 - PARADE MAGAZINE   PARADE MAGAZINE - NOVEMBER 20, 1983 - PAGE 7

PARADE MAGAZINE   SPRING 1983

Outdoor Pleasures
BY ELIZABETH GAYNOR

What To Do, What's New

Looking for a way to have fun, stay fit and enjoy the great weather? You can have it all this summer—all of you—young or old, athlete or not, in town or out. Read on for a roundup of what's in, outside.

Riding Sky High

Why would someone want to stand in a wicker basket and float off into heaven with an $8 tank of propane as his only power source? "There's no telephone," replies Alan Blount, president of the Balloon Federation of America. Indeed, hot-air ballooning offers spectacular fulfillment of the great escape fantasy. Quietly, as if by magic, one lifts off at sunrise from a dewy field directed only by the will of the wind. But the principles that govern the flight are down-to-earth. A gas burner heats air trapped in the house-size balloon so that it's lighter than the surrounding air and thus rises.

This summer will be a choice one for balloonists, spectators and anyone wishing to ride with a licensed pilot (see the Yellow Pages, "Balloons—Manned," for local groups). It's the Air and Space Bicentennial, commemorating the first manned flight, when two Frenchmen took off in the balloon that ushered in the age of flying. Theirs was made of varnished linen and paper! For listings of national and international events, contact the Balloon Federation (P.O. Box 346, Indianola, Iowa 50125).

PARADE - MAY 1, 1983 - PAGE 21

247

Art Directors	Ira Yoffe, Christopher Austopchuk
Designers	Ira Yoffe, Christopher Austopchuk
Photographer	Michael Jang
Writer	Dick Schaap
Client	Parade Publications, Inc.
Editor	Walter Anderson
Publisher	Carlo Vittorini
Publication	Parade Magazine, New York

248

Art Directors	Ira Yoffe, Christopher Austopchuk
Designers	Ira Yoffe, Christopher Austopchuk
Photographer	Aurness
Writer	Elizabeth Gaynor
Client	Parade Publications, Inc.
Editor	Walter Anderson
Publisher	Carlo Vittorini
Publication	Parade Magazine, New York

THE SOPHISTICATED TRAVELER

THE NEW YORK TIMES MAGAZINE/ PART 2/ MARCH 13, 1983

Copyright © 1983, The New York Times

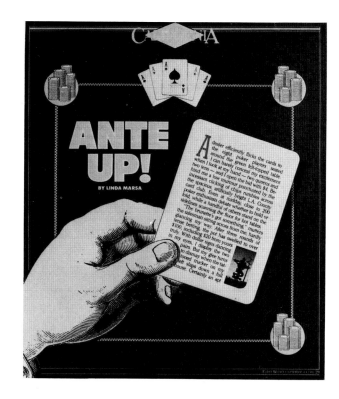

249

Art Directors	**Louis Silverstein, Walter Bernard**
Designer	**Walter Bernard**
Artist	**Seymour Chwast**
Client	**The New York Times**
Editor	**Mike Leahy**
Publisher	**The New York Times, New York**
Publication	**The New York Times**

250

Art Director	**Rick Stark**
Designer	**Rick Stark**
Director	**Altemus**
Publication	**Family Weekly, New York**

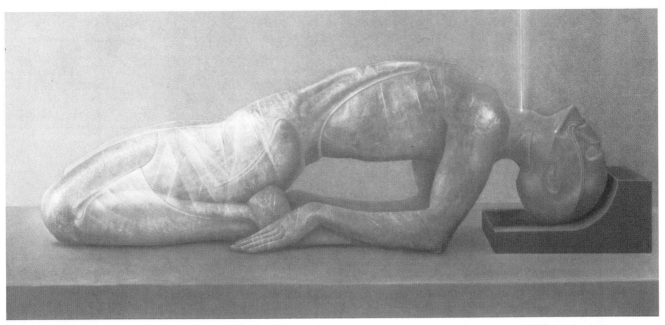

GOLD AWARD

—— **251** ——

Art Director **Elizabeth Woodson**
Designer **Liz Siroka, Patrick
Deffenbaugh**
Artist **Michel Henricot**
Publication **Omni Publications Int'l
Ltd., New York**

V.P./Graphics
Director **Frank M. DeVino**

THE SHORT
AND
HAPPY
FLIGHT
OF A
SPY
ON THE RUN

BY DAVID JACKSON

When energy runs low we'll
import plasma from the nearest star

MOTHER
SUN

BY EDWARD REGIS, JR

It's A.D. 2600, and the solar system has been gob-
bled up, plundered. The planets from Mercury to
Jupiter, their satellites, even the rings of Saturn
have been cannibalized. Humanity has spread
itself out across the solar system as if on a vast
spider's web, and there are far more people living
off Earth than on it. Space settlement is old hat,
with people on the moon, on what's left of the
planets and their remaining satellites, and in the
s homes—space homes—that have proliferated
like splitting bacteria. Sol's entire planetary sys-

PHOTOGRAPH BY DAN MORRILL

252

Art Director	**Bob Ciano**
Designer	**Nora Sheehan**
Photographer	**Wayne Sorce**
Writer	**David Jackson**
Editors	**Richard B. Stolley,**
	Judith Daniels
Publisher	**Time Inc.**
Publication	**LIFE Magazine, New York**

253

Art Director	**Elizabeth Woodson**
Designer	**Regina Dombrowski**
Photographer	**Dan Morrill**
Publication	**Omni Publications Int'l Ltd., New York**
V.P./Graphics Director	**Frank M. DeVino**

IT'S
JUST
ANOTHER

DAY

*Who
says the only
life worth
living goes
according
to plan?*

*by
Prudence
Mackintosh*

Pollution on Tap
How to Find Pure Water

*You can make sure it's safe—with these tips
on lab tests, bottled brands and home filters*
By Gerald Lanson

When Rich Christie decided to test the
drinking water of Rockaway Town-
ship, NJ, for contaminants, he didn't
expect to find any. As chief environmental officer for the wooded, residential community, Christie had read
reports of bad water elsewhere and
set out "to prove we didn't have a
problem in this pristine wilderness."
He was wrong.

	254		255
Art Director	Fred Woodward	Art Directors	Will Hopkins, Ira Friedlander
Designer	Fred Woodward	Designers	Will Hopkins, Ira Friedlander
Artist	Andrzej Dudzinski	Photographer	Pete Turner
Client	Texas Monthly	Writer	Gerald Lanson
Editor	Greg Curtis	Editor	T. George Harris
Publisher	Texas Monthly Inc., Austin	Publisher	Owen Lipstein
Publication	Texas Monthly	Publication	American Health, New York

A TALE OF TWO CITIES

SHANGHAI

In China, change is the only constant

AND IN THE DISTANCE, THROUGH THE PORTHOLE, THERE stood China.

Of course, wherever you are in the world, China stands *figuratively* there, a dim, tremendous presence somewhere across the horizon, sending out its coded messages, exerting its ancient magnetism over the continents. I had been prowling and loitering around it for years, often touched on the shoulder by its long, long reach—watching the Chinese-Americans shadowbox in San Francisco, say, or being dragged, screaming and kicking, to the Chinese opera somewhere, or interviewing renegade patriots in Taiwan, or debating whether to go to the fish-and-chip shop or the Cantonese takeout in Dublin. It had always seemed to me the land of the grand simplicities, pursuing its own mighty way through history, impassive, impervious, where everything was more absolute than it was elsewhere and the human condition majestically overrode all obstacles. I had wondered and marveled at it for half a lifetime, and here I was, at last, on my way to meet it face to face on a less than spanking Chinese steamship, rust-streaked, off-white, red flag at the stern, steaming northward through the blue-green China Sea.

My fellow passengers assiduously prepared me for the encounter. They showed me how best to suck the goodness out of the smoked black carp at dinner. They taught me to count to ten in Mandarin. They drew my attention to an article in *China Pictorial* about the propagation of stinkbugs in Guangdong Province. Mrs. Wang, returning from a visit to her sister in Taiwan, vividly evoked for me her hysterectomy by acupuncture. ("When they slit me open, oh, it hurt very bad, but after, it was a very *strange* feeling, very *strange*....) A bureaucrat, returning from an official mission to Hong Kong, thoroughly explained to me the Three Principles of Chinese Government Policy.

Around us, the sea was like a Chinese geography lesson, too. It was never empty. Sometimes, apparently abandoned sampans wallowed in the swell; sometimes, flotillas of trawlers threshed about the place. Red-

BY JAN MORRIS

In the early mornings, I used to go wandering....Only by peering through the half-open gates can you glimpse the tangled, crowded life within.

OLYMPICS '84
AMERICA GETS SET

By P. S. Wood

THE NUCLEAR KNOT

IN DIPLOMATIC TIES

by Gary L. Browning

Recently my family and I enjoyed a vacation in Arches National Park. When we arrived and while the older children and I unloaded the car, our younger daughters explored their fascinating new surroundings. Katie Jane, age two, soon came running to Joan from a nearby water faucet where she had just seen her first live lizards. "Mommie," she shrieked, "come quick. I show you baby alligators!" Katie Jane, we would all agree, had made an error in identifying full-grown lizards as baby alligators. Yet, given her tender years, her naivete was harmless and entirely forgivable.

The situation is more serious, however, when we adults commit and stubbornly persist in error, when we ignore or distort common experience and our deepest feelings, or mangle reality under the weights pestle of our prejudices. In some important ways we have done this with the Russians, and have created out of a great nation "an impossible and foolish fancy," a chimera. In Greek mythology, Chimera was a fire-breathing she-monster usually represented as a composite of a lion, a goat, and a serpent or dragon. Like prejudices, a chimera arises not from enlightened observation of real life, but from the imagination, from fantasy.

The Russian stereotype, a menacing chimera assailing the minds of many Americans, is a demeaning caricature of the Russian people. It alleges that Russians are generally ill-mannered and swaggering; bellicose and militaristic; unreliable, deceitful, cunning, and atheistic; they trample on all that is humane, on respect for the individual, on tolerance for dissent, on compassion for the suffering, on spiritual refinement; and, like a bear, they are dull-witted but powerful, and only respond to displays of superior

Dr. Browning is an associate professor of Russian and dean of Honors Education at BYU. He has visited the U.S.S.R. six times and studied at the University of Moscow. Professor Browning recently returned from leading a trip of American ranchers to the Soviet Union. This article is an edited amalgam of talks first presented at a BYU forum and at the First Market of Ideas.

force, and even then with belligerence.

Let me also share with you my understanding of the Soviet stereotype of Americans. It is inaccurate, unfair, demeaning, and self-serving. But, with their wand of class-consciousness, the Soviets tend to divide Americans into a large group of poor workers oppressed by a smaller clique of the evil wealthy, especially those financiers, manufacturers, and suppliers of armaments.

In the Soviet stereotype, the capitalist American is opportunistic, exploitative, and ruthless; he is intellectually shallow, irreverent toward his heritage, and obsessed with an amoral technology; he is permissive and narcissistic, and he is easily satisfied with the trivial and tawdry in the arts, and uncritically swayed by charisma and rhetoric in politics. Most important, he is naive, inconstant, and, thus, dangerous in his behavior. That is, he is capable of unpredictable and illogical responses which, on the international plane, may well risk war and even the future of mankind to protect his position and ego. This stereotype fits Americans little better than does our Russian stereotype their people, but both, underlie much thinking, and behavior.

How do these unfortunate misperceptions arise among intelligent human beings, and how are they perpetuated? Of course the answer lies largely in inadequate, unreliable information. The Soviet media distort the truth, principally from ideological and chauvinistic motivations, the American media, though ostensibly free, are also influenced by powerful forces, some chauvinistic, some ideological, but mostly commercial. "What should the public know?" is too often superseded by "What does the public want?" Of course we are only free to the degree that we know the truth. Frequently we are content to follow the wretched path of established prejudice, rather than clear the way of the mental undergrowth obscuring true objectivity and lucid thinking. The value of an open society is diminished when the minds of its

people are closed.

In an effort to acquire more accurate information, I traveled to the U.S.S.R. last December with five American ranchers from the Western states. The ranchers' purpose in going there was to see that country with their own eyes, to talk directly with Soviet citizens, to learn their perspectives on life, their attitudes toward the United States, and their commitment to peace and disarmament. The ranchers are intelligent, well-read, and articulate, and they were eager to learn.

They did not return to America as experts after 15 days abroad, but they now know much more than most Americans do about the Soviet Union. Since not all citizens of our two countries can visit the other, I would like to share with you some of the discoveries the ranchers made.

Russians are more like Americans than different

First and foremost, the ranchers learned after talking with scores of Soviets on several levels that they are less Russian, Ukrainian, or citizens from the other 13 republics than they are human: women, men, and children. They have the full range of human features, emotions, aspirations, and failings. Each has good qualities and weaknesses. But given the opportunity and incentives, most prefer to be upright, generous, trustworthy, and peace-loving. However, almost any of them can be mean and even vicious, especially when insulted or frightened. These masses are a mirror of American masses, of you and me, too better, no worse.

The ranchers recognized that among Russians and Americans there is roughly the same distribution of the capable and the weak, the compassionate and the barbaric, the moral and the unprincipled, and, in summary, the good and the evil. Are we not far more alike than we are different?

We all witnessed the need for the people

May 1983 BYU Today Page 1

SILVER AWARD

258

Art Director **Bryan L. Peterson**
Designer **Bryan L. Peterson**
Artist **Mark Robison**
Writer **Gary L. Browning**
Client **Brigham Young University**
Editor **Ken Shelton**
Publisher **Brigham Young University, Provo, UT**

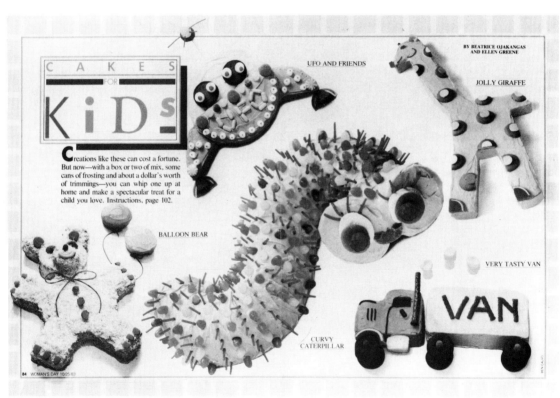

259

Art Director **Lloyd Ziff**
Designer **Lloyd Ziff**
Artist **Fernando Botero**
Writer **Gabriel Garcia Marquez**
Editor **Richard Locke**
Publisher **Conde Nast Publications, Inc., New York**
Publication **Vanity Fair**

260

Art Director **Brad Pallas**
Photographer **Ben Calvo**
Editor **Ellen Green**
Publication **Woman's Day, New York**

A SHORT HISTORY OF THE PHAETON

Featuring the 1934 Packard 1108 Sport Phaeton by LeBaron

	261		262
Art Director	**David W. Bird II**	Art Director	**Derek Ungless**
Photographer	**Roy Query**	Designer	**Steven Doyle**
Writer	**Ron Santucci**	Photographer	**David Bailey**
Publication	**Automobile Quarterly Magazine, Princeton, NJ**	Publication	**Rolling Stone Magazine, New York**
		Photo Editor	**Laurie Kratochvil**

SCOTT GLENN

A fter he gave up the freeways of L.A. for the mountain roads of Idaho, Glenn's career took off. Now the tough men of Urban Cowboy and Personal Best has really hit high gear, he's starring in The Right Stuff and The Keep.

When you interview Scott Glenn, you don't do it in the Polo Lounge in Beverly Hills. Glenn may have a thriving Hollywood acting career going, but he's *not* a creature of Lotusland. The man who tangled with John Travolta in *Urban Cowboy* and toughened Mariel Hemingway in *Personal Best* has leads in two of this fall's big Hollywood movies—*The Right Stuff* and *The Keep*. But he remains firmly and permanently domiciled in Ketchum (pop. 1,400), a cultural haven in southern Idaho. How can he live in Ketchum and still find work in Hollywood? With great success; ironically, Glenn didn't become a force in the movies until, fed up with L.A., he turned his back on the movie capital.

By Bart Mills. Photography by Mark Hanauer.

A BOOM IN BULBS

Dutch tulip merchants have transformed a sixteenth-century curiosity into a flourishing twentieth-century industry. The value comes not from the flowers but from the bulbs.

By Jon and Marianne Swan

263		264	
Art Director	Andrew J. Epstein	Art Director	Mary Shapiro
Designer	Andrew J. Epstein	Designer	Mary Shapiro
Photographer	Mark Hanauer	Photographer	Dennis Stock/Magnum
Writer	Bart Mills	Writers	Jon and Marianne Swan
Client	Moviegoer Magazine	Client	Connoisseur Magazine
Editor	Frank Finn	Editor	Philip Herrera
Publisher	13-30 Corporation, Knoxville, TN	Publisher	Connoisseur Magazine/ Hearst Corp., New York
Publication	Moviegoer Magazine	Photo Research	Laurie Platt Winfrey and Diane Raines Keim

265

Art Director	**Frances Reinfeld**
Designer	**Roger Gorman**
Editor	**Ingrid Sischy**
Publisher	**Anthony Korner, Amy Baker Sandback**
Design Firm	**Reiner Design Consultants, New York**

266

Art Director	**David Herbick**
Designer	**David Herbick**
Artists	**Joe Lertola, David Herbick**
Writer	**Ken Robbins**
Publisher	**Playboy Enterprises, Inc.**
Publication	**GAMES Magazine, New York**

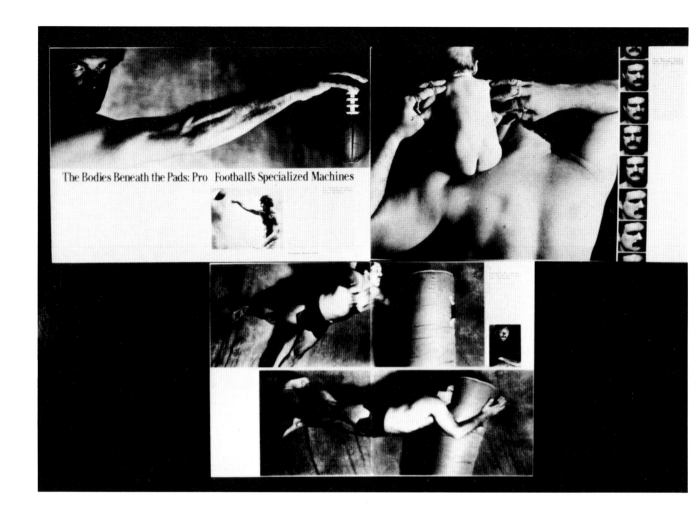

The Bodies Beneath the Pads: Pro Football's Specialized Machines

GOLD AWARD

267

Art Director	**Bob Ciano**
Designer	**Bob Ciano**
Photographer	**Michael O'Neill**
Writer	**Steve Robinson**
Editors	**Richard B. Stolley, Steve Robinson**
Publisher	**Time Inc.**
Publication	**LIFE Magazine, New York**

RUDI GERNREICH
Designer

268

Art Director	**Bob Ciano**
Designer	**Charles W. Pates**
Photographer	**John Loengard**
Writer	**Tod Brewster**
Editors	**Richard B. Stolley, Mary Simons**
Publisher	**Time Inc.**
Publication	**LIFE Magazine, New York**

269

Art Director	**Nancy Butkus**
Designer	**Nancy Duckworth**
Photographer	**Bonnie Schiffman**
Writer	**Terry McDonell**
Client	**California Magazine**
Editor	**Nancy Butkus**
Publisher	**Alan Bennett**
Publication	**California Magazine, Beverly Hills**

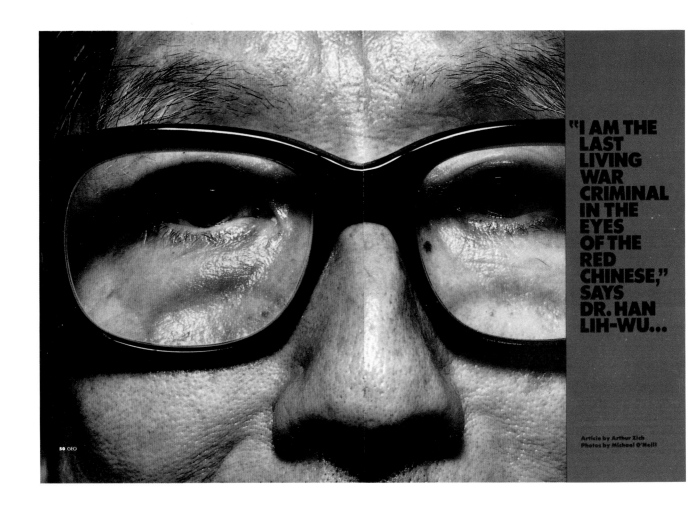

"I AM THE LAST LIVING WAR CRIMINAL IN THE EYES OF THE RED CHINESE," SAYS DR. HAN LIH-WU...

Article by Arthur Zich
Photos by Michael O'Neill

50 GEO

◦ **GOLD AWARD**

270

Art Director	**Mary K. Baumann**
Designer	**Mary K. Baumann**
Photographer	**Michael O'Neill**
Editor	**John Tarkov**
Publisher	**Knapp Communications, Corp.**
Publication	**GEO Magazine, New York**

June, 1983

A NEW WAY OF SEEING

Five years and 60 issues ago this month, a small group of us launched a magazine designed around a new way of seeing photography. It was our belief then, as now, that a magazine about photographers and their photographs (as opposed to yet another about cameras and craft) would bring a new literature to the language of photography.

In that first issue I stated that we perceived the photography universe as being made up of five constituencies: fashion, fine art, historical, photojournalistic and commercial photography. But for this special anniversary issue we decided to look at photographs in terms of the senses they convey, those which serve photographers and through which photographers reach their audience.

Of the thousands of photographs we've published, we selected 60—one for each issue—and divided the pictures into what we are calling the five senses of photography: style, time, being, place and nonsense.

Great pictures are always more than literal representations of people, places and facts. They have shadings and resonances of their own, like the tones and textures of a complex symphony. Leafing through the score of the five movements that follow, you are invited to interpret, question and perceive photographs in a new way, one which we hope once again will broaden and enrich the language of photography. —Sean Callahan

48

NO ONE LIVES FOR MORE THAN A CENTURY WITHOUT ACQUIRING A SINGULAR WISDOM.

GEO**PEOPLE**

Columnist George Will, writing recently about the death of 119-year-old ex-slave Bo Ward, asserted that "anyone who manages to live through 100 or more years—including years prodigicd by such terrors as nuclear weapons and processed cheese, has done something remarkable." Will added: "Such longevity is a triumph not just of physiology but of the spirit."

Each of the Americans whose words and photos appear on these pages is an affirmation of such spiritual resilience. It is not that some of them aren't extraordinary in their own right: Joel Hildebrand, a professor of chemistry, provided research that made modern deep-sea diving possible; Olga Ulke was a former glamour girl and star of the Broadway hit *Babes in Toyland*; Harry Lieberman, celebrated Jewish folk artist, grew up in the Hasidic Mystery Ecstasy sect in Poland. Yet they, and the other centenarians interviewed for this article—a mere handful of the estimated 13,200 people over 100 years old in the United States—are remarkable for more than their individual accomplishments, for more even than their triumph over the actuarial odds (it has been estimated that for identical twins such as Lucy Brown Coleman and her sister to reach the century mark together is a 700-million-to-1 shot). They are unique, pungently individual survivors not only of time but of what George Will calls "historical vertigo."

Modern societies have notably short attention spans. As essayist Susan Sontag recently pointed

out, we now measure cultural epochs in terms of decades when we once used centuries; there is simply no gauge that can meaningfully measure a hundred years' worth of change at today's rates without skittering instantly off scale. To be confronted, then, with people who actually remember the nineteenth century is a trifle unnerving. For example, Mary Duckworth, 121 years old, spent her childhood in slavery in Taylorsville, Mississippi. When she was born, Victor Hugo was writing *Les Misérables*; Ivan Turgenev, *Fathers and Sons*. In her youth, Dickens, Tolstoy, Twain, Longfellow and Flaubert were putting the finishing touches on new works: Gregor Mendel, Louis Pasteur and Alfred Nobel were perfecting their discoveries. When she was a teenager, Alexander Graham Bell demonstrated his telephone, and Thomas Edison was displaying his first phonograph.

Had they lived to enjoy as ripe an old age as the people on these pages, such figures as Lenin, Henry Ford, H.G. Wells, Marconi and Einstein would be among us still.

These centenarians do not have uniformly keen memories; indeed, their senses are often noticeably faded. Yet each has something to say to us—something about a sense of self that is less encumbered by the concerns about appearance, status and accomplishment by which most of us regard ourselves. Harry Lieberman, pictured opposite with his great-granddaughter, Sarah, begins the tale on page 24. —*Marc Barasch*

GEO **23**

BREAKING

DISTINCTIVE MERIT

270A		271A	
Art Director	**Will Hopkins**	Art Director	**Mary K. Baumann**
Designer	**Will Hopkins**	Designer	**Mary K. Baumann**
Writer	**Sean Callahan**	Photographer	**Max Aguilera–Hellweg**
Editor	**Sean Callahan**	Writer	**Marc Barasch**
Publisher	**Gary Fisher**	Editor	**Ken Labich**
Publication	**American Photographer/CBS Magazines, New York**	Publisher	**Knapp Communications, Corp.**
		Publication	**GEO Magazine, New York**

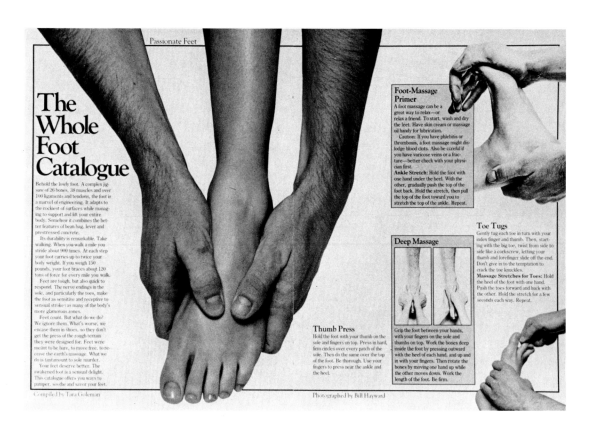

271

Art Directors **Will Hopkins, Ira Friedlander**
Designers **Will Hopkins, Ira Friedlander**
Photographer **Bill Hayward**
Writer **Tara Goleman**
Editor **T. George Harris**
Publisher **Owen Lipstein**
Publication **American Health, New York**

272

Art Director **Fred Woodward**
Designer **Fred Woodward**
Photographers **Matthew Savins, Jim Cammack, Will van Overbeek**
Artists **Gary Kelley, Ray-Mel Cornelius, Jose Cruz, Alexa Grace, Melissa Grimes, LeeLee Brazeal**
Client **Texas Monthly**
Editor **Greg Curtis**
Publisher **Texas Monthly Inc.**
Publication **Texas Monthly, Austin**

IT TAKES TWO

In ballet, great partnerships are extraordinarily rare. When they happen, they become legends.

NATALIA MAKAROVA AND ANTHONY DOWELL
Each emerged as an international star in the 1960s, she at Leningrad's Kirov Ballet, he at England's Royal Ballet. After her defection in 1970, they formed a luminous alliance, complementing each other's superb style in such classics as Tchaikovsky's *Swan Lake*.

272A	
Art Director	**Mary K. Baumann**
Designer	**John Tom Cohoe**
Writer	**Anita Finkel**
Editor	**David Bourdon**
Publisher	**Knapp Communications**
Publication	**GEO Magazine, New York**

273A	
Art Director	**Bob Ciano**
Designer	**Bob Ciano**
Photographer	**Wendy Watriss**
Writers	**George Colt, Donna Haupt**
Editors	**Richard B. Stolley, Jeff Wheelwright**
Publisher	**Time Inc.**
Publication	**LIFE Magazine, New York**

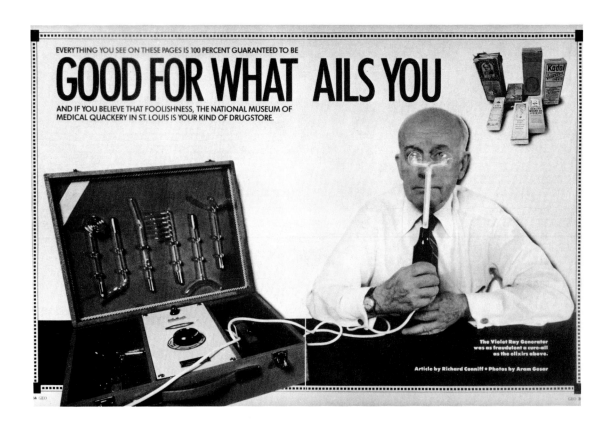

	273		274
Art Director	**Mary K. Baumann**	Art Director	**Bob Ciano**
Designer	**Lori Barra**	Designer	**Nora Sheehan**
Photographer	**Aram Gesar**	Photographer	**Annie Leibowitz**
Writer	**Richard Conniff**	Editors	**Richard B. Stolley, Mary**
Editor	**John Tarkov**		**Steinbauer**
Publisher	**Knapp**	Publisher	**Time Inc.**
	Communications	Publication	**LIFE Magazine, New**
Publication	**Geo Magazine, New**		**York**
	York		

Chris Rainier

As photographic assistant to Ansel Adams, Chris Rainier has spent the past two years making prints from the master photographer's 30,000-negative file, curating his exhibits, researching his books and testing his equipment. When Rainier began his own work, he was apprehensive that he might be tempted to follow too closely in Adams's footsteps, and he will be the first to admit that the pastoral serenity of his early photographs is characteristic of work by many Adams disciples. However, he believes that his immersion in Adams's photography "served as a catalyst" to help him define his own style. Both photographers are drawn to the landscape and to environmental issues, but the younger is more attuned to nature's dark

side. These fallen limbs, tangled roots and timeworn surfaces are reminders of nature's changeability rather than its endurance.

An avid environmentalist, Rainier is involved in various conservation-related projects, among them researching photos for a recent publication by the International Union for Conservation of Nature and Natural Resources (IUCN), and making pictures for a forthcoming book on international parks in danger. Though he plans to travel more extensively for this project, Rainier made many of his recent photos of nature's symbolic response to man's inhumanity in the American Southwest.

Social commentary in landscape photography has largely been the prov-

ince of urban photographers who depict such blatant man-made subjects as shopping malls, superhighways or discarded beer cans. But Rainier comments on the wilderness by using a unique approach to classic motifs. Although the promontory scenes that his photographs with a 4 x 5 view camera are made far from a visible human presence, they inspire a dramatic realization of the precarious relationship between man and the earth. Rainier's photographs possess a tension and power that elicit our fear for the sanctity of the remaining wilderness. In the light, forms and textures of these portentous places he has found signs that the true "spirit of the land" may be more vulnerable than we know.—Kathryn Livingston

Portentous and vulnerable landscapes.

Tumbleweed and ravine, Utah, 1982

GEO**ARCHIVE**

CONEY ISLAND
BALLYHOO AND INNOCENCE
VINTAGE PHOTOGRAPHS SHOW WHAT AMERICA'S FIRST AMUSEMENT PARK LOOKED LIKE WHEN IT AND THE NATION WERE YOUNG.

88 GEO

274 A

Art Director	**Will Hopkins**
Designer	**Louis F. Cruz**
Photographer	**Chris Rainier**
Writer	**Kathryn Livingston**
Editor	**Sean Callahan**
Publisher	**Gary Fisher**
Publication	**American Photographer/CBS Magazines, New York**

275A

Art Director	**Mary K. Baumann**
Designer	**Lori Barra**
Writer	**Jeffrey Simpson**
Editor	**David Bourdon**
Publisher	**Knapp Communications, Corp.**
Publication	**GEO Magazine, New York**

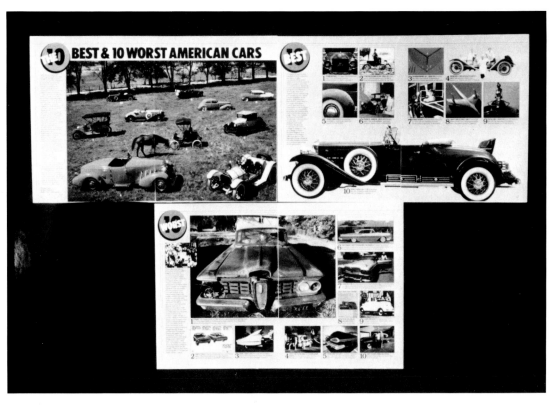

	275
Art Director	Bob Ciano
Designer	Charles W. Pates
Photographers	Philippe Halsman, Paul Schutzer, Cornell Capa, Stanley Tretick, Toni Frissell, Jacques Lowe, Robert L. Knudsen, Cecil Stoughton
Writer	Ann Bayer
Editors	Richard B. Stolley, Mary Steinbauer
Publisher	Time Inc.
Publication	LIFE Magazine, New York

	276
Art Director	Bob Ciano
Designer	Bob Ciano
Photographer	Michael Melford
Writers	Joe Pointdexter, Linda Gomez
Editors	Richard B. Stolley, Mary Steinbauer
Publisher	Time Inc.
Publication	LIFE Magazine, New York

DISTINCTIVE MERIT

276A

Art Director	**Bob Ciano**
Designer	**Bob Ciano**
Photographer	**Bob Adelman**
Writers	**George Colt, Joseph Pointdexter**
Editors	**Richard B. Stolley, Mary Steinbauer**
Publisher	**Time Inc.**
Publication	**LIFE Magazine, New York**

277A

Art Director	**Elizabeth Woodson**
Designer	**Elizabeth Woodson**
Photographer	**Jeffrey Rotman**
Publication	**Omni Publications Int'l Ltd., New York**
V.P./Graphics Director	**Frank M. DeVino**

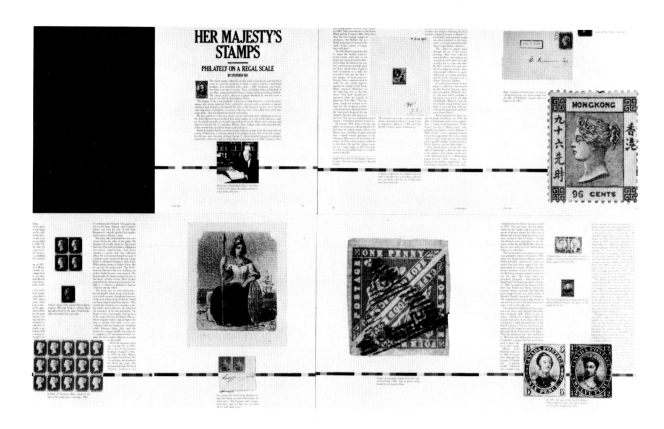

277		278	
Art Director	**Carla Barr**	Art Director	**Will Hopkins**
Designer	**Carla Barr**	Designer	**Will Hopkins**
Photographer	**Geoffrey Shakerly**	Photographer	**David Burnett**
Writer	**Stephen Fay**	Writer	**Laurence Shames**
Client	**Connoisseur Magazine**	Editor	**Sean Callahan**
Editor	**Thomas Hoving**	Publisher	**Gary Fisher**
Publisher	**The Hearst Corporation**	Publication	**American**
Publication	**Connoisseur Magazine, New York**		**Photographer/CBS Magazines, New York**
Editor	**Eve Auchincloss**		

THE INTIMATE VISION OF EVELYN CAMERON

In 1889, a well-born British woman and her husband forsook the stately life for the hard, barren frontiers of eastern Montana. Her diaries, her letters, her photographs and the texture of her life and thinking leave us an unforgettable portrait of the Old West that really was.

Evelyn Cameron exploring the badlands of Montana—and mounting photographs inside her ranch house.

GEO 67

279		280	
Art Director	**Mary K. Baumann**	Art Director	**Bob Ciano**
Designer	**John Tom Cohoe**	Designer	**Ellen A. Kostroff**
Photographer	**Evelyn Cameron**	Photographer	**Bert Stern**
Writer	**Donna L. Lucey**	Writer	**Ann Bayer**
Editor	**John Tarkov**	Editors	**Richard B. Stolley, Jim Watters**
Publisher	**Knapp Communications, Corp.**	Publisher	**Time Inc.**
Publication	**GEO Magazine, New York**	Publication	**LIFE Magazine, New York**

To the Lakes with Love

Colwith Force is a waterfall near Elterwater.

Inspired by England's Lake District, Coleridge, Wordsworth and Southey linked man and the nourishing wilderness in poems that never die.

There was a time when meadow, grove,
and stream,
The earth and every common sight,
To me did seem
Apparelled in celestial light,
The glory and the freshness of a dream.
William Wordsworth
"Intimations of Immortality"

Celestial light—or something very close to it—still cloaks the massive mountains of Cumbria, the English Lake District. It picks out the daffodil and celandine, the lonely reaches of upland pond and hidden vale celebrated by William Wordsworth, Samuel Taylor Coleridge and Robert Southey, the Lake Poets of the early nineteenth century. Wandering clouds, lonely or otherwise, still cast their shadows over the lakes these poets immortalized—Grasmere, Rydal Water, Esthwaite Water, Brothers' Water. The cataracts, as Wordsworth wrote, still "blow their trumpets from the steep." You don't have to care about poetry to love the lakes, but it certainly helps.

Every year, thousands of people are drawn to the district who care nothing for dactyl or spondee and have long forgotten what they may have known of Romantic poetry. They come to hike and camp and wind surf, escaping from a world that, as Wordsworth saw, "is too much with us."

Cumbria, the new name for the old counties of Cumberland and Westmorland, curves outward from the northwestern coast of England between Wales and Scotland. It contains England's highest peaks (Scafell Pike, Skiddaw, Helvellyn, all over 3,000 feet) and some of the oldest mountains in the world, a few are 400 million years old. Wordsworth described the region in his best-selling *Guide to the Lakes* (1810) as being shaped like a wheel, with the lakes for spokes: Windermere, Coniston, Haweswater and Thirlmere (now reservoirs), Ullswater, Grasmere, Derwentwater, Crummock Water, Buttermere, Loweswater, Ennerdale Water and Wastwater, as well as innumerable smaller bodies of water called tarns and

GEO **53**

Art & Crafts

Perhaps nothing ever made by the hand of man is as reassuring as a boat. Created primarily as a means of transportation, a boat is at the same time a safe haven in an innately hostile environment. As long as we are in the boat, and the boat is sound, we are okay. The feeling of well-being that comes from knowing that a boat can be depended on must be as old as civilization itself.

Another reassuring thing about boats is that fundamentally they don't change. Their function predetermines their form, and though sail has given way to steam, which in turn has given way to internal combustion, boats still have bow and stern and gunwales, always in the same place.

The rowboat is one of the most dependable and satisfying of all boats, a humble and venerable craft that can move steadily through the water whether or not there is wind or fuel, as long as a pair of arms and a back are in working order. The thoroughly decent nature of the rowboat tends to attract the sort of artisans to whom excellence of workmanship and integrity of design mean more than speed or technological wizardry, men and women who view change for its own sake as foolish. They know that the way two strips of spruce decking dovetail says more about a boat's soul than a .04 percent increase in performance through the use of Fiberglas. Rowboat people tend to be enlightened fogies, both old and young, whose feeling for what constitutes art is a lot closer to home than the Mona Lisa.

Allan Weitz, a photographer from landlocked Princeton, New Jersey, has never built a boat, but his ideas about art in photography often involve the cut of a jib or the set of an oar. For the last few years Weitz has done the bulk of his editorial work for a handsome publication called *Nautical Quarterly*, photographing everything from 70mph power boats to the interiors of floating townhouses. Along the way, Weitz has developed a special affection for rowing boats, whether the latest in state-of-the-art sliding seat shells or the oldest seat-of-the-pants dories. With a connoisseur's loving eye, Weitz has assembled his pictorial armada, giving each carefully wrought craft its proper place in the sun, and on the sea.

Allan Weitz assembles his pictorial armada.

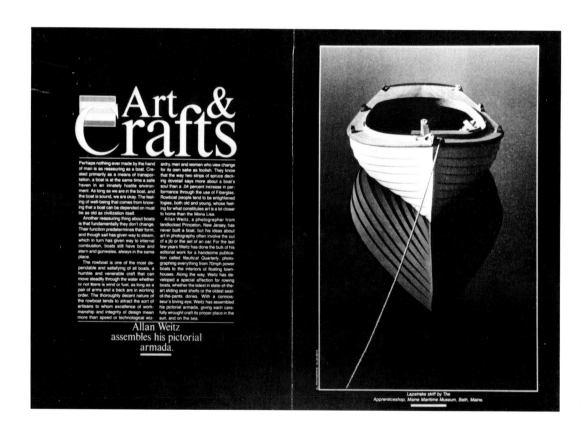

Lapstrake skiff by The Apprenticeshop, Maine Maritime Museum, Bath, Maine.

	281		282
Art Director	**Mary K. Baumann**	Art Director	**Will Hopkins**
Designer	**Mary K. Baumann**	Designer	**Louis F. Cruz**
Photographer	**Denis Waugh**	Photographer	**Allan Weitz**
Writer	**Erla Zwingle**	Writer	**Owen Edwards**
Editor	**David Bourdon**	Editor	**Sean Callahan**
Publisher	**Knapp Communications**	Publisher	**Gary Fisher**
Publication	**GEO Magazine, New York**	Publication	**American Photographer/CBS Magazines, New York**

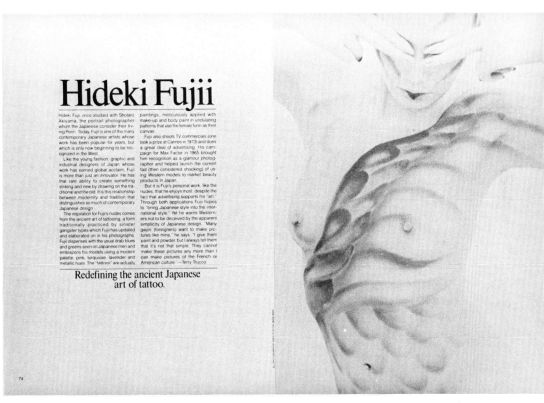

283		284	
Art Director	**Bob Ciano**	Art Director	**Will Hopkins**
Designer	**Nora Sheehan**	Designer	**Louis Cruz**
Photographer	**Robert Vavra**	Photographer	**Hideki Fujii**
Writer	**Anne Fadiman**	Writer	**Terry Trucco**
Editors	**Richard B. Stolley, Mary Steinbauer**	Editor	**Sean Callahan**
		Publisher	**Gary Fisher**
Publisher	**Time Inc.**	Publication	**American Photographer/CBS Magazines, New York**
Publication	**LIFE Magazine, New York**		

THE ISSUE IS LIFE AND death, nothing less. The last-minute stay that spared J. D. Autry dramatized the dilemma of the death penalty and raised again the question of whether Autry and the 1,230 other residents now on death row would ever be executed.

TO DIE OR NOT TO DIE

O nce again Alvin Bronstein sat patiently in a deserted alcove of the Supreme Court, waiting for a chance to save the life of a killer he had never met. As the American Civil Liberties Union's senior lawyer in Washington, it repeatedly fell to him to search for a high-court justice willing to stay an executioner's hand. In six earlier cases, he had failed; there is seldom much ammunition left at this stage of a case. Last week looked like a macabre reprise: 1,200 miles away James David Autry lay stretched out on a Texas prison gurney, already tethered to an intravenous tube that would deliver a fatal dose of poison in less than an hour.

Just after midnight (11 p.m. Texas time), Bronstein got word that three appellate judges had turned down Autry's latest plea. Now, literally past the 11th hour, Bronstein sprang into action. Coolly, but with little private hope, he dashed off another few lines to his handwritten petition—emphasizing an unsettled issue about the fairness of Autry's sentence. Court clerks grabbed his three pages of yellow foolscap and dispatched them to Associate Justice Byron R. White. Again Bronstein waited. Twenty minutes later the phone rang. It was his ACLU colleagues in Houston. Bronstein was amazed that they seemed so pleased.

"How did you do it?" one of them cried.

"What are you talking about?" he replied. Even as he said it, he understood. But elation waited until he saw White's official order. "We saved somebody's life today," he sighed.

The last-minute reprieve of J. D. Autry was just that—a reprieve, a delay, a chance to re-examine and reargue the question of whether a killer should die or should not die. It means that not only Autry but all the death-row inmates in Texas and California, who account for about one-quarter of the nation's condemned population, may not even be considered for execution until the spring of 1984. The Supreme Court will hear arguments next month in a case from California that poses the question of whether a condemned prisoner is entitled to a judicial review of his sentence to determine whether it is "proportional" to those of criminals who committed similar crimes. In effect, Byron

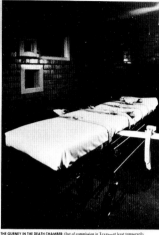

THE GURNEY IN THE DEATH CHAMBER: Out of commission in Texas—at least temporarily

Kane's
Kids

What would possess a photographer more associated with beautiful babies than burping babies to make portraits of these bite-sized bundles of joy?

It was an assignment, of sorts, although Art Kane will be the first to tell you that the concept was entirely his. Asked by the Johnson & Johnson Baby Products Company to create photographs to decorate its sleek new I.M. Pei-designed headquarters, the able Kane envisioned an "international portrait gallery of faces." He sent a team of scouts and assistants scurrying around the streets of New York to find babies of every color, flavor and ethnic origin available in this melting crib of minorities and majorities. Likely kids were immortalized on Polaroid film, and then brought back to the master's studio. If Kane liked the face, the parents got a letter from J&J asking them to bring their child in for a sitting.

Kane photographed each baby in an identical, minimal setting. The only unusual element was the absorbent cotton batting used to cover the table on which his models posed. The sophisti-

cated style that Kane achieved through the use of stark lighting and simple settings shows us babies in a whole new way. By departing from the traditional approach to baby portraits, Kane challenges the notion of the generic baby. We are reminded that babies have personalities—like adults, only more so. These faces are the expression of unspoiled characters; miniature people with mannerisms unaffected by any knowledge of Brooke Shields or Shirley Temple, and minds oblivious to the fact that they are wetting themselves in front of a very famous photographer.

At the same time, we can read into these faces certain adult qualities: the French girl looks sweet and seductive; the Japanese girl appears clever and tenacious, capable of bringing honor to her family; and the Irish girl is clearly a fine broth of a colleen. Kane's kids show more of themselves than most adults ever do in formal portrait sittings. The camera and the photographer disappear, and the viewer is left in the presence of pure, unadulterated child.
—Amy Schiffman

The "melting-crib"
theory of baby photography.

Hungarian

50

285		286	
Art Director	Margaret Joskow	Art Director	Will Hopkins
Designer	Margaret Joskow	Designer	Will Hopkins
Photographer	Wally McNamee	Photographer	Art Kane
Writer	Peter Goldman	Writer	Amy Schiffman
Publisher	Washington Post Co.	Editor	Sean Callahan
Publication	Newsweek, New York	Publisher	Gary Fisher
		Publication	American Photographer/CBS Magazines, New York

1919-1933
In the Eye of the Storm

Germany's national upheaval propelled a revolution in the arts and the birth of photography's avant-garde.
by Bonnie Barrett Stretch and David Markus

The great *Film und Foto* exhibit in Stuttgart in 1929—whose famous poster (below) depicts the photographer as colossus bestriding the world—celebrated a decade of astonishing changes in photography: changes that irrevocably transformed the ways in which we perceive our lives. Nowhere were these events more dramatic than in Germany, where in the turbulent years between the two World Wars, photography tore loose from its nineteenth-century origins and embraced the multiple functions it fills today. Photojournalism, industrial and architectural photography, micrography, stop-motion, aerial photography, advertising and political propaganda

all had their first full flourishing in Germany of the 1920s.

Germany's defeat in the First World War left the country in a shambles; its economy was ruined, its people dispirited, its future mortgaged to the banks of its former enemies. Artists could only look to the future for inspiration, and the avant-garde seized on photography as the perfect union of art and technology, the quintessential form of modern expression. Unexpected angles, revolutionary subjects, smaller cameras, eye-twisting distortions, all burst the old pictorial boundaries and produced what was widely hailed as the New Vision.

In the years of the Weimar Republic

arts and intellectual life in Germany flourished as never before. Yet the forces of reaction did not disappear. The clash between left and right, tradition and modernism, continued with a vengeance. Hitler rose to prominence only to fall and rise again. Popular tastes in literature see-sawed between the nostalgic eloquence of Thomas Mann and the anti-bourgeois dramas of Bertolt Brecht. "It was modernism under pressure," noted one observer of the day. "It tasted of the future."

In this volatile environment photography was embraced by some of the most creative artists of the time. Using techniques like precipitous perspective, foreshortening, superimposition, blur and cut, extreme closeup and fragmented cropping, they set out to create entirely new ways of seeing. Convinced that the camera could expand the capacity not only to observe but to understand, the avant-garde used photography to subvert visual tradition and to symbolize the accelerating flow and altered perception of space. Only in the mid-Thirties, with the final rise of Hitler, did the brightness of their enthusiasm begin to flicker, later to be extinguished by the wave of Nazi repression.

Last July an exhibit of avant-garde photos curated by Van Deren Coke for the San Francisco Museum of Modern Art completed an 18-month tour of the United States. What follows is a montage using pictures from that show as well as other reproductions from the period, a kind of memory book of the energy, anger, creativity and joy that animated the whirlwind years during which photography's New Vision was born.

A revolutionary way of seeing (opposite page) is embodied in this photogram by Laszlo Moholy-Nagy. The Hungarian-born artist's experiments with light, montage and diagonals are crucial to the avant-garde's transformation of photography

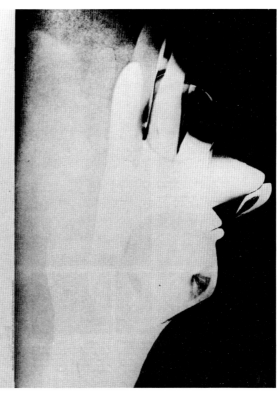

287	
Art Director	**Will Hopkins**
Designer	**Will Hopkins**
Writer	**David Markus**
Editor	**Sean Callahan**
Publisher	**Gary Fisher**
Publication	**American Photographer/CBS Magazines, New York**

288	
Art Director	**Bob Ciano**
Designer	**Bob Ciano**
Photographer	**Alen MacWeeney**
Writer	**Drew Greenland**
Editors	**Richard B. Stolley, Mary Steinbauer**
Publisher	**Time Inc.**
Publication	**LIFE Magazine, New York**

DIANA: AMERICAN BALLAD

A giver, a beauty, a woman of style, a woman: Diana Ross. In the tradition of the mid-twentieth-century love balladeer, with her voice she conveys warmth, lyric and totally feminine; with her all-stops-out delivery of a song, she suggests a vulnerability all the world's glamour cannot defend. For the voiceless millions, she sings their song. Captions by Jeanine Larmoth.

Dress: her own design. Harry Winston diamonds. From Revlon: ColorCreme Eyeshadows, Jungle Violet and Spirited Rose. Hair and make-up in this portfolio: Akira Mitani.

Photographs by Skrebneski/Produced by Nancy Tuck Gardiner

GEO**ARTS**

LIVING TREASURES OF **JAPAN**

JAPAN HAS A UNIQUE WAY OF HONORING ITS TRADITIONAL ARTISTS AND ENSURING THAT THEIR SKILLS LIVE ON.

Some nations make a commendable effort to honor their cultural heroes. The British, for instance, reward an eminent poet by naming him poet laureate, a title that also qualifies him as a salaried member of the royal household. In France, litterateurs fiendishly vie with one another to gain admission to the 40-member Académie Française, Europe's most prestigious literary academy. In Japan, the government honors the artist-craftspeople who preserve the nation's traditional crafts by designating them as "Holders of Important Intangible Cultural Properties." These individuals (there are rarely more than 70 at a time) are commonly referred to as "Living National Treasures." The accolade is of relatively recent origin, dating only from the early 1950s, when the government, concerned by the sacrifice of Japan's classic arts to the onrush of modernism and westernization, decided to preserve its cultural roots by encouraging traditional Japanese crafts. One of the most revered Living National Treasures is Gonroku Matsuda (opposite), an artist who designed a lacquered tea caddy, the lid of which (above) is inlaid with eggshell and gold dust. The tea caddy represents the artist's impression of Mount Fuji, Japan's sacred mountain and the symbol of the highest cultural aspirations of the Japanese spirit. Like Matsuda, all Living National Treasures are accomplished artists who stand at the peak of their country's cultural traditions.

GEO 67

	289		**290**
Art Director	**Melissa Tardiff**	Art Director	**Mary K. Baumann**
Designer	**Mary Rosen**	Designer	**Lori Barra**
Photographer	**Skrebneski**	Photographer	**Tom Jacobi**
Publication	**Town & Country Magazine, New York**	Writer	**Peter Grilli**
		Editor	**David Bourdon**
		Publisher	**Knapp Communications, Corp.**
		Publication	**GEO Magazine, New York**

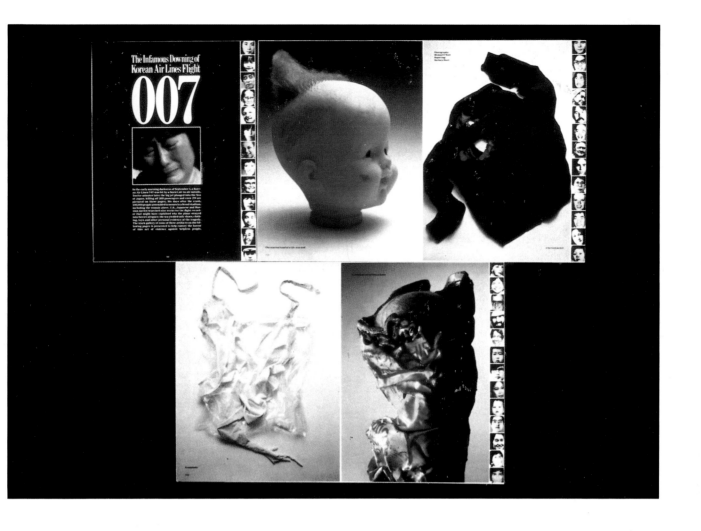

GOLD AWARD

291

Art Director	**Bob Ciano**
Designer	**Bob Ciano**
Photographer	**Michael O'Neill**
Writer	**Joseph Pointdexter**
Editors	**Richard B. Stolley, Mary Steinbauer**
Publisher	**Time Inc.**
Publication	**LIFE Magazine, New York**

292

Art Director	**Carla Barr**
Designer	**Carla Barr**
Photographers	**Sandi Fellman,**
	Toby Sanford
Writer	**Andrea DiNoto**
Client	**Connoisseur Magazine**
Editor	**Thomas Hoving**
Publisher	**The Hearst Corporation**
Publication	**Connoisseur Magazine,**
	New York

293

Art Director	**Bob Ciano**
Designers	**Charles Pates, Nora Sheehan, Ellen Kostroff, Lou Valentino**
Writer	**Staff**
Editors	**Richard B. Stolley, Mary Steinbauer**
Publisher	**Time Inc.**
Publication	**LIFE Magazine, New York**

294

Art Director	**Laura Duggan**
Editor	**Terry McDonell**
Publisher	**Washington Post Co.**
Publication	**Newsweek, New York**

An angle of the grand
salon with its subtle
harmonies between the
walls and the floor
tiles. Two eighteenth-
century Italian arm-
chairs in wood painted
gray-green and picked
out in rose: their
original colors.
Overleaf left: Passage
between the salon and
the library in the
director's apartment. A
handsome seventeenth-
century Florentine
desk in waxed wood,
and eighteenth-century
Genoese painted
yellow chairs with their
original brown leather
upholstery. *Overleaf
right:* False window in
the two-story grand
salon in the central part
of the building. Its
door opens onto the
garden loggia, and its
balcony overlooks Rome.

295		296	
Art Directors	**Lloyd Ziff, Ruth Ansel**	Art Director	**Lloyd Ziff**
Designer	**Lloyd Ziff**	Designer	**Lloyd Ziff**
Photographer	**Evelyn Hofer**	Photographers	**Evelyn Hofer, Richard Avedon, George Platt Lynes**
Writer	**Jean Leymarie**		
Editor	**Lou Gropp**		
Publisher	**Conde Nast Publications, Inc.**	Writer	**Elizabeth Bishop**
		Editor	**Richard Locke**
Publication	**House & Garden, New York**	Publisher	**Conde Nast Publications, Inc.**
		Publication	**Vanity Fair, New York**

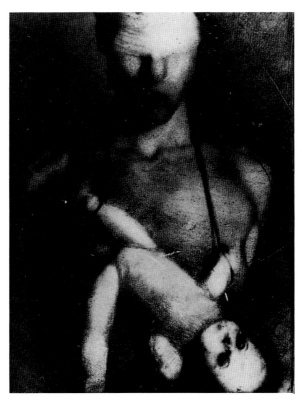

297

Art Director	**Barbara Koster**
Designer	**Barbara Koster**
Photographer	**William Coupon**
Writer	**Deborah Vajda Goertz**
Client	**Trans World Airlines**
Editor	**Bonnie Blodgett**
Publisher	**Jack Burkam**
Publication	**TWA AMBASSADOR Magazine, St. Paul**
Producer	**Diana Stoianovich**

298

Art Director	**Rudolph Hoglund**
Designer	**Irene Ramp**
Artist	**Matt Mahurin**
Publisher	**John A. Meyers/Time Magazine, New York**

299

Art Director	Roger Gorman
Designer	Frances Reinfeld
Editor	Ingrid Sischy
Publisher	Anthony Korner, Amy Baker Sandback
Design Firm	Reiner Design Consultants, New York

BAZAAR'S ALL-STARS

You deserve the best of everything. That's why, on these 24 pages, we're bringing you the most entertaining personalities, the most exciting events coming up in this pre-holiday season. The celebration begins with Barbra Streisand, whose movie *Yentl* promises to be a stunner, and continues right through the hard-charging Islanders to the movies' hottest actress. They're all here ... and they're all stars!

THE BEST IN ENTERTAINMENT
BARBRA
STREISAND

THE BEST OF THE BEST BETTE
DAVIS

With a film career that's lasted over 50 years and includes two Academy Awards, this legendary actress is commanding the home screen this season as the owner of a first-class San Francisco hostelry in ABC's *Hotel*, and then starring with James Stewart in this month's *Right of Way* on HBO.

Two-time Academy Award winner Meryl Streep throws herself completely into her role—even if it means cutting off her signature blonde hair. And so she did in her role as Karen Silkwood, a plutonium plant worker who died mysteriously. With co-stars Kurt Russell and Cher, Streep turns in a stellar performance, making *Silkwood* a prime candidate for movie of the year.

THE BEST IN FILM MERYL
STREEP

She seems to appear out of nowhere. But in December, sexy 25-year-old Joanna Pacula will be making her American debut in the much-awaited film adaptation of best-selling mystery thriller *Gorky Park*. She plays the beautiful Soviet lover, Irina, of box office hero William Hurt. The two become entangled in a web of intrigue involving three Moscow murders—and the outcome promises to be explosive!

THE BEST THAT'S YET TO COME
JOANNA
PACULA

300

Art Directors	**Robert Flora, Ron Albrecht**
Designer	**Ron Albrecht**
Photographers	**Francesco Scavullo, Mary Ellen Mark, Glariano**
Editor	**Anthony T. Mazzola**
Publisher	**The Hearst Corporation**
Publication	**Harper's Bazaar Magazine, New York**

A century later, the
flagship of
British sailing photography is
still a family named

Beken of Cowes

They were the "greyhounds of the sea," the magnificent racing yachts of the English Channel at the turn of the century. The J-class boats — vessels of two to four hundred tons, carrying as much as 12,000 square feet of sail borne by masts of solid wood as high as 150 feet — were the pride of royalty and the passion of Alfred Edward Beken, a chemist from Canterbury, England and photographic hobbyist. In 1888, Beken moved his family to Cowes, the center of British yachting on the Isle of Wight, where he gradually began selling his pictures on the side. His pastime became the foundation of a thriving fourth-generation family business. Beken of Cowes.

Today, Kenneth Beken pursues what the family has always considered "maritime portraiture." Out in his launch armed with his Hasselblad, he will shoot sparingly, rarely taking more than six shots of a boat. Knowledge of sailing helps of course, in choosing and framing his subjects, but more fundamental is his sense that he is recording not

(Above) Frank Beken with his camera. (At right) Valkyrie I, 1891, was built to challenge for the America's Cup, but never did. Note the mastheadman halfway up the rigging, to clear the foresails during tacking. (Overleaf) Sonya, Moyana and Britomart, August, 1905. An early morning calm slows the start of a race.

60

SILVER AWARD

301

Art Director	**Will Hopkins**
Designer	**Louis F. Cruz**
Photographers	**Eric Schweikardt, Allan Weitz, Beken of Cowes**
Writer	**Erla Zwingle**
Editor	**Sean Callahan**
Publisher	**Gary Fisher**
Publication	**American Photographer/CBS Magazines, New York**

Pie Town, N.M., 1940

Forty-three years ago, Russell Lee visited a tiny western settlement where some real pioneering was still going on, and created a seminal work of photojournalism.

by F. Jack Hurley

A few years ago, any writer proposing to deal with the documentary tradition in American photography could get through the 1930s by discussing Walker Evans in detail, with perhaps a nod or two in the direction of Dorothea Lange or Arthur Rothstein. Evans was elevated into the pantheon of "Art" very early because his work looked like art to art historians. To a lesser extent Lange and Rothstein shared a similar advantage. But today we are becoming aware that the Thirties spawned another, very different approach to documentary photography, one that was almost anti-artistic in its lean, spare understatement. The creator of this very direct, deceptively simple style was Russell Lee.

Forty-three years ago, when the pictures in this es-

(Above) Entrance to hotel, where Lee resided and developed his film. (Right) Mr. Keele, merchant, at the store.

say were made, Lee was working as a photographer for the Farm Security Administration. This small federal agency was supposed to help improve the lives of the poorest one-third of the nation's farmers, the migrant fruit pickers, the sharecroppers, the tenants and those farmers who owned their land but had worn it out through ignorance or neglect. If the agency was to do its job however, a certain amount of "selling" had to be done. Under Roy Stryker's direction, the pictures that were taken by Russell Lee, Walker Evans, Dorothea Lange and all the rest were designed to be part of that selling effort. Their broad mandate was to go out and photograph rural and small-town culture in the United States. Was it propaganda? Undoubtedly. But it was also visual history in the making, and all the photog

Mrs. Bill Stagg with a quilt. The Lees were deeply interested in how the settlers used their time and resources.

DISTINCTIVE MERIT

302

Art Director	**Will Hopkins**
Designer	**Will Hopkins**
Editor	**Sean Callahan**
Publisher	**Gary Fisher**
Publication	**American Photographer/CBS Magazines, New York**

303

Art Director	**Michael Grossman**
Designers	**Marianne Gaffney, Timothy McCarthy, Michael Delevante**
Photographers	**Ronald G. Harris, Dan Nelken, Eric Richmond, Michael Watson, various stock**
Illustrators	**Ajin, A. Grace, H. Ihara, H. Lewis, B. Rakita, G. Ruddell, P. Scheuer, P. Thorpe, M. Witte**
Editors	**Kevin Curran, Peter Gaffney, Fred Graver, Sean Kelly**
Copy Editor	**Diane Giddis**
Mgng. Editor	**Glenn Eichler**
Publication	**National Lampoon, New York**
Prod. Artist	**Tracey L. Glick**

VOLCANO!

VOLCANO!

For Notes on the Pictures, see page 32

VOLCANO!

304

Art Director	**Shinichiro Tora**
Designer	**Shinichiro Tora**
Photographer	**Eric Meola**
Writer	**Miriam Berkley**
Editor	**Arthur Goldsmith**
Publisher	**Ziff Davis Publishing Co.**
Publication	**Popular Photography, New York**

GEO**SPHERE**
News of the World and Beyond: September 1983

Ice Sheets Are Not Melting as Once Feared

New evidence debunks the alarming, much publicized reports that the polar ice caps are melting—and worldwide sea levels rising dramatically—because the burning of fossil fuels is causing temperatures to rise.

According to reports first issued two years ago, at most 1 million square miles of sea ice in the Antarctic Ocean melted during the 1970s. Some scientists have predicted that if sea ice and the ice sheets themselves were to continue melting at such a rapid rate, the world's oceans could rise by as much as 25 feet over the next few centuries, inundating low-lying areas and displacing millions of people.

But researchers at the Goddard Space Flight Center in Greenbelt, Maryland, now report that the amount of sea ice in the Antarctic is increasing again. Polar scientist Claire Parkinson and the other researchers, who base their findings on satellite data and ship reports, have also discovered that most of the decline occurred in the Ross Sea and the Weddell Sea, and that ice actually increased in some other areas, indicating that the 1970s melt was caused

Widespread predictions that coastal cities will soon be submerged as the polar ice sheets melt have been refuted by the discovery that Antarctic ice is increasing.

not by overall global warming but by temporary changes in ocean circulation patterns and other isolated phenomena.

World's Clocks Are Set Back by One Second

The minute beginning at 7:59 P.M., Eastern Daylight Time, June 30, 1983, was 61 seconds long. At that moment, the International Bureau

GEO **105**

GEO**SPHERE**
News of the World and Beyond: February 1983

Panic of Animals Before Earthquakes Laid to Ions In the Air

The release of highly charged particles from the ground prior to earthquakes may explain the often observed but mystifying behavior quirks of animals in the hours before quakes occur. Chickens, hogs and cows refuse to enter their pens;

snakes flee their burrows; birds take to flight and do not return to their nests; fish, dogs and cats are jumpy.

Helmut Tributsch, professor of physical chemistry at the Free University of Berlin, speculates in his recently published book, *When Snakes Awake: Animals and Earthquake Prediction* (MIT Press), that pressure electricity, created when pressure is applied along certain axes of quartz crystals in the earth, is the underlying cause of the animals' behavior. If even a small amount of quartz is present in a granite

Electrically charged ions released in the air are thought to cause the pre-earthquake jitters observed in many animals.

crust formation, as much as 100,000 volts of electricity per meter could be generated before and during a moderately severe earthquake. This would cause electrically charged ions, or aerosols, to escape from the ground.

Animals are more sensitive to the electrostatic charges than humans are, because their body surfaces

are drier. Tributsch's theory is consistent with observed phenomena, such as fluctuations in the power of magnets and the eerie glow that is occasionally seen during earthquakes (see GEO: August 1982, page 119).

Man May Be Mining the Moon by Year 2000

Recent experiments proving that the moon can easily be mined for metals and miner-

GEO 119

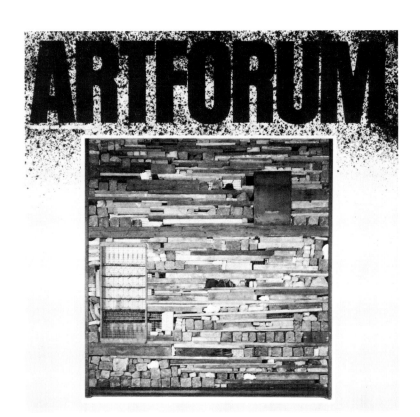

305		306		307	
Art Director	John Tom Cohoe	Art Director	John Tom Cohoe	Art Director	Frances Reinfeld
Writers	John Berendt, Stephen Brewer	Designer	John Tom Cohoe	Designer	Roger Gorman
		Writers	John Berendt, Stephen Brewer	Editor	Ingrid Sischy
Editors	John Berendt, Stephen Brewer			Publishers	Anthony Korner, Amy Baker Sandback
		Editors	John Berendt, Stephen Brewer	Design Firm	Reiner Design Consultants, New York
Publisher	Knapp Communications, Corp.	Publisher	Knapp Communications, Corp.		
Publication	GEO Magazine, New York	Publication	GEO Magazine, New York		

Art Director **Nancy Steiny**
Designer **Nancy Steiny**
Photographer **Robert Elias**
Client **Shape Magazine,**
Woodland Hills, CA

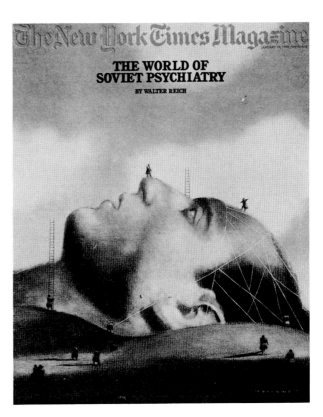

309

Art Director	Carla Barr
Designer	Carla Barr
Photographer	Gregory Heisler
Client	Connoisseur Magazine
Editor	Thomas Hoving
Publisher	The Hearst Corporation
Publication	Connoisseur Magazine, New York

310

Art Directors	Roger Black, Ken Kendrick
Designers	Ken Kendrick, Michael Valenti
Artist	Brad Holland
Writer	Walter Reich
Client	The New York Times
Editor	Ed Klein
Publisher	The New York Times
Publication	The New York Times Magazine, New York

311

Art Director	Fred Woodward
Designer	Fred Woodward
Artist	Tom Curry
Client	Texas Monthly, Inc.
Editor	Greg Curtis
Publisher	Texas Monthly, Inc.
Publication	Texas Monthly, Austin

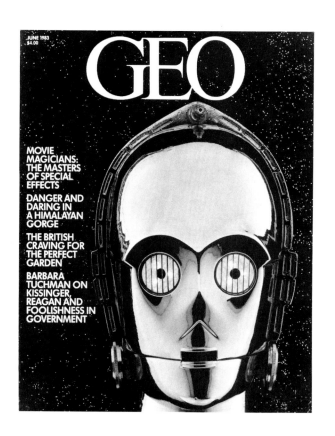

312

Art Director   **Mary K. Baumann**
Photographer   **Terry Chostner**
Editor   **David Maxey**
Publisher   **Knapp Communications**
Publication   **GEO Magazine, New York**

313

Art Director   **Rudolph Hoglund**
Designer   **Tom Bentkowski**
Artist   **Kinuko Craft**
Publisher   **John A. Meyers/Time Magazine, New York**

314

Art Director   **Rudolph Hoglund**
Designer   **Irene Ramp**
Artist   **Matt Mahurin**
Publisher   **John A. Meyers/Time Magazine, New York**

315

Art Director	**Rudolph Hoglund**
Sculptor	**George Segal**
Publisher	**John A. Meyers/Time Magazine, New York**

316

Art Director	**Rudolph Hoglund**
Designer	**Nigel Holmes**
Artist	**James Marsh**
Publisher	**John A. Meyers/Time Magazine, New York**

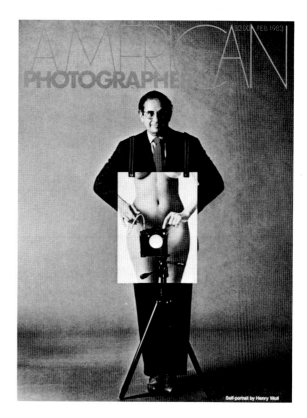

317

Art Director	Mary K. Baumann
Photographer	Micheal O'Neill
Editor	David Maxey
Publisher	Knapp Communications, Corp.
Publication	GEO Magazine, New York

318

Art Director	Will Hopkins
Photographer	Henry Wolf
Editor	Sean Callahan
Publication	American Photographer/CBS Publications, New York

319

Art Director	Will Hopkins
Designer	Will Hopkins
Photographer	Hideki Fujii
Editor	Sean Callahan
Publisher	Gary Fisher
Publication	American Photographer/CBS Magazines, New York

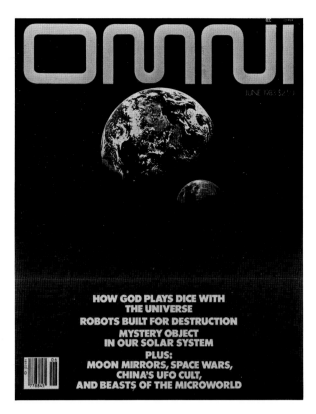

320		321		322	
Art Director	Elizabeth Woodson	Art Director	Elizabeth Woodson	Art Director	Lloyd Ziff
Designer	Liz Siroka	Photographer	Ken Cooper	Photographer	Oberto Gili
Artist	Paul Wunderlich	Client	Omni Magazine	Editor	Lou Gropp
Publication	Omni Publications Int'l Ltd., New York	Publisher	Bob Guccione	Publisher	Conde Nast Publications, Inc.
V.P./Graphics		Publication	Omni Publications Int'l Ltd., New York	Publication	House & Garden, New York
Director	Frank M. DeVino				

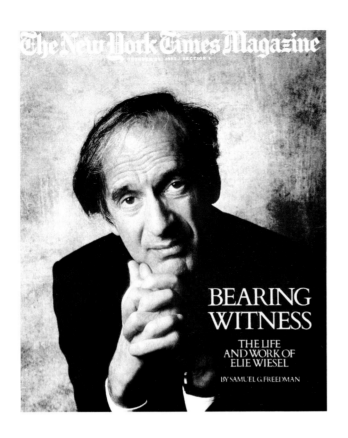

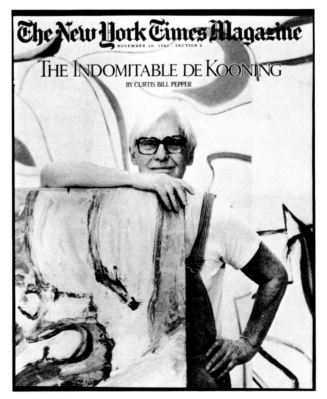

	323		324		325
Art Director	Roger Black	Art Directors	Roger Black, Ken Kendrick	Art Director	Roger Black
Designer	Roger Black			Designer	Ken Kendrick
Photographer	William Coupon	Designer	Ken Kendrick	Photographer	Arnold Newman
Writer	Samuel G. Freedman	Artist	Barry Root	Writer	Curtis Bill Pepper
Client	The New York Times	Writer	Marie Winn	Client	The New York Times
Editor	Ed Klein	Client	The New York Times	Editor	Ed Klein
Publisher	The New York Times	Editor	Ed Klein	Publisher	The New York Times
Publication	The New York Times Magazine, New York	Publisher	The New York Times	Publication	The New York Times Magazine, New York
		Publication	The New York Times Magazine, New York		

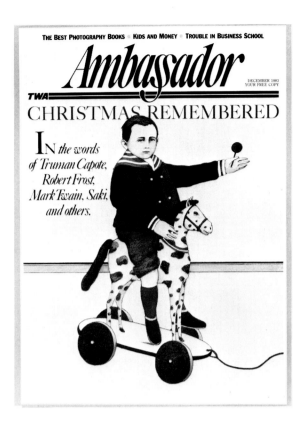

	326		**327**		**328**
Art Directors	Louis Silverstein, Walter Bernard	Art Director	Marcia Wright	Art Director	Altemus
Designer	Walter Bernard	Designer	Marcia Wright	Designer	Altemus
Artist	Seymour Chwast	Artist	Dagmar Frinta	Artist	Kathy Staico Schorr
Client	The New York Times	Client	Trans World Airlines	Publication	Family Weekly, New York
Editor	Mike Leahy	Editor	Bonnie Blodgett		
Publisher	The New York Times	Publisher	Jack Burkam		
Publication	The New York Times, New York	Publication	TWA AMBASSADOR Magazine, St. Paul		

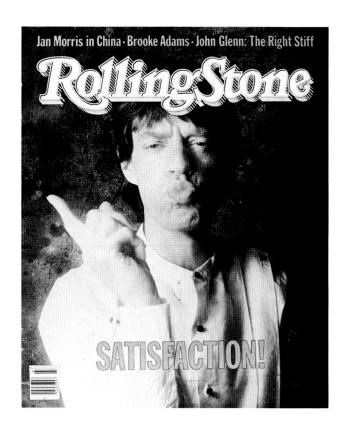

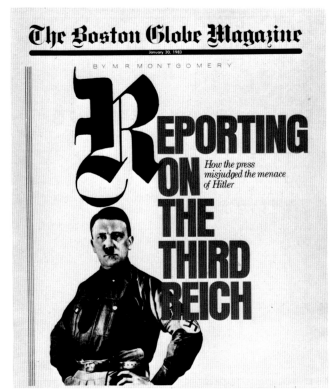

329

Art Director	**Judy Garlan**
Photographer	**Esther Bubley**
Writer	**Nicholas Lemann**
Editor	**William Whitworth**
Publisher	**The Atlantic Monthly Co.**
Publication	**The Atlantic Monthly, Boston**

330

Art Director	**Derek Ungless**
Designer	**Derek Ungless**
Photographer	**William Coupon**
Editor	**David Rosenthal**
Publication	**Rolling Stone Magazine, New York**
Photo Editor	**Laurie Kratochvil**

331

Art Director	**Ronn Campisi**
Designer	**Ronn Campisi**
Editor	**Michael Larkin**
Publisher	**The Boston Globe, Boston**

By Katherine Sheehy Hussy, Contributing Editor

The story of a 12-year-old who is growing bigger than anyone expected.

The paralegal profession we know today is really only 12 years old.

But we've been more successful, faster, than anyone would have predicted, thanks to the determination, high standards and hard work of those of you who helped get this business started.

If you had been a little less professional, or less smart, where might the rest of us be today? Thanks.

In June of 1971, a graduating college senior spotted a poster announcing a recruiter on campus who was offering training to become a "Lawyer's Assistant." She had never known anyone who had done that sort of work. She had never heard of the school. But the law had always had an attraction. Maybe this was a way to experience working in a law office before making the depth of commitment required for a 3-year law school program. Little did she realize the depth and importance of the commitment she made that day.

Just twelve years ago this commitment was almost unknown. It entailed a 3-month stay in a strange city and a strenuous new course of study. But a job placement was virtually guaranteed; tuition would even be refunded if the student were not placed in a job! Although virtually unknown, it did look like a challenging opportunity. And challenging opportunities were sparse for the highly intelligent, female liberal arts graduate twelve years ago. If she were not inclined toward teaching, graduate school, or starting in the business world as a secretary, opportunities for women of that day were obscure.

It is not surprising that an institution such as the Institute for Paralegal Training in Philadelphia was successful in recruiting some highly outstanding students, nearly all women, to populate its classes. It was certainly no accident that the Institute selected individuals likely to do well; the better the performance of the early practitioners in this new profession, the stronger would be the demand for such trained legal assistants. Occasionally, the interests of a private institution parallel those of the public at large, and this was such a time. Those highly intelligent, serious students, recruited from all over the country, were rigorously and thoroughly trained. They were placed in paralegal positions throughout the country, pioneering the paralegal profession from San Francisco and Los Angeles to Washington, D.C., and of course, Philadelphia. Their experiences and capabilities made them welcome new contributors to the legal services team.

This pioneering paralegal had few contemporaries in 1971. Her employer had little idea of the range of her capabilities and no prior experience with legal assistants. There were no paralegal groups or professional guidelines. If she had begun poorly trained, careless or irresponsible, that employer would not have hired another. The early experiences with legal assistants must have been largely very positive; look what has happened since then?

Despite the claims of the early administrators and staff at the Institute in Philadelphia, however, they are not exclusively responsible for the creation and growth of the legal assistant profession. Movement toward using nonlawyers as assistants to lawyers began before 1970. Nonlawyers had been used in some capacity during most of the 20th Century, sometimes almost as assembly-line workers. In the late 1940's lay advocates began to represent individuals in various federal agencies. But not until the 1960's did the idea of using nonlawyers more extensively begin to take hold. Charles A. Williams of the Kentucky Bar, in 1960, urged the delegation of duties by lawyers to nonlawyers; he suggested systematizing tasks so they could be handled by a good secretary. He must have startled his lawyer readers by declaring, "There is no requirement, legally or ethically, that a lawyer should be a researcher or fact-gatherer." He also suggested that many tasks were assumed by an attorney "because he has no one else to whom to assign them." The tasks he was ready to turn over to nonlawyers included some of those now routinely undertaken by legal assistants: investigation, preparation of exhibits, and accumulation of facts and interviewing.

A Missouri Economic Survey in 1962 predicted that more use would be made of nonlawyer personnel by law offices, because lawyers would be buried under an avalanche of work if the Bar did not begin to accept new procedures.

Still early in this movement, a 1966 article challenged the legal profession to face facts:

"The public needs, seems to want, is asking for more, better and perhaps more economical legal services than we apparently have provided. If experience is any guide, the public will get what it wants with or without us. The question is whether we shall experience a bloody revolution or a peaceful evolution."

Clearly, the quality of the early members of the profession and the degree of training which prepared them, the willingness of the Bar to accept this profession and make good use of it, and the openness which has characterized the movement, has made this transition more of a "peaceful evolution" than a "bloody revolution."

One of the "extreme" solutions proposed in this 1966 article was "the creation of a subprofessional class comparable to medical technicians." As extreme as that idea may have seemed to be, that phrase does not come close to describing the breadth, depth and professionalism achieved by legal assistants since 1966. We have certainly surpassed those expectations. But the concept of legal assistants constituting a profession and undergoing specific training did not really evolve until the late 1960's and early 1970's.

The Poor Provided Impetus

The need for delivery of affordable legal services to the poor played an important part in the serious attention that was finally paid to development of this new position on the legal services team. The movement was responsive to, and nurtured by, the social consciousness of the '60's. Some early paralegal courses offered in Denver, Colorado, are reflective of this trend. In the Fall of 1968, the Denver College of Law offered a 20-hour "paralegal course" to 20 housing specialists from the Metro Denver Fair Housing Center, covering the areas of housing law, welfare law, employment law, domestic relations and criminal law. In May of 1969, students and professors at that University, together with local attorneys, offered a 25-hour

Continued on page 28

19

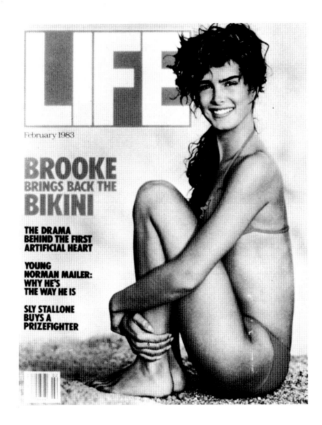

February 1983

BROOKE BRINGS BACK THE BIKINI

THE DRAMA BEHIND THE FIRST ARTIFICIAL HEART

YOUNG NORMAN MAILER: WHY HE'S THE WAY HE IS

SLY STALLONE BUYS A PRIZEFIGHTER

332		333	
Art Director	Jim Jacobs	Art Director	Bob Ciano
Designer	Jim Jacobs	Designer	Bob Ciano
Artist	Jim Jacobs	Photographer	Bruce Weber
Writer	Katherine Sheehy Hussy	Writer	Margot Dougherty
Client	Legal Assistant Today Magazine	Editors	Richard B. Stolley, Mary Simons
Editor	Ann Hall	Publisher	Time Inc.
Publisher	Legal Assistant Today	Publication	LIFE Magazine, New York
Publication	Legal Assistant Today Magazine, Dallas		

Phineas T. Barnum established himself as the most innovative and celebrated showman ever to flourish in the United States. Barnum was born in Bethel, Connecticut, on July 5, 1810. He was 15 years old when his father died, and the support of his mother and his five sisters and brothers fell on his shoulders. After holding a variety of jobs, he became publisher of a Danbury, Connecticut, weekly newspaper, Herald of Freedom. Arrested three times for libel, he enjoyed his first taste of notoriety. In 1829, at the age of 19, Barnum married a 21-year-old Bethel girl, Charity Hallet, who was to bear him four daughters. In 1834 he moved to New York City, where he found his vocation as a showman one year later when he presented Joice Heth, a wizened black lady whom he advertised as the 161-year-old nurse to Gen. George Washington. This human relic, on her death, was exposed as a hoax. He later out-manoeuvred wealthier bidders to acquire Scudder's American Museum, in New York City, a five-story marble structure filled with stuffed animals, wax-work figures, and similar conventional exhibits. Barnum scoured the world for curiosities, living or dead, genuine or fake. By means of outrageous repetitive advertising stunts, and exaggerated publicity, he rapidly transformed the museum into a carnival of live freaks, beauty contests, and other sensational attractions.

P.T. Barnum called himself the Prince of Humbugs. He dwelt in a three-story mansion, on a 17-acre estate in Bridgeport, Connecticut, where he hosted to such notables as Mark Twain and Horace Greeley. Close friends regarded him as good-natured as well as egotistical. After serving two terms in the Connecticut state legislature, he was elected mayor of Bridgeport, in which post he fought prostitution and discrimination against Negroes. One daughter was dropped from his will for her committing adultery. In 1855 he published his autobiography, The Life of P.T. Barnum, Written by Himself. Barnum placed his autobiography in the public domain, allowing anyone to print and sell it without copyright infringement. "There's a sucker born every minute" has long been attributed to Barnum. Disappointed because he had no male heir, Barnum left a sizable bequest to a grandson on the condition that he agree to use the name Barnum. After 44 years of marriage, Charity died in 1873. The following year, Barnum, who was then 64, took the 24-year-old Nancy Fish for his second wife. In his 81st year, Barnum fell gravely ill. A New York newspaper, at his request, published his obituary in advance so that he might enjoy it. Two weeks later, on April 7, 1891, after inquiring about the box office receipts of the circus, Barnum died in his Connecticut mansion.

This spread was set in ITC Franklin Gothic and is available at Plinc.

Adapted with permission from Encyclopaedia Britannica, 15th Edition © 1982

TYPOGRAPHY

Many voluminous books have been written and printed on the subject of typography, and more are in preparation, but things that the busy graphic designer needs to know about the use of type in advertising can be condensed into a few short sentences. The first and foremost thing that should be kept in mind is that your catalogue, or booklet, or folder—whatever is to be printed from the type you are selecting or approving—is to be issued for the purpose of selling a product to people perhaps not too willing to read what you have to say about it; and the essential thing, therefore, is that the story should be easy to read. To make a book or other advertisement easy to read, there are three primary requirements that must be observed: 1. The type selected must be legible. 2. It must be suited to the size and shape of the space in which it is to be set. 3. It must be properly arranged. The intrinsic legibility of the type is, of course, the most important thing. No amount of skillful arrangement will make an advertisement easy to read if the type has not been properly selected in the first place.

AVOID FANCY FACE JOBS

Beautiful and legible typefaces are available in great variety, and there is no excuse whatever for sacrificing easy readability, as is so often done, in the mistaken effort to secure an "artistic" effect. Artistic effects are often desirable as a means of giving an advertisement the proper "atmosphere," but the designer or type director should make sure that the "atmosphere" does not tend to become a fog. Art is never good salesmanship if it makes the selling talk more difficult to comprehend. Designers, therefore, can not be urged too strongly or too often to avoid the habitual use of the fancy typefaces which are now being exploited so extensively. These fancy faces are all right in their place, and they have their legitimate uses, but it is pretty safe to assert that they have spoiled more layouts than they have ever made, and they should never be considered, if at all, for any but the very briefest announcements. For catalogues, booklets, etc. or, any advertisement that requires the serious and sustained attention of the reader, they are utterly unsuited.

DON'T USE SMALL TYPE

Do not allow your layout to be set in an unnecessarily small size of type. An examination of any representative collection of such advertisements will as a rule disclose several that could have been made much more readable by the use of a larger type-size. The reason for this is when the typographers are required to set matter to fill a certain space, they naturally pick a size that they are sure will allow them to get everything in without crowding. If it comes short of filling the space, they have only to "lead it out"—that is, insert leading between the lines—whereas if there were too much matter, part or all of it would have to be reset. Both contingencies can be avoided by careful figuring, and if necessary by setting an experimental page before the size of type is decided upon. The size and shape of the space in which the type is set is the second important factor to be considered in designing a readable and attractive layout. Proper arrangement of the type is an important factor in determining the readability of an advertisement, though it is less vital than the selection of a legible typeface of the proper size and shape for the prescribed space. Enough depends upon the actual typesetting, however, to make it worthwhile for the advertiser to see that the following points are observed:

ABUSE OF ITALICS & CAPS

Italics, small capitals and capitals are used to give emphasis to important words or phrases in the text of an advertisement. The principle to be applied in employing them is the same that applies to emphasizing the spoken word—"If it is emphasized too much, it isn't emphasized at all." Just as the too-vociferous speaker fails to impress the audience, so the italic or capital besprinkled page defeats its own purpose. The readers become so accustomed to the frequent recurrence of emphasis that they either pay no attention to it whatever, or it serves merely as an irritant. It is the quiet-talking person, the individual of reserve force, who makes an occasional emphasis count, and it is precisely so with an advertisement. Italics or capitals achieve their purpose if they are used sparingly, and not otherwise. Incidentally, it is to be noted that good copy, as a rule, does not require frequent emphasis. If the argument is inherently sound and forceful, it will for the most part carry its own emphasis. Words, phrases and sentences can be emphasized by underscoring, by setting in boldface type, and by printing in a color different from that in which the balance of the text is printed. Underscoring is little used in up-to-date advertising, and has little to recommend it. Compared with other methods it is expensive, and it spoils the typographic appearance of the text. It is sometimes justifiable where suitable italic type is not available, but seldom otherwise. Boldface type is preferable to underscoring in most cases where choice must be made between the two, as it is less expensive to use, and produces stronger emphasis with less detriment to the typographical appearance of the text. Color is often used as a means of securing emphasis, and is very effective in display advertising, but is hardly more effective then boldface type when used in the text of catalogues and booklets, and is at the same time much more expensive, since it entails separation of the type-forms in make-up. Even where a book is printed in two or more colors, it adds considerably to the cost to print different portions of the text in different colors. Headings, marginal references and initial letters can be separated more readily than occasional words and phrases in the text, and can usually be displayed effectively in a separate color. Display advertising is ubiquitous these days, and scarcely requires definition. Readers of any magazine or newspaper can see for themselves in what manner and to what extent it differs from straight reading matter. They can see that a variety of typefaces and a variety of arrangements have been utilized for the purpose of giving character to the individual advertisements, and also, in many cases, to differentiate the several sections of a single advertisement, giving emphasis to important words, phrases, sentences, etc.

ADAPT TYPE TO THE SPACE

Avoid unnecessary letterspacing—that is, spacing between the letters of a word, and remember that most such spacing is unnecessary, except in setting title pages. As a rule, letterspacing has a tendency to make display lines less attractive and more difficult to read. Larger or more extended type can nearly always be substituted.

USE OF HAND LETTERING

Where handlettering is preferable to type, it is usually for either one of two reasons: 1. It offers greater opportunities for decorative treatment and elaboration. 2. It is more flexible, giving a great deal more latitude in the arrangement of words and phrases, and even of the individual letters in a word, than is possible with type. The second of these reasons, strange as it will seem to some readers, is the more important of the two. The decoration and elaboration of a piece of text, though often highly desirable, is never necessary. The proper arrangement of the text, on the other hand, is absolutely essential, if the advertisement is to be attractive and effective. It is therefore not the advertiser with a taste for decorative treatment in advertising matter, or who can use decorative treatment to good advantage, who most needs to appreciate the considerations which should determine the employment of handlettering. It is rather the customary user of plain printing who needs to understand that they must occasionally use handlettering if they wish the ad to be properly displayed.

This article from the 1915 volume "Direct Advertising" was reprinted with written permission from The Beckett Paper Company, Hamilton, Ohio.

Text was set in 12 on 13 Pacella Royale, style number 6814, and is available exclusively at Plinc.

A-Z shadow alphabet with screened background was handlettered by Ed Benguiat.

334

Art Director **Ed Benguiat**
Designer **Ed Benguiat**
Writer **Encyclopaedia Britannica**
Client **Photo-Lettering Inc., New York**

335

Art Director **Ed Benguiat**
Designer **Ed Benguiat**
Artist **Ed Benguiat**
Client **Photo-Lettering Inc., New York**

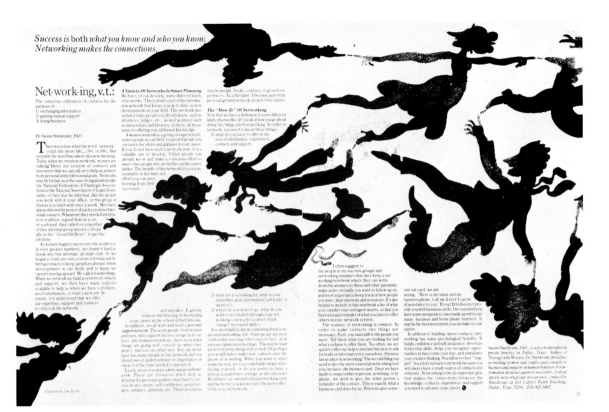

336

Art Director	**Jim Jacobs**
Designer	**Jim Jacobs**
Artist	**Jim Jacobs**
Writer	**Susan Sturdivant**
Client	**Legal Assistant Today Magazine**
Editor	**Ann Hall**
Publisher	**Legal Assistant Today**
Publication	**Legal Assistant Today Magazine, Dallas**

337

Art Director	**James T. Walsh**
Artist	**Robert Goldstrom**
Editor	**Alan Fitch**
Publication	**Emergency Medicine Magazine, New York**

338

Art Director	**James T. Walsh**
Artist	**Frank Riccio**
Publisher	**Mr. Steve Fischer**
Publication	**Emergency Medicine Magazine, New York**

339

Art Director	**Jason Calfo**
Designer	**Jason Calfo**
Photographer	**Salvatore Ficara**
Writer	**Louis F.D. Kelley**
Client	**World Typeface Center, Inc.**
Editor	**Jason Calfo**
Publisher	**World Typeface Center, Inc., New York**
Agency	**Carnase, Inc.**
Publication	**Ligature**

QUINTESSENCE
THE QUALITY OF HAVING *IT*

BY BETTY CORNFELD AND OWEN EDWARDS
DESIGN BY JOHN C JAY

The Oreo Cookie

Oh, Oh, Oreo.
Nabisco claims it's the world's most popular cookie, and why not? The Oreo has been around since 1913, when it made its debut as the Oreo Biscuit. In 1921 it was renamed the Oreo Sandwich and

renamed yet again in 1948, when it became the 'Oreo Creme Sandwich,' its current designation.

The Oreo is more than a cookie (as profound a thing as a cookie is), it is a form of personal expression. You can eat it straightforwardly as a sandwich (invisible), or you can lift the top off, eat that, then scrape the sweet white stuff off the second wafer with your front teeth, then give the bottom wafer to someone you're not that crazy about. Or you can eat the top wafer and then the cream and second wafer together. Or you can eat the cream first and throw the cookie away. Or you can

The quintessentiality of the Oreo is mysteriously and precariously balanced: witness the failure of the spin-off Oreo Double Stuff, the 'Jaws 3' of cookies, in which the white cream is laid on twice as thickly as it ought to be, a classic case of fixing something that isn't broken. The real Oreo, having twice the biscuit as long, brilliantly fulfills a fundamental requirement for the quintessential cookie; it absolutely demands to be eaten with milk.

The Spalding Rubber Ball

A ball, in order properly to be a ball, must be round and must bounce. Nothing seems quite so round and bouncy as a Spalding pink rubber ball. Its size is perfect for hands large or small, its appearance at rest or at play charms the eye with pure functional simplicity. Made of unadorned hard rubber, the ball

is firm, which gives it sincerity, the promise of a true and noble bounce. And, of no small importance, it makes a satisfying *thwok* on sidewalk or stoop. There's no knowing how many great baseball careers have started with the wonderful rightness of the little pink ball.

The Spalding Company manufactures other things besides the pink rubber ball, and everything else the company makes is said to be a Spalding this or a Spalding that. But the pink rubber ball—and only the pink rubber ball—is a Spaldeen (spelled 'Spalding' in elegant script on the ball itself). And anyone who doesn't know that can't really know why the Spaldeen is The Ball.

340

Art Director   John C. Jay, New York
Photographer   Dan Kozan
Writers   Owen Edwards,
Betty Cornfeld
Editor   Pam Thomas

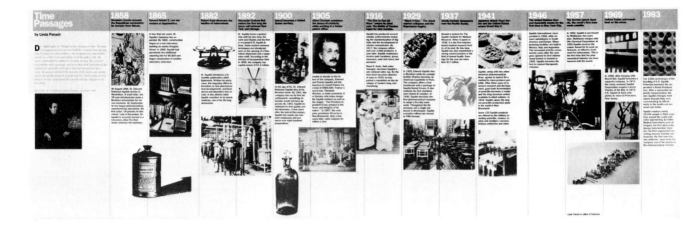

1858 | 1865 | 1882 | 1892 | 1900 | 1905 | 1916 | 1929 | 1937 | 1941 | 1946 | 1957 | 1969 | 1983

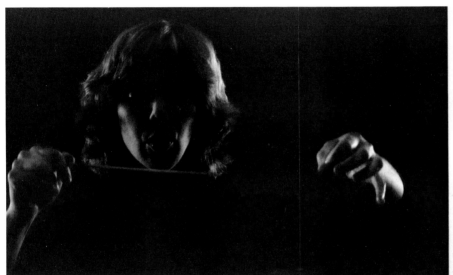

Although male charisma and power have traditionally been seen as prerequisites for leading symphony orchestras, many women are beginning to succeed in this difficult field with help from an Exxon-aided program.

Pioneers on the podium

by Heidi Waleson
Photographs by Erich Hartmann

In 1970, eight conductors were selected to spend a month working with the St. Louis Symphony Orchestra. Eve Queler, the only woman in the group, remembers male colleagues predicting that she would have an easier time making a career as a conductor than they would.

Queler recalls, "One of the men said, 'No one will forget if they saw you conduct,' because you're a woman, and it's an event.' We men just fade into the woodwork.' As it turned out, a newspaper did do a big color spread on me, but when the other orchestra in town was looking for guest conductors, they made offers to each of the men. I was the only person in the program who was not invited for an interview."

Queler has since gained recognition as a distinguished conducting and recording artist. Her credits include work with the New York City Opera and with the Fort Wayne Symphony Orchestra. In 1967, she founded the Opera Orchestra of New York and continues to serve as its conductor.

While a handful of women like Eve Queler are beginning to gain more opportunities to assert their leadership capabilities, the positions of music director and conductor of major American symphony orchestras still remain out of reach for most. According to the American Symphony Orchestra League, of over 180 orchestras in its top three budget categories—from $850,000 to over $3.25 million—all of the music directors are men. In the 150 orchestras at the next level, only three have women music directors, and of the 420 conductors indexed in the Musical America Annual, only 15 are females.

The principal reason for this situation, many in the field say, is tradition: audiences and orchestra members alike have long been accustomed to the charisma associated with such celebrated male conductors as Zubin Mehta and Herbert von Karajan. But all that may eventually become history as new opportunities open for women.

Helping to promote such opportunities is a 10-year-old program funded by Exxon and the National Endowment for the Arts, with the cooperation of leading orchestras and opera companies throughout the country. Administered by Affiliate Artists Inc., a non-profit group that assists in the career development of American performing artists of all disciplines, the Exxon/Arts Endowment program seeks to identify and aid in the development of promising music directors for American symphony orchestras.

Victoria Bond, directing the Empire State Youth Orchestra in Albany, New York, says "it's the rapport between the conductor and the orchestra that helps you achieve the quality of sound you're aiming for." She served from 1978-1980 in the Exxon/Arts Endowment program with the Pittsburgh Symphony.

EDITOR'S NOTE: *Freelancer Heidi Waleson writes on the arts for* The New York Times, Opera News, Ballet News *and other publications.*

19

341

Art Director — Anthony Russell
Designer — Kevin McPhee
Client — E.R. Squibb & Sons
Editor — Eric Sauter
Agency — Anthony Russell, Inc., New York
Publication — Squibbline

342

Art Director — Elton Robinson
Designer — Elton Robinson
Photographer — Erich Hartmann, Magnum
Editor — Ernest Dunbar
Publisher — Exxon Corporation, New York
Publication — The Lamp

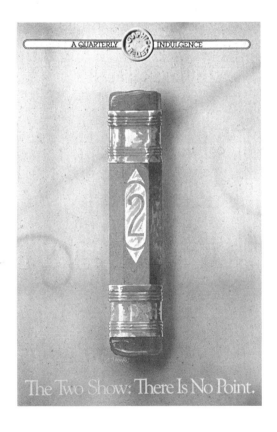

343	
Art Directors	**Bob Farber, Mike Quon**
Designers	**Bob Farber, Mike Quon**
Artist	**Mike Quon**
Writer	**Marion Muller**
Client	**Upper & Lower Case**
Publisher	**International Typeface Corp.**
Agency	**Mike Quon Design Office, Inc., New York**

344	
Art Director	**David Brier**
Designer	**David Brier**
Photographer	**Bill Dolce**
Artist	**Andrea Baruffi**
Writer	**Nancy Baxter**
Client	**David Brier Design Works/Sterling Roman Press**
Publisher	**David Brier Design Works, New York**
Publication	**Graphic Relief**

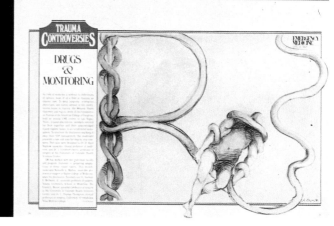

SILVER AWARD

345

Art Director   **James T. Walsh**
Artist   **Geoffrey Moss**
Editor   **John Heinegg**
Publication   **Emergency Medicine**
Magazine, New York

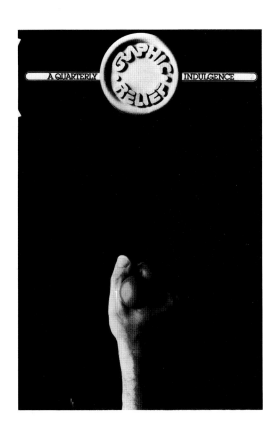

POLAROID **CLOSE·UP**

<table>
<tr><td colspan="2" align="center">346</td></tr>
<tr><td align="right">Art Director</td><td>**David Brier**</td></tr>
<tr><td align="right">Designer</td><td>**David Brier**</td></tr>
<tr><td align="right">Photographer</td><td>**Bill Dolce**</td></tr>
<tr><td align="right">Client</td><td>**David Brier Design Works/Sterling Roman Press**</td></tr>
<tr><td align="right">Publisher</td><td>**David Brier Design Works, New York**</td></tr>
<tr><td align="right">Publication</td><td>**Graphic Relief**</td></tr>
</table>

<table>
<tr><td colspan="2" align="center">347</td></tr>
<tr><td align="right">Art Director</td><td>**Constance Sullivan**</td></tr>
<tr><td align="right">Designer</td><td>**Katy Homans**</td></tr>
<tr><td align="right">Editor</td><td>**Constance Sullivan**</td></tr>
<tr><td align="right">Publisher</td><td>**Polaroid Corporation, Cambridge, MA**</td></tr>
</table>

DISTINCTIVE MERIT

	348		**349**		**350**
Art Director	Everett Halvorsen	Art Director	Everett Halvorsen	Art Director	Carole Palmer
Designers	Roger Zapke and	Designer	Everett Halvorsen	Designer	Carole Palmer
	Ronda Kass	Artist	Chas. B. Slackman	Photographers	Wolfgang Hoyt, ESTO
Artist	Kinuko Craft	Writer	Barbara Rudolph	Editor	Donald Canty
Writer	James Cook	Editor	James W. Michaels	Publisher	The American Inst. of
Editor	James W. Michaels	Publisher	Forbes, Inc., New York		Architects/SC
Publisher	Forbes, Inc., New York	Publication	Forbes	Publication	AIA Journal,
Publication	Forbes				Washington, D.C.

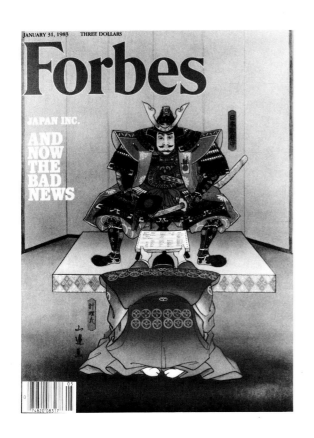

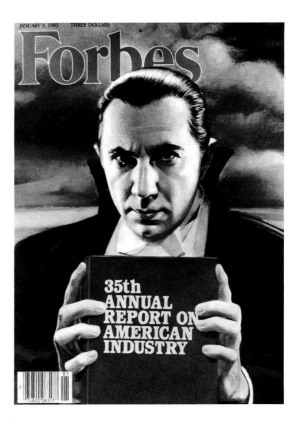

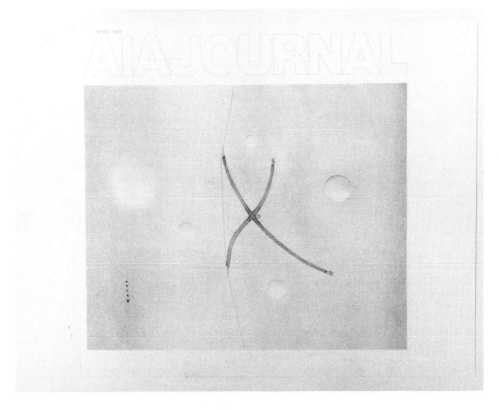

351		352		353	
Art Director	Everett Halvorsen	Art Director	Everett Halvorsen	Art Director	Carole Palmer
Designer	Ronda Kass	Designer	Roger Zapke	Designer	Carole Palmer
Artist	Kinuko Craft	Artist	Alan Reingold	Artist	
Writer	Norman Gall	Writer	Staff	Watercolor	Jean-Michel Folon
Editor	James W. Michaels	Editor	James W. Michaels	Editor	Donald Canty
Publisher	Forbes, Inc., New York	Publisher	Forbes, Inc., New York	Publisher	The American Inst. of
Publication	Forbes	Publication	Forbes		Architects/SC
				Publication	AIA Journal,
					Washington, D.C.

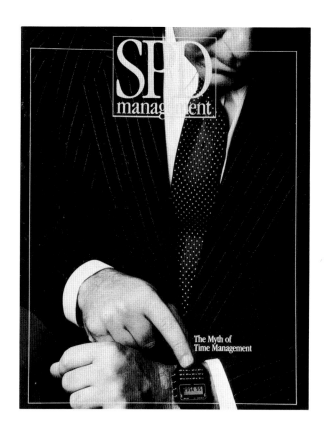

354

Art Directors	**Will Hopkins,**
	Ira Friedlander
Designers	**Will Hopkins,**
	Ira Friedlander
Photographer	**Brownie Harris**
Client	**IBM**
Agency	**Will Hopkins Group,**
	New York
Publication	**SPD Management**

355

Art Directors	**Faye Eng, Anthony Yee**
Designers	**Faye Eng, Anthony Yee**
Photographer	**Ken Hicks**
Editor	**Joan G. Lowenthal**
Publisher	**Museum of American**
	Folk Art, New York
Publication	**The Clarion**

356

Art Directors	**Robert K. Cassetti,**
	Michael R. Orr
Designer	**Robert K. Cassetti**
Photographer	**Don Albern**
Writer	**Z.P. Henderson,**
	S. S. Lang
Client	**Media Services at**
	Cornell University
Editor	**James Titus**
Publication	**Human Ecology Forum**
Design Firm	**Micheal Orr +**
	Associates Inc.,
	Corning, NY

357		358		359	
Art Director	**Robert E. Cargill**	Art Director	**Ken Godat**	Art Directors	**Craig Bernhardt, Janice**
Designer	**Art Riser**	Photographer	**Barbara Karant,**		**Fudyma**
Photographer	**Neal Higgins**		**Karant Associates**	Designer	**Ron Schankweiler**
Client	**IBM**	Editor	**John Dixon**	Artist	**Roger Huyssen**
Agency	**Cargill & Associates,**	Publication	**Progressive**	Client	**Maxwell House**
	Inc., Atlanta		**Architecture,**	Editor	**Nan Haley Redmond**
			Stamford, CT	Agency	**Bernhardt/Fudyma**
					Design, New York

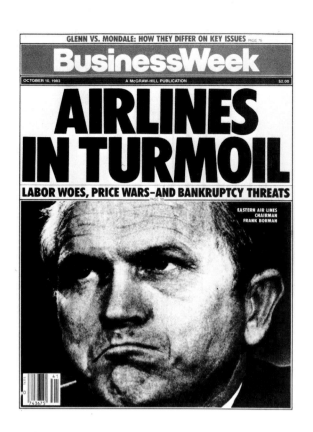

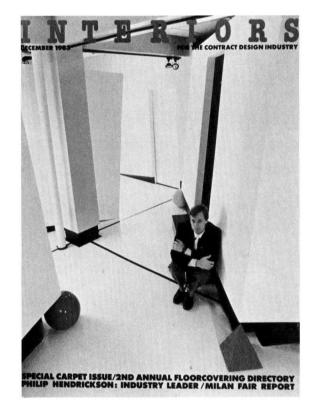

360		**361**		**362**	
Art Director	John R. Vogler	Art Directors	Malcolm Frouman/	Art Director	Peter Deutsch
Designer	John R. Vogler		John R. Vogler	Photographer	Langdon Clay
Photographer	UPI	Designer	John R. Vogler	Editor	Beverly Russell
Client	Business Week	Artist	Victor Juhasz	Publication	Interiors Magazine,
Publisher	James R. Pierce/	Client	Business Week		New York
	McGraw Hill, New York	Publisher	James R. Pierce/		
Design Concept	Martin Pedersen		McGraw Hill, New York		
		Design Concept	Martin Pedersen		

363	
Art Director	**James Pavlovich**
Designer	**James Pavlovich**
Artist	**Patrick Blackwell**
Editor	**Mary Jane Patrone**
Publisher	**The Boston Globe, Boston**

364	
Art Director	**Mark Lichtenstein**
Designer	**Mark Lichtenstein**
Artist	**Bob Conge**
Writer	**Jan Christensen**
Client	**Rochester Society of Communicating Arts**
Agency	**Lichtenstein Marketing Communications, Rochester, NY**

365	
Art Director	**Jack Lefkowitz**
Designer	**Jack Lefkowitz**
Artist	**Virginia Strnad**
Writer	**David Ritchey**
Client	**Institute of Industrial Launderers**
Editor	**David Ritchey**
Publisher	**Institute of Industrial Launderers**
Agency	**Jack Lefkowitz Inc., Leesburg, VA**
Publication	**Industrial Launderer**

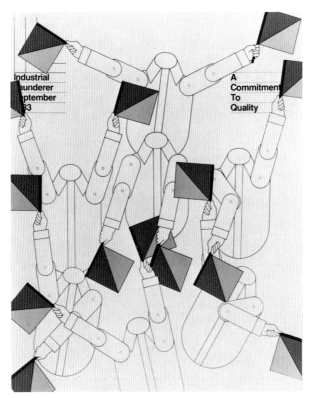

366		367		368	
Art Director	**Jack Lefkowitz**	Art Director	**Jack Lefkowitz**	Art Director	**Jack Lefkowitz**
Designer	**Jack Lefkowitz**	Designer	**Jack Lefkowitz**	Designer	**Jack Lefkowitz**
Artist	**Pamela Kipp–Lefkowitz**	Artist	**Virginia Strnad**	Artist	**Virginia Strnad**
Writer	**David Ritchey**	Writer	**David Ritchey**	Writer	**David Ritchey**
Client	**Institute of Industrial Launderers**	Client	**Institute of Industrial Launderers**	Client	**Institute of Industrial Launderers**
Editor	**David Ritchey**	Editor	**David Ritchey**	Editor	**David Ritchey**
Publisher	**Institute of Industrial Launderers**	Publisher	**Institute of Industrial Launderers**	Publisher	**Institute of Industrial Launderers**
Agency	**Jack Lefkowitz Inc., Leesburg, VA**	Agency	**Jack Lefkowitz Inc., Leesburg, VA**	Agency	**Jack Lefkowitz Inc., Leesburg, VA**
Publication	**Industrial Launderer**	Publication	**Industrial Launderer**	Publication	**Industrial Launderer**

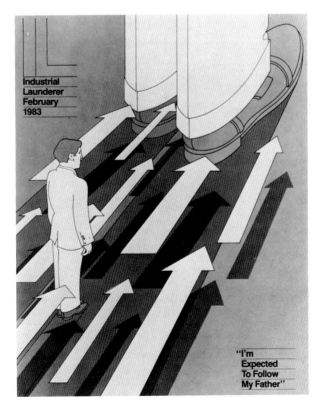

369		370		371	
Art Director	**Jack Lefkowitz**	Art Director	**Jack Lefkowitz**	Art Director	**Jack Lefkowitz**
Designer	**Jack Lefkowitz**	Designer	**Jack Lefkowitz**	Designer	**Jack Lefkowitz**
Artist	**Pamela Kipp-Lefkowitz**	Artist	**Jack Lefkowitz**	Artist	**Pamela Kipp-Lefkowitz**
Writer	**David Ritchey**	Writer	**David Ritchey**	Writer	**David Ritchey**
Client	**Institute of Industrial Launderers**	Client	**Institute of Industrial Launderers**	Client	**Institute of Industrial Launderers**
Editor	**David Ritchey**	Editor	**David Ritchey**	Editor	**David Ritchey**
Publisher	**Institute of Industrial Launderers**	Publisher	**Institute of Industrial Launderers**	Publisher	**Institute of Industrial Launderers**
Agency	**Jack Lefkowitz Inc., Leesburg, VA**	Agency	**Jack Lefkowitz Inc., Leesburg, VA**	Agency	**Jack Lefkowitz Inc., Leesburg, VA**
Publication	**Industrial Launderer**	Publication	**Industrial Launderer**	Publication	**Industrial Launderer**

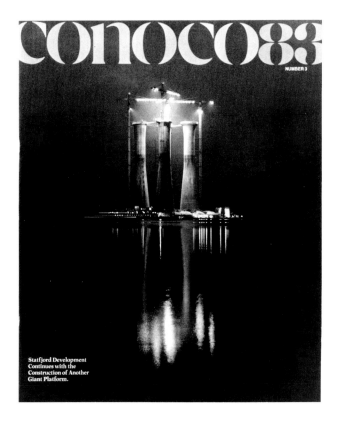

	372		373		374
Art Director	**Elton Robinson**	Art Director	**Elton Robinson**	Art Director	**Milt Simpson**
Designer	**Elton Robinson**	Designer	**Elton Robinson**	Designer	**Anne Giacalone**
Photographer	**Michael St. Maur Sheil**	Photographer	**Brian Brake**	Photographers	**Kyllingstad and Fuenes A/S**
Editor	**Ernest Dunbar**	Editor	**Ernest Dunbar**	Client	**Conoco Inc.**
Publisher	**Exxon Corporation, New York**	Publisher	**Exxon Corporation, New York**	Editor	**Maury Bates, Jr.**
Publication	**The Lamp**	Publication	**The Lamp**	Agency	**Johnson & Simpson Graphic Designers, Newark, NJ**
				Publication	**Conoco 83 Number 3**

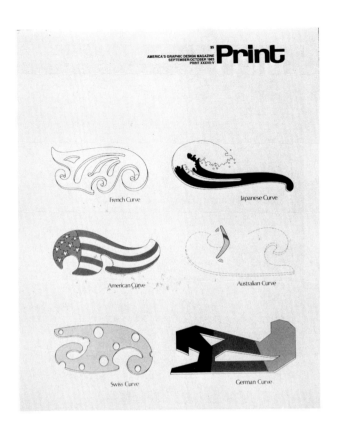

	375
Art Director	**Andrew Kner**
Designer	**Crystal Neal**
Artist	**Crystal Neal**
Client	**Print Magazine**
Editor	**Martin Fox**
Publisher	**R.C. Publications**
Publication	**Print Magazine, New York**

	376
Art Director	**Andrew Kner**
Designer	**Andrew Kner**
Artist	**David Wilcox**
Client	**Print Magazine**
Editor	**Martin Fox**
Publisher	**R.C. Publications**
Publication	**Print Magazine, New York**

	377
Art Director	**Anthony Russell**
Designer	**Kevin McPhee**
Photographer	**Charlotte Raymond**
Client	**E.R. Squibb & Sons**
Editor	**Eric Sauter**
Agency	**Anthony Russell, Inc., New York**
Publication	**Squibbline**

Montepulciano

Poggibonsi
Matera

378		379	
Art Director	Constance Sullivan	Art Director	Ed Benguiat
Designer	Katy Homans	Designer	Ed Benguiat
Editor	Constance Sullivan	Client	Photo-Lettering Inc.,
Publisher	Polaroid Corporation,		New York
	Cambridge, MA		

DECEMBER 1983
$2.95

HOW
TO JOIN
THE FRENCH
FOREIGN
LEGION

DEATH
AND GOLD
IN THE
SUPERSTITION
MOUNTAINS

DEFENDING
CLAUS VON
BÜLOW,
JEAN HARRIS
AND SMUT

ANTHONY
BURGESS
ON A TOWN
HE CAN'T
FORGET

GOLD AWARD

380

Art Director **Mary K. Baumann**
Designers **Mary K. Baumann, John Tom Cohoe, Lori Barra**
Editor **David Maxey**
Publisher **Knapp Communications, Corp.**
Publication **GEO Magazine, New York**

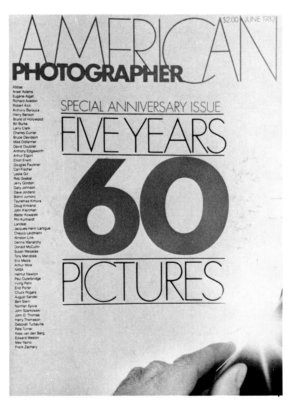

DISTINCTIVE MERIT

381		382	
Art Director	Bob Ciano	Art Director	Will Hopkins
Designers	Charles Pates, Nora Sheehan, Ellen Kostroff, Lou Valentino	Designer	Will Hopkins
		Editor	Sean Callahan
Writer	Staff	Publisher	Gary Fisher
Editors	Richard B. Stolley, Mary Steinbauer	Publication	American Photographer/CBS Magazines, New York
Publisher	Time Inc.		
Publication	LIFE Magazine, New York		

ILLUSTRATED BY DAVE CALVER

	383		384
Art Director	Elton Robinson	Art Director	Robert Best
Designer	Margaret Wollenhaupt	Designers	Patricia Bradbury, Don Morris
Photographer	Various		
Artist	Eugene Mihaesco	Client	New York Magazine
Editor	Rose DeNeve	Publication	New York Magazine, New York
Publisher	American Institute of Graphic Arts		
Publication	AIGA Journal of Graphic Design, New York		

DISTINCTIVE MERIT

385

Art Director	**David Boss**
Designer	**Carl Seltzer**
Photographer	**Various**
Editor	**David Boss**
Publisher	**David Gray Gardner**
Director	**Jean Gardner**
Agency	**Cross Associates, Los Angeles**
Publication	**Picture Magazine**
Printers	**Gardner/Fulmer Lithograph**

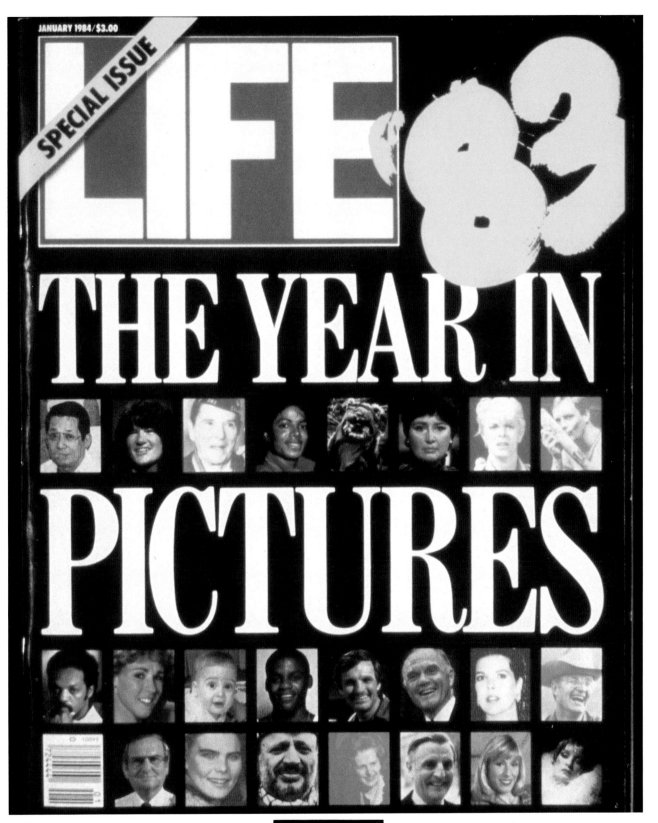

JANUARY 1984/$3.00

SPECIAL ISSUE

LIFE '83

THE YEAR IN PICTURES

SILVER AWARD

386

Art Director	**Bob Ciano**
Designers	**Charles Pates, Nora Sheehan, Ellen Kostroff, Lou Valentino**
Writer	**Staff**
Editors	**Richard B. Stolley, Mary Steinbauer**
Publisher	**Time Inc.**
Publication	**LIFE Magazine, New York**

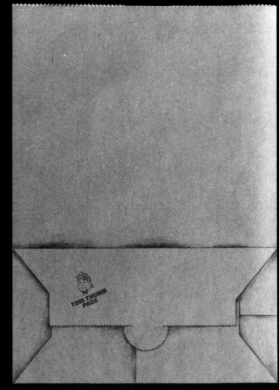

387

Art Director   **Louis Allison**
Writer   **Marsha Tunnel**
Client   **Tom Thumb-Page**
Agency   **Arnold Harwell
McClain & Assoc.,
Dallas**

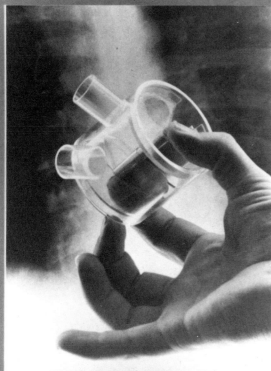

Art Director   **Robert J. Rytter**
Designer   **Jane Polanka**
Photographer   **Don Carstens**
Client   **Dr. Barbara W. Cahn/**
University of Maryland
Medical System
Agency   **R.S. Jensen, Inc.,**
Baltimore

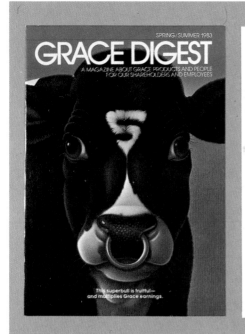

SILVER AWARD

389

Art Directors   **Craig Bernhardt, Janice Fudyma**

Designers   **C. Bernhardt, J. Fudyma, D. Duerr, R. Gorman, J. Sobczak**

Photographer   **Various**

Artist   **Various**

Writer   **Various**

Client   **W.R. Grace & Co.**

Editor   **Joyce Cole**

Agency   **Bernhardt/Fudyma Design, New York**

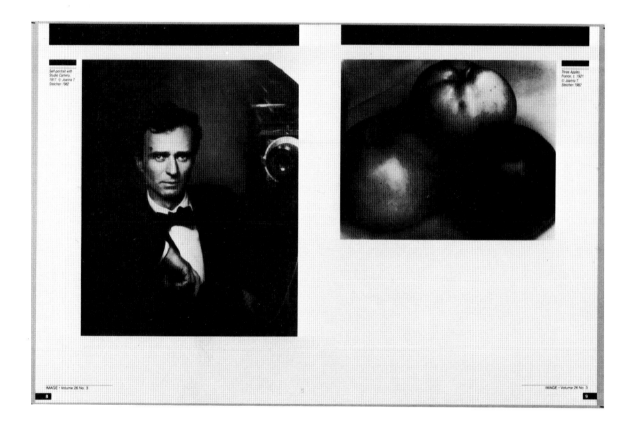

DISTINCTIVE MERIT

390		391	
Art Director	**Paul Hardy**	Art Director	**Robert Meyer**
Designer	**Peter Deutsch**	Designer	**Julia Wyant**
Editor	**Beverly Russell**	Writer	**Joanna T. Steichen**
Publication	**Interiors Magazine, New York**	Client	**International Museum of Photography at George Eastman House**
		Publication	**Image, Rochester, NY**

392

Art Director   **Don Kubly**
Designer   **John Hoernle**
Artist   **Beverly Lazor**
Writer   **Cornelia Emerson**
Client   **Art Center College of Design**
Publication   **At Art Center, Pasadena, CA**

393

Art Director	**Michael Mabry**
Designer	**Michael Mabry**
Photographer	**Michele Clement**
Artist	**Georgia Deaver**
Client	**Pacific School of Religion**
Editor	**Judy Rapp Smith, Judy Dodd**
Agency	**Michael Mabry Design, San Francisco**

PROMOTION & GRAPHIC DESIGN

B. Martin Pedersen

Tony Cappiello
Robert Cipriani
Molly Epstein
Blanche Fiorenza
Dick Hess
Chris Hill
Nigel Holmes
Elizabeth Kim
Norma Kwan
Geoffrey Moss
Susan Niles
Jerry Philips
Woody Pirtle
Sherry Pollack
Brenda Preis
Chuck Queener
Robert Reed
Bennett Robinson
Anthony Russell
James Sebastian
Dugald Stermer
John Vogler
Ken White
Cynthia Wojdyla

A century ago, the vineyards of
Europe were fast approaching ruin,
the French wine industry was on
the verge of collapse. The phylloxera
bug had come to the continent, ravaging grape plants wherever it traveled. But by the year 1900, the
phylloxera epidemic was under control, and the vineyards were saved
— thanks largely to the efforts of a
viticulturist from Texas.

Thomas Volney Munson came
to Denison and the Red River country in 1873 and found a remarkable
and established the many varieties
of grape indigenous to the region.
Before long, he developed a hybrid
immune to the phylloxera attack.
By grafting this hardy strain on
the vulnerable European roots,
France's viticulture recovered from
ruin and began to thrive again.

For his expertise and his
work, T. V. Munson was awarded the
French Legion of Honor. He also wro-
ote several books, one of which
in several languages, and brought
his simple flourish to Europe
this day.

So there is to T. V. Munson, the
Texas pioneer who rescued the
French wine industry.

sur·viv·al

\sər-ˈvī-vəl\ n 1 a: a living or continuing longer
than another person or thing b: the continuation
of life or existence <problems of~in arctic condi-
tions> 2: one that survives.

California
Human Development
Corporation

Annual Report
1982

Criminal justice system
services

FIGHTING CRIME

EARLY ON

A return from the dead and the unneeded $196,000

During 1982, Project Inter-
cept revived its once-dead services to Sonoma
County, California, its offenders and served
toll enrollees with our normal diversion services, terminating 444 of them successfully. We
also reduced expenses by moving to shared
quarters and demonstrated that PI's services
saved local taxpayers an estimated $196,000
during the year.

Project Intercept does what its name implies: it
intercepts certain accused first-time mis-
demeanants after they have obtained legal
counsel but before a he enters a plea. Instead
of trying the defendant, the Court refers him or
her to Project Intercept to determine their
eligibility for our services. If the defendant
agrees that PI offers a viable opportunity, s/he
signs an agreement to complete certain tasks
while enrolled. Next comes a record check to
confirm eligibility, and staff sends a letter to
Court requesting both a trial continuance and
that the defendant be formally referred to
Project Intercept for a minimum of 90 days.

During that time, a client may be assigned a
high or low service level, a decision made on

the basis of the client's need and whether or not
s/he is employed full time, among other factors. A low service level client may be required
to come to the office for an initial screening, an
initial counseling appointment, and a final
counseling session. During the interim, s/he
will be required to report monthly by mail
regarding their current status. Those assigned a
high service level may be required to make
weekly phone or in-person contact with their
counselor, to complete a number of volunteer
hours in the community, to attend workshops,
or to obtain their GED. Other possibilities include financial counseling, participation in
anger control groups, parenting groups,
involvement with the law workshops, or
interaction with other community resources,
e.g., mental health or substance abuse centers.

Funds for the above come from the County of
Sonoma and from fees we service from the
clients themselves.

Besides intercepting clients
during the year, PI served a different population with a formerly discontinued but now
revitalized component called simply the Jail Pro-

Criminal justice system
services

...does Project Intercept
work? Is it worth taxpayer
funds? Consider this:
historically, 30% of PI's
diversion clients indicate
that, were our services not
available, they would opt
for a trial—at an average
cost to taxpayers of $2,000
per proceeding. Given
1982's 444 successful diver-
sions, then, roughly 133
trials (30%) would other-
wise have ensued—at a
cost to taxpayers of
$266,000. PI's 1982
budget, in contrast, was
slightly under $70,000.

394

Art Director	**Alan Spaeth**
Designer	**Alan Spaeth**
Photographer	**Gary McCoy**
Writer	**Larry Sisson**
Client	**Texas Federal Savings**
Agency	**Robert A. Wilson Assoc. Inc., Dallas**

395

Art Director	**Wayne D. Gibb**
Designer	**Wayne D. Gibb**
Photographer	**Ken Light**
Writer	**Wayne D. Gibb**
Editor	**Wayne D. Gibb**
Publisher	**California Human Development Corporation, Santa Rosa**
Printing	**Northwestern Graphics, Santa Rosa, CA**
Typesetting	**Digi-Type, Inc., Santa Rosa, CA**

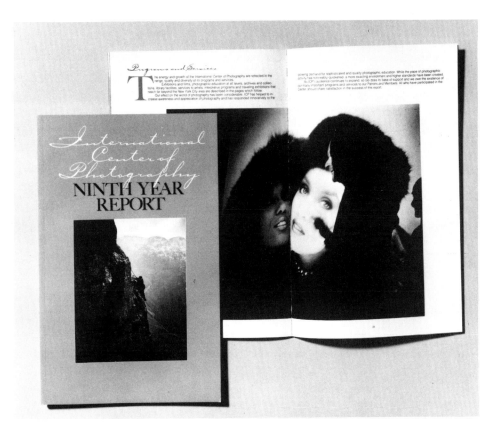

396		397	
Art Director	**Lou Dorfsman**	Art Director	**Lou Dorfsman**
Designer	**Ted Andresakes**	Designer	**Ira Teichberg**
Photographer	**CBS Photo**	Client	**International Center of**
Writer	**J. Garrett Blowers**		**Photography, New York**
Client	**CBS Inc., New York**	Editor	**Ann Doherty**
		Printer	**Sterling Roman Press**

GOLD AWARD

398

Art Director	**Kit Hinrichs**
Designers	**Kit Hinrichs, Barbara Vick**
Photographers	**Tom Tracy, Paul Fusco**
Artists	**Will Nelson, Justin Carroll**
Writer	**Delphine Hirasuna**
Client	**Potlatch Corp.**
Printer	**Anderson Lithograph**
Design Firm	**Jonson Pedersen Hinrichs & Shakery, San Francisco**

E ven in a world of rapid change, the home remains a focal point of peoples' lives. Family members still prefer to spend much of their free time with one another and to pursue their leisure activities at home. Reaching the home and providing increasingly important home-related products and services is the business of American Can's Specialty Retailing sector.

Fingerhut Corporation, including the operations of Figi's, Inc., has posted record sales and earnings over the past seven years, and represents one of the largest and most profitable general merchandise mail-order marketing operations in the country. Using sophisticated computer technology, Fingerhut's targeted marketing approach offers selected household, apparel and food products to its more than eight million customers. Illustrative of the scope of Fingerhut's operations, it maintains purchasing information on 18 million households, and last year mailed approximately 600 million promotional pieces and processed seven million orders. In spite of the overall weakness in the economy and generally sluggish retail sales environment, direct marketing has proven much more recession-resistant than the overall retailing industry. This trend should continue, paralleling the growing consumer demand for convenient, time-saving shopping options.

The Musicland Group is a leader in marketing products for the expanding home entertainment industry. With more than 420 specialized retail stores nationwide, Musicland is the world's largest retailer of pre-recorded music, and is broadening its product line to capitalize on the growth in home computer and video software. Musicland and Sam Goody stores are generally situated in modern, high-traffic malls. They successfully service the home entertainment market using creative store design and layout as well as the optimum mix of audio and video products. This expertise in product merchandising is also put to work for department stores and mass merchandisers through the sector's Pickwick Distribution Companies.

Pickwick is one of the largest rack jobbers in the country and provides a full range of merchandising services to thousands of retail outlets throughout the U.S.

The Specialty Retailing sector, with 1982 sales of more than $800 million, is expected to be a major vehicle for the future growth of American Can. In addition to internal growth through the expansion of Fingerhut's customer base, acquisitions are planned that will capitalize on the sector's unique combination of information-based marketing and retailing skills.

As information replaces capital as the premier resource of the 80's, the Specialty Retailing sector is well positioned for growth, based on a strong presence in home-oriented businesses and demonstrated expertise in targeted marketing.

Specialty
Retailing

Information-based marketing skills enable American Can to channel home entertainment products and shop-at-home services to millions of households.

Texas Industries, Inc. 1983 Annual Report

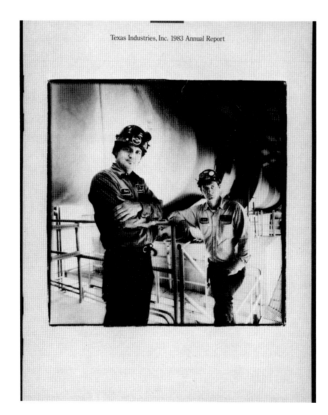

399	
Art Director	**Bennett Robinson**
Designer	**Bennett Robinson,**
	Paula Zographos
Photographers	**Bob Day, Bruce**
	Davidson, Jay Maisel
Artist	**Geoffrey Moss**
Client	**American Can**
	Company
Design Firm	**Corporate Graphics**
	Inc., New York

400	
Art Director	**Alan Spaeth**
Designer	**Alan Spaeth**
Photographer	**Robert Latorre**
Writer	**Robert Wilson**
Client	**Texas Industries Inc.**
Agency	**Robert A. Wilson Assoc.**
	Inc., Dallas

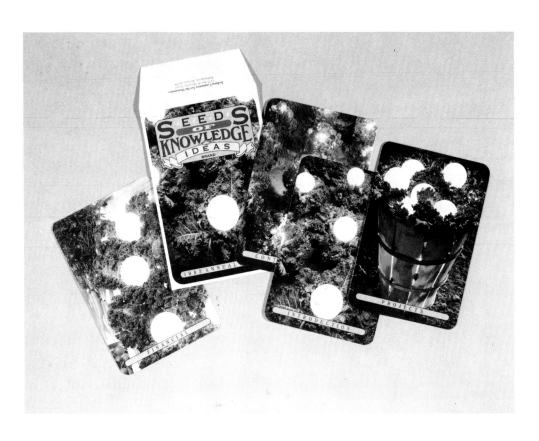

401		**402**	
Art Director	**Dean C. Eller**	Art Director	**Lawrence Bender**
Designer	**Dean C. Eller**	Designer	**Linda Brandon**
Photographer	**Dick Spahr**	Photographer	**Tom Tracy**
Writer	**Dorane Fredland**	Writer	**Ann Fenimore**
Client	**Indiana Committee for the Humanities**	Client	**Priam Corporation**
Agency	**DesignMark Inc., Indianapolis**	Agency	**Lawrence Bender & Associates, Palo Alto, CA**

403

Art Director	**Lawrence Bender**
Designers	**Margaret Hellman, Peter Oberdorf**
Photographer	**Various**
Writer	**Simon Public Relations**
Client	**Ramtek Corporation**
Agency	**Lawrence Bender & Associates, Palo Alto, CA**

404

Art Director	**Ken Bloomhorst**
Designer	**Ken Bloomhorst**
Artist	**Dave Lesh**
Client	**Merchants National Corporation**
Agency	**McQuade Bloomhorst & Story, Inc., Indianapolis**

LUBY'S CAFETERIAS, INC
1982 ANNUAL REPORT
FUTURE GENERATIONS

ENTREPRENEURIAL SPIRIT DRIVES OUR GROWTH

Our success at Luby's is, we believe, largely attributable to the strong entrepreneurial tradition behind our founding and growth. The first cafeteria, begun by Robert M. Luby and Charles R. Johnston in 1947, served menu selections gathered from a discriminating circle of family and friends. They enlarged upon the skills of the traditional family kitchen and marketed them in a special way. The need they saw among the public for excellent food, attractively priced, became a business opportunity. And thus was launched the enterprise that today is Luby's Cafeterias, Inc.

That original effort was an experiment that worked well. Accordingly, the goal of our famous training program has been to pass on to every succeeding cafeteria manager the skills and the outlooks that created that early success. Through instruction and guided experience, managers-to-be strengthen and prove their ability to carry on in the founding tradition. Ultimately, each one who stays with our company becomes responsible for the success of his or her own Luby's cafeteria. Every opening remains as rich in potential as the very first.

But our origins are well known. What is perhaps less often realized is that the entrepreneurial spirit that gave shape to our founding continues to characterize the activity of the entire Luby's organization. With the passage of time, we refined our entrepreneurial model into a method that works extremely well for us and is unique in the restaurant industry.

In our growth, for example, we have learned the benefits of expanding into those areas where our reputation has preceded us. There are objective data to be taken into account, of course. But being able subjectively to judge just when the moment is right, and where a cafeteria should be built, in either a new city or an established major market, relies on more than demographic studies. How we assess the intangible elements peculiar to each location is part of our continuing story.

To grow in the measured manner, we coordinate expansion plans closely with our training program and with advantageous methods of financing. Thus, when we are ready to expand, the funds to build and a seasoned team to manage are ready at hand. The timing and coordination of this system have resulted from a disciplined combination of trial, experience, and planning.

Net Income
(in millions of dollars)

At the time Secretary of State Marshall proposed that the U.S. help rebuild Europe, the first Luby's cafeteria opened its doors in downtown San Antonio. The idea wasn't new in 1947. Cafeterias just hadn't been operated that well before. So while the baby boom was beginning quietly, Luby's opened to enthusiastic, but well-mannered applause.

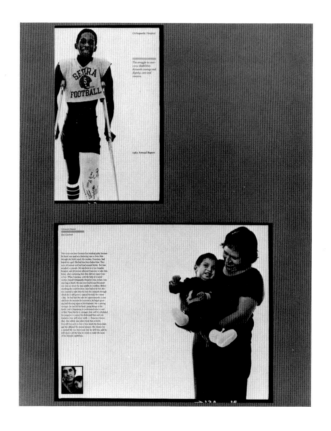

405		406	
Art Director	**Janis Koy**	Art Directors	**Robert Miles Runyan & Associates**
Designer	**Janis Koy**	Designer	**Doug Oliver**
Photographer	**Steve Brady**	Photographer	**Bob Pacheco**
Writer	**Steve Barnhill**	Writer	**Anita Bennett**
Client	**Luby's Cafeterias, Inc.**	Client	**Orthopaedic Hospital**
Printer	**Heritage Press**	Agency	**Robert Miles Runyan & Associates, Playa Del Rey, CA**
Typographer	**ProType of San Antonio**		
Production	**Peter Szarmach**		
Design Firm	**Koy Design Inc., San Antonio, TX**		

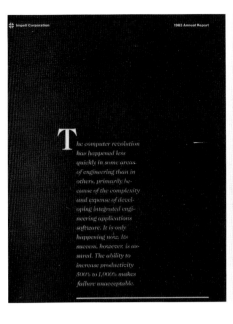

407		408	
Art Directors	Michael Barile, Richard Garnas	Art Director	D.J. Stout
Designers	Michael Barile, Richard Garnas, Gene Clark	Designer	D.J. Stout
		Photographer	Robert Latorre
Photographer	Michael K. Nichols	Writer	Larry Sisson
Client	Impell Corporation	Client	Wyly Corporation
Design Firm	Barile/Garnas Design, Oakland, CA	Agency	Robert A. Wilson Assoc, Inc., Dallas

Fiscal 1983 Annual Report

Schlumberger Annual Report 1982

	409		**410**		**411**
Art Director	Thomas D. Morin	Art Director	Stephen Miller	Art Director	Milton Glaser
Designer	Thomas D. Morin	Designer	Stephen Miller	Designer	Karen Skelton
Artists	J. Hablitzel, H. Goerke, K. Maruyama	Photographer	Greg Booth	Artist	James McMullan
Writer	Elaine Vail	Writers	Mark Perkins, Jess Hay	Writers	André Misk, Seth McCormick, Jean-Claude Comert
Client	Clabir Corporation	Client	Lomas & Nettleton Financial Corp.	Client	Schlumberger, Ltd.
Editor	David Downes	Agency	Richards, Brock, Miller, Mitchell-The Richards Group, Dallas	Agency	Milton Glaser Inc., New York
Agency	Jack Hough Assoc., Inc., Norwalk, CT				
Publication	1983 Annual Report				
Printer	Lebanon Valley Offset				
Typesetter	Production Typographers				

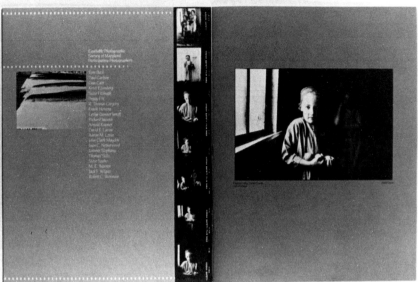

412		413	
Art Director	**Jerry Dadds**	Art Director	**B. Martin Pedersen**
Designer	**Jerry Dadds**	Designers	**B. Martin Pedersen,**
Photographer	**Equitable Photographic**		**Adrian Pulfer**
	Survey of Maryland	Photographers	**Neil Selkirk, Cheryl**
Artist	**Nancy Johnston**		**Rossum, Robin Moyer**
Writer	**William Amelia &**	Writer	**Lawrence A. Armour**
	Associates, Inc.	Client	**Dow Jones & Co.**
Client	**Equitable**	Agency	**Jonson, Pedersen,**
	Bancorporation		**Hinrichs & Shakery,**
Design Firm	**Eucalyptus Tree Studio,**		**New York**
	Inc., Baltimore		
Printer	**Schneidereith & Sons,**		
	Inc.		

414

Art Director	**Milt Simpson**
Designer	**Lynn Keffer**
Photographers	**Todd Weinstein, William Rivelli, Bill Cadge, Dick Luria, Faustino**
Writer	**F. Robert Kniffin**
Client	**Johnson & Johnson**
Design Firm	**Johnson & Simpson Graphic Designers, Newark, NJ**
Publication	**Johnson & Johnson 1982 Annual Report**

415

Art Director	**Diana Graham**
Designer	**Diana Graham**
Photographer	**Greg Heisler, Bob Colton**
Writer	**Francis X. Piderit**
Client	**Johnson & Higgins, Inc.**
Agency	**Gips + Balkind + Associates, New York**
Publication	**1983 Annual Review**

416

Art Director	**Ron Sullivan**
Designer	**Ron Sullivan**
Photographers	**Greg Booth/Andy Post**
Writer	**Mark Perkins**
Client	**Lomas & Nettleton Mortgage Investors**
Publisher	**Heritage Press**
Agency	**Richards, Brock, Miller & Mitchell/The Richards Group, Dallas**

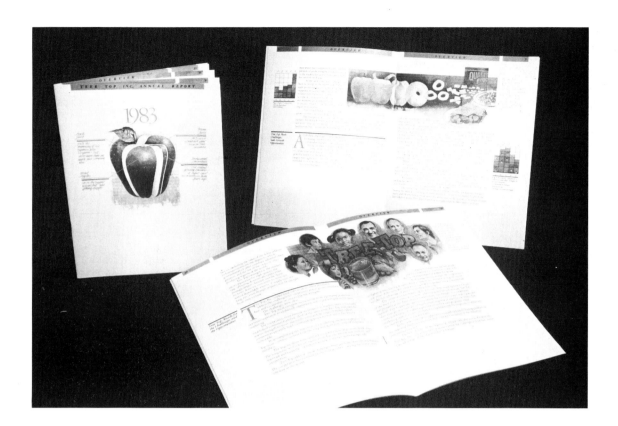

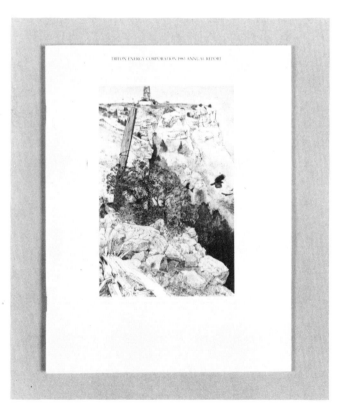

<table>
<tr><td colspan="2">

417

Art Director **John Hornall**
Designer **Andrea Sames**
Artist **Jim Hayes**
Writer **Tom McCarthy**
Client **Tree Top, Inc.**
Design Firm **John Hornall Design Works, Seattle**

</td></tr>
</table>

417	418
Art Director **John Hornall**	Art Director **Stephen Miller**
Designer **Andrea Sames**	Designer **Stephen Miller**
Artist **Jim Hayes**	Artist **Jack Unruh**
Writer **Tom McCarthy**	Writer **Mike McInearney**
Client **Tree Top, Inc.**	Client **Triton Energy Corp**
Design Firm **John Hornall Design Works, Seattle**	Agency **Richards, Brock, Miller, Mitchell-The Richards Group, Dallas**

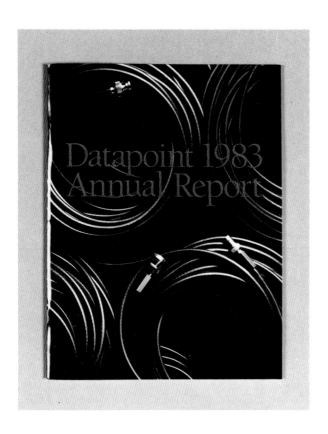

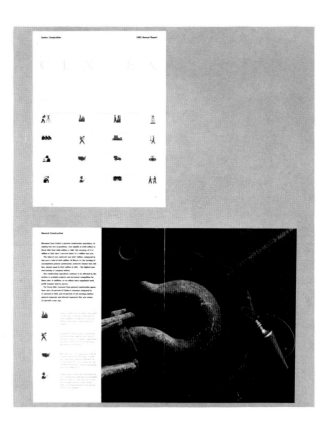

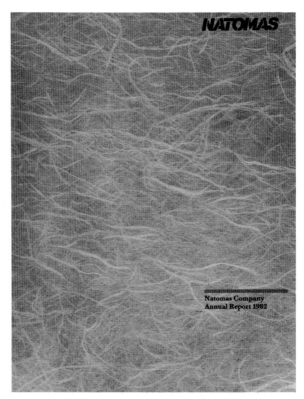

419		420		421	
Art Director	**Chris Rovillo**	Art Director	**Woody Pirtle**	Art Director	**Stephen Stanley**
Designer	**Chris Rovillo**	Designer	**Woody Pirtle, David**	Designer	**Stephen Stanley**
Photographer	**Andy Post**		**Kampa**	Photographers	**Michael K. Nichols,**
Client	**Jack Milne, Datapoint**	Photographer	**Arthur Meyerson**		**Tom Lea, Various**
	Corporation	Artist	**David Kampa**	Writer	**James A. Campbell**
Agency	**Richards, Brock, Miller,**	Writer	**Sheila Gallager**	Client	**Natomas Company**
	Mitchell & Assoc./The	Client	**Centex Corporation**	Design Firm	**Stephen Stanley**
	Richards Group, Dallas	Publisher	**Centex Corp.**		**Graphic Design, San**
Printer	**Bordnax Printing**	Agency	**Pirtle Design, Dallas**		**Francisco**

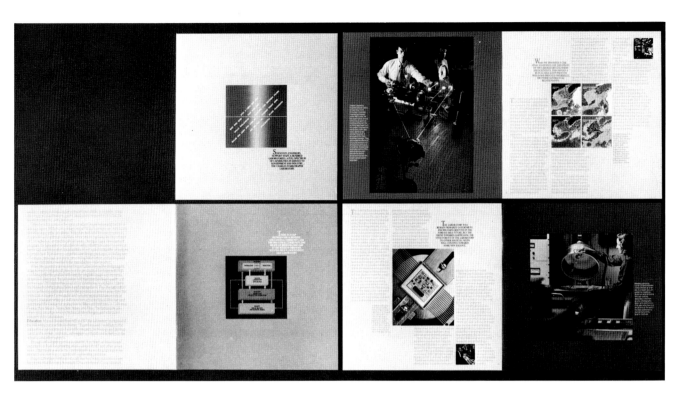

	422		423
Art Director	**Robert Cipriani**	Art Director	**Vance Jonson**
Designer	**Robert Cipriani**	Designer	**Vance Jonson**
Photographer	**Steve Dunwell**	Artist	**Dave Lesh**
Writer	**Catherine Flannery**	Writer	**Judith Greer**
Client	**The Charles Stark Draper Laboratory, Inc.**	Client	**Grow Group, Inc.**
Agency	**Cipriani Advertising, Inc., Boston**	Agency	**Jonson Pedersen Hinrichs & Shakery, Rowayton, CT**
Project Supervisor	**J. Dustin Thomas**		

424

Art Director	Thomas Ryan
Designer	Thomas Ryan
Photographer	McGuire
Writers	Matt Hamilton, Dan Evins
Client	The Cracker Barrel Old Country Store
Agency	Corporate Communications, Inc., Nashville

425

Art Director	Robert Miles Runyan & Associates
Designer	Robert Miles Runyan & Associates
Photographer	Lon Harding
Writer	Getty Oil Company
Client	Getty Oil Company
Agency	Robert Miles Runyan & Associates, Playa Del Ray, CA

426

Art Director	Stephen Ferrari
Client	Federal Express Corporation
Agency	The Graphic Expression, Inc., New York

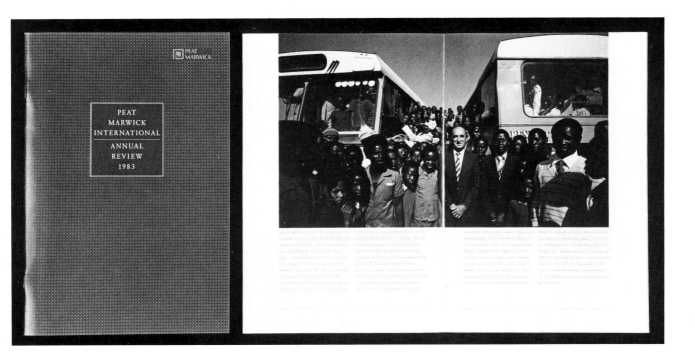

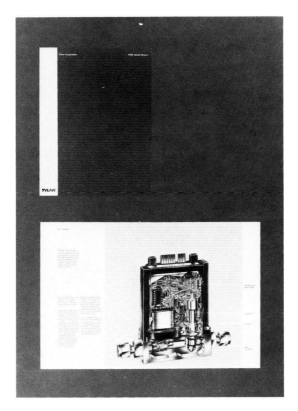

427		**428**	
Art Director	**Peter Harrison**	Art Director	**Douglas Joseph**
Designer	**Susan Hochbaum**	Designer	**Douglas Joseph**
Photographer	**Neil Slavin**	Artist	**David Kimble**
Writer	**Gerry Barry**	Writer	**Craig Parsons**
Client	**Peat Marwick**	Client	**Tylan Corporation**
	International	Agency	**Douglas Joseph, Los**
Director	**Chris Rubin**		**Angeles**
Design Firm	**Pentagram Design, Ltd.,**		
	New York		

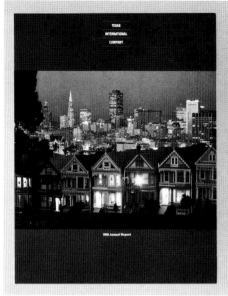

429		430	
Art Director	**Richard Kilmer**	Art Director	**Richard Hess**
Designer	**Richard Kilmer**	Designer	**Richard Hess**
Photographer	**Various**	Client	**Champion**
Writer	**Russell Burget**		**International**
Client	**Texas International**		**Corporation, Stamford**
	Company		**CT**
Agency	**Ben Carter &**	Editor	**David R. Brown**
	Associates, Bellaire, TX		

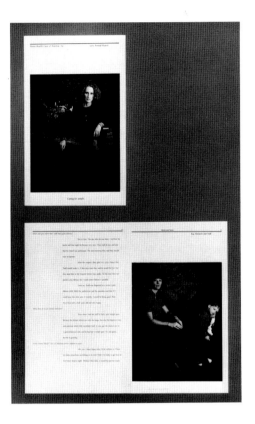

431		432		433	
Art Director	James Cross	Art Director	Jim Berte	Art Directors	Rob Carter, Timothy H. Priddy
Designer	Carl Seltzer	Designer	Jim Berte	Designers	Rob Carter, Timothy H. Priddy
Photographer	Ken Whitmore	Photographer	Deborah Meyer	Photographer	Various
Writer	Ronald J. Meder	Writer	Dave Johnson	Writer	J. Michael Welton
Client	Lockheed Corporation	Client	Home Health Care of America, Inc.	Client	Best Products Co., Inc., Richmond, VA
Design Firm	Cross Associates, Los Angeles	Agency	Robert Miles Runyan & Associates, Los Angeles	Editor	Edwin J. Slipek, Jr.
Printer	Anderson Lithography Co.				

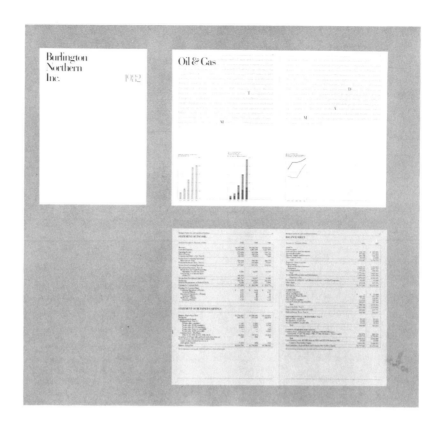

434

Art Director	John Van Dyke
Designer	John Van Dyke
Client	Philip Scheetz, Burlington Northern
Agency	Van Dyke Company, Seattle

435

Art Director	Janis Koy
Designer	Janis Koy
Photographer	E.O. Goldbeck
Writer	Suzy Lawton
Client	1776, Inc.
Design Firm	Koy Design, Inc., San Antonio
Typographer	ProType of San Antonio

Directing the Self Against Disease

A master key for the immune system.
  The possibilities for therapy seem endless since immune processes now appear to have some involvement in almost all chronic diseases. The key, however, is complex in the extreme. It should open many doors, but only after long and arduous research.
  Cytokines are some fifty to one hundred naturally occurring compounds that direct the immune system. They work through complex interactions among themselves and with the system's specialized cellular components. If we understood cytokines completely, we could cause the immune system to attack or undermine conditions ranging from cancer and arthritis to multiple sclerosis, rejection of transplanted organs, and, perhaps, even the aging process itself.
  Research on cytokines is so new that only one subgroup, called interferons, has been completely purified and produced in any quantity. Reports of work at various laboratories, however, are promising. For example, hybrid cytokines, produced by combining segments from two of these substances, have been much more effective in laboratory tests than their naturally occurring counterparts.
  At present, scientists are seeking at least three types of drugs in this new area of immunology: single cytokines or several used together, hybrid versions of these natural substances, and compounds that either mimic or interfere with normal cytokine activity.
  Any of these approaches could produce dramatic new therapies for a broad range of diseases. Together they could eventually give us a master key to the immune system.

	436		437
Art Director	Bennett Robinson	Art Director	Robin Jahncke
Designers	Bennett Robinson, Naomi Burstein	Designer	Doug May/Carnase Inc.
Artist	Robert Giusti	Photographer	Fred Maroon
Client	Eli Lilly And Company	Printer	Stephenson Inc.
Design Firm	Corporate Graphics, Inc., New York	Client	E.F. Hutton & Co. Inc.
		Publisher	E.F. Hutton & Co. Inc.
		Production Coordinator	Bill Block
		Agency	E.F. Hutton Corporate Advertising
		Typographer	Carnase Typography Inc., New York

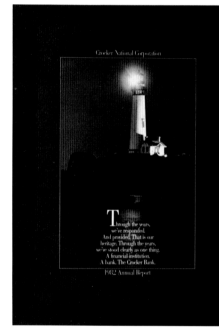

438		439	
Art Director	Neil Shakery	Art Director	Kit Hinrichs
Designers	Neil Shakery, Sandra McHenry	Designers	Kit Hinrichs, Lenore Bartz
Photographer	Various	Photographers	Terry Heffernan, Light Language/Chad Ehlers (cover)
Artists	Bill Dodge (cover), Elaine Keenan (tinting)		
Writer	Harry Matte	Writer	Dave Sanson
Client	Amfac, Inc.	Client	Crocker Bank
Printer	Graphic Arts Center	Printer	Graphic Arts Center
Design Firm	Jonson Pedersen Hinrichs & Shakery, San Francisco	Design Firm	Jonson Pedersen Hinrichs & Shakery, San Francisco

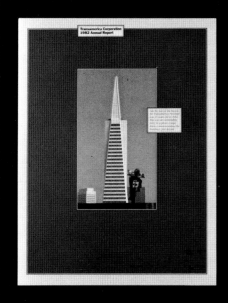

440

Art Director	**Linda Hinrichs**
Designers	**Linda Hinrichs, Karen Berndt**
Photographers	**John Blaustein, Jon Brenneis, Jennifer Feldman (cover)**
Artist	**Gary Pierazzi**
Writer	**Candy Kessler**
Client	**Transamerica Corp.**
Printer	**Graphic Arts Center**
Design Firm	**Jonson Pedersen Hinrichs & Shakery, San Francisco**

441

Art Director	**Alan Fletcher**
Designer	**Seymour Chwast**
Artist	**Seymour Chwast**
Client	**Geers Gross**
Agency	**Pushpin Lubalin Peckolick, New York**

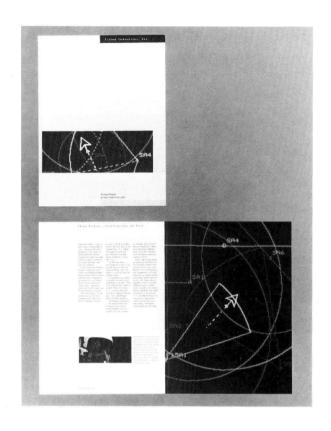

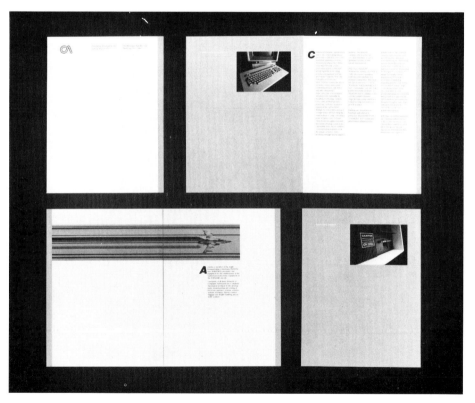

442		443		444	
Art Director	Robert Miles Runyan & Associates	Art Director	Anthony Rutka	Art Director	Kevin O'Neill
Designer	Robert Miles Runyan & Associates	Designer	Anthony Rutka	Designers	Kevin O'Neill, Steve Quinn
Photographer	Mark Joseph	Photographers	Burt Glinn, Doug Barber	Photographer	Gregory Gorfkle
Writer	John Tuffy	Artist	Werner Mueller	Writer	Vivian Hunter
Client	Litton Industries, Inc.	Writer	Jo Clendenon	Client	Computer Automation, Inc.
Agency	Robert Miles Runyan & Associates, Los Angeles	Client	The Johns Hopkins Medical Institutions	Design Firm	Tandem Design Group, Inc., Denver
		Editors	Leslye Sugar, Elaine Freeman		
		Agency	Rutka & Weadock, Baltimore		

	445		**446**		**446A**
Art Director	Richard Danne/Danne & Blackburn, Inc., New York	Art Director	Nancy Hoefig	Art Director	Linda Hinrichs
		Designer	Nancy Hoefig	Designers	Linda Hinrichs, Sandra McHenry
Designers	Gary Skeggs and Richard Danne	Photographer	Greg Booth	Photographer	John Blaustein
Photographers	Alex Webb, Magnum	Artist	Amon Carter Museum The Bettman Archives	Artists	Greg Spalenka, Ellen Jacobs, John Mattos, David Monteil
Clients	AmeriTrust Corporation, Robert F. Miller	Writer	Mark Perkins	Writer	Issac Grazian
		Client	L&N Housing Corp.	Client	Syntex Corp.
Agency	Edward Howard & Company, John T. Bailey	Agency	Richards, Brock, Miller & Mitchell, The Richards Group, Dallas	Printer	George Rice & Sons
Printer	The Hennegan Company			Design Firm	Jonson Pedersen Hinrichs & Shakery, San Francisco

GOLD AWARD

447

Art Director	**James Sebastian**
Designers	**James Sebastian, Michael McGinn, Jim Hinchee**
Photographer	**Bruce Wolf**
Client	**Martex/West Point Pepperell**
Design Firm	**Designframe, Inc., New York**

448

Art Director **John R. Kleinschmidt,
New York**
Designer **Bessen and Tully, Inc.**
Photographer **Susan Wood**
Writer **Michael Teague**
Client **Wamsutta Home
Products**

449

Art Director **Lowell Williams**
Designers **Lowell Williams, Bill
Carson**
Photographers **Ron Scott, Arthur
Meyerson, Bob Haar**
Client **Gerald D. Hines
Interests**
Agency **Lowell Williams
Design, Inc., Houston**

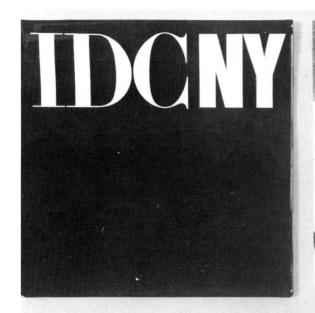

450

Art Director	Massimo Vignelli
Designer	Michael Bierut
Writer	Edward Colquhoun
Client	Lazard Development Corporation
Design Firm	Vignelli Associates, New York

451

Art Director	Carnet, O'Mary
Designer	Jean Carnet
Photographer	Jean Carnet
Writer	Sandra Carnet
Client	Jim Byrd, Wilma Realty Services
Design Firm	Carnet & Associates, Atlanta

453		454	
Art Director	**Peter Laundy**	Art Director	**Lowell Williams**
Photographer	**Ambrose Cucinotta**	Designers	**Lowell Williams,**
Client	**Jean Solomon,**		**Bill Carson**
	Solomon Equities	Photographer	**Ron Scott**
Design Firm	**Vignelli Associates,**	Writer	**Lee Herrick**
	New York	Client	**Rose Associates, Inc.**
Photographer	**ESTO**	Agency	**Lowell Williams**
			Design, Inc., Houston

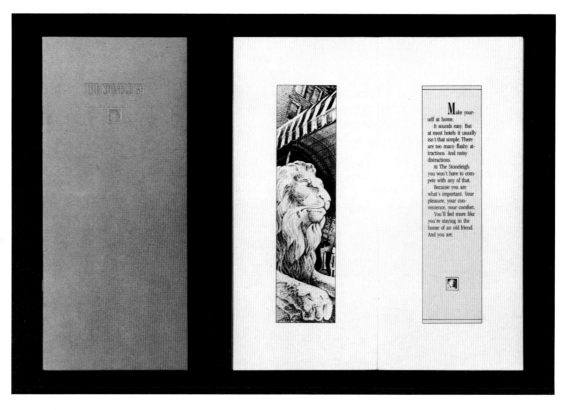

	455		**456**
Art Director	Lowell Williams	Art Directors	Glenn Dady,
Designers	Lowell Williams,		Tom Gilmore
	Bill Carson	Designers	Glen Dady,
Photographer	Joe Baraban		Tom Gilmore
Artists	Lana Rigsby,	Artist	Genevieve Meek
	Barry Parker	Writer	Kerry Hersh
Client	The George Hederhorst	Client	Stoneleigh Hotel
	Company	Agency	The Richards Group,
Agency	Lowell Williams		Dallas
	Design, Inc., Houston	Production	
		Manager	Dave Cole

Harbour Ridge

457

Art Director	**Robert E. Cargill**
Designer	**Bonnie Lovell**
Photographer	**Bill Weema**
Client	**Harbour Ridge**
Agency	**Cargill & Associates, Inc., Atlanta**

458

Art Director	**Jann Church Partners**
Designers	**Jann Church, Lea Pascoe**
Photographer	**O.E. Studios**
Artist	**Jann Church Partners**
Writer	**McDargh**
Client	**Leighton French Co.**
Agency	**Jann Church Partners, Inc., NewPort Beach, CA**

459

Art Directors	**Jim Huckabay, Focus Design Group, Inc.**
Photographer	**Tim Harper**
Artist	**John Cook**
Writer	**Dan Baldwin**
Design Firm	**Focus Design Group, Inc., Shreveport, LA**
Printer	**Mid South Press, Inc.**

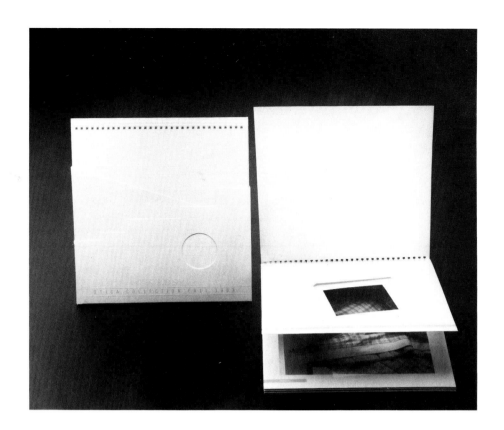

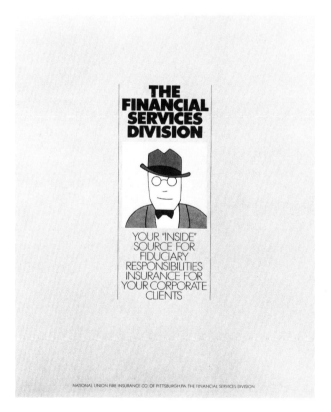

	460		**461**
Art Director	Dick Solay	Art Director	Leslie Schecht
Designer	Philip Badal	Designer	Alan Peckolick
Photographer	Robert Grant	Artists	Seymour Chwast, Kevin Gatta
Client	J.P. Stevens	Writer	Peter Borrell
Design Firm	Solay/Hunt, Inc., New York	Editor	American International Group
		Agency	Pushpin Lubalin Peckolick, New York

Biofitness. Inside and Out.

The Parkway   A Master Plan

464

Art Directors	**Seymour Chwast, Alan Peckolick**
Designer	**Seymour Chwast**
Artist	**Seymour Chwast**
Client	**Christian Joyce, Biofitness Institute**
Agency	**Pushpin Lubalin Peckolick, New York**

465

Art Director	**Felix Rhymes**
Photographer	**Steve Brady**
Writer	**Skip Jordan**
Client	**Holmes Investments**
Agency	**LargeRhymes, Houston**

GOLD AWARD

———— **466** ————

Art Directors **David Edelstein, Nancy Edelstein, Lanny French**
Designers **David Edelstein, Nancy Edelstein, Lanny French**
Photographers **Jim Cummins, Rocky Salskov**
Writer **David Edelstein**
Client **Generra Sportswear**
Agency **Edelstein Associates, Inc., Seattle**
Production Co. **Wilkins & Peterson**

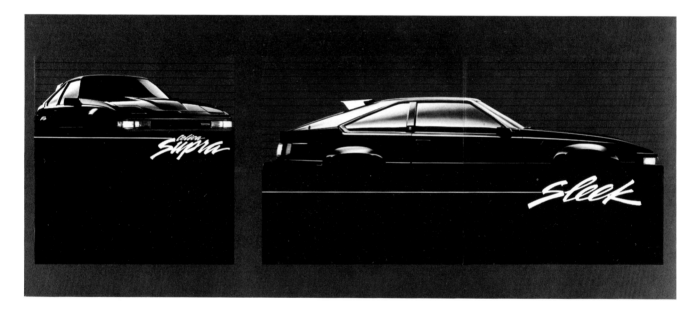

467

Art Director	**Jim Jacobs**
Designer	**Jim Jacobs**
Artist	**Jim Jacobs**
Writer	**Jim Jacobs**
Client	**Anne McGilvray**
Design Firm	**Jim Jacobs' Studio, Inc., Dallas**

468

Art Director	**Jim Doyle**
Designer	**Jim Doyle**
Photographer	**Boulevard Photographic**
Writer	**Bob Nathan**
Client	**Toyota Motor Sales/ USA, Inc.**
Creative Director	**Bill Hamilton**
Agency	**Dancer Fitzgerald Sample, Inc./Southern California**
Group Head	**Jim Lodge**

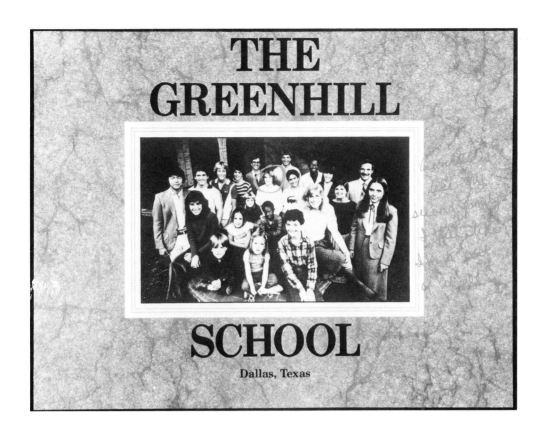

469		470	
Art Director	D.J. Stout	Art Director	Kurt Meinecke
Designer	D.J. Stout	Designer	Kurt Meinecke
Photographer	Gary Bishop	Photographer	Von
Writer	Larry Sisson	Writer	Donald Manelli
Client	Greenhill School	Client	The Color Market
Agency	Robert A. Wilson Assoc. Inc., Dallas	Agency	Group/Chicago, Inc.

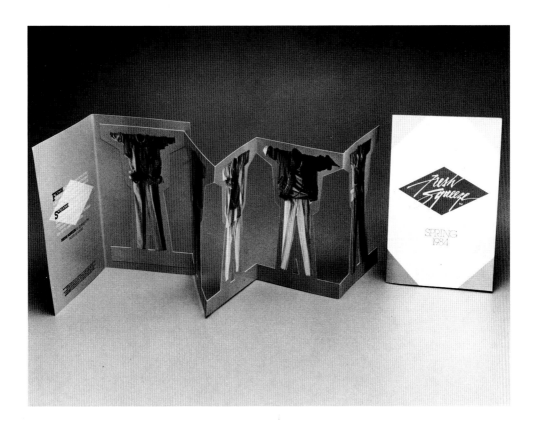

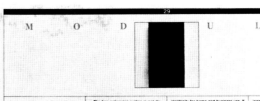

471		472	
Art Directors	David Edelstein, Nancy Edelstein, Lanny French	Art Directors	Michael David Brown, Donald Lynn
Designers	David Edelstein, Nancy Edelstein, Lanny French	Designers	Charles Gallis, Kathleen Wilmes Herring
Photographer	Jim Cummins	Artist	Michael David Brown
Writers	David Edelstein, Ron Koliha	Client	Internal Revenue Service
Client	Fresh Squeeze Sportswear	Design Firm	Michael David Brown, Inc., Rockville, MD
Agency	Edelstein Associates, Inc., Seattle		
Production Co.	Wilkins & Peterson		

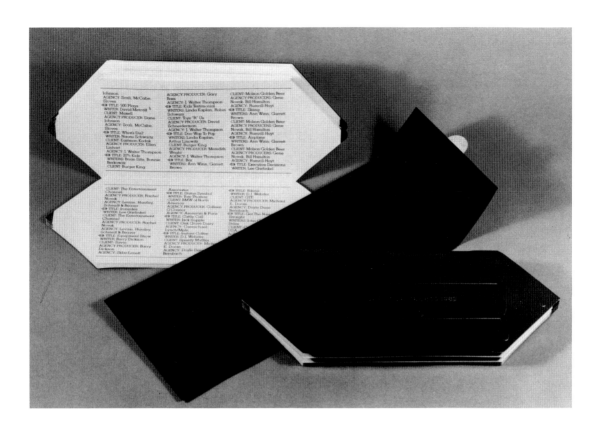

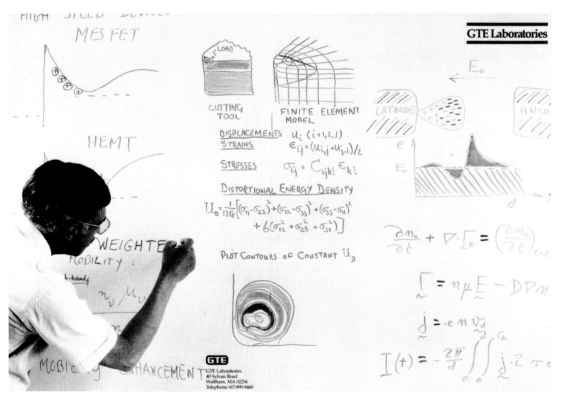

473		474	
Art director	**Tom Schwartz**	Art Director	**John Milligan**
Client	**The One Club**	Designers	**Lydna Fishbourn,**
Agency	**Scali, McCabe, Sloves,**		**John Milligan**
	New York	Photographer	**John Earle**
		Writer	**Brian Flood**
		Client	**GTE Laboratories**
		Agency	**John Milligan Design**
			Inc., Boston

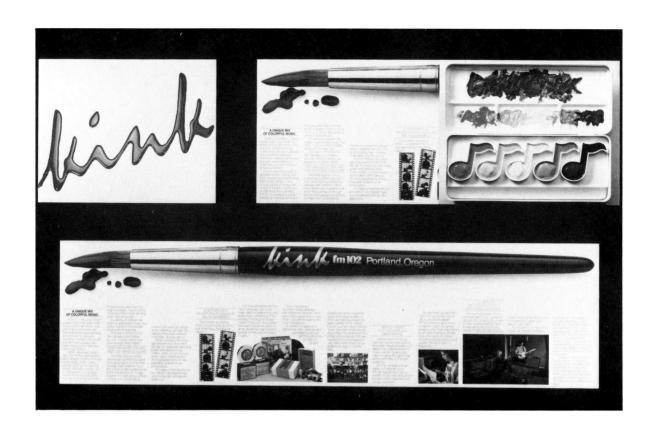

	475		476
Art Director	**Warren Eakins**	Art Director	**Mike Campbell**
Designer	**Warren Eakins**	Designers	**Mike Campbell,**
Photographer	**Jerry LaRocca**		**Jim Jacobs**
Artist	**Tim Kilian**	Artist	**Jim Jacobs**
Writer	**Bill Borders**	Writer	**Jim Jacobs**
Client	**KINK-FM**	Client	**Anne McGilvray**
Agency	**Borders, Perrin &**	Design Firm	**Jim Jacobs' Studio, Inc.,**
	Norrander, Inc.,		**Dallas**
	Portland		

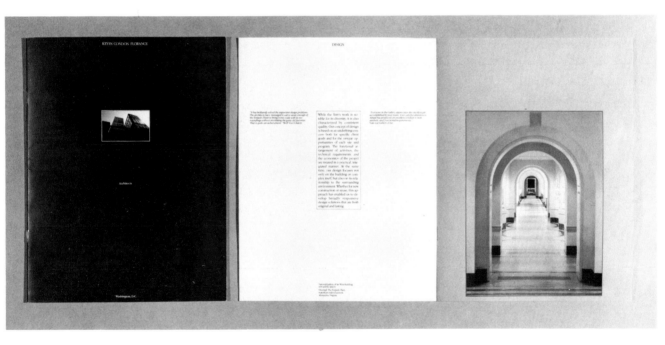

	477		**478**
Art Director	Walter J. Ender	Art Director	David A. Ashton
Designer	Walter J. Ender	Designer	David A. Ashton
Photographers	Arnold Zann, Greg Hursley, Gary Blockley, John Rogers, Rick Alexander, William Burwell, Judd Haggard, Robert Cook	Photographer	Gary Fleming
		Writer	Douglass B. Forsyth
		Client	Keyes Condon Florance
		Agency	Ashton-Worthington, Inc., Baltimore
Writers	JPJ Architects, Rominger Agency		
Client	JPJ Architects		
Agency	Ender Associates Advertising Inc., Dallas		

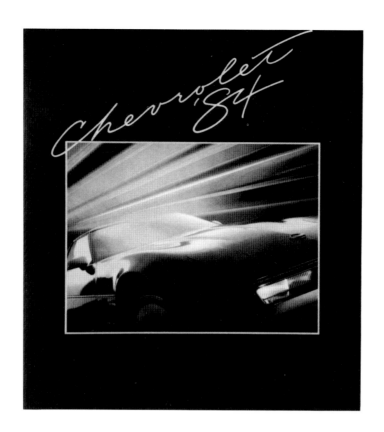

479

Art Director	**Ron Tosh**
Writer	**Lawrence Dolph**
Client	**Chevrolet Motor Division**
Studio	**McNamara Associates, Inc.**
Director	**Gene Butera**
Agency	**Campbell-Ewald Company, Warren, MI**
Creative Director	**Sean K. Fitzpatrick**

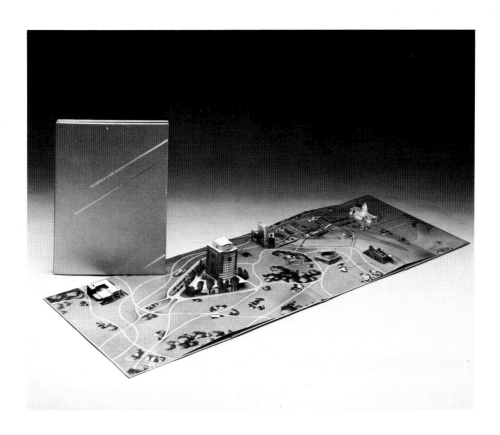

The Xerox Software Solution

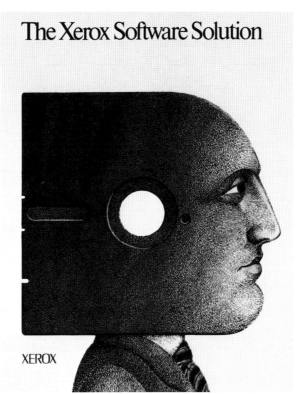

XEROX

480		481	
Art Director	Hanna Mayer	Art Director	Al Weintraub
Cover Design	Rick Myerchalk	Writer	Bob Ingwersen
Artist	B.J. Johnson	Agency	Crume & Associates,
Writer	Terry Coveny		Inc., Dallas
Client	Olmsted Foundation	Creative	
	Building	Director	Ben Vergati
Agency	Abramson Associates,		
	Inc., Washington, DC		
Paper			
Engineering	I.B. Penick/Structural		
	Graphics		

482
Art Director Victor Liebert
Writer Larry Miller
Client Hoechst Fibers
Industries
Agency Ina Kahn Trevira-In-
House, New York

483
Art Director Seymour Chwast
Designer Seymour Chwast
Artist Seymour Chwast
Client New York State Dept. of
Social Welfare
Agency Pushpin Lubalin
Peckolick, New York

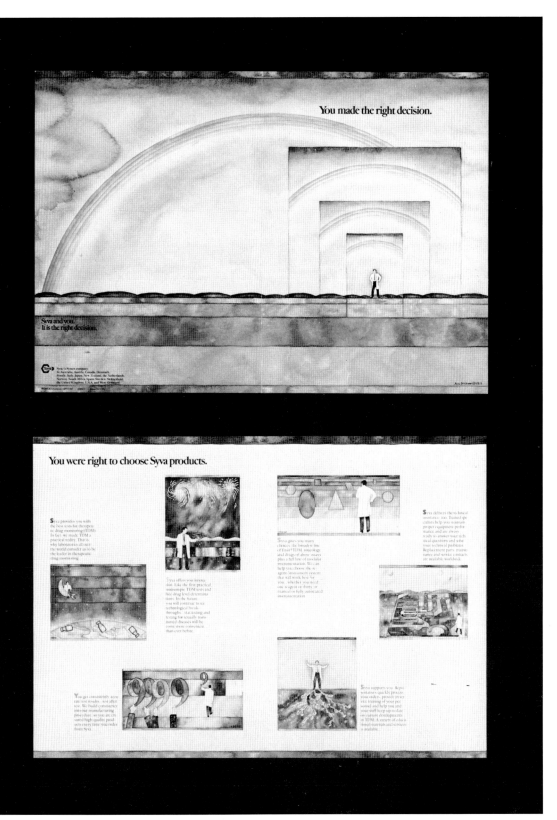

484

Art Director **Donna Perzel**
Designer **Donna Perzel**
Artist **Alice Brickner**
Writer **Maris Hochman**
Client **Syva Company**
Editor **Wilma Sharken**
Agency **Gross Townsend Frank, Inc., New York**
VP Production **Clare Macken**

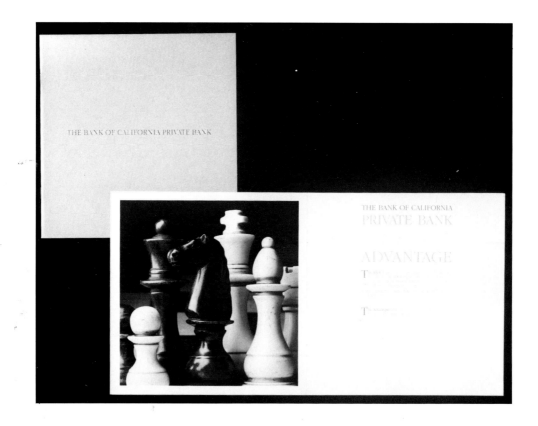

485		486	
Art Director	**Edd Mangino**	Art Directors	**David November,**
Designer	**Peter Mock**		**Marie-Christine**
Photographer	**Arthur Beck**		**Lawrence**
Writer	**Jill Murray**	Designers	**Susan Borgen, David**
Client	**Bank of California**		**November**
Agency	**Mangino/Murray Inc.,**	Photographer	**Don Huntstein**
	San Francisco	Writers	**Barbara Coulter, David**
			November
		Client	**CBS Television Network**
			Sales, New York

California
State Capitol
Restoration

487		488	
Art Director	**Pat Davis Design**	Art Director	**Marjorie Greene**
Designers/		Designer	**Marjorie Greene**
Calligrapher	**Brenda Walton Design, Sacramento, CA**	Photographer	**Steve Marsal**
		Artist	**Tyler Peppel/MIT Visual Language Workshop**
Writer	**Lynn G. Marlowe**		
Client	**California State Legislature, Joint Committee on Rules**	Writer	**Brian Flood**
		Client	**Interactive Training Systems**
Editors	**John C. Worsley, FAIA; Dale E. Dwyer, AIA**	Editor	**Bev MacDonald**
Printer	**Graphic Center**	Publisher	**Interactive Training Systems**
Typographer	**Ad Type Graphics**	Design Firm	**Gunn Associates, Boston**

489

Art Directors **Bob Dennard, Ken Koester**
Designer **Ken Koester**
Artist **Lee Lee Brazeal**
Writer **John Crawley**
Client **Paul Broadhead & Associates, Inc.**
Agency **Dennard Creative, Inc., Dallas**
Creative Director **Bob Dennard**

490		491	
Art Director	James Sebastian	Art Director	Tom Poth
Designers	James Sebastian, Michael McGinn, Jim Hinchee	Designer	Tom Poth
		Photographers	Michael Patrick, Ave Bonar
Photographer	Bruce Wolf	Writer	Guy Bommarito
Client	Martex/West Point Pepperell	Client	St. David's Community Hospital
Design Firm	Designframe, Inc., New York	Editor	Melinda Muse
		Publisher	Printmasters, Inc.
		Agency	HIXO, Inc., Austin

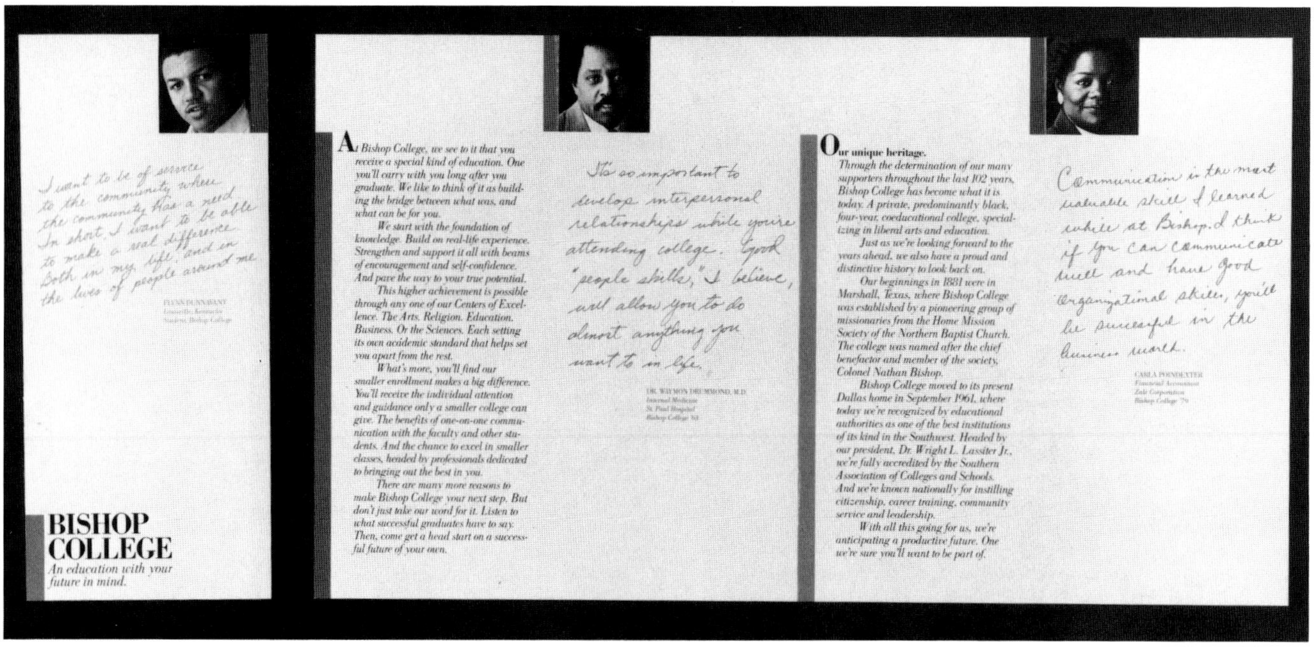

BISHOP COLLEGE

An education with your future in mind.

(handwritten testimonial panels)

At Bishop College, we see to it that you receive a special kind of education. One you'll carry with you long after you graduate. We like to think of it as building the bridge between what was, and what can be for you.

We start with the foundation of knowledge. Build on real-life experience. Strengthen and support it all with beams of encouragement and self-confidence. And pave the way to your true potential.

This higher achievement is possible through any one of our Centers of Excellence. The Arts. Religion. Education. Business. Or the Sciences. Each setting its own academic standard that helps set you apart from the rest.

What's more, you'll find our smaller enrollment makes a big difference. You'll receive the individual attention and guidance only a smaller college can give. The benefits of one-on-one communication with the faculty and other students. And the chance to excel in smaller classes, headed by professionals dedicated to bringing out the best in you.

There are many more reasons to make Bishop College your next step. But don't just take our word for it. Listen to what successful graduates have to say. Then, come get a head start on a successful future of your own.

Our unique heritage.

Through the determination of our many supporters throughout the last 102 years, Bishop College has become what it is today. A private, predominantly black, four-year, coeducational college, specializing in liberal arts and education.

Just as we're looking forward to the years ahead, we also have a proud and distinctive history to look back on.

Our beginnings in 1881 were in Marshall, Texas, where Bishop College was established by a pioneering group of missionaries from the Home Mission Society of the Northern Baptist Church. The college was named after the chief benefactor and member of the society, Colonel Nathan Bishop.

Bishop College moved to its present Dallas home in September 1961, where today we're recognized by educational authorities as one of the best institutions of its kind in the Southwest. Headed by our president, Dr. Wright L. Lassiter Jr., we're fully accredited by the Southern Association of Colleges and Schools. And we're known nationally for instilling citizenship, career training, community service and leadership.

With all this going for us, we're anticipating a productive future. One we're sure you'll want to be part of.

ARTS & BUSINESS COUNCIL, INC. 1982

492		493	
Art Director	**Tim Varner**	Art Director	**Alan Peckolick**
Designer	**Tim Varner**	Designer	**Alan Peckolick**
Photographer	**Dennis Murphy**	Artist	**Seymour Chwast**
Writer	**Julie Gardner**	Client	**Arts & Business**
Client	**Bishops College**		**Council, Inc.**
Agency	**Levenson, Levenson &**	Agency	**Corpcom Services Inc.,**
	Hill, Dallas/Ft. Worth		**New York**

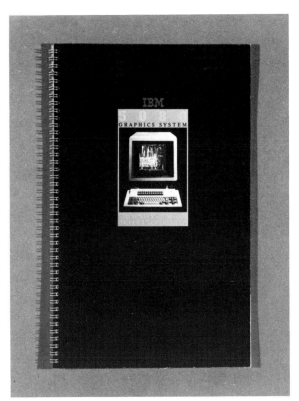

	494		495
Art Director	**Jerold Fox Jr.**	Art Director	**B. Martin Pedersen**
Designer	**Jerold Fox Jr.**	Designers	**B. Martin Pedersen,**
Artists	**Jerold Fox Jr., Dorothea**		**Adrian Pulfer**
	Trecroce-Fox	Photographer	**Mike Djir Djirian**
Client	**David Eyler**	Writer	**Bill Littlefield**
Agency	**Roth & Associates,**	Client	**IBM**
	Bloomfield, NJ	Director	**Rolf Sauer**
		Agency	**Jonson Pedersen**
			Hinrichs & Shakery,
			New York

S T . A N D R E W S

B O C A · R A T O N

SILVER AWARD

496

Art Director	**Philip Gips**
Designer	**Philip Gips**
Artist	**Chuck Wilkinson**
Writer	**Francis X. Piderit**
Client	**St. Andrews Development Co. of Boca Raton, Inc.**
Agency	**Gips+Balkind+ Associates, New York**
Publication	**St. Andrews Boca Raton Brochure**
Creative Director	**Ruth Ansel**

497		498	
Art Director	**Dean Hanson**	Art Directors	**Robin Rickabaugh,**
Designer	**Dean Hanson**		**Heidi Rickabaugh**
Photographers	**Tom Back, Marvy**	Designer	**Robin Rickabaugh**
	Photography	Photographer	**Lawrence Hudetz**
Writer	**Tom McElligott**	Writer	**Marilyn Musick**
Client	**Vander Zanden, Inc.**	Client	**SRG Partnership**
Agency	**Fallon McElligott Rice,**	Design Firm	**Rickabaugh Design,**
	Minneapolis		**Portland**

	499		500
Art Director	Tetsuya Matsuura	Art Director	Sharon L. Tooley, Houston
Designer	Tetsuya Matsuura	Designer	Sharon L. Tooley
Photographers	Various	Photographer	Frank White
Artist	Gerard Huerta	Writer	Paule Sheya Hewlett
Writer	Hal Alterman	Client	S.T.UDIO
Client	NBC Marketing, New York		

JUNE 16, 1982 NEW YORK, NEW YORK

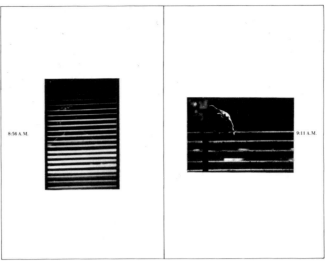

8:56 A.M.

9:11 A.M.

2:12 P.M.

2:40 P.M.

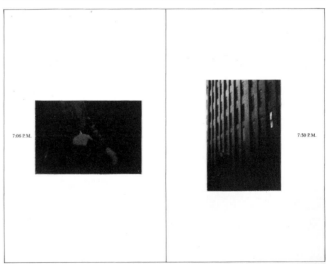

7:06 P.M.

7:50 P.M.

501

Art Director **Chris Hill**
Designer **Chris Hill**
Photographer **Chris Hill**
Writer **Chris Hill**
Client **Chris Hill**
Agency **Hill/A Graphic Design
Group, Houston**

502		503	
Art Director	**Danny Kamerath**	Art Directors	**Bob Dennard, Glyn Powell**
Designer	**Danny Kamerath**	Designer	**Glyn Powell**
Artist	**Danny Kamerath**	Artist	**Glyn Powell**
Writer	**Mark Perkins**	Writer	**Liza Orchard**
Client	**Monarch Paper**	Client	**Natural Resource Management**
Agency	**Richards, Brock Miller & Mitchell/The Richards Group, Dallas**	Agency	**Dennard Creative, Inc., Dallas**
		Creative Director	**Bob Dennard**

504

Art Director **Bob Salpeter**
Designer **Bob Salpeter**
Artist **Eugene Mihaesco**
Writer **Bill Littlefield**
Client **Rolf Sauer IBMA/FE**
Agency **Salpeter Paganucci Inc., New York**

505

Art Director **James Miho**
Designer **James Miho**
Photographer **Sally A. Bruce**
Client **Champion International Corporation, Stamford, CT**
Editor **Marian Jill Sendor**

506

Art Director **James Cross**
Designer **James Cross**
Photographers **Various**
Artists **Various**
Writers **James Cross, Laurence Pearson, William Junkin**
Client **Cross Asssociates**
Agency **Cross Associates, Los Angeles**
Printer **Gardner/Fulmer Lithograph**

507		508	
Art Director	Sharon L. Tooley, Houston	Art Director	Robert L. Whiting
Designer	Sharon L. Tooley	Photographer	Andy Olenick
Photographer	Frank White	Aritst	Vicki Wehrman
Writer	Paule Sheya Hewlett	Client	James Clarke/Xerox Corporation
Client	Index Incorporated, A Design Firm	Design Firm	Bob Wright Creative Group, Rochester, NY

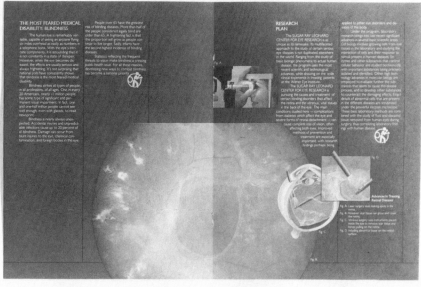

	509		510
Art Directors	**Jack Anderson, Terri Small**	Art Director	**Byron Tucker**
Designers	**Cliff Chung, Jack Anderson**	Designers	**Byron Tucker, Janet Fishbein**
Artist	**Susan Ryan**	Photographer	**Allan Charles**
Client	**HealthPlus**	Writer	**John Elder**
Agency	**John Hornall Design Works, Seattle**	Client	**Wilmer Eye Institute/ Johns Hopkins Hospital**
		Editor	**Leslye Donner Sugar**
		Agency	**Trahan, Burden & Charles, Inc., Baltimore**

DISTINCTIVE MERIT

511		512	
Art Director	**Henry Wolf, New York**	Art Directors	**D.C. Stipp, Brent Croxton, Ron Sullivan**
Designer	**Henry Wolf**	Designers	**D.C. Stipp, Brent Croxton**
Photographer	**Henry Wolf**	Photographers	**Various**
Director	**Caroline Hightower**	Artists	**Various**
		Writer	**Mark Perkins**
		Client	**The Dallas Symphony**
		Agency	**Richards, Brock, Miller & Mitchell/The Richards Group, Dallas**

513

Art Director   **Bob Pitt**
Writer   **John Mattingly**
Client   **Kimberly-Clark Corporation**
Agency   **Cargill, Wilson & Acree, Atlanta**

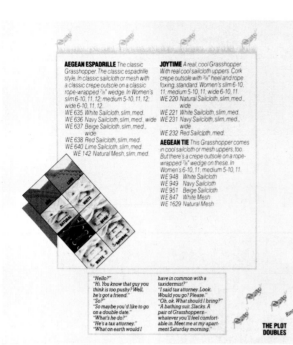

AEGEAN ESPADRILLE The classic Grasshopper. The classic espadrille style. In classic sailcloth or mesh with a classic crepe outsole on a classic rope-wrapped ⅞" wedge. In Women's slim 6-10, 11, 12; medium 5-10, 11, 12; wide 6-10, 11, 12.
WE 635 White Sailcloth, slim, med.
WE 636 Navy Sailcloth, slim, med., wide
WE 637 Beige Sailcloth, slim, med., wide
WE 638 Red Sailcloth, slim, med.
WE 640 Lime Sailcloth, slim, med.
WE 142 Natural Mesh, slim, med.

JOYTIME A real, cool Grasshopper. With real cool sailcloth uppers. Cork crepe outsole with ⅞" heel and rope foxing, standard. Women's slim 6-10, 11, medium 5-10, 11, wide 6-10, 11.
WE 220 Natural Sailcloth, slim, med., wide
WE 221 White Sailcloth, slim, med.
WE 231 Navy Sailcloth, slim, med., wide
WE 232 Red Sailcloth, med.

AEGEAN TIE This Grasshopper comes in cool sailcloth or mesh uppers, too. But there's a crepe outsole on a rope-wrapped ⅞" wedge on these. In Women's 6-10, 11; medium 5-10, 11.
WE 948 White Sailcloth
WE 949 Navy Sailcloth
WE 951 Beige Sailcloth
WE 847 White Mesh
WE 1629 Natural Mesh

"Hello?"
"Hi. You know that guy you think is too pushy? Well, he's got a friend."
"So?"
"So maybe you'd like to go on a double date."
"What's he do?"
"He's a tax attorney."
"What on earth would I have in common with a taxidermist?"
"I said tax attorney. Look. Would you go? Please."
"Oh, ok. What should I bring?"
"A bathing suit. Slacks. A pair of Grasshoppers—whatever you'll feel comfortable in. Meet me at my apartment Saturday morning."

Ring-ring-ring.

THE PLOT DOUBLES

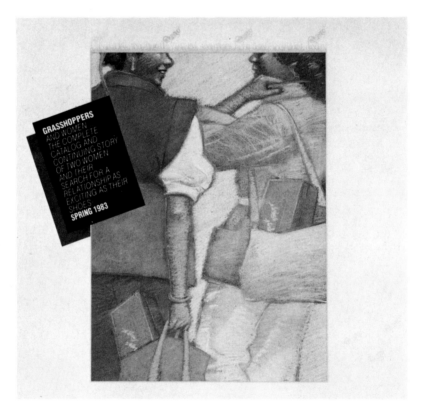

GRASSHOPPERS AND WOMEN. THE COMPLETE CATALOG AND CONTINUING STORY OF TWO WOMEN AND THEIR SEARCH FOR A RELATIONSHIP AS EXCITING AS THEIR SHOES. SPRING 1983

514

Art Director   **Cheryl Heller**
Designer   **Cheryl Heller**
Artist   **Gary Kelly**
Writer   **Bill Heater**
Client   **Keds Corporation**
Agency   **Humphrey Browning MacDougall, Inc., Boston**

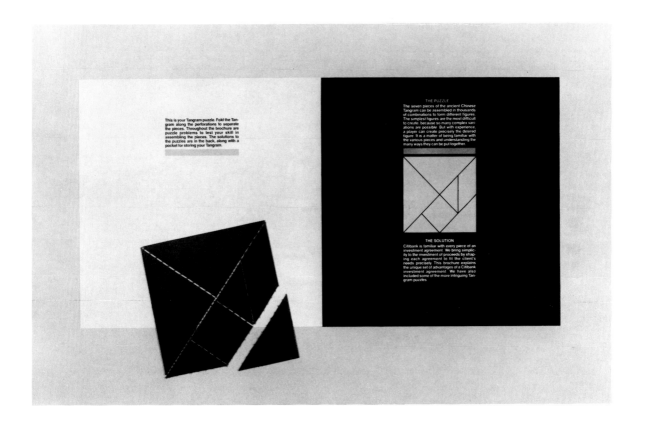

515		516	
Art Director	**Craig Bernhardt**	Art Director	**Bob Paganucci**
Designers	**Craig Bernhardt, Janice Fudyma**	Designer	**Bob Paganucci**
		Artist	**Dave Leash**
Writer	**Michael Starks**	Writer	**Phillip Sweedar**
Client	**Citibank/Leslie Lynn**	Client	**Contel**
Design Firm	**Bernhardt/Fudyma Design, New York**	Director	**Norm Brust**
		Agency	**Salpeter Paganucci, New York**

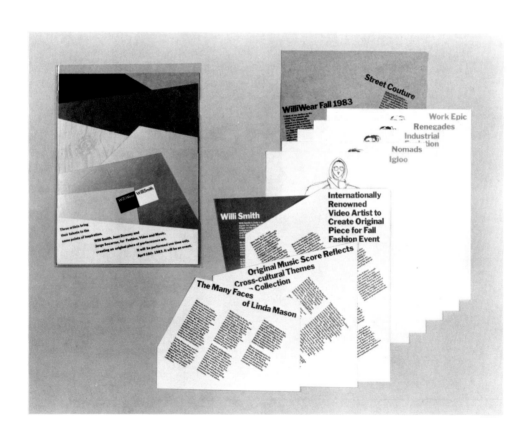

517
ARt Director   **Lou Dorfsman**
Designer   **Ira Teichberg**
Writer   **Naomi Andrews**
Client   **CBS Television Stations, New York**
Typography   **Brian Epp**

518
Art Director   **Bill Bonnell**
Designer   **Bill Bonnell**
Writers   **Willi Wear, Willi Smith**
Client   **Willi Wear/Willi Smith**
Agency   **Bonnell Design Associates, Inc., New York**

519		520	
Art Director	**Dennis Benoit**	Art Director	**Hinsche + Associates**
Artist	**Jack Unruh**	Designer	**Hinsche + Associates**
Writer	**Bill Baldwin**	Photographer	**Gerry Traficanda**
Client	**Rosewood Properties**	Client	**Sparcraft**
Design Firm	**Ben-Wah Design, Inc.,**	Agency	**Hinsche + Associates,**
	Dallas		**Santa Monica, CA**

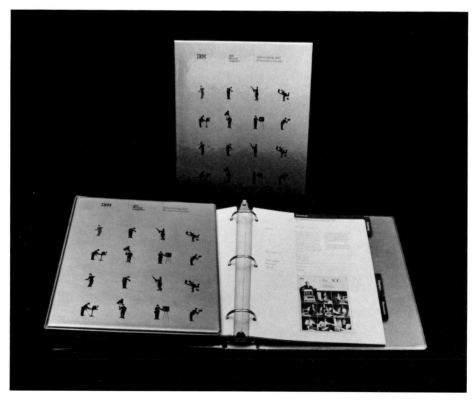

DISTINCTIVE MERIT

521	
Art Director	**Julia Pepper**
Designer	**Julia Pepper**
Artists	**Julia Pepper, Mark Moore**
Writer	**Steve Barnhill & Company, Inc.**
Client	**Criterion Funds**
Design Firm	**Savage Design Group, Inc., Houston**

522	
Art Director	**Toni Schowalter**
Designers	**Scott Baker, Toni Schowalter**
Illustrator	**David FeBland**
Writer	**Don Kaufman**
Client	**Gary Conrad/IBM**
Agency	**Muir Cornelius Moore, New York**
Div. Design Director	**Lou Fiorentino**

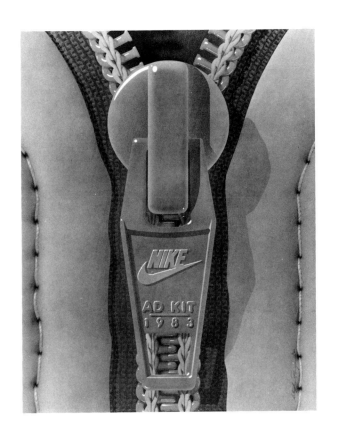

523

Art Director	**David Kennedy**
Artist	**Steve Derringer**
Client	**Nike, Inc.**
Agency	**Wieden & Kennedy, Portland**

524

Art Director	**David Kennedy**
Artist	**Steve Perringer**
Client	**Nike, Inc.**
Agency	**Wieden & Kennedy, Portland**

525

Art Director	**Charles V. Blake**
Designer	**Glazer/Kalayjian**
Photographers	**Various**
Artist	**Gerard Huerta**
Writer	**Steve Jaffe**
Client	**NBC Marketing, New York**

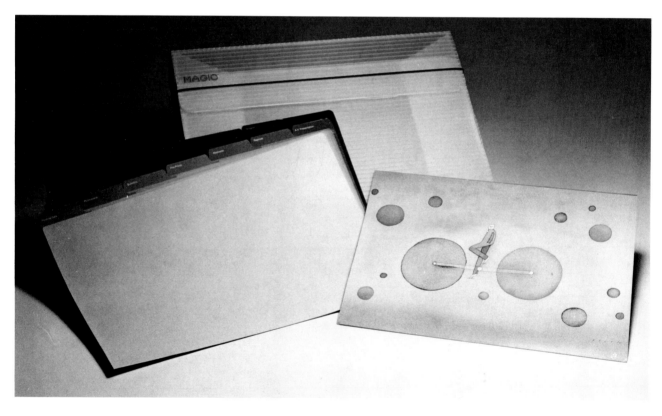

	526		527
Art Director	**Chris Pullman**	Art Director	**Kathleen Forsythe**
Photographers	**Roger-Viollet, Larry Burrows**	Designer	**Kathleen Forsythe**
		Artist	**Folon**
Writer	**Sara Altherr**	Client	**Corning Medical**
Client	**WGBH Educational Foundation, Boston**	Agency	**Lehman Millet Incorporated, Boston**

DISTINCTIVE MERIT

	528		529
Art Director	**Rex Peteet**	Art Directors	**Florence Mayers, Rocco**
Designer	**Rex Peteet**		**Campanelli**
Artists	**Rex Peteet, Don Sibley,**	Photographer	**Phil Mazzurco**
	Waleo Horton	Writers	**Brad Londy, Alan Glass**
Writer	**Sherry Anderson**	Client	**P.H. Glatfelter**
Client	**Schroder Real Estate**	Agency	**David Deutsch**
Design Firm	**Sibley/Peteet Design,**		**Associates, Inc., New**
	Inc., Dallas		**York**

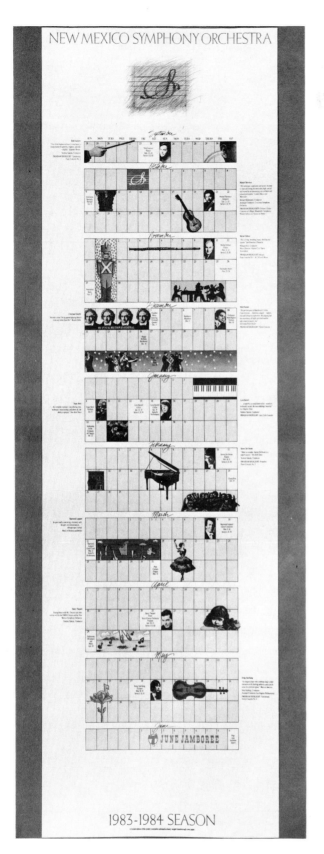

530

Art Directors	**Rick Vaughn, Steven Wedeen**
Designer	**Vaughn/Weeden Creative, Inc.**
Artists	**Kevin Tolman, Rick Vaughn, Steven Wedeen**
Client	**New Mexico Symphony Orchestra**
Agency	**Will Sherwood & Company, Albuquerque, NM**

531

Art Director	**Dean Narahara**
Artist	**Lee Lee Brazeal**
Writer	**Mary Langridge**
Client	**Berman Films**
Design Firm	**Narahara Creative Services, Houston**

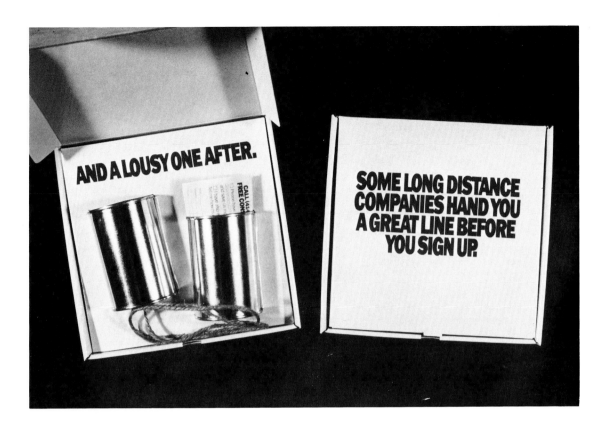

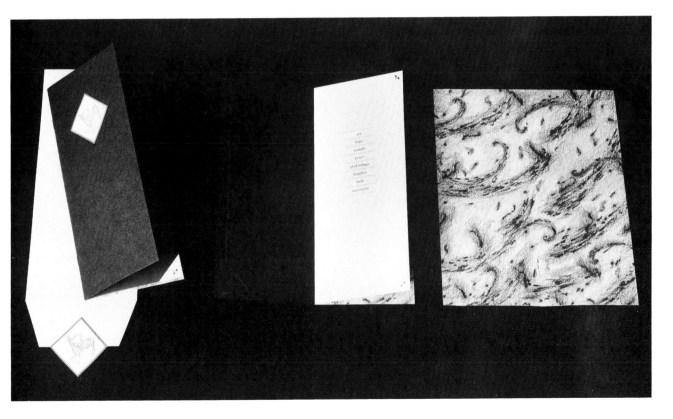

532

Art Director **John Morrison**
Designer **John Morrison**
Writer **Rod Kilpatrick**
Client **American Sharecom**
Agency **Fallon McElligott Rice,
Minneapolis**

533

Art Director **Karen D. Forkner**
Designer **Karen D. Forkner**
Artist **Karen D. Forkner**
Writer **Karen D. Forkner**
Client **Savage Design Group,
Inc., Houston**

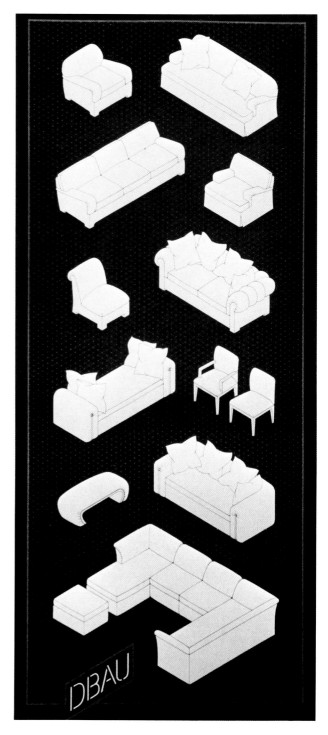

534

Art Director	**Jaclynn Carroll**
Designer	**Jaclynn Carroll**
Photographer	**Erica Lennard**
Writer	**Elizabeth Forbes**
Client	**Paul Stuart**
Agency	**Chillingworth/Radding Inc., New York**

535

Art Directors	**Frank Nichols, Jim Jacobs**
Designer	**Frank Nichols**
Artist	**Amy Luedke**
Client	**Rob Jones**
Design Firm	**Jim Jacob's Studio, Inc., Dallas**

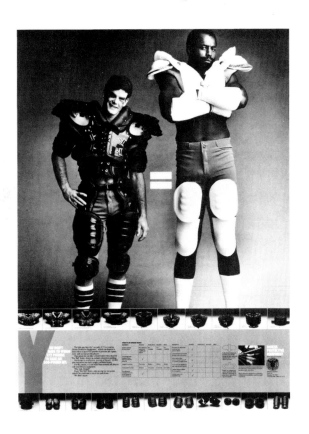

536		537	
Art Director	Dennis S. Juett	Art Director	Gayl Ware
Designer	Jeffrey D. Lawson	Designer	Gayl Ware
Artist	Jeffrey D. Lawson	Photographer	Chuck Untersee
Client	Dennis S. Juett &	Writer	Bob Miller
	Associates Inc.	Client	Donzis Protective
Agency	Dennis S. Juett &		Equipment
	Associates Inc., Los	Agency	Rives Smith Baldwin
	Angeles		Carlberg + Y&R,
			Houston
		Creative	
		Director	Chuck Carlberg

538
Art Director	**Richard A. DeOlivera**
Designer	**Steve Jones**
Client	**DeOlivera Creative, Inc.**
Agency	**DeOlivera Creative, Inc., Denver**

539
Art Director	**Cabell Harris**
Designer	**Cabell Harris**
Photographer	**West/Edwards**
Writer	**Barbara Ford**
Client	**Mobil**
Agency	**The Martin Agency, Richmond, VA**

The Marina at Bay Street Landing, St. George, Staten Island

DISTINCTIVE MERIT

540		541	
Art Director	**Steve Erenberg**	Art Director	**Lowell Williams**
Writer	**Words and Company**	Designers	**Lowell Williams, Bill**
Client	**Bay Street Landing**		**Carson**
Agency	**Pace Advertising**	Photographer	**Bob Haar**
	Agency, New York	Writer	**Mary Langridge**
		Client	**Gerald D. Hines**
			Interests
		Agency	**Lowell Williams**
			Design, Inc., Houston

	542		543
Art Director	**Bill Bouley**	Art Director	**Nancy Rice**
Photographer	**Pat Pollard**	Designer	**Nancy Rice**
Writer	**Philip Clement**	Artist	**Edvard Munch, RIP**
Client	**Ad Club of Greater Hartford/Red Cross of Greater Hartford**	Writer	**Tom McElligott**
		Client	**Advertising Federal of Minnesota**
Agency	**Naftzger & Kuhe, Inc., Farmington, CT**	Agency	**Fallon McElligott Rice, Minneapolis**

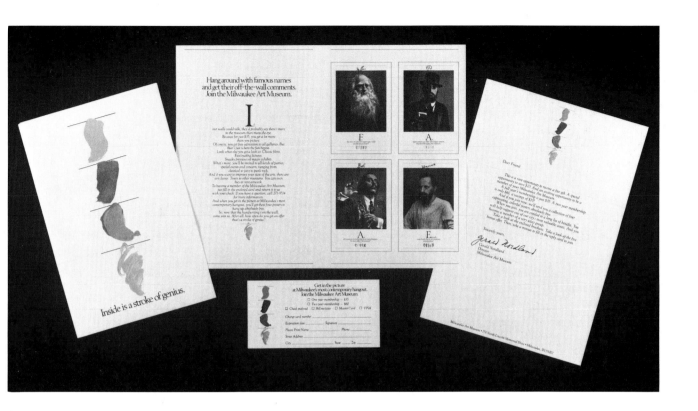

544		545	
Art Director	**Rachel Stephens**	Art Director	**Dennis Gagarin**
Writer	**Robin Reynolds**	Designer	**Dennis Gagarin**
Client	**Milwaukee Art Museum**	Photographer	**Dow, Clement &**
Agency	**Frankenberry, Laughlin**		**Simison**
	& Constable,	Writer	**Chuck Lebo**
	Milwaukee	Client	**Public Relations**
			Society of America
		Director	**Del Tycer**
		Agency	**Tycer-Fultz-Bellack,**
			Palo Alto, CA

546	547
Art Director **Frank Roehr**	Art Director **Paul Regan**
Photographer **Ed Dull**	Artist **Larry Johnson**
Writer **Judge Schonfeld**	Writer **Seumas McGuire**
Client **Young & Roehr, Inc.**	Client **New England Broadcast**
Agency **Young & Roehr, Inc., Portland**	**Assoc.**
	Agency **Hill, Holliday, Connors, Cosmopulos, Inc., Boston**
	Printer **Rand Typographer/ Nat'l Bickford Foremost**

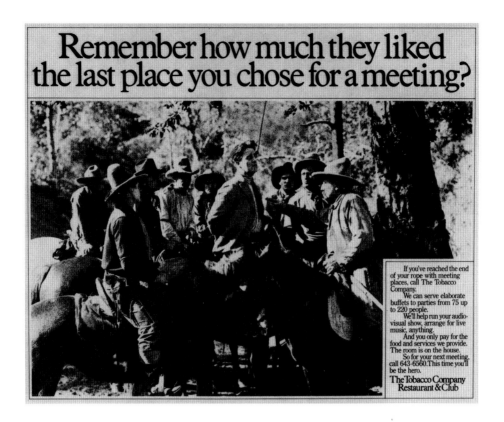

548		549	
Art Director	Wayne Gibson	Art Director	Chris Overholser
Writers	Kerry Feuerman, Bill Westbrook	Photographer	Scott Barrow
		Writer	Mel Bryant
Client	The Tobacco Company	Client	The Virginia Peninsula Economic Development Council
Agency	Westbrook, Inc., Richmond, VA	Agency	The Smyth Agency, Glen Allen, VA

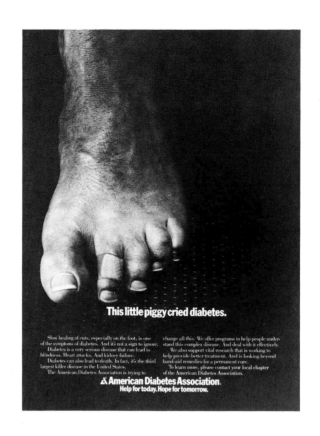

This little piggy cried diabetes.

Slow healing of cuts, especially on the foot, is one of the symptoms of diabetes. And it's not a sign to ignore.
Diabetes is a very serious disease that can lead to blindness. Heart attacks. And kidney failure.
Diabetes can also lead to death. In fact, it's the third largest killer disease in the United States.
The American Diabetes Association is trying to change all this. We offer programs to help people understand this complex disease. And deal with it effectively.
We also support vital research that is working to help provide better treatment. And is looking beyond band-aid remedies for a permanent cure.
To learn more, please contact your local chapter of the American Diabetes Association.

American Diabetes Association.
Help for today. Hope for tomorrow.

550		551	
Art Director	**Dave Martin**	Art Director	**Hoi L. Chu**
Designer	**Dave Martin**	Designers	**Hoi L. Chu, Gary**
Photographer	**Gary Hanlon**		**Stilovich**
Writer	**Pete Faulkner**	Photographer	**Gary Stilovich**
Client	**American Diabetes**	Artists	**Gary Stilovich,**
	Association		**Benjamin Perez**
Agency	**Doyle Dane Bernbach**	Writer	**David Konigsberg**
	Inc., New York	Client	**Champion**
			International
			Corporation
		Editor	**Tony McDowell**
		Agency	**H.L. Chu & Company,**
			Ltd., New York

Most people don't recognize diabetes when they see it.

Diabetes can appear right under your nose.

The Psychology Of Sales

552		553		554	
Art Director	**Dave Martin**	Art Director	**Dave Martin**	Art Director	**Diane Cook Tench**
Designer	**Dave Martin**	Designer	**Dave Martin**	Designer	**Diane Cook Tench**
Photographer	**Jim McLoughlin**	Photographer	**Jim McLoughlin**	Artist	**Scott Wright**
Writer	**Pete Faulkner**	Writer	**Pete Faulkner**	Writer	**Andy Ellis**
Client	**American Diabetes Association**	Client	**American Diabetes Association**	Client	**Advertising Club of Richmond**
Agency	**Doyle Dane Bernbach Inc., New York**	Agency	**Doyle Dane Bernbach Inc., New York**	Agency	**Siddall, Matus & Coughter Inc., Richmond, VA**

555		556	
Art Director	**Gerry Rosentswieg**	Art Director	**Terry Briley**
Writer	**Sally Ann Hotson**	Designers	**Dan Stables, Terry**
Client	**The Rouse Company**		**Briley**
Agency	**The Graphics Studio,**	Artist	**Terry Briley**
	Los Angeles	Writers	**Fran Hoover, Lynne**
			Marek
		Client	**Banctec/Directions**
		Agency	**Briley Creative Inc.,**
			Dallas

Serendipity is the faculty of making fortuitate and unexpected discoveries by accident. Blimps were developed primarily for the purpose of military observation. Now they exist solely to be observed, to communicate, delight, and astound. With Warren Flokota, delightful results are no accident. The unique stock bulks larger than life, combining a substantial look with the potential for substantial savings... the illusion of weight with the reality of economy. Not at all illusory, however, is the value-to-weight ratio of Flokota. In fact, the higher the basis weight of Flokota, the greater the value. Compare Flokota Bookweight to equivalent calendered sheets.

Flokota Bulk 47 Ilvers
70# 10
80# 18
004# 24

Calendered Bulk 47 Ilvers
70# 14
80# 15
004# 19

The Flokota Advantage
70# .... 7% more bulk
80# .... 10% more bulk
004# .... 25% more bulk

The Facts of Light

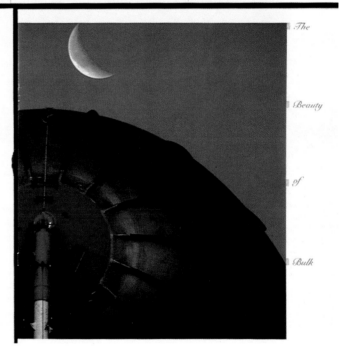

The Beauty of Bulk

GOLD AWARD

557

Art Director	**Cheryl Heller**
Designer	**Cheryl Heller**
Photographer	**Clint Clemens**
Writer	**Peter Caroline**
Client	**S.D. Warren**
Agency	**Humphrey Browning MacDougall, Inc., Boston**

Houston Ballet
Ben Stevenson, Artistic Director

In the beginning, man was made to dance.

By 1800, the first Classic Period waned as heroes and gods lost popularity. The Romantic Era dawned... to glorify the human spirit.

La Sylphide was a milestone in 1832... followed by decades of Romantic ballets... *Papillon, Giselle*. Women began to dance en pointe.

In the mid-1800's, the second great Classical Era emerged from Imperial Russia, ignited by the brilliance of Diaghilev and the *Ballets Russes*.

"I BELONG BEHIND BARS."

Gary Mountjoy, Bartender.
Just call 875-1123.

558		559	
Art Directors	Jay Loucks, Julie Ray	Art Director	Jim Mountjoy
Designer	Paul Huber	Writer	Steve Lasch
Artist	Charles Schorre	Client	Gary Mountjoy
Writer	Julie Ray	Agency	Loeffler Marley
Client	Houston Ballet		Mountjoy, Charlotte, NC
Agency	Taylor Brown & Barnhill, Houston		

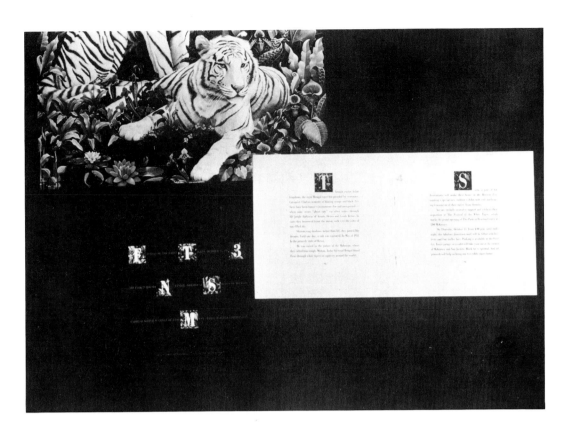

560		561	
Art Director	**Lowell Williams**	Art Director	**Jessica Welton**
Designers	**Bill Carson, Lana Rigsby**	Designer	**Jessica Welton**
		Photographer	**Brent Cavedo**
Artist	**Heather Cooper**	Writer	**Andy Ellis**
Writer	**Lee Herrick**	Client	**Advertising Club of Richmond**
Client	**Cadillac Fairview, Texas Eastern, Zoological Society of Houston**	Agency	**Siddall, Matus & Coughter Inc., Richmond, VA**
Agency	**Lowell Williams Design, Inc., Houston**		

THESE MEN ARE DOING EVERYTHING IN THEIR POWER TO DISRUPT THE NEXT MEETING OF AD FED.

Bernard Kalb, Jim Cummins, Bonnie Anderson and Bill Monroe will all be speaking at the next Ad Fed luncheon Monday, October 24 at the Hyatt Regency Hotel. Then again, they may not. As NBC news correspondents, they have to go where the stories are. Whenever they happen. But, barring a coup in Libya or a documented reappearance of Generalissimo Franco, you can hear about the American image abroad from our foreign field correspondents. Similarly, you should learn a thing or two about the Reagan administration's dealing with the press from the national correspondents. That is, if Mr. Reagan lets them. ★ Cocktails start at 11:30. Lunch is at noon. Tickets are $11.00 members, $12.50 others. To reserve your place, call 379-1645. If a Russian answers, hang up.

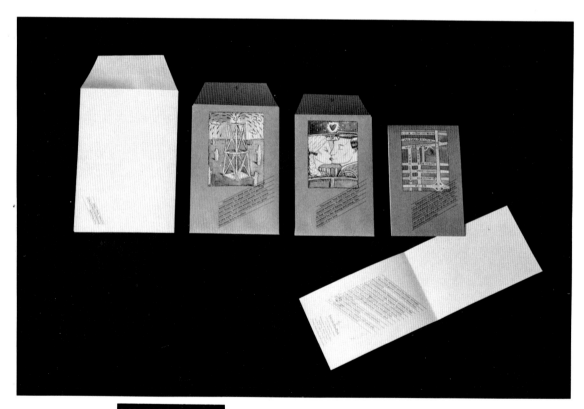

DISTINCTIVE MERIT

<table>
<tr><td colspan="2">562</td><td colspan="2">563</td></tr>
<tr><td>Art Director</td><td>Dean Hanson</td><td>Art Director</td><td>Julia Pepper</td></tr>
<tr><td>Designer</td><td>Dean Hanson</td><td>Designer</td><td>Julia Pepper</td></tr>
<tr><td>Photographers</td><td>U.P.I., Stock</td><td>Artist</td><td>Regan Dunnick</td></tr>
<tr><td>Writer</td><td>Jarl Olsen</td><td>Writer</td><td>Steve Barnhill & Company, Inc.</td></tr>
<tr><td>Client</td><td>Advertising Federation of Minnesota</td><td>Client</td><td>Inn on the Park</td></tr>
<tr><td>Agency</td><td>Fallon McElligott Rice, Minneapolis</td><td>Agency</td><td>Savage Design Group, Inc., Houston</td></tr>
</table>

564		565	
Art Director	**Steve Freeman**	Art Director	**Hoi L. Chu**
Designer	**Steve Freeman**	Designers	**Hoi L. Chu, Steve**
Writer	**Doug Speidel**		**Jenkins, Benjamin**
Client	**March of Dimes**		**Perez**
Agency	**Media**	Photographer	**Morton/Riggs**
	Communications,	Artists	**Benjamin Perez, Hoi L.**
	Austin		**Chu**
		Writer	**David Konigsberg**
		Client	**Champion Intl Corp**
		Editor	**Tony McDowell**
		Agency	**H.L. Chu & Company,**
			Ltd., New York

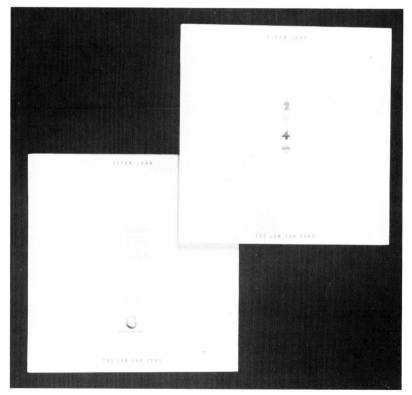

DISTINCTIVE MERIT

566

Art Director	**Ken Harris**
Photographer	**Hornick/Rivlin Studio**
Writers	**John DiCocco, Allyson Gray, Ken Harris**
Client	**Art Directors Club of Boston**
Design Firm	**Grand Design, Boston**
Printer	**Merchants Press**

DISTINCTIVE MERIT

567

Art Director	**Jaclynn Carroll**
Designer	**Jaclynn Carroll**
Photographers	**John Stember, Robert Grant**
Writer	**Edith Myers**
Client	**Paul Stuart**
Agency	**Chillingworth/Radding Inc., New York**

568

Art Directors	**Rod Dyer, Bernie Taupin**
Designers	**Clive Piercy, Rod Dyer**
Client	**Geffen Records**
Agency	**Dyer/Kahn, Inc., Los Angeles**
Recording Artist	**Elton John**

<table>
<tr><td colspan="2">

569

Art Director **Nancy Donald**
Artist **René Magritte**
Client **Gladys Knight and the Pips on Columbia Records**
Agency **CBS Records, Los Angeles**

</td><td>

570

Art Director **Allen Weinberg**
Artist **Marshall Arisman**
Client **CBS Records, New York**

</td><td>

571

Art Director **John Berg**
Artist **Don Wilson**
Client **CBS Records, New York**

</td></tr>
</table>

572		573		574	
Art Director	**Karen Katz**	Art Director	**Art Chantry**	Art Directors	**Tony Lane, Nancy Donald**
Artist	**Gene Greif**	Designer	**Art Chantry**		
Client	**Atlantic Records, New York**	Writer	**R. Bruce Smith**	Designer	**Timothy Eames**
		Design Firm	**Art Chantry Design, Seattle**	Photographers	**Galen Rowell, Welden Andersen**
		Airbrush Photo Re-Touching	**Gary Jacobsen**	Client	**Silver Condor on Columbia Records**
				Agency	**CBS Records, Los Angeles**

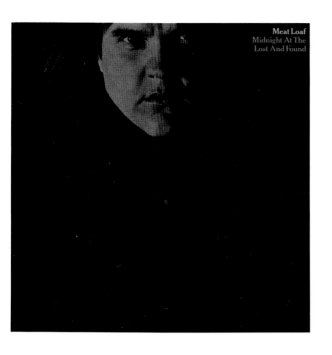

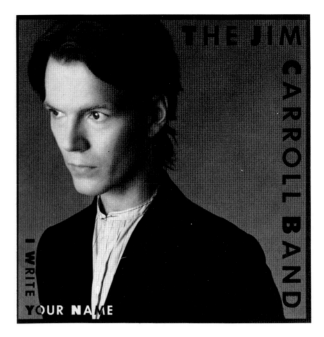

575
Art Director **John Berg**
Photographer **Skrebneski**
Client **CBS Records, New York**

576
Art Director **Lynn Dreese Breslin**
Photographer **Curtis Knapp**
Client **Atlantic Records, New York**

577
Art Director **Peter Andrew Alfieri**
Client **CBS Records, New York**
Hand Coloring **Ken Robbins**

578

Art Director	**Christopher Lione**
Client	**CBS Records, New York**

579

Art Director	**Douglas Joseph**
Designer	**Douglas Joseph**
Artist	**Cliff Boule**
Client	**Montage Records**
Agency	**Douglas Joseph, Los Angeles**
Manager	**Jerry Heller**

580

Art Director	**Christopher Lione**
Client	**CBS Records, New York**
Lettering	**Georgina Lehner**

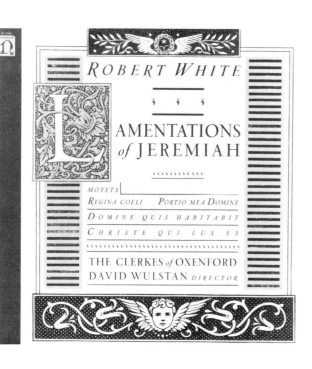

581
Art Directors **Stan Evenson, Norm Ung**
Designer **Stan Evenson**
Client **Nonesuch Records**
Agency **Stan Evenson Design, Inc., Los Angeles**

582
Art Director **Henrietta Condak**
Artist **Robert Van Nutt**
Client **CBS Records, New York**

583
Art Director **Allen Weinberg**
Artist **Robert Goldstrom**
Client **CBS Records, New York**

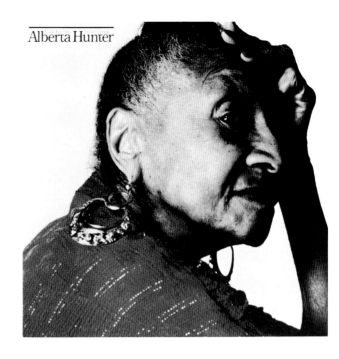

584		585		586	
Art Directors	**Peter Nomura, Stan Evenson, Los Angeles**	Art Director	**Allen Weinberg**	Art Director	**Edward Kahler, Lancaster, PA**
Designer	**Peter Nomura**	Photographer	**Bill King**	Designer	**Edward Kahler**
Client	**Jerry Luby/Nautilus Recordings**	Client	**CBS Records, New York**	Photographer	**Brian Tolbert/BRT Photos**
Creative				Artist	**Edward Kahler**
Director	**Jeffrey Weber**			Client	**Doug Phillips/The Sharks**

SILVER AWARD

587

Art Director	**Mark Anderson**
Designers	**Steve Tolleson, Michael Kunisaki, Tony Milner, Sue Cretarolo**
Artist	**Tony Milner**
Writer	**Ron Perotta**
Client	**Apple Computer, Inc.**
Publisher	**Container Corporation of America**
Agency	**Mark Anderson Design, Palo Alto, CA**

DISTINCTIVE MERIT

588		589	
Art Director	Dan Stewart	Art Director	Richard Holmes
Designer	Dan Steward	Designer	Ronald K. Morris
Client	Kelly Technical Coatings	Artist	Kevin Davidson
Agency	Stewart Winner Inc., Louisville, KY	Writers	Jack Marble, Richard Holmes
		Client	Mrs. Gooch's Ranch Markets
		Agency	The Holmes Organization, Newport Beach, CA

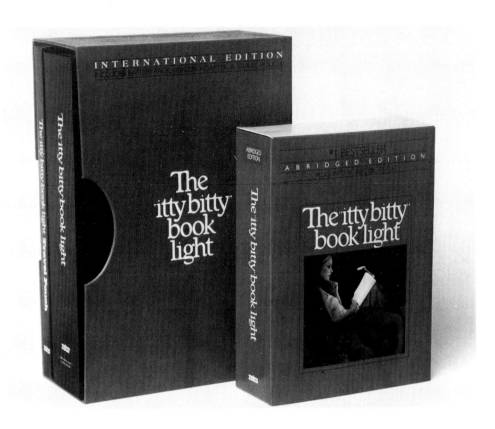

590		591	
Art Director	**Fabian Melgar**	Art Directors	**Richard Manzo, Mary Finalborgo**
Photographer	**Fabian Melgar**	Designers	**Richard Manzo, Mary Finalborgo**
Writer	**Robert Singer**	Client	**Ladies' Home Journal**
Client	**Noel Zeller, Zelco Industries, Inc.**	Agency	**Manzo/Finalborgo Assoc., Inc., New York**
Agency	**Melgar Nordlinger, Inc., New York**	Promotion Director	**Esther Laufer**
		Printer	**Kenner Printing Co. Inc.**

GOLD AWARD

592

Art Director **Peter Good**
Designer **Peter Good**
Writer **Tom Mann**
Client **Champion International Corporation, Stamford, CT**

DISTINCTIVE MERIT

593		594	
Art Director	**Barry Deutsch, Steinhilber Deutsch & Gard**	Art Director	**Richard Nodine**
Designer	**Barry Deutsch**	Designer	**Max Seabaugh**
Photographer	**Larry Keenan**	Artist	**Max Seabaugh**
Writer	**Jeff Goodby**	Client	**Macy's California**
Client	**Electronic Arts**	Agency	**Macy's Graphic Design, San Francisco**
Agency	**Goodby, Berlin and Silverstein, San Francisco**		
Calligraphy	**Georgia Deaver**		

595		596	
Art Director	**Charles V. Blake**	Art Directors	**James R. Stitt, M.J. Rosenthal**
Designers	**Glazer/Kalayjian**		
Photographers	**Various**	Designers	**James R. Stitt, M.J. Rosenthal**
Artist	**Gerard Huerta**		
Writer	**Steve Jaffe**	Artist	**James R. Stitt**
Client	**NBC Marketing, New York**	Client	**Tepusquet Vineyards-Al Gagnon, Louis Lucas**
		Agency	**Wine Industry Research—Ed Everett, John Gay**
		Design Firm	**James Stitt & Company, Sausalito, CA**

597	598
Art Directors **Frank Roehr, Martin Rupert**	Art Director **Cary Schroeder**
Designers **Frank Roehr, Martin Rupert**	Designers **Cary Schroeder, Brenda Brown**
Photographer **Ed Dull**	Photographer **Will Ryan**
Artist **Martin Rupert**	Client **Godiva Chocolatier, Inc.**
Writer **JoAnn Lunt**	Agency **Margeotes-Fertitta & Weiss, New York**
Client **Graphic Arts Center**	
Agency **Young & Roehr, Inc., Portland**	

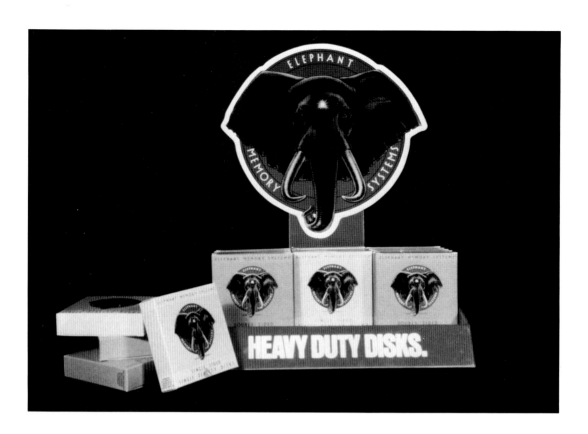

	599		600
Art Directors	John Filosi, Rollin Binzer	Art Director	Henry Beer
Designers	John Filosi, Rollin Binzer	Designer	David Shelton
		Client	Trizec Properties, Inc.
Artist	Bob Hickson	Agency	Communication Arts, Inc., Boulder
Writer	Ray Welch	Printer	D & K Printing
Client	Leading Edge		
Agency	Welch, Currier, Smith, Boston		

601		602	
Art Director	Jill Korostoff	Art Director	Barry Deutsch
Graphic		Designer	Myland McRevey
Designer	Jill Korostoff	Photographer	Terry Heffernan
Client	The Museum of Modern	Writers	Mary Beth Mader &
	Art, New York		Robin Raj, Ogilvy &
Editor	George Beylerian		Mather
Publisher	Magnaform	Client	Convergent
	Corporation		Technologies
Director	George Beylerian	Agency	Steinhilber Deutsch &
			Gard, San Francisco

GOLD AWARD

	603		604
Art Director	Eric Nord	Art Director	Milton Glaser, New York
Designer	Marjorie Greene	Designer	Milton Glaser
Artists	Gene Lemery, Charles Linnett	Artist	Milton Glaser
Writer	Michael Howell	Writer	Milton Glaser
Client	Infocom	Client	Zanders Feinpapiere, A.G.
Editor	David Haskell		
Director	Giardini Russell		
Agency	Giardini Russell, Boston		
Typography	Sam Petrucci/Martina Mikulka		

<table>
<tr><td colspan="2" align="center">605</td></tr>
</table>

Art Director	**Lou Fiorentino**
Designer	**Lou Fiorentino**
Photographers	**Lou Fiorentino, Helen Soper Fiorentino**
Artist	**Frank Cueco**
Writer	**Helen Soper Fiorentino**
Client	**Tri Arts Press**
Agency	**Visual Communications, New York**
Consultant	**Michael Reinitz**

<table>
<tr><td colspan="2" align="center">606</td></tr>
</table>

Art Director	**Chris Vice**
Designer	**Chris Vice**
Writer	**Jane Lamensdorf-Bucher**
Client	**Northrup King**
Agency	**Carmichael-Lynch, Minneapolis**

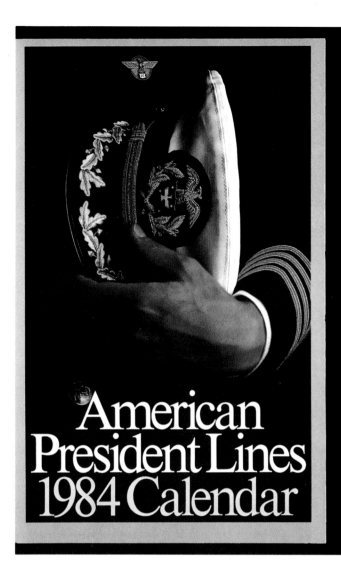

SILVER AWARD

607

Art Director	**Kit Hinrichs**
Designers	**Kit Hinrichs, Nancy Koc**
Photographer	**Terry Heffernan, Light Language**
Writer	**Peterson & Dodge**
Client	**American President Lines**
Printer	**Dai Nippon, Japan**
Design Firm	**Jonson Pedersen Hinrichs & Shakery, San Francisco**

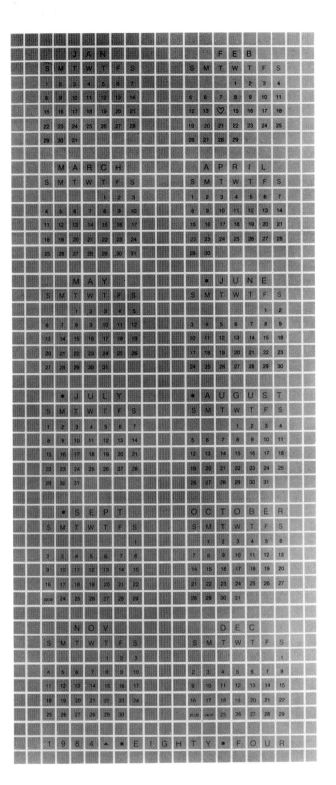

608

Art Director   **KB Heineman**
Design Firm   **KB Heineman Squeegee!, Rhinecliff, NY**
Design Consultant   **Jerome Frankel**

609

Art Director   **Rod Dyer**
Designer   **Hoi Ping Law**
Client   **Jon Gould/Paramount Pictures Corporation**
Agency   **Dyer/Kahn, Inc., Los Angeles**

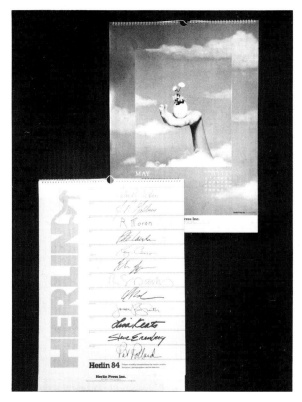

610

Art Director **Arthur Beckenstein**
Writer **Susan Bidel**
Client **PEOPLE Magazine,
New York**
Design Director **Dick Martell**

611

Art Director **Herlin Press**
Designers **Peter Orkin, Jon
Gallucci, Robert E.
Moran, Peter Landa,
Ray Cicero, Kristina
Jorgenson, Richard
Sparks, David Rushlow,
Jesse R. Smith, Lisa
Keats, Steve Erenberg,
Pat Pollard**
Client **Herlin Press, Inc., West
Haven, CT**

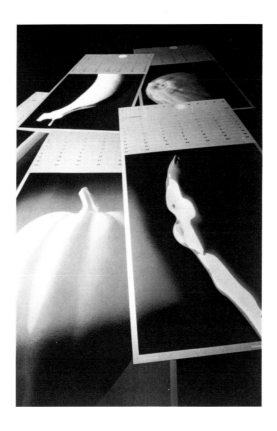

612		613	
Art Directors	**366 individual art directors**	Art Directors	**Jeff Barnes, Dennis Manarchy**
Designer	**Steven Liska**	Designer	**Jeff Barnes**
Client	**Fiat & Associates**	Photographer	**Dennis Manarchy**
Editor	**Randi Fiat**	Client	**Kieffer Nolde**
Design Firm	**Fiat & Associates, Chicago**	Publisher	**Kieffer Nolde**
		Agency	**Barnes Design Office, Chicago**

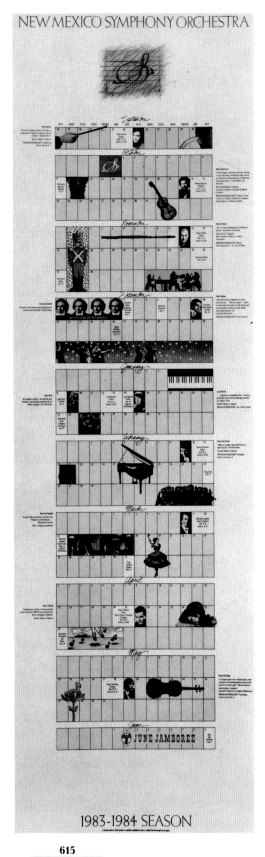

	614
Art Director	**Yvonne Tocquigny**
Designer	**Yvonne Tocquigny**
Artist	**Kim Stewart**
Writer	**Guy Bommarito**
Client	**The Dominion**
Agency	**McBride Advertising/ Tocquigny Design, Austin**

	615
Art Directors	**Rick Vaughn, Steven Wedeen**
Designer	**Vaughn/Wedeen Creative, Inc.**
Artists	**Kevin Tolman, Rick Vaughn, Steven Wedeen**
Client	**New Mexico Symphony Orchestra**
Agency	**Will Sherwood & Company, Albuquerque, NM**

Here's your invitation to the event you've waited 20 years for...

1963

Here's your invitation to the event you've waited 20 years for...

1983

SILVER AWARD

616

Art Director	**Ken Pugh**
Designer	**Ken Pugh**
Client	**Garland High School Class of 1963**
Design Firm	**Pugh & Company, Dallas**

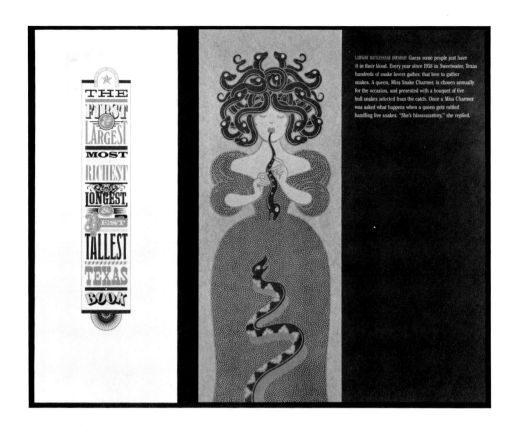

	617		**618**
Art Directors	**Rex Peteet, Marianne Tombaugh**	Art Directors	**Forrest & Valerie Richardson**
Designers	**Rex Peteet, Ken Shafer**	Designers	**Forrest & Valerie Richardson**
Artist	**Jerry Jeanmard**	Writers	**Forrest & Valerie Richardson**
Writer	**Rex Peteet**		
Client	**Lomas & Nettleton**	Client	**Brian Landauer**
Agency	**Hay Agency**	Agency	**Richardson or Richardson, Phoenix**
Design Firm	**Sibley/Peteet Design, Inc., Dallas**		

BERNHARDT FUDYMA DESIGN GROUP

619		620	
Art Directors	Dick Krogstad, Jim Nancekivell	Art Directors	Craig Bernhardt, Janice Fudyma
Designer	Jim Nancekivell	Designers	Craig Bernhardt, Janice Fudyma
Writer	Nancy Wellinger	Client	Bernhardt/Fudyma Design
Client	First Street Station Restaurant	Agency	Bernhardt/Fudyma Design, New York
Agency	Krogstad Design Associates, Inc., Minneapolis		

621		622	
Art Directors	**Scott Eggers, D.C. Stipp**	Art Directors	**Linda Eissler, Arthur**
Designers	**Scott Eggers, D.C. Stipp**		**Eisenberg**
Writer	**Mark Perkins**	Designer	**Linda Eissler**
Client	**Heritage Press**	Writer	**Linda Eissler**
Agency	**Richards, Brock, Miller**	Client	**Mike and Claudia**
	& Mitchell-The		**Montgomery**
	Richards Group, Dallas	Design Firm	**Eisenberg, Inc., Dallas**
Printer	**Heritage Press**		

SILVER AWARD

623

Art Director	**Luis Acevedo**
Designer	**Luis Acevedo**
Artist	**Luis Acevedo**
Writer	**T.G.I. Friday's, Inc.**
Client	**T.G.I. Friday's, Inc.**
Publisher	**T.G.I. Friday's, Inc.**
Agency	**Pirtle Design, Dallas**
Creative Director	**Woody Pirtle**

Typeworks. On Wednesday, November 23, we'll be packed up, loaded up, geared up, and moving up to 1100 North Post Oak Road, Suite 210, Houston 77055. Give us a call at 682-6666. By Monday morning our familiar faces will be set and ready to deliver.

Donna Hill

ME

Mike Baugh

E

E

E

WE

Donna and Mike Baugh

Charlie and Jean Hill
Announce the Marriage
of Their Daughter
Donna Joanne Hill
to
John Michael Baugh
January 29, 1983
2:00 PM
904 East 9th Street
Bonham, Texas

624

Art Directors	**Mark Geer, Richard Kilmer**
Designers	**Mark Geer, Richard Kilmer**
Photographer	**Arthur Meyerson**
Writer	**Linda Bradford**
Client	**Typeworks, Inc.**
Agency	**Kilmer/Geer Graphic Design, Bellaire, TX**

625

Art Director	**Chris Hill**
Designer	**Chris Hill**
Writer	**Chris Hill**
Client	**Mike & Donna Baugh**
Agency	**Hill/A Graphic Design Group, Houston**

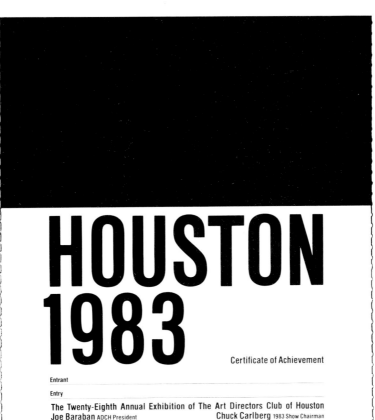

626

Art Director	Yvonne Tocquigny
Designers	Yvonne Tocquigny, Kim Stewart
Artist	Melissa Grimes
Writer	Guy Bommarito
Client	The Dominion
Agency	McBride Advertising/ Tocquigny Design, Austin

627

Art Director	Joe Rattan
Designer	Chris Hill
Writer	Joe Rattan
Client	Art Directors Club of Houston
Agency	Hill/A Graphic Design Group, Houston

SILVER AWARD

628

Art Director **Brian Boyd**
Designer **Brian Boyd**
Artist **Brian Boyd**
Writer **Mark Perkins**
Client **Skyline High School
Class of '73**
Agency **Richards, Brock, Miller,
Mitchell-The Richards
Group, Dallas**

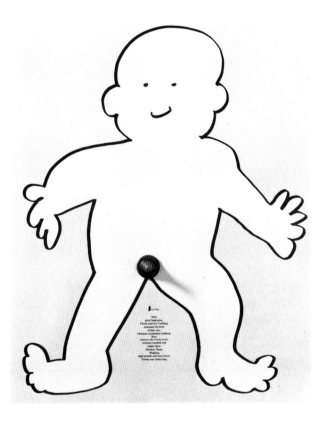

<table>
<tr><td colspan="2">629</td><td colspan="2">630</td></tr>
</table>

Art Director	**Don Grimes**	Art Directors	**Gayl Ware, Chuck Carlberg**
Designer	**Don Grimes**	Designers	**Gayl Ware, Chuck Carlberg**
Artist	**Don Grimes**	Artist	**Gayl Ware**
Writer	**Bebra Tidwell**	Writer	**Gayl Ware**
Client	**Joe & Tony Gray**	Client	**The Carlbergs**
Agency	**Don Grimes Design, Inc., Dallas**	Agency	**Rives Smith Baldwin Carlberg + Y&R, Houston**
		Model	**Chris Carlberg**

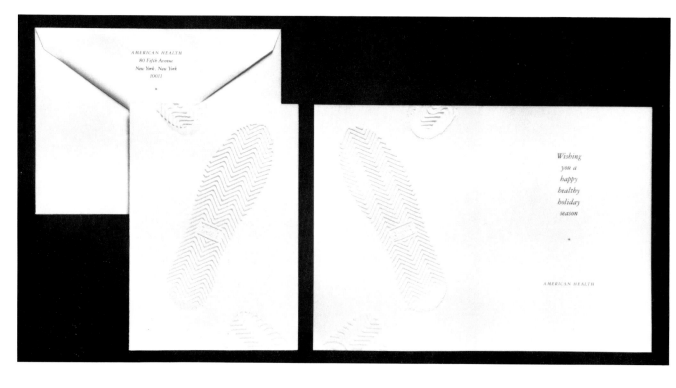

631		632	
Art Director	Anne Shaver	Art Directors	Louis F. Cruz, John Baxter
Artist	Sandra Papke	Designers	Louis F. Cruz, John Baxter
Writer	Jane Foreman	Artist	John Baxter
Client	J. Walter Thompson	Writer	John Baxter
Agency	J. Walter Thompson, Atlanta	Client	American Health
		Publisher	Owen J. Lipstein
		Director	Susan J. Boyd
		Agency	Cruz Baxter Design, Brooklyn, NY
		Publication	American Health Magazine

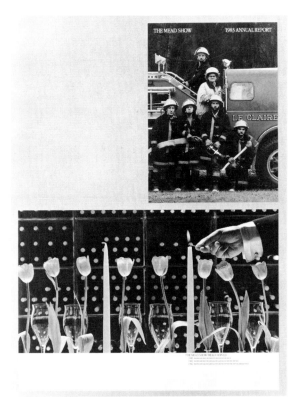

633		634	
Art Director	John Donaghue, San Francisco	Art Director	Ward G. Pennebaker, Houston
Designer	John Donaghue	Designer	Ward G. Pennebaker
Writer	John Donaghue	Photographer	Joe Baraban
Client	John & Roberta Donaghue	Writer	Randy Elia
		Client	Clampitt Paper Company
		Separations/Printing	The Olivet Group

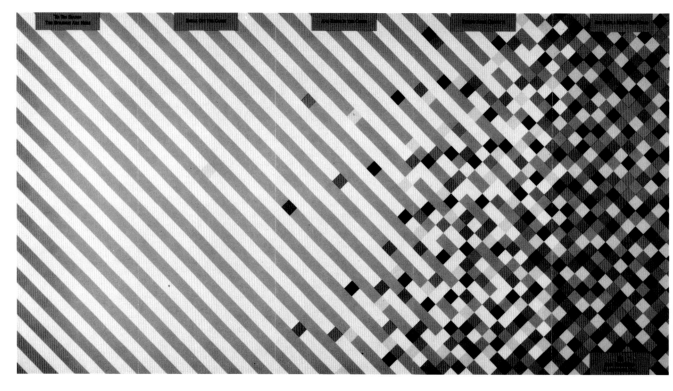

635		636		637	
Art Director	**Chris Rovillo**	Art Director,	**Ken Martin, Dallas**	Art Director	**Jan Wilson**
Designer	**Chris Rovillo**	Designer	**Ken Martin**	Designer	**Jan Wilson**
Writer	**Mark Perkins**	Photographer	**Hank Benson**	Artist	**Jan Wilson**
Client	**Dallas Society of Visual**	Writer	**Vanita Halliburton**	Writers	**Liza Orchard, Bob**
	Communications	Client	**Alan and Vanita**		**Dennard**
Agency	**Richards, Brock, Miller**		**Halliburton**	Client	**Paul Broadhead &**
	& Mitchell/The	Typographers	**Chiles & Chiles**		**Associates**
	Richards Group, Dallas			Agency	**Dennard Creative, Inc.,**
Printer	**Padgett Printing**				**Dallas**
				Creative	
				Director	**Bob Dennard**

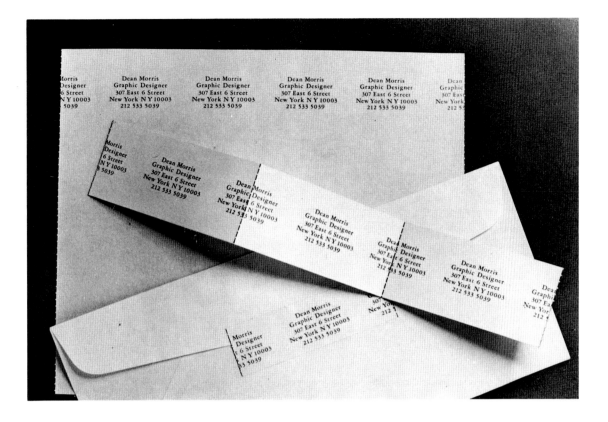

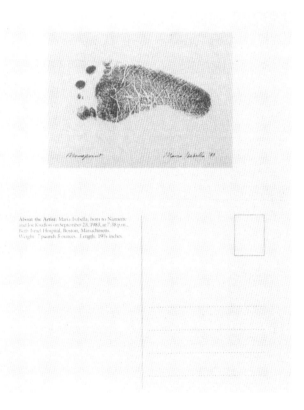

	638			639
Art Director	**Dean Morris, New York**		Art Directors	**Nannett Gonzalez, Joe**
Designer	**Dean Morris**			**Kredlow**
Printer	**A Printing**		Designer	**Nannette Gonzalez**
Production			Artist	**Maria Isabella G.**
Manager	**Mark Grogan**			**Kredlow**
			Agency	**Kredlow & Gonzalez,**
				Cambridge, MA
			Printer	**Hy Greenbaum/Court**
				Square Press

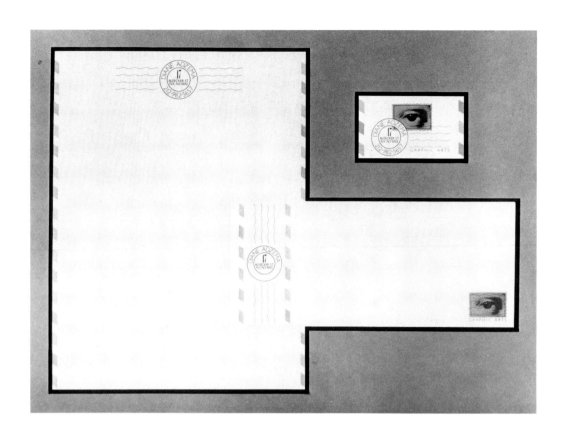

<table>
<tr><td colspan="2">640</td><td colspan="2">641</td></tr>
</table>

Art Director	**Diane Adzema, New York**	Art Director	**Alan Lidji**
Designer	**Diane Adzema**	Designer	**Alan Lidji**
Client	**Diane Adzema**	Artist	**Alan Lidji**
Printer	**Jack Eigen/Corinne Offset**	Client	**Madelyn Miller Inc.**
		Agency	**Cunningham & Walsh, Dallas**
		Production Director	**Ms. Bobby Larson**

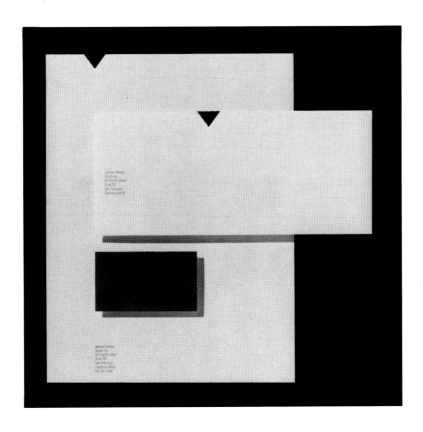

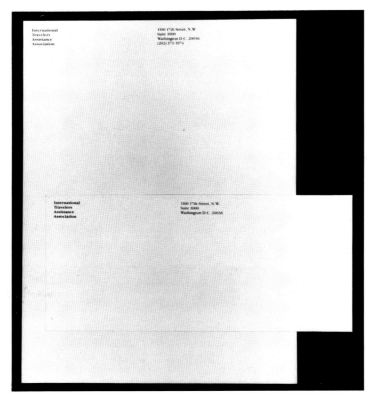

642		643	
Art Director	**Michael Mabry**	Art Director	**Janet Nebel**
Designer	**Michael Mabry**	Designer	**Janet Nebel**
Artist	**Margie Eng-Chu**	Artist	**Michael Wilson**
Client	**Jackson Vereen**	Agency	**The Woods Group,**
Design Firm	**Michael Mabry Design,**		**Baltimore**
	San Francisco		

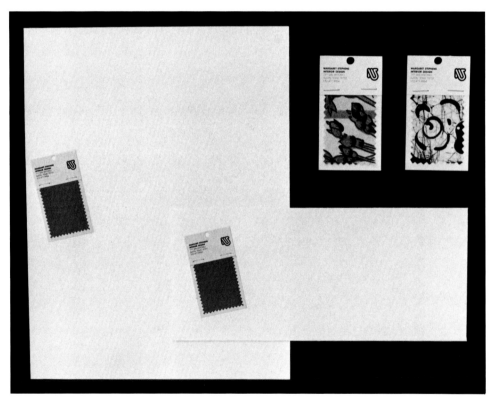

644		645		646	
Art Directors	Woody Pirtle, David Kampa	Art Director	Don Grimes	Art Director	Mike Hicks
Designer	David Kampa	Designer	Don Grimes	Designer	Mike Hicks
Artist	David Kampa	Writers	Don Grimes, Lisa Gray	Artist	Harrison Saunders
Client	David Griffin & Company	Client	Lisa Gray, Inc.	Client	Margaret Stephens Interior Design
Publisher	David Griffin & Co.	Agency	Don Grimes Design, Inc., Dallas	Publisher	Printmasters, Inc.
Agency	Pirtle Design, Dallas			Agency	HIXO, Inc., Austin

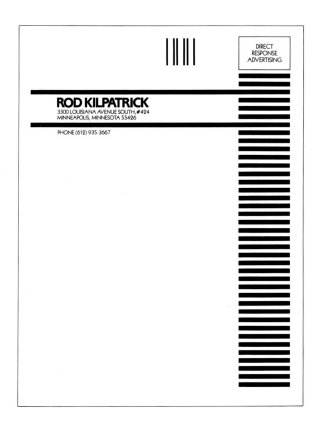

Highlander Eyewear, Inc. Two Northside 75. Atlanta. Georgia 30318 404-355-4930

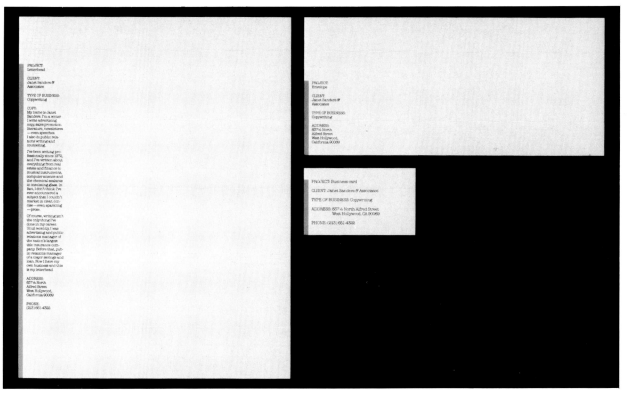

647		648		649	
Art Director	**Bob Barrie**	Art Director	**Sheila McCaffery**	Art Director	**Joanne Tepper**
Designer	**Bob Barrie**	Client	**Highlander, Inc.**	Designer	**Joanne Tepper**
Artist	**Bob Barrie**	Agency	**McCaffery & Ratner,**	Writer	**Janet Sanders**
Client	**Rod Kilpatrick**		**Inc., New York**	Client	**Janet Sanders & Assoc.**
Agency	**Fallon McElligott Rice,**			Design Firm	**Tepper/Myers Graphic**
	Minneapolis				**Design Assoc. Inc.,**
					Venice, CA
				Printer	**Adco Graphics**

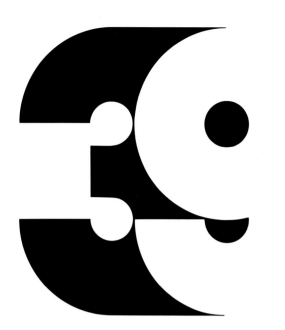

650

Art Directors **Waleo Horton, Jim Frazier**
Designer **Waleo Horton**
Artist **Waleo Horton**
Client **Channel 39 TV**
Agency **Arnold, Harwell, McClain & Associates**
Design Firm **Sibley/Peteet Design, Inc., Dallas**

651

Art Director **Sachi Kuwahara**
Designer **Sachi Kuwahara**
Artist **Sachi Kuwahara**
Client **Sawcheese Studio**
Design Firm **Sawcheese Studio, Los Angeles**

652

Art Director **Neville Smith**
Designer **Neville Smith**
Artist **Neville Smith**
Client **Black Cat Cafe**
Design Firm **Neville Smith Graphic Design, Ottawa**

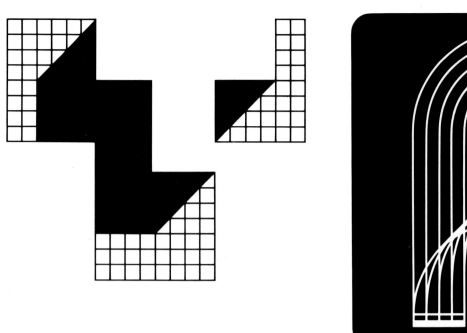
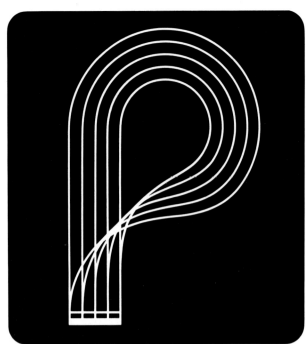
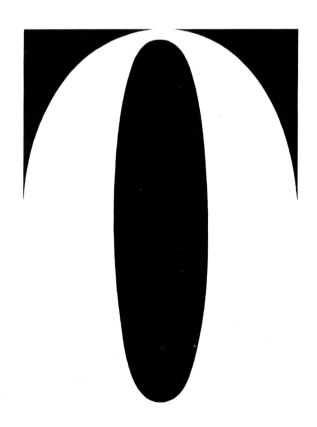

	653		654		655
Art Director	**Gregory Thomas**	Designer	**Ford, Byrne & Associates**	Art Director	**Terry O'Connor**
Designer	**Vanig Torikian**	Artist	**Ford, Byrne & Associates**	Designer	**Terry O'Connor**
Client	**TeleTech Communications**	Client	**Judith Karp, The Philadelphia Orchestra**	Client	**Terry O Communications Inc.**
Agency	**Thomas & Associates, Los Angeles**	Agency	**Ford, Byrne & Associates, Philadelphia**	Agency	**Terry O Communications Inc., Toronto**

JOE'S
HOT
TEXAS
CHILE

656		**657**	
Art Director	**Robert D. Frink**	Art Director	**David J. Chomowicz,**
Designer	**Robert D. Frink**		**Westfield, NJ**
Photographer	**Bill Gale**	Designer	**David J. Chomowicz**
Artist	**Rockford Mjos**	Artist	**David J. Chomowicz**
Writer	**Donald Phillips**	Client	**Joseph Flagg**
Client	**Bang & Olufsen of America**		
Agency	**Donald Phillips & Assoc.**		
Studio	**Frink Chin Casey Inc., Minneapolis**		

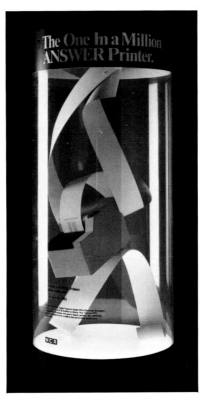

658		659	
Art Director	**Mike Murray**	Art Director	**Michael R. Orr**
Photographer	**Kerry Peterson/Marvy Photography**	Designers	**Robert K. Cassetti, Michael R. Orr**
Writer	**Bill Miller**	Writer	**Robert K. Cassetti**
Client	**International Multifoods**	Client	**Georgie Vogel/NCR Corporation**
Agency	**Chuck Ruhr Advertising, Minneapolis**	Design Firm	**Michael Orr + Associates, Corning, NY**

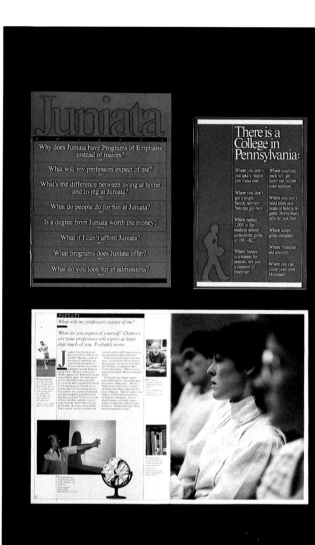

SILVER AWARD

660

Art Director   **Claude Skelton**
Designer   **Amy Knoell**
Photographers   **Paul Fetters, Doug Barber**
Artists   **Whitney Sherman, Rebecca Lee**
Writer   **David Treadwell**
Client   **Juniata College**
Agency   **The Barton-Gillet Co., Baltimore**

GOLD AWARD

661

Art Director	**Robert E. Demougeot**
Artist	**Joel Lenecker**
Writer	**Nancy L. Gallagher**
Client	**The Kanthal Corporation**
Editor	**Thomas W. Mills**
Director	**James J. Hoverman**
Agency	**Sundberg, Mills & Demougeot, Ridgefield, CT**

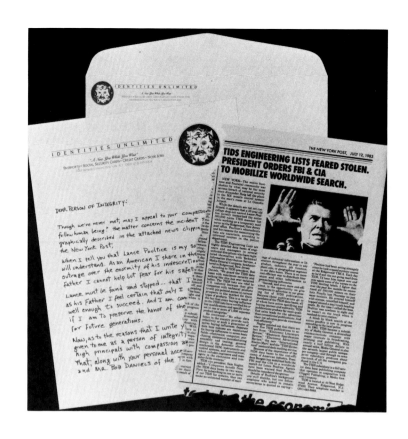

662		**663**	
Art Director	**Dick Grider**	Art Director	**Felix Rhymes**
Writer	**Jack Warner**	Artist	**John Collier**
Client	**Technical Information**	Writer	**Skip Jordan**
	Distribution Service	Client	**Holmes Investments**
Agency	**Warner Bicking &**	Agency	**LargeRhymes, Houston**
	Fenwick, Inc., New York		

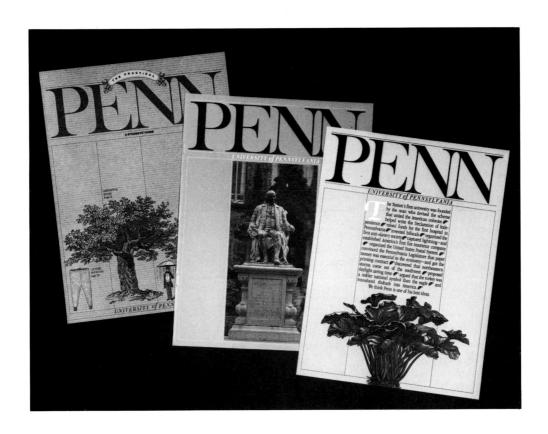

DISTINCTIVE MERIT

	664		665
Art Directors/ Designers	Elizabeth G. Clark, Domenica Genovese	Art Directors	George Pierson, Etta Siegel, Guy Augeri
Artist	Carolyn McIntyre	Designer	Guy Augeri
Writers	Jewell Vroonland, Anne Bailey	Photographer	Herb Ritts
Client	U of PA Publications	Artist	Guy Augeri—logo, Gary Dueno—record
Editors	Anne Bailey, Donna Avergun	Client	Home Box Office
Publisher	Univ. of Pennsylvania	Agency	HBO Creative Services, New York
Director	Ann J. Duffield		
Agency	The North Charles St. Design Org., Baltimore		

SILVER AWARD

666

Art Director **Cap Pannell**
Designer **Cap Pannell**
Writer **Cap Pannell**
Client **Southwestern Bell**
Agency **Cap Pannell &
Company, Dallas**

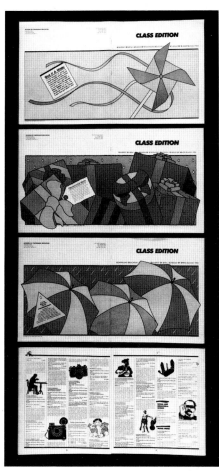

DISTINCTIVE MERIT

	667		668
Art Director	**Mark Anderson**	Art Director	**Micheal Richards**
Designers	**Steve Tolleson, Micheal**	Designer	**Bill Swensen**
	Kunisaki, Tony Milner,	Artist	**Bill Swensen**
	Sue Cretarolo	Client	**Univ. of Utah Student**
Artist	**Tony Milner**		**Health Services, Salt**
Writer	**Ron Perotta**		**Lake City**
Client	**Apple Computer, Inc.**		
Publisher	**Container Corporation**		
	of America		
Agency	**Mark Anderson Design,**		
	Palo Alto, CA		

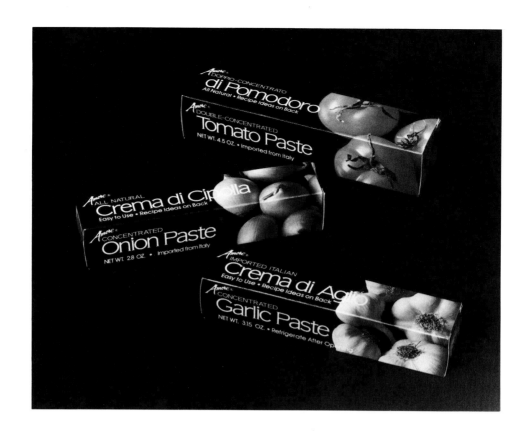

669		670	
Art Directors	**Millie Falcaro, Mary Tiegreen**	Art Director	**Mark Anderson**
Designers	**Millie Falcaro & Mary Tiegreen**	Designer	**Steven Tolleson**
Photographer	**Michael Zens**	Artist	**Steven Tolleson**
Client	**Universal Foods Corp.**	Client	**Mad Computer, Inc.**
Agency	**Falcaro & Tiegreen Ltd., New York**	Publisher	**Petersen & Strong Inc.**
Clients	**Ted Koran, William Skure/Universal Foods**	Agency	**Mark Anderson Design, Palo Alto, CA**

	671		672
Art Director	**Timothy J. Musios**	Art Director	**Keith Bright**
Designer	**Lori Houseworth-Uhmeyer**	Designer	**Ray Wood**
Artist	**Chiu Li**	Artist	**Ray Wood**
Client	**Avon Products, Inc., New York**	Writer	**Carnation Company**
		Client	**Carnation Company**
		Agency	**Bright & Associates, Los Angeles**

673		674	
Art Director	**Peter Windett**	Art Director	**Peter Windett**
Designer	**Peter Windett**	Designer	**Peter Windett**
Artist	**Judy Clifford**	Artist	**Judy Clifford**
Client	**Scarborough and Company, Wilton, NH**	Client	**Scarborough and Company, Wilton, NH**
Box Printer	**Laurino Packaging Corporation**	Box Printer	**Laurino Packaging Corporation**

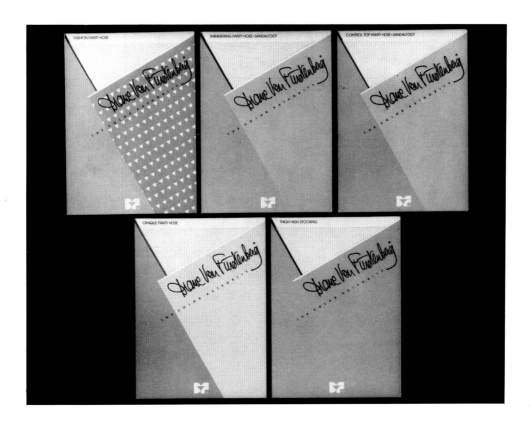

675		676	
Art Director	**Pat Garling**	Art Director	**Barry Deutsch**
Designer	**Pat Garling**	Designer	**Myland McRevey**
Client	**Diane Von Furstenberg**	Photographer	**Various**
	Studio	Writers	**Mary Beth Mader &**
Director of			**Robin Raj, Ogilvy &**
Advertising	**Michael Smith**		**Mather**
Agency	**Diane Von Furstenberg**	Client	**Convergent**
	Studio, New York		**Technologies**
		Agency	**Steinhilber Deutsch &**
			Gard, San Francisco

	677		678
Art Director	**Jill Dubin, Atlanta**	Art Director	**Richard Nodine**
Designer	**Jill Dubin**	Designer	**Fortunato Fong**
Client	**Anna Lou McCalister/**	Client	**Macy's California**
	Lulabelle's Gourmet	Agency	**Macy's California, San**
	Cookies		**Francisco**
Creative			
Director	**Clark Dubin**		

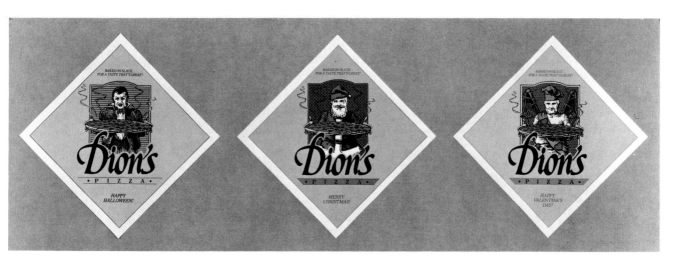

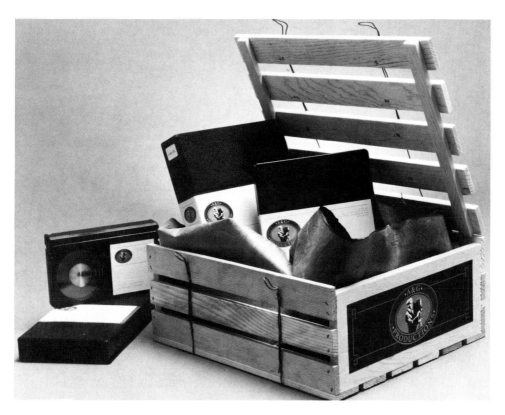

679		680	
Art Directors	**Steven Wedeen, Rick Vaughn**	Art Directors	**Clem & Bonnie Schwartz**
Designer	**Vaughn/Wedeen Creative, Inc.**	Designers	**Clem & Bonnie Schwartz**
Artists	**Russ Ball, Steven Wedeen**	Artists	**Joyce Kitchell, Linda Lockowitz**
Client	**Dion's Pizza**	Client	**A&G Productions**
Agency	**Vaughn/Wedeen Creative, Inc., Albuquerque, NM**	Agency	**Clem & Bonnie Schwartz Graphic Design, San Francisco**

681		682	
Art Director	**Muts Yasumura**	Art Directors	**Thom Marchionna,**
Designer	**Regina Rubino**		**Dennis Caldwell**
Photographer	**Steven Mark Needham**	Designers	**Thom Marchionna,**
Client	**The Dannon Company,**		**Dennis Caldwell**
	Inc.	Photographers	**Tom Landecker, Bruce**
Director	**Joe Gregory**		**Ashley**
Agency	**Yasumura & Associates/**	Writers	**Mark Aulman, Mary**
	CYB, New York		**Perry**
Printer	**Miner Container**	Client	**Waveform Corporation**
	Printing, Inc.	Agency	**Carter Callahan, Inc.,**
			San Jose, CA

THE BIRTH OF AN OCEAN LINER.

THE NIEUW AMSTERDAM.

GOLD AWARD

683

Art Director	**Keith Bright**
Designers	**Gretchen Goldie, Greg Berman**
Photographer	**Rien Bassen**
Artists	**Doug Johnson, David Kimble, Dusty Deyo, Ken Parkhurst, Steve Curry, Ray Wood, Richard Pietruska**
Writer	**John Salvati**
Client	**Holland America**
Agency	**Bright & Associates, Los Angeles**

684		**685**	
Art Director	**Peter Windett**	Art Director	**Jeff Pienkos**
Designer	**Peter Windett**	Designer	**Jeff Pienkos**
Client	**Scarborough and**	Photographer	**William K. Sladcik**
	Company, Wilton, NH	Writer	**Charlie AuBuchon**
Agency	**Peter Windett and**	Client	**Jeff Pienkos Design,**
	Associates		**Mundelein,IL**
Box Printer	**Creative Printers**		

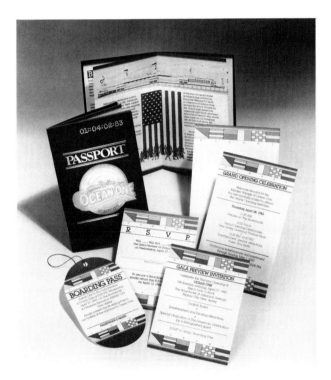

686

Art Director   **Robert Probst**
Designer   **Robert Probst**
Photographer   **Joel Conison**
Client   **Joel Conison
Photography**
Agency   **Schenker, Probst &
Barensfeld, Cincinnati**
Printer   **Young & Klein**

687

Art Director   **Seth Blum**
Designer   **Seth Blum**
Writer   **Lawrence Becker**
Agency   **Becker Kanter, Cherry
Hill, NJ**

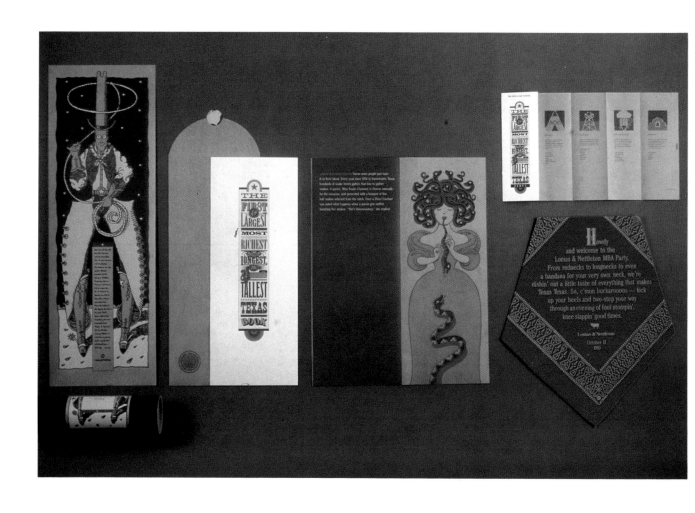

SILVER AWARD

689

Art Director	**Marianne Tombaugh**
Designers	**Rex Peteet, Michael Landon**
Artists	**Rex Peteet, Michael Landon, Jerry Jeanmard**
Writers	**Rex Peteet, Carol St. George, Marianne Tombaugh**
Client	**Lomas & Nettleton Financial Corporation**
Agency	**The Hay Agency, Inc., Dallas**

688

Art Director   **Lou Dorfsman**
Designer   **Sharon Gresh**
Client   **The Rose Restaurant**
Publisher   **CBS Inc., New York**

690

Art Director   **Marianne Tombaugh**
Designer   **Marianne Tombaugh**
Writer   **Marianne Tombaugh**
Client   **The Mental Health Association in Texas**
Agency   **The Hay Agency, Inc., Dallas**

691		**692**	
Art Director	**Martin Solomon, New York**	Art Director	**Rod Dyer**
Designer	**Martin Solomon**	Designer	**Hoi Ping Law**
Writer	**Martin Solomon**	Photographer	**Bret Lopez**
Client	**Royal Composing Room**	Client	**Barbara Goldman - Malibu Art & Design**
		Agency	**Dyer/Kahn, Inc., Los Angeles**

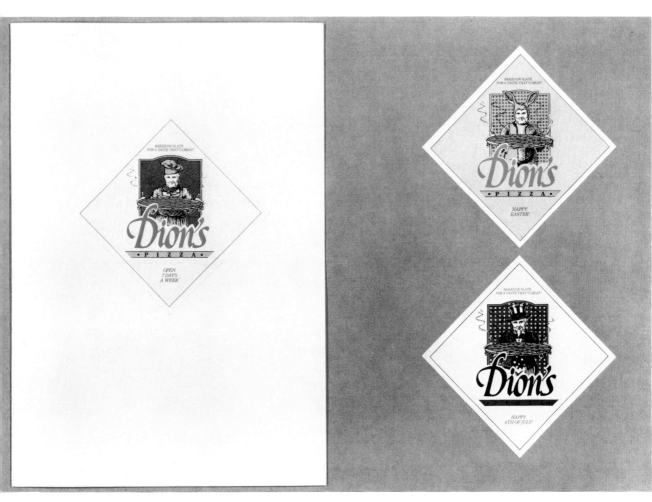

	693		694
Art Director	Richard Danne/Danne & Blackburn, Inc.	Art Directors	Steven Wedeen, Rick Vaughn
Designer	Richard Danne	Designer	Vaughn/Wedeen Creative, Inc.
Photographer	Jeff Perkell	Artists	Russ Ball, Steven Wedeen
Client	South Street Seaport Museum/Sallie Stutz	Writer	Steven Wedeen
Publisher	Perkell/Danne & Blackburn, New York	Client	Dion's Pizza
Printer	Froelich-Greene Litho Corp.	Agency	Vaughn/Wedeen Creative, Inc., Albuquerque, NM

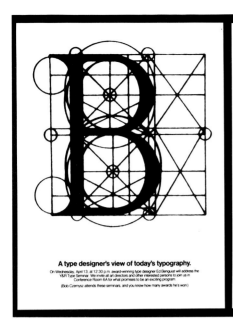

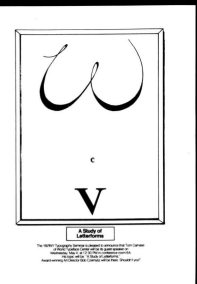

695		696	
Art Director	**Chuck Anderson**	Art Director	**Gerald Millet**
Designers	**Chuck Anderson, Alan Zwiebel**	Designers	**Lark Carrier, Jeffrey Boortz, Mark Feldman**
Writer	**Alan Zwiebel**	Client	**Corning Medical**
Agency	**Young & Rubicam Inc., New York**	Agency	**Lehman Millet Incorporated, Boston**
Type Director	**Roy Zucca**		

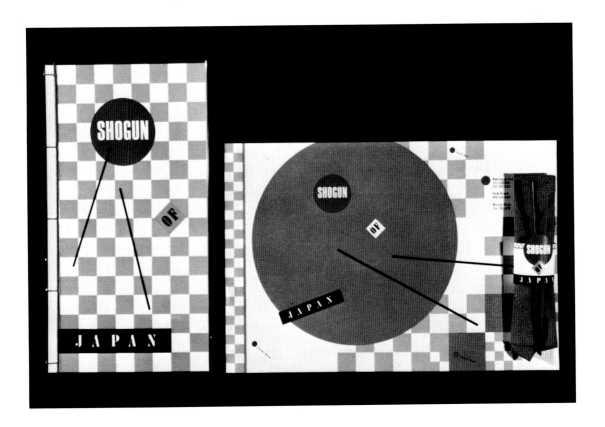

697

Art Director   **Deborah Sussman**
Designer   **Debra Valencia**
Artist   **Felice Matare'**
Client   **Maguire/Thomas & Associates, Shogun of Japan**
Agency   **Sussman/Prejza & Company, Santa Monica, CA**

698

Art Director   **Phil French**
Designer   **Linny Heagy**
Artist   **Bill Greer**
Writer   **Nordeen Willard**
Client   **Neiman-Marcus, Dallas**

<table>
</table>

699		700	
Creative		Creative	
Director	Howard York	Director	Howard York
Design		Design Director	John Wanek
Director/		Client	Hills Bros. Coffee, Inc.
Designer	Michael Mills	Agency	S&O Consultants, San
Client	The Arts Commission of		Francisco
	San Francisco		
Agency	S&O Consultants, San		
	Francisco		

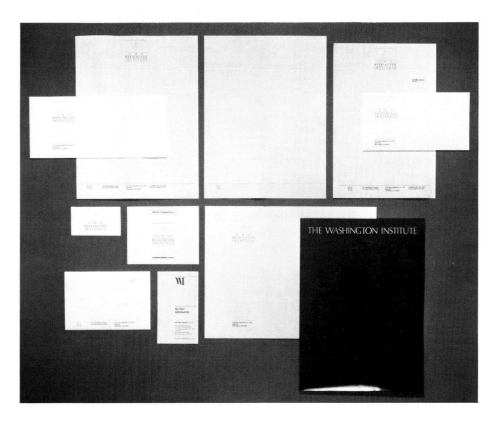

	701		702
Art Director	**John Clark**	Art Director	**Sheila Freeman**
Designer	**John Clark**	Designers	**Jim Nuttle, Sheila**
Photographers	**Eric Schweikhart,**		**Freeman**
	Myron, Bruce Laurence	Artist	**Jim Nuttle**
Writer	**Steve Rzymski**	Client	**The Washington**
Client	**Gant Clothing Corp.**		**Institute**
Agency	**Jason Grant Assoc.,**	Agency	**Freeman Design**
	Providence, RI		**Incorporated,**
			Washington, DC

GOLD AWARD

703

Art Director	**Lowell Williams**
Designers	**Lowell Williams, Bill Carson**
Photographers	**Ron Scott, Bob Haar, Richard Payne**
Artist	**Tom McNeff**
Writer	**Lee Herrick**
Client	**Gerald D. Hines Interests**
Agency	**Lowell Williams Design, Inc., Houston**

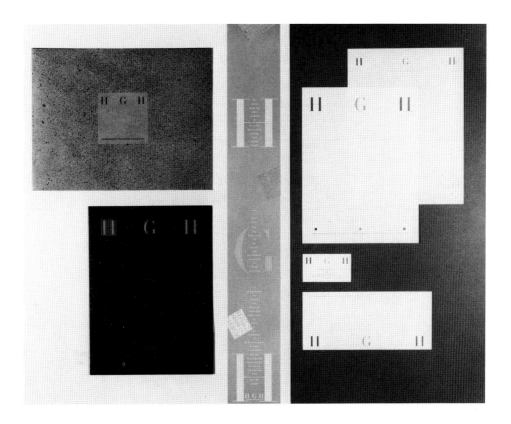

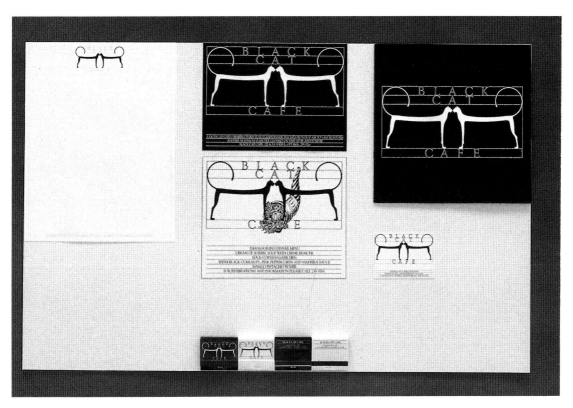

	704		705
Art Directors	**Larry Kazal, KC Witherell**	Art Director	**Neville Smith**
		Designer	**Neville Smith**
Clients	**Harlan G. Hoffman, Frederick Norton**	Client	**Black Cat Cafe**
Agency	**Larry Kazal/KC Witherell Inc., New York**	Design Firm	**Neville Smith Graphic Design, Ottawa**
		Printer	**M.O.M. Printing, Ottawa**

BOOKS

Sam Antupit

Bascove
Guy Billout
Peter Bradford
Louise Fili
Alvin Grossman
Steven Heller
Steve Miller
Martin Moskof
Holly Nelson
Stephanie Tevonian
Susan Trowbridge

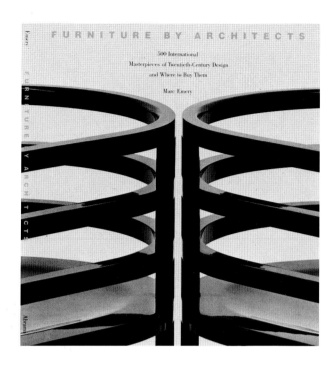

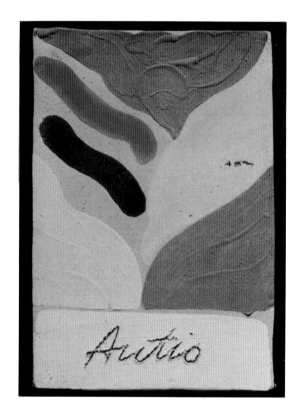

DISTINCTIVE MERIT

DISTINCTIVE MERIT

706

Art Director	**Samuel N. Antupit**
Designer	**Patrick Cunningham**
Photographer	**Various**
Writer	**Marc Emery**
Editor	**Anne Yarowsky**
Publisher	**Harry N. Abrams, Inc., New York**

707

Art Directors	**Seymour Chwast, Steven Heller**
Designer	**Seymour Chwast**
Artist	**Various**
Writer	**Various**
Editors	**Seymour Chwast, Steven Heller, Margaret Donovan**
Publisher	**Harry N. Abrams, Inc., New York**
Producer	**Steven Heller**
Project Manager	**Samuel N. Antupit**

708

Art Director	**James Miho**
Designer	**James Miho**
Client	**Champion International Corporation, Stamford, CT**
Editor	**Sallie B. Vandervort**

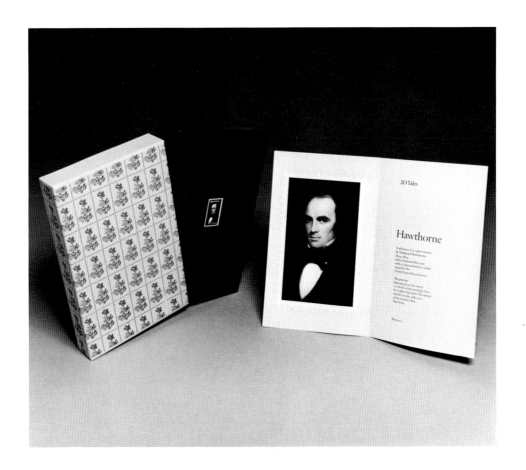

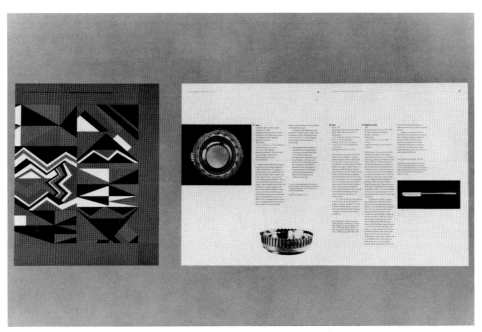

DISTINCTIVE MERIT

709		**710**	
Art Directors	**Marie T. Raperto,**	Art Director	**Karen Salsgiver**
	Bradbury Thompson	Designer	**Karen Salsgiver**
Writer	**Nathaniel Hawthorne**	Author	**Karen Davies**
Publisher	**Westvaco Corporation,**	Client	**Pat Kane/Curator of**
	New York		**American Decorative**
			Arts, Yale University Art
			Gallery
		Agency	**Homans/Salsgiver, New**
			York
		Printer	**John Gambell, Yale**
			University Printing
			Service

PAUL JENKINS

ANATOMY OF A CLOUD

PAUL JENKINS **ANATOMY OF A CLOUD**

ABRAMS

SILVER AWARD

711

Art Director	**Samuel N. Antupit**
Designers	**Will Hopkins and Ira Friedlander**
Artist	**Paul Jenkins**
Writers	**Paul Jenkins and Suzanne Donnelly Jenkins**
Editor	**Joan E. Fisher**
Publisher	**Harry N. Abrams, Inc., New York**

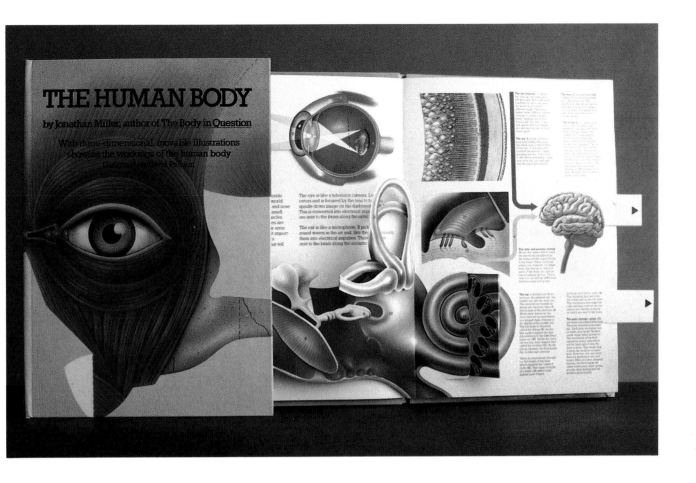

GOLD AWARD

712

Art Director   **David Pelham**
Designer   **David Pelham**
Artist   **Harry Willock**
Authors   **Jonathan Miller, Jeremy Cox**
Publisher   **Viking Penguin Inc., New York**
Paper
Engineers   **Vic Duppa-Whyte, David Rosendale**

713	
Art Director	Nathan Garland
Designer	Nathan Garland
Artist	Juan Gris
Writer	Mark Rosenthal
Clients	Abbeville Press and U of CA Art Museum
Editors	N. Grubb, A. Karlstrom, M. Rosenthal
Publishers	Abbeville Press and University Art Museum U of CA, Berkeley
Design Firm	Nathan Garland Graphic Design, New Haven, CT

714	
Art Director	Constance Sullivan
Designer	Logowitz & Moore Associates, Boston, MA
Editor	Jacqueline Twarog
Publisher	Focal Press

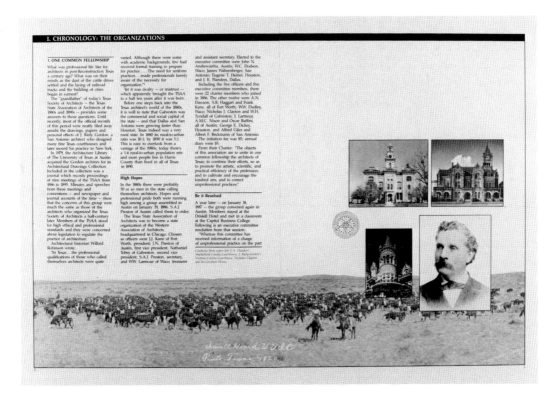

715

Art Director   **Yvonne Tocquigny**
Designer   **Yvonne Tocquigny**
Artists   **Kim Stewart/Kathy Green/Kelly Leahy**
Writer   **Hank Smith**
Client   **Texas Society of Architects**
Editor   **Larry Paul Fuller**
Agency   **Tocquigny Design, Inc., Austin**

716

Art Directors   **Mark Anderson, Kathy Price**
Designer   **Steven Tolleson**
Photographer   **David Monley**
Artists   **Kathy McHale, Steven Tolleson**
Writer   **David Alexander**
Client   **Ultratech Stepper**
Publisher   **National Press**
Agency   **Mark Anderson Design, Palo Alto, CA**

717

Art Director	**John Sapp**
Designer	**David Haddock**
Writers	**Alicia Stamm, C. Ford Peatross**
Client	**Dana Pratt**
Editor	**Evelyn Sinclair**
Publisher	**Library of Congress**
Director	**Louis R. Glessmann**
Agency	**U.S. Government Printing Office, Washington, DC**

718

Art Director	**Karen A. Schell**
Designer	**Joan Peckolick**
Photographer	**Carl Doney**
Publisher	**Rodale Press Inc., Emmaus, PA**

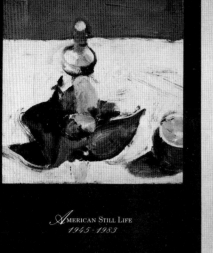

JACK BEAL

THOMAS HART BENTON

DISTINCTIVE MERIT

	719		720
Art Director	**Eric Morrell**	Art Director	**Louise Fili**
Designer	**Cinda Debbink**	Designer	**Louise Fili**
Client	**Contemporary Arts Museum**	Artist	**Claude Monet**
Agency	**Creel Morrell Inc., Houston**	Writer	**Eva Figes**
		Publisher	**Pantheon Books, New York**

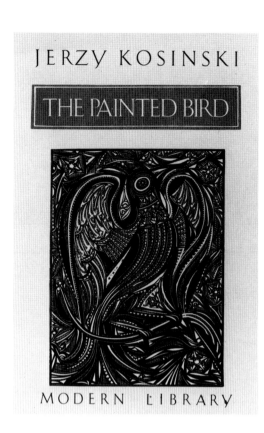

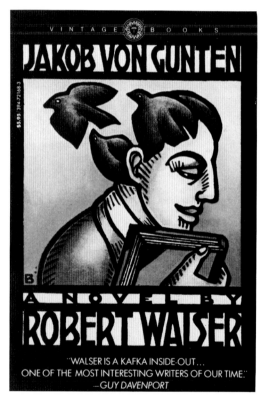

DISTINCTIVE MERIT

721

Art Director	**R.D. Scudellari**
Designer	**R.D. Scudellari**
Artist	**Stephen Alcorn**
Client	**Modern Library**
Editor	**John Glusman**
Publisher	**Modern Library, New York**

DISTINCTIVE MERIT

722

Art Director	**Judith Loeser**
Designer	**Bascove**
Artist	**Bascove**
Writer	**Robert Walser**
Client	**Vintage**
Editor	**Melanie Fleishman**
Publisher	**Vintage/Random House, New York**

DISTINCTIVE MERIT

723

Art Director	**Judith Loeser**
Designer	**Bascove**
Artist	**Bascove**
Writer	**Robert Walser**
Client	**Vintage**
Editor	**Melanie Fleishman**
Publisher	**Vintage/Random House, New York**

724

Art Director **Leslee Avchen**
Designer **Leslee Avchen**
Client **Department of German/University of Minnesota**
Editor **Thomas G. Plummer**
Agency **Leslee Avchen Design, Minneapolis**

725

Art Director **Gael Towey Dillon**
Artist **Bascove, New York**
Writer **William Goyen**
Editor **Carol Southern**
Publisher **Clarkson N. Potter, Inc.**

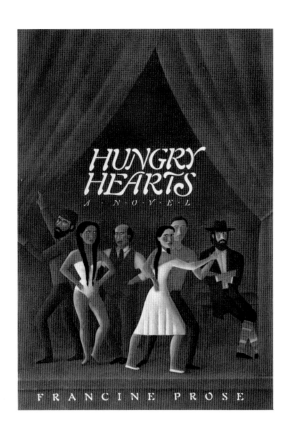

DISTINCTIVE MERIT

	726		727		728
Art Director	**Louise Fili**	Art Director	**Louise Fili**	Art Director	**Louise Fili**
Designer	**Louise Fili**	Designer	**Fred Marcellino**	Designer	**Louise Fili**
Artist	**Susan Walp**	Artist	**Fred Marcellino**	Artist	**John Martinez**
Writer	**Francine Prose**	Writer	**Peter Schneider**	Publisher	**Pantheon Books, New York**
Publisher	**Pantheon Books, New York**	Publisher	**Pantheon Books, New York**		

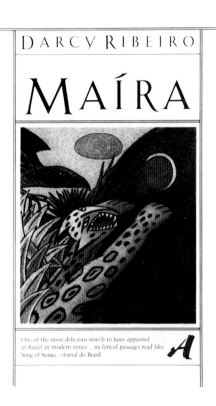

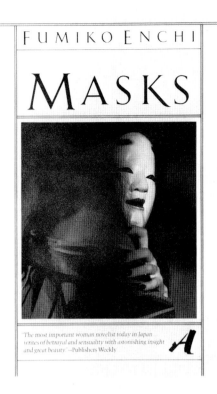

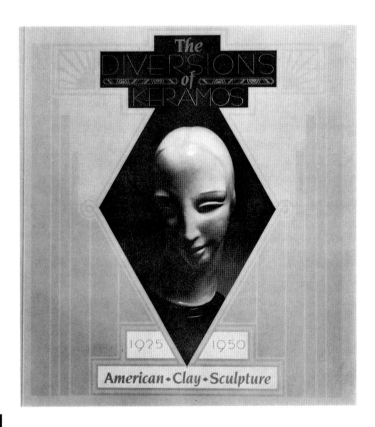

DISTINCTIVE MERIT

	729		730		731
Art Director	**Judith Loeser**	Art Director	**Judith Loeser**	Art Director	**CW Pike**
Designer	**Keith Sheridan**	Designer	**Keith Sheridan**	Designer	**CW Pike**
Artists	**Melanie Marder Parks, Dagmar Frinta, Daniel Maffia**	Photographer	**Kenneth McGowan**	Photographer	**Courtney Frisse**
		Artists	**Marshall Arisman, Wendy Hoile**	Writers	**Ross Anderson, Dr. Barbara Perry**
Writers	**Darcy Ribeiro, Grusa, Manlio Argueta**	Writers	**Fumiko Enchi, Thomas Bernhard, Wole Soyinka**	Client	**Everson Museum of Art**
Client	**Aventura**	Client	**Aventura**	Publisher	**Everson Museum of Art**
Editor	**Erroll McDonald**	Editor	**Erroll McDonald**	Agency	**The Great Northern Pikes, Fayetteville, NY**
Publisher	**Aventura, New York**	Publisher	**Aventura, New York**	Printer	**Salina Press**

POSTERS

Malcolm End
Tony Gill
Jean Govoni
Brian Harrod
Thom Higgins
Lawrence Miller
Seymon Ostilly
Elissa Querze
Richard Radke
Bob Reitzfeld
Marion Sackett
Bob Wilvers
Tom Wolsey
Mary Baumann
Robert Best
Mike Brock
Bill Cadge
Frank DeVino
Paul Hardy
Kristina Jorgensen
David Levy
Frank Rothmann
Neil Shakery
Lou Silverstein
Melissa Tardiff
Adrian Taylor

Pete Turner
Rodney Williams
Tony Cappiello
Robert Cipriani
Molly Epstein
Blanche Fiorenza
Dick Hess
Chris Hill
Nigel Holmes
Elizabeth Kim
Norma Kwan
Geoffrey Moss
Susan Niles
Jerry Philips
Woody Pirtle
Sherry Pollack
Brenda Preis
Chuck Queener
Robert Reed
Bennett Robinson
Anthony Russell
James Sebastian
Dugald Stermer
John Vogler
Ken White
Cynthia Wojdyla

DISTINCTIVE MERIT

732

Art Director **Jim Lacey**
Writer **Pete Smith**
Client **Minneapolis Star & Tribune**
Agnecy **Bozell & Jacobs, Inc., Minneapolis**
Publication **Outdoor**

DISTINCTIVE MERIT

733

Art Director **Carlton Gunn**
Designer **Carlton Gunn**
Artist **Lu Matthews**
Writer **Carlton Gunn**
Client **WRVQ Radio**
Agency **The Paxton Group, Richmond, VA**

734		735	
Art Director	Bob Kwait	Art Director	Philip Gips
Designer	Ron VanBuskirk	Designers	Philip Gips, Gina Stone
Artist	Darrel Milsap	Photographer	Gail Harvey
Writer	Bob Kwait	Writer	Kate Carroll Cox
Client	San Diego Zoo	Client	Home Box Office, Inc.
Agency	Phillips-Ramsey, San Diego	Agency	Gips + Balkind + Associates, New York

GOLD AWARD

736

Art Directors   **Gary Johns, Lee Clow**
Writer   **Jeff Gorman**
Client   **Nike, Inc.**
Agency   **Chiat/Day, Los Angeles**

"MOMMY, I'M PREGNANT."

Call 869-7221 for care and counseling.
The DePelchin/Crittenton Center

MOBIL MASTERPIECE THEATRE PRESENTS

THE IRISH R·M·

A BRITISH RESIDENT MAGISTRATE WHO HAD TO LEARN THE LORE TO ADMINISTER THE LAW

STARRING: PETER BOWLES AND BRYAN MURRAY

BEGINS SUNDAY, JANUARY 29   9PM CHANNEL 13 PBS   HOST: ALISTAIR COOKE

Mobil

737		738	
Art Directors	Chuck Carlberg, Matthew Gleason	Art Director	Seymour Chwast
Designer	Chuck Carlberg	Designer	Seymour Chwast
Writer	Carol Miller	Artist	Stan Zagorski
Client	DePelchin/Crittendon Center	Client	Sandra Ruch, Mobil
Agency	Rives Smith Baldwin Carlberg + Y&R, Houston	Agency	Pushpin Lubalin Peckolick, New York
Creative Director	Chuck Carlberg		

AN EXPERIENCE OF ASTRONOMICAL PROPORTIONS.

The Minneapolis Planetarium
300 Nicollet Mall Phone 372-6644

THOUSANDS OF STARS PERFORMING DAILY.

The Minneapolis Planetarium
300 Nicollet Mall / Phone 372-6644

739	
Art Director	**Bob Barrie, Richfield, MN**
Designer	**Bob Barrie**
Artist	**Bob Barrie**
Writer	**Jim Newcombe**
Client	**Minneapolis Planetarium**
Agency	**Advertising Au Gratin**

740	
Art Director	**Bob Barrie, Richfield, MN**
Designer	**Bob Barrie**
Writer	**Jim Newcombe**
Client	**Minneapolis Planetarium**
Agency	**Advertising Au Gratin**

In Focus

VANITY FAIR

741

Art Director	**Robert Barthelmes**
Designer	**Younghee Choi**
Photographer	**Annie Leibovitz**
Writer	**Wendy Smith**
Publisher	**The Condé Nast Publications, New York**
Publication	**Vanity Fair**
Executive Editor	**Katherine Mountain**

742

Art Director	**David Gauger**
Designer	**Jeanne Kimmel**
Artist	**Jeanne Kimmel**
Client	**Dicor Development Corporation**
Agency	**Gauger Sparks Silva, Inc., San Francisco**
Sign Painters	**Horizon Signs**

	743		744		745
Art Director	Bob Appleton, West Hartford, CT	Art Director	Dean Hanson	Art Director	Dave Martin
Designer	Bob Appleton	Designer	Dean Hanson	Designer	Dave Martin
Artist	Bob Appleton	Writer	Tom McElligott	Photographer	Jim McLoughlin
Writer	Judith Pryor	Client	Vander Zanden, Inc.	Writer	Pete Faulkner
Client	The Womens Committee of the Wadsworth Atheneum	Agency	Fallon McElligott Rice, Minneapolis	Client	American Diabetes Association
Publisher	The Womens Committee of the Wadsworth Atheneum			Agency	Doyle Dane Bernbach Inc., New York
Design Studio	William Wondriska Associates				

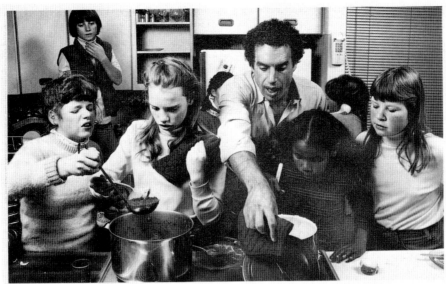

Are you man enough to be a Girl Scout?

GIRL SCOUTS

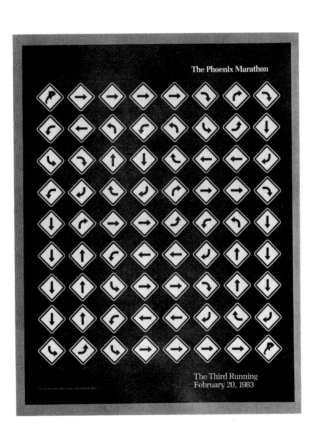

The Phoenix Marathon

The Third Running
February 20, 1983

746		747	
Art Director	Lisbeth Rokicki	Art Director	Forrest Richardson, Phoenix, AZ
Photographer	Michael Malyszko	Designer	Forrest Richardson
Artist	Lisbeth Rokicki	Writer	Forrest Richardson
Writer	David Wecal	Client	The Phoenix Marathon
Client	Patriots' Trail Girl Scout Council	Agency	KPHO Television/ Meredith Corp.
Agency	Schneider Parker Jakuc, Inc., Boston		

"For the price of your last supper, you could join the art museum."

"An art museum membership is an unreal bargain. So don't dilly-Dali around."

POWERED**FLIGHT**DAY

December 17, 1983
Bradley Air Museum

	748		749		750
Art Director	**Rachel Stephens**	Art Director	**Rachel Stephens**	Art Director	**Robert J. Goehring**
Photographers	**Peter Amft, Don Wilson**	Photographers	**Peter Amft, Don Wilson**	Designer	**Bob Appleton**
Writer	**Kirk Ruhnke**	Writer	**Robin Reynolds**	Artist	**Bob Appleton**
Client	**Milwaukee Art Museum**	Client	**Milwaukee Art Museum**	Writer	**Robert J. Goehring**
Agency	**Frankenberry, Laughlin & Constable, Milwaukee**	Agency	**Frankenberry, Laughlin & Constable, Milwaukee**	Client	**Pratt & Whitney Aircraft**
		Production Manager	**Paula A. Rothe**	Design Studio	**Appleton Design, West Hartford, CT**

751

Art Director   **Rachel Stephens**
Photographers   **Peter Amft, Don Wilson**
Writer   **Robin Reynolds**
Client   **Milwaukee Art Museum**
Agency   **Frankenberry, Laughlin
& Constable,
Milwaukee**

752

Art Director   **Rachel Stephens**
Photographers   **Peter Amft, Don Wilson**
Writer   **Kirk Ruhnke**
Client   **Milwaukee Art Museum**
Agency   **Frankenberry, Laughlin
& Constable,
Milwaukee**

Production
Manager   **Paula A. Rothe**

753

Art Director   **Franklin J. Ross**
Designer   **Franklin J. Ross**
Artist   **Sheryl Nelson Lauder**
Agency   **Franklin Ross &
Associates,
Louisville, KY**

754		755	
Art Directors	**Whendie Wolfinger Cerminaro, Judith Shear**	Art Director	**Michael Mabry**
Designer	**Whendie Wolfinger Cerminaro**	Designer	**Michael Mabry**
Artist	**Whendie Wolfinger Cerminaro**	Artist	**Michael Mabry**
Writer	**Lori Wise**	Client	**Rudolph Schaffer School of Design**
Client	**CertainTeed Corporation**	Agency	**Michael Mabry Design, San Francisco**
Agency	**CertainTeed Communication Services, Valley Forge, PA**		

The Language
of
Michael Graves

September 9 - October 15.
1 9 8 3
Moore College of Art

THE
WRONG
STUFF
★

When the future stopped.

	756		757
Art Director	**William Longhauser**	Art Director	**Bill Caldwell**
Designer	**William Longhauser**	Designer	**Bill Caldwell**
Client	**Elsa Weiner, Director, Moore College of Art Gallery**	Photographer	**Bob Grove**
		Artist	**Bill Caldwell**
		Writer	**Bill Caldwell**
Agency	**William Longhauser Design, Philadelphia**	Client	**Grass Roots Graphics**
		Editor	**Bill Caldwell**
Printer	**Michael Becotte**	Publisher	**Just Imagine**
		Director	**Bill Caldwell**
		Agency	**Just Imagine, McLean, VA**

758		759		759A	
Art Director	**Milton Glaser**	Art Director	**Michael McGinn**	Art Director	**Bob Kwait**
Designer	**Milton Glaser**	Designer	**Sharon Gresh**	Designer	**Ron VanBuskirk**
Artist	**Milton Glaser**	Writer	**Marie Avona**	Artist	**Darrel Millsap**
Writer	**Peter Matthiessen**	Client	**Pratt Institute/Joseph**	Writer	**Bob Kwait**
Client	**New York Zoological**		**Azzinaro, Brooklyn, NY**	Client	**San Diego Zoo**
	Society			Agency	**Phillips-Ramsey, San**
Agency	**Milton Glaser, Inc.,**				**Diego**
	New York				

760		761	
Art Director	Eddie H.S. Lee, Boston	Art Director	Milton Glaser
Designer	Eddie H.S. Lee	Designer	Milton Glaser
Artist	Eddie H.S. Lee	Artist	Milton Glaser
Client	Asian American Resource Workshop	Client	Proscenium, Inc.
		Publisher	Ann Bohlen
		Agency	Milton Glaser Inc., New York

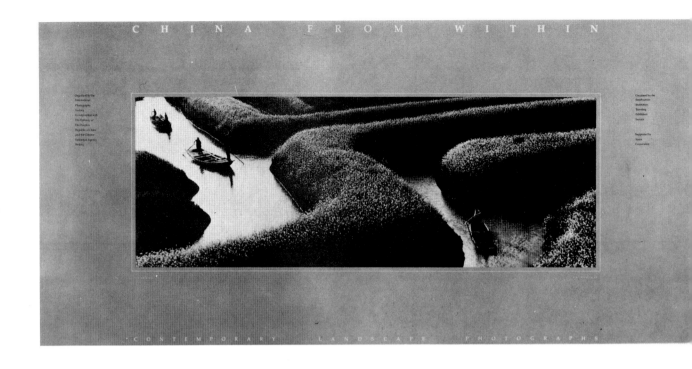

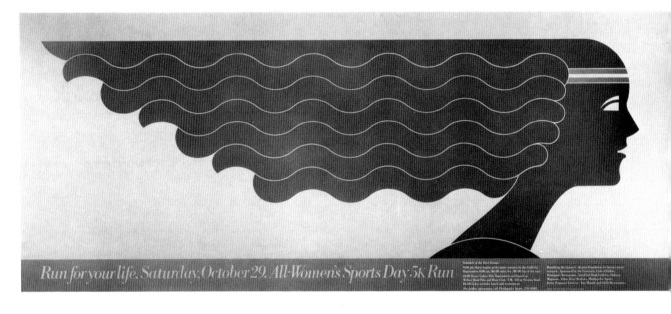

762		763	
Art Director	**Ethel Kessler**	Art Directors	**Bob Dennard, Glyn Powell**
Designer	**Ethel Kessler**		
Photographer	**Lu Hou-Min**	Designer	**Glyn Powell**
Client	**Smithsonian Institution Traveling Exhibition Service**	Artist	**Glyn Powell**
		Writers	**Liza Orchard, Glyn Powell**
Agency	**Ethel Kessler Design, Washington, DC**	Client	**Susan G. Komen Foundation**
Coordinator	**Andrea Stevens**	Agency	**Dennard Creative, Inc., Dallas**
		Creative Director	**Bob Dennard**

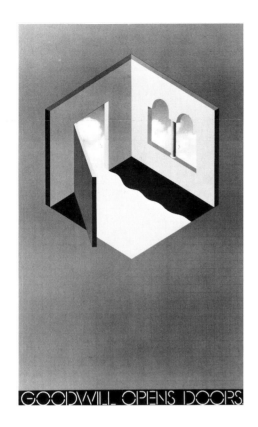

764		765		766	
Art Director	**Alan Lidji**	Art Director	**Chuck Byrne**	Art Director	**James Lienhart**
Designer	**Alan Lidji**	Photographers	**Vince Leo, Kerry Schuss**	Designer	**James Lienhart**
Photographer	**Laynie Lidji**	Client	**The Taft Museum**	Writer	**Jim Carey**
Artist	**Alan Lidji**	Agency	**Colophon, Cincinnati**	Client	**Museum of Science and**
Writer	**Alan Lidji**	Collector	**Chris Steele**		**Industry**
Client	**Goodwill Industries Inc.**			Agency	**James Lienhart Design,**
Agency	**Cunningham & Walsh,**				**Chicago**
	Dallas				
Production					
Director	**Ms. Bobby Larson**				

DOMESTIC ISSUES

BY Corinne Jacker   ADAPTED BY Eve Merriam

WITH
Michael Ayr   Joyce Reehling Christopher   Caroline Kava   Glynnis O'Connor   James Pickens, Jr.   Robert Stattel

Set by David Potts   Costumes by Joan E. Weiss   Lighting by Dennis Parichy
Production Stage Manager Jody Boese   Sound by Chuck London Media/Stewart Werner

March 2   April 3

767

Art Director	**Robert Petrick, Rochester, NY**
Designer	**Robert Petrick**
Photographer	**Ron Wu**
Client	**Circle Repertory Co.**
Marketing Director	**Tom Thompson, Circle Repertory Co.**

768

Art Director	**Paul Black**
Designers	**Paul Black, Ellen Hales**
Artist	**Paul Black**
Writer	**Paul Black**
Client	**Eastfield College**
Agency	**Hale/Black Design, Dallas**

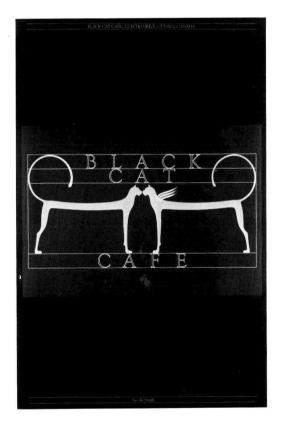

<table>
<tr><td colspan="2">769</td><td colspan="2">770</td></tr>
</table>

769		770	
Art Director	Glenn Dady	Art Director	Neville Smith
Photographer	Dennis Murphy	Designer	Neville Smith
Writer	Melinda Marcus	Client	Black Cat Cafe
Client	Dallas Area Rapid Transit (DART)	Design Firm	Neville Smith Graphic Design, Ottawa
Agency	The Richards Group, Dallas	Screen Printing	Viki Ball, Ottawa
Production Manager	Martin Bybee		

771		772		773	
Art Director	Stephen Frykholm	Designers	B.J. Krivanek,	Art Director	Lila Sternglass
Designer	Stephen Frykholm		R. Christine Hershey	Designer	Seymour Chwast
Artist	Stephen Frykholm	Photographer	Rick Brian	Artist	Seymour Chwast
Client	Herman Miller, Inc.	Writer	Victoria Miller	Writer	Art Winters
Agency	Herman Miller, Inc.,	Client	Art Directors Club of	Client	New York City Opera
	Zeeland, MI		Los Angeles	Agency	Rumrill Hoyt
Printer	Continental	Studios	B.J. Krivanek Art &		Advertising, New York
	Identification Products		Design, Los Angeles,		
			Hershey Dale &		
			Associates		
		Stylist	Barry Curtis		

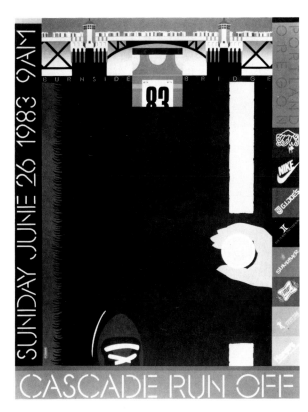

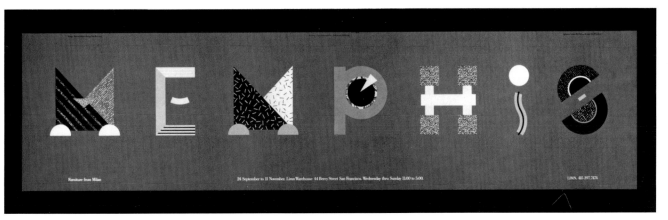

774	775	776
Art Director **Pam Conboy**	Art Director **Ann Marra, Portland**	Art Director **Michael Mabry**
Writer **Luke Sullivan**	Artist **Ann Marra**	Designer **Michael Mabry**
Client **Radisson Hotel Corporation**	Client **Cascade Run Off**	Artists **Michael Mabry, Peter Soe**
Agency **Bozell & Jacobs, Inc., Minneapolis**	Agency **Bowler & Associates**	Client **LIMN**
		Agency **Michael Mabry Design, San Francisco**

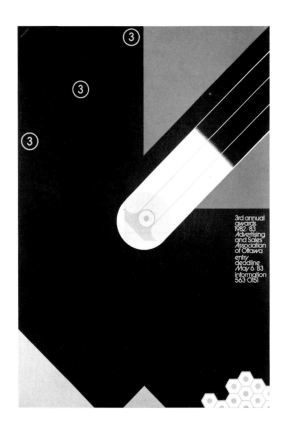

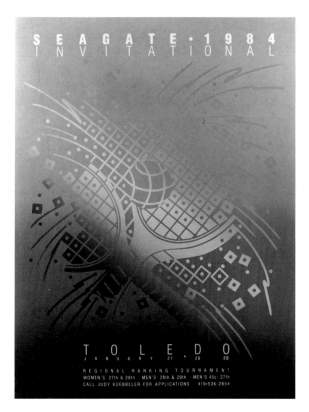

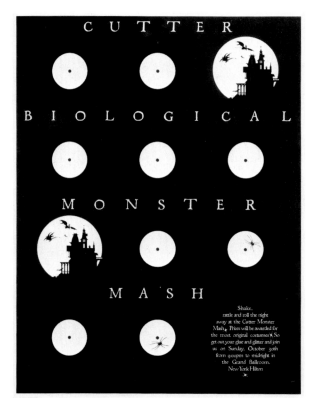

777

Art Director   **Neville Smith**
Designer   **Neville Smith**
Client   **The Advertising and Sales Association of Ottawa '83**
Design Firm   **Neville Smith Graphic Design, Ottawa**
Screen Printing   **Viki Ball, Ottawa**

778

Art Director   **Vyto Bendoraitis**
Designer   **Vyto Bendoraitis**
Artist   **Vyto Bendoraitis**
Client   **Seagate Platform Tennis Association**
Agency   **Fahlgren & Ferriss, Toledo, OH**

779

Art Director   **David Frank**
Designer   **Julie Loane**
Artist   **David FeBland**
Writer   **Marietta Abrams**
Client   **Cutter Biological**
Editor   **Wilma Sharken**
Agency   **Gross Townsend Frank, Inc., New York**
Production Manager   **David Brune**

780

Art Director **Stephen Frykholm**
Designer **Stephen Frykholm**
Artist **Stephen Frykholm**
Client **Tulip Time Festival**
Agency **Herman Miller, Inc.,
Zeeland, MI**
Printer **Continental
Identification Products**

781

Art Director **Andrew Kner**
Designer **Andrew Kner**
Artist **Bill Nelson**
Writer **Louise Francke**
Client **The New York Times**
Publisher **The New York Times,
New York**

THE DAY AFTER ...beyond imagining

An ABC Theatre Production On The ABC Television Network • November 20, 1983 • 8:00 p.m. EST

H O T

The Salty Seventh WHALE Auction

Saturday, March 26th, 10:00 A.M.

Champagne Preview

782

Art Director **Ken Petreeti**
Designer **Martha Grossmann**
Artist **Richard Hess**
Client **ABC Visual Communication, New York**

783

Art Directors **Linda Eissler, Arthur Eisenberg, Dallas**
Designer **Linda Eissler**
Photographer **John Katz**
Writer **Linda Eissler**
Client **Uncle Tai's Chinese Restaurant**
Agency **The Cherri Oakley Company**

784

Art Director **Tom Corey**
Designer **Tom Corey**
Client **Waterfront Historical Area League**
Design Firm **Corey & Company: Designers, Boston**

785	
Art Director	**John Jay**
Designer	**Michael Doret**
Artist	**Michael Doret**
Client	**Le Train Bleu Restaurant**
Publisher	**ProCreations Publishing Company**
Agency	**Michael Doret, Inc., New York**
Printer	**George C. Miller & Son, Inc.**

786	
Art Director	**A. Doyle Moore**
Artist	**Shozo Sato**
Client	**Krannert Center for Performing Arts**
Publisher	**Oren Johnson, Printer**
Agency	**School of Art and Design, University of Illinois, Champaign**
Typographer	**4C Typography**

Hartford Symphony Orchestra
40th Anniversary Season 1983~84

Arthur Winograd,
Music Director

Thanks to
United Technologies
for this poster

VM · THE WAVE OF THE FUTURE

787

Art Director	**Peter Good**
Designer	**Peter Good**
Artists	**Janet Good & various**
Clients	**Hartford Symphony Orchestra, United Technologies**
Design Firm	**Peter Good Graphic Design, Chester, CT**

788

Art Director	**Brenda Kilmer**
Designer	**Brenda Kilmer**
Client	**Zaisan**
Publisher	**Specialty Press**
Design Firm	**Kilmer Design, Houston**

789

Art Director	**Judy Kirpich**
Artist	**Bradley O. Pomeroy**
Client	**VM Software**
Agency	**Grafik Communications, Ltd., Alexandria, VA**

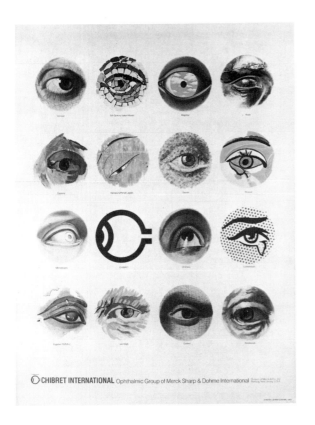

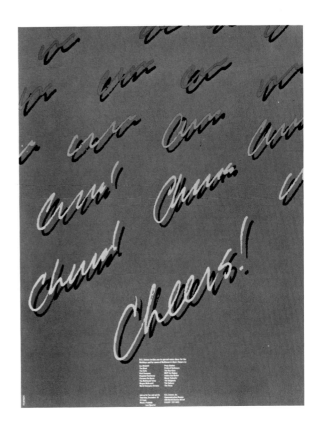

790

Art Director **Arthur Ludwig**
Artist **William Teason**
Clients **Merck Sharp & Dohme Int'l., Chibret Int'l Division**
Agency **Sudler & Hennessey, Inc., New York**

791

Art Director **Robert J. Rytter**
Designer **Robert J. Rytter, Scott Markman**
Client **R.S. Jensen, Inc.**
Agency **R.S. Jensen, Inc., Baltimore**
Printer **Britannia, Ltd.**

792

Art Director **Bill Heatley**
Photographer **Al Satterwhite**
Writer **Rob Feakins**
Agency **Ted Bates Advertising, New York**

793		794		795	
Art Director	**Christopher Garland**	Art Director	**Keith Bright**	Art Director	**Pier Anselmo**
Artist	**David Csicsko**	Designer	**Doug Johnson**	Designer	**Pier Anselmo**
Client	**Barry Bursak, City**	Artist	**Doug Johnson**	Artist	**Pier Anselmo**
Design Firm	**Xeno, Chicago**	Client	**Holland America**	Client	**SIN Television Network,**
Printer	**P & A Century Graphics**	Agency	**Bright & Associates,**		**New York**
			Los Angeles		

796		797		798	
Art Director	**David G. Foote**	Art director	**Peter Good**	Art Director	**Colin Forbes**
Artist	**Steven Tarantel**	Designer	**Peter Good**	Designer	**Colin Forbes**
Client	**U.S. Postal Service, Washington, DC**	Photographer	**David Hays**	Client	**Simpson Paper**
		Artist	**Peter Good**	Agency	**Cross Associates**
		Writer	**David Hays**	Design Firm	**Pentagram Design, Ltd., New York**
		Client	**National Theatre of the Deaf, IBM**		
		Design Firm	**Peter Good Graphic Design, Chester, CT**		

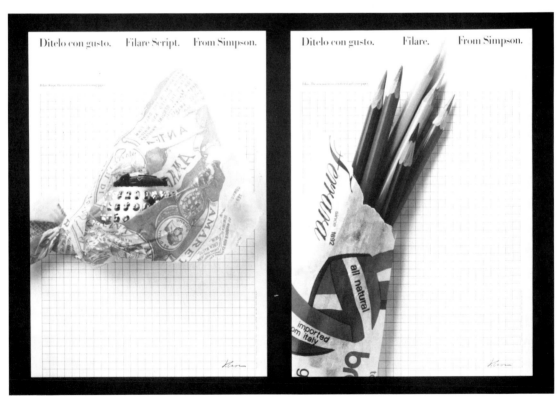

	799		**800**
Art Director	**Woody Pirtle**	Art Director	**James Cross**
Designers	**Alan Colvin, Woody Pirtle**	Designer	**James Cross**
Photographers	**Joe Baraban, Arthur Meyerson**	Photographer	**Michael Going**
Artist	**Alan Colvin**	Client	**Simpson Paper Company**
Client	**Houston Chapter/AIA**	Agency	**Cross Associates, Los Angeles**
Publisher	**Houston Chapter/AIA**	Printer	**Anderson Lithograph**
Agency	**Pirtle Design, Dallas/ Taylor Brown & Barnhill**		

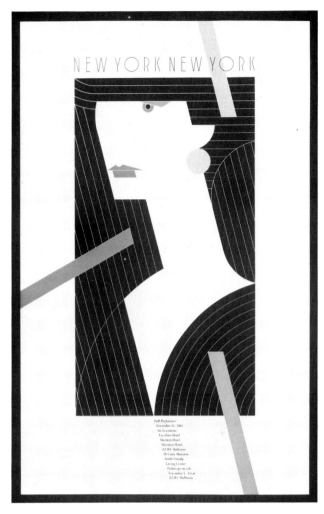

	801
Art Directors	**Gene Bramson, Harold Burch**
Designers	**Gene Bramson, Doug Brotherton**
Artist	**Charles Pigg**
Client	**M. David Paul & Associates**
Agency	**Bramson & Associates, Los Angeles**

	802
Art Director	**McRay Magleby**
Designer	**McRay Magleby**
Photographer	**McRay Magleby**
Writer	**McRay Magleby**
Client	**Brigham Young University, Provo, UT**
Agency	**Graphic Communications**

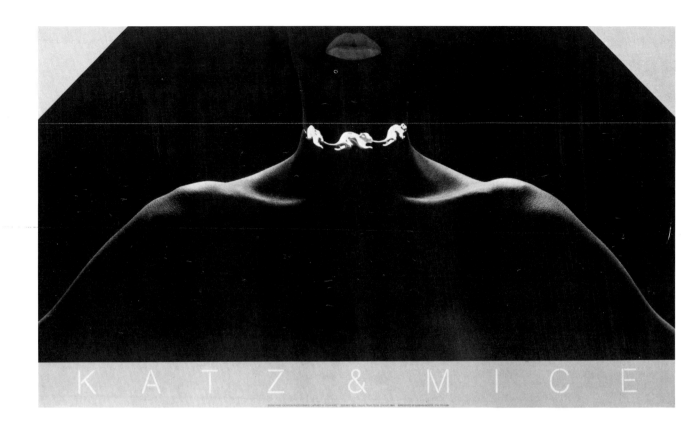

K A T Z & M I C E

803

Art Director	Woody Pirtle
Designer	Woody Pirtle
Photographer	John Katz
Artist	Ken Shafer
Writer	Woody Pirtle
Client	John Katz Photography
Publisher	John Katz
Agency	Pirtle Design, Dallas

804

Art Director	Lowell Williams
Designers	Lowell Williams, Bill Carson
Artist	Heather Cooper
Clients	Cadillac Fairview, Texas Eastern, Zoological Society of Houston
Agency	Lowell Williams Design Inc., Houston

805		806		807	
Art Director	**Robert Blue**	Art Director	**Woody Pirtle**	Art Director	**Micheal Richards**
Artist	**Brian Davis**	Designer	**Woody Pirtle**	Designers	**Micheal Richards, Bill Swensen**
Client	**The Huntington Museum Library**	Artist	**David Kampa**	Artists	**Bill Swensen, Micheal Richards, Scott Greer**
Design Firm	**Davis-Blue Artwork, Inc., Culver City, CA**	Client	**Tango/Shannon Wynne**	Writers	**Joan Levy, Polly Richman**
Printers	**Gore Graphics**	Publisher	**Shannon Wynne**	Client	**Univ. of Utah Division of Continuing Education, Salt Lake City**
		Agency	**Pirtle Design, Dallas**		
		Type Designer	**Mike Schroeder**		

808		809	
Art Director	**David Bartels**	Art Directors	**Scott Eggers, Ron Sullivan**
Artist	**Alex Murawski**		
Client	**Bruce Bendinger**	Designer	**Scott Eggers**
Design Firm	**Bartels & Company, Inc., St. Louis**	Photographer	**Andy Post**
		Writer	**Scott Dytch**
Lettering &		Client	**The Rouse Company**
Mechanical	**Michael Simpson**	Agency	**Richards, Brock, Miller, Mitchell-The Richards Group, Dallas**
		Printer	**Brodnax Printing**

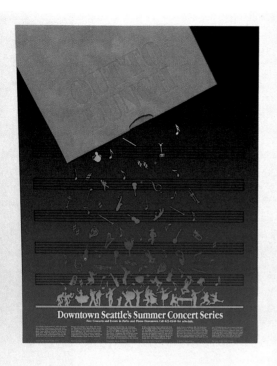

SILVER AWARD

810

Art Director	**Jack Anderson**
Designers	**Cliff Chung, John Hornall**
Artist	**Nancy Gellos**
Client	**Downtown Seattle Association**
Agency	**John Hornall Design Works, Seattle**

DISTINCTIVE MERIT

811		812		812A	
Art Director	Pat Burnham	Art Director	Joel Goldstein	Art Director	Bob Kwait
Designer	Pat Burnham	Designer	Joel Goldstein	Designer	Ron VanBuskirk
Artist	Charlie Brown	Photographers	Michael Pateman,	Artist	Darrel Millsap
Writer	Mike Lescarbeau		Frank Whitney (Image	Writer	Bob Kwait
Client	Control Data		Bank), Dick Durrance	Client	San Diego Zoo
	Corporation		II	Agency	Phillips-Ramsey, San
Agency	Fallon McElligott Rice,	Writer	Tim Fenton		Diego
	Minneapolis	Client	Todd Middleton/Avis		
		Agency	McCaffrey and McCall,		
			Inc., New York		
		Account			
		Executive	Sam Fertig		

THOUSANDS OF STARS PERFORMING DAILY.

The Minneapolis Planetarium
300 Nicollet Mall Phone 372-6644

DON'T LET THIS BE YOUR KID'S ONLY VIEW OF OUTER SPACE.

The Minneapolis Planetarium
300 Nicollet Mall Phone 372-6644

AN EXPERIENCE OF ASTRONOMICAL PROPORTIONS.

The Minneapolis Planetarium
300 Nicollet Mall Phone 372-6644

DISTINCTIVE MERIT

813

Art Director	**Bob Barrie, Richfield, MN**
Designer	**Bob Barrie**
Artist	**Bob Barrie**
Writer	**Jim Newcombe**
Client	**Minneapolis Planetarium**
Agency	**Advertising Au Gratin**

Most people don't recognize diabetes when they see it.

Blurred vision is one of the symptoms of diabetes. And it's not a sign to ignore.

Diabetes is a very serious disease that can lead to blindness. Heart attacks. And kidney failure.

Diabetes can also lead to death. In fact, it's the third largest killer disease in the United States.

The American Diabetes Association is trying to change all this. We offer programs to help people understand this complex disease. And deal with it effectively.

We also support vital research that gives not only hope of better treatment. But the promise of bringing the cure for diabetes into sharp focus.

To learn more, please contact your local chapter of the American Diabetes Association.

△ American Diabetes Association.
Help for today. Hope for tomorrow.

GOLD AWARD

814

Art Director   **Dave Martin**
Photographers   **Gary Hanlon, Jim McLoughlin**
Writer   **Pete Faulkner**
Client   **American Diabetes Association**
Agency   **Doyle Dane Bernbach Inc., New York**

da Vinci

"**F**or
the price of your last supper, you could
join the art museum."

"**A**rt
appreciation can make you a bigger person.
Join the Milwaukee Art Museum."

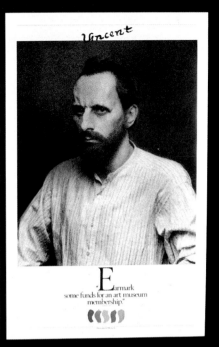

Vincent

"**E**armark
some funds for an art museum
membership."

SILVER AWARD

——— 815 ———

Art Director	**Rachel J. Stephens**
Photographers	**Peter Amft, Don Wilson**
Writers	**Robin Reynolds, Kirk Ruhnke**
Client	**Milwaukee Art Museum**
Agency	**Frankenberry, Laughlin & Constable, Milwaukee**

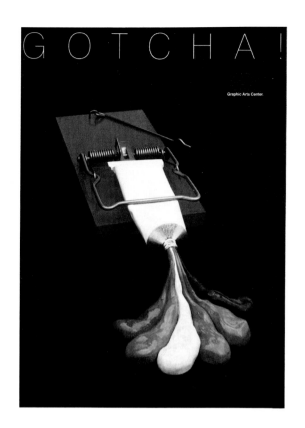

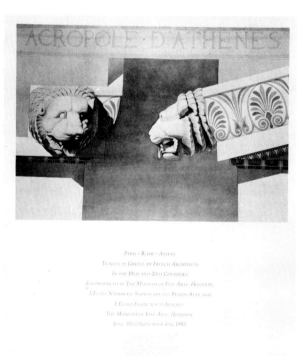

816		817		818	
Art Director	Frank Roehr	Art Director	Don Sibley	Art Director	Amy Werfel
Designer	Frank Roehr	Designer	Don Sibley	Designer	Amy Werfel
Photographer	Ed Dull	Artists	Don Sibley, Rex Peteet	Writers	Larry Sisson, Barry Wells
Writer	JoAnn Lunt	Client	Dallas Theater Center	Client	Linbeck Construction
Client	Graphic Arts Center	Design Firm	Sibley/Peteet Design, Inc., Dallas	Agency	Robert A. Wilson Assoc. Inc., Dallas
Agency	Young & Roehr, Inc., Portland				

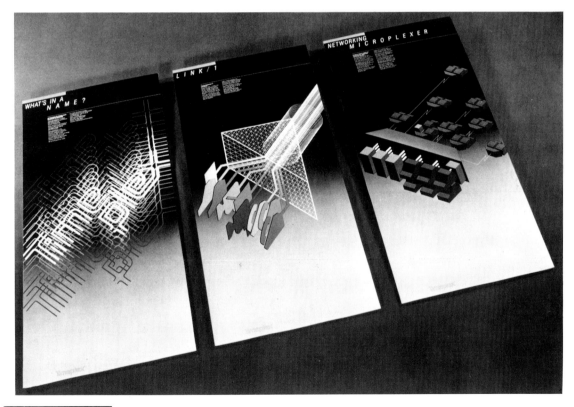

DISTINCTIVE MERIT

819

Art Director	**McRay Magleby**
Designer	**McRay Magleby**
Artist	**McRay Magleby**
Writer	**Norman A. Darias**
Client	**Brigham Young University, Provo, UT**
Agency	**Graphic Communications**

820

Art Director	**Cooper/Copeland, Inc., Atlanta**
Designer	**M.C. Akers**
Photographers	**various**
Writers	**various**
Client	**Turner Broadcasting System/Vivian Lawand**
Agency	**Turner Broadcasting System**

821

Art Director	**Lou Fiorentino**
Designer	**Russ Tatro**
Artists	**Marty Gilsenberg, Yuri Yarmolinsky**
Client	**Timeplex, Inc.**
Agency	**Muir Cornelius Moore, New York**

SILVER AWARD

822

Art Director   **Tyler Smith,**
           Providence, RI
Designer   **Tyler Smith**
Photographers   **Ira Garber, Clint**
           Clemens, Kurt Stier
Writer   **Gail Welch**
Client   **National Bickford**
           Foremost Printers

SILVER AWARD

823

Art Director	**McRay Magleby**
Designer	**McRay Magleby**
Artist	**McRay Magleby**
Writer	**Norman A. Darias**
Client	**Brigham Young University, Provo, UT**
Agency	**Graphic Communications**

824		825	
Art Director	Chris Blum	Art Director	David Gauger
Artists	Brain Honkawa, Kinuko	Designer	Mary Rudnicki Orr
	Craft, Sahara Claire	Photographers	George Lowe, John
Client	Levi Strauss		Horvers, Gordon
Agency	Foote, Cone & Belding,		Wittsie, Galen Rowell
	San Francisco	Artists	Marge Clennon, Jeanne
			Kimmel
		Writers	S. Goldstein, D. Gauger,
			M. Rudnicki Orr
		Client	Sierra Designs
		Agency	Gauger Sparks Silva,
			Inc., San Francisco
		Printer	Dai Nippon

826		827	
Art Director	**Jud Smith**	Art Director	**Lowell Williams**
Photographer	**Steve Umland**	Designers	**Lowell Williams, Bill Carson**
Writer	**Tom Van Steenhoven**	Artist	**Tom McNeff**
Client	**Polaris Industries Inc.**	Writer	**Pat Harris**
Agency	**Carmichael-Lynch, Minneapolis**	Client	**Gerald D. Hines Interests**
		Agency	**Lowell Williams Design, Inc., Houston**

ART/ILLUSTRATION/PHOTOGRAPHY

Malcolm End
Tony Gill
Jean Govoni
Brian Harrod
Thom Higgins
Lawrence Miller
Seymon Ostilly
Elissa Querze
Richard Radke
Bob Reitzfeld
Marion Sackett
Bob Wilvers
Tom Wolsey
Mary Baumann
Robert Best
Mike Brock
Bill Cadge
Frank DeVino
Paul Hardy
Kristina Jorgensen
David Levy
Frank Rothmann
Neil Shakery
Lou Silverstein
Melissa Tardiff
Adrian Taylor

Pete Turner
Rodney Williams
Tony Cappiello
Robert Cipriani
Molly Epstein
Blanche Fiorenza
Dick Hess
Chris Hill
Nigel Holmes
Elizabeth Kim
Norma Kwan
Geoffrey Moss
Susan Niles
Jerry Philips
Woody Pirtle
Sherry Pollack
Brenda Preis
Chuck Queener
Robert Reed
Bennett Robinson
Anthony Russell
James Sebastian
Dugald Stermer
John Vogler
Ken White
Cynthia Wojdyla

828

Art Director	**Jerelle Kraus**
Designer	**Jerelle Kraus**
Artist	**Marshall Arisman**
Writer	**A.J.P. Taylor**
Client	**The New York Times**
Editor	**Robert Semple**
Publisher	**The New York Times, New York**
Publication	**The New York Times Op-Ed page**

829

Art Director	**Jerelle Kraus**
Designer	**Jerelle Kraus**
Artist	**Brad Holland**
Writer	**Zbigniew Brzezinski**
Client	**The New York Times**
Editor	**Robert Semple**
Publisher	**The New York Times, New York**
Publication	**The New York Times Op-Ed page**

830

Art Director	**Jerelle Kraus**
Designer	**Jerelle Kraus**
Artist	**Jerelle Kraus**
Client	**The New York Times**
Editor	**Bob Semple**
Publisher	**The New York Times, New York**
Publication	**The New York Times**

A STROKE AHEAD OF THE REST

CATCH OF THE DAY

831

Art Director **Thomas Corcoran**
Artist **Vladimir Kordic**
Client **Thomas B. Thomas**
Agency **Busch Creative Services Corp., St. Louis**
Production **Gary Kodner**

832

Art Director **Thomas Graves**
Designer **Thomas Corcoran**
Artist **Donald L. Kueker**
Client **Thomas B. Thomas**
Agency **Busch Creative Services Corp., St. Louis**
Production **Ken Froeschner**

SILVER AWARD

833

Art Director	**Frank C. Lionetti**
Designers	**Frank C. Lionetti, Diane McNamee, Condict Freeman**
Artist	**Braldt Bralds**
Writer	**Ciaran McCabe**
Client	**Trefoil Development Company**
Agency	**Frank C. Lionetti Design, Old Greenwich, CT**
Publication	**Real Estate Forum**

ASSETS

Freshly baked hot kuchen and the Wall Street Journal at breakfast each morning.
Mouth watering desserts prepared daily. At the Marten House we're justly proud of our cooking.
And our relaxed, pleasant surroundings add to your meals; from our bright Bluebird coffee shop, to the
rich luxury of Sir John Sexton's, one of Indianapolis' premier restaurants. Enjoy before dinner drinks
in the brass and wood 1890's atmosphere of our Gondola Vista lounge. For business guests, our
Professional Lounge serves food and drink in the distinctive atmosphere of an English Gentlemen's
club. Wherever you dine with us, you can taste the care we put into every meal.

marten house

More personal than a hotel. The Marten House.

1801 West 86th Street • Indianapolis, Indiana 46260 • On Indianapolis' Northside near St. Vincent's Hospital
Call toll free 800-428-1235 • In Indiana, 800-732-1375 • In Indianapolis, 872-4111

SILVER AWARD

834

Art Director	**Dawn Keller**
Designer	**Dawn Keller**
Artist	**Mark Braught, Terre Haute, IN**
Writer	**Siobhan Magee**
Client	**Marten House**
Agency	**Caldwell-Van Riper**

835

Art Director **Peggy McDaniel**
Designer **Peggy McDaniel**
Artist **Ed Lindlof, Austin**
Client **Gary L. Cutsinger
Company**
Agency **The Hinckley Group**

836

Art Director **Warren Weilbacher**
Artist **Gary Viscupic**
Writer **Dan Cryer**
Client **Newsday Books**
Editor **Nina King**
Publisher **Newsday, Inc.,
Melville, NY**
Director of
Design **Paul Back**

Stands head and antlers above the rest.

IMPORTED MOOSEHEAD. BREWED BY CANADA'S OLDEST INDEPENDENT FAMILY BREWERY.

Without teamwork, nothing works.

Teamwork is the reason why Showtime is the country's second largest pay TV network.

By working closely with our affiliates, we have developed some of the most revolutionary programming and marketing ideas in the industry.

Our team effort began when we introduced the concept of multi-pay marketing and then developed Core Packaging to help make it more profitable for our affiliates.

And over the years, we have been first to respond to their need

for bold, new, innovative programming. In fact, we were the first pay network to offer made-for-pay movies, continuing dramatic series, Broadway shows and comedy series.

And when our affiliates need us, we're there with sophisticated and effective marketing materials, support programs and a responsive regional staff, ready to adapt to the ever changing multi-pay environment.

Showtime is committed to teamwork, because it works. Join us!

All eyes turn for SHOWTIME

RECORDS

Randy Newman: sourpuss in utopia

TROUBLE IN PARADISE
RANDY NEWMAN
Warner Bros.
★★★★

BY CHRISTOPHER CONNELLY

837		838		839

837
Art Director — Jim Clarke
Artist — Birney Lettick
Writer — Richard Wagman
Client — All Brand Importers
Agency — The Bloom Agency, New York
Creative Director — Stuart Bresner

838
Art Director — Paul Lepelletier
Artist — Guy Billout
Writer — Glen Bentley
Agency — Benton & Bowles, New York
Group Head — Graham Griffiths

839
Art Director — Derek Ungless
Designer — Steven Doyle
Artist — Tom Woodruff
Publication — Rolling Stone Magazine, New York

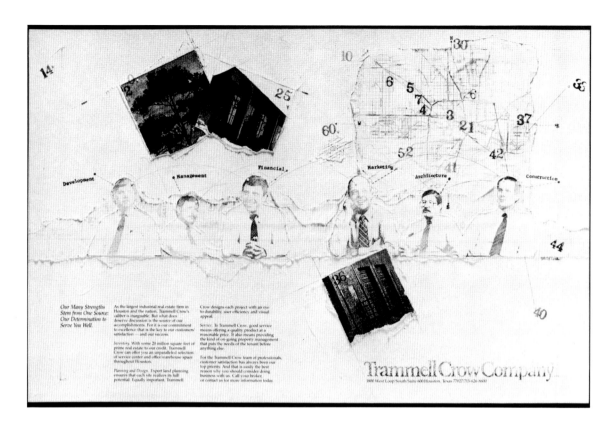

Our Many Strengths Stem from One Source: Our Determination to Serve You Well.

As the largest industrial real estate firm in Houston and the nation, Trammell Crow's caliber is inarguable. But what does deserve discussion is the source of our accomplishments. For it is our commitment to excellence that is the key to our customers' satisfaction — and our success.

Inventory. With some 20 million square feet of prime real estate to our credit, Trammell Crow can offer you an unparalleled selection of service center and office/warehouse space throughout Houston.

Planning and Design. Expert land planning ensures that each site realizes its full potential. Equally important, Trammell

Crow designs each project with an eye to durability, user efficiency and visual appeal.

Service. To Trammell Crow, good service means offering a quality product at a reasonable price. It also means providing the kind of on-going property management that puts the needs of the tenant before anything else.

For the Trammell Crow team of professionals, customer satisfaction has always been our top priority. And that is easily the best reason why you should consider doing business with us. Call your broker, or contact us for more information today.

Trammell Crow Company

1800 West Loop South Suite 600 Houston, Texas 77027/713-626-8600

THIS TICKER TAPE DESERVES A SPECIAL CELEBRATION. ONE FROM THE HEART.

Some of the things we're doing in cardiology these days would have been considered miracles not that long ago.

Like coronary transluminal angioplasty — a simple procedure that uses a catheter with a balloon-like tip to destroy life-threatening obstructions in the heart's vessels. It can sometimes spare a seriously ill patient the trauma and expense of open heart surgery.

Or a "wonder drug" enzyme that dissolves clots almost instantly. For some patients, a timely injection of streptokinase can arrest damage to the heart muscle.

And a computerized imaging lab that offers safe, painless, and very accurate ways of viewing and diagnosing heart conditions.

Still, with all our technology, nothing *we* can do is as important as one thing *you* can do: if you experience any kind of heart problem, *seek medical attention immediately.* Because in matters of the heart, every second counts.

STATE OF THE HEART CARE.

MORTON F. PLANT HOSPITAL

323 Jeffords Street · Clearwater, FL 33517 · 813-461-8000

840		841	
Art Director	**Karen Abney**	Art Director	**Lisa Hill**
Artist	**David Lesh, Indianapolis**	Artist	**Lisa Hill**
Client	**Trammel Crow Inc.**	Writer	**Nora Minor**
Agency	**Diane Butler & Associates**	Client	**Morton F. Plant Hospital**
		Agency	**Wood + Cohen, Tampa, Fl**

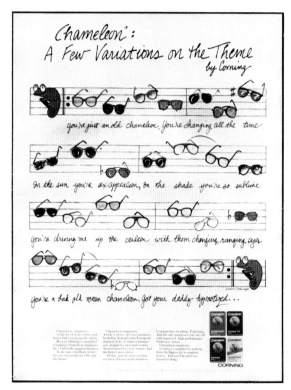

SILVER AWARD

842	843	844
Art Director **Cody Newman Calhoun**	Art Director **Curt Chuvalas**	Art Director **Meredith Spenser**
Designer **Cody Newman Calhoun**	Designer **Curt Chuvalas**	Artist **Doris Ettlinger**
Artist **Ed Lindlof, Austin**	Artist **Mark Braught, Terre**	Writer **David Liemer**
Client **Spring Creek**	**Haute, IN**	Client **Corning Glass Works**
Investments	Client **Indianapolis Parks &**	Agency **Foote, Cone & Belding,**
Agency **Rosenberg & Company**	**Recreation**	**New York**

845		846	
Art Director	**Dick Henderson**	Art Director	**Jeffrey Walker**
Designers	**Dick Henderson, Alan E. Cober**	Designer	**Michael Schwab**
		Artist	**Michael Schwab**
Artist	**Alan E. Cober, Ossining, NY**	Client	**Wilkes Bashford**
		Agency	**Michael Schwab Design, San Francisco**
Client	**Fox River Valley Adv. Assoc.**		

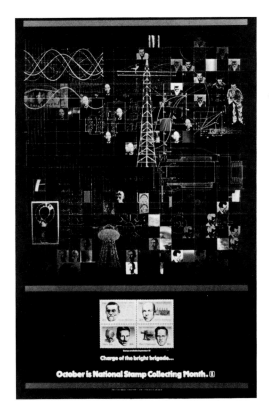

847

Art Director   **David G. Foote**
Designer   **Terrence W. McCaffrey**
Artist   **Jerry Pinkney**
Client   **U.S. Postal Service,
Washington, DC**

848

Art Director   **David G. Foote**
Artist   **Fred Otnes**
Client   **U.S. Postal Service,
Washington, DC**

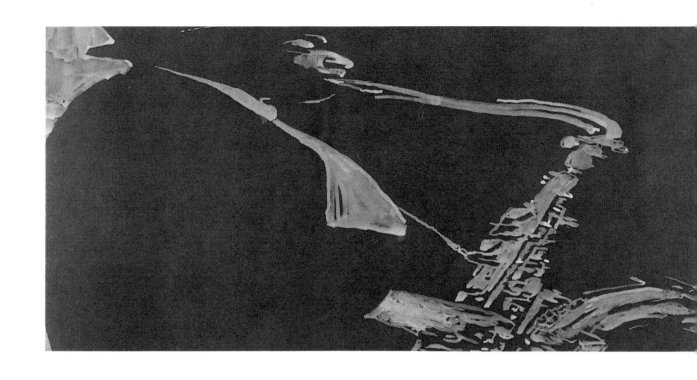

SILVER AWARD

849

Art Director   **Glenn Batkin, N. White Plains, NY**
Artist   **Glenn Batkin**
Client   **Lord, Geller, Federico, Einstein**
Editor   **Yvette Hill**

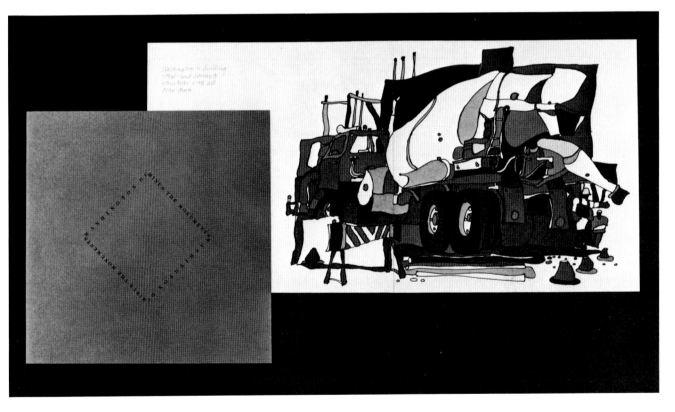

850

Art Directors	**Bill Nelson, C. Randall Sherman**
Designer	**C. Randall Sherman**
Artist	**Bill Nelson**
Writer	**Don Pierce**
Client	**Palmer Paper Co.**
Agency	**Loucks Atelier Inc., Houston**

851

Art Director	**Andrew Kner**
Designer	**Emil Micha**
Artist	**William Low**
Client	**The New York Times**
Publisher	**The New York Times, New York**

852

Art Directors	**Michael David Brown, Kathleen Wilmes Herring**
Designer	**Kathleen Wilmes Herring, Michael David Brown**
Artist	**Michael David Brown, Rockville, MD**
Client	**MDB Communications**

EYE TO EYE WITH MR. T

*we went after america's latest cultural phenom with a simple
question—what's going on here, anyway?*

By D. KEITH MANO

A TASTE FOR THE LATIN

BY · IRENE · FISCHL

853

Art Director	**Tom Staebler**
Designer	**Skip Williamson**
Artist	**Brad Holland**
Writer	**D. Keith Mano**
Client	**Playboy Magazine**
Editor	**Jim Morgan**
Publisher	**Playboy Enterprises, Inc., Chicago**
Publication	**Playboy Magazine**

854

Art Directors	**Janet Froelich, Thomas P. Ruis**
Artist	**Marcos Oksenhendler**
Client	**New York Sunday News Magazine, New York**

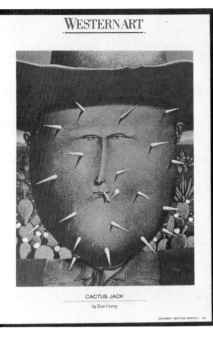

WESTERN ART

CACTUS JACK
by Tom Curry

WESTERN ART

STAMPEDE
by Marshall Arisman

WESTERN ART

RAWHIDE
by José Cruz

APRIL 1983   THE ATLANTIC MONTHLY   PAGE 87

TIME LINE   BY GUY BILLOUT

855

Art Director	Fred Woodward
Designer	David Kampa
Artists	Marshall Arisman, Jose Cruz, Tom Curry
Client	Texas Monthly
Editor	Greg Curtis
Publisher	Texas Monthly, Inc., Austin
Publication	Texas Monthly

856

Art Director	Judy Garlan
Artist	Guy Billout
Editor	William Whitworth
Publisher	The Atlantic Monthly Co., Boston
Publication	The Atlantic Monthly

THE RUSH TO DEREGULATE

Government is unraveling an entire skein of health and safety protections.

By Martin Tolchin and Susan J. Tolchin

THE EVIDENCE WAS CLEAR. Thousands of infants had suffered convulsions and brain damage when they were fed commercial formulas lacking essential nutrients. Congress reacted by adopting the Infant Formula Act of 1980, and the Food and Drug Administration promptly proposed stringent rules to enforce the law. In 1981, however, the newly installed Reagan Administration delayed those regulations, studied the matter for 18 months (during which time three million cans of flawed formula were sold) and finally produced a new set of rules. According to Jim Greene, a spokesman for the F.D.A., the new standards meet "all the requirements needed to protect the consumer." According to a staff report prepared for the Oversight Subcommittee of the House Energy and Commerce Committee, the new rules "adopted, virtually in every respect, the suggestions of the infant-formula industry to relax the proposed rules and add 'flexibility.'"

Representative Albert Gore Jr., Democrat of Tennessee and author of the original legislation, believes that the revised rules are so flexible that dangerous products can still be marketed. "This Administration's No. 1 priority," he says, "is to make certain that no industry is in any way displeased or even slightly disconcerted by any action of Government."

Only recently, in the wake of the scandal over the Environmental Protection Agency (E.P.A.), has the public begun to glimpse the depth and scope of President Reagan's deregulation initiative — the most comprehensive overhaul of the regulatory process in the history of the republic. The goal is to reduce Government involvement in business, leaving the free market free so that American business can produce a new age of prosperity. But deregulation's most dramatic result has been the dangerous unraveling of an entire skein of health, safety and other citizen protections that has been decades in the making.

At the Occupational Safety and Health Administration (OSHA), for example, the number of inspections of workplaces dropped 17 percent in the first two years of the Reagan Administration, and the penalties levied on companies plummeted 78 per-

Martin Tolchin reports on Congress for The New York Times. Susan J. Tolchin, his wife, is Professor of Public Administration, George Washington University. This article is adapted from "Dismantling America — The Rush to Deregulate," to be published this fall by Houghton Mifflin.

cent. At the Department of Agriculture, regulations were rescinded that required labels stating that pulverized tissue, bone and bone marrow were used in processed meats such as frankfurters. ("A little bit of bone or whatever you're going to get isn't going to hurt you in the least," says John McClung of the agency's Food Safety and Inspection Service. "The industry argued that the label was so frightening to consumers that they wouldn't buy the product.")

Some aspects of this regulatory overhaul have become familiar: the trims in agency budgets, for instance, that have forced program cutbacks; or the appointments to key agency posts of people hostile to the mission of their agencies. What has escaped general notice has been the primary means to the President's deregulatory ends: He has elevated the Office of Management and Budget (O.M.B.) to the position of chief regulator, challenging Congress's traditional influence over the agencies and the independence of the agencies themselves. Deregulation has been achieved, not by obtaining the repeal or revision of the laws on which the regulations were based, but by administrative fiat.

During recent months, the constitutional issues raised by this approach to regulation have been addressed in decisions by the United States Supreme Court and lower Federal courts. And O.M.B.'s resounding success — the wholesale reduction in regulations that protect the environment and the public's health and safety — may be a campaign issue in the Presidential election next year.

THE FOUNDING FATHERS gave Congress jurisdiction over commerce, and as the nation industrialized, it was Congress that created regulatory agencies, primarily to protect the interest of the business community. As a result of the consumer and environmental movements of the late 1960's, Congress set up three new agencies — the E.P.A., OSHA and the Consumer Product Safety Commission — and strengthened the powers of many other regulatory agencies. The goal was to protect the public and the worker in seeking safe workplaces, safe products and a healthy environment. One result was to increase the power of Congress and the agency bureaucrats over social policy, at the expense of the White House.

The foundation for the Reagan Administration's reversal of that situation was laid by Jimmy Carter. Confronted by a spiraling inflation rate, President Carter listened to those who insisted that regulations were a major cause of higher prices. (A steel company required to improve the air-quality equipment in its plant, for example, would simply

add that extra cost to the price it charged for girders.) In 1978, he issued Executive Order 12044, improving Government Regulations, and soon thereafter created the Regulatory Analysis Review Group, the first significant attempt to give the White House power over the day-to-day operations of the regulatory agencies.

Mr. Carter also initiated the extensive use of cost-benefit analysis as a key tool for the assertion of this power, once again providing Mr. Reagan with a precedent he would follow. Cost-benefit analysis seeks to compare the cost of a factory's new air-quality equipment, for example, to the cost of doing without that equipment in terms of the workers' health and the price society would pay for a sustained illness.

It is a much-debated approach. Mark Green, a public-interest advocate, has commented, "The child-labor laws would never have passed a cost-benefit test."

One of the advantages of creating the review group, Carter aides felt, was political: the group would serve as a lightning rod for attacks from those forces angered by deregulation moves. The President himself would be above the fray. These hopes proved false when Mr. Carter tried to relax the standards set by the Department of Labor on the amount of cotton dust permitted in textile plants. The dust causes byssinosis, a serious lung disease. Labor unions and health groups attacked the change as inhumane and the textile industry attacked it as too small a step in the right direction. Eventually the Supreme Court upheld the standards, but meanwhile Mr. Carter backed down and never again intervened directly in a regulatory issue. In the process, he lost some important political capital.

FEW PRESIDENTS HAVE ENtered the White House with more ambitious and well-defined goals than Ronald Reagan. His central objective was to reverse the direction of government, and the scaling back of the regulatory agencies was high on his list.

Some experts thought he could hardly make a dent in the huge bureaucracy, but he was helped by the swing to the right in the country. The public seemed ready for change. What's more, he and his aides had plenty of ammunition in the form of regulatory excesses.

Just as the early agencies such as the Interstate Commerce Commission had favored their corporate constituencies, so had the later agencies such as OSHA become identified with public-interest groups. The new agencies were staffed with men and women who had worked with Ralph Nader and other public-interest advocates, and their zeal —

GOLD AWARD

857

Art Directors	Roger Black, Ken Kendrick
Designer	Ken Kendrick
Artist	Brad Holland
Writers	Martin Tolchin, Susan J. Tolchin
Client	The New York Times
Editor	Ed Klein
Publisher	The New York Times, New York
Publication	The New York Times Magazine

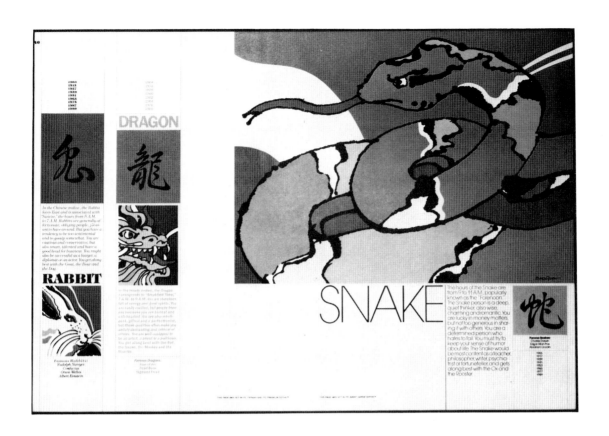

858
Art Director	**Mike Quon, New York**
Designer	**Mike Quon**
Artist	**Mike Quon**
Client	**Mike Quon/Upper & Lower Case**
Publisher	**International Typeface Corp.**
Publication	**U & lc**

859
Art Director	**David M. Seager**
Artist	**Davis Meltzer**
Client	**National Geographic Society, Washington, DC**

<table>
</table>

860		861	
Art Director	David M. Seager	Art Director	Sanae Yamasaki
Artist	Robert Hynes	Artist	Thomas B. Allen,
Client	National Geographic		Lawrence, KS
	Society, Washington,DC	Writer	Frank Deford
		Client	People Magazine

AMERICA'S GLOBAL LIE DETECTOR

As the Russians move troops and equipment and test new weapons, we're watching from space, sky, sea and land.

BY MICHAEL KREPON AND BARRY BLECHMAN; Illustrated by John Berkey

Last September, when the Soviet Union shot down a Korean Air Lines jumbo jet, Japanese and American officials quickly reported the incident in great detail. This information came from intelligence-gathering methods that reconstructed the movements of Russian aircraft and even tapped into the Soviet air-to-ground communications system. By vividly presenting this evidence, an immediate indictment against Russia followed. The Far Eastern network used to reconstruct the fate of the airliner was just part of the worldwide system now in place to protect American security and monitor existing treaty compliance by the Russians. The following article, written by two experts in the field, provides us with non-classified details on how the system works.

Reconnaissance photos taken over a few weeks reveal unusual truck movement into the Soviet missile test

Artist's conception shows Big Bird satellite over the Soviet Union. Satellite takes photos and listens in on Soviet communications. Also shown are TR-1 spy plane and Hawkeye plane with radar dome. A 10-story radar station follows Soviet activities from air-to-sea to land. Similar radar is carried aboard a Navy cruiser.

Ambassador
DECEMBER 1983

STORIES of CHRISTMAS PAST *A Celebration of the Holiday Season, in Words & Pictures*

As is often the case with the compilation of more ordinary Christmas shopping lists, assembling this selection of holiday literature proved a considerable undertaking. Not to put too fine a point on it, there have simply been too many wonderful words written about Christmas, over too great a period of time. Poets and essayists, humorists and short-story writers, novelists and, of course, even little Virginia — all have had their say. ¶ It's our hope that our little Christmas package gives some sense of this, that it conveys a variety of holiday sentiments as they have been expressed by different writers working at different times in different countries and styles. Above all, we hope it appeals to the sentiments of *these* times, and of this special time. Season's greetings.

DECEMBER 1983 TWA AMBASSADOR 33

ILLUSTRATED BY DAGMAR FRINTA

DECEMBER 1983 TWA AMBASSADOR 47

862		863	
Art Director	Bryan Canniff	Art Director	Marcia Wright
Artist	John Berkey	Designer	Marcia Wright
Editor	Dennis Eskow	Artists	Dagmar Frinta, Alexa
Publication	Popular Mechanics, New York		Grace, Steven Guarnaccia, Michael Witte, Andrzej Dudzinski
		Writer	A Collection of Stories
		Client	Trans World Airlines
		Editor	Bonnie Blodgett
		Publisher	Jack Burkam
		Publication	TWA AMBASSADOR Magazine, St. Paul

The Warner Mob

by Neil Hickey and Edward Sorel

With the Depression pushing the studio toward bankruptcy, Warner Brothers had to resort to crime— and crime paid so well that the company was able to recruit the toughest guys that ever shot up a sound stage.

JACK WARNER RAN HIS organization the same way Al Capone ran his ruthlessly. The problem was that, unlike Capone, he couldn't simply wipe out the competition. In 1930 Jack and his two older brothers, Sam and Harry, owned one-quarter of all the movie houses in the United States, plus the Warner Brothers studio and fifty-one subsidiary companies. But their theaters were now frighteningly empty. Millions were out of work, and the novelty of talking pictures, which had started with Warner's Vitaphone process, had lost its drawing power. Warner's profits came crashing down along with the stock market—$14 million in 1929, $7 million in 1930, and losses of $8 million anticipated for 1931.

Jack could not be consoled by the knowledge that other Hollywood studios were in trouble too. MGM was the exception, but MGM's movies had opulent sets, high-key lighting, lush scores, large casts. The Warner assembly line was not equipped to turn out that sort of luxury product. Something else was called for, something fast—and cheap.

The man who would supply it was Darryl F. Zanuck. He had come to Warner's in 1924 to write screenplays for the canine star Rin Tin Tin (the only actor for whom Jack Warner had a good word) but soon graduated to more ambitious projects. In his first six years he turned out so many scripts that he had to adopt various pseudonyms. By 1930 Zanuck was head of production for the entire studio. He was then twenty-eight years old and convinced he knew the formula for bringing Depression audiences back into the movie theater: crime.

There was nothing new about gangster films. They had been around ever since D. W. Griffith made *The Musketeers of Pig Alley* in 1912, but few in recent years had shown strength at the box office. Jack Warner was not enthusiastic

The Mob by Sorel. Clockwise from lower left: Humphrey Bogart, George Raft, Eduardo Ciannelli, Jack Warner, Barton MacLane, John Garfield, Edward G. Robinson, James Cagney.

32   33

864		865	
Art Director	**Murray Belsky**	Art Director	**Everett Halvorsen**
Designer	**Murray Belsky**	Designer	**Everett Halvorsen**
Artist	**Edward Sorel, New York**	Artist	**Chas. B. Slackman**
Writers	**Edward Sorel, Neil Hickey**	Writer	**Barbara Rudolph**
		Editor	**James W. Michaels**
Client	**American Heritage**	Publisher	**Forbes, Inc., New York**
Editor	**Byron Dobell**	Publication	**Forbes**
Publisher	**Byron S. Hollingshead**		
Publication	**American Heritage**		

KISSINGER
trium-
phant

BY GARRY WILLS

He won the Nobel Peace Prize
for a war that never ended.
Watergate left him unscathed.
The sovereign schemer somehow
manages to turn each defeat into
a personal victory. But, we ask
you, is this diplomacy?

How does Henry Kissinger do it? He strolls from scene to scene, tinkering with structures that collapse behind him; he is sniped at from the left and from the right; he wiretaps his friends and accumulates enemies—yet all the while he is moving from strength to strength. An Al Capp character used to travel under his own private rain cloud of attendant trouble; Kissinger seems to walk through storms, through earthquakes, through apocalypses, in a protective spotlight of sunshiny luck.

He is one of the few men who palled around with the tar baby of Watergate yet did not get stuck to it. He picked up a Nobel Peace Prize for a war that never ended. He mocked Third World concerns and is now asked to preside over them. Others talk of success just barely eluding them. He manages to have failure skitter endlessly out of his grasp.

This mysterious not-quite-success story is explained hyperbolically by both friend and foe. To his supporters he remains Super-K, history's Mister Fix-It. To critics like Seymour Hersh, he is diabolical, a colossal liar and schemer, a vindictive egomaniac.

176 GQ/DECEMBER

FICTION

*The contestants in a game
of mind manipulation find they are caught
in their own malicious trap*

CARRION
COMFORT

BY DAN SIMMONS

Nina was going to take credit for the death of that Beatle, John. I thought that was in very bad taste. She had her scrapbook laid out on my mahogany coffee table, newspaper clippings neatly arranged in chronological order, the bold statements of death recording all of her Feedings. Nina Drayton's smile was radiant, but her pale-blue eyes showed no hint of warmth.

"We should wait for Willi," I said.

"Of course, Melanie. You're right, as always. How silly of me. I know the rules." Nina stood and began walking around the room, idly touching the furnishings or exclaiming softly over a ceramic statuette or piece of needlepoint. This part of the house had once been the conservatory, but now I used it as my sewing room. Green plants still caught the morning light. The light made it a warm, cozy place in the daytime, but now that winter had come the

The piece is the first section of a two-part novelette

PAINTING BY ROBIN MULLER

866

Art Director	**Rochelle Udell**
Designer	**Rochelle Udell**
Artist	**Edward Sorel, New York**
Writer	**Gary Wills**
Client	**Gentlemen's Quarterly**
Editor	**Art Cooper**
Director	**Steven Florio**
Publication	**Gentlemen's Quarterly (Conde Nast)**

867

Art Director	**Elizabeth Woodson**
Designer	**Liz Siroka**
Artist	**Robin Muller**
Publication	**Omni Publications Int'l Ltd., New York**
V.P., Graphics Director	**Frank M. DeVino**

FICTION

THE CIRCUS ANIMALS' DESERTION

BY SCOTT RUSSELL SANDERS

A lone in his go-house after fucking the beasts in their lairs for the night, Orlando Spinks was stitching a tear in

PAINTING BY MICHAEL PARKES

FICTION

It was a typical suburban cocktail party, with its shoptalk and a hint of illicit sex

DURING THE JURASSIC

BY JOHN UPDIKE

W aiting for the first guests, the iguanodon gazed along the path and beyond toward the monotonous cycad forests and the low volcanic hills. The landscape was everywhere interpenetrated by the sea, a kind of metallic blue rottenness that daily breathed in and out. Behind him, his wife was assembling the hors d'oeuvres. As he watched her, something unintended, something grossly solemn in his expression made her laugh, displaying the leaf-shaped teeth lining her cheeks. Like him, she was an ornithischian, but much smaller—a compsognathus. He wondered watching her race bipedally back and forth among the scraps of food (dragonflies wrapped in ferns, cephalopods on toast) how he had ever found her

PAINTING BY ROLAND CAT

868		869	
Art Director	**Elizabeth Woodson**	Art Director	**Elizabeth Woodson**
Designer	**Liz Siroka**	Designer	**Victor Chan**
Artist	**Michael Parkes**	Artist	**Roland Cat**
Publication	**Omni Publications Int'l Ltd., New York**	Publication	**Omni Publications Int'l Ltd., New York**
V.P., Graphics Director	**Frank M. DeVino**	V.P., Graphics Director	**Frank M. DeVino**

FICTION

KALEIDOSCOPE

BY CHERRY WILDER

In the closing years of the twentieth century, the artist Gus Rocca was living down on Parker's Key. He had everything he needed. He had never been a great consumer of anything but red wine, and now, at fifty-five, he couldn't take too much of that anymore. The launch brought in food and the magazines he needed for his collages. He walked along the beach each morning and evening looking for found objects.

Parker's Key was a small island, dull and sullen, with few interesting features. After a month Gus decided the place was like a *jolie-laide*, a beautiful, ugly woman. He lived in a low, gray, weathered house among scrawny palms. There was a shack at the other end of the beach, and it was prettier, covered with bougainvillea, the purple bracts clustered on its sagging roof like a swarm of butterflies.

A woman lived in this shack, and Gus, watching her at first with the naked eye, hoped for another *jolie-laide* at least. But Sophie Moller was something more like a female counterpart of Gus himself, and when he looked through his binoculars he was disappointed. Damn, she

PAINTING BY CHARLES PFAHL

THE ULTIMATE HOTEL

A Fantasy

by Roy Strickland
and
James Sanders

This is a hotel as you have always imagined hotels to be. It stands by the sea, at the confluence of great boulevards and canals, and overlooks mountains. Its guest list is long and proud and includes billionaires, great artists and raconteurs, and the tragic heroes of fiction. It has been designed by architects and poets and is at once historic and visionary. Its cuisine is unsurpassed—and stimulates desire.

A Spanish architect, famous for his unfinished cathedral, envisioned its dining room's celestial, star-studded ceiling. A German expressionist director gave its lobby a magical shape that would capture passers-by from the streets of a city about to be plunged into war. F. Scott Fitzgerald described it as being "on the pleasant shore of the French (continued on page 131)

THE GUESTS (from left to right)

Cary Grant / Alfred Hitchcock
Ernest Hemingway / Luchino Visconti
Mick Jagger / Dorothy Parker
Joan Crawford / Marlene Dietrich
Twiggy / David Hockney
Greta Garbo / Andy Warhol
Mohammad Ali / Noël Coward

THE VIEWS (from left to right)

From the Gritti Palace, Venice
The Corvo Run, St. Moritz
Chrysler Building, New York City

THE FIXTURES

Chairs, tables, and chandeliers from the George V, Paris
Pillar from the Kurhaus, Baden-Baden
Bar from the Observation Lounge, RMS Queen Mary

86

870

Art Director **Elizabeth Woodson**
Designer **Patrick Deffenbaugh**
Artist **Charles Pfahl**
Publication **Omni Publications Int'l Ltd., New York**
V.P., Graphics Director **Frank M. DeVino**

871

Art Director **Lloyd Ziff**
Designer **Lloyd Ziff**
Artist **Julian Allen**
Writers **Roy Strickland, James Sanders**
Editor **Don David Guttenplan**
Publisher **Conde Nast Publications, Inc., New York**
Publication **Vanity Fair**

Are the rites of
passage on the right track ... or have
they taken a detour?

LOSING IT IN THE EIGHTIES

BY MARJORIE ROSEN

"I was always such a jerk about sex. When I finally lost
my virginity last year, I was too macho and too ashamed to tell the woman
I was with that it was my first time."
Jimmy, an eighteen-year-old college freshman from suburban
Connecticut who now plays quarterback on a leading college football
team, laughs sheepishly, then shrugs his muscular
shoulders. "I was your typical high school stud. The football
hero who'd been around and who seemed to know everything. Well, that's what

PAINTING BY PIERRE LACOMBE

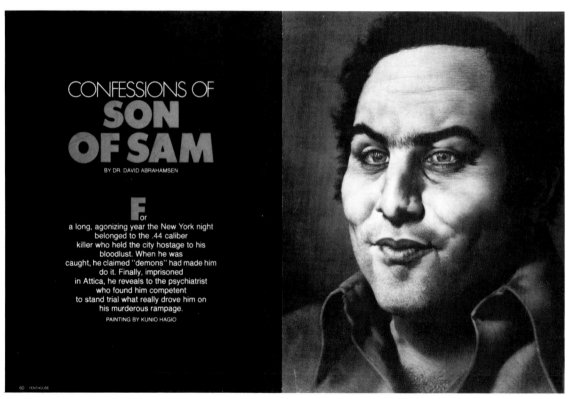

CONFESSIONS OF
SON
OF SAM

BY DR. DAVID ABRAHAMSEN

For
a long, agonizing year the New York night
belonged to the .44 caliber
killer who held the city hostage to his
bloodlust. When he was
caught, he claimed "demons" had made him
do it. Finally, imprisoned
in Attica, he reveals to the psychiatrist
who found him competent
to stand trial what really drove him on
his murderous rampage.

PAINTING BY KUNIO HAGIO

60 PENTHOUSE

<table>
<tr><td colspan="2">872</td><td colspan="2">873</td></tr>
<tr><td>Art Director</td><td>Richard Bleiweiss</td><td>Art Director</td><td>Richard Bleiweiss</td></tr>
<tr><td>Designer</td><td>Pablo Rodriguez</td><td>Designer</td><td>Richard Bleiweiss</td></tr>
<tr><td>Artist</td><td>Pierre LaCombe</td><td>Artist</td><td>Kunio Hagio</td></tr>
<tr><td>Writer</td><td>Marjorie Rosen</td><td>Client</td><td>Penthouse</td></tr>
<tr><td>Client</td><td>Penthouse</td><td>Editor</td><td>Peter Bloch</td></tr>
<tr><td>Editor</td><td>Peter Bloch</td><td>Publisher</td><td>Bob Guccione</td></tr>
<tr><td>Publisher</td><td>Bob Guccione</td><td>Publication</td><td>Penthouse, New York</td></tr>
<tr><td>Publication</td><td>Penthouse, New York</td><td>Graphics</td><td></td></tr>
<tr><td>Graphics</td><td></td><td>Director</td><td>Frank M. DeVino</td></tr>
<tr><td>Director</td><td>Frank M. DeVino</td><td></td><td></td></tr>
</table>

PART ONE

Yoko Ono's psychic
and tarot card reader reveals for the first time his account
of the temper tantrums
and strange disappearances that characterized rock music's
most bizarre and
tumultuous marriage. John and Yoko. If only they could
give peace a chance.

JOHN AND YOKO: THE FINAL YEARS

BY JOHN GREEN

I first met John Lennon on Groundhog Day of 1975. I had been lured out of my Fifth Avenue burrow for the occasion by Yoko. It was, she said, an emergency.

I was used to Yoko's emergencies. They happened day and night. They came in two varieties: routine and titanic. "The cat is under the sofa and what should we do?" was a routine emergency. A $60 million lawsuit was the other kind.

The phone call came at an atypically civilized hour, 6:47 P.M. I immediately assumed the worst. Having been conditioned by long months of 2:00 A.M. calls waking me from a dead sleep to ask if I

had some time," I instinctively mistrusted the convenience of the hour. Convenient emergencies are generally the worst kind.

"John's home!" Yoko rasped.

This might not have qualified as an "emergency," but it certainly qualified as news. Fifteen months earlier, in October 1973, John had walked out the front door saying he was going for a paper. There had been a few phone calls since then, but for the most part his exact whereabouts during that time had been more or less a mystery. According to Yoko, his return was as sudden and unexpected as his departure. Apparently he simply showed up

PAINTING BY KUNIO HAGIO

HOFMEKLER

Ori Hofmekler, a brilliant, young Israeli artist, virtually unknown in the United States, is barely thirty years old. Yet his trenchant wit, laserlike perceptions, and incandescent talent have already won him universal recognition abroad as one of the world's very best and brashest socio-political satirists. This month, a collection of his recent portraits, entitled Hofmekler's People, is being published by Holt, Rinehart & Winston. Also this month, in keeping with our policy of finding and securing world-class talent, Penthouse is delighted to welcome this latter-day Honoré Daumier and his provocative, etched-in-acid paintings in what will become the first of a regular, exclusive, and long-term series.

125

	874		**875**
Art Director	**Richard Bleiweiss**	Art Director	**Richard Bleiweiss**
Designer	**Sheila Lynn**	Designer	**Richard Bleiweiss**
Artist	**Kunio Hagio**	Artist	**Ori Hofmekler**
Client	**Penthouse**	Client	**Penthouse**
Editor	**Peter Bloch**	Editor	**Peter Bloch**
Publisher	**Bob Guccione**	Publisher	**Bob Guccione**
Publication	**Penthouse, New York**	Publication	**Penthouse, New York**
Graphics Director	**Frank M. DeVino**	Graphics Director	**Frank M. DeVino**

CHILD
MOLESTERS AND
THEIR VICTIMS
CLOSE ENCOUNTERS
OF THE
WORST KIND
BY ALLAN SONNENSCHEIN

They're not all dirty old men who lurk
in the corners of schoolyards. In fact, most child
sex abusers are "ordinary" people from
all walks of life . . . some of whom actually organize
to promote their abnormal behavior.

PAINTING BY GOTTFRIED HELNWEIN

SUICIDE SIGNALS

A substance in the
brain identifies those likely
to kill themselves.

by Maya Pines

Taking one's life appears to be a conscious decision that only human beings can make. Only humans can think about the future and deliberately override the powerful will to live. Yet strong evidence is emerging that suicide is heavily influenced by one's genes and one's biology.

By measuring the level of a certain chemical in the spinal fluid of depressed and suicidal patients, researchers at Sweden's Karolinska Hospital in Stockholm have been able to identify which patients are most likely to kill themselves. Their discovery, which meshes nicely with several other strands of research in the United States and abroad, may help scientists identify potential suicides and intervene to save their lives.

In the early 1970s Marie Asberg, a psychiatrist, and her associates at the Karolinska were looking for chemical markers in the cerebrospinal fluid of patients with severe depression. These patients felt that life was no longer worth living. Steeped in self-blame or thoughts of death, they could neither sleep, eat, nor work normally. Severe depression can be treated more successfully than most mental disorders, but there are several forms of it, and picking the right treatment in a particular case is often a matter of guesswork. The researchers hoped that chemical markers would help them identify some of the subgroups of depression so that the most effective treatment could be provided.

One marker had been found: About a third of the 68 patients had particularly low levels of a chemical called 5HIAA (5-hydroxyindoleacetic acid) in their spinal fluid. This difference seemed promising because 5HIAA is a metabolite, or breakdown product, of serotonin, a key chemical messenger in the brain that affects mood and emotion, among other things.

The research took a dramatic and unexpected turn on June 13, 1975, when the staff heard shocking news about one of their depressed patients. The man had been admitted to the psychiatric ward after a suicide attempt, Asberg recalls. He was treated with antidepres-

Illustrations by Dagmar Frinta

55

876

Art Director	**Richard Bleiweiss**
Designer	**Richard Bleiweiss**
Artist	**Gottfried Helnwein**
Client	**Penthouse**
Editor	**Peter Bloch**
Publisher	**Bob Guccione**
Publication	**Penthouse, New York**
Graphics Director	**Frank M. DeVino**

877

Art Director	**Rodney Williams**
Designer	**Mary Challinor**
Artist	**Dagmar Frinta**
Writer	**Maya Pines**
Client	**SCIENCE 83/Amer. Assoc. for the Advancement of Science, Washington, DC**
Editor	**Allen L. Hammond**
Publisher	**William D. Carey**
Publication	**SCIENCE 83**

THE TELLTALE METABOLISM OF ALCOHOLICS

A new interpretation of
standard blood tests may lead to
early diagnosis.

by Michael Watterlond

When she speaks of her old self, her "drinking self," it is as though she is talking about another girl who stood off in the shadows, a confused girl she hardly knew.

"I thought the big problem in my life was geography," she says. "I lost things. One year I reported my car stolen three times. The police would find it abandoned somewhere between my house and wherever I'd been drinking.

"Eventually, I moved to this little resort town where the bars were within walking distance. That solved my stolen car problem.

"It never once occurred to me that I was an alcoholic. I was only 23. I thought I drank just like everyone else."

"Most alcoholics have absolutely no idea what drinking is like for normal people," says Morris Hill, director of the Arlington Hospital Alcoholism Treatment Unit in Arlington, Virginia. "And that is the major stumbling block to early diagnosis of alcoholism."

According to many physicians and health experts, alcoholism is the most urgent public health problem in the country. Three to 10 percent of the population will become alcoholic at one time or another in their lives.

affecting one out of three families. But the exact number of alcoholics at any given time is impossible to determine. For one thing, doctors are understandably hesitant to stamp a patient's record with a diagnosis of alcoholism.

Although alcoholism is a disease that causes progressive physical damage, society often perceives it only in terms of its secondary symptoms—the baffling, troublesome behavior of the alcoholic. And researchers approach the problem from a number of angles, because it is characterized by a jigsaw of factors that can be organized roughly into three areas: biological (how alcohol affects the body), psychological (how it affects the mind), and sociological (how alcohol is provided and consumed in society).

A specific cause for the disease, unfortunately, has not been found. But the host of primary physiological symptoms are all too familiar to treatment specialists. They include a high tolerance for alcohol, impaired nutrition due to poor eating habits, digestive problems, inflammation of the liver and pancreas, anemia, and impotence. All too often the symptoms are ignored or excused by the alcoholic until there is major internal damage.

"Unfortunately," says James R. Milam, a Seattle treatment specialist, author, and lecturer, "alcoholism is not considered a medical diagnosis by most people. It is considered a personal slur."

TALES OF AN ELUSIVE
ANCESTOR

Was evolution's first attempt
to shape the human species a creature
known as *Ramapithecus?*

*by Allen L. Hammond
photographs by Margo Crabtree*

In 1971 Peter Andrews was a graduate student working in Nairobi at Kenya's National Museum. He knew that bits of fossil bone picked up during excavations are often misclassified. So he was sorting through some ape specimens to see if anything interesting turned up, and sure enough, he found a lower jawbone that seemed unusual. It was from the Kenyan site of Fort Ternan, where anthropologist Louis Leakey had found an upper jaw and some teeth belonging to a 14-million-year-old animal called *Ramapithecus.* This creature was believed to show the earliest hint of evolutionary change away from the apes and toward humans.

Andrews tried fitting the odd lower jaw into the upper jaw of Leakey's *Ramapithecus* specimen. To his astonishment, it fit almost per-

NOVEMBER

Living eyes once peered from the bony sockets of this Chinese ramapith skull.

fectly. In fact, the only thing that didn't fit was a tooth that Leakey had found separately and glued into the upper jaw—improperly, it turned out. When Andrews reglued the tooth less deeply into the socket, the upper and lower jaws meshed nicely enough to make an orthodontist smile.

The unmistakable fit of the jaws startled the paleoanthropology community, the small band of scientists who study human origins, because it showed very apelike dental features in this supposed human ancestor. Perhaps *Ramapithecus* was not a hominid, or member of the human lineage, but just an ancient ape. Perhaps it was neither ape nor hominid but ancestral to both. The implications for the earliest stages of human evolution were intriguing.

Ever since Darwin, biologists have assumed that the human lineage split off from that of the apes. Apes, after all, look and act surprisingly human. And, as later investigators showed, the ancestors of today's apes were the dominant primates for most of the last 90 million years. Monkeys, though more numerous now, have achieved their

Art Director	**Rodney Williams**
Designer	**Rodney Williams**
Artist	**David Lesh**
Writer	**Michael Watterloud**
Client	**SCIENCE 83/Amer. Assoc. for the Advancement of Science, Washington, DC**
Editor	**Allen L. Hammond**
Publisher	**William D. Carey**
Publication	**SCIENCE 83**

879

Art Directors	**Joyce Black, Rodney Williams**
Designer	**Joyce Black**
Artist	**Kinuko Craft**
Writer	**Allen L. Hammond**
Client	**SCIENCE 83/Amer. Assoc. for the Advancement of Science, Washington, DC**
Editor	**Allen L. Hammond**
Publisher	**William D. Carey**
Publication	**SCIENCE 83**

Grazing in a field at Langford, near Bristol, England, are 12 lambs—six sets of twins. They appear to be normal, contented members of the St. Kilda breed, except that one of each pair is about 15 percent taller than its twin. This came about not through chance, differences in nutrition, or some feat of futuristic breeding. Instead, Langford's extraordinary sheep were the products of a novel attempt to immunize the body against one of its own hormones—in this case, the hormone that slows growth. But similar methods of immunization are being used to probe and regulate several other physiological processes.

Those in charge of the Langford experiments, Stuart Spencer and Diane Williamson, are animal physiologists with the Agricultural Research Council's Meat Research Institute. They knew the

THE NEW SHEPHERDS OF ST. KILDA

By finessing the immune system, researchers are growing bigger sheep, halting sperm production in mice, and creating voracious rats.

by Bernard Dixon
Illustrations by Geoffrey Moss

ON BECOMING HUMAN

THE NATURE–NURTURE DEBATE II

The steps toward human nature are built of culture *and* genes.

by Boyce Rensberger

Edward O. Wilson has a theory about what makes people act the way they do. He thinks that broad categories of human behavior—things such as male dominance, incest taboos, and other patterns such as male dominance, incest taboos, and other patterns perpetuated by tradition and cultural practice—are not merely cultural inventions. Instead Wilson believes that social behaviors like these are under a degree of genetic control built into the brain. He thinks these behaviors have been shaped by a special kind of evolution in which genes and culture—the forces of nature *and* nurture—worked together.

But in the two years that Wilson has been promoting his provocative theory, he has learned that many humans find it hard to accept the idea of any genetic control of their behavior. So he likes to explain his theory by taking people on an imaginary trip to another galaxy. There he shows them two species of intelligent beings—the Eidylons and the Xenidrins, who represent extreme examples of the two possible ways of explaining the forces that might govern human behavior.

Eidylons and Xenidrins both look rather human, but they differ in one respect. The Eidylons (Greek for "skilled ones") behave strictly according to genetic control. The Xenidrins (from the Greek for "strangers") act only according to cultural influence.

Eidylons are as intelligent as Earthlings, but they can respond only one way to a given set of circumstances. During embryonic development Eidylon genes build brains that are "hard wired" and thus capable of learning only one set of social behaviors. All Eidylon societies have the same political and economic systems. Details of language, art, and other elements of their culture may vary, but the basic structures are unchangeable. At Eidylon festivals ritual hymns stir feelings of deep pleasure in the audience; but the music is always the same, note for note. Eidylons teach and learn all that they know, but they are capable of learning only one thing in each category—one language, one creation myth, one courtship ritual. Like the white-crowned sparrows of California, they must hear the song of their species in order to learn it, but it is the only song they can learn.

At the opposite end of the spectrum are the Xenidrins, who are born with minds that are truly blank slates. Their every behavior is shaped by their culture. Like Eidylons, they must be taught in order to learn, but they can learn any form of behavior. In some Xenidrin societies the culture leads men to dominate women, but in as many others the culture leads women to dominate men. Some prohibit incest; others encourage it. Smiles are not the universal language among the Xenidrins; in some Xenidrin cultures the tradi-

880

Art Director   **Joyce Black, Rodney Williams**
Designer   **Joyce Black**
Artist   **Geoffrey Moss**
Writer   **Bernard Dixon**
Client   **SCIENCE 83/Amer. Assoc. for the Advancement of Science, Washington, DC**
Editor   **Allen L. Hammond**
Publisher   **William D. Carey**
Publication   **SCIENCE 83**

881

Art Director   **Rodney Williams**
Designer   **Wayne Fitzpatrick**
Artist   **Brad Holland**
Writer   **Boyce Rensberger**
Client   **SCIENCE 83/Amer. Assoc. for the Advancement of Science, Washington, DC**
Editor   **Allen L. Hammond**
Publisher   **William D. Carey**
Publication   **SCIENCE 83**

Directing the Self Against Disease

A master key for the immune system.

The possibilities for therapy seem endless since immune processes now appear to have some involvement in almost all chronic diseases. The key, however, is complex in the extreme. It should open many doors, but only after long and arduous research.

Cytokines are some fifty to one hundred naturally occurring compounds that direct the immune system. They work through complex interactions among themselves and with the system's specialized cellular components. If we understood cytokines completely, we could cause the immune system to attack or undermine conditions ranging from cancer and arthritis to multiple sclerosis, rejection of transplanted organs, and, perhaps, even the aging process itself.

Research on cytokines is so new that only one subgroup, called interferons, has been completely purified and produced in any quantity. Reports of work at various laboratories, however, are promising. For example, hybrid cytokines, produced by combining segments from two of these substances, have been much more effective in laboratory tests than their naturally occurring counterparts.

At present, scientists are seeking at least three types of drugs in this new area of immunology: single cytokines or several used together, hybrid versions of these natural substances, and compounds that either mimic or interfere with normal cytokine activity.

Any of these approaches could produce dramatic new therapies for a broad range of diseases. Together they could eventually give us a master key to the immune system.

GIUSTI

882

Art Director	**Bennett Robinson**
Designers	**Bennett Robinson, Naomi Burstein**
Artist	**Robert Giusti**
Client	**Eli Lilly and Company**
Design Firm	**Corporate Graphics, Inc., New York**

883

Art Director	**Fred Woodward**
Designer	**Fred Woodward**
Artists	**Blair Drawson, Sean Earley, Thomas Woodruff**
Client	**Texas Monthly**
Editor	**Greg Curtis**
Publisher	**Texas Monthly, Inc., Austin**
Publication	**Texas Monthly**

BY MONIKA MAECKLE

TROPICAL ROMANCE

FOR U.S. RETIREES AND COSTA RICAN WOMEN, THE NAME OF THE GAME IS LET'S MAKE A DEAL

ILLUSTRATION BY DAVID GAMBALE

Texas, a Long, Long, Long, Long Time Ago

Some people look over the land-scape and see the ghosts of cowboys past. Wann Langston sees dinosaurs and the eerie swamps where they once lived.

BY LAWRENCE WRIGHT

884

Art Director	**Fred Woodward**
Designer	**Fred Woodward**
Artist	**David Gambale**
Writer	**Monika Maeckle**
Editors	**Ande Zellman, Chris Wohlwend**
Publisher	**Dallas Times Herald**
Publication	**Westward Magazine, Dallas Times Herald, Dallas**

885

Art Directors	**Fred Woodward, Nancy E. McMillen**
Designers	**Fred Woodward, Nancy E. McMillen**
Artist	**Jack Unruh**
Client	**Texas Monthly**
Editor	**Greg Curtis**
Publisher	**Texas Monthly, Inc., Austin**
Publication	**Texas Monthly**

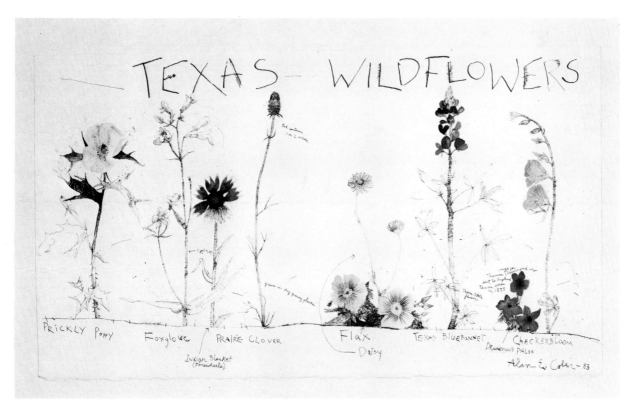

886

Art Director	**Fred Woodward**
Designer	**Fred Woodward**
Artist	**Alan E. Cober,**
	Ossining, NY
Writer	**Jay Lewis**
Publication	**Westward Magazine**

887

Art Director	**Fred Woodward**
Designer	**Alan E. Cober**
Artist	**Alan E. Cober,**
	Ossining, NY
Publication	**Westward Magazine**

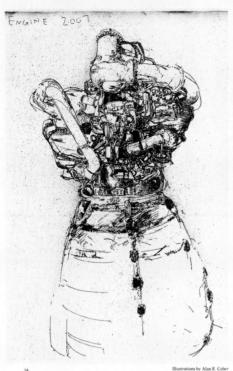

ENGINE 2007

Engine-uity

To the mechanically minded, engines are a source of endless fascination and delight. To those not-so-inclined, they can be a baffling, often maddening array of pistons, cylinders and valves moving in mysterious ways and speaking in a completely foreign tongue. Their rapid development in this century has changed society, opening up horizons undreamt of by their inventors. From the time, less than 100 years ago, when the piston-driven automobile made its debut, technology has created engines that can fly us to the moon. If we have had to give up the mythical "man in the moon" so treasured in our childhood days, we have the great new wonder called astronautics as recompense. The latter has been the focus of an immense scientific effort, yielding dazzling results. For example, the space shuttle *Columbia* traveled more than 10 million miles, orbited the earth 396 times and spent almost 25 days in space. One of the *Columbia's* three main engines, shown at left, is part of a portfolio of etchings made by artist Alan E. Cober during visits to engine builders.

Space shuttle

Gas turbine

The EXXON brand is widely associated with gasoline. But the company also manufactures a wide range of "behind-the-scenes" products to service both today's increasingly diverse and sophisticated engines and the craft they power. The *Columbia's* solid-fuel boosters were cleaned with Exxon's LIQUA-BLASTER water-jetting system, while our TERESSTIC oils are used to lubricate industrial equipment which includes the large General Electric Company gas turbine at right.

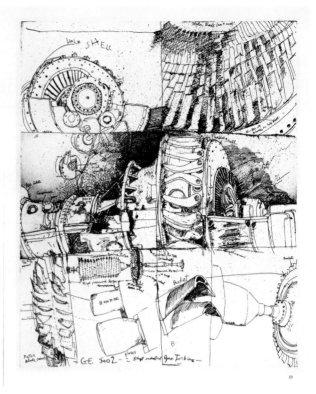

HALF SHELL

G.E. 5002 – 2 shaft industrial gas turbine

18 — Illustrations by Alan E. Cober — 19

Industry's hidden helpers

Exxon's petroleum specialty products have been used in everything from medicines and cosmetics to locomotives and space vehicles.

by Lawrence Locke
Illustrations by Bill Charmatz

Tribology is the study of friction, and while history does not record the names of the first tribologists, archaeological evidence suggests that they must have been at work in Egypt as early as 1400 B.C. Artifacts from that period show that animal fat had been slathered on the axles of chariots and other vehicles to reduce rubbing.

Today's tribologist is still studying what happens when surfaces rub against each other. From such contacts have sprung today's $15-billion-plus-a-year petroleum specialties field which provides both consumers and industry with a broad range of helpful

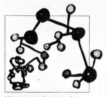

Axle grease for all types of vehicles

lubricants, process oils, greases and waxes.

"Petroleum specialty products are critical to performance in many important processes and pieces of modern machinery," says Raphael ("Ray") H. Beresford, vice president of Exxon's petroleum products department. "As their name suggests, specialty products are carefully designed for particular kinds of uses," he says. "Some are formulated to function under extreme heat, cold or pressure. Some are designed to be removed immediately after they have done their work. Others are made to remain in place for a decade or more."

What does a petroleum specialty product look like? "You name it," says Beresford. "They run the gamut from wood-hard blocks of certain greases to very light mineral oils."

The petroleum specialties industry, in which Exxon is the largest single producer, has developed over the last 100 years. For centuries before that, tallow was the chief lubricant. Only in the 1860s, with the coming of crude oil refining, did more effective and durable petroleum-based lubricants begin to emerge. As the manufacture, distribution and transportation of goods became increasingly mechanized, their use expanded rapidly. Petroleum lubricants found application on thousands of factory spindles, delivery wagon axles and in the

moving mechanisms of many other transportation vehicles of the period.

As the Industrial Age advanced in the 19th century, other specialized petroleum products joined lubricants in the oil industry's effort to supply the multitude of industries, such as textiles and shoes, that were producing the necessities of life.

When railroads began crisscrossing the nation, not only did their moving parts need lubricants but their headlamps consumed special oil. And at each railroad crossing in thousands of cowtowns, villages and major cities stood a signal whose light burned a special type of oil.

Oil for railroad crossing signals

Under more than 1,000 trademarks from various manufacturers, an array of oils and greases were offered to the buying public.

For horses, there were hoof, harness and belt-dressing oils, to mention only a few products. More than 75 different types of grease were made, with railroads and steel mills consuming, by far, the lion's share. By the early 1900s, another fresh batch of new, custom-designed lubricants was needed to keep diesel and gasoline engines and automobile chassis in good condition.

Exxon has been making and selling petroleum specialties since 1885, when it was known as Standard Oil Company of New Jersey. The first product was grease. By 1892, Jersey Standard owned two lubricant plants, two others that produced pressed paraffin oils and held interests in a number of other companies that manufactured and marketed lubricants.

Waxes, too, had many uses in those days. In 1900, Jersey alone made 300 grades and sizes of candles, six grades of petrolatum—an ointment similar to petroleum jelly—and 20 different types of paraffin wax. In the home, paraffin was widely used in containers to preserve foods.

New machinery required new petroleum products. The advent of refrigeration in the mid-19th century, the development of high-pressure and high-temperature manufacturing processes and of high-speed precision machinery demanded special fluids.

Today, Exxon makes and markets more than 600 different petroleum specialty products worldwide, totaling over three million gallons each day. They yield annual earnings above $250 million. To be sure, some of these products are greases and lubricants that still help to turn the "wheels of industry." But others are important ingredients used in pharmaceutical prod-

High-purity grease for space vehicles

ucts, cosmetics and even space vehicles.

Raw materials for petroleum specialty products are called lube basestocks and are produced at 11 Exxon refineries throughout the world. Some basestocks are transported to company specialties plants, like the one at Bayonne, New Jersey, where lubricating oils and additives are blended into finished products for shipment to customers. Additives are customized chemicals which impart unique properties to such products as lubricants, transmission fluids, fuels and many varieties of industrial oils.

The PARAMINS product line of additives is made by Exxon Chemical Company for customers worldwide. One of the first of these products—a pour depressant that helps motor oils flow at low temperatures—was introduced more than 50 years ago and is still being manufactured today in Bayonne, New Jersey.

Produced in 13 Exxon Chemical plants around the world, PARAMINS supply more than one-fourth of the lubricant additives

12 — 13

888

Art Director	**Elton Robinson**
Designer	**Elton Robinson**
Artist	**Alan Cober**
Editor	**Ernest Dunbar**
Publisher	**Exxon Corporation, New York**
Publication	**The Lamp**

889

Art Director	**Elton Robinson**
Designer	**Elton Robinson**
Artist	**Bill Charmatz**
Editor	**Ernest Dunbar**
Publisher	**Exxon Corporation, New York**
Publication	**The Lamp**

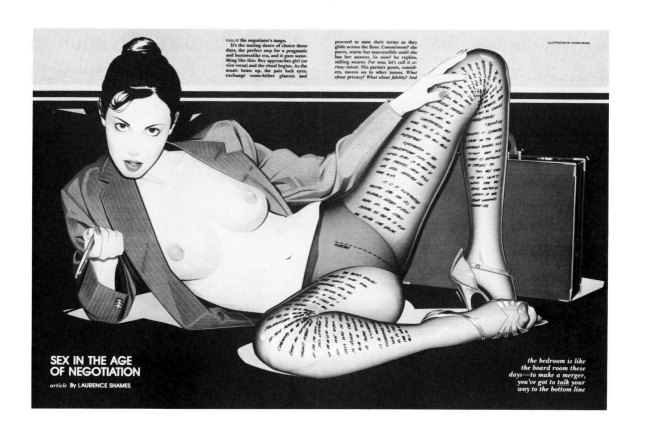

SEX IN THE AGE
OF NEGOTIATION

article By LAURENCE SHAMES

CALL IT the negotiator's tango. It's the mating dance of choice these days, the perfect step for a pragmatic and businesslike era, and it goes something like this: Boy approaches girl (or vice versa) and the ritual begins. As the music heats up, the pair lock eyes, exchange come-hither glances and proceed to state their terms as they glide across the floor. *Commitment?* she purrs, warm but inaccessible until she has her answer. *So soon?* he replies, sidling nearer. *For now, let's call it serious intent.* His partner pouts, considers, moves on to other issues. *What about privacy? What about fidelity? And*

the bedroom is like the board room these days—to make a merger, you've got to talk your way to the bottom line

ILLUSTRATION BY DENNIS MUKAI

	890		891
Art Director	**Tom Staebler**	Art Director	**Lloyd Ziff**
Designer	**Len Willis**	Designer	**Lloyd Ziff**
Artist	**Dennis Mukai**	Artist	**Robert Risko**
Writer:	**Laurence Shames**	Editor	**Richard Locke**
Client	**PLAYBOY Magazine**	Publisher	**Conde Nast**
Editor	**Jim Morgan**		**Publications, Inc.,**
Publisher	**PLAYBOY Enterprises,**		**New York**
	Inc., Chicago	Publication	**Vanity Fair**
Publication	**PLAYBOY Magazine**		

MR. MIKE'S AMERICA

a funny thing happened to macabre comedy master michael o'donoghue on his way from coast to coast—he found a country as weird as himself

personality By PAUL SLANSKY

IT WAS A TIME when people walked the nation's streets with orange-foam pads clamped to their ears and antennae bouncing above their heads. The newspapers of the day told of several thousand men and women who had allowed themselves to be paired off and married by the leader of a religious cult, while on television there was a show that featured actual couples discussing their actual sexual problems with an actual therapist. Hundreds of consumers mistook a dishwashing liquid for lemon juice and squirted it into their drinks.

A gold designer handgun was available to the public, as was a breakfast cereal that claimed to taste like doughnuts. The Post Office boasted of its plan for post-nuclear-war mail delivery, which seemed to depend heavily on the distribution of emergency change-of-address cards. The President, who was known far and wide as a man who loved to laugh, communicated his displeasure with a foreign country by posing for a photograph with a representative of that country and refusing to smile.

And it was a time when, from a pay phone in the mental hospital to which he'd been committed, a would-be Presidential assassin told a reporter that he regretted putting a bullet through the brain of an unintended victim. "I just honestly wish I could go back before the shooting," the young man said, "and let him move two inches out of the way."

It was the beginning of last summer, and I was about to drive across the country with the dark prince of black comedy, Michael O'Donoghue, also known as Mr. Mike.

"I've never been one of those snotty New York writers who sneer at L.A.," says O'Donoghue, turning his BMW into the Holland Tunnel in Lower Manhattan and heading for New Jersey. "I think the concept of a sybaritic culture is terrifying to a lot of people from the Northeast, but not to me." Not to

a 42-year-old man who gets really cranky if he goes too long without a bubble bath.

O'Donoghue has been talking about moving to Los Angeles for years, and now he is doing it. He is leaving the faded elegance of his Greenwich Village brownstone to live, for an indefinite period, in a rented house in the Hollywood Hills. Since there are certain amenities—art, music, fine silverware and silk dressing gowns, to name a few—that a civilized man cannot be expected to give up, O'Donoghue has packed those into the rear of his car and is moving them West himself. It is his first cross-country drive in more than 20 years.

It's already past noon on Wednesday, June 30th, and O'Donoghue wants to celebrate the Fourth of July in L.A., so there aren't any leisurely encounters with Mr. Bubble on his immediate schedule. Not to worry: he has drugs. He reaches behind his seat and pulls out a blue Right Guard aerosol can. He unscrews the false bottom and casually displays the contents: 35 perfectly rolled joints, a dozen Precodans (he gets migraine headaches) and a little something special to help with the late-night driving.

"A friend of mine has this theory about my comedy that has to do with my migraines," O'Donoghue says as we move through the eerie light of the tunnel, "which is, if *I'm* gonna get migraines, *they're* gonna get migraines, and I'll just have to give 'em to them."

O'Donoghue, as any serious comedy fan knows, was present at the creation of the two dominant comic institutions of the Seventies: the *National Lampoon* and *Saturday Night Live*. As a performer on the latter, he clawed his way into the national psyche with his "impressions" of how Mike Douglas, Tony Orlando, Elvis Presley and the Mormon Tabernacle Choir might react if 18-inch-long steel needles were suddenly plunged into their eyes. As it

113

ILLUSTRATION BY SANDRA HENDLER

THE LITTLE DRUMMER GIRL

the israeli mission: kidnap and interrogate a palestinian terrorist—it was not so simple as it seemed

fiction

By JOHN LE CARRÉ

author of Smiley's People

"HE's a serious young man, this Yanuka," Lenny pleaded valiantly. "Tradesman admire him. Friends admire him. That is a likable, popular person, Marty. Studies liked to enjoy himself, talk a lot, he's a sensate fellow, with healthy appetites. Catching Kurtz's eye, he became a little foolish. "Now and then, it's hard to believe in this other side of him, Marty, trust me."

Kurtz offered Lenny that he fully understood. Heart over crackers, cheese and tea, the three professional men's audiences gave Kurtz the full tour of Yanuka's already quite disregarding the fact that his works man, Kurtz had been playing every small acquisition a primo Yanuka's photos call it and on; as the final verdict, his fast words, Lenny was highest and kind and a holy duty of people he was ordered to tap. He had only ears and set aside in ordinances'; and perhaps that way why he kept it from the hard gaze of the world. He once a tiny gray, hovered someone, like those men by other commentators. Kurtz would stay, he listed very quickly, but he required Lenny and paid the closest attention to everything he said, nodding, congratulating, picking

all the right expressions for him. Lace curtains hung across the window of the high-gabled gingerbread house right at the heart of fashionable Munich. It was dusk in the street and dusk in the flat also, and the place was pervaded with an air of sad neglect. An array of electronic and optical devices was crowded among the fake Biedermeier furniture, including indoor aerials of varying designs. But in the falling light, these spectral shapes only added to the mood of bereavement.

"Want to take a look, Marty?" Lenny suggested hopefully. "I can see by Joshua's smile there that he has a very nice perception of Yanuka tonight. Want too long, he'll draw the curtain on us. What do you see, Joshua? Is Yanuka all dolled up for going out tonight? Who does he speak to on the telephone? A girl, for certain."

Gently, pushing Joshua aside, Kurtz ducked his big head so the binoculars. And he remained a long time that way, hunched like an old sea dog in a storm, hardly seeming to breathe, while he studied Yanuka, the half-grown suckling.

"See his books there in the background?" Lenny asked. "That boy reads like my father."

"Yes, have a fine boy there," Kurtz agreed finally, with his iron-hard smile, as he slowly straightened himself. "A good-looking kid, no question." Picking his gray raincoat from the chair, he selected a sleeve and pulled it tenderly over his arm. "Just be sure you don't marry him to your daughter. The next thing you know, she'll be planting bombs for him or his big brother."

Lenny looked even more foolish than before, but Kurtz was quick to console him: "We should be thankful to you, Lenny. And so we are, no question."

Having shaken hands with each man in turn, Kurtz added an old blue beret to his costume and, thus disabled against the handle of the rush hour, strode vigorously into the street.

The lady of Kurtz's hastily assembled Munich team was Oded, a 23-year-old graduate of the prestigious Sayeret. The grandfather was a 50-year-old Georgian

79

Art Director	**Tom Staebler**
Designer	**Skip Willamson**
Artist	**Sandra Hendler**
Writer	**Paul Slansky**
Client	**PLAYBOY Magazine**
Editor	**Jim Morgan**
Publisher	**PLAYBOY Enterprises, Inc., Chicago**
Publication	**PLAYBOY Magazine**

893

Art Director	**Tom Staebler**
Designer	**Kerig Pope**
Artist	**Phillipe Weisbecker**
Writer	**John Le Carré**
Client	**PLAYBOY Magazine**
Editor	**Alice Turner**
Publisher	**PLAYBOY Enterprises, Inc., Chicago**
Publication	**PLAYBOY Magazine**

FRIENDSHIP
IN THE CITY

J OYCE JOHNSON HAS JUST SAID "LET'S
have lunch" to a woman with whom she
would like to be friends. They are at a
crowded book party, Perriers in hand,
pens at the ready. Jotting down Johnson's office and home numbers, the
other woman nods in vigorous agreement. "Yes, let's," she replies.

The two women have a lot in common. Both
are writers and editors, both are divorced, and
both have raised an only child to adolescence.
They've discovered that they share a number of
casual friends, and even one close one. They
have read and—more to the point—liked each
other's books. Johnson's *Minor Characters*, a
reminiscence about being a literary groupie in
the fifties, has just been published, and the
woman she is speaking with has revealed that
she, too, once hung out with some of the figures
in Johnson's memoir. What's more, the women
have learned that they held the same job at
Partisan Review, albeit two years apart, and they
shared—they are quick to note it was at different periods in his life—the same boyfriend.
They are amazed at the way their many experiences have overlapped, at their obvious
mutuality of taste and temperament. "We *must*
have lunch," says Johnson. "We *must*," echoes
the other woman.

It is the twelfth time in six years they've had
this conversation. And the twelfth time in those
six years they have jotted down each other's
phone numbers.

But for all their sincere enthusiasm about
each other, Johnson and the woman have never
gotten together except at parties, never actually
made a lunch date or any other appointment. "If
we lived anywhere but New York, we'd have
become friends the first time we met. We are
truly fond of one another," Johnson says. "But
friendship in New York is different from friendship elsewhere. Everyone here is working so
drivingly, and everyone already knows so many
people, that you really have to think long and
hard about whether you can afford to undertake
a new friendship."

**The New York
friendship is
as intense as
friendship in a
small town. But
it's different.
It can be
complicated,
even cruel.**

∎

By
Linda Wolfe

J OHNSON'S OBSERVATION IS ACCURATE
enough, but it is also testimony to the
fact that friendship in New York is thriving. Many New Yorkers are reluctant to
start new friendships not because they
are aloof but because they already have
so many friends of one sort or another.
But New Yorkers are not, as out-of-towners so
often imagine them to be, drifters whose social
relationships are fleeting and superficial. As I
was to discover after dozens of interviews, the
New York friendship is every bit as intense as
friendship in a small town or suburb. Perhaps
more so.

This isn't to say that making and keeping
friends here doesn't pose problems. Some of the
difficulties are not peculiar to New York: Distance and lack of time create problems everywhere. And everywhere—perhaps even more in
the suburbs than in the city—people report
having been abandoned after a divorce. But in
New York, where professional connections generate so many eventual friendships, many people say they mistake sociability for intimacy.
Some say they have trouble distinguishing the
professional contact from the true friend. Some
report "friendships" that were initiated for
predatory motives, for self-aggrandizement or
favors. And many have had the experience of
being dropped by friends whose power or pres-
tige suddenly outstripped theirs. The New York
friendship can be complicated, even cruel.

Y OU DON'T HAVE TO BE A PSYCHOLOGIST
to know that friendship in a metropolis
like New York is different from friendship elsewhere, but social scientists
have documented the phenomenon.
"What's important about large numbers of people—what we sociologists
call 'critical mass'—is that they result in an
intensity and a structure to social life that is
unique," says Claude S. Fischer, perhaps the
country's leading authority on personal networks in towns and cities. Fischer is an expo-
nent of the "subcultural theory" of city life,

894

Art Director	**Robert Best**
Designers	**Patricia Bradbury, Don Morris**
Illustrators	**Guy Billout, Vivienne Flesher, Alan Reingold, Seth Jaben, Dave Calver**
Client	**New York Magazine, New York**

BANANA SLUG

· Ariolimax columbianus ·

18.5 to 20 cm
in length

895

Art Director	**Robyn Ricks**
Artist	**Dugald Stermer,**
	San Francisco
Writer	**Rick Gauger**
Client	**Pacific Northwest**
	Magazine
Editor	**Peter Potterfield**
Publisher	**Harriet Bullitt**
Publication	**Pacific Northwest**
	Magazine

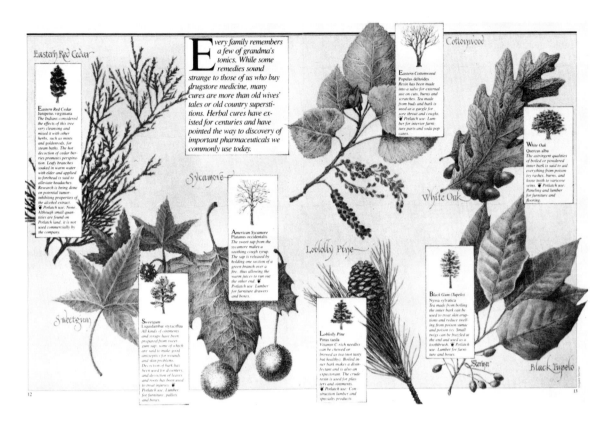

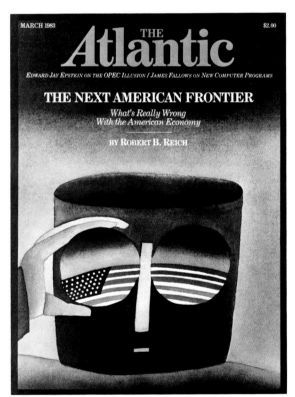

896

Art Director	**Kit Hinrichs**
Designers	**Kit Hinrichs, Lenore Bartz**
Artist	**Dugald Stermer, San Francisco**
Writer	**Holly Hutchins**
Client	**Potlatch Papers**
Editor	**Delphine Hirasuna**
Agency	**Jonson Pederson Hinrichs & Shakery**
Publication	**The Potlatch Story**

897

Art Director	**Terry Brown**
Artist	**Jean-Michel Folon**
Writer	**Robert B. Reich**
Editor	**William Whitworth**
Publisher	**The Atlantic Monthly Co., Boston**
Publication	**The Atlantic Monthly**

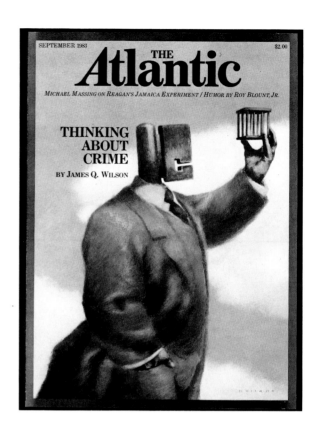

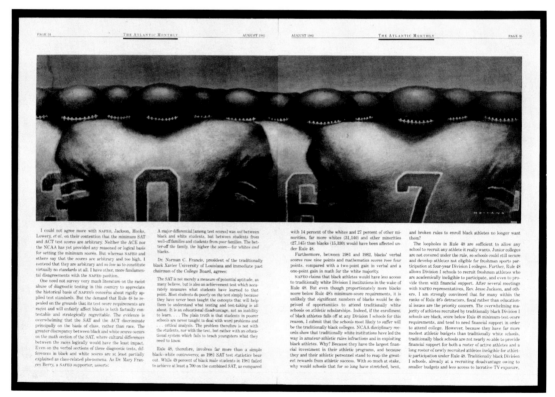

898	899	900
Art Director Judy Garlan	**Art Director** Judy Garlan	**Art Director** Judy Garlan
Artist David Wilcox	**Artist** Brad Holland	**Artist** Brad Holland
Writer Jane Smiley	**Writer** James Q. Wilson	**Writer** Harry Edwards
Editor William Whitworth	**Editor** William Whitworth	**Editor** William Whitworth
Publisher The Atlantic Monthly Co., Boston	**Publisher** The Atlantic Monthly Co., Boston	**Publisher** The Atlantic Monthly Co., Boston
Publication The Atlantic Monthly	**Publication** The Atlantic Monthly	**Publication** The Atlantic Monthly

ber, and petrochemical industries (and the other high-volume industries that depend on them) are becoming uncompetitive in the world. Second, now that production can be fragmented into separate, globally scattered operations, whole segments of other American industries are becoming uncompetitive. Whatever the final product, those parts of its production requiring high-volume machinery and unsophisticated workers can be accomplished more cheaply in developing nations.

Automation, far from halting this trend, has accelerated it. Sophisticated machinery is readily moved to low-wage countries. Robots and computerized machines further reduce the need for semiskilled workers in high-volume production (except for workers with easily learned maintenance and programming skills). For example, robots in the automobile industry are replacing workers at more semiskilled jobs, such as welding and spot welding, than unskilled jobs. Meanwhile, automated inspection machines are reducing the cost of screening out poor-quality components—thereby encouraging firms in industrialized nations to farm out the production of standardized parts to developing nations.

W HAT BEGAN IN THE 1960s AS A GRADUAL SHIFT became by the late 1970s a major structural change in the world economy. Assembly operations were being established in developing countries at a rapid clip, and America's manufacturing base was eroding precipitously. The recession of the past two years has stalled growth around the globe and plunged several developing nations into near bankruptcy. But it is important to distinguish these short-term phenomena—brought on by a temporary oil glut and high interest rates—from long-term trends that have been growing for two decades and surely will resume.

Other industrialized nations have faced the same competitive threat. Since the mid-1960s, European industries have faced an ever-greater challenge from low-wage production in developing countries. And since the late 1970s, Japan has been challenged as well. Japan is no longer a low-wage nation—the real earnings of Japanese workers are approaching those of their European and American counterparts.

Japan, West Germany, France, and other industrialized countries have sought to meet this challenge by shifting their industrial bases toward products and processes that require skilled workers. Skilled labor is the only dimension of production where these countries retain an advantage. Technological innovations can be bought or imitated by anyone. High-volume, standardized-production facilities can be established anywhere. But production processes that depend on skilled labor must stay where the skilled labor is.

The fate of British industry over the past twenty-five years illustrates this new reality. Britain has consistently led the world in major technological breakthroughs, such as continuous casting for steel, monoclonal antibodies, and CAT-scan devices. But because British businesses lacked the organization and their workers lacked the skills necessary to incorporate these inventions into production processes quickly enough, the British have reaped no real competitive advantage from them. These inventions were commercialized in Japan and the United States.

Industrialized countries are therefore moving into precision castings, specialty steel, special chemicals, and sensor devices, as well as the design and manufacture of fiber-optic cable, fine ceramics, lasers, large-scale integrated circuits, and advanced aircraft engines. Emerging industries such as these hold promise of generating new wealth and employment as their markets expand.

Some of these products or processes require precision engineering, complex testing, and sophisticated maintenance. Others are custom-tailored to the special needs of customers. The remainder involve technologies that are changing rapidly. All three are relatively secure against low-wage competition.

These product categories—precision-manufactured, custom-tailored, and technology-driven—have a great deal in common. They all depend on the sophisticated skills of their employees, skills that are often developed within teams. And they all require that traditionally separate business functions (design, engineering, purchasing, manufacturing, distribution, marketing, sales) be merged into a highly integrated system that can respond quickly to new opportunities. In short, they are premised on *flexible systems* of production.

Flexible-system production has an advantage over high-volume, standardized production whenever solving new problems is more important than routinizing the solution of

---

FIRST ENCOUNTERS

ROBERT LOUIS STEVENSON AND HENRY ADAMS

It was never easy being an Adams. For Henry Adams it was burdensome—in Quincy, in Boston, in the elegant custom-built Washington house—and, finally, in Samoa.

In 1890, Adams, accompanied by the American artist John La Farge, set out on a South Seas junket that was half adventure, half escape. He had just completed his nine-volume history of the Jefferson and Madison administrations, and felt in need of a complete break. Samoa offered that; still, Adams had scarcely disembarked before he was seeking out the island's famous writer-in-residence—Robert Louis Stevenson.

That November, Stevenson and his American wife, Fanny, were just settling in at Vailima, a wild, almost inaccessible estate chosen for the salubrious effect of its altitude on Stevenson's advanced tuberculosis. Adams and La Farge plodded upward on horseback to come out upon a temporary iron-roofed shanty surrounded by the charred stumps of trees. From it emerged their surprised host, nearly a foot taller than Adams, thin to emaciation. The scene was *Treasure Island* incarnate. Stevenson wore striped pajamas tucked into coarse-knit stockings, one brown, one purple. His face was streaked with soot.

But it was Adams, not Stevenson, who was embarrassed. To Adams, who was always correctly dressed, who had not moved into his house until the last rug was placed and picture hung, celebrity implied obligation. An Adams understood obligation. Stevenson seemed preoccupied with other matters. Besides, there was the distressing fact that although Stevenson had recognized La Farge, he had obviously not a clue who Adams was.

The Americans were on Samoa for some weeks. Adams enjoyed Stevenson's company, but conversation inclined to wild tales of native practices, with little occasion for his own wry witticisms. Adams envied the fame of which Stevenson, twelve years his junior, was so careless. He felt himself a "straggler." Because his *Education* was not published until after his death, he never knew how magnificently he caught up.
       —Nancy Caldwell Sorel

901

Art Director	**Terry Brown**
Artist	**Jean-Michel Folon**
Writer	**Robert B. Reich**
Editor	**William Whitworth**
Publisher	**The Atlantic Monthly Co., Boston**
Publication	**The Atlantic Monthly**

902

Art Director	**Judy Garlan**
Artist	**Edward Sorel**
Writer	**Nancy Caldwell Sorel**
Editor	**William Whitworth**
Publisher	**The Atlantic Monthly Co., Boston**
Publication	**The Atlantic Monthly**

THE NAKED VULTURE AND THE THINKING APE

BY KENNETH BROWER

IT ARRIVES AS A GIANT, OVATE-ELLIPSOIDAL EGG OF the palest green or blue. The egg meets the planet with a small calcareous click, for its nest is no nest at all, just the bare rock floor of some high cave, cleft, or pothole. Nudged gently by great beaks hooked for tearing corpses, straddled by clawed feet the size of human hands, warmed by breast feathers as black as the nights outside the cave, the egg incubates. In close to sixty days, the lip of a new beak, smaller but hooked like the others, pips out into the world. The nostrils sample aromas much like those that greeted the first life on Earth. The rest of the California condor smells of ammonia and rock dust, and fishy.

The chick struggles free and sprawls on the rock, wet and bedraggled, the rarest of birds. Each condor hatched now, late in the twentieth century, is the most recent in a line that goes back to the Pleistocene age; each one stands a chance of being the very last of its kind.

The chick dries and expands into a yellowish ball of woolly down. It opens a brown eye. Its parents work shifts feeding it—a gastric vasopepsic extract of rabbit, rarely aged ears of Hereford, deer, coyote, sheep. The down turns dark gray. The chick preens, bounds around the cave, hiccups mightily, perks at eggshells, toys with mottled feathers. It stretches its wings, reddles them, stretches them again. It fans them, sending small windstorms scurrying through the down and malted feathers and loose

Pets. We feed and care for them. Many of us choose to share a large portion of our lives with them. In April we even observe a Pets Are Wonderful Month. Why?

Whatever creates the need to have a pet, it's been going on for thousands of years. The affection humans have for their pets is paralleled by the history of pets' loyalty to and affection for their owners.

A Story from Pompeii

In the Pompeii Museum commemorating the great Mt. Vesuvius eruption 1,900 years ago two figures lie side by side: a small boy and his dog. Around the dog's neck is the outline of a collar bearing an inscription which translates:

"Thrice has this dog saved his little master from death: once from fire, once from flood, once from thieves." Again this dog was loyal to his master. Virtually no animals, save those stabled or tethered, were caught in the lava. Warned by their instincts, most fled to safety. This little dog, though, chose to stay with his master rather than escape.

In a Nottinghamshire, England, garden stands a small monument inscribed, "To mark a friend's remains, these stones arise: I never knew but one and here he lies." That friend was Boatswain, the beloved Newfoundland dog belonging to Lord Byron. The two were inseparable and, although it was never fulfilled, it was the wish of the great Romantic poet that his own remains lie beside those of his Boatswain.

Devotion between owner and pet is as much in evidence today as it was then. Pets Are Wonderful Month was the creation of the Pets Are Wonderful (PAW) Council. Founded in 1981, PAW is a not-for-profit, public service organization

PETS and PEOPLE

903		904	
Art Director	**Judy Garlan**	Art Director	**Don Johnson**
Artist	**Braldt Bralds**	Designer	**Bonnie Berish**
Writer	**Kenneth Brower**	Artist	**Alice Brickner**
Editor	**William Whitworth**	Client	**Nabisco Brands, Inc.**
Publisher	**The Atlantic Monthly Co., Boston**	Editor	**Dana Lee Wood**
Publication	**The Atlantic Monthly**	Agency	**Johnson & Simpson Graphic Designers, Newark, NJ**
		Publication	**NB Eye, Spring 1983**

905
Art Director **Judy Garlan**
Artist **David Wilcox**
Writer **William Lanouette**
Editor **William Whitworth**
Publisher **The Atlantic Monthly Co., Boston**
Publication **The Atlantic Monthly**

906
Art Director **Derek W. Ungless**
Artist **Guy Billout, New York**
Client **Rolling Stone**

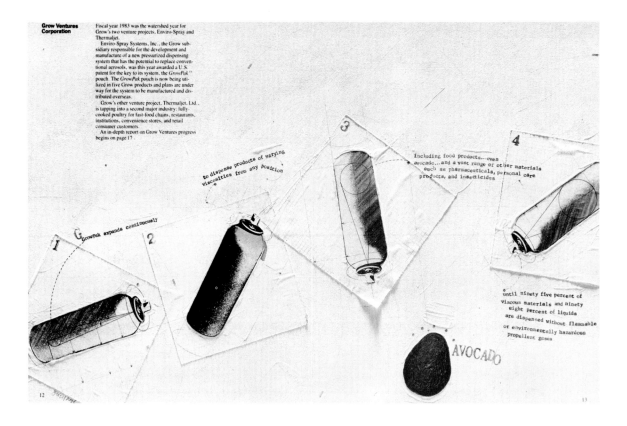

Grow Ventures Corporation

Fiscal year 1983 was the watershed year for Grow's two venture projects, Enviro-Spray and Thermaljet.

Enviro-Spray Systems, Inc., the Grow subsidiary responsible for the development and manufacture of a new pressurized dispensing system that has the potential to replace conventional aerosols, was this year awarded a U.S. patent for the key to its system, the *GrowPak™* pouch. The *GrowPak* pouch is now being utilized in five Grow products and plans are under way for the system to be manufactured and distributed overseas.

Grow's other venture project, Thermaljet, Ltd., is tapping into a second major industry: fully-cooked poultry for fast-food chains, restaurants, institutions, convenience stores, and retail consumer customers.

An in-depth report on Grow Ventures progress begins on page 17.

GrowPak expands continuously to dispense products of varying viscosities from any position including food products...even avocado...and a vast range of other materials such as pharmaceuticals, personal care products, and insecticides until ninety five percent of viscous materials and ninety eight percent of liquids are dispensed without flammable or environmentally hazardous propellent gases

AVOCADO

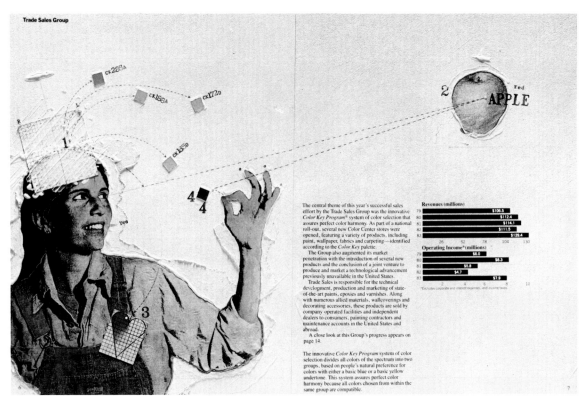

Trade Sales Group

The central theme of this year's successful sales effort by the Trade Sales Group was the innovative *Color Key Program®* system of color selection that assures perfect color harmony. As part of a national roll-out, several new Color Center stores were opened, featuring a variety of products, including paint, wallpaper, fabrics and carpeting—identified according to the *Color Key* palette.

The Group also augmented its market penetration with the introduction of several new products and the conclusion of a joint venture to produce and market a technological advancement previously unavailable in the United States.

Trade Sales is responsible for the technical development, production and marketing of state-of-the-art paints, epoxies and varnishes. Along with numerous allied materials, wallcoverings and decorating accessories, these products are sold by company operated facilities and independent dealers to consumers, painting contractors and maintenance accounts in the United States and abroad.

A close look at this Group's progress appears on page 14.

The innovative *Color Key Program* system of color selection divides all colors of the spectrum into two groups, based on people's natural preference for colors with either a basic blue or a basic yellow undertone. This system assures perfect color harmony because all colors chosen from within the same group are compatible.

red APPLE

Revenues (millions)
79 $106.5
80 $112.4
81 $114.1
82 $111.5
83 $120.4

Operating Income* (millions)
79 $6.0
80 $6.3
81 $5.8
82 $4.7
83 $7.9

907
Art Director Vance Jonson
Designer Vance Jonson
Artist David Lesh,
Indianapolis, IN
Client Grow Group Inc.

908
Art Director Vance Jonson
Designer Vance Jonson
Artist David Lesh,
Indianapolis, IN
Client Grow Group Inc.

	909		910
Art Director	**Ken Bloomhorst**	Art Director	**Don Nelson**
Designer	**Ken Bloomhorst**	Designer	**Don Nelson**
Artist	**David Lesh, Indianapolis, IN**	Artist	**David Lesh, Indianapolis, IN**
Client	**Merchants National Corporation**	Client	**Notre Dame Magazine**

911		912	
Art Director	**Jan Adkins**	Art Director	**Jan Adkins**
Artist	**Barron Storey**	Artist	**Barron Storey**
Editor	**Wilbur E. Garrett**	Editor	**Wilbur E. Garrett**
Publication	**National Geographic, Washington, DC**	Publication	**National Geographic, Washington, DC**

As many students turn to religion for spiritual and social guidance, some evangelical churches are winning converts with effective recruiting tactics, then demanding strict obedience to church doctrine.

HARD-SELL RELIGION

BY RASA GUSTAITIS

avid Pallas was in the cancer-research lab until 6 a.m. today, and he will be there tomorrow until 5 a.m.; he's completing his doctoral work in biochemistry. He has already passed his orals and is due to defend his Ph.D. thesis at the Massachusetts Institute of Technology (MIT) in three months. Time is precious, and his pale face is witness to his fatigue and lack of sleep.

But Pallas, 27, still had time for church yesterday; on Tuesday he will have time to lead a Bible-study group; and he will be there for both the discipleship group and the devotional on Friday night.

The Lexington Church of Christ in Boston, Massachusetts, demands a great deal of Pallas' time—about 15 hours a week. He says it speaks to his needs; it brings meaning and order into his life, and he believes it is a source of God-given strength.

The Lexington Church of Christ is part of a phenomenon with mounting influence on college campuses: hard-sell Chris-

The names of some former church members mentioned in this article have been changed to protect their identities.

BONUS HOLIDAY GIFT GUIDE

Christmas Memories That Live Forever | How Charitable is Indianapolis? The Answer May Surprise You

Indianapolis magazine

December 1983/$1.50

THE CAT BURGLAR

Learning how he thinks may help protect you

913

Art Director	**Ken Smith**
Designer	**Su Pogany**
Artist	**Brad Holland**
Writer	**Rasa Gustaitis**
Client	**Nutshell Magazine**
Editor	**Keith Bellows**
Publisher	**13-30 Corporation, Knoxville, TN**
Publication	**Nutshell Magazine**

914

Art Director	**Jeff Laramore**
Artist	**Jeff Laramore**
Client	**Indianapolis Magazine**
Agency	**Young & Laramore, Indianapolis**

	915		916
Art Director	**Shelley Williams**	Art Director	**Jan Adkins**
Designer	**Debbie Smith**	Artist	**Barron Storey**
Artist	**Seymour Chwast**	Editor	**Wilbur E. Garrett**
Writers	**Various**	Publication	**National Geographic,**
Client	**Pet Information Center**		**Washington, DC**
Editors	**Wendy Lowe, Hope**		
	Dlugozima, Denise		
	Graveline		
Publisher	**13-30 Corporation,**		
	Knoxville, TN		
Publication	**Pet Information Center**		

FINANCE'83

NEW STRATEGIES
in a new era

How Small Banks Plan to Avoid Getting Trampled

*A new trough of profits
is strengthening the independents
in the race for market share.*

By John Craddock

The red Porsche 944 sitting in front of an upscale suburban home in St. Petersburg marks its owner as an upper income professional with a taste for high-ticket items. Though this $20,000 bauble sparkles in the driveway like an expensive charm, almost any working Joe could afford the payments. The small bank that carried the loan required nothing down and interest-only installments of $208 per month.

Switch scenes to rural Florida, and the shaded lanes of Live Oak in Suwannee County. A rattly Chevy rolls to a stop in front of the local bank and an elderly woman emerges. In the bank, she corners a loan officer and asks to see the vault "to check on her money," as she puts it. She looks at the cash and leaves, her curiosity satisfied.

Whether providing fast-lane financing or going the extra mile to keep a customer happy, small banks in Florida have been gearing up to stay in the financial race of the 1980s. At first glance, the banks would have seemed sure candidates to be run over. Larger bank holding companies have expanded rapidly in-state and seem capable of flattening their smaller counterparts with an ever-broadening range of services, technological refinements and sheer financial muscle. Holding company executives, in fact, confidently predict that small banking operations will go the way of the corner grocery. "Mom and Pop stores were driven out because customers

Gary Kelley illustration

PHYSICAL GEOLOGY

SPENCER

ADDISON
WESLEY

ISBN 0-201-06423-5

6423

DISTINCTIVE MERIT

917

Art Directors	**Steve Duckett, Gary Bernloehr**
Designer	**Gary Bernloehr**
Artist	**Gary Kelley**
Publication	**Florida Trend Magazine, St. Petersburg, FL**

918

Art Director	**Geri Davis**
Designers	**Richard Hannus/ Hannus Design Associates**
Artist	**Alan Magee**
Publisher	**Addison - Wesley Company, Inc., Reading, MA**
Color Separator	**Color Response, Inc.**

LOVE
GONE WRONG

Loving and being loved—the simplest things in the world and often the hardest. On these pages, two writers explore the far boundaries of our strongest emotion: how it feels to be the object of an uncontrollable passion and how to survive when love is over. Both have something to tell us about the true nature of love that lasts.

BY LOVE OBSESSED

He won't take "no" for an answer. He says he can't live without you. Does he really love you that much or are you just playing a part in some strange fantasy of his own?

When John Hinckley, Jr., lay in his hospital bed, wavering between life and death after his third suicide attempt, once again the sorry young loser who shot the President had made himself the focus of our unwilling attention. The whole nation knows that he shot President Reagan in a bizarre attempt to win the admiration of the young woman he thought he loved—a woman whom he did not even know. John Hinckley had seen actress Jodie Foster in the film *Taxi Driver*, just like millions of other moviegoers. On that slight / turn to page 122

BY ANNIE GOTTLIEB

ILLUSTRATION BY GUY BILLOUT

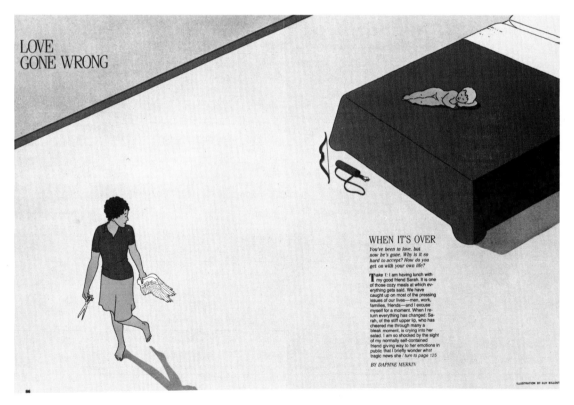

LOVE
GONE WRONG

WHEN IT'S OVER

You've been in love, but now he's gone. Why is it so hard to accept? How do you get on with your own life?

Take 1: I am having lunch with my good friend Sarah. It is one of those cozy meals at which everything gets said. We have caught up on most of the pressing issues of our lives—men, work, families, friends—and I excuse myself for a moment. When I return everything has changed. Sarah, of the stiff upper lip, who has cheered me through many a bleak moment, is crying into her salad. I am so shocked by the sight of my normally self-contained friend giving way to her emotions in public that I briefly wonder what tragic news she / turn to page 125

BY DAPHNE MERKIN

ILLUSTRATION BY GUY BILLOUT

919

Art Director	**Modesto Torre**
Designers	**Min Jae Hong, Mary Lynn Blasutta**
Artist	**Guy Billout**
Writers	**Annie Gottlieb, Daphne Merkin**
Client	**McCall's Magazine**
Publisher	**McCall Publishing Company, New York**

Vincent van Gogh Visits New York

Greg
Constantine

920		921	
Art Director	R.D. Scudellari	Art Director	Michael Mendelsohn
Designer	R.D. Scudellari	Designer	Jane Heelan
Artist	Greg Constantine	Artist	Miro Malish
Writer	Greg Constantine	Writers	The Brothers Grimm
Client	Alfred A. Knopf	Client	The Franklin Library
Editor	Robert Gottlieb	Editor	Bob Daniels
Publisher	Alfred A. Knopf/ Random House, New York	Publisher	The Franklin Library, New York
		Bindery	The Sloves Organization
		Production Manager	Renee Guilmette

George W. Bomar

TexasWeather

	922		923		924
Art Director	**Michael Mendelsohn**	Art Director	**Michael Mendelsohn**	Art Director	**George Lenox**
Designer	**Jennifer Dossin**	Designer	**Maria Epes**	Designer	**George Lenox**
Artist	**David Frampton**	Artist	**Jarmila Maranova**	Artist	**Ed Lindlof**
Writer	**Walt Whitman**	Writer	**Franz Kafka**	Client	**University of Texas**
Client	**The Franklin Library**	Client	**The Franklin Library**		**Press**
Editors	**Peter Wilkie, Jana**	Editor	**Christine Valentine**	Publisher	**University of Texas**
	Durham	Publisher	**The Franklin Library,**		**Press, Austin**
Publisher	**The Franklin Library,**		**New York**		
	New York	Bindery	**The Sloves**		
Bindery	**The Sloves**		**Organization**		
	Organization	Production			
Prod. Mngrs.	**Janet Sessa, Jo Anne**	Managers	**Janet Sessa, Jo Anne**		
	Milana		**Milana**		

925

Art Director	**Lidia Ferrara**
Designer	**Braldt Bralds**
Artist	**Braldt Bralds**
Writer	**Marian Zimmer Bradley**
Client	**Alfred A. Knopf**
Editor	**Robert Gotlieb**
Publisher	**Alfred A. Knopf, New York**

926

Art Director	**Matt Tepper**
Artist	**Donna Pacinelli**
Publication	**Avon Books, New York**

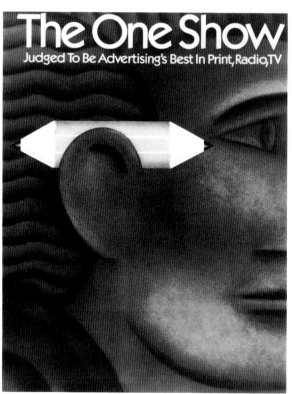

927

Art Director   **Lidia Ferrara**
Designer   **Carlin Goldberg**
Artist   **Edward Sorel**
Writer   **Hugh Kenner**
Client   **Alfred A. Knopf**
Editor   **Charles Elliott**
Publisher   **Alfred A. Knopf,
New York**

928

Art Director   **Seymour Chwast**
Designer   **Michael Aron**
Artist   **Michael Aron**
Client   **American Showcase**
Editor   **Chris Curtis**
Agency   **Pushpin Lubalin
Peckolick, New York**

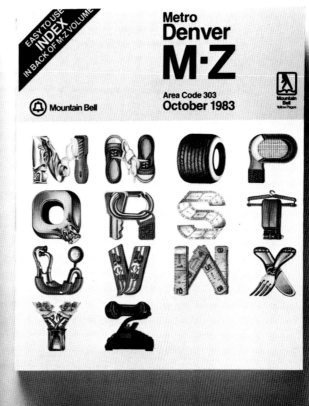

929

Art Director **Tim Hannell**
Designer **Tim Hannell**
Artist **Jözef Sumichrast**
Client **Mountain Bell Yellow Pages**
Agency **Tracy-Locke/BBDO, Englewood, CO**

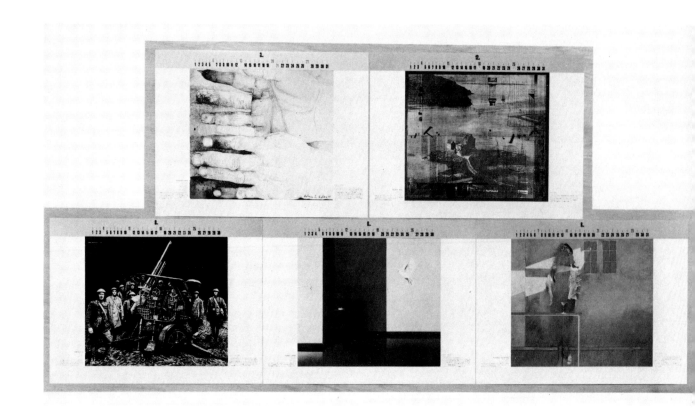

930

Art Directors   Shinichiro Tora/U.S.A.
Mitsutoshi Hosaka,
Japan
Designer   Mitsuo Katsui
Artists   Alan E. Cober, Braldt
Bralds, Gerald
McConnell, Robert
Hindel, Fred Otnes
Client   Hotel Barmen's
Association
Agency   Dai Nippon Printing Co.
CDC, New York

A world of magical causality
where pencils and green peppers float
through imaginary mindscapes

HIDDEN CONNECTIONS

PAINTINGS BY DONALD ROLLER WILSON

The children are playing in the attic, dressing up in fancy old clothes, acting out dramas of their own devising in scenes of great purity and silliness. The artist is also there, an unseen presence, and he, too, is playing. In these games there's always something moving and unfixed—a smoking cigarette, a twister seen through the window, green peppers, or a yellow pencil suspended miraculously in thin air.

The artist plays at being children playing at being apes, nuns, dogs, and cats. The attic is full of interesting things, props for the children's dramas. The artist plays with what the children find, and invents what they need: teeth, smoke, plumed hats, shoes, skulls, baby carriages, baboons, bulldogs, and olives stuffed with pimientos. The paradoxical images are koans inviting true response, stifling the obvious. Feel the painting with your mind. Touch it with your sensibility. Your reward will be a little satori, interrupting the dreary thingness of the everyday world

TEXT BY ROBERT SHECKLEY

931		932	
Art Director	Elizabeth Woodson	Art Director	Beverly Littlewood
Designer	Patrick Deffenbaugh	Designer	Turk Winterrowd
Artist	Donald Roller Wilson	Artist	Turk Winterrowd
Publication	Omni Publications Int'l Ltd., New York	Client	WNBC-TV, New York
V.P., Graphics Director	Frank M. DeVino		

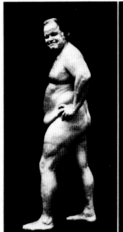

HOW MUCH WEIGHT DO YOU HAVE TO LOSE BEFORE YOUR INSURANCE COMPANY NOTICES IT?

Anyone who's ever tried knows that losing weight can be a real struggle. You go to bed hungry. You wake up hungry. You learn to despise lettuce. You exercise until you ache.

The good news is that according to recent studies, people who stay trim and exercise regularly live longer and are better life insurance risks. So now, ITT Life has come up with a Good Health Bonus® for non-smokers and people who are trim and

fit. Which means that if you don't smoke, you could earn a 65% insurance bonus. *With no increase in your insurance premiums.*

If you stay trim and don't smoke, you could get a 100% life insurance bonus. And over half of the non-smokers who apply meet the special underwriting criteria for the Good Health Bonus.

Look. You work very hard to keep your body trim. Isn't it about time you got the trimmer life insurance premiums you deserve?

For more details call free: **1-800-328-2193** and ask for operator 901. In Minnesota call us at 612-545-2100. Or mail the coupon to us today.

ITT Life Insurance Corporation **ITT**

L'ORÉAL
PARIS · NEW YORK

Now. Shadow Riche. Powdered Satin.

It's staggering.
The effect.
L'Oréal
has developed
a satin powder
capable of blending
like layers of light
to form the most
eyeopening
results.

GOLD AWARD

933		934	
Art Director	**Dean Hanson**	Art Director	**George D'Amato**
Designer	**Dean Hanson**	Photographer	**Irving Penn**
Photographer	**Bob Adelman**	Writer	**Herb Green**
Writer	**Tom McElligott**	Client	**Beatrice Dautresme/**
Client	**ITT Life Insurance**		**L'Oreal/COSMAIR**
	Corporation	Agency	**McCann-Erickson,**
Agency	**Fallon McElligott Rice,**		**New York**
	Minneapolis		
Publication	**American Health**		

GOLD AWARD

935

Art Director	**George D'Amato**
Photographer	**Irving Penn**
Writer	**Herb Green**
Client	**Beatrice Dautresme/ L'Oreal/COSMAIR**
Agency	**McCann-Erickson, New York**

GOLD AWARD

936

Art Director	**George D'Amato**
Photographer	**Irving Penn**
Writer	**Herb Green**
Client	**Beatrice Dautresme/ L'Oreal/COSMAIR**
Agency	**McCann-Erickson, New York**

ITT LIFE BELIEVES A BEAUTIFUL BODY SHOULD BE WORTH MORE THAN A FEW WHISTLES AT THE BEACH.

When you're young, a beautiful body may be something you take for granted. As you grow older, however, keeping your body beautiful takes work.

For those of you who haven't given in to rich foods, cigarettes, and gravity, however, ITT Life has good news: the ITT Life Good Health Bonus. This is a life insurance plan which truly recognizes that people who exercise regularly and don't smoke live longer on the average and, therefore, are better life insurance risks.

ITT Life rewards them for those good habits.

If you don't smoke, the Good Health Bonus could be worth a 65% insurance bonus to you. For example, your $50,000 policy would be increased to $82,500. *With no increase in premiums.*

If you don't smoke and you also exercise regularly, you could earn a 100% life insurance bonus — *double the protection without any increase in premiums.* And over half of the non-smokers who apply are meeting the special underwriting criteria for the Good Health Bonus.

Isn't it time you began getting the beautiful insurance rates your beautiful body deserves?

For details call free **1-800-328-2193** and ask for operator 599. In Minnesota: 612-545-2100. Or mail the coupon.

ITT
ITT Life Insurance Corporation

GINKO

For catalog of complete gift line, call 415-777-4450, 486 Brannan Street, San Francisco, CA 94107

937	
Art Director	**Nancy Rice**
Designer	**Nancy Rice**
Photographer	**Dick Jones**
Writer	**Tom McElligott**
Client	**ITT Life Insurance Corporation**
Agency	**Fallon McEligott Rice, Minneapolis**
Publication	**MAC Gopher**

938	
Art Director	**Phil Toy**
Photographer	**Phil Toy**
Client	**Ginko**
Agency	**Phil Toy Photography, San Francisco**

Vertigo... *going... gone*

*Indications: Based on a review of this drug by the National Academy of Sciences - National Research Council and/or other information. FDA has classified the indications as follows:
Effective: Management of nausea and vomiting, and dizziness associated with motion sickness.
Possibly Effective: Management of vertigo associated with diseases affecting the vestibular system.
Final classification of the less than effective indications requires further investigation.
Contraindications: Previous hypersensitivity.
Warnings: Drowsiness may occur, patients should be warned of this possibility and

cautioned against driving a car or operating dangerous machinery. Patients should avoid alcoholic beverages while taking this drug.
Due to its potential anticholinergic action, this drug should be used with caution in patients with asthma, glaucoma, or enlargement of the prostate gland.
Usage in Children. Safety and effectiveness in children have not been established; usage is not recommended in children under 12 years of age.
Usage in Pregnancy. Pregnancy Category B. Reproduction studies in rats have shown cleft palates at 25-50 times the human dose. Epidemiological studies in pregnant women, however, do not indicate that meclizine

increases the risk of abnormalities when administered during pregnancy. Despite the animal findings, it would appear that the possibility of fetal harm is remote. Nevertheless, meclizine, or any other medication, should be used during pregnancy only if clearly necessary.
Adverse Reactions: Drowsiness, dry mouth, and blurred vision have been reported.

Before prescribing or administering, please see package circular.

ROERIG *Pfizer*

A division of Pfizer Pharmaceuticals
New York, New York 10017

Antivert/50
(meclizine HCl) 50 mg Tablets

Dosage for vertigo*: The recommended dose is 25 mg to 100 mg daily in divided dosage.

Also available
Antivert* (meclizine HCl) 12.5 mg Tablets • Antivert*/25 (meclizine HCl) 25 mg Tablets

*This drug has been evaluated as possibly effective in the management of vertigo associated with diseases affecting the vestibular system. See Brief Summary.

For Prescribing Information, please see last tab in Compendium.

939

Art Director	**Frank O'Blak**
Photographer	**David Attie**
Writer	**Norman Franklin**
Client	**Roerig Div. of Pfizer**
Agency	**Robert A. Becker Inc., New York**
Client	**Richard Fulmer**

940

Art Director	**Chris Hill**
Photographer	**Arthur Meyerson**
Client	**Steven Interiors**
Agency	**Media Communications, Inc., Houston**

941		942	
Art Director	**Harry De Zitter, New York**	Art Director	**Harry De Zitter, New York**
Designer	**De Zitter/Wilson**	Designer	**De Zitter/Wilson**
Photographer	**De Zitter**	Photographer	**De Zitter**
Client	**De Zitter Photography**	Client	**De Zitter Photography**
Publisher	**Beith**	Publisher	**Beith**

943		944	
Art Director	**Harry De Zitter,** **New York**	Art Director	**Harry De Zitter,** **New York**
Designer	**De Zitter/Wilson**	Designer	**De Zitter/Wilson**
Photographer	**De Zitter**	Photographer	**De Zitter**
Client	**De Zitter Photography**	Client	**De Zitter Photography**
Publisher	**Beith**	Publisher	**Beith**

DE ZITTER LANDSCAPES

945

Art Director   **Harry De Zitter,**
New York
Designer   **De Zitter/Wilson**
Photographer   **De Zitter**
Client   **De Zitter Photography**
Publisher   **Beith**

DE ZITTER LANDSCAPES

GOLD AWARD

946

Art Director **Harry De Zitter,
New York**
Designer **De Zitter/Wilson**
Photographer **De Zitter**
Client **De Zitter Photography**
Publisher **Beith**

**IT IS A
COLLECTION
BEYOND
ANY MEASURE
OF WORLDLY
VALUE.**

sect plague to the most remote reaches of war-torn China and then, on the eve of the Communist victory, removed from the mainland entirely and taken to their present home on the Nationalists' island redoubt, Taiwan. "In all that time, over all those miles," says Dr. Han Lih-wu, the Nationalists' retired minister of education and one of the three men still living who were most responsible for the removal of the treasures, "there was not so much as a teacup broken."

It is a collection that is quite beyond assessment of worldly value. Amassed in the eighteenth century during the reign of the Ch'ing Dynasty's Ch'ien-lung emperor—one of China's greatest patrons of the arts—the trove includes no fewer than 6,411 paintings and pieces of calligraphy, some of which date back to the Chin Dynasty, 1,700 years ago; 23,780 porcelains from as far back as the Southern Sung Dynasty, 700 years ago; 4,402 bronzes and 3,894 pieces of jade that go all the way back to the Shang era, more than 10 centuries before Christ. Says Stanford University Chinese art historian John

La Plante, "In the realm of paintings, calligraphy and porcelains, the Taipei collection is utterly matchless." James Cahill, Chinese art historian at the University of California at Berkeley, calls the collection "incomparable."

A portion of the collection fills the National Palace Museum, a block-long pagoda-roofed building nestled in a mountainside outside Taipei. The rest—2,345 cratefuls—is stored in two bombproof concrete tunnels that

The Mongol emperor Genghis Khan (in portrait at top) conquered much of northern China in the early thirteenth century.

The art treasures have shaped the entire adult life of Na Chih-liang (above). Retired, he still lives on the National Palace Museum grounds.

wind 127 and 181 yards into the mountain itself. The tunnels are equipped with temperature and humidity controls, a secret electronic security system and emergency escape doors. So much is stored in them that museum authorities claim they can change their entire display every six months and not repeat themselves for 30 years.

The trove's political value is just as immense. The treasures are *not*, as they have sometimes been called, China's crown jewels. But their possession does carry with it an aura of dynastic legitimacy, enhancing if not confirming Nationalist claims to being the rightful rulers of China. The Communists, for their part, consider the entire collection stolen goods. In 1965, Han now delights in relating, Peking issued a blanket amnesty to all but four members of Taiwan's Nationalist regime: President Chiang Kai-shek, his vice-president, his finance minister—and Dr. Han Lih-wu. To Peking, says 82-year-old Han, he is the last living "war criminal."

It was Japan's 1931 conquest of Manchuria and the threat it posed to

The Sung Dynasty was one of China's richest artistic periods. The porcelain Ting ware vase at right is an elegant work from that time.

54 GEO

DISTINCTIVE MERIT

	947		948
Art Director	John Kleinschmidt, New York	Art Director	Mary K. Baumann
Designer	Bessen & Tully Inc.	Designer	Mary K. Baumann
Photographer	Susan Wood	Photographer	Michael O'Neill
Client	Wamsutta Mills	Editor	John Tarkov
		Publisher	Knapp Communications
		Publication	GEO Magazine, New York

DISTINCTIVE MERIT

	949
Art Director	**Glenn Staada**
Photographer	**Dennis Gottlieb**
Client	**L.P. Thebault Co.**
Design Firm	**Dennis M. Gottlieb, New York**
Cover Design	**Jon Grondahl**

	950
Art Director	**Mary K. Baumann**
Designer	**John Tom Cohoe**
Photographer	**Reinhart Wolf**
Artist	**Douglas Day**
Editor	**Stephen Brewer**
Publisher	**Knapp Communications, Corp.**
Publication	**GEO Magazine, New York**

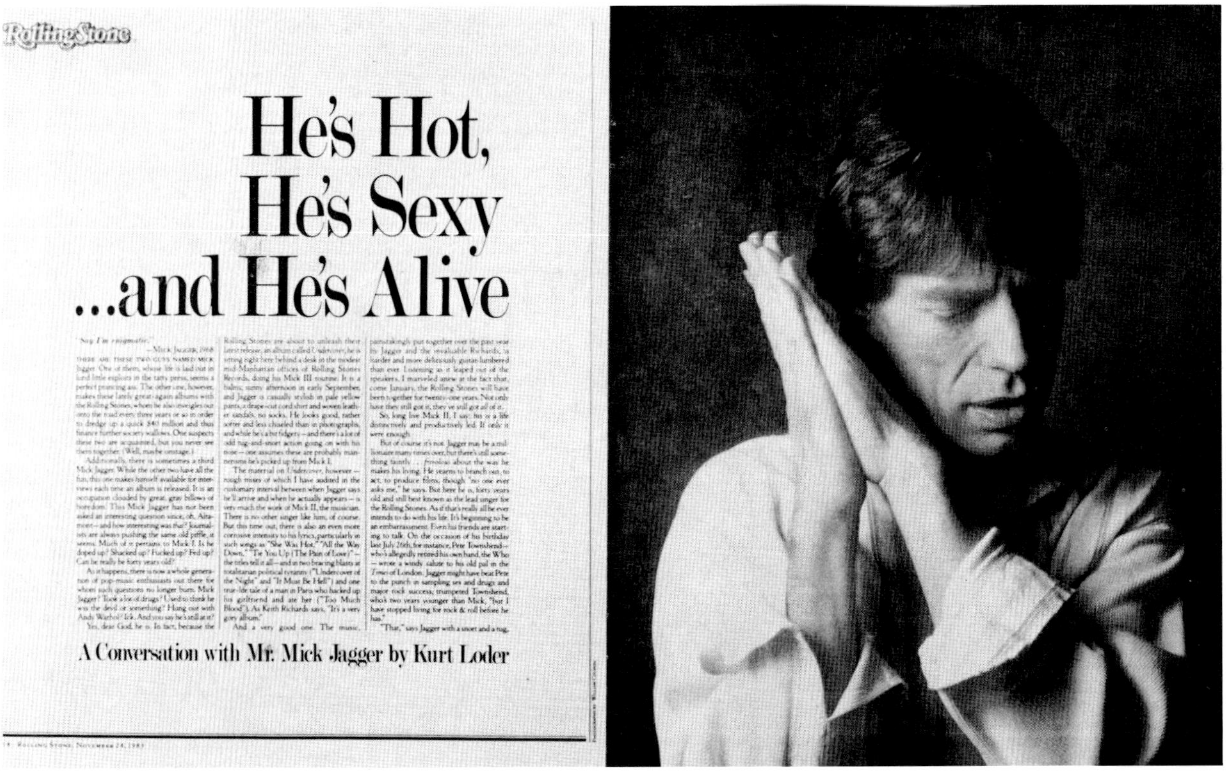

Rolling Stone
He's Hot,
He's Sexy
...and He's Alive
A Conversation with Mr. Mick Jagger by Kurt Loder

PASSAGE TO MALABAR
South of Bombay, the coast of India holds places whose very names — Calicut and Mangalore, Goa, Cochin and Trivandrum — are scented by the history of the spice trade, when the West first realized its great dream of finding a sea route to the fabled riches of the Orient.
Santha Rama Rau

951

Art Director **Derek Ungless**
Designer **Elizabeth Williams**
Photographer **William Coupon**
Publication **Rolling Stone Magazine, New York**
Photo Editor **Laurie Kratochvil**

952

Art Directors **Louis Silverstein, Walter Bernard**
Designer **Walter Bernard**
Photographer **Mitch Epstein**
Writer **Santha Rama Rau**
Client **The New York Times**
Editor **Mike Leahy**
Publisher **The New York Times, New York**
Publication **The New York Times Sophisticated Traveler**

SILK IS AS LUXURIOUS AS OTHER FIBERS ARE practical. Something that is forbidden is always that much more desirable, as silk was in Rome under Julius Caesar, who passed an edict restricting silk exclusively to his use and to the purple stripes on the togas of certain officials. It's no wonder silk had such cachet: It was worth its weight in gold.

It wasn't until 550 A.D. that the Western world produced its own silk. For almost three thousand years after its legendary discovery, the Chinese guarded the secret of silk and its production to such a degree that, under imperial decree, the person who disclosed it to the outside world would be put to death by torture. The story goes that the Emperor Huang-ti, who ruled China around 2640 B.C., assigned to his fourteen-year-old wife the task of studying the blight that was ravaging the imperial mulberry grove. Tiny white worms were eating the leaves, then attaching themselves to the stems and spinning pale cocoons. She brought a handful of cocoons into her room and accidentally dropped one into a basin of hot water, where the filament began to unwind from the cocoon. She pulled it into the air and began to unwind it.

If the legend is true, it unwound for a long time, because a single filament from a cultivated silkworm is from 800 to 1,300 yards long. A single filament is also stronger than a like filament of steel, and can stretch twenty percent beyond its length and spring back without breaking.

The fact that silk is so strong and long-lasting made it ideal for use as a writing material. Up until about 300 A.D. the Chinese wrote on silk because it was lightweight and could be easily rolled into scrolls. But it was so expensive that it was eventually replaced by paper and other substances.

Silk still is expensive because of the intensive skilled hand-labor it requires. The pinhead-sized eggs of the *Bombyx mori* must be tested for disease before they are cultivated, and put into cold storage until spring. From an hour after the worms are born they are fed fresh mulberry leaves every two or three hours for five weeks, during which time they grow to about 70 times their original size. They then spin cocoons by attaching themselves to a twig and moving their heads back and forth in a figure eight, building a wall held together by a gummy substance called sericin. Hence the word "sericulture," the raising of silk worms and the production of raw silk.

MIRIAM HSIA, bureau chief, picture editor, Time/Life Books, in silk clothes by Nancy Feldman.

POPULAR PHOTOGRAPHY
NOVEMBER 1983

VOLCANO!

Steeped in lava and dodging debris, Eric Meola photographs Kilauea's eruption in spectacular detail

By Miriam Berkley

The temperature is in the mid-eighties and the humidity is nearly 100 percent. In addition to water vapor, you breathe sulphur dioxide and other substances so noxious you can pass out after a few seconds if you're not careful. Hot, sometimes sharp, pellets rain down from the sky; if one touches your skin, it can burn or cut you.

Walking, you may sink as far down as a foot into the ground, and raising your legs again is an effort. What's more, you've got to tread very carefully, or you may find your boots starting to melt from the fires beneath your feet. Around you, trees and other vegetation are scorched. The air hisses with steam. The sky has a fiery glow.

Sound like a nightmare? These are the conditions under which New York photographer Eric Meola created these stunning pictures of Hawaii's Kilauea volcano. It was an experience he'd waited a decade for.

The story began in 1972 when Meola, then 25, read a newspaper account of volcanic activity in Iceland. Without sufficient financial resources of his own, he asked the picture editor at *Time* magazine, where he'd occasionally worked, to send him there on assignment to photograph the eruptions. The editor refused; the volcano quieted down.

Then, last February, Meola read that Kilauea located in the southeast of the

---

953

Art Director	**Barbara Koster**
Designer	**Barbara Koster**
Photographer	**William Coupon**
Writer	**Deborah Vajda Goertz**
Client	**Trans World Airlines**
Editor	**Bonnie Blodgett**
Publisher	**Jack Burkam**
Publication	**TWA Ambassador Magazine, St. Paul**
Producer	**Diana Stoianovich**

954

Art Director	**Shinichiro Tora**
Photographer	**Eric Meola**
Picture Editor	**Monica Cipnic**
Publication	**Popular Photography, New York**

A PHOTOGRAPHER ANGLES IN ON THE STATUE OF LIBERTY

TORCH SONG

These golf-scene views of the venerable lady were taken by a photographer-mountaineer named Peter B. Kaplan. He perched on her upheld torch to obtain the top of her massive nose. The close-up of her hand-reach fingertipped is bigger than a human face: came from hanging out a window in the spiked crown. Admiring her a feat of heights, Kaplan, 42, has captured St. Patrick's Cathedral from its steeple cross,

and the Empire State Building from its TV antenna. Although much of the Statue of Liberty is off-limits to the public, Kaplan recently was granted rare access by a colossal commission, set up to raise funds for the statue's badly needed overhaul. It is scheduled to begin later this year. Her copper exterior and iron framework have been corroded by the salt air in New York harbor, and she is all but falling apart.

Kaplan's pictures will be used to help raise the $30 million it will take to rejuvenate Miss Liberty, a gift from the French, in time for her 1986 centennial. Over the next three years Kaplan expects to spend as much as 400 hours photographing the statue from every conceivable vantage point. "I'm come to think of her as almost human," he says. "It saddens me to see her in this state of decay."

That's Kaplan in the window at top. To learn how he took this picture, turn to page 14.

"I PUT MY MIND 17 FEET AWAY AND SEE THE IMAGE FROM THERE"

To obtain this lofty perspective of the Statue of Liberty's torch, Kaplan used what he calls a pole shot. He attached his camera to one end of a 17-foot aluminum pole (right) and, standing on the torch's circular walkway (closed to tourists since 1916), held the pole straight above his head. The camera had to be operated by a 35-foot wire stretched from the pole to a specially made remote-control box. Once Kaplan got the camera into position, he shouted, "Fire!" and his assistant pressed a button in the box to activate the camera. Having studied under landscape photographer Ansel Adams, Kaplan uses Adams's concept of "previsualization" for his pole shots. "I put my mind seventeen feet away," says Kaplan, "and see the image from there." The idea first came to him while photographing atop Manhattan's World Trade Center. He tried extending his tripod as far over the edge as it would go and was delighted with the results. It was the pole that enabled him to photograph the statue head-on (top of page 12). The pole's shadow is barely visible along the left side of that noble face.

Leaning out a window in the statue's crown, Kaplan wields his camera-tipped pole. Top: the tip of the torch with aluminum Manhattan in the background.

To photograph the statue's right foot, Kaplan aimed his camera through a hole in her dress.

Art Director **Bob Ciano**
Photographer **Peter B. Kaplan**
Publication **Life Magazine, New York**

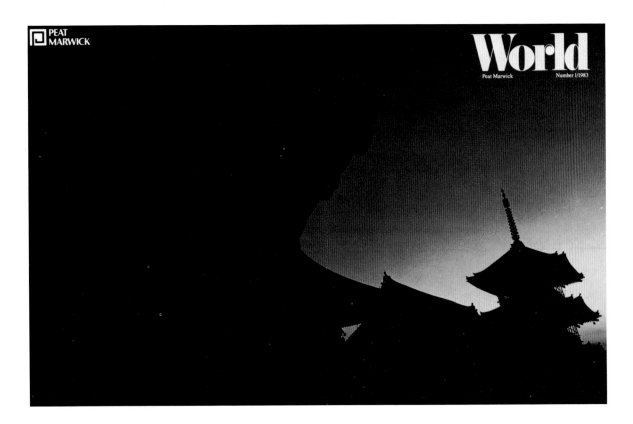

PEAT MARWICK

World
Peat Marwick   Number I/1983

GEO IN RANGOON
THE EIGHT
HAIRS
OF THE
BUDDHA
FOR A PLACE
THAT
HOUSES ANCIENT
RELICS,
RANGOON'S
SHWE DAGON
PAGODA
IS AMAZINGLY
MODERN.

956		957	
Art Director	**Charles Curtis**	Art Director	**Mary K. Baumann**
Photographer	**Camille Vickers**	Designer	**Lori Barra**
Writer	**Will Peterson**	Photographer	**Michael O'Neill**
Client	**Peat Marwick**	Writer	**Michael John Weber**
Editor	**Jerry Bowles**	Editor	**Kevin Buckley**
Publication	**Peat Marwick World Magazine, New York**	Publisher	**Knapp Communications Corp.**
		Publication	**GEO Magazine, New York**

A Fashionable
Hegira to

**THE FABLED
VALES OF
YEMEN**

Produced by
Mary Louise
Norton and
Rebecca
McDermott.
Photographs by
Joel Baldwin.

*Travelers in an
ancient land,
Claudia and
Adriana Oliveri,
daughters of Am-
bassador and
Sra. Angel M
Oliveri of Buenos
Aires and New
York, encounter
Yemen. Here,
overlooking ter-
races for crops at
Alhagra. Outfits
by Tudaomi. At
Bonwit Teller,
NYC; Frost Bros.
Frank Olive hats.
Kai Yin Lo jewel-
ry. Maud Frizon
shoes. Hair and
make-up. Leo-
nardo de Vega.*

AFTER-DARK DAZZLE
BEAUTY

Photographs by Skrebneski/Produced by Nancy Tuck Gardiner/Artwork by Joe Eula

Brilliant, gem-like colors bring fantasy to autumn. This season of first nights and twilight din- ners à deux comes alive in a swirl of social events that demand presence and panache. The drama of light-en- hancing shades and gems of rare quality adds elegance and mystery. Here, for Town & Country, the great designers of dazzling jewelry and cos- metics present Fall Evenings of Splen- dor. Eric Bertrand's iridescent pearls frame the face, near right, aglow with Christian Dior's Feux Follets make-up collection. Her eyes, luminous with "Blue/Violet" from Ombre Poudre 4- colour Eyeshadow, gaze upon the beauty radiant in Cartier's canary dia- monds and Visage/Chanel Nouveau Maquillage, featuring a meld of Nou- veau Red and Nouveau Pink Lipsticks. All hair and make-up designed by Akira Mitani. Nails by Anna Foley.

958	959
Art Director **Melissa Tardiff**	Art Director **Melissa Tardiff**
Designer **Mary Rosen**	Designer **Mary Rosen**
Photographer **Joel Baldwin**	Photographer **Skrebneski**
Publication **Town & Country Magazine, New York**	Publication **Town & Country Magazine, New York**

<table>
<tr><td colspan="2">960</td></tr>
<tr><td>Art Director</td><td>Mary K. Baumann</td></tr>
<tr><td>Photographer</td><td>Jon Ortner</td></tr>
<tr><td>Writer</td><td>Jon Ortner</td></tr>
<tr><td>Client</td><td>GEO Magazine</td></tr>
<tr><td>Photo Editor</td><td>Elisabeth Biondi</td></tr>
<tr><td>Managing</td><td></td></tr>
<tr><td>Editor</td><td>Kevin Buckley</td></tr>
<tr><td>Publication</td><td>GEO Magazine, New York</td></tr>
</table>

<table>
<tr><td colspan="2">961</td></tr>
<tr><td>Art Director</td><td>Fred Woodward</td></tr>
<tr><td>Designer</td><td>Fred Woodward</td></tr>
<tr><td>Photographer</td><td>Jim Myers</td></tr>
<tr><td>Artist</td><td>Janice Ashford</td></tr>
<tr><td>Client</td><td>Texas Monthly</td></tr>
<tr><td>Editor</td><td>Greg Curtis</td></tr>
<tr><td>Publisher</td><td>Texas Monthly, Inc.</td></tr>
<tr><td>Publication</td><td>Texas Monthly, Austin</td></tr>
</table>

Flowers for the Feast

From sweet to spicy, these edible blossoms are a treat for the palate
By Steven Brewer

Lavender's *young leaves give a pleasant bite to salads.*

Carnation *petals add spice to desserts, sauces and cordials.*

Rose *petals lend their fragrance to salads, jams, teas and honeys.*

Violet *petals, like roses, make fragrant salads; crystalized, they sweeten the sweetest dessert.*

Nasturtium *blossoms, leaves and stems impart a peppery flavor to salads; petals form the base for an exotic vinegar.*

962

Art Directors	**Will Hopkins, Ira Friedlander, New York**
Designers	**Will Hopkins, Ira Friedlander**
Photographer	**Susan Wood**
Client	**American Health Partners**

963

Art Directors	**Lloyd Ziff, Ruth Ansel**
Designer	**Cathy Hall**
Photographer	**Deborah Turbeville**
Editor	**Lou Gropp**
Publisher	**Conde Nast Publications, Inc.**
Publication	**House & Garden, New York**

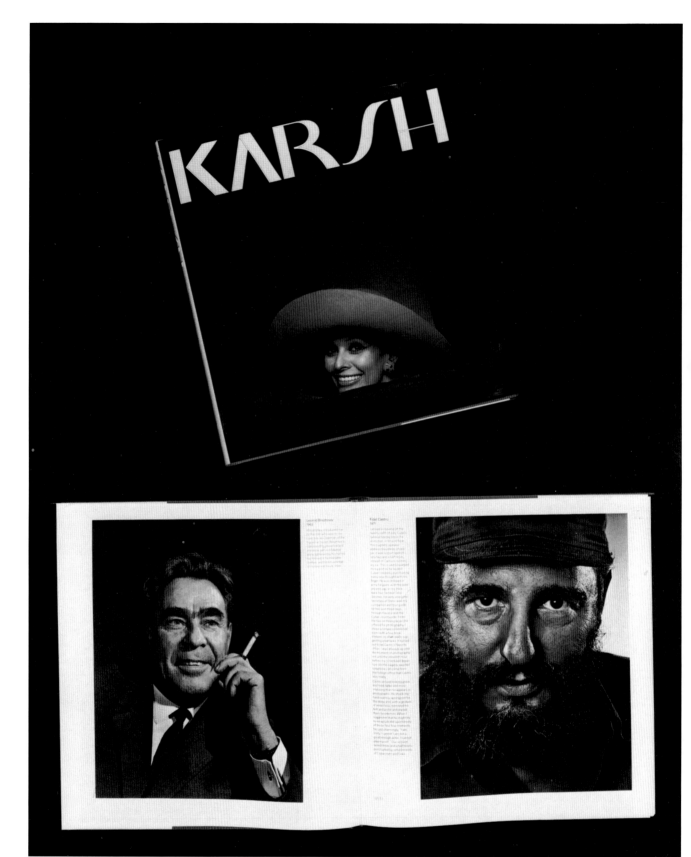

964

Art Director Nan Jernigan
Designer Carl Zahn
Photographer Yousuf Karsh
Writers Yousuf Karsh, Estrellita
Karsh
Editor Betty Childs
Publisher New York Graphic
Society/Little, Brown
and Co., Boston

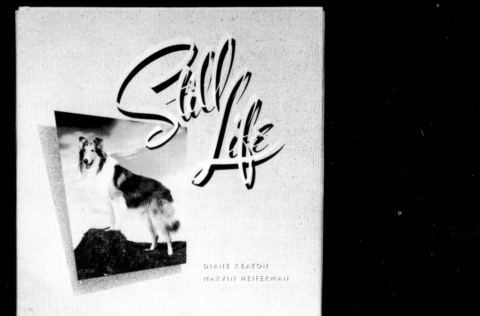

_____965_____

Art Director   Lloyd Ziff
Designers   Lloyd Ziff, Mick
  Haggerty, Marvin
  Heiferman, Nicholas
  Callaway, Diane Keaton
Photo Editors   Marvin Heiferman,
  Diane Keaton
Artist   Mick Haggerty
Writer   Diane Keaton, Marvin
  Heiferman
Publisher   Callaway Editions,
  New York
Publication   Still Life

966

Art Director   **Shinichiro Tora**
Designer   **Shinichiro Tora**
Photographer   **Yuten Konishi**
Writer   **Arthur Goldsmith**
Editor   **Arthur Goldsmith**
Publisher   **Ziff Davis Publishing Co.**
Publication   **Popular Photography, New York**

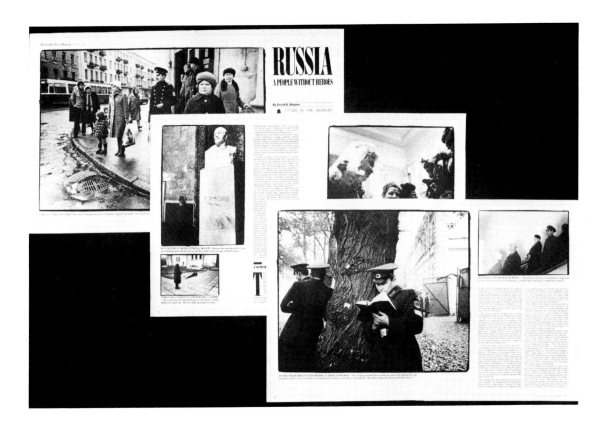

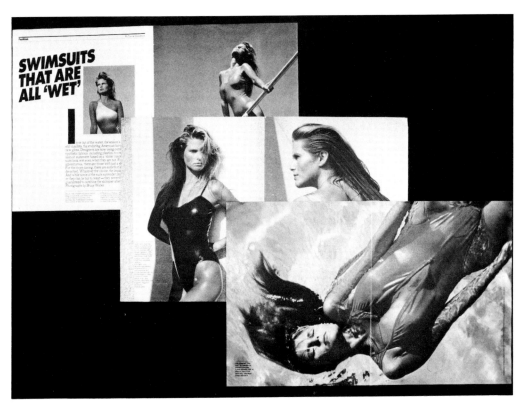

967

Art Directors **Roger Black, Ken Kendrick**
Designer **Martine Winter**
Photographer **Carrie Boretz**
Writer **David K. Shipler**
Client **The New York Times**
Editor **Ed Klein**
Publisher **The New York Times, New York**
Publication **The New York Times Magazine**

968

Art Director **Roger Black**
Designer **Ken Kendrick**
Photographer **Bruce Weber**
Writer **Tonne Goodman**
Client **The New York Times**
Editor **Ed Klein**
Publisher **The New York Times, New York**
Publication **The New York Times Magazine**

TELEVISION

Harvey Gabor

Norman Black
Don Blauweiss
Morty Dubin
Aaron Ehrlich
Stu Hyatt
Tana Klugherz
Stuart Pittman
Don Pojednik
Sam Reed
Tana Roten
Jerry Siano
Bob Smith
Norman Tannen
William Wurtzel

YOUR EYES, YOUR LIPS, YOUR RIBS
10-second
SFX: PIANO CHORD
WOMAN (VO)(SEXY VOICE): "Your eyes . . .
Your lips . . .
Your ribs."
SFX: PIANO
ANNCR (VO): Rudolph's Bar-B-Que at Franklin and Lyndale,
Minneapolis.

WALL OF WATER
10-second
ANNCR (VO): Don't just sit there.
Raging Waters is coming.
SFX: CRASH OF WATER COMING THROUGH WALL.

969

Art Director **Sue T. Crolick**
Designer **Sue T. Crolick**
Artist **Rod Pierce**
Director of Photography **Kent Severson**
Director **Jim Kosmas**
Client **Rudolph's Bar-B-Que**
Agency **Kosmas Advertising, Inc.,
Minneapolis/Jim Kosmas**
Production Company **Action Visuals/Gil Mann**

970

Art Director **Jordin Mendelsohn**
Writer **Jeff Gorman**
Directors **Jeff Gorman, Jordin
Mendelsohn**
Client **Raging Waters Park**
Agency **Mendelsohn Advertising,
Los Angeles**

TV KID
10-second
GIRL (OC): Thanks to People Express, even grown-ups can
fly at kids prices.
Oh Dad, behave yourself!

BOAT DOCK
10-second
FADE UP MUSIC
ANNCR (VO): Make a splash with Timex SportsQuartz.
Water resistant to 100 meters.
Another Timex Quartz Value.
FADE OUT MUSIC.

971
Art Director   Bob Phillips
Writer   Peri Frost
Client   People Express Airlines
Agency   Plapler & Associates, New
                York

972
Art Directors   Jeff Hill, Louis Hernandez
Writer   Jim Morrissey
Editor   Larry Plastrik
Director   Richard Greenberg
Client   Timex Corporation
Agency   Grey Advertising, Inc., New
                    York/Nancy Axthelm
Production Company   R. Greenberg Assoc./Robert
                    Greenberg

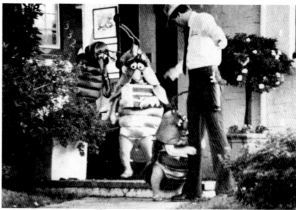

ZAP
10-second
ANNCR: You could win $10,000 playing Instant Lotto.
MAN: I got a better chance being struck by lightning.
SFX: ZAAAAAAAAAP.
MAN: One ticket please.
SUPER: Somebody's going to win, why not you?

BAD BUGS
10-second
ANNCR: No matter how bad the bugs, we'll make your problems go away.
Terminix. No more bugs.
No more worries.

973
Art Director	**Gary Wolfson**
Writer	**Jim Gorman**
Director	**Marty Lieberman**
Client	**Michigan Lottery**
Agency	**Shelley Cowan/W.B. Doner & Company, Southfield, MI**

974
Art Director	**Bill Smith**
Writer	**Mike Faems**
Director	**Bob Eggers**
Client	**Terminix International**
Agency	**Young & Rubicam/Chicago**
Production Company	**Eggers Films**
Agency Producer	**Enid Katz**

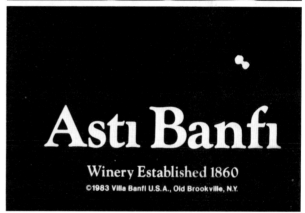

BOXER
10-second
BOXER: Play 7-Eleven's Pepsi Big Gulp Peel and Win Game
and you could win a trip for two to the fights. Y' just peel off
this little thing here . . . y' just . . . just . . .
FX: POW.

POP YOUR CORK
10-second
Asti . . .
(Sound Effect: POP)
Banfi . . .
(Sound Effect: POP)
The premium Asti
with the taste that will pop your cork.
Asti . . . (POP)
Banfi. (POP)

<table>
<tr><td colspan="2" align="center">975</td></tr>
<tr><td align="right">Art Directors</td><td>Jeff Roll, Greg Clancey</td></tr>
<tr><td align="right">Writer</td><td>Dale Richards</td></tr>
<tr><td align="right">Editors</td><td>Larry Chernoff, Charlie Chubak</td></tr>
<tr><td align="right">Director</td><td>Mark Coppos</td></tr>
<tr><td align="right">Client</td><td>7-Eleven</td></tr>
<tr><td align="right">Agency</td><td>Chiat/Day, Los Angeles/ Francesca Cohn</td></tr>
<tr><td align="right">Production Company</td><td></td></tr>
<tr><td align="right">Producer</td><td>Bill Bratkowski</td></tr>
</table>

<table>
<tr><td colspan="2" align="center">976</td></tr>
<tr><td align="right">Art Director</td><td>Bill Wurtzel</td></tr>
<tr><td align="right">Designer</td><td>Bill Wurtzel</td></tr>
<tr><td align="right">Artist</td><td>Rebecca Singer Studio</td></tr>
<tr><td align="right">Director of Photography</td><td>Richard Shore</td></tr>
<tr><td align="right">Writer</td><td>Bill Wurtzel</td></tr>
<tr><td align="right">Editor</td><td>Sue Demsky</td></tr>
<tr><td align="right">Director</td><td>Bill Wurtzel</td></tr>
<tr><td align="right">Client</td><td>Villa Banfi, USA</td></tr>
<tr><td align="right">Agency Producer</td><td>Susan Terlemezian/Hicks & Greist, New York</td></tr>
<tr><td align="right">Production Company</td><td>Gerry Gilman, Inc.</td></tr>
<tr><td align="right">Account Supervisor</td><td>Charles Skoog</td></tr>
<tr><td align="right">Account Executive</td><td>Tony Lacitignola</td></tr>
</table>

KIDS HILL
10-second
KIDS: Bogey! Miss Piggy! Snoopy! Pammy! Kermit!
ANNCR (VO): Nothing's as fun as a Timex watch.
DOG: Arf!

MASTERPIECES BY FRATELLI
10-second
ANNCR: This commercial was made possible by a grant from
Fratelli's . . . the ice cream of the crop.

977

Art Directors **Jeff Hill, Louis Hernandez**
Motion Control Photography **Randy Balsmeyer**
Director of Photography **James Szalapski**
Writer **Jim Morrissey**
Editor **Larry Plastrik**
Director **Richard Greenberg**
Client **Timex Corporation**
Agency **Grey Advertising/Nancy Axthelm**
Production Company **R/Greenberg Associates, Inc., New York/Robert M. Greenberg**
Optical Director **Joel Hynek**

978

Art Director **Bob Camuso**
Client **Fratelli Corporation**
Agency **Asher Camuso & Gibbs, Seattle**
Production Company **Hill Film**

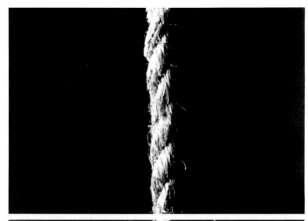
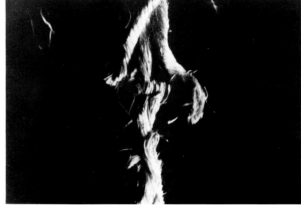

POLE VAULTER
10-second
He has spent nine . . . years on the runway . . . for . . . two seconds of flight. That's the Spirit of . . . the Games. adidas.

ROPE
10-second
SFX: DRONE THROUGHOUT, CRACKING SOUNDS
(VO): Sometimes stress can be too much to bear.
(VO): Call the StressCenter.
(VO): We can't make your problems go away, but we can show you how to live with them.
SFX: DRONE ENDS

979

Art Directors	**Brett Shevack, Joel Sobelson**
Artist	**R. Greenberg Productions**
Writer	**Robby Goolrick**
Editor	**Ed Friedman**
Creative Director	**Brett Shevack**
Client	**Adidas, U.S.A.**
Agency Producer	**Ellen Goldschmidt/LCF&S, New York**
Production Co Producers	**Ron Dexters, Sharon Starr**

980

Art Directors	**Jim Hallowes, Peter Brown**
Director of Photography	**Henry Sandbank**
Writers	**Peter Brown, Jim Hallowes**
Editor	**Charlie Chubak/Film Core**
Director	**Henry Sandbank**
Client	**Comprehensive Care Corporation (Stress Center)**
Agency	**Doyle Dane Bernbach Inc., Los Angeles/Elaine Lord**
Production Company	**Sandbank Films/J. Kamen**
Music	**H.K. Sounds**
Voice Over	**Peter Thomas**

MARATHON CHRISTMAS
10-second
MUSIC BEGINS
AVO (VO): This Christmas give the Timex Marathon Runners Quartz. For under $30.00.
SFX: PING
AVO (VO): Happy holidays one and all.

TWO REASONS
10-second
(VO): During the Country Cash give-away on K-102, you've got two reasons to give us a listen.
Money that talks . . . . .
And disc jockeys that don't.
More music. Less Bull. FM Country K-102.

981

Art Directors	**Jeff Hill, Louis Hernandez**
Writer	**Jim Morrissey**
Editor	**Larry Plastrik**
Director	**Richard Greenberg**
Client	**Timex Corporation**
Agency	**Grey Advertising, Inc., New York/Nancy Axthelm**
Production Company	**R. Greenberg Assoc./Robert Greenberg**

982

Art Director	**Kurt Tausche**
Writer	**Pete Smith**
Director	**Harry Allen**
Client	**Malrite Communications**
Agency	**Bozell & Jacobs, Inc., Minneapolis**
Production Company	**Sight & Sound - Richard Henry**

WHITE WATER CANYON
10-second
(WAGNERIAN MUSIC THROUGHOUT)
ANNCR (VO): Kings Dominion's new White Water Canyon.
Bring your family.
ANNCR (VO): Bring your friends. Bring a towel.
(MUSIC ENDS)

WET RAT SHOPPER
30-second
ANNCR: Before you go get it
See if they've got it
SHOPPER: Do you have . . .
CLERK: No, we don't.
ANNCR: Phone first.

983
Art Director **Hal Tench**
Designer **Hal Tench**
Writer **Craig Bowlus**
Director **Jimmy Collins**
Client **Vicki Sutton**
Agency Producer **Craig Bowlus/Martin Agency, Richmond, VA**
Production Co Producer **Jayan**

984
Art Director **Bill Hesterberg**
Writer **Allen Cohn**
Client **Bob Campbell/Illinois Bell**
Agency Producer **Sue Thompson/NW Ayer, Inc., Chicago**
Creative Directors **Bill Hesterberg, Allen Cohn**

MIX
30-second
ANNCR (VO): Which iced tea mix has no artificial color, no artificial flavor, no artificial nothin'?
SINGERS: CLEARLY NESTEA
      COLD, CRISP, CLEAN, BRISK
      CLEARLY NESTEA
      CLEAR, FRESH, COOL, WET
      LET'S GET NESTEA
      SPLISH SPLASH
      A PURE BLAST
      NATURALLY ZESTY
      CLEARLY NESTEA
      CLEARLY NESTEA
ANNCR (VO): Nestea iced tea mix has no artificial color, no

HOT/COLD
30-second
SINGERS: WHEN YOU'VE GOT A REAL HOT SUMMER THIRST, WHICH ICED TEA DO YOU THINK OF FIRST?
CLEARLY NESTEA
DRY THIRST, WET BURST
CLEARLY, NESTEA
HEAT WAVE, COLD WAVE
WE CRAVE NESTEA
HOT RAYS, COOL SPRAYS
ALWAYS ZESTY
CLEARLY NESTEA, CLEARLY NESTEA
BRIGHT SUN, WET ONE
HAVE SOME NESTEA
TASTES GREAT, CAN'T WAIT

	985
Art Director	**Greg Weinschenker**
Director of Photography	**Jeff Kimball**
Writer	**Linda Kaplan**
Editor	**Bobby Smalheiser**
Director	**Adrian Lyne**
Client	**Nestle Co./Nestea**
Agency Producer	**Meredith Wright/J.W.T., New York**
Production Company	**Jennie & Co./Paul Esposito**
Production Mgr.	**Mindy Goldberg**

	986
Art Director	**Greg Weinschenker**
Director of Photography	**Jeff Kimball**
Writers	**Linda Kaplan, Robin Schwarz**
Editor	**Michael Swerdloff**
Director	**Adrian Lyne**
Client	**Nestle Co./Nestea**
Agency Producer	**Meredith Wright/J.W.T., New York**
Production Company	**Jennie & Co./Paul Esposito**
Production Mgr.	**Mindy Goldberg**

DANCING BOTTLES
30-second
SINGING THROUGHOUT:
BACKGROUND: Milgurt flavored fruit drink
Milgurt flavored fruit drink
LEAD SINGER: 6 fruit flavors in bottles of fun . . .
a great snack drink for everyone . . . it's fruity
BACKGROUND: Milgurt
LEAD: What a beauty
BACKGROUND: Milgurt flavored fruit drink
LEAD: So sweet
BACKGROUND: Milgurt
LEAD: What a treat
BACKGROUND: Milgurt flavored fruit drink
LEAD: 6 tangy tastes so good you'll see, you'll flip your lid

NIKE
30-second
ANNCR: There's only one problem with having a great idea.
ANNCR: It just leads to more ideas.
ANNCR: One after another.
ANNCR: After another.
ANNCR: You try to be more critical.
ANNCR: But the innovations keep on coming.
ANNCR: And coming.
ANNCR: And then . . .
ANNCR: . . . When you finally reach the end of the line . . .
ANNCR: . . . You realize . . .
ANNCR: . . . It's only the beginning.

987

Art Director	**Scott Kane**
Writer	**Mark Patton**
Client	**Milgurt**
Agency	**Hakuhodo Advertising America, Los Angeles**
Production Company	**Coast Productions**
Creative Director	**Taka Arai**

988

Art Director	**David Kennedy**
Writer	**Dan Wieden**
Director	**Phil Marco**
Client	**Nike, Inc.**
Agency	**Wieden & Kennedy, Portland**

ROOM
30-second
ANNCR (VO): These days, a lot of airlines are crowding more seats into their planes . . . leaving less room for people.
But on Alaska Airlines, we don't cramp your style. That way you can sit back, relax, and fly with a happy face.

ALEX THE DOG
30-second
POKER PLAYER: I'd sure like another Stroh's.
HOST: No, wait. (To the dog) Alex, (DOG BARKS) two cold Stroh's.
(DOG BARKS AGAIN)
(To his buddies) Wait till you see this.
(SFX REFRIGERATOR DOOR OPENING)
He just opened the Refrigerator.
(SFX BOTTLE OPENING)

GOLD AWARD

_____
989
_____

Art Director	**Jerry Box, VP**
Writer	**Jim Copacino, VP**
Client	**Alaska Airlines**
Agency Producer	**Virginia Pellegrino, VP**
Production Company	**Sedelmaier Productions**
Agency	**Livingston & Company, Seattle**

_____
990
_____

Art Director	**Gary Ennis**
Director of Photography	**Rick Levine**
Writer	**Seth Werner**
Editor	**Len Mandelbaum**
Director	**Rick Levine**
Client	**The Stroh Brewery**
Agency	**The Marschalk Company, Inc., New York/Paula Dwoskin**
Production Company	**Levine, Pytka Prod./Cindy Akins**
Dog	**Pepper**
Trainer	**Alvin Mears**

HEARTBEAT
30-second
SFX: Heartbeat.
Shot of empty road. Cut to hand opening door.
SUPER: Introducing the 1984 Volkswagen Scirocco.
(Graphic shots and fast cuts follow as the Scirocco speeds
down various roads and curves. All the while, the heartbeat
gets faster and faster and faster. As both the heartbeat and
Scirocco are going full blast another super appears.)
SUPER: You get the idea.
(The Scirocco vanishes off into the distance.)
SUPER AND VO: Scirocco. It's not a car. It's a Volkswagen.

SILVER AWARD

_____ 991 _____

Art Director	**Gary Goldsmith**
Director of Photography	**Hugh Johnson**
Writer	**Steven Landsberg**
Editor	**Pierre Kahn**
Director	**Willie Patterson**
Client	**Volkswagen**
Agency Producer	**Jim deBarros/Doyle Dane Bernbach Inc., New York**
Production Company	**Fairbanks Film/R. Goldberg**

CHIPPENDALE
30-second
ANNCR: Now the Chicago Tribune gives you a new way to
advertise. Target Classified.
SFX: (Arrow hitting man's head)
MAN: Honey, did you see . . .
WOMAN: The Chippendale . . .
ANNCR: You can advertise in one zone, all six or any combi-
nation. And reach people, for less, where it will do you the
most good.
MAN: Hi, we came about the Chippendale
WOMAN: Dining room set?
SELLER: Sure.
SELLER: Right over here . . .
ANNCR: Tribune Target Classified.

_____ 992 _____

Art Director	**Cary Cochrane**
Writer	**Lisa Kleckner**
Editor	**Michael Curran**
Director	**Mark Story**
Client	**The Chicago Tribune**
Agency	**Ogilvy & Mather, Chicago/ Phil Bodwell**
Production Company	**Pfeifer-Story/Christina Ritzman**
Creative Director	**Doug Mc Clatchy**

ANGEL EYES
30-second
SFX: ANGEL EYES MUSIC
Pretty little angel eyes
Pretty little angel eyes
Pretty little
Pretty little
Pretty little angel
Angel eyes I really love you so
Because I love you, my darling angel eyes.
Pretty pretty little angel eyes.
VO: Want your eyes to be noticed, angel?
Bring 'em to D.O.C.

ORANGE BOX
30-second
ANNCR (VO): You can eat an orange, or you can drink it.
Introducing Sunkist Fruit Juice Drinks.
Taste the real fruit flavor of Sunkist.
Experience the refreshment of Sunkist.
All 100% Natural.
There's orange, grape, fruit punch and apple.
Taste the real fruit flavor that could only come from Sunkist.
New Sunkist Fruit Juice Drinks.

DISTINCTIVE MERIT

993

Art Directors	Steve LaGattuta, Dan Hackett
Writers	Bruce Broder, John DeCerchio
Client	D.O.C. Optics Corporation
Agency Producer	Sheldon Cohn/W.B. Doner & Company, Southfield, MI

994

Art Director	Sam Gulisano
Writer	Mike Bookman
Editor	Craig Warnick
Director	Phil Marco
Client	Thomas J. Lipton
Agency	Foote, Cone & Belding, New York/Steve Friedman
Production Co Producer	Phil Marco

NOSEY271-GASS
30-second
ANNCR: One of the most effective safety warning devices in the world is right in the middle of your face.
If you smell a strong gas odor, or suspect gas, immediately take your family outdoors and call APS from a neighbor's phone.
Don't call from your own phone; don't operate light switches; and don't light a match.
Natural gas is a safe, dependable fuel. Being nosy can make it even safer.

CREWCUT
30-second
MUSIC: INSTRUMENTAL LEAD
SONG: PUT YOUR . . .
HEAD ON MY SHOULDER.
(MUSIC)
SONG: HOLD ME IN YOUR ARMS, BABY.
(MUSIC)
(MUSIC)
(MUSIC)
(MUSIC)
ANNCR (VO): Sharing a special closeness . . . without worry of dandruff. That's the promise of Head & Shoulders.
And that's beautiful!
SONG: PUT YOUR HEAD ON MY SHOULDER.

995

Art Director	**Chris Poisson**
Writer	**Gregg Cebulski**
Director	**Bruce Dorn**
Client	**Arizona Public Service**
Agency	**Phillips-Ramsey, San Diego/David Hoogenakker**
Production Company	**Studio b**

996

Art Directors	**Ken Kimura, Jeff Turek**
Writer	**Mary Jo Leverette**
Editor	**John Cary**
Director	**Catherine Lefebvre**
Client	**Procter & Gamble**
Agency Producer	**John Schneider**
Production Company	**N. Lee Lacy/Assoc.**
Agency	**Tatham-Laird & Kudner, Chicago**

1984
30-second
For today we celebrate the first glorious anniversary of the Information Purification Directives. We have created, for the first time in all history, a garden of pure ideology, where each worker may bloom secure from the pests of contradictory and confusing truths.
Our Unification of Thought is more powerful a weapon than any fleet or army on earth.
We are one people. With one will. One resolve. One cause. Our enemies shall talk themselves to death. And we will bury them with their own confusion.
We shall prevail.

UNDERWATER
30-second
ANNCR (VO): This woman is putting HTH pool chlorinator through a truly grueling test. A test designed to prove how easy it can be to have the most crystal-clear water. Everyday. You see, no chlorine in any form—is stronger, more effective than HTH. Here's the proof.
(SFX: EFFECT)
WOMAN: Is your pool clear enough that they could have filmed this commercial in it?
ANNCR (VO): HTH. Water so clear
(SFX) It's startling.

SILVER AWARD

	997
Art Directors	**Brent Thomas, Lee Clow**
Writer	**Steve Hayden**
Editor	**Pam Powers**
Director	**Ridley Scott**
Client	**Apple Computer**
Agency	**Chiat/Day, Los Angeles/ Richard O'Neill**
Production Co Producer	**Richard Goldberg**

	998
Art Directors	**Richard Kushel, Bill Shea**
Writer	**David Weinman**
Editors	**Karina Friend, Rita Sitnick**
Director	**Mike Zingale**
Client	**Olin Corporation**
Agency	**Grey Advertising, Inc., New York/Nick Lemesh**
Production Company	**EUE/Screen Gems/Dessa Kay**

LAMBERT RIDES
30-second
ANNCR: Jack Lambert has taken on Cowboys, Redskins,
Raiders, and Vikings.
Now he's gonna take on Kennywood Park.
MUSIC & SFX Grunts & Groans Up
Jack Lambert (sync sound) threateningly
I'll get you next time Kennywood!!
ANNCR: Kennywood Park—The undefeated rollercoaster
capital of the world.

KNIFE SHARPENER
30-second
MUSIC/SFX
CHEF: "Ho cho - tomato"
CHEF: "Oh boy!"
ANNCR: "Introducing the easiest way yet to make a dull
knife sharp -
ANNCR: the Fiskars Two-Stage Knife Sharpener
ANNCR: An honorable new American invention."

SILVER AWARD

999

Art Director	**Vann Jennings**
Writer	**Edward Fine**
Editor	**Jim Humphrey**
Director	**Jim Humphrey**
Client	**Kennywood Park**
Agency	**Marc & Company, Inc., Pittsburgh**
Production Company	**TPC Communications, Inc.**

DISTINCTIVE MERIT

1000

Art Director	**George Halvorson**
Writer	**John Francis**
Client	**Fiskars Manufacturing**
Agency	**George Halvorson Advertising, Edina, MN**
Production Company	**James Productions**

AMTRAK
30-second
MUSIC THROUGHOUT
ANNCR (VO): Next time you're planning to fly somewhere . . .
Consider going with a carrier
. . . who has spent the last six and a half years . . .rebuilding
its entire fleet.
A fleet that now offers you some of the newest, most techno-
logically advanced equipment in the world.
Not surprisingly, it's also some of the most comfortable.
Next time, see what a thrill it is to fly . . . on a train.
CONDUCTOR: ALL ABOARD!
SINGERS: "All aboard, all aboard, all aboard Amtrak."

RUNNER
30-second
ANNCR (VO): In the 1984 Los Angeles Olympics, every athlete will be running at the speed of light.
Thanks to a lightwave communications system developed by
Western Electric and Bell Labs. It converts voice, data and
images into light impulses carried over glass fibers.
Who will help bring the Olympics to every corner of the
globe, including the corner of your living room?
WE will. We're Western Electric. Working with your phone
company to bring the Information Age home to you.

<table>
<tr><td colspan="2" align="center">**1001**</td></tr>
<tr><td align="right">Art Director</td><td>**Paul Frahm**</td></tr>
<tr><td align="right">Writer</td><td>**Michael Robertson**</td></tr>
<tr><td align="right">Client</td><td>**National Railroad Passenger Corporation**</td></tr>
<tr><td align="right">Agency</td><td>**Needham, Harper & Steers, New York**</td></tr>
</table>

<table>
<tr><td colspan="2" align="center">**1002**</td></tr>
<tr><td align="right">Art Director</td><td>**Maurice Mahler**</td></tr>
<tr><td align="right">Writer</td><td>**Ted Littleford**</td></tr>
<tr><td align="right">Director</td><td>**Steven Goldblatt**</td></tr>
<tr><td align="right">Client</td><td>**Western Electric**</td></tr>
<tr><td align="right">Agency</td><td>**Foote, Cone & Belding, New York/Ken Yagoda**</td></tr>
<tr><td align="right">Production Company</td><td>**LoFaro & Associates**</td></tr>
</table>

TROPHY
30-second
ANNCR: Imagine, just for a moment . . .
ANNCR: . . . That you held the world record . . .
ANNCR: . . . For the 800 meters.
ANNCR: That you were also the world's fastest miler. That, in fact, you held the world record for every long distance running event . . .
ANNCR: . . . Up to and including the marathon . . . now if you were really that good, could you keep it a secret?
ANNCR: We couldn't either.

CHRISTMAS W/O TIMEX SUPER
30-second
MUSIC FADES UP WITH SLEIGH BELLS UNDER THROUGHOUT.
ANNCR: Timex wishes everyone . . . Happy Holidays, with incredible innovation at a Timex price.
Timex for men's gifts . . .
. . . for kids gifts.
. . . for women's gifts.
with over 200 styles to choose from.
There's a Timex gift for everyone.
SFX: PING
ANNCR: Happy Holidays one and all.
MUSIC FADES OUT.

1003	
Art Director	**David Kennedy**
Writer	**Dan Wieden**
Director	**Phil Marco**
Client	**Nike, Inc.**
Agency	**Wieden & Kennedy, Portland**

1004	
Art Directors	**Jeff Hill, Louis Hernandez**
Writer	**Jim Morrissey**
Editor	**Larry Plastrik**
Director	**Richard Greenberg**
Client	**Timex Corporation**
Agency	**Grey Advertising, Inc., New York/Nancy Axthelm**
Production Company	**R. Greenberg Assoc./Robert Greenberg**

RIGHT UNDER YOUR NOSE
30-second
SINGERS:
It's right here under your nose.
A place where the whole world goes
The San Diego Zoo
Is so close to you.
So don't just sit and wonder
What the world is coming to.
Come on along, to where you belong
In the San Diego Zoo.
Hey you,
Belong in the Zoo
ANNCR: The world's greatest zoo is right under your nose.
Live Tag

DURO IT RIGHT/HOME
30-second
(Music Up)
ANNCR: Brilliant repair job!
Very clever!
That's inventive!
Duro Fix-It products
salute all you Americans
who devise ingenious
temporary solutions
to unfortunately permanent problems.
But now it's time to . . .
SINGERS: DURO IT RIGHT!
	GLUE IT.
	FILL IT.

1005

Art Director	**Bob Kwait**
Writers	**Hal Maynard, Rich Badami**
Editor	**Chris Kern**
Director	**Eric Saarinen**
Client	**San Diego Zoo**
Agency	**Phillips-Ramsey, San Diego/David Hoogenakker**
Production Company	**Coast Productions**
Music	**Sunny Blueskyes/AdMusic**

1006

Art Directors	**John Kamerer, Jay Dederick, Marshall Taylor**
Director of Photography	**Bob Porche**
Writer	**Bruce Palmer, Arnold Ostrower**
Editor	**Steve Schrieber**
Director	**Andrew Field**
Client	**William Cherry/Loctite Corp.**
Agency Producer	**David Schneiderman/ J.W.T., New York**
Production Company	**Field & Wall/Andrew Field**

CHALLENGES PORSCHE
30-second
JAMES EARL JONES (VO):
Laser.... XE Chrysler's new turbo sports car.... challenges Porsche 944.
In high speed cornering and acceleration, Porsche leads.
Front-wheel-drive laser beats Porsche in the slalom...
Matches it in braking. But Laser XE has advanced electronics,
and with Mark Cross leathers added, is still thousands less.
Laser has a 5 year/50,000 mile protection plan. Porsche doesn't. Chrysler Laser XE.
Because we knew the competition was good.

PRO KEDS
30-second
(ORIGINAL MUSIC THROUGHOUT)
AVO: Pro-Keds.
We come to play for basketball, field, running and tennis.
Pro-Keds. And a bag to put them in.

1007	
Art Directors	Ron DeVito, Ken Duskin
Director of Photography	William Fraeker
Writer	Bruce Montgomery
Editor	Morty Perlstein
Director	Rod Davis
Client	Chrysler Corporation
Agency	Kenyon & Eckhardt, New York/Burns Patterson
Production Company	Robert Abel & Assoc./ Melinda Block
Creative Director	Ken Duskin

1008	
Art Director	Dick Gage
Writer	Ron Lawner
Director	Ian Leach
Client	Keds Corporation
Agency	Humphrey Browning MacDougall, Boston/Jerry Kreeger
Production Company	Ian Leach Assoc.

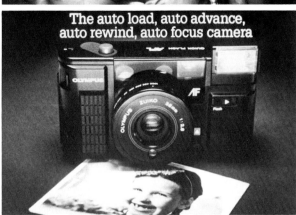

QUICK FLASH AFL
30-second
Mother's VO: Keep smiling. The flash is almost ready.
Song: Smile though your mouth is aching.
　　　Smile though your face is breaking.
VO: For all those frozen smiles waiting for flashes to re-
charge, we've introduced the Olympus Quick Flash. The
world's only 35mm auto focus camera that flashes every 1½
seconds. So when those unexpected pictures happen, you're
ready. The Olympus Quick Flash. The auto load, auto advance auto rewind, auto focus camera from Olympus.

HATS
30-second
To run the Hat of the Month Club in a businesslike way, the
boss has to keep the books, organize the files, write the let-
ters, be creative and still keep on top of things.
The boss could bring home a tool for modern times, the IBM
Personal Computer.
It can help the businessperson wear many hats, and sell
even more.
The IBM Personal Computer.
Try one on at a store near you.

	1009
Art Director	**Marty Weiss**
Director of Photography	**Richard Henry**
Writer	**Barbara Siegel**
Editors	**Dick Stone/Stonecutters**
Director	**Michael Ulick**
Client	**Olympus**
Agency	**The Marschalk Co., Inc., New York/Martha Pfeffer**
Production Company	**Michael Ulick Prod./Liz Kramer**

	1010
Art Director	**Bob Tore**
Writers	**Arlene Jaffe, Tom Mabley**
Client	**IBM Corp.**
Agency Producer	**Robert L. Dein/Lord, Geller, Federico, Einstein, New York**
Production Company	**H.I.S.K.**
Creative Director	**Tom Mabley**

DURO IT RIGHT/CAR
30-second
(Music up)
ANNCR: Ingenious repair job!
That's clever!
Nice . . . try!
Duro Fix-It products salute . . .
all you Americans who
devise brilliant temporary solutions
to unfortunately permanent problems.
But now it's time to
SINGERS: DURO IT RIGHT!
       GLUE IT!
       FILL IT!
       MEND IT!

BURGER KING/PEPSI TOGETHER AT LAST
30-second
(MUSIC UNDER)
ANNCR: Burger King presents a love story. Separately they
won the hearts of America. Now finally they have found each
other. Burger King and Pepsi—two winning tastes together
at last.
SINGERS: HAVE A PEPSI AT BURGER KING NOW!

1011

Art Directors	John Kamerer, Jay Dederick, Marshall Taylor
Director of Photography	Bob Porche
Writers	Bruce Palmer, Arnold Ostrower
Editor	Steve Schreiber
Director	Andrew Field
Client	William Cherry/Loctite Corp.
Agency Producer	David Schneiderman/ J.W.T., New York
Production Company	Field & Wall/Andrew Field

1012

Art Directors	Howie Cohen, Frank Perry
Director of Photography	Steve Horn
Writers	Hal Friedman, Brian Sitts
Editor	Bob Derise
Director	Steve Horn
Client	Burger King/Kyle Craig
Agency Producer	Gary Bass/J.W.T., New York
Prod'n Co Producer	Linda Houston Horn/Steve Horn, Inc.
Creative Director	Jim Patterson

DA VINCI
30-second
ANNCR: We have been fascinated from the beginning.
ANNCR: As a machine, the human body remains the supreme invention. To unlock its potential, we offer Soloflex. Simple. And efficient. Like the body itself.
ANNCR: Which may explain why Soloflex looks less like a machine . . .
ANNCR: . . And more like a work of art.

REFRESHER COURSE
30-second
MUSIC UP
SPOKESMAN (OC): Today a refresher course in sore throats. There's the one from smoking.
SFX: COUGH
SPOKESMAN (OC): The dry tickley kind.
SFX: COUGH   The burning sore throat.
SFX: COUGH
SPOKESMAN (OC): Fortunately, there's great tasting Luden's cough drops.
SPOKESMAN (VO): Luden's help replace pain . . with pleasure. They quickly dissolve to coat irritated, inflamed tissue with soothing, cooling relief.
SPOKESMAN (OC): So for minor sore throat problems

1013

Art Director	**David Kennedy**
Writer	**Dan Wieden**
Client	**Soloflex**
Agency	**Wieden & Kennedy, Portland**
Production Company	**Richard Williams**

1014

Art Director	**Alan Chalfin**
Directors of Photography	**Geoff Mayo, Herb Loebel**
Writer	**Larry Vine**
Editor	**Morty Ashkinos**
Director	**Geoffrey Mayo**
Client	**Ludens/Al Ciaramella**
Agency Producer	**Dorothy Franklyn/Geers Gross, New York**
Production Company	**Geoffrey Mayo Films**

AL THE COMPUTER/GENERIC NEW
30-second
DAVE: Al?
AL: Yes Dave?
DAVE: Yeah, listen. You helped Jimmy with his algebra, and eh, when Helen redecorated, *you* suggested the fishtank.
AL: I like to look at the fish, Dave.
DAVE: Alright, alright. But what about managing our money, Al?
AL: We have a Choice Card Dave. It's new.
DAVE: Another credit card, Al?
AL: It's more than a credit card, Dave.
Choice has rebates, loans, cash advances, no fee, even a savings plan.
DAVE: You mean we've been saving money, Al?

BOSS TYPES
30-second
CHARMER: Hi there Doll! These are for typing that report . . . again.
BEGGAR: Miss Smith . . . please type in one itsy bitsy change, please, please, please. . . .
ANNCR: No matter what type of boss you have, with a Panasonic 708 Electronic Typewriter you won't have to retype.
Its 8K memory stores what you've typed. Type in the corrections and it does the retyping for you.
So when your boss . . .
SCREAMER: Brenda!!!
ANNCR: Requests the work
SCREAMER: Where's that

1015

Art Director	**Bob Hinden**
Writer	**Seth Werner**
Editor	**Dennis Hayes**
Director	**Michael Ulick**
Client	**Citicorp Choice Card**
Agency	**The Marschalk Co., Inc., New York/Mindy Gerber**
Production Company	**Michael Ulick Prod./Bobby Fisher, Liz Kramer**

1016

Art Director	**Martin Rosen**
Writer	**Joel Tretin**
Director	**Jim Johnston**
Client	**Panasonic**
Agency Producer	**Stuart Raffel/Ted Bates, New York**

SITTING PRETTY
30-second
SFX: DISCORDANT SOUNDS OF SYMPHONY ORCHESTRA
WARMING UP.
BATON TAP.
VO: Ladies and gentlemen please be seated . . . The Pontiac
performance is about to begin.
SFX: (MUSIC) MARCHE DES CONTREBANDIERS BY BIZET
BEGINS.

SHRINKING WORLD
30-second
ANNCR (VO): The world has been shrinking. Big clocks have
evolved.
MUSIC: THROUGHOUT.
ANNCR (VO): into paper-thin watches.
Size has been subtracted from calculators. While accuracy
has multiplied. Computers have proven you don't have to be
big to have brains. And stereo components have been reduced to about the size of a record jacket with Pioneer's
Progression IV. Never has the expression "It's a small world"
been more accurate.

	1017
Art Director	**Stanislaus M. Shibinsky**
Designer	**Stanislaus M. Shibinsky**
Director of Photography	**Brian Thomson**
Writer	**Stanislaus M. Shibinsky**
Editor	**Michelle Jones**
Director	**Peter Thomson**
Client	**General Motors of Canada Limited**
Agency	**Foster Advertising Ltd., Toronto**
Production Company	**Boardwalk Motion Pictures Ltd./Sue Percival**
Music	**Mort Ross Productions**

	1018
Art Director	**Gary Johns**
Writer	**Jeff Gorman**
Editor	**Gayle Grant**
Director	**Mark Coppos**
Client	**Pioneer Electronics**
Agency	**Chiat/Day, Los Angeles/ Richard O'Neill**
Prod'n Co Producer	**Bill Bratkowski**

SINGING RAIN
30-second
(SFX: Man hums "It's Raining, It's Pouring")
ANNCR: The long dry spell is over. Finally, high technology
has come to lawn and garden watering products. Introducing Gardena. A revolutionary line of spray guns, innovative
click-on connectors, and the world's most advanced sprin-
klers. Precision tooled and turbo driven for years of more
natural coverage. Gardena watering products. There's nothing like them on earth . . . except maybe rain.

RELIEF PITCHER
30-second
MAN #1: This bartender is an ex-big league pitcher, and he
loves to serve fire-brewed Stroh's.
(SFX: ONE BEER SLIDING IN.)
(SFX: BEERS TWO AND THREE SLIDING IN.)
MAN #1: See what I mean.
That was his fast ball.
MAN #1: That was the curve.
Look out, wild pitch!
(SFX: Pitcher sliding by)
LAUGHTER
MAN #3: What was that?
MAN #1: Relief pitcher.
BAR CROWD SINGS: FROM ONE BEER LOVER TO

	1019
Art Director	**Frank Haggerty**
Director of Photography	**Eric Young**
Writer	**Ron Sackett**
Director	**Jim Lund**
Client	**Gardena, Inc.**
Agency	**Carmichael-Lynch, Minneapolis**
Production Company	**James Productions**

	1020
Art Director	**Gary Ennis**
Director of Photography	**Ed Martin**
Writer	**Seth Werner**
Editor	**Morty Schwartz**
Director	**Fred Levinsin**
Client	**The Stroh Brewery**
Agency	**The Marschalk Co., Inc., New York/Paula Dwoskin**
Production Company	**Fred Levinsin Prod./Bob Ramsey**

THE BAND WAGON
30-second
SFX: A BAND PLAYING IN THE DISTANCE . . . NOT VERY
WELL.
RUMBLE OF THUNDER.
THE MUSIC BEGINS TO FALTER.
MUSIC STOPS. HISS AND SPATTER OF RAIN.
ANNCR: Introducing the new Peugeot wagon. A station wa-
gon that is bigger than the best-selling imported or Ameri-
can wagons.
A wagon that will carry over half a ton of . . . almost anything.
SFX: RAIN ON ROOF.
ANNCR: The Peugeot 505S.
Perhaps the most comfortable wagon in the world today.
SFX: FUNNY NOTE FROM TUBA.

FOOD
30-second
FLIGHT ATTENDANT: Munchie time!
PASSENGER: This is it?
ANNCR (VO): Has your airline lost its taste for food?
PASSENGER: This is it? This is it?
PASSENGER: Evidently, this is it.
ANNCR (VO): Next trip try Alaska Airlines Gold Coast
Service.
It'll leave a good taste in your mouth.

<table>
<tr><td colspan="2" align="center">1021</td></tr>
<tr><td align="right">Art Director</td><td>**Alan Sprules**</td></tr>
<tr><td align="right">Writer</td><td>**Roger Proulx**</td></tr>
<tr><td align="right">Editor</td><td>**Frank Cioffredi**</td></tr>
<tr><td align="right">Director</td><td>**Norman Griner**</td></tr>
<tr><td align="right">Client</td><td>**Peugeot Motors of America**</td></tr>
<tr><td align="right">Agency Producer</td><td>**Bernie Wesson/Ogilvy & Mather, New York**</td></tr>
<tr><td align="right">Production Company</td><td>**Griner Cuesta & Assoc.**</td></tr>
<tr><td align="right">Creative Director</td><td>**Jay Jasper**</td></tr>
</table>

<table>
<tr><td colspan="2" align="center">1022</td></tr>
<tr><td align="right">Art Director</td><td>**Jerry Box, VP**</td></tr>
<tr><td align="right">Writer</td><td>**Jim Copacino, VP**</td></tr>
<tr><td align="right">Client</td><td>**Alaska Airlines**</td></tr>
<tr><td align="right">Agency Producer</td><td>**Virginia Pellegrino, VP**</td></tr>
<tr><td align="right">Production Company</td><td>**Sedelmaier Productions**</td></tr>
<tr><td align="right">Agency</td><td>**Livingston & Company, Seattle**</td></tr>
</table>

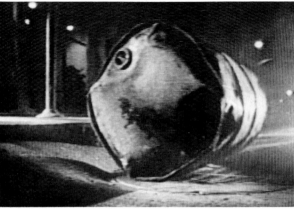

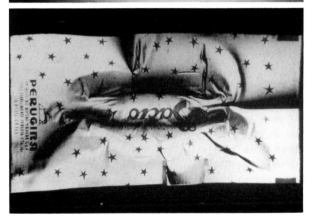

DIOXIN: IN SEARCH OF A KILLER
30-second
ANNCR: This is the anatomy of a *murderer*.
The true story of a villian no longer far away . . . a potent
poison working its way into our community. Toxic chemical
waste that threatens the *health* of you and your family.
What is it?
What does it do?
Who can stop it?
Ernie Anastos investigates.
Dioxin - In Search of a Killer on Eyewitness News all this
week at 6 PM only on Channel 7.

CHOCOLATE DANCE/ELITE
30-second
More Great Taste from Italy

	1023
Art Director	**Michael Grasso**
Director of Photography	**Ruland Hardy**
Writer	**Angie Gordon**
Director	**Michael Grasso**
Client	**WABC-TV, New York**
Agency Producer	**Angie Gordon**
Production Company	**Grasso Productions, Inc., San Francisco**
Client Producer	**Tim Miller**

	1024
Art Director	**Phil Marco**
Designer	**Phil Marco**
Director of Photography	**Phil Marco**
Writer	**Al Kaplan**
Editor	**Bob Lynch**
Director	**Phil Marco**
Client	**Perugina Chocolates & Confections, Inc.**
Agency	**Cannon Advertising Associates, Inc., New York**
Production Company	**Phil Marco Productions, Inc.**

JANNY/NEW
30-second
ANNCR (VO): Nestle introduces the Peanut Butter . . . burst cookie. Made with new morsels so peanut buttery, we wonder . . .
JANNY: Whoa!
ANNCR (VO): Have we gone too far?
JANNY: Yeah!
ANNCR (VO): Are they too creamy? Too smooth?
JANNY: Yeah!
ANNCR (VO): Too peanut buttery?
JANNY: Yeah!
ANNCR (VO): Nestle's new Peanut Butter Morsels . . . give you a smooth, creamy burst of peanut butter flavor so far from ordinary . . . it's overwhelming.

	1025
Art Director	**Bob Sears**
Writer	**Matt Gunn**
Editor	**Chris Claeys**
Client	**Nestle**
Agency	**Leo Burnett, Chicago/ Cathy Nelson**
Production Company	**Ron Finley Films/Ron Finley**

GOOD, CLEAN FUN
30-second
MUSIC: YAMAHA THEME MUSIC UP THEN UNDER VOICE OVER.
FATHER: Our Saturdays sure have changed.
Used to be, all I'd see of Kelly was the back of his head in front of the T.V. . . .
And all he'd see of me was the front page of the morning paper. Then we got a couple of shaft drive three wheelers from Yamaha.
We go almost every weekend now. And you know what? Since we've started riding, I've realized something—Kelly doesn't know much about the generation gap.
Neither do I.
MUSIC: BUILT FOR THE FUN OF IT THEME MUSIC UP

	1026
Art Director	**Houman Pirdavari**
Writer	**Brent Bouchez**
Editor	**Charlie Chubak**
Director	**Mark Coppos**
Client	**Yamaha Motor Corporation**
Agency	**Chiat/Day, Los Angeles/ Morty Baran**
Prod'n Co Producer	**Bill Bratkowski**

MOSES
30-second
SFX: ECHO OF BALL BOUNCING AND GRUNTS OF MAN.
MALONE: At the age of 14, I discovered the secret. Pick the one thing you do best. And work at it.
So, while every other kid was trying to be the next Ice Man, I was hitting at the boards. Because I figured if you ain't got the ball . . .
SFX: SLAM OF BALL BEING DUNKED.
MALONE: you can't shoot the ball.

OLD MAN
30-second
MUSIC UP AND UNDER.
MAN: Me and this old Hunter Fan been together since I was a boy.
Seen lots of good times. Entertained some lovely ladies on warm summer nights.
Played many a game of poker with the boys. Lots of fine cigars too.
But, after 60 years, I figured that fan may outlast me . . .
and then again, maybe it won't.
I'm keeping my eye on it.

<table>
<tr><td colspan="2" align="center">1027</td></tr>
<tr><td align="right">Art Director</td><td>Gary Johns</td></tr>
<tr><td align="right">Writer</td><td>Jeff Gorman</td></tr>
<tr><td align="right">Editor</td><td>Charlie Chubak</td></tr>
<tr><td align="right">Director</td><td>Bob Giraldi</td></tr>
<tr><td align="right">Client</td><td>Nike, Inc.</td></tr>
<tr><td align="right">Agency</td><td>Chiat/Day, Los Angeles/
Morty Baran</td></tr>
<tr><td align="right">Prod'n Co Producer</td><td>Ralph Cohen</td></tr>
</table>

<table>
<tr><td colspan="2" align="center">1028</td></tr>
<tr><td align="right">Art Director</td><td>John Sapienza</td></tr>
<tr><td align="right">Writer</td><td>Richard M. Coad</td></tr>
<tr><td align="right">Director</td><td>Bob Reagan</td></tr>
<tr><td align="right">Client</td><td>Robbins & Myers</td></tr>
<tr><td align="right">Agency</td><td>Young & Rubicam/Chicago</td></tr>
<tr><td align="right">Agency Producer</td><td>Lee Lunardi</td></tr>
</table>

INT'L FRENCH FRY
30-second
You start with a potato
Our very best potato
It's a peeling, peeling feeling
McDonalds takes it
McDonalds makes it
French fries
Fry 'em hot
Turn 'em brown
Cook 'em up
Shake 'em round
Salt 'em good
Good and hot
Nice and crisp

FRISKIES NUTCRACKER SUITE
30-second
ANNCR (VO): This commercial is dedicated to new Friskies
with the frisky new taste . . . that has cats dancing in the
aisles and jumping for joy.
New Friskies have a friskier taste because the flavor is baked
right in.
Give your cat new Friskies . . . and you will have a very satisfied cat.

1029	
Art Director	**Rick Rogers**
Writer	**Cathy Altman**
Director	**Alex Fernbach**
Agency	**Chuck Kessler/Leo Burnett, Chicago**
Production Company	**Sunlight Pictures/Julie Ryder**

1030	
Art Director	**Joe Shelesky**
Designers	**Dana Jones, Joe Shelesky**
Director of Photography	**Ralph Devito**
Writer	**Dana Jones**
Editor	**Marc Cerutti**
Director	**Ralph Devito**
Client	**Carnation**
Agency	**SSC&B, New York/Vito Barbara**
Production Company	**Devito Productions**

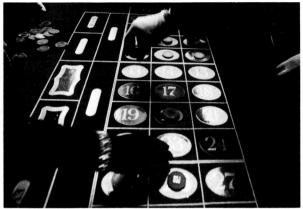

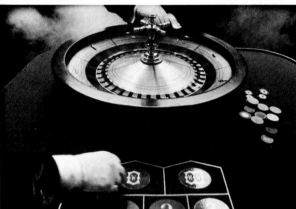

MYSTERY ILLNESSES
30-second
MUSIC: EERIE ELECTRONIC TONE (UP TO ESTABLISH,
THEN UNDER, RISING AGAIN AT END)
SFX: AMBIENT CASINO NOISES (UNDER THROUGHOUT)
THE GRIM CROUPIER (VO):
Ladies and gentlemen, place your bets.
Round and round and round they go,
Who will get them? Nobody knows . . .
Round and round and round they go,
Who will cure them? Nobody knows . . .
ANNCR (VO): Diseases . . . for which there are no known
causes or cures. What are the odds your number will come
up? Find out. Watch "Mystery Illnesses." This week at six on
Channel Seven.

SIZZLER - PRODUCT LINE GENERIC
30-second
WOMAN #1: "Sizzler!"
WOMAN #2: "Light!"
MAN #1: "Lean."
MAN #2: "Sizzler."
WOMAN #1: "Fresh."
WOMAN #3: "Crunch."
WOMAN #4: "Cheers."
MAN #1: "The Steak . . ."
WOMAN #2: ". . . Seafood . . ."
WOMAN #3: ". . . Salad . . ."
MAN #1)
WOMAN #2) ". . . Sizzler!"
WOMAN 3)

1031	
Art Director	**Clyde Hogg**
Director of Photography	**Jordan Cronenweth**
Writer/ACD	**Rob Ingalls**
Editor	**Larry Bridges**
Director	**Paul Henman**
Client	**KGO-TV, Channel 7 News**
Agency Producer	**Randy Rennolds/Davis, Johnson, Mogul & Colombatto, Inc., San Francisco**
Prod'n Co Producer	**David Dwiggins**

1032	
Art Director	**Stan Jones**
Writer	**Elizabeth Hayes**
Editor	**Rob Kirsner**
Director	**Elbert Budin**
Client	**Sizzler International Restaurants**
Agency	**BBDO/West/Jim Baier**
Prod'n Co Producer	**Bill Curren**

UMPIRE
30-second
ANNCR: Why do business fliers choose United?
LUCIANO: In my business consistency was always
important.
SFX: (BASEBALL GAME NOISE) You're out!
LUCIANO: Game after game . . .
SFX: (BASEBALL GAME NOISE) Safe!
LUCIANO: Time after time . . .
SFX: (BASEBALL GAME) Y'er out!
LUCIANO: I was always right.
SFX: (BASEBALL GAME) Go!
LUCIANO: Now when I travel on business I still make the
right call. United. I can always count on United for the things
that make a great flight: comfortable planes, good service,

THUMB REVEAL
30-second
(MUSIC UNDER)
ANNCR (VO): This imported beer is all that you'd expect. It
has a rich full bodied, imported flavor—as you'd expect.
(SFX)
And a deep golden color to match its quality taste—
as you'd expect.
But here's one thing you probably won't expect . . .
It's light. Amstel Light Bier.
SINGERS: 95 CALORIES NEVER TASTED SO IMPORTED . . .
ANNCR (VO): Amstel Light Bier.
Imported by Van Munching and Company, New York.

	1033
Art Director	**Greg King**
Writer	**Jeff Sherman**
Editor	**John Montgomery**
Client	**United Airlines**
Agency	**Joe Mangan/Leo Burnett, Chicago**
Production Company	**Bean/Kahn Films/Bob Bean**
Agency Exec. Producer	**Al Lira**

	1034
Art Director	**Doris Latino**
Writer	**Daniel Sheehan**
Producer	**Eric Brenner**
Editor	**Joe Leone/Spot Shop**
Director/Cameraman	**John Bonanno**
Music	**H.E.A.**
Client	**Van Munching & Co.**
Agency	**SSC&B, Inc., New York**

TROUBLE FOR CHARLIE
30-second
VO: In the race to put personal computers in the office, Wang introduces the winning formula: The Wang Professional Computer.
In Data Processing, it's faster than any personal computer tested.
Only Wang offers you the best selling word processing in the world.
And only Wang gives you all this plus unbeaten communications.
The Wang Professional Computer. In the race to office automation, it leaves the competition in the dust.

COMMUNICATION
30-second
JOHN HUSTON (VO): Today, many companies are shocked to find their electronic office machines can't communicate. But at Exxon Office Systems, our products speak the same language.
So everyone can send and receive information . . . to and from everyone else.
Even to . . . large central computers . . . and other systems.
It's freedom of speech . . . for the electronic office.
Exxon Office Systems. It's the future . . . without the shock.

_____ 1035 _____
Art Director   **Dick Pantano**
Writer   **Doug Houston**
Client   **Wang Office Automation**
Agency   **HHCC, Boston/Ann Finucane**
Production Company   **Ulick Productions**

_____ 1036 _____
Art Director   **Ted McNeil**
Artist   **Phil Kimmelman**
Writer   **Paul Levett**
Agency   **Marsteller Inc., New York/ Sam Milgrim**

BUILD UP
30-second
When a Tour pro chooses his ball, he's looking for the same things that could make you a better golfer . . . Consistent distance and accuracy ball, after ball, after ball. That's why most pros play the only ball that can pass the 32 performance checks it takes to be a Titleist . . . Consistent distance and accuracy is why most pros play Titleist. And that can make a world of difference in your game.

BURGER KING
30-second
ANNCR: Due to the suggestive nature of the following Burger King commercial, viewers are advised to watch at their own risk.
SINGERS: OOH THAT HOT AND SIZZLIN' BACON
ANNCR: The bacon double cheeseburger is intended for mature audiences only.
SINGERS: TWO JUICY FLAME BROILED BURGERS, MMM WITH MELTED CHEESE
ANNCR: This is your last warning.
SINGERS: AREN'T YOU HUNGRY? AREN'T YOU HUNGRY? AREN'T YOU HUNGRY FOR BURGER KING NOW?
ANNCR: The bacon double cheeseburger has been rated PD—perfectly delicious!

	1037
Art Director	**Bill Boch**
Writer	**Chuck Matzell**
Director	**Lear Levin**
Client	**Acushnet Company**
Agency	**Humphrey Browning MacDougall, Boston/ Brenda Smeriglio**
Production Company	**Lear Levin Productions**

	1038
Art Director	**Howie Cohen**
Director of Photography	**Simon Ramsley**
Writers	**Hal Friedman, Laurie Birnbaum**
Editors	**Jack Coddington, Gary Sharfin**
Director	**Patrick Morgan**
Client	**Burger King/Kyle Craig**
Executive Producer	**Don Brown/J.W.T., New York**
Prod'n Co Producer	**Richard Goldberg/ Fairbanks Films**
Creative Director	**Jim Patterson**

MISTLETOE
30-second
SINGERS:
BETTER WATCH OUT WHEN YOU'RE STEALING A KISS
CAUSE I'M GONNA GET YOU WITH THE KODAK DISC I'M
GONNA GET YOU WITH THE KODAK DISC SURE AS SHOO-
TIN' I'M NOT GONNA MISS NOT WHEN IT'S AS EASY AS
THIS I'M GONNA GET YOU WITH THE KODAK DISC
VO: The Kodak disc camera is easy to load advances auto-
matically, and has a built-in flash. You want a camera that's
easier and more fun than that? You're not gonna get it!
SINGERS:
THIS IS ONE KISS
I'M NOT GONNA MISS
I'M GONNA GET YOU WITH THE KODAK DISC

TEACHER
30-second
TEACHER: A very gifted student sat here. She knew Shakespeare, Shelley, Keats. And could she write. But the day before graduation she was in a car crash. They said if she'd
been wearing a safety belt, she might have had a few bruises
. . . not brain damage. Now she won't read or write or ever
think again.
When you're 17, you don't think about those things. You think
you're going to live forever. She was 17.

	1039
Art Directors	**Beth Pritchett, Greg Weinschenker**
Writers	**Cathy McMahon, Linda Kaplan, Bonnie Berkowitz, Robin Schwarz**
Editor	**Tony Siggia**
Director	**Joe Hanwright**
Client	**Eastman Kodak/Roger Morrison**
Agency	**J.W.T., New York/Sid Horn**
Production Company	**Kira Films/Lisa Peglessi**

	1040
Art Director	**Al Zerries**
Writer	**Al Zerries**
Editor	**Norman Levine**
Director	**Steve Horn**
Client	**National Highway Traffic Safety Administration**
Agency	**Grey Advertising, Inc., New York/Maura Dausey**
Production Company	**Steve Horn Prod.**

MAGFORCE TV
30-second
ANNCR: Daiwa introduces the most advanced baitcasting reel ever to surface. Graphite Magforce with Autocast. (SUPER: Model PMA 33): The lightweight reel that helped Larry Nixon win the Bass Masters Classic. With Daiwa's new Autocast control that lets you cast one-handed, and cover the water faster. Plus a 5.36 to 1 retrieve that's the fastest in fishing. Get Daiwa's new Magforce with Autocast. And get a jump on the fish.

SAX
30-second
LOCKER ROOM MANAGER: You're early. You don't have to be on the field 'til 4:30. Now, if you have any aches or pains, I want you to see the trainer just as soon as you come in. Mail box is back over there . . . And, eh, no no. . . This is you here.
Kinda nervous, eh? Butterflies?
Take some advice. When that feeling goes away?
. . . quit.

	1041
Art Director	Bob Kwait
Writer	Tony Durket
Editor	Benedict Coulter
Director	Paul Henman
Client	Daiwa Corporation
Agency	Phillips-Ramsey, San Diego/David Hoogenakker
Production Company	Kaleidoscope Film & Tape
Music	T.J. Knowles/The Knowles Group

	1042
Art Director	Houman Pirdavari
Writer	Brent Bouchez
Editor	Charlie Chubak
Director	Bob Giraldi
Client	Nike, Inc.
Agency	Chiat/Day, Los Angeles/ Morty Baran
Prod'n Co Producer	Ralph Cohen

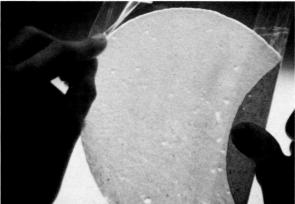

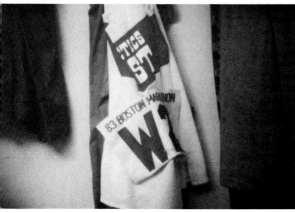

JOANIE
30-second
SFX: ALARM BUZZING
RADIO: Good morning. It's 5:24 a.m., no make that 5:25.
Twenty five minutes past five in downtown Portland. This is
the Doctor smiling at you. Eight lucky people are going to
win a couple of tickets to the show . . . if you haven't got your
entry in, get it in here today. We've got to have it.
Remember the oldies show at 9 p.m. is only right here on
music radio. And coming right up another 30 minutes of
commercial-free music. Well, our own Joan Benoit won the
Boston Marathon Monday with a woman's world record in
2:22:42.
Hey, if you're listening, way to go Joanie.

RIPPING FRUIT
30-second
MUSIC AND SFX.
MUSIC AND SFX.
MUSIC AND SFX.
MUSIC AND SFX (RRRRIIIIPPPP!)
ANNCR (VO): New Sunkist Fruit-Rolls.
Made with real fruit . . .
. . . and other wholesome ingredients pressed flat . . .
. . . and rolled onto cellophane . . .
SFX: (RRRRIIIIPPPPP!)
So you can eat them . . .
anytime . . .
anywhere. Sunkist Fruit Rolls.
Made with real grapes . . .

<table>
<tr><td colspan="2">1043</td></tr>
<tr><td>Art Director</td><td>Gary Johns</td></tr>
<tr><td>Writer</td><td>Jeff Gorman</td></tr>
<tr><td>Editor</td><td>Charlie Chubak</td></tr>
<tr><td>Director</td><td>Bob Giraldi</td></tr>
<tr><td>Client</td><td>Nike, Inc.</td></tr>
<tr><td>Agency</td><td>Chiat/Day, Los Angeles/
Morty Baran</td></tr>
<tr><td>Prod'n Co Producer</td><td>Ralph Cohen</td></tr>
</table>

<table>
<tr><td colspan="2">1044</td></tr>
<tr><td>Art Director</td><td>Sam Gulisano</td></tr>
<tr><td>Artist</td><td>Rod McCall</td></tr>
<tr><td>Writer</td><td>Rob Austin</td></tr>
<tr><td>Editor</td><td>Harry Chang</td></tr>
<tr><td>Directors</td><td>Phil Marco, Rod McCall</td></tr>
<tr><td>Client</td><td>Thomas J. Lipton</td></tr>
<tr><td>Agency</td><td>Foote, Cone & Belding, New
York/Lewis Kuperman</td></tr>
<tr><td>Production Company</td><td>Phil Marco Productions/
McCall Coppola</td></tr>
<tr><td>Prod'n. Co Producers</td><td>Kathy Bromley, Adele
Solomon</td></tr>
</table>

POLICEMAN
30-second
(SFX: CARS GOING BY ON HIGHWAY, BIRDS . . .)
POLICEMAN: No matter how tough a policeman thinks he is, he's never ready for the first highway fatality he sees. Mine was here 11 years ago. I had a six-year old die in my arms. It still wakes me up some nights. She'd be about 17 today if her mother had her wear her safety belt. Safety belts can save more than 16,000 lives each year. In all those 11 years, I've never once unbuckled a dead man.

YEP
30-second
(COUNTRY MUSIC UP AND UNDER . . .)
VO: So you're on the radio.
JOCK: Yep.
VO: But you don't talk much.
JOCK: Nope.
VO: You play country music.
JOCK: Yep.
VO: But you don't talk much.
JOCK: Nope.
VO: FM Stereo?
JOCK: Yep.
VO: But you don't talk much.
JOCK: Nope.

1045

Art Director	**Al Zerries**
Writer	**Al Zerries**
Editor	**Norman Levine**
Director	**Steve Horn**
Client	**National Highway Traffic Safety Administration**
Agency	**Grey Advertising, Inc., New York/Maura Dausey**
Production Company	**Steve Horn Prod.**

1046

Art Director	**Kurt Tausche**
Writer	**Pete Smith**
Director	**Harry Allen**
Client	**Malrite Communications**
Agency	**Bozell & Jacobs, Inc., Minneapolis**
Production Company	**Sight & Sound/Richard Henry**

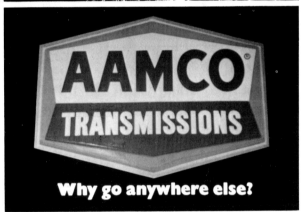

FEVER
30-second
ANNCR (VO): Maybe more people listen to Y96 than any station of its kind because we listen to you.
MEDLEY: EVERYDAY PEOPLE LIP-SYNCING POPULAR SONGS
At Y96, we do local music surveys to find out exactly what you want to hear. WLTY/FM. We Listen To You.

NO APPOINTMENT NECESSARY
30-second
ANNCR. (VO): You can't get anything done these days without an appointment.
WIFE (TO HUSBAND): He says he's very sorry, but he can't make it till next week.
WIFE: The dentist says he'll be able to fit you in on the eleventh.
WIFE: Thursday? He says he'll be right over next Thursday.
VO: But if the transmission on your foreign car breaks down, there's no appointment necessary at AAMCO. We'll get to it right away and get it back to you fast. Call AAMCO.
WIFE: He says bring it right over.
VO: AAMCO. (BEEP-BEEP) Why go anywhere else?

1047
Art Director	**Jeff France**
Writer	**Bruce Mansfield**
Director	**Bill Randall**
Client	**WLTY/FM**
Agency	**Lawler Ballard Advertising, Norfolk, VA/Jeff France, Bruce Mansfield**
Production Company	**Associated Filmakers International**

1048
Art Director	**Michael Withers**
Writer	**Hy Abady**
Director	**Joe Sedelmaier**
Client	**AAMCO Transmissions**
Agency Producer	**Frank DiSalvo/Calet, Hirsch & Spector, Inc., New York**
Production Company	**Sedelmaier Films**
Creative Director	**Peter Hirsch**

HANDS
30-second
ANNCR (VO): What company sold the most small copiers in the U.S. last year?
MAN #1: Oh, I'd say Xer . . . .
MAN #2: Number 1 huh? Let's see, how about IB . . . . MMMMMMMMMMM.
MAN #3: Number 1 small copier? Sharp.
ANNCR: (SURPRISED) Right. How'd you know?
MAN #3: Simple. I sell copiers. So I know Sharp doesn't cut corners to cut space. Their small copiers do big jobs . . . . so, they sell big.
ANNCR: You don't seem very happy about it.
MAN #3: I'm not. I sell CAN . . . . ONNNNNN.
ANNCR: Sharp. The #1 company in small copiers.

1049	
Art Director	**Bob Musachio**
Designer	**Howard Barker**
Writer	**Rick Meyer**
Editor	**Tony Lover**
Director	**Tony Lover**
Client	**Sharp Electronics Corp.**
Agency	**Rosenfeld, Sirowitz & Lawson, New York/Nancy Braunstein**
Production Company	**Liberty Studio/Jim Kowalski**
Creative Director	**Len Sirowitz**

911
30-second
ANNCR: Someday, when you see a fire, you'll be able to call a new type of 911 number.
Thanks to new Western Electric software systems being installed in many communities.
Systems that automatically flash the exact location of the emergency service nearest to you and the exact location of your call.
So that someday, when you dial 911, who will make sure nobody has to ask "Where's the fire?"
WE will.
We're Western Electric. Working with your phone company to bring the Information Age home to you.

1050	
Art Director	**Maurice Mahler**
Writer	**Ted Littleford**
Client	**Western Electric**
Agency	**Foote, Cone & Belding, New York/Ken Yagoda**
Production Company	**Lofaro & Assoc.**
Special Effects	**Apogee/L.A.**

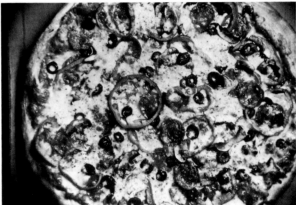

JOAN COLLINS "FIRE"
30-second
JOAN COLLINS: It takes . . . something black.
Something brilliant.
Something cool.
Something hot.
Something Scoundrel. My favorite fragrance.
It's sophisticated and elegant. And there's something sexy about it, too.
Then, when something happens, and it will, you can always say,
"It wasn't me. It was my Scoundrel."
ANNCR: Scoundrel. From Revlon.
MAN: Somebody here report a fire?

BOX
30-second
SFX THROUGHOUT: New York street noises, Honking, screeching, etc.
PIZZA (VO): Hey, welcome to New York. Ain't you ever . . . seen a real New York style thin crust pizza before? Numero Uno makes this delicious crust from . . . hand-stretched dough. So it's kind-a-soft. So's you can fold it. So fold me. Good. That's the Flatbush Fold. The Radio City Roll. The Brooklyn Bend. Very chichi. The Holland Funnel. Some tasty sauce, heh guy!
Ciao!
ANNCR (VO): Get a real taste of New York at Numero Uno today.
PIZZA (VO): What crust!

<table>
<tr><td colspan="2" align="center">1051</td></tr>
<tr><td align="right">Art Director</td><td>**Michael Koulermos**</td></tr>
<tr><td align="right">Writer</td><td>**Maryellen Flynn**</td></tr>
<tr><td align="right">Editor</td><td>**Larry Feinstein**</td></tr>
<tr><td align="right">Director</td><td>**Richard Heiman**</td></tr>
<tr><td align="right">Client</td><td>**Revlon, Inc.**</td></tr>
<tr><td align="right">Agency</td><td>**Grey Advertising, Inc., New York/John Greene**</td></tr>
<tr><td align="right">Production Company</td><td>**RHA/Howie Title**</td></tr>
</table>

<table>
<tr><td colspan="2" align="center">1052</td></tr>
<tr><td align="right">Art Director</td><td>**Darryl Shimazu**</td></tr>
<tr><td align="right">Writer</td><td>**Elaine Cossman**</td></tr>
<tr><td align="right">Client</td><td>**Numero Uno Pizzeria**</td></tr>
<tr><td align="right">Agency Producer</td><td>**Penny Webber/Gumpertz/ Bentley/Fried, Los Angeles**</td></tr>
</table>

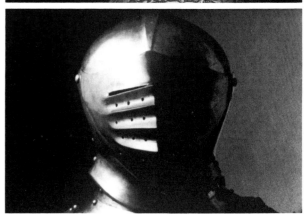

DISASTERS
30-second
ANNCR: Pacific Northwest Bell is constantly working to keep your telephone constantly working. No matter what problem befalls you . . .
. . .we're there. With the people, the equipment, and the service:
Where you need it, when you need it
Pacific Northwest Bell. Above and beyond the call.

ART OF CHIVALRY
30-second
ANNCR (VO): The Art of Chivalry.
The armor, arms, and armaments.
See it all at the Minneapolis Institute of Arts.
It will knock you out.

1053

Art Director	Terri Small
Writer	Jim Copacino, VP/Kevin Threadgold
Client	Pacific Northwest Bell
Agency Producer	Virginia Pellegrino, VP
Production Company	Midocean Motion Pictures
Agency	Livingston & Company, Seattle

1054

Art Director	Doug Lew
Designer	Doug Lew
Writer	Bob Thacker
Editor	Bob Wickland
Director	Doug Lew
Client	Minneapolis Institute of Arts
Agency	Chuck Ruhr Advertising, Minneapolis/Arleen Kulis
Production Company	John Harvey/Wilson-Griak

MEGABUCKS
30-second
(SFX: CONFERENCE ROOM AMBIANCE; PHONE)
1ST. VP: Who . . . who . . . who called this meeting.
ALL VPS: (MUMBLED AND CONFUSED) Not me. I don't
know. I don't know.
(SFX: DOOR OPENS AND CLOSES)
WOMAN JANITOR: I did.
ALL VPS: She did. She did. She did.
WOMAN JANITOR: Have you all heard of Megabucks?
ALL VPS: Megabucks? Megabucks? Megabucks? Oh,
Megabucks.
ANNCR: In the lottery's Megabucks game the jackpot keeps
growing every week until someone wins.
WOMAN JANITOR: Gentlemen I've enjoyed working for all of

CONVENIENCE
30-second
MAN: Hi! You're new here, I'm Adam. I'm the Social Director.
WOMAN: Eve Taylor, fashion consultant.
MAN: I see we have a lot in common.
WOMAN: We do?
MAN: You look good in tortoise shell.
WOMAN: They're not too dressy?
MAN: No!
WOMAN: Oh! Wish I had sunglasses. Hey, where'd you
get yours?
MAN: I had them all the time.
WOMAN: Where'd you keep them?
MAN: They have Corning lenses that change from eyeglasses
to sunglasses in less than 60 seconds.

<table>
<tr><td colspan="2" style="text-align:center">1055</td></tr>
<tr><td>Art Director</td><td>**Frank Sobocienski**</td></tr>
<tr><td>Writer</td><td>**Seumas McGuire**</td></tr>
<tr><td>Director</td><td>**Joe Sedelmaier**</td></tr>
<tr><td>Client</td><td>**Massachusetts State Lottery**</td></tr>
<tr><td>Agency</td><td>**HHCC, Boston/Maggie Hines, Steve Fox**</td></tr>
<tr><td>Production Co Producer</td><td>**Peggy DeLay**</td></tr>
</table>

<table>
<tr><td colspan="2" style="text-align:center">1056</td></tr>
<tr><td>Art Director</td><td>**Peter Hirsch**</td></tr>
<tr><td>Writer</td><td>**Ken Majka**</td></tr>
<tr><td>Director</td><td>**Bob Giraldi**</td></tr>
<tr><td>Client</td><td>**Corning Glass Works, Optical Division**</td></tr>
<tr><td>Agency Producer</td><td>**Frank DiSalvo/Calet, Hirsch & Spector, Inc., New York**</td></tr>
<tr><td>Production Company</td><td>**Bob Giraldi Productions**</td></tr>
<tr><td>Creative Director</td><td>**Peter Hirsch**</td></tr>
</table>

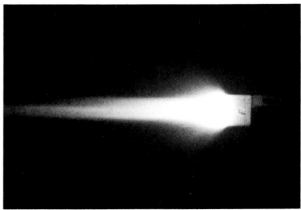

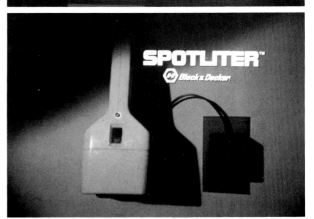

FLASH
30-second
ANNCR (VO): Maybe more people listen to Y96 than any station of its kind because we listen to you.
MEDLEY: EVERYDAY PEOPLE LIP-SYNCING POPULAR SONGS
At Y96, we do local music surveys to find out exactly what you want to hear. WLTY/FM. We Listen To You.

SPLIT THE DARK
30-second
It splits the dark with a beam so powerful it projects 125 yards.
Spotlighter from Black and Decker.
Built of high impact polymers, it can withstand a 6 foot drop to concrete.
It mounts in its own recharging base, storing all the power you need.
So on a moments notice it gives you light.
Light for your safety, light for your peace of mind. Light as dependable as the name Black & Decker Spotlighter. The one rechargeable light that does more than just shine.

1057

Art Director	**Jeff France**
Writer	**Bruce Mansfield**
Director	**Bill Randall**
Client	**WLTY/FM**
Agency	**Lawler Ballard Advertising, Norfolk, VA/Jeff France, Bruce Mansfield**
Production Company	**Associated Filmakers International**

1058

Art Director	**Tony Lamonte**
Writer	**Michael Shevack**
Director	**Alex Fernbach**
Client	**Black & Decker**
Agency Producer	**Russel Hudson/BBDO**
Production Company	**Sunlight Pictures, New York/Dianne Miller**

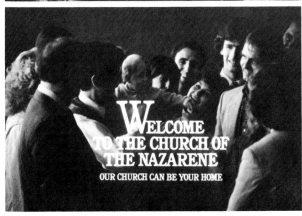

PASADENA
30-second
ANNCR (VO): We dedicate this child to God.
The child of a stranger in trouble.
His mother came to our church from another state.
With no job, pregnant and unmarried.
And the people here reached out to her.
They took her home and welcomed her into their families.
And when this baby was born, he was their child too.
And they gave him all the love in their hearts.
Welcome to the Church of the Nazarene. Our church can be your home.

JIMMY CONNORS
30-second
BURGESS MEREDITH (VO); Investing these days is a little like . . . you playing tennis against Jimmy Connors. You're going to need all the professional help you can get.
Paine Webber (SFX: CROWD CHEERS) can supply that help. A full range of services. And, the financial advice to help you make those difficult decisions. Because at Paine Webber we believe . . . the quality of life just might depend on the quality of your investments.
CONNORS: Hey, great match
CLIENT: Thanks, Jimmy. Thank you, Paine Webber.
PAINE WEBBER: You're welcome!
CONNORS: Next time I want those guys on my team, okay?

1059	
Art Director	**Lila Sternglass**
Director of Photography	**Jack Churchill**
Writer	**Bill Hamilton**
Editor	**Salamandra Films**
Director	**Chuck East**
Client	**Church of the Nazarene**
Agency Producers	**Marilyn Cook, Matthew Borzi**
Production Company	**Iris Films**
Agency	**Rumril-Hoyt Advertising, New York**

1060	
Art Director	**Shelley Schachter**
Director of Photography	**Dan Quinn**
Writer	**Kurt Willinger**
Editor	**Richard Nuchow**
Director	**Bob Giraldi**
Client	**Paine Webber - John Lampe**
Agency Producer	**Tim Devitt for Compton Advertising, New York**
Prod'n Co Producer	**Barbara Michaelson**

WORKING GIRL
30-second
(MUSIC: UNDER. CARMINA BURANA, "FORTUNA")
VO: She's a working girl. An athlete. She makes men sing. She's tough. She's soft. She flies by night. She dances in Carmina Burana.
October 13 through 30 at The Colonial Theatre. Call 542-3945 for tickets now.
This season, The Boston Ballet is too, too much.

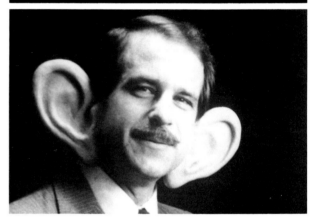

NOSE
30-second
VO: You've seen what plastic surgery can do for people. But have you seen what it can do for plastic? This is a Stick Up concentrated air deodorizer before plastic surgery. Stick Ups air deodorizers now have a slimmer, trimmer design and a controlled release system to last longer, up to 6 weeks. Well?
GUY: Ahhhh
GUY: This is a good place for a Stick Up
GUY: Isn't it wonderful what plastic surgery can do?

1061

Art Directors	**Frank Sobocienski, Dick Pantano**
Writer	**Maryann Barone**
Director	**Dan Driscoll**
Client	**The Boston Ballet**
Agency	**HHCC, Boston/Maggie Hines**
Production Company	**September/William Trautvetter**

1062

Art Director	**Paul Jervis**
Writer	**Neil Drossman**
Editor	**The Editors**
Director	**Paul Jervis**
Client	**Airwick Industries**
Agency Producer	**Rhoda Malamet/Drossman Marino Reveley, Inc.,**
Production Company	**Tulchin Studios**

AIRPORT
30-second
VO: Once upon a time people went all the way to Las Vegas looking for a big win.
PRINCIPAL: Haaayy - Vaayygus!
VO: Then along came Atlantic City.
PRINCIPAL: Haaayy - Atlantic City!
VO: But now, there's a new route to riches. Instant Jackpot. The new lottery game with the biggest instant prize in the whole world. Up to $200,000. Right here in Massachusetts. So play Instant Jackpot today. Before the crowds get out of line.

VROOM VROOM CHILD
30-second
BKGD: (SFX OF CARS - Vroom, Vroom, etc . . .)
VO: Indulge your fantasies . . . "Automagic". The First Hamilton International Auto Show. October 13th through 16th at the Hamilton Convention Centre.

	1063
Art Directors	**Frank Sobocienski, Andy Dijak**
Writers	**Seumas McGuire, Vashti Eifler**
Editor	**David Doob**
Director	**Dan Driscoll**
Client	**Massachusetts State Lottery**
Agency	**HHCC, Boston/Maggie Hines**
Production Company	**September/Bill Trautvetter**

	1064
Art Director	**Stanislaus M. Shibinsky**
Designer	**Stanislaus M. Shibinsky**
Director of Photography	**Bob Perks**
Writer	**Stanislaus M. Shibinsky**
Editor	**Traver Lalonde**
Director	**Bob Perks**
Client	**Hamilton Automobile Dealers' Association**
Agency Producer	**Stanislaus M. Shibinsky/ Foster Advertising Limited, Toronto**
Production Company	**Dalton/Fenske & Friends**

CHEATING
30-second
My first time was in a motel room. I figured why not? Every-
one else does it. It was all downhill from there. Before long I
was taking on the big guys.
How low could I sink?
My husband won't be at work today. He's very sick. Goodbye.
Right then and there I vowed never to cheat anyone again.
Watch cheating - our newest addiction. Beginning Tuesday
on Eyewitness News at eleven. Only on Channel 7.

FIRST CHOICE
30-second
VO: From the rancher in Pendleton . . .
To the electronics technician in Portland . . .
To the fisherman in Coos Bay
. . . Twice as many Oregonians count on one health insur-
ance company over any other. It's an Oregon company—its
headquarters are here. Blue Cross and Blue Shield of Ore-
gon . . .
Oregon's first choice.

<table>
<tr><td colspan="2" align="center">1065</td></tr>
<tr><td align="right">Art Director</td><td>**Michael Grasso**</td></tr>
<tr><td align="right">Director of Photography</td><td>**Roland Harding**</td></tr>
<tr><td align="right">Writer</td><td>**Angie Gordon**</td></tr>
<tr><td align="right">Director</td><td>**Michael Grasso**</td></tr>
<tr><td align="right">Client</td><td>**WABC-TV, New York**</td></tr>
<tr><td align="right">Agency Producer</td><td>**Angie Gordon**</td></tr>
<tr><td align="right">Production Company</td><td>**Grasso Productions, Inc.**</td></tr>
<tr><td align="right">Client Producer</td><td>**Tim Miller**</td></tr>
</table>

<table>
<tr><td colspan="2" align="center">1066</td></tr>
<tr><td align="right">Art Director</td><td>**Tom Stoneham**</td></tr>
<tr><td align="right">Writer</td><td>**Barry Pullman**</td></tr>
<tr><td align="right">Director</td><td>**Mike McNamara**</td></tr>
<tr><td align="right">Client</td><td>**Blue Cross/Blue Shield of Oregon**</td></tr>
<tr><td align="right">Agency</td><td>**Borders, Perrin & Norrander, Portland/Tom Kelly**</td></tr>
</table>

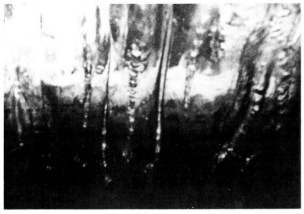

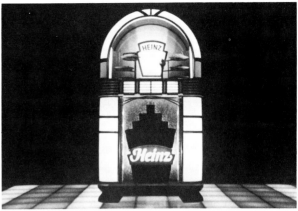

MAKING WAVES
30-second
VO: Before Cub Foods came to town, things were reasonably calm in the supermarket business. Oh, every once in a while, someone made a ripple with a special price on one thing or another. But Cub offers the lowest overall prices everyday. Lower than any supermarket . . . lower than any warehouse market . . . Lower than anyone. So, any claim of lower prices . . . other than Cub Foods . . . simply doesn't hold water.

YOU'RE THE TOP/JUKEBOX
30-second
(MUSIC: STYLE OF TACO/PUTTIN ON THE RITZ)
You're the top,
You're the crowning glory.
You're the top
to every hot dog story.
So of course you'd perk up an everyday
grilled cheese.
Scrambled eggs adore you
Everytime I pour you
You sure do please.
You add zest
to macaroni dinner.
You're the best

<table>
<tr><td colspan="2" align="center">1067</td></tr>
<tr><td align="right">Art Director</td><td>**Mike Murray**</td></tr>
<tr><td align="right">Writer</td><td>**Terry Bremer**</td></tr>
<tr><td align="right">Editor</td><td>**Steve Sheperd**</td></tr>
<tr><td align="right">Director</td><td>**Eric Young**</td></tr>
<tr><td align="right">Client</td><td>**CUB Foods**</td></tr>
<tr><td align="right">Agency</td><td>**Chuck Ruhr Advertising, Minneapolis**</td></tr>
<tr><td align="right">Production Company</td><td>**Wilson-Griak/Mike Monten**</td></tr>
<tr><td align="right">Special Effects</td><td>**Sam Mancino**</td></tr>
</table>

<table>
<tr><td colspan="2" align="center">1068</td></tr>
<tr><td align="right">Art Director</td><td>**Carol Livingston Knox**</td></tr>
<tr><td align="right">Writer</td><td>**Wendie Scott Davis**</td></tr>
<tr><td align="right">Client</td><td>**H.J. Heinz Company of Canada Ltd.**</td></tr>
<tr><td align="right">Agency</td><td>**Carder Gray Advertising Inc., Toronto**</td></tr>
</table>

CARL LEWIS
30-second
CARL: My first jump was a joke. Nine feet even. But I said to myself "don't give up". In high school, I kept coming in second. I could have called it quits. But I believe you should never
give up.
When that's your philosophy, there's no telling how far you can go.

WHEN YOU NEED US
30-second
SFX: THUNDER. BABY CRYING.
MOTHER (VO): It's okay. It's just thunder. You're okay.
ANNCR (VO): We're there when you need us. We're Texas Power & Light.

	1069
Art Director	**Gary Johns**
Writer	**Jeff Gorman**
Editor	**Charlie Chubak**
Director	**Mark Coppos**
Client	**Nike, Inc.**
Agency Producer	**Morty Baran/Chiat/Day, Los Angeles**
Prod'n Co Producer	**Bill Bratkowski**

	1070
Art Director	**Gary Gibson**
Director of Photography	**Robert Latorre**
Writer	**John Crawley**
Director	**Roger Flint**
Client	**Texas Power & Light**
Agency	**The Richards Group, Dallas/George Klein**
Production Company	**Flint Productions**

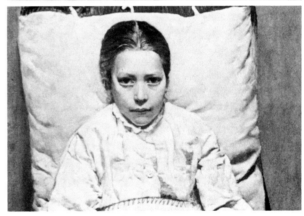

BUS STOP
30-second
TAMMY GRIMES: Every morning, millions of women get up
and go to work. Which means, every morning, millions of
women have to choose an outfit to go to work *in*.
In the twin cities, many of them choose clothes by Russ from
Powers . . . for their style, for their comfort and for their
versatility. And because clothes by Russ not only look beautiful *on* the job . . . they look beautiful on the way *to* the job.
Clothing by Russ. From Powers.

NORTHERN LIGHT
30-second
(MUSIC - "SIBELIUS" - UNDER AND THROUGHOUT)
VO: Haunting said
SUPER: "Haunting"
The N.Y. Times
VO: Trembles with erotic yearning said Newsweek.
SUPER: "Trembles with erotic yearning" Newsweek
VO: So good it's scary said the Washington Post.
SUPER: "So good it's scary." Washington Post
SUPER: Northern Light Feb. 6 -April 10
VO: Northern Light. One hundred paintings from Scandina-
via that will stop you, hold you and leave your senses shaken.
See it at the Minneapolis Institute of Arts.
SUPER: Minneapolis Institute of Arts

	1071
Art Director	**Kurt Tausche**
Designer	**Kurt Tausche**
Director of Photography	**Don Paul**
Writer	**Kurt Tausche**
Editor	**Gene Borman**
Director	**Don Paul**
Client	**Powers Department Stores**
Agency	**One Man Band, Inc., Minneapolis**
Production Company	**Fresh Pictures**

	1072
Art Director	**Doug Lew**
Writer	**Bob Thacker**
Editor	**Steve Shepherd**
Director	**Steve Griak**
Client	**Minneapolis Institute of Arts**
Agency	**Chuck Ruhr Advertising, Minneapolis**
Production Company	**Wilson-Griak/Mike Monten**

Coming soon. Bikinis.

Eat cottage cheese.

CALIFORNIA MILK ADVISORY BOARD

Ship Greyhound

BIKINI
30-second
SINGERS: One, two, three, four
        tell the people what she wore . . .
        It was an itsy bitsy teeny weeny
        yellow polka dot bikini
        that she wore for the first time today.
        And in her itsy bitsy
        teeny weeny yellow polka dot bikini
        she brought the boys to their knees.
ANNCR: Hey, bikinis are coming. Eat cottage cheese.

SAME DAY/$10
30-second
MUSIC UP THEN UNDER.
VO: In the race to get your package there faster . . . guess who's broken the overnight barrier . . .
SFX: (MUSIC UP) WHOOSH.
VO: Greyhound Package Express.
VO: Greyhound Priority Service can get your package there the *same* day . . .
VO: . . . to cities within 200 miles . . .
VO: . . . for a flat rate of only ten dollars . . . for packages up to ten pounds.
VO: So ship Greyhound Priority . . . And don't wait 'til tomorrow . . . for a package you could have there today . . .
SFX: WHOOSH

1073

Art Director	**Ralph Price**
Writers	**Jack Foster, Michael Wagman**
Editor	**Jacques Dury**
Director	**Harold Becker**
Client	**California Milk Advisory Board**
Agency	**FCB/LA/Len Levy**
Prod'n Co Producer	**N. Lee Lacy**
Creative Director	**Michael Wagman**

1074

Art Director	**Ron Fisher**
Client	**Greyhound Package Express**
Agency	**Bozell & Jacobs, Inc., Dallas-Ft. Worth**
Agency Producer	**Sally Hotchkiss**

GREAT TASTE
30-second
ANNCR (VO): OK, America, which iced tea has the great taste which refreshes you most?
SINGERS: CLEARLY NESTEA
      SPLASH, POOL, ICY, COOL
      CLEARLY NESTEA
      WET, CRISP, CLEAN, BRISK
      LIKE THIS NESTEA
      SPLISH SPLASH
      A TALL GLASS
      A TASTE BLAST
      CLEARLY NESTEA, CLEARLY NESTEA
      COLD DRINK, CLINK CLINK
      JUST THINK NESTEA

STONEFACE
30-second
ANNCR (VO): For years, banks and savings and loans have been singing the same old song.
MUSIC: "I Can't Give You Anything But Love, Baby."
They tell you how much they love you, but they never seem able to loan you money. At Minnesota Federal we love you, too, but we also have money to loan at very competitive rates.
SFX: MUSIC UP
Minnesota Federal. Money to loan . . . without the song and dance.

	1075
Art Director	**Greg Weinschenker**
Director of Photography	**Jeff Kimball**
Writer	**Linda Kaplan**
Editor	**Bobby Smalheiser**
Director	**Adrian Lyne**
Client	**Nestle Co./Nestea**
Agency Producer	**Meredith Wright/J.W.T., New York**
Production Company	**Jennie & Co./Paul Esposito**
Production Mgr.	**Mindy Goldberg**

	1076
Art Director	**Dean Hanson**
Writer	**Tom McElligott**
Editor	**Bobby Smalheiser**
Director	**Steve Steigman**
Client	**Minnesota Federal Savings & Loan**
Agency	**FMR, Minneapolis/Judy Carter**
Production Company	**Steve Steigman Prod.**

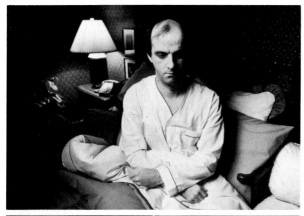

APPETITE
30-second
ANNCR (VO): Do you ever wake up with an appetite that's so
big, you just can't control it?
SFX: CRUNCH
At Country Kitchen we understand big appetites. That's why
we're offering . . .
. . . three new hearty skillet breakfasts . . . steak and omelet
skillet . . .
. . . skillet scramble . . .
. . . and Southern skillet.
Country Kitchen's newest skillet breakfasts.
Big breakfasts . . .
. . . for big appetites . . .
SFX: CRUNCH

TANK
30-second
(SFX: MUSIC, NATURAL SFX)
ANNCR (VO): When it comes to handling money, a lot of
people are over their heads.
And unless you have an awful *lot* of money . . . getting the
attention of your banker isn't always easy.
At Minnesota Federal, we believe you deserve clear, straight-
forward answers to your financial questions.
We call it Plain Talk banking.
Next time you've got a question, call Minnesota Federal . . .
before you take a dive.

	1077
Art Director	**Pat Burnham**
Writer	**Tom McElligott**
Editor	**Steve Shepherd**
Director	**Jim Hinton**
Client	**Country Kitchen International**
Agency	**FMR, Minneapolis/Judy Carter**
Production Company	**Wilson-Griak**

	1078
Art Director	**Dean Hanson**
Writer	**Tom McElligott**
Editor	**Tony Fischer**
Director	**Jim Lund**
Client	**Minnesota Federal Savings and Loan**
Agency	**FMR, Minneapolis/Judy Carter**
Production Company	**James Productions**

VICTORY
30-second
(MUSIC OVER)
Time again for Gold'n Plump news.
(VO): All across the Midwest citizens flock to the streets to greet the victorious Gold'n Plump armies.
(MUSIC UNDER)
VO: . . . Knowing that they can now serve fresher, plumper, tastier Gold'n Plump Chickens.
(MUSIC UNDER)
SFX: (CROWD CHEERS, TANK SOUNDS)
VO: . . . They celebrate their liberation from ordinary chicken.
VO: . . . And vow never again to fall prey to Southern birds.
(MUSIC BUILDS)

MONEY
30-second
ANNCR (VO): These days, a lot of banks and savings and loans are *very* confusing.
BANKER: "I Can't Give You Anything But Love, Baby."
ANNCR (VO): They tell you they have money to loan . . . but somehow they never want to give it to you.
At Minnesota Federal, things are simpler. We not only *have* money to loan, but we *want* to loan it to you.
SFX: MUSIC UP
Minnesota Federal . . . money to loan without the song and dance.

	1079
Art Director	**Nancy Rice**
Writer	**Tom McElligott**
Editor	**Bob Wickland**
Director	**Jim Hinton**
Client	**Gold'n Plump Poultry, Inc.**
Agency	**FMR, Minneapolis/Judy Carter**
Production Company	**Wilson-Griak**
News Reel Footage	**Bob DeFlores**

	1080
Art Director	**Dean Hanson**
Writer	**Tom McElligott**
Editor	**Bobby Smalheiser**
Director	**Steve Steigman**
Client	**Minnesota Federal Savings And Loan**
Agency	**FMR, Minneapolis/Judy Carter**
Production Company	**Steve Steigman Prod.**

NOT THE SAME OLD THING
30-second
SFX: SNORING.
FRANK PERDUE (VO): No matter how well you dress up the same old things,
WOMAN: Boeuf a la Camouflage!
FRANK PERDUE (VO): they're still the same old things.
MAN: Pot roast.
WOMAN: Terrine de Groucho!
MAN: Meat Loaf.
FRANK PERDUE: So try Perdue Cornish Game Hens. They're tender, delicious and easy to make. But best of all, they make a welcome surprise.
SFX: SNORING.
WOMAN: Cornish a la Frank!

THE TEAM
30-second
MUSIC & VO UP:
The Coca-Cola Company would like to salute all the 1984 Olympic athletes.
The Italians, the English, the Germans, the Swedes, the Africans, the Irish.
The Chinese, the Portuguese.
The Brazilians,
the Greeks,
the French, the Poles.
All those athletes, of every heritage, who will wear the uniform of the United States Olympic team. To Coca-Cola . . . to all of America . . . you are it.

1081

Art Director	**Sam Scali**
Writer	**Ed McCabe**
Client	**Perdue Farms, Inc.**
Agency	**Scali, McCabe, Sloves, New York/Carol Singer**

1082

Art Directors	**Robert Conlan, Frank Marrone**
Writer	**Frank Marrone**
Editor	**Randy Illwott/First Edition**
Director	**Steve Horn**
Client	**Coca-Cola Co.**
Agency Producer	**Robert Conlan/McCann Erickson, New York**
Prod'n Co Producer	**Steve Horn**
Creative Director	**John Bergin**

GRANT WOOD-THE TAKE OFF
30-second
(MUSIC THROUGHOUT)
ANNCR (VO): American Gothic by Grant Wood. No other
painting in the world has been so plagiarized. Now that
you've seen all the rip-offs, come see the original.
The Grant Wood Show at the Minneapolis Institute of Arts.

HOMESTYLE DINNERS
30-second
GRANDFATHER: (Singing) MOONLIGHT, STARLIGHT
DA DA DA DA DA DA
WE'RE GOING OUT TONIGHT
GRANDMOTHER: My dinner?
ANNCR: Dinner at Perkins. Hearty . . . wholesome . . . and
now something new. As always, served with touches of
home.
GRANDFATHER: WELL, WHAT ABOUT YOUR DINNER?
GRANDMOTHER: Good.
GRANDFATHER: Good.

	1083
Art Director	Doug Lew
Writer	Bob Thacker
Editor	Charles Diercks, Teleproducers
Director	Charles Diercks
Client	Minneapolis Institute of Arts
Agency	Chuck Ruhr Advertising, Minneapolis
Production Company	Teleproducers

	1084
Art Director	Doug Lew
Writer	Terry Bremer
Editor	Bob Wickland
Director	Steve Griak
Client	Perkins Restaurants
Agency	Chuck Ruhr Advertising, Minneapolis
Production Company	Wilson-Griak/Mike Monten

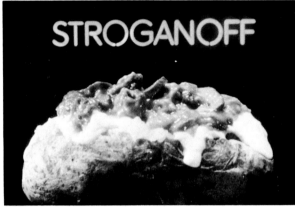

MORE HOT STUFF
30-second
SFX: CYMBAL.
SINGERS: More (rim shot)
　　　　　Hot (snare hit)
　　　　　Stuff (aah)
ANNCR: Wendy's has potatoes stuffed 3 new ways.
SINGERS: New stuff is hot!
ANNCR: Chicken Ala King ought to hit the spot.
ANNCR: Stroganoff with beef. You're gonna like it alot.
SINGERS: Wendy's is hot!
ANNCR: Or veggies stuff and a sauce with cheddar cheese.
When you want new hot stuff Wendy's has three.
MAN: That's big news to me.
ANNCR: New hot stuffed baked potatoes, for Wendy's kind

MOTHERS DAY/BABY
30-second
(MUSIC UNDER)
SONG: It's your first year . . .
　　　　as a mother . . .
　　　　and I want
　　　　to thank you dear . . .
　　　　for the love
　　　　you shared with him and me . . .
　　　　All through the year . . .
　　　　so I'm giving you this HALLMARK . . .
MOTHER: Is that for me?
SONG: . . . and I hope
　　　　that you will see . . .
　　　　what I'm really

<hr>

1085

Art Director	**George Cinfo**
Designer	**Cathy Edwards**
Writer	**Arthur Bijur**
Editor	**New York Film Experience**
Director	**Ben Somoroff**
Client	**Wendy's**
Agency	**DFS, New York/John Lacey**
Production Company	**Elite**

<hr>

1086

Art Director	**Greta Carlstrom**
Writer	**Roger Feuerman**
Editor	**FilmBillders**
Director	**Bob Brooks**
Client	**Hallmark Cards**
Agency Producers	**Mootsy Elliot/Wendy Noll/ Y&R, New York**
Production Company	**Brooks, Fulford, Cramer, Seresin**
Music Director	**Hunter Murtaugh, Y&R**

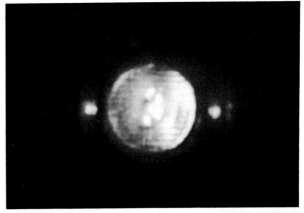

CLOTHESPIN
30-second
(MUSIC UNDER)
ANNCR (VO): If you think aerosol fumes are the price you have to pay to get your oven clean, good news. You're wrong. Introducing the new S.O.S. Oven Cleaning Pad. It has no aerosol fumes. It has no aerosol. And the new S.O.S. Oven Cleaning Pad is this easy . . . this fast . . . and best of all . . . this good. So next time avoid the little difficulties of an aerosol. Get the new S.O.S. Oven Cleaning Pad. For a really clean oven with no fumes.

RED
30-second
OPEN ON RED FLASHING LIGHT TO THE RHYTHM OF MUSIC SCORE.
VO: Nothing gets your attention like red.
SERIES OF CUTS FOLLOW: RED FIRE ALARM, RED STREET LIGHTS, RED PAINT, RED PHONE ETC.
VO: And now, you can get the power of red in your GTE yellow pages ad.
ARROW HITS RED BULLSEYE; PULL BACK REVEALING YELLOW PAGE AD.
DISSOLVE TO LOGO.

1087
Art Director	**Ervin Jue**
Writer	**Cynthia Beck**
Editor	**Joe Pelicano**
Director	**John Danza**
Client	**Miles Laboratories**
Agency Producer	**Jill Gordon/Doyle Dane Bernbach Inc., New York**
Production Company	**Danza Prod.**

1088
Art Director	**Ervin Jue**
Writer	**Hank Volker**
Editor	**David Dee**
Director	**Andy Wall**
Client	**GTE**
Agency Producer	**Rosemary Barre/Doyle Dane Bernbach Inc., New York**
Production Company	**Field & Wall**

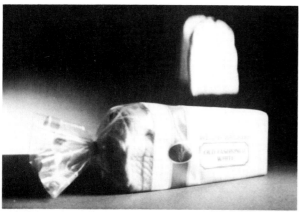

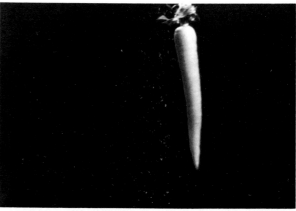

RHAPSODY IN BREAD
30-second
ANNCR (VO): Presenting bread from Weight Watchers. White, the old-fashioned way: Freshly baked . . . without any artificial preservatives. Just like our new Soft Light Rye. Oh-so-light, and full of whole-grain good taste . . . along with new Wholesome Cracked Wheat. So if you love bread, now you can indulge in Weight Watchers. It makes a great beginning to a very tasteful sandwich.

CARROT
30-second
VO: Almost irresistible . . .
Those money market interest rates . . .
the banks have been dangling.
Some gave 20% in December . . .
for a few weeks. (SFX: CRUNCH)
Then in January . . . less. (SFX: CRUNCH)
February . . . even less. (SFX: CRUNCH)
March . . .
April . . . (SFX: CRUNCH)
Not so much to bite at anymore.
Aren't you better off now in a Money Market Mutual Fund?
There's no come on . . . plus other benefits the banks don't offer.

1089

Art Director	**Marion Sackett**
Director of Photography	**Santiago Suarez**
Writer	**Ms. Perri Feuer**
Editor	**Joe Laliker**
Director	**Santiago Suarez**
Client	**Kevin Conner**
Agency Producer	**Ms. Lee Weiss/Doyle Dane Bernbach, Inc., New York**

1090

Art Director	**Paul Maurer**
Designer	**Paul Maurer**
Director of Photography	**William Helburn**
Writer	**Paul Zoellner**
Editor	**Pierre Kahn/Pelco**
Director	**William Helburn**
Client	**ICI**
Agency Producer	**Will Wilcox/Doyle Dane Bernbach, Inc., New York**

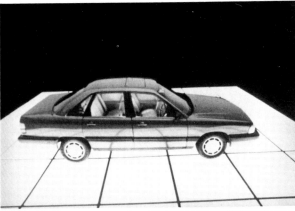

SCREENS
30-second
(MUSIC UNDER)
VO: Audi introduces the luxury sedan voted "Car of the Year"
by Europe's motor press. The new Audi 5000S. Years ahead
in German technology. Wind tunnel designed to be the
world's most aerodynamic luxury sedan.
(MUSIC)
With self-diagnostic electronics. Extraordinary quiet and
performance. The new 5000S. From Audi. The art of
engineering.

CIGNA CORPORATE
30-second
MUSIC UNDER.
VO: At INA, a CIGNA company we've insured hospitals . . .
. . . and Doctors.
We've covered fathers, . . .
. . . and Suns . . .
. . . and corporate giants . . .
. . . of all kinds.
We've written insurance on Mercury.
And we've even designed coverage for satellites. So, if you
need property or casualty insurance . . . remember our people at . . .
CIGNA. After all . . .
accidents happen.

1091

Art Director	**William Taubin**
Designer	**Skip Wildes**
Writer	**Ed Smith**
Director	**Rich Clemente**
Client	**Porsche/Audi**
Agency Producer	**Jim Callan/Doyle Dane Bernbach Inc., New York**
Production Company	**Intercom/Dave Russell**

1092

Art Director	**Harvey Baron**
Designer	**Harvey Baron**
Writer	**Diane Rothschild**
Director	**Geoffrey Mayo**
Client	**CIGNA**
Agency Producer	**Cheryl Nelson/Doyle Dane Bernbach Inc., New York**

HUGE ADVANTAGE
30-second
If you only knew what your finger goes through every time you push your old fashioned dial around and around and around when you could be pushing these. Convenient Touch Calling is the most advanced way of making a call. Besides being just plain fun. So get General Telephone's Touch Calling service today. And someday you'll be able to shop by phone, bank, even get the news by phone. But you won't be able to do any of those things if you're still hanging on to your rotary dial . . .
MAN: Aaaagh!!!

EVERY WHICH WAY BUT DOWN
30-second
Of all the means of transportation available, the fastest, most efficient, most economical way for business people to go from one place . . . to another . . . is still the telephone. So for your next business trip why not use the phone instead?

1093
Art Director	**Andy DeSantis**
Writer	**Nicole Cranberg Crosby**
Editor	**Ciro**
Director	**Alan Brooks**
Client	**GTE**
Agency Producer	**Bob Samuel/Doyle Dane Bernbach Inc., New York**
Prod'n Co Producer	**Ed Christie**

1094
Art Director	**Joe Delvecchio**
Designer	**Joe Delvecchio**
Director of Photography	**Stock**
Writer	**Peter Bregman**
Editor	**Pelco**
Client	**GTE**
Agency Producer	**Stuart Raffael/Doyle Dane Bernbach Inc., New York**
Production Company	**Film Search**

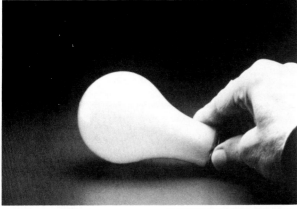

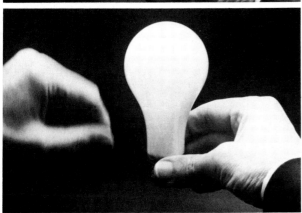

RUNNING ON EMPTY
30-second
You're about to see an extra ordinary line of light bulbs.
Sylvania Energy Pinchers. (KACHICK) They're engineered to
use a lot less energy (KACHICK) yet still shine just as
brightly
(KACHICK) as ordinary bulbs. In fact, (KACHICK) Sylvania
Energy Pincher light bulbs use so little energy they seem to
run (KACHICK) . . . on nothing. Energy Pincher light bulbs.
E-S-P energy saving products from Sylvania. (KACHICK)

DESERT
30-second
(MUSIC UNDER)
VO: Audi introduces the luxury sedan voted "Car of the Year"
by Europe's motor press. The new Audi 5000S. Years ahead
in German technology. Smooth and slippery to the wind, it is
the world's most aerodynamic luxury sedan. If you think it's
the most beautiful, all the better. The 5000S. From Audi. The
art of engineering.

1095

Art Director	Joe Delvecchio
Designer	Joe Delvecchio
Director of Photography	Matthew Brady
Writer	Peter Bregman
Editor	Pelco
Director	Matthew Brady
Client	GTE
Agency Producer	Stuart Raffel/Doyle Dane Bernbach Inc., New York
Production Company	Matthew Brady Films

1096

Art Director	William Taubin
Designer	Skip Wildes
Writer	Ed Smith
Director	Rich Clemente
Client	Porsche/Audi
Agency Producer	Jim Callan/Doyle Dane Bernbach Inc., New York
Production Company	Intercom/Dave Russell

SON OF AUSGEZEICHNET
30-second
(MUSIC UNDER)
GERMAN (VO): The German engineers who built the
Volkswagen Scirocco . . . were obsessed with aerodynamics
. . . and passionate about precision . . .
They also looked forward to a pleasant Sunday drive.
(MUSIC)
(MUSIC)
(MUSIC)
HEAD ENGINEER (KNOWINGLY): "Ausgezeichnet?"
ASSISTANT (IN AWE): Ausgezeichnet!

CLAIROL NICE 'N EASY
30-second
MUSIC THROUGHOUT
ANNCR (VO): Color and condition that should have been
yours . . . can be. Make it happen. Nice 'N Easy.
It sells the most . . .
(SFX: DOOR OPENING)
. . . it conditions the most.
(SFX: DOOR CLOSING)
MALE VOICE: Hi, how's it going?
(MUSIC OUT)

1097

Art Director	**Dom Marino**
Designer	**Dom Marino**
Director of Photography	**Michael Werk**
Writer	**Deanna Cohen**
Editor	**Pelco**
Director	**John St. Clair**
Client	**Volkswagen**
Agency Producer	**Mark Sitley/Doyle Dane Bernbach Inc., New York**
Production Company:	**Peterson Prod.**

1098

Art Director	**Robert Starr**
Designer	**Robert Starr**
Writer	**Sue Brock**
Editor	**Pelco**
Director	**Michael Ulick**
Client	**Clairol/Nice n' Easy**
Agency Producer	**Cheryl Nelson/Doyle Dane Bernbach Inc., New York**
Production Company	**Michael Ulick Productions**
Music Composition	**Don Hall**

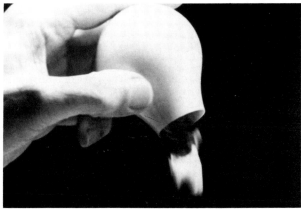

PRESTO CHANGE-O
30-second
MUSIC UNDER
This is a new Sylvania Energy Pincher. It looks like an ordinary light bulb. Shines just as bright. And lasts as long. But it also saves 5 watts of energy. Which means by the time it burns out . . . you'll get back a lot of money to use toward your next one. Energy Pincher Light bulbs. E-S-P energy saving products from Sylvania.
(KACHICK)

COWS
30-second
(MUSIC UNDER)
ANNCR (VO):
Dave Shriver is well known in these parts. He's in the animal husbandry business. Specifically, artificial insemination.
(COW MOOS)
Dave drives a Volkswagen Rabbit - 7 days a week . . . 52 weeks a year. And he's never missed a day, because of mechanical failure. (CALF MOOS)
To date, Dave's Rabbit has traveled over 355,000 miles. And it's still going strong. (COW MOOS) Rabbit. It's not a car. It's a Volkswagen.

	1099
Art Director	**Joe Delvecchio**
Designer	**Joe Delvecchio**
Director of Photography	**Matthew Brady**
Writer	**Peter Bregman**
Editor	**Pelco**
Director	**Matthew Brady**
Client	**GTE**
Agency Producer	**Stuart Raffael/Doyle Dane Bernbach Inc., New York**
Production Company	**Matthew Brady Films**

	1100
Art Director	**Charles Piccirillo**
Designer	**Charles Piccirillo**
Director of Photography	**Dick James**
Writer	**Tom Yobbagy**
Editor	**Pierre Kahn**
Director	**Dick James**
Client	**Volkswagen**
Agency Producer	**Rosemary Barre/Doyle Dane Bernbach Inc., New York**
Production Company	**James Stern Productions/ Greg Stern**

SUPERMARKET
30-second
(MUSIC AND SFX UNDER)
ANNCR (VO): Ever notice when you run out of cash, how
ugly things can get? Well, running out of cash is a thing of
the past with Barney . . . CBT is putting Barney right where
you need him most. Everywhere from supermarkets to department stores. So when you run out of cash, you don't have
to run to the bank . . .
OLD WOMAN: Nice move, sonny!
ANNCR (VO): Because CBT's bringing the bank to you. CBT's
Barney. It's like having a bank right in your pocket.

A MAN AND A WOMAN
30-second
(MUSIC THROUGHOUT)
MAN: She'll never understand.
WOMAN: I knew why he had to have this car.
MAN: My very own Quantum.
WOMAN: It's so responsive.
MAN: Front wheel drive.
WOMAN: Skiing in the Alps.
MAN: A patented rear axle that thinks.
WOMAN: *This* car is *very* adult.
MAN: This car is *very* adult.
WOMAN: He's such a little boy.
VO: The German engineered Volkswagen Quantum.
It's very adult.

1101
Art Director	**Steven McMacken**
Designer	**Steven McMacken**
Writer	**Dik Haddad**
Director	**William Gove**
Client	**Connecticut Bank & Trust**
Agency	**Mintz & Hoke Inc., Avon, CT/Mary Ann Gates**
Production Company	**Harvest Moon**

1102
Art Directors	**Charley Rice, John Eding**
Writer	**Jane Talcott**
Director	**Michael Serecin**
Client	**Volkswagen**
Agency Producer	**Regina Ebel/Doyle Dane Bernbach Inc., New York**
Production Company	**Fuller, Creamer, Wolford, Serecin**

FREDDIE LAKER REV.
30-second
VO: Hello, I'm Freddie Laker, the chap who tried to get you Yanks overseas for as little as possible. It was a good idea, now I've found another way—by telephone.
You can dial a one-minute call from the states to the United Kingdom for only $1.25. Each additional minute is only 76 cents. If you've got family and friends in the U.K. who'd like to hear from you, fly Bell . . . I mean try Bell. Call them.
ANNCR (VO): Bell brings the world closer.

OLDER BROTHER REV.
30-second
BOY #1: Bet you're glad your brother finally went away to school.
BOY #2: Yeah.
BOY #1: You get his room, his bike, and everything. What a deal.
BOY #2: Yeah.
BOY #1: And just think . . . no one to call you peeper anymore.
BOY #2: Yeah.
MOTHER: David, your brother's on the phone. He wants to talk to you.
BOY #2: Brian? For me? Oh boy!
BOY #2: Hi, Brian!

1103
Art Director	**Rene Kuypers**
Writer	**Dolores Hanan**
Editor	**H. Lazarus**
Director	**Norman Griner**
Client	**AT&T Communications Residence/Kim Armstrong**
Agency	**NW Ayer Incorporated, New York/Liz Krauss**
Production Company	**Griner/Cuesta & Assoc.**
Creative Director	**Ron Salzberg**

1104
Art Director	**Diane Campbell**
Writer	**Beth McLure**
Editor	**H. Lazarua**
Director	**Steve Horn**
Client	**AT&T Comm. Res-Kim Armstrong, Phil Shyposh**
Agency	**NW Ayer Incorporated, New York/Gaston Braun**
Production Company	**Steve Horn Inc./Linda H. Horn**
Creative Director	**Ron Salzberg**

Exclusively from Avon

FANTASQUE
30-second
(MUSIC)
(MUSIC UNDER)
LOUIS FÉRAUD: I am Louis Féraud.
(MUSIC)
LOUIS FÉRAUD: The clothes I design transform a woman.
My fragrance from Avon, Fantasque, does the same thing.
Fantasque lets a woman experience intensely her power
to excite.
(MUSIC)
LOUIS FÉRAUD: Fantasque.
WOMAN (VO): Exclusively from Avon.

RIGHT
30-second
VO: Ever notice, when some designer outlets have just the
right clothes.
SALESWOMAN: It's you.
VO: They're just the wrong size. And when they're just the
right size.
SALESWOMAN: Perfect.
VO: They're just the wrong clothes. That's why we created
Practically Wholesale.
You'll find a full range of the latest fashions and designer
creations. In a full range of colors and sizes. And private
dressing rooms . . . to try on just the right clothes in just the
right size.
At last, all the benefits of retail at Practically Wholesale.

	1105
Art Director	**Alistair Proctor**
Writer	**Veronica Nash**
Editors	**Film Editors-London/**
	Dennis Hayes-New York
Director	**Howard Guard**
Client	**Avon Products**
Agency Producer	**Nancy Perez/Ogilvy &**
	Mather, New York
Prod'n Company Producer	**Maxine Tabak**
Creative Director	**Malcolm End**

	1106
Art Director	**Allen Kay**
Writer	**Lois Korey**
Editor	**Morty Ashkinos**
Director	**Allen Kay**
Client	**Practically Wholesale/**
	Richard Pollack
Agency Producer	**Milda Misevicius/Korey,**
	Kay & Partners, New York
Production Company	**Korey, Kay Films**

OLYMPIC EXCELLENCE
30-second
ANNCR: Dale Brynestad is a soldier with a dream. The '84 Olympics. His sport the modern pentathlon. Five grueling events. The Army is full of people who are striving to be all they can be. For specialist Dale Brynestad that means striving to be the best in the world.
SINGERS: Be All That You Can Be.
You Can Do It In The Army.

COMPLETE COMPUTER
30-second
CUSTOMER: Yea, I'd like to buy this twelve-hundred dollar computer.
SALESMAN 1: That'll be fifty-three hundred dollars, complete.
CUSTOMER: Fifty-three hundred dollars?
SALESMAN 1: What with monitor, software, disc drives . . .
SALESMAN 2: Etcetera, etcetera, etcetera.
CUSTOMER: Oh, how much is that thousand dollar computer?
SALESMAN 1: Ah, forty-four hundred.
CUSTOMER: Uhhh, how much is that fourteen-hundred dollar computer?
SALESMAN 1: Thirty-nine hundred.

<table>
<tr><td colspan="2" align="center">1107</td></tr>
<tr><td align="right">Art Director</td><td>John Byrnes</td></tr>
<tr><td align="right">Writer</td><td>Susan McFeatters</td></tr>
<tr><td align="right">Editor</td><td>Jerry Bender</td></tr>
<tr><td align="right">Director</td><td>Rolf Bode</td></tr>
<tr><td align="right">Client</td><td>United States Army/Maj. Gen. Jack Bradshaw</td></tr>
<tr><td align="right">Agency</td><td>NW Ayer Incorporated, New York/Jim McMenemy</td></tr>
<tr><td align="right">Production Company</td><td>Lofaro & Assoc./Houston Winn</td></tr>
<tr><td align="right">Creative Directors</td><td>Walter Burek, Ted Regan</td></tr>
</table>

<table>
<tr><td colspan="2" align="center">1108</td></tr>
<tr><td align="right">Art Director</td><td>Joe Sedelmaier</td></tr>
<tr><td align="right">Writer</td><td>Jim Weller</td></tr>
<tr><td align="right">Editor</td><td>Peggy DeLay</td></tr>
<tr><td align="right">Director</td><td>Joe Sedelmaier</td></tr>
<tr><td align="right">Client</td><td>Kaypro Computers</td></tr>
<tr><td align="right">Agency</td><td>Della Femina Travisano, Los Angeles</td></tr>
<tr><td align="right">Production Company</td><td>Sedelmaier Film Prod.</td></tr>
</table>

CUCKOO
30-second
MOTHER: Lester! It's so good to hear your voice!
ANNCR (VO): The happiness of a person receiving a long-distance call is matched only by . . . the concern of the person making that call with how long he's on the line.
Well, if you dial direct any weekday after five PM, you'll save 40%.
If you call after eleven PM, or on the weekend, you'll save 60%.
And you'll be able to carry on a normal conversation without driving yourself . . .
CLOCK: CUCKOO!

YOUNG WARNER
30-second
ANNCR (VO): Early in his life, Warner Wolf, showed an avid interest in sports . . .
RADIO (VO): Five seconds left and they're gonna run out the clock. But the ball is stolen. One second to go, he puts it up from the midcourt line and he made the BASKET!
YOUNG WARNER: Swish!!!
ANNCR (VO): And an unusual grasp of the language.
RADIO (VO): It's a long one, deep into right field. It's a HOMERUN!
YOUNG WARNER: Boom!!!
ANNCR (VO): Nobody speaks sports like Warner Wolf . . .
RADIO (VO): Ball at the 25, 13 seconds left in the half.
There's the snap. It's a quarterback sneak. He breaks free.

1109

Art Director	**Lester Feldman**
Writer	**Mike Mangano**
Editor	**Joe Pellicano**
Director	**Michael Ulick**
Client	**GTE**
Agency Producer	**Stuart Raffel/Doyle Dane Bernbach Inc., New York**
Production Company	**Ulick Productions**

1110

Art Director	**Lou Zaffos**
Writer	**Dean Weller**
Editor	**Morty Ashkinos**
Director	**Michael Ulick**
Client	**WCBS-TV/Paula McCorkle**
Agency	**Korey, Kay & Partners, New York/Milda Misevicius**

FLYING CARS
30-second
(MUSIC THROUGHOUT)
VO: It takes more than high octane to keep your car perform-
ing well.
That's why these world famous stunt drivers rely on Mobil
Detergent Gasoline. They know a car with a clean carbure-
tor performs better.
It's as simple as that.
Mobil Detergent Gasoline.
For your everyday driving needs.

ROOF
30-second
VO: Sometimes it's reassuring to know your car will
perform well.
That's why stunt driver Buzz Bundy relies on Mobil Deter-
gent Gasoline.
After all, a clean carburetor performs better.
It's as simple as that.
Mobil Detergent Gasoline.
For your everyday driving needs.

<table>
<tr><td colspan="2">1111</td></tr>
<tr><td>Art Director</td><td>Roy Grace</td></tr>
<tr><td>Designer</td><td>Roy Grace</td></tr>
<tr><td>Director of Photography</td><td>Henry Sandbank</td></tr>
<tr><td>Writer</td><td>John Noble</td></tr>
<tr><td>Editor</td><td>Dick Stone/Stone-Cutters</td></tr>
<tr><td>Director</td><td>Henry Sandbank</td></tr>
<tr><td>Client</td><td>Mobil Oil Corporation</td></tr>
<tr><td>Agency</td><td>Doyle Dane Bernbach Inc., New York/Susan Calhoun</td></tr>
<tr><td>Production Company</td><td>Sandbank Films, Inc.</td></tr>
</table>

<table>
<tr><td colspan="2">1112</td></tr>
<tr><td>Art Director</td><td>Roy Grace</td></tr>
<tr><td>Designer</td><td>Roy Grace</td></tr>
<tr><td>Director of Photography</td><td>Henry Sandbank</td></tr>
<tr><td>Writer</td><td>John Noble</td></tr>
<tr><td>Editor</td><td>Dick Stone/Stone-Cutters</td></tr>
<tr><td>Director</td><td>Henry Sandbank</td></tr>
<tr><td>Client</td><td>Mobil Oil Corporation</td></tr>
<tr><td>Agency</td><td>Doyle Dane Bernbach Inc., New York/Susan Calhoun</td></tr>
<tr><td>Production Company</td><td>Sandbank Films, Inc.</td></tr>
</table>

RABBITS REDUX-UM
30-second
CLARA: Ed, I think we need a bigger place . . . I better rent a truck.
ANNCR: It's easy to move yourself with a Jartran truck or trailer. Jartran vans even have automatic transmission and power steering.
CLARA: Ed, don't forget the chair.
ANNCR: Right now, along with a low price, you get unlimited mileage on one-way moves.
CLARA: Ed dear, we're here. Ed? Ed? I musta forgot him.
ANNCR: Jartran. For long moves. Or short hops.

DAVE EPPLEY
30-second
MUSIC UNDER
Good afternoon sports fans and welcome to the fourth weekly mowing of Dave Eppley's lawn. Tension mounts as Dave boards the incredible John Deere 318.
Down the drive he goes, the extra wide mower cutting time in the straights.
Into the first turn he flies, feeling the power of all eighteen horses.
And the 318 with power steering mows up the back stretch in record time . . .
Proof, once again, that nothing runs like a . . .
Dear?
MUSIC UP

1113

Art Director	**Cindy Perego**
Director of Photography	**Josef Sedelmaier**
Writer	**Tom McNeer**
Editor	**Henry Hoda**
Director	**Josef Sedelmaier**
Client	**Jartran, Inc.**
Agency	**Bozell & Jacobs, Atlanta/ Tom McNeer**
Production Company	**Sedelmaier Films**

1114

Art Director	**Brian Kelly**
Writer	**Stephen Fortier**
Editor	**Jerrry Hastings**
Director	**John Panza**
Client	**Deere & Company**
Agency	**NW Ayer, Inc., Chicago/ Hank Sabian**
Production Company	**Levine/Pytka**
Creative Dirs.	**Dennis French, Larry Sommerville**

MAMMOTH
30-second
MUSIC UP.
VO: At the dawn of history man ran, primarily for his health!
CAVEMAN: Je suis fini!
MUSICAL ACCENT.
VO: But he could . . . revive himself at the spring we now call Perrier.
CAVEMAN: Un miracle!
RUNNING MUSIC.
VO: Today . . .man has discovered the joy of running . . . and the sparkling reward of naturally salt-free Perrier.
VO: Earth's first soft drink.

MANY CANS
30-second
MUSIC IN SYNC WITH CHANGING CANS.
VO: Do you know how many of these motor oils would love to make this claim?
Well, this one can.

1115

Art Director	Joe LaRosa
Artist	R.O. Blechman
Writers	Joe LaRosa, Francesca Blumenthal
Client	Great Waters of France, Inc.
Agency	Waring & LaRosa, Inc., New York
Production Company	The Ink Tank/R.O. Blechman

1116

Art Director	Roy Grace
Designer	Roy Grace
Director of Photography	Henry Sandbank
Writer	John Noble
Editor	Dick Stone/Stone-Cutters
Director	Henry Sandbank
Client	Mobil Oil Corporation
Agency	Doyle Dane Bernbach Inc., New York/Susan Calhoun
Production Company	Sandbank Films, Inc.

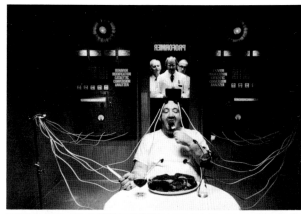

DO YOU KNOW ME/TOM LANDRY
30-second
LANDRY: Do you know me? I'm one of the best known cowboys in Texas.
But a lot of people don't recognize me in a cowboy hat.
So I just carry the American Express Card.
It can help you out in plenty of tough situations.
Because you never know when you're gonna be surrounded.
By Redskins . . . Howdy.
ANNCR: To apply for the card, look for this display and take one.
LANDRY: The American Express Card. Don't leave home without it.

BEHAVIOR MODIFICATION
30-second
ANNCR (VO): It seems like clinical tests have proven that everything you like is hazardous to your health.
As a result, people are being required to modify their habits.
But there is an alternative. Really Naturals. The delicious all-natural snack. No additives. No preservatives.
No warning labels.

1117
Art Director	F. Paul Pracilio
Writer	Jeff Atlas
Client	American Express Company
Agency Producer	Nancy Perez/Ogilvy & Mather, New York

1118
Art Director	Joe Sedelmaier
Writer	Jeff Gorman
Editor	Peggy DeLay
Director	Joe Sedelmaier
Client	Really Naturals/Confection Group
Agency	Marketing Communications, Chicago
Production Company	Sedelmaier Film Prod.

PHONE JACK
30-second
ANNE: I'd like a phone jack.
PHIL: The name's Phil.
ANNE: How do you do?
PHIL: Oh, it's easy. You just connect this to the wires in your wall. Anybody can do it. And you save money.
ANNE: Thank you, Phil, you've been very helpful.
PHIL: Er . . . listen, drop in to the Phone Mart again—if you need new service—touch calling—anything.
You can even bring your phones in here for repair, Miss er . . .
ANNE: Sorry, Phil, it Mrs. Er . . . Uh.
(MUSIC UNDER)
SINGERS: Get it all at General Telephone.
(MUSIC OUT)

JOHN CLEESE ALTERNATE VERSION
30-second
JOHN CLEESE: Hello, John Cleese here.
(Yells)
I'd like to explain to you how life works.
You're born, you grow up, you go to school, you get a decent job, and then you apply for the American Express Card. It's a marvelous thing.
BUTLER: You howled sir?
JOHN CLEESE: Ah, thank you Dobbs.
Now, these applications are to be found in posh shops, ritzy restaurants, hoity-toity hotels—they're everywhere. So do apply.
Ah, Dobbs has and they've accepted him. Hmm!
BUTLER: Perhaps you should try again sir.

<table>
<tr><td colspan="2" align="center">1119</td></tr>
<tr><td align="right">Art Director</td><td>Lester Feldman</td></tr>
<tr><td align="right">Director of Photography</td><td>John Fleckenstein</td></tr>
<tr><td align="right">Writer</td><td>Mike Mangano</td></tr>
<tr><td align="right">Editor</td><td>Joe Pellicano</td></tr>
<tr><td align="right">Director</td><td>Bob Giraldi</td></tr>
<tr><td align="right">Client</td><td>GTE</td></tr>
<tr><td align="right">Agency Producer</td><td>Stuart Raffel/Doyle Dane Bernbach Inc., New York</td></tr>
<tr><td align="right">Production Company</td><td>Giraldi Productions</td></tr>
</table>

<table>
<tr><td colspan="2" align="center">1120</td></tr>
<tr><td align="right">Art Director</td><td>Candace Van Stryker</td></tr>
<tr><td align="right">Designer</td><td>F. Paul Pracilio</td></tr>
<tr><td align="right">Client</td><td>American Express Company</td></tr>
<tr><td align="right">Agency Producer</td><td>Laure Ann Carroll/Ogilvy & Mather, New York</td></tr>
</table>

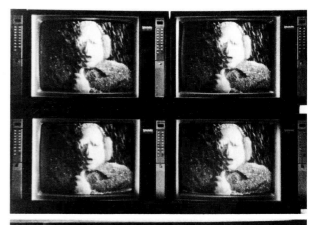

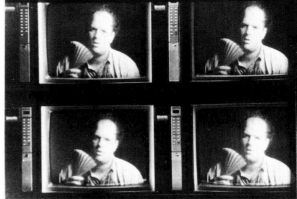

TRIBUTE
30-second
This is a tribute to Fred Lowenhar's seven year old London Fog raincoat. It's seen 483 downpours and snowstorms.
It's been used as a pillow 55 times on late night flights.
It's been worn over business suits, tuxedos and pajamas with equal style and grace.
And, because it's a London Fog, even the buttons have stayed on.
But after seven long years—perhaps it's time to get a new one.
SUPER: LONDON FOG.

TORTURE TEST
30-second
(MUSIC UNDER)
ANNCR (VO): Here at the Sharp reliability test center for television, we turn the temperature down to minus 4 degrees. And then we turn it up to 104 degrees. This one is about to go for a little ride . . . to find out how tough he really is.
And finally, the aging test . . . to make sure they last and last.
At Sharp, sure we play rough with our TV's, but that's only so they play nice for you.
From Sharp minds come Sharp products.

1121

Art Director	**Bruce Bloch**
Director of Photography	**Henry Holtzman**
Writer	**Patty Rockmore**
Client	**Londontown Corporation**
Agency	**AC&R Advertising, New York/Linda Becker, Robert Goldblatt**
Production Company	**N. Lee Lacy**

1122

Art Director	**Mark Yustein**
Cameraman	**Adam Hollander**
Writer	**Rita Senders**
Editor	**Jeff Dell Editorial**
Director	**Mark Story**
Client	**Sharp Electronics**
Agency	**Della Femina, Travisano, New York/Linda Tesa**
Production Company	**Pfeiffer/Story, Piccolo/Christine Ritzmann**

FREEFALL/DAR ROBINSON
30-second
ANNCR: On June 3, 1981, professional stuntman, Dar Robinson, performed a stunt so dangerous, no one else in the world would even try it. Now he's about to attempt new "Freefall" at Great Adventure . . . It takes you up . . . 13 stories above the earth. And then drops you off . . . without anything to cushion your fall.
"Freefall."
Only at Six Flags.
Because everyone needs a Great Adventure.

BUILDING
30-second
ANNCR (VO): Maybe the only way to improve the postal system is to build a new one. Introducing MCI Mail. It lets you use practically any electronic typewriter, home computer work station or telex to send mail to anyone, anywhere. Even to people without equipment.
MCI Mail can work instantly, in hours, or overnight . . . and can cost up to 90% less than overnight mail.
MCI Mail.
The nation's new postal system.

1123

Art Director	**Ron Travisano**
Writer	**Jim Weller**
Editors	**Filmcore/Charlie Chubak**
Director	**Werner Hlinka**
Client	**Great Adventure**
Agency	**Della Femina, Travisano, New York/Peter Yahr**
Production Company	**THT Prod./Mark Romanski**

1124

Art Director	**Ron Arnold**
Prop Design	**Eric Chamberlain**
Motion Control Photography	**Randy Balsmeyer**
Director of Photography	**James Szalapski**
Writer	**Hal Altman**
Editor	**Larry Plastrik**
Director	**Richard Greenberg**
Client	**MCI Mail**
Agency	**Ally & Gargano, New York/ Mark Sitley**
Production Company	**R/Greenberg Associates, Inc./Robert M. Greenberg**

SYSTEM 3100/THE BOSS
60-second
SFX: PHONE RINGS.
SECRETARY: (Calling to Boss) Mr. Oakner, it's time for your conference call.
OAKNER: (OFF CAMERA, SHOUTING) OK. Get me Jackson in Peoria. And find Olsen.
SECRETARY: Olsen's no longer with us.
OAKNER: Then get me Bromley!
SECRETARY: Mr. Bromley!
ANNCR (VO): Even in small businesses today, office phone systems have to do more than handle calls.
So ITT created the System 3100 digital business communication system.
OAKNER: (OFF CAMERA, AS PART OF ON-GOING DIA-

1125

Art Director	**Howard Benson**
Writers	**Barry Biederman, Larry Oakner**
Editor	**Tony Siggia**
Client	**John L. Lowden/ITT Corporation**
Agency	**NHS/Issues & Images, New York/Jean Galton, Howard Benson**
Production Company	**Johnston Films**

KIDS/ADULTS
60-second
SINGERS: WATCH OUT KIDS
I'M GOING CLICK, CLICK, CLICK
I'M GONNA GET YOU WITH THE KODAK DISC
I'M GONNA GET YOU WITH THE KODAK DISC
SURE AS SHOOTIN' I'M NOT GONNA MISS
KNOW WHEN IT'S EASY AS EASY AS THIS
I'M GONNA GET YOU WITH THE KODAK DISC
I'M GONNA GET EVERY DOGGONE SHOT
I'M GONNA GET YOU CATCH YOU TILL YOU'RE CAUGHT
I'M GONNA GET YOU READY OR NOT
I'M GONNA GET YOU WITH THE KODAK DISC
KISS KISS

1126

Art Directors	**Beth Pritchett, Greg Weinschenker**
Writers	**Cathy McMahon, Linda Kaplan, Bonnie Berkowitz, Robin Schwarz**
Editor	**Tony Siggia/First Edition**
Director	**Joe Hanwright**
Client	**Eastman Kodak/Roger Morrison**
Agency	**J.W.T., New York/Sid Horn**
Production Company	**Kira Films/Lisa Peglessi**

HATS
60-second
(MUSIC THROUGHOUT)
ANNCR (VO): In these modern times, the person who goes to work . . . may not have far to go. But at the Hat of the Month Club, the boss better keep moving . . . to keep the books, organize the files, write the letters, check out the inventory, find time to create and still keep on top of things. Yet even a thriving business
(SFX: DOORBELL)
can reach a point of diminishing returns . . . a good time to learn about the IBM Personal Computer. With this tool for modern times, a person can quickly master such jobs as accounting or word processing, even use the IBM Personal Computer to forecast growth.

WATSON
60-second
(MUSIC UNDER)
ANNCR: In 1876 Alexander Graham Bell started a communications revolution.
MAN: Watson, come here. I want you!
WOMAN: Washington, Willoughby, Woodhall and Watson.
MAN: Good morning, Watson.
(MUSIC)
ANNCR: Today there's a new revolution from AT&T Information Systems.
MAN: Glad you could join us Mr. Watson. (MUSIC)
WOMAN: Oops!(MUSIC)
MAN: We still on for lunch Watson? (MUSIC)
MAN: Good-bye for now, Watson. (MUSIC)

	1127
Art Director	**Bob Tore**
Writers	**Arlene Jaffe, Tom Mabley**
Client	**IBM Corp.**
Agency Producer	**Robert L. Dein/Lord, Geller, Federico, Einstein, New York**
Production Company	**H.I.S.K.**
Creative Director	**Tom Mabley**

	1128
Art Director	**Thom Higgins**
Director of Photography	**Peter Brown**
Writer	**Kirk Citron**
Editor	**Dennis Hayes Editorial**
Directors	**Thom Higgins, Mark Coppos**
Client	**AT&T Information Systems**
Agency	**Ogilvy & Mather, New York/ Skip Allocco**
Production Company	**Director's Consortium**

CAMP NIPPERSINK
60-second
KID (VO): Dear Mom and Dad-
I'm having a great time here at Camp Nippersink—there's
lots to do—
SING: WHAT I REALLY WANNA SAY IT'S BEEN RAININ'
EVERY DAY.
KID (VO): Canoeing, swimming . . .
SING: ALL COUPED UP, NO TELEPHONE, MAYBE I
SHOULD COME ON HOME . . .
SFX: WHISTLE
CAMP COUNSELOR: Nippersinkers! We're going to town for
lunch.
SONG: MCDONALD'S AND YOU . . .
JUST AROUND THE BEND MCDONALD'S

EVOLUTION
60-second
ANNCR: From day one . . .
ANNCR:. . . Runners have taken their sport . . .
ANNCR:. . . Rather seriously.
ANNCR: Once things got a little better organized, people
started taking notes.
ANNCR: Analyzing how they ran.
ANNCR: And how they could run even faster.
ANNCR: Today, at Nike, we know even more.
ANNCR: We developed one of the most sophisticated sports
research labs in the world . . .
ANNCR: . . . To let us see, in detail, the peculiarities of style . . .
ANNCR: . . . The dynamics of footstrike.
ANNCR: And we're putting that knowledge to work.

1129

Art Director	**Gene Mandarino**
Writer	**Jack Smith**
Client	**McDonald's**
Agency	**Leo Burnett, Chicago/**
	Glant Cohen

1130

Art Director	**David Kennedy**
Writer	**Dan Wieden**
Client	**Nike, Inc.**
Agency	**Wieden & Kennedy,**
	Portland
Production Company	**Griner/Cuesta**

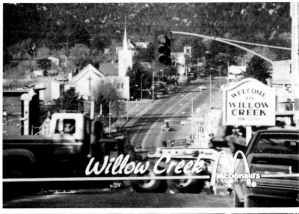

WILLOW CREEK III
60-second
SFX: DIESEL TRUCK ON HIGHWAY
SING: SOMETHING IS COMING . . . A PLACE ALL YOUR
OWN.
BARBER: Heard what they're building up the street?
CUSTOMER: Isn't that something!
SFX: CONSTRUCTION WITH BULLDOZER AND CREW.
SIDEWALK MAN #1: They said it was a choice between
building it here, or building it over in Pleasant Valley.
MAN #2: Poor old Pleasant Valley.
SFX: CONSTRUCTION
KID: And they got the greatest french fries!
KIDS: Yeahhhh!
WOMAN: Guess who won't be cooking dinner every night?

GREEN MARINE
60-second
SING: YOU'RE NOT JUST ANOTHER FACE, ALONG THE
WAY TO ANOTHER PLACE.
AGENT: Where are you headed today, Private (pause)
Zeleski?
MARINE: Home!
AGENT: Home . . . that's one of our most popular
destinations.
SING: YOU'RE THE PRIDE OF UNITED'S FRIENDLY SKIES.
MARINE: Thank you, sir.
SING: SO BEFORE YOU GO MY FRIEND, WE WANT YOU TO
KNOW MY FRIEND
YOU'RE NOT JUST FLYIN, YOU'RE
FLYIN' THE FRIENDLY SKIES.

_____

1131

Art Director **Bob Engel**
Writer **Rory Monaghan**
Client **McDonald's**
Agency **Leo Burnett, Chicago/Jim
McAward**

_____

1132

Art Director **Mary Martin**
Writer **Mary Ann Quick**
Client **United Airlines**
Agency **Leo Burnett, Chicago/
Michael Birch**

MONSTER I
60-second
(SFX: OF GAMEPLAY)
(SFX: MUSIC THROUGHOUT)
SINGERS: (WHISPERING) "CENTIPEDE".
SINGERS: (WHISPERING) "CENTIPEDE".
SINGERS: (WHISPERING) "CENTIPEDE".
SINGERS: (WHISPERING) "CENTIPEDE"
SINGERS: (WHISPERING) "CENTIPEDE".
(SFX: SCREAMING)
ANNCR: Centipede from Atari, it could change your life.
BOY: HELP! Somebody call the exterminator.

MONSTER II
60-second
SPOOKY MUSIC
PERCUSSION STARTS.
MAN: Aaaaahhhhh!!!!
BLOND: Eeeeehh!!!!
BUM: Aaauuuggghhh!!!
VO: Welcome to the Club Centipede. With Tommy Pede and
his leg quartet.
SINGERS: Come on down,
          come on down.
VO: Come on down, everybody.
SINGERS: We got more feet than
          you can count.
          We pick 'em up,

<table>
<tr><td colspan="2" align="center">1133</td></tr>
<tr><td align="right">Art Director</td><td>Charley Rice</td></tr>
<tr><td align="right">Writer</td><td>D.J. Webster</td></tr>
<tr><td align="right">Editor</td><td>Pierre Kahn</td></tr>
<tr><td align="right">Director</td><td>Jim Johnston</td></tr>
<tr><td align="right">Client</td><td>Atari</td></tr>
<tr><td align="right">Agency Producer</td><td>Graciela Vidal/Doyle Dane Bernbach Inc., New York</td></tr>
<tr><td align="right">Production Company</td><td>Johnston Films</td></tr>
</table>

<table>
<tr><td colspan="2" align="center">1134</td></tr>
<tr><td align="right">Art Director</td><td>Charley Rice</td></tr>
<tr><td align="right">Writer</td><td>D.J. Webster</td></tr>
<tr><td align="right">Editor</td><td>Pierre Kahn</td></tr>
<tr><td align="right">Director</td><td>Jim Johnston</td></tr>
<tr><td align="right">Client</td><td>Atari</td></tr>
<tr><td align="right">Agency Producer</td><td>Graciela Vidal/Doyle Dane Bernbach Inc., New York</td></tr>
<tr><td align="right">Production Company</td><td>Johnston Films</td></tr>
</table>

INTERVIEW
60-second
(SFX: HELICOPTER) (MUSIC IN)
(SFX: CAMERA CLICKING)
ANNCR (VO): You know how to get at the facts.
REPORTER: Welcome to America Mr. . . .
ANNCR (VO): You're a Professional.
ANNCR (VO): You live, eat . . .
ANNCR (VO): and breathe information . . .
REPORTER: I really want to thank you for allowing us this
interview.
MAN: If we could . . .
ANNCR (VO): But as good as you are . . .
ANNCR (VO): You can't do it alone.
REPORTER: Let's go we got a deadline to meet.

SEE THE MUSIC REV.
60-second
ANNCR: RCA Stereo VideoDisc wants you to see the music.
MUSIC: SEE THE MUSIC—
    SEE THE MUSIC ANYTIME AT ALL.
    SEE THE MUSIC—SEE THE MUSIC.
    HEAR THAT PICTURE CALL.
ANNCR (VO): RCA VideoDisc brings your TV and your stereo
together . . . for music like you've never seen it, video like
you've never heard it, anytime you want it.
MUSIC: SEE THE MUSIC. SEE THE MUSIC.
And now, to get you into it, when you buy an RCA Stereo
VideoDisc Player . . . we'll give you a six-pack of great video-
discs. A one-hundred fifty dollar value. Free. Featuring Flash-
dance and more.

<hr>

1135

Art Director	**Rebecca Cooney**
Director of Photography	**Danny Quinn**
Writer	**Andy Edelstein**
Editor	**Dick Langenbach - Splice is Nice**
Director	**Bob Giraldi**
Client	**Digital Equipment Corp.**
Agency	**Benton & Bowles, New York/Paul McDonough**
Production Company	**Giraldi Prod./Ralph Cohen**
Creative Group Head	**Mary Jo Clayton**

<hr>

1136

Art Director	**Kim Richardson**
Writer	**Allen Klein**
Client	**RCA**
Agency	**Leo Burnett, Chicago/Bob Davis**

GOOD HEALTH
60-second
VO: Eckerd Drugs dedicates the next 60 seconds to the most
important thing in your life . . . your health.
GIRL: Can you play something fast?
SAXOPHONIST: Sure.
VO: The old saying happens to be true—"You're only as
young as you feel." And that's why keeping you in good
health is the most important thing we do. Your Eckerd
pharmacist.

PHONE BOOTH
60-second
The telephone.
You've got to agree it's one of the most significant inventions
in history.
But if it isn't connected to another phone, it's just a useless
piece of technology.
And that's true of office machines. Once they're connected to
a system, they can be a lot more productive.
Now the scientists at Xerox figured that out ten years ago
when they invented a network they called Ethernet.
Today, Ethernet is an accepted international standard.
With it you can connect Xerox personal computers, word
processors, professional work stations, even electronic
printers.

1137

Art Director	**Dan Hackett**
Writers	**Bruce Broder, John DeCerchio**
Client	**Eckerd Drugs**
Agency	**Mary Beth Langenhorst**
Producer	**W.B. Doner & Company, Southfield, MI**

1138

Art Director	**Robert Cox**
Director	**Neil Tardio**
Client	**Xerox Corporation**
Agency	**Needham, Harper & Steers, New York**

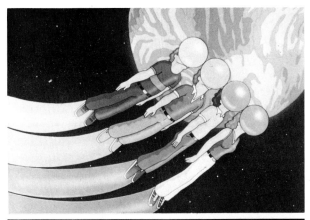

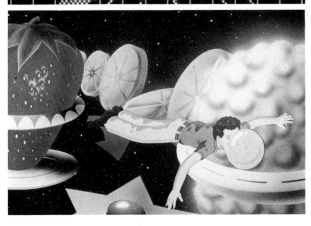

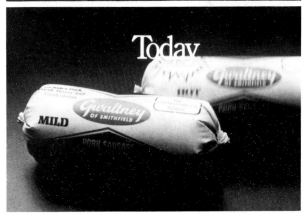

FLY AWAY
60-second
SFX: EXPLOSION
VOICE: Fly away. Fly away. Fly away to a flavor fantasy.
Bubblicious.
SINGERS: BUBBLICIOUS! THE ULTIMATE BUBBLE HAS
THE ULTIMATE FLAVOR.
VOICE: Timeless space fills your mind. Flavor deep flavor
wide. Your mouth can't resist it. Nor can your mind. Come on
a funky flavor ride. Flavor that blows you away. It's your fla-
vor fantasy.
ELECTRONIC VOICE: So delicious!
SINGERS: BUBBLICIOUS HAS THE ULTIMATE FLAVOR.
IT'S GOT THE TASTE YOU JUST CAN'T RESIST!
BUBBLICIOUS!

1139	
Art Director	**Mike Scherfen**
Writer	**Karen Boss**
Director	**Jane Simpson**
Client	**Bubblicious/Warner-Lambert**
Agency	**Ted Bates, New York**
Production Company	**Harold Friedman Consortium**

MORNINGS
60-second
ANNCR (VO): Good mornings . . . from Gwaltney.
(MUSIC UP)
Since 1870, mornings have been getting off to a sizzling start
with famous Gwaltney bacon and sausage.
And it's just as true today. 'Cause anything that's been a
breakfast favorite for that long is a lot more than just a flash
in the pan.
Gwaltney. Over 100 years later, we're still the choice.

1140	
Art Director	**Jeff France**
Writer	**Bruce Mansfield**
Editor	**Jimmy Smyth/Optimus**
Director	**Richard Foster**
Client	**Gwaltney of Smithfield**
Agency	**Lawler Ballard Advertising, Norfolk, VA/Jeff France, Bruce Mansfield**
Production Company	**Richard Foster Productions**

HUNCHBACK
60-second
BELLRINGER: Dahtahpember! Dahtahpember!
CROWD: Dahtahpember? What does he mean? What is he saying?
BELLRINGER: Dahtahpember! Hey gimme a Dahtahpember! Dahtahpember! Dahtah!
BELLRINGER: Ah, thank you. Pooey! Watch my lips. DR PEPPER. DR PEPPER.
MUSIC: Hold out for the out of the ordinary. Hold out for DR PEPPER. Don't be sold out, it's a taste that's extraordinary . . .
GIRL: Shall we ring some bells?
MUSIC: There's no doubt, it's DR PEPPER. Hold out . . .

1984
60-second
For today we celebrate the first glorious anniversary of the Information Purification Directives.
We have created, for the first time in all history, a garden of pure ideology, where each worker may bloom secure from the pests of contradictory and confusing truths.
Our Unification of Thought is more powerful a weapon than any fleet or army on earth.
We are one people. With one will. One resolve. One cause. Our enemies shall talk themselves to death. And we will bury them with their own confusion.
We shall prevail.

SILVER AWARD

1141

Art Director	**Roy Tuck**
Writer	**Bill Appelman**
Editor	**Lanny Friedman**
Director	**Manny Perez**
Client	**Dr. Pepper/Regular**
Agency Producer	**Roseanne Horn/Young & Rubicam, New York**
Production Company	**Film Fair**
Music Director	**Hunter Murtaugh, Y&R**

GOLD AWARD

1142

Art Directors	**Brent Thomas, Lee Clow**
Writer	**Steve Hayden**
Editor	**Pam Powers**
Director	**Ridley Scott**
Client	**Apple Computer**
Agency	**Chiat/Day, Los Angeles/ Richard O'Neill**
Prod'n Co Producer	**Richard Goldberg**

COPS
60-second
BKG SFX: OFFICE AMBIENCE, PHONE RINGING, TYPE-
WRITER, OUTSIDE SIREN.
COP #2: Devlin, biggest game of the year and you couldn't
get tickets.
COP #1: (SINGING) Welcome . . .
COP #1: to Miller Time . . .
COP #4 (VO): he didn't
COPS #2,3,3: He DID!!!!!!!
all right, let's go . . . . .
MUSIC INTRO BUILDS
MUSIC INTRO PEAKS
SONG: WELCOME . . .
    to Miller Time . . . .

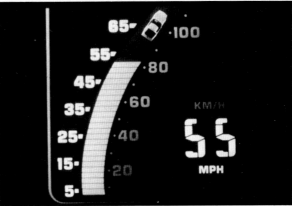

NEVER BEFORE
90-second
MUSIC: HEROIC/MODERN THROUGHOUT
ANNCR (VO): It began as genius . . . and grew to be legend
. . . and has become at long last the most advanced produc-
tion car on the planet.
SINGERS: YOU'VE NEVER SEEN ANYTHING LIKE THIS
BEFORE.
ANNCR: A new Chevrolet Corvette like never before.
SINGERS: NEVER BEFORE.
ANNCR: A Corvette superb in its engineering and technolo-
gy, and defiant in its performance.
SINGERS: YOU'VE NEVER FELT ANYTHING LIKE THIS
BEFORE.
ANNCR: Feel the performance of the world's first computer-

1143

Art Director	**John Lucci**
Writer	**Roger Feuerman**
Agency	**Backer & Spielvogel, New York/Eric Steinhauser**

1144

Art Director	**Jim Nicoll**
Creative Directors	**Sean K. Fitzpatrick, James I. Bernardin**
Director of Photography	**Jordon Croneweth**
Writer	**Jim Nicoll**
Editor	**Kathy Campbell**
Director	**Robert Abel**
Client	**Chevrolet Motor Division**
Agency	**Campbell-Ewald, Warren, MI/Jim Nicoll**
Production Company	**Robert Abel & Assoc./Alan Devebrois**
Director of Broadcast	**Dennis H. Plansker**

LIGHTHOUSE - MAINE
60-second
(MUSIC UNDER)
BOY: Watcha doin', mister?
HAL: Hi. I'm takin' pictures of that lighthouse.
BOY: That's my grandpa's lighthouse.
HAL: It is? Well, I'd like to put your grandpa's lighthouse in
my book.
GRANDPA: Sounds interestin'. Want to see the inside? We got
some hot coffee brewin'.
HAL: I could go for that.
BOY: Grandma, this is Hal & Duke. Hal's a real photographer.
GRANDMA: Hello Hal. You're just in time for coffee.
(MUSIC)
GRANDPA: So, you're photographing Maine.

WEDDING
60-second
SFX: CHURCH BELLS.
SFX: FAMILY CHEERS.
MUSIC: WEDDING RECESSIONAL.
MUSIC: WEDDING RECESSIONAL HITS A FLAT OR DIS-
CORDANT NOTE.
MOM (DV): How far does a Mom have to go to get weddin'
kids clean?
CHORUS OF KIDS (VO): "All the way to Tide country!"
MAN SINGS: Where you can dress 'em for a wedding day . . .
WOMAN SINGS: But don't expect they'll stay that way.
MAN SINGS: There's an usher sittin' on a supper -
WOMAN SINGS: Sauce on baby's bib and tucker -
MOM (DV): Extra-action wedding kids need extra-action

1145

Art Director	**Charles Gennarelli**
Director of Photography	**Leslie Dektor**
Writer	**Jerry McGee**
Editor	**Mel Cohen/DJM**
Director	**Leslie Dektor**
Client	**General Foods**
Agency Producer	**Jill Paperno/Ogilvy & Mather, New York**
Production Company	**Associates & Toback**

1146

Art Director	**Barbara John**
Director of Photography	**Ralph Bode**
Writer	**Cynthia Webber**
Editor	**Richard Nuchow**
Director	**Murray Bruce**
Client	**Procter & Gamble**
Agency	**Compton Advertising, Inc., New York**
Prod'n Co Producers	**Billy Hassel, David Caldwell**

NORTHERN LIGHT
60-second
(MUSIC - "SIBELIUS" -UNDER AND THROUGHOUT)
VO: Haunting said the New York Times.
SUPER: "Haunting" The New York Times
VO: Dark. Turbulent. Said Vogue.
SUPER: "Dark . . . Turbulent" Vogue
VO: Trembles with erotic yearning said Newsweek.
SUPER: "Trembles with erotic yearning." Newsweek
VO: So good, it's scary said the Washington Post.
SUPER: "So good it's scary" Washington Post
VO: Northern Light. Come bask in the beauty of 100 paint-
ings from Scandinavia that will stop you, hold you and leave
your senses shaken.
SUPER: Northern Light

1147

Art Director	**Doug Lew**
Writer	**Bob Thacker**
Editor	**Steve Sheperd**
Director	**Steve Griak**
Client	**Minneapolis Institute of Arts**
Agency	**Chuck Ruhr Advertising, Minneapolis**
Production Company	**Wilson-Griak/Mike Monten**

CONFUSED
60-second
SUPER: c1983, Home Savings of America, a Federal Savings
and Loan Association.
SUPER: Based on a true story.
MAN: I can't believe I did this. I took the morning paper to a
Home Savings Counselor, showed her the 23 ads for money
markets and T-Bills and variable rates and fixed rates and
said "If you don't help me, I'm going to put all my money in a
mattress." Well, after *the* most lucid financial conversation I
ever had, I opened a Money Market Account and a 6-month
term account. And told Sally she had a customer for life.
ANNCR (VO): It's people like Tom McKay who make Home
Savings $19 billion strong.
COUNSELOR: It's funny how I get some of my Home Savings

1148

Art Directors	**Yvonne Smith, Richard Crispo**
Writers	**Bill Hamilton, Dave Butler**
Editor	**Gayle Grant**
Director	**Norm Griner**
Client	**Home Savings of America**
Agency	**Chiat/Day, Los Angeles/ Morty Baran**
Prod'n Co Producer	**Phil Payton**

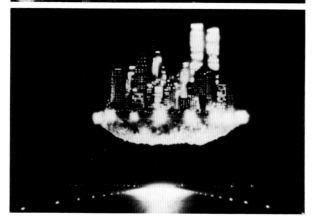

MANHATTAN LANDING
90-second
LONDON AIR TRAFFIC CONTROLLER: Roger, Manhattan continue descent to F.L. eight 0 . . .
CO-PILOT: Roger, Heathrow, descending to F.L. eight 0 . . .
SFX: QUIET, SLIGHTLY SPOOKY MUSIC, SIMILAR TO "CLOSE ENCOUNTERS."
LONDON AIR TRAFFIC CONTROLLER: Manhattan, that's correct, contact radar director on one-two-0-point four . . . .
LONDON AIR TRAFFIC CONTROLLER: Roger, Manhattan, continue to 2,000 feet. Reduce speed to one-seven-0 knots . . .
STRAIGHT VO: Every year British Airways fly more people to more countries than any other airline.
STRAIGHT VO: In fact, each year we fly more people across the Atlantic than the entire population of Manhattan.

<table>
<tr><td colspan="2" align="center">1149</td></tr>
<tr><td align="right">Art Director</td><td>Phil Mason</td></tr>
<tr><td align="right">Designer</td><td>Phil Harrison</td></tr>
<tr><td align="right">Writer</td><td>Rita Dempsey</td></tr>
<tr><td align="right">Editor</td><td>Keith Daniels</td></tr>
<tr><td align="right">Director</td><td>Richard Loncraine</td></tr>
<tr><td align="right">Client</td><td>British Airways, Derek Dear</td></tr>
<tr><td align="right">Agency Producer</td><td>Jon Staton/Compton Advertising, Inc., New York</td></tr>
<tr><td align="right">Production Company</td><td>James Garratt & Partners, Inc., David Fanthorpe</td></tr>
<tr><td align="right">Opticals</td><td>Mike Uden</td></tr>
</table>

HERITAGE
60-second
SFX: THUNDER AND RAIN
MAN (VO): (FROM CAR UNDER SFX) Now we're *really* lost!
MAN AND WOMAN IN UNISON: Didn't you get the directions?
MAN: I'll go see if that farmhouse we just passed has a telephone.
ANNCR (VO): In a world where anything can go wrong, it's nice to know there's something you can depend on that can help make it go right.
MAN: (TIMIDLY) Excuse me, sir, do you have a telephone?
MAN: (IN HOME BOASTING) Sure do!
MAN: Oh swell! I think . . . that we're a little lost . . .
CONCIERGE: (SHAKING HEAD) Sorry, sir, no honeymoon

<table>
<tr><td colspan="2" align="center">1150</td></tr>
<tr><td align="right">Art Director</td><td>Gary Goldstein</td></tr>
<tr><td align="right">Writer</td><td>Joel Maliniak</td></tr>
<tr><td align="right">Editor</td><td>Michael Charles</td></tr>
<tr><td align="right">Director</td><td>Norm Griner</td></tr>
<tr><td align="right">Client</td><td>New York Telephone</td></tr>
<tr><td align="right">Agency Producer</td><td>Mootsy Elliot/Young & Rubicam, New York</td></tr>
<tr><td align="right">Production Company</td><td>Griner/Cuesta</td></tr>
<tr><td align="right">Music</td><td>Barbara Tager, Y&R</td></tr>
</table>

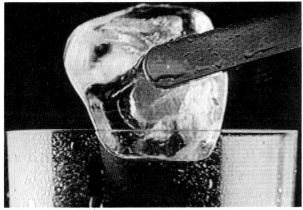
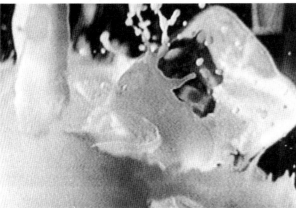
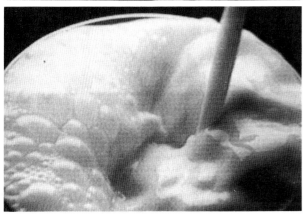

MILK ON ICE
60-second
SFX: ICE CRASHING. OCEAN SOUNDS.
ANNCR (VO): Just a reminder, nothing tastes better than an ice cold glass of Oak Farms Milk. How about right now? Oak Farms Milk at your 7-Eleven store.

NELL CARTER
60-second
NELL CARTER: Hello, ladies—I'm Nell Carter. If you're a woman, black and *somewhere* between 29 and 99—but still sweet, and sort of sassy—I'm talking to you. About Breast Cancer. How to *detect* it—Early—And protect yourself. Oh, I know, I know, you don't want to hear it. And you think it's gonna hurt. Well, honey it's not the *exam* that hurts. A breast exam only takes one half hour, once a year. It's that fast. That easy. And it's free. And you can get it at the Breast Examination Center in the Harlem State Office Building. Ladies, I'm doing it for *my* health. You should do it for yours. 'Cause the truth is, early detection is the best protection—the *only* protection we have. So if you don't have your breasts examined—maybe you should have your *head* examined.

1151

Art Directors	**Glenn Dady, Phil Marco**
Director of Photography	**Phil Marco**
Writer	**Melinda Marcus**
Editor	**Larry Plastrick**
Director	**Phil Marco**
Client	**Southland Dairies Group**
Agency	**The Richards Group, Dallas/Brad Christian**
Production Company	**Phil Marco Inc./Michael Kass**

1152

Art Director	**Cathy Edwards**
Writer	**Sherry Nemmers**
Director	**Neil Tardio**
Client	**Harlem Breast Exam Center**
Agency Producer	**Jack Smart/DFS, New York**
Procuction Company	**Lovinger, Tardio, Melsky,Inc.**

DETECTIVE
60-second
DETECTIVE (VO): It was late, very late. But I had no place to go. The pulse of the city was electric but for me things were looking dim. Then she walked in.
SHE: Please . . . I have no where else to turn . . .
VO: I offered her the usual . . .
SHE: No thanks.
SHE: UH UH!
VO: She turned down my java too . . .
SHE: You must help me.
VO: She didn't look like she needed help . . . but I offered her a diet cola anyway.
SHE: UH UH!
VO: Then it hit me. This was no ordinary dame.

MARIE ANTOINETTE
60-second
CROWD: Roar!
MAN: Ssh! Be quiet! Go away!
CROWD: No!
MAN: Contain yourself. What is it you want?
CROWD: We're thirsty.
MAN: Then go back to your villages.
CROWD: No!
MAN: You're going to get Marie out here . . . so we're . . .oh!
MARIE: Now what do they want?
MAN: Well, Marie, there's a great thirst in the land.
MARIE: Oh come now, there is plenty to drink.
CROWD: No there's not!
MARIE: Perhaps they would like some scrumptious

	1153
Art Director	**Roy Tuck**
Writer	**Bill Appelman**
Editor	**Allen Rozek**
Director	**Manny Perez**
Client	**Dr Pepper/Sugar Free**
Agency Producer	**Roseanne Horn/Young & Rubicam, New York**
Production Company	**Film Fair**
Music Director	**Hunter Murtaugh, Y&R**

	1154
Art Director	**Roy Tuck**
Writer	**Bill Appelman**
Editor	**Lanny Friedman**
Director	**Manny Perez**
Client	**Dr Pepper/Regular**
Agency Producer	**Roseanne Horn/Young & Rubicam, New York**
Production Company	**Film Fair**
Music Director	**Hunter Murtaugh, Y&R**

TOWN SQUARE REV.
60-second
(MUSIC THROUGHOUT)
1ST MAN: What's that Fred's getting?
2ND MAN: A computer
1ST MAN: What's he know about computers?
2ND MAN: They taught him everything he needs to know.
1ST MAN: He can't even drive a car; he's gonna run a computer.
2ND MAN: Yup, they sent him to a special class to learn how.
1ST MAN: Hope he did better in theirs than he did in ours.
2ND MAN: There's a special phone number he can call if he has any questions.
1st Man: He'll keep them busy.
2ND MAN: And if there's a problem they'll come right here

BROTHERS-IT FIGURES
60-second
STEVE: So, little brother, did you have a good year?
BROTHER: I'm surprised Steve, the business really took off!
STEVE: Surprised? I'm not surprised. Remember when everyone else had a regular lemonade stand, you had lemonade on wheels and you even did your own advertising.
BROTHER: I was only six years old.
STEVE: Oh come on, when you needed the money to buy a bike you started a newspaper delivery service.
Ollie, Willie and Sam delivered for you and you called it
BOTH: All bark and no bike!
STEVE: And you even worked an extra year.
Because you had to have the best bike. You always knew what you wanted.

	1155
Art Director	**John Caggiano**
Designer	**John Caggiano**
Writer	**Iva Silver**
Editor	**Pelco**
Director	**Rick Levine**
Client	**IBM**
Agency Producer	**Bob Samuels/Doyle Dane Bembach Inc., New York**
Production Company	**Levine/Pytka**

	1156
Art Director	**John Caggiano**
Designer	**John Caggiano**
Writer	**Iva Silver**
Editor	**Pelco**
Director	**Michael Ulick**
Client	**IBM**
Agency Producer	**Regina Ebel/Doyle Dane Bernbach Inc., New York**
Production Company	**Michael Ulick Productions**

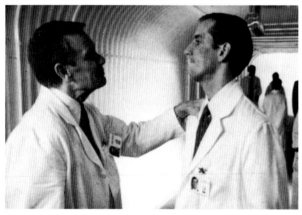

NOBEL PRIZE REVISED
60-second
(MUSIC UNDER THROUGHOUT)
VO: More than 50 years ago, a scientist at AT&T's Bell Laboratories discovered the principle that led to all solid state technology. His discovery won him the 1937 Nobel Prize. Nineteen years later, the Nobel Prize was again awarded to Bell Labs' scientists for the transistor . . . the key that opened the entire computer age.
The creativity of AT&T people has been recognized with more Nobel Prizes than any other company on earth.
Over the years, people have come to expect a lot from us. And now . . . you can expect even more.
We're the new AT&T. And we're reaching out to find even newer ways to improve your life.

POOL
60-second
(MUSIC THROUGHOUT)
Some people were meant for each other.
Some people were meant for Kent.

	1157
Art Director	**Bob Needleman**
Writer	**Jim Murphy**
Editor	**H. Lazarus**
Director	**Steve Horn**
Client	**AT&T Corporate/David Shaver**
Agency	**NW Ayer Incorporated, New York/Gaston Braun**
Production Company	**Steve Horn Inc./Linda H. Horn**
Creative Directors	**Jim Murphy, Bob Needleman**

	1158
Art Director	**Saskia Mossel**
Writer	**Stephen Baer**
Client	**Brown & Williamson International**
Agency Producer	**Sandra Breakstone/Ogilvy & Mather, New York**

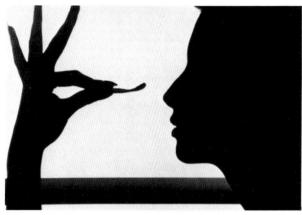

STORE
60-second
(MUSIC UNDER)
WOMAN: When you see Avon now, you'll say Avon wow!
WOMEN SING: We've got the twist, we've got the mist, we've got the bangles for your wrist. We've got the sheen, we've got the clean, we've got the moisturizing cream. Fragrance candles glow, clever colors flow.
WOMAN: Avon's got it.
WOMEN SING: Avon now.
WOMAN: Avon, wow!
WOMEN SING: Avon brings just what you need and all of it is guaranteed to raise a smile or with a shout.
WOMAN: That's what Avon's all about.
WOMEN SING: We've got your style, we make you smile,

COSMETICS
60-second
(MUSIC UNDER)
WOMAN: In the 50's, there was one way to wear make-up, just like everyone else.
In the 60's the look changed, but there was still only one look.
And remember the 70's? Well now, Avon announces the end of the cookie cutter face.
WOMAN SINGS: Colors from demure to wild we've got a collection that's just your style with Avon . . .
The face of the 80's is yours.
We've got a look that's right for you so you can do anything you want to do.
WOMEN SING: With Avon . . .

1159
Art Director **Ann Phares**
Writer **Susan Parenio**
Director **Bruce Dowad**
Client **Avon Products**
Agency Producer **Ann Marcato/Ogilvy & Mather, New York**
Production Co Producer **Alex Myer**
Creative Director **Malcolm End**

1160
Art Director **Mark Shap**
Designer **David Brockhurst**
Writer **Veronica Nash**
Editors **Barry Stillwell, Dennis Hayes Ed.**
Director **Howard Guard**
Client **Avon Products**
Agency Producer **Elaine Keeve/Ogilvy & Mather, New York**
Prod'n Co Producer **Maxine Tabak**
Creative Director **Malcolm End**

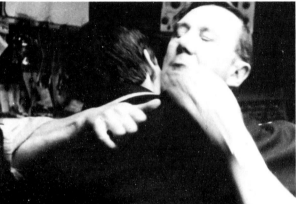

DART
60-second
(MUSIC THROUGHOUT)
Some people were meant for each other.
Some people were meant for Kent.

FATHER & SON
60-second
FATHER: I thought you had practice today.
SON: Nah, the field was too wet. Dad, do you have a minute?
FATHER: What's up?
SON: Dad I've decided . . .
SFX: WHIRR OF TV
DAD: What?
SON: I've decided to join the Army.
DAD: Wooa!
SON: I think it's right for me.
DAD: What about college.
SON: I'm still gonna go to college after the Army.
DAD: I thought you wanted to be an electrical engineer.
SON: I'll be learning about electronics and that will help me

<table>
<tr><td colspan="2" align="center">1161</td></tr>
<tr><td align="right">Art Director</td><td>Saskia Mossel</td></tr>
<tr><td align="right">Writer</td><td>Stephen Baer</td></tr>
<tr><td align="right">Client</td><td>Brown & Williamson International</td></tr>
<tr><td align="right">Agency Producer</td><td>Sandra Breakstone/Ogilvy & Mather, New York</td></tr>
</table>

<table>
<tr><td colspan="2" align="center">1162</td></tr>
<tr><td align="right">Art Director</td><td>Mickey Tender</td></tr>
<tr><td align="right">Writer</td><td>Susan McFeatters</td></tr>
<tr><td align="right">Editor</td><td>Mark Polycan/The Tape House</td></tr>
<tr><td align="right">Director</td><td>Neil Tardio</td></tr>
<tr><td align="right">Client</td><td>United States Army/Major Gen. Jack Bradshaw</td></tr>
<tr><td align="right">Agency</td><td>NW Ayer Incorporated, New York/Jim McMenemy</td></tr>
<tr><td align="right">Production Company</td><td>Lovinger, Tardio, & Melsky/ Nan Simmons</td></tr>
<tr><td align="right">Creative Directors</td><td>Walter Burek, Ted Regan</td></tr>
</table>

THIRTY MPH/SEATBELTS/PASSENGER
10-second
WOMAN: Some people don't think 30 miles per hour is very
fast.
SFX: ZOOOOOOM!
WOMAN: I'd wear a seatbelt.
SUPER: SEATBELTS. A SIMPLE FACT OF LIFE.

LITTLE GTI/DRIVEWAY/HEARTBEAT
30-second
MUSIC
MUSIC
MUSIC
MUSIC
MUSIC UNDER
SINGERS: Kleiner GTI.
Du siehst prima aus.
Ich, liebe sie zu fahren.
Hol'die lestung 'raus.

DISTINCTIVE MERIT

1163
Art Director   Gary Yoshida
Writer   Bob Coburn
Client   American Honda Motor
Company, Inc.
Agency   Needham, Harper & Steers,
Los Angeles/Helmut
Dorger

1164
Art Directors   Jim Scalfone, Mark Hughes,
Gary Goldsmith
Writers   Penny Kapousouz, Steve
Landsberg, Neil Gomberg
Client   Volkswagen of America
Agency   Doyle Dane Bernbach Inc.,
New York/Jim DeBarros,
Sheldon Levy
Production Company   Johnston, Fairbanks

FLYING CARS/EXPLOSIVE/ROOF
30-second
(MUSIC THROUGHOUT)
V/O: It takes more than high octane to keep your car
performing well.
That's why these world famous stunt drivers rely on
Mobil Detergent Gasoline. They know a car with a
clean carburetor performs better.
It's as simple as that.
Mobil Detergent Gasoline.
For your everyday driving needs.

HOT COLD/GREAT TASTE/MIX
30-second
SINGERS: When you've got a real hot summer thirst,
Which iced tea do you think of first?
CLEARLY NESTEA
DRY THIRST, WET BURST
CLEARLY, NESTEA
HEAT WAVE, COLD WAVE
WE CRAVE NESTEA
HOT RAYS, COOL SPRAYS
ALWAYS ZESTY

SILVER AWARD

1165

Art Director	**Roy Grace**
Designer	**Roy Grace**
Director of Photography	**Henry Sandbank**
Writer	**John Noble**
Editor	**Dick Stone/Stone-Cutters**
Director	**Henry Sandbank**
Client	**Mobil Oil Corporation**
Agency	**Doyle Dane Bernbach Inc., New York/Susan Calhoun**
Production Company	**Sandbank Films, Inc.**

DISTINCTIVE MERIT

1166

Art Director	**Greg Weinschenker**
Director of Photography	**Jeff Kimball**
Writers	**Linda Kaplan, Robin Schwarz**
Editors	**Bobby Smalheiser, Michael Swerdloff**
Director	**Adrian Lyne**
Client	**Nestle Co./Nestea**
Agency Producer	**Meredith Wright/J.W.T., New York**
Production Company	**Jennie & Co./Paul Esposito**
Production Mgr.	**Mindy Goldberg**

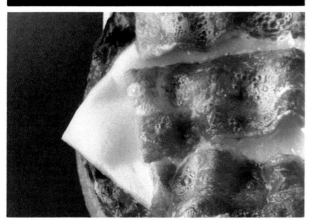

**II BACON DOUBLE CHEESE VIEWER
DISCRETION/TICK TICK REV./ULTIMATE WEAPON**
30-second
ANNCR: Due to the suggestive nature of the following Burger King commercial, viewers are advised to watch at their own risk.
SINGERS: OOH THAT HOT AND SIZZLIN' BACON
ANNCR: The bacon double cheeseburger is intended for mature audiences only.

CARL LEWIS/MOSES/JOANIE
30-second
CARL: My first jump was a joke. Nine feet even. But I said to myself "don't give up". In high school, I kept coming in second. I could have called it quits. But I believe you should never give up.
When that's your philosophy, there's no telling how far you can go.

SILVER AWARD

1167

Art Directors	**Howie Cohen, Frank Perry, Deyna Vesey**
Directors of Photography	**Simon Ramsley, Bob Balin**
Writers	**Hal Friedman, Brian Sitts, Laurie Birnbaum, Jim Patterson**
Editors	**Jack Coddington, Gary Sharfin, Steve Schreiber**
Directors	**Patrick Morgan, Jim Johnston**
Client	**Burger King/Kyle Craig**
Agency Producers	**Gary Bass/Executive Prod.- Don Brown/J.W.T., New York**
Prod'n Co Producers	**Richard Goldberg/ Fairbanks Films, Dan Deitchman/Johnston Films**
Creative Director	**Jim Patterson**

GOLD AWARD

1168

Art Director	**Gary Johns**
Writer	**Jeff Gorman**
Editor	**Charlie Chubak**
Director	**Bob Giraldi**
Client	**Nike, Inc.**
Agency	**Chiat/Day, Los Angeles/ Morty Baran**
Prod'n Co Producer	**Ralph Cohen**

MONKEY/COUPLE/FROG
30-second
MUSIC: What would you do for a Klondike Bar?
ANNCR (VO): Would you make monkey sounds?
MAN: Monkey sounds? Gee, I don't think so.
VO: Got the Klondike right here . . . rich vanilla ice cream . . .
smothered in thick chocolate . . .
MAN: (ATTEMPTS SOUND)
VO: Nah, that's a baboon.
MAN: (ATTEMPTS SOUND)
VO: I think you've drifted into gorilla.
MAN: (SUCCESSFUL SOUND)
VO: That's got it.
SONG: FOR THAT CHOCOLATE COATED, ICE-CREAM
LOADED, BIG AND THICK . . . NO ROOM FOR A STICK . . .

LAUREL & WHO/HONEYMOONERS
30-second
VO: HARPER & GANNON IN FAMOUS COMEDY TEAMS.
COSTELLO: Alright, tell me Who's on first?
ABBOTT: Yes.
COSTELLO: The man's name?
ABBOTT: Who.
COSTELLO: The guy playing first.
ABBOTT: WHO.
COSTELLO: The guy playing first base.
ABBOTT: Who is on first.
COSTELLO: I don't know! What are you asking me for?
ELWOOD: We've got a full tank of gas, a half a pack of ciga-
rettes, it's dark out and we're wearing sunglasses?

1169
Art Director	**Steve Perrin**
Writer	**James M. Dale**
Director	**Harry Hamburg**
Client	**The Isaly Co., Klondike Bars, Griff Dixcy**
Agency	**W.B. Doner & Co., Baltimore/Bonnie Herman**
Production Company	**N./Lee Lacy Assoc./ Madeline Curtis**

1170
Art Director	**Larry Zuger**
Designer	**Larry Zuger**
Director of Photography	**Patrick Cragin**
Writers	**Chato Hill, Jim Harper, Steve Gannon**
Director	**Chato Hill**
Client	**WNIC Radio**
Agency	**DeLeeuw Hill & Associates, Inc., Southfield, MI**
Production Company	**Patrick Cragin Productions**

SOVIET CONSULATE/COCAINE/MYSTERY ILLNESSES
30-second
MUSIC: "SANTA CLAUS IS COMING TO TOWN" (UP TO ES-
TABLISH, THEN UNDER)
ANNCR (VO): Everywhere in the world, even on San Francis-
co's very own Green Street, the Soviets are dreaming of a red
Christmas.
If they could, they would change our way of life.
To them, nothing is sacred.
SFX: EXPLOSION (UP, THEN OUT)
MUSIC: OUT WITH EXPLOSION
ANNCR: Watch "Green Street Reds."
This week at eleven on Channel Seven.
SFX: WIND WHISTLING
SUPERS: GREEN STREET REDS

AMITYVILLE III/OUTDOOR ANSWER BOOTH/ SZLUB II
30-second
SFX: CRICKETS
ANNCR (VO): Recently, John Fixx at 22 Birdie Lane pur-
chased some plumbing and electrical supplies to remodel an
upstairs bath.
SFX: FRANKENSTEIN CRACKLES
He could have saved money on a wider selection at Knox.
SFX: FLUSHER, SONAR
More importantly, he could have signed up for a Knox semi-
nar and learned how to do plumbing and wiring.
SFX: RUSHING WATER
But, John insisted on figuring that out for himself.
SFX: EXPLOSIONS
What possessed him, we'll never know.

<table>
<tr><td colspan="2" align="center">1171</td></tr>
<tr><td align="right">Art Director</td><td>Clyde Hogg</td></tr>
<tr><td align="right">Artists</td><td>Tom Roth, Jim George</td></tr>
<tr><td align="right">Director of Photography</td><td>Jordan Cronenweth</td></tr>
<tr><td align="right">Writer/ACD</td><td>Rob Ingalls</td></tr>
<tr><td align="right">Editors</td><td>Larry Bridges, Editel</td></tr>
<tr><td align="right">Directors</td><td>Paul Henman, Jean Maxime Perramon</td></tr>
<tr><td align="right">Client</td><td>KGO-TV, Channel 7 News</td></tr>
<tr><td align="right">Agency</td><td>R. Rennolds/Davis, Johnson, Mogul & Colombatto, Inc., San Francisco</td></tr>
<tr><td align="right">Prod'n Co Producers</td><td>David Dwiggins, Elizabeth Reed</td></tr>
</table>

<table>
<tr><td colspan="2" align="center">1172</td></tr>
<tr><td align="right">Art Director</td><td>Pat Burnham</td></tr>
<tr><td align="right">Director of Photography</td><td>Eric Young</td></tr>
<tr><td align="right">Writer</td><td>Jarl Olsen</td></tr>
<tr><td align="right">Editor</td><td>Tony Fischer</td></tr>
<tr><td align="right">Director</td><td>Jim Lund</td></tr>
<tr><td align="right">Client</td><td>Knox Lumber Company</td></tr>
<tr><td align="right">Agency</td><td>Judy Carter/Fallon McElligott Rice, Minneapolis</td></tr>
<tr><td align="right">Production Company</td><td>James Productions</td></tr>
</table>

I AM/FIRST CLASS/EXECUTIVE
30-second
I am Eilean Donan Castle on the shores of Loch Alsh.
I am the proud regiment of the Queen's household Cavalry.
I am the words of Jane Austen.
I am the footsteps of William Shakespeare along the River
Avon.
I am the tradition that has always been.
I am the warmth and smiles of an island people.
I am the airline that never forgets you have a choice.
I am the best of Great Britain.
I am British Caledonian Airways.

	1173
Art Director	**Ed Kennard**
Directors of Photography	**Quentin Masters, R. Robson**
Writers	**Ed Kennard, Michael McKeever**
Editor	**Andy Walter**
Director	**Quentin Masters**
Client	**British Caledonian Airways**
Agency	**Winius-Brandon Advertising, Bellaire, TX/ Ed Kennard**
Production Company	**James Garrett Prod./John Byrne**
Audio	**E.J. Nowinski**

TRAINING CAMP/MARCH/VICTORY
30-second
(MUSIC OVER)
Time again for Gold'n Plump news.
VO: As America turns to better chickens, Gold'n Plump steps
up to meet the demand.
(MUSIC UNDER)
Here, truckloads of hopeful recruits arrive at Camp Gold'n
Plump. (MUSIC UNDER)
For eight intense weeks, these select birds will be the best
fed, best housed chickens in the world. (MUSIC UNDER)
One final inspection, and it's back on the truck for a quick
ride to your supermarket.
(MUSIC BUILDS)
Gold'n Plump chickens . . . freshness marches on!

	1174
Art Director	**Nancy Rice**
Writer	**Tom McElligott**
Editor	**Bob Wicklund**
Director	**Jim Hinton**
Client	**Gold'n Plump Poultry, Inc.**
Agency	**Judy Carter/Fallon McElligott Rice, Minneapolis**
Production Company	**Wilson-Griak**
News Reel Footage	**Bob DeFlores**

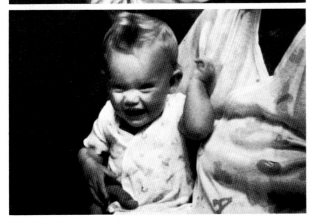

T-SHIRT/SLEEPER/TRAINING PANTS
30-second
Ed: I'm Ed Hinds from Curity, and I may look silly in this undershirt.
But I think it's a lot sillier to talk about a product without first-hand experience. So I had this Curity undershirt made. Believe me, these seamless underarms are really comfortable.
So's this soft, preshrunk cotton fabric. And this style makes getting dressed a snap.
VO: Buy three Curity shirts, or training pants and get a white T-shirt free.
ALTERNATE (VO): The best reasons for Curity are little ones.

CLOUDS/HANGAR/RAINY DAY
30-second
ANNCR (VO): Guess who can take you to more places than American, TWA, United and Delta combined. Who's on-time record has improved nearly 40%.
And who has rebuilt its entire fleet, adding some of the newest, most technologically advanced equipment in the world. We'll give you one clue: it isn't an airline.
SINGERS: ALL ABOARD ALL ABOARD ALL ABOARD AMTRAK!!

	1175
Art Directors	**Jan Hawkins, Mary Moore**
Writer	**Karen Larson**
Directors	**George Gomes, Peter Cooper**
Client	**Kendall Company**
Agency	**Humphrey Browning MacDougall, Boston/Lisa Page, Amy Mizner**
Prod'n Co Producer	**Gomes Lowe/Cooper & Co.**

	1176
Art Director	**Paul Frahm**
Writer	**Michael Robertson**
Client	**National Railroad Passenger Corporation**
Agency	**Needham, Harper & Steers, New York**

40% AUNT CHARISE/WELDERS/CLEVELAND
30-second
LANDESBERG: (TO TELEPHONE) Ring . . .!
(TO CAMERA.) Hi. For those of you that didn't get the message the first time, you can save up to 40% on any long distance call in the United States. That's right, you can call anybody, save 40%.
Call your Aunt Charise in New York . . . (NEW YORK ACCENT) Yes? Well why you calling now, do you need money, what is it? I can't listen, I can't send you anymore money, thank you, goodbye.
You don't have to call her, you can call anybody, you must have some . . . just call, call me, call them, anybody.
LANDESBERG: Did you know right now you could call long distance anywhere in the United States and save up to 40%?

LOANS/MONEY/STONEFACE
30-second
ANNCR (VO): For years banks and savings and loans have been singing the same old song.
BANKER 1: "I Can't Give You Anything but Love, Baby.
BANKER 2: "That's the one thing I've got plenty of, baby."
ANNCR (VO): They tell you how much they love you, but they never seem able to loan you money.
At Minnesota Federal we love you, too, but we also have money to loan . . . at very competitive rates.
BANKER: "I Can't Give You Anything But Love."
SFX: MUSIC UP
ANNCR (VO): Minnesota Federal. Money to loan without the song and dance.

————— 1177 —————
Art Director **Ron Sandilands, VP**
Writer **Bernie Hafeli**
Director **George Gomes**
Client **Pacific Northwest Bell**
Agency Producer **Virginia Pellegrino, VP**
Production Company **Gomes/Loew**
Agency **Livingston & Company, Seattle**

————— 1178 —————
Art Director **Dean Hanson**
Writer **Tom McElligott**
Editor **Bobby Smalheiser**
Director **Steve Steigman**
Client **Minnesota Federal Savings and Loan**
Agency Producer **Judy Carter/Fallon McElligott Rice, Minneapolis**
Production Company **Steve Steigman Prod.**

ALEX THE DOG/RELIEF PITCHER/THREE WISHES
30-second
POKER PLAYER: I'd sure like another Stroh's.
HOST: No, wait. (To the dog) Alex, (DOG BARKS) two cold Stroh's.
(DOG BARKS AGAIN)
(To his buddies) Wait till you see this.
(SFX REFRIGERATOR DOOR OPENING)
He just opened the Refrigerator.
(SFX BOTTLE OPENING)
He just opened one bottle.
(SFX BOTTLE OPENING)
He opened the other.
(SFX STROH'S BEING POURED.)
Now he's pouring yours.

POLICEMAN/TEACHER/YOUNG BOY
30-second
(SFX: CARS GOING BY ON HIGHWAY, BIRDS . . .)
POLICEMAN: No matter how tough a policeman thinks he is, he's never ready for the first highway fatality he sees. Mine was here 11 years ago. I had a six-year old die in my arms. It still wakes me up some nights. She'd be about 17 today if her mother had her wear her safety belt.
Safety belts can save more than 16,000 lives each year. In all those 11 years, I've never once unbuckled a dead man.

	1179
Art Directors	**Gary Ennis, Andrew Langer**
Writers	**Seth Werner, Marshall Karp**
Editors	**Len Mandelbaum, Morty Schwartz, Bob Jubin**
Directors	**Rick Levine, Fred Levinson, Steve Horn**
Client	**The Stroh Brewery**
Agency Producers	**The Marschalk Co., Inc., New York/Paula Dwoskin, Alice Mintzer; Levine, Pytka Prod.**
Production Companies	**Fred Levinson Prod., Steve Horn Prod.**

	1180
Art Director	**Al Zerries**
Writer	**Al Zerries**
Editor	**Norman Levine**
Director	**Steve Horn**
Client	**National Highway Traffic Safety Administration**
Agency	**Grey Advertising, Inc., New York/Maura Dausey**
Production Company	**Steve Horn Prod.**

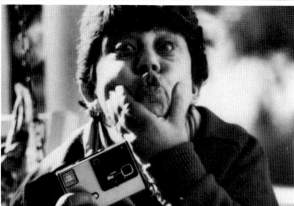

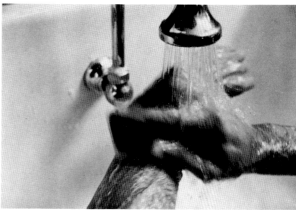

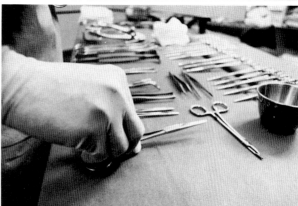

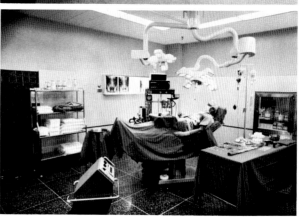

PETS/KIDS ADULTS/MISTLETOE
30-second
SINGERS: WATCH OUT WORLD
I'M GOING CLICK, CLICK, CLICK
I'M GONNA GET YOU WITH THE KODAK DISC
I'M GONNA GET YOU WITH THE KODAK DISC
AS SURE AS SHOOTIN' I'M NOT GONNA MISS.
NOT WHEN IT'S AS EASY AS THIS
I'M GONNA GET YOU WITH THE KODAK DISC!
(VO): The Kodak disc camera, with it's automatic advance
and built-in flash is just about the easiest camera in the
world to use. No matter who you want to hound. Smile.
SINGERS: YOU CAN OINK, YOU CAN MOO, YOU CAN COCK
A DOODLE DO.
I'M GONNA GET YOU WITH THE KODAK DISC!

**OPERATING ROOM/SKID ROW BUM/BIRTHDAY
CANDLES**
30-second
SFX: DRONE AND HEARTBEAT THROUGHOUT:
BEGIN HERE AND OTHERS AS APPROPRIATE
THROUGHOUT
(VO): When you're suffering . . .
(VO): . . . from a disease, you seek . . .
(VO): . . . professional medical care.
(VO): But unfortunately,
(VO): . . . there's one disease that 14 . . .
(VO): . . . million Americans insist
(VO): on treating themselves.
(VO): The disease is alcoholism.
(VO): And treating it yourself makes as much sense as . . .

1181	
Art Directors	**Beth Pritchett, Greg Weinschenker**
Writers	**Kathy McMahon, Linda Kaplan, Bonnie Berkowitz, Robin Schwarz**
Editors	**Tony Siggia, First Edition**
Director	**Joe Hanwright**
Client	**Eastman Kodak/Roger Morrison**
Agency Producer	**Sid Horn/J.W.T., New York**
Production Company	**Kira Films/Lisa Peglessi**

1182	
Art Directors	**Jim Hallowes, Peter Brown**
Director of Photography	**Henry Sandbank**
Writers	**Peter Brown, Jim Hallowes**
Editor	**Charles Chubak/Film Core**
Director	**Henry Sandbank**
Client	**Comprehensive Care Corp. (CareUnit)**
Agency	**Doyle Dane Bernbach Inc., Los Angeles/Elaine Lord**
Production Company	**Sandbank Films/John Kamen**
Music	**H.K. Sound**
VoiceOver	**Peter Thomas**

BEST WURST/FALLING OBJECT/SPECIAL AUTO
30-second
(VO): Sid and Sammy's Sub Shop had a big slice of the sandwich market.
SID: Must be your salami, Sammy!
WAITRESS: I'm waitin'.
(VO): They wanted to get into knackwurst, bratwurst, yachtwurst, and liverwurst.
S&S: In the worst way!
(VO): But a refrigeration failure turned their best wurst into the world's worst wurst . . .
S&S: Oy!
(VO): Fortunately they had a Business Owner's Special Policy from Sentry Insurance.
SAM: So we didn't have to swallow our losses.

1183

Art Director	John Constable
Writers	Steve Laughlin, Dennis Frankenberry, Karen Ninnemann
Editors	Bob Blanford, Mike Losurdo
Director	Lee Lacy
Client	Sentry Insurance
Agency Producers	Steve Laughlin, Kirk Ruhnke, John Constable
Prod'n Co Producer	Carol Emmerich
Agency	Frankenberry, Laughlin, Constable, Milwaukee

BACHELOR WEEKEND REV./OLDER BROTHER/ TRUCKER
30-second
GUY 1: Hey, a whole week without women.
GUY 2: And no responsibility.
GUY 1: I think I'll grow a beard.
GUY 3: You think we'll survive?
GUY 4: It'll be tough.
GUY 1: Hey, no dishes to wash.
GUY 3 Fishing all day.
GUY 2: Yeah, cards all night.
GUY 5: And I feel lucky!!
GUY 2: Hi honey, ya miss me?
MUSIC AND LYRICS: Reach out, reach out and touch someone.

1184

Art Directors	Diane Campbell, Elliott Manketo, Ed Di Benedetto
Writers	Beth McLure, Judy Craven, Pat O'Connor
Editor	H. Lazarus
Director	Steve Horn
Client	AT&T Communications Residence/Kim Armstrong, Phil Shyposh
Agency	NW Ayer Incorporated, New York/Gaston Braun
Production Company	Steve Horn Inc.
Creative Director	Ron Salzberg

RANGER PRIDE REV. 800/BRADLEY/FATHER & SON
30-second
(VO): A Ranger never takes the easy way out.
Singers: You're reaching deep inside you for things you've never known.
(VO): Go.
(VO): That's why getting into the rangers is tough . . . and the training is tough.
Singers: Be All That You Can Be.
(VO): So it makes me feel like I'm part of something special . . .
Singers: Be All That You Can Be
(VO): And I'm not the only one. Hi Mom!
Singers: You can do it in the Army.

ONE STEP BEHIND/COUNTRY HOUSE/PHOTO-DESIRE
30-second
LYRIC: Open my heart up.
Silhouette, you make love right.
ANNCR: Silhouette Books captures love like no other novels.
LYRIC: Silhouette, you make love right.
WOMAN: I've been expecting you.
ANNCR: Open your heart to a Silhouette Special Edition.
LYRIC: Silhouette, you make love right.

1185

Creative Directors	**Walter Burek, Ted Regan**
Art Directors	**Mickey Tender, John Byrnes**
Writer	**Susan McFeatters**
Editors	**Mark Polycan, Jerry Bender**
Directors	**Neil Tardio, Lear Levin, Don Guy**
Client	**United States Army**
Agency	**NW Ayer Incorporated, New York/Jim McMenemy**
Production Cos	**Lovinger, Tardio & Melsky, Lear Levin Productions, Dennis, Guy & Hirsch**

1186

Art Director	**Mark Shap**
Designer	**Ken Davis**
Writer	**Michael Zambrelli**
Editor	**Frank Ciofreddi**
Director	**Tony Scott**
Client	**Silhouette Books**
Agency	**Ogilvy & Mather, New York/Sue Chiafullo**
Prod'n Co Producer	**Jack Provost/Fairbanks Films**

ATHLETES AFRICA/GERMANY/USA
30-second
ANNCR (VO): In 1984, people will leave their homelands to attend the largest peacetime event in the history of the world.
10,000 athletes, from almost every country on earth.
And Transamerica Insurance and Transamerica Occidental Life will support the dreams of every athlete by insuring the Olympic games.
Because our business is ensuring people's dreams.
SUPER: Transamerica.
Insurance.
Finance.
Manufacturing.
Transportation.

1187	
Art Director	**Ron Travisano**
Writer	**Jim Weller**
Editors	**Jim Edwards, Ace & Edie II**
Director	**Werner Hlinka**
Client	**Transamerica Corp.**
Agency	**Della Femina, Travisano, New York/Peter Yahr**
Production Company	**THT Productions/Mark Romanski**
Music	**Carmine Coppola**

DO YOU KNOW ME TOM LANDRY/ROGER MILLER/ JAMES GALWAY
30-second
(MUSIC UNDER)
LANDRY: Do you know me? I'm one of the best known cowboys in Texas.
But a lot of people don't recognize me in a cowboy hat.
So I just carry the American Express Card.
It can help you out in plenty of tough situations.
Because you never know when you're gonna be surrounded.
By Redskins . . . Howdy.
ANNCR: To apply for the card, look for this display and take one.

1188	
Art Director	**F. Paul Pracilio**
Writers	**Jeff Atlas, Robert Neuman**
Client	**American Express Company**
Agency	**Sandra Breakstone, Ann Marcato/Ogilvy & Mather, New York**

CHANGING PICTURE/EXCHANGING IDEAS/
25 YEARS IN SPACE
30-second
ANNCR (VO): Did you ever notice that just when you think
you see the whole picture, the picture changes.
Technology from a company called TRW lets us look at our
world in fresh ways.
Because there's more to everything than meets the eye.
(WINK)
Tomorrow is taking shape at
A Company Called TRW.

NORTHERN LIGHT X 3
60-second
(MUSIC- "SIBELIUS" - UNDER AND THROUGHOUT)
(CU SWEEPS AND DISSOLVES OF PAINTINGS IN THE
NORTHERN LIGHT EXHIBITION EDITED TO THE MUSIC)
(VO): Haunting said the New York Times.
SUPER: "Haunting"
The N.Y. Times
(VO): Dark. Turbulent. Said Vogue.
SUPER: "Dark . . . Turbulent"
Vogue
(VO): Trembles with erotic yearning said Newsweek.
SUPER: "Trembles with erotic yearning,"
Newsweek
(VO): So good, it's scary said the Washington Post.

	1189
Art Director	Tom Smith
Designers	Tom Smith, Ken Mirman
Artist	Ken Mirman
Writer	Chuck Withrow
Editor	Lenny Mandelbaum
Director	Henry Sandbank
Client	TRW, Inc.
Agency Producer	Donna Baltas/Wyse Advertising, Cleveland
Production Company	Henry Sandbank Films

	1190
Art Director	Doug Lew
Writer	Bob Thacker
Editor	Steve Sheperd
Director	Steve Griak
Client	Minneapolis Institute of Arts
Agency	Chuck Ruhr Advertising, Minneapolis
Production Company	Wilson-Griak/Mike Monten

BREAKFAST/BASKETBALL/SOLOIST
60-second
MUSIC: THROUGHOUT.
ANNCR (VO): The way some business people spend
their time has very little to do with a clock.
ANNCR (VO): At Apple, we understand that "business
as usual" isn't anymore. That's why we make the most
advanced personal computers in the world.
And why, soon, there'll be just two kinds of people.
GUY: Hi.
ANNCR (VO): Those who use computers
GUY: Yeah. I'll be home for breakfast
ANNCR (VO): and those who use Apples.

WE'VE GOT THE TOUCH LOVE/WORK/PLAY
60-second
(MUSIC UNDER)
Singer: We've got a way of showing love.
Here in the U.S.A. A certain style.
A certain flair. That comes through every day.
Chorus: You've got the touch, America, and you're comin' on
with all the best.
We've got the touch, America, you and CBS.
Singer: You're tuned to us. We're tuned to
you. With stars to touch you through
and through. A touch of love. A touch of tears. With friends
you've known for years.

GOLD AWARD		SILVER AWARD	
1191		**1192**	
Art Directors	**Brent Thomas, Lee Clow**	Art Director	**Alan Friedlander**
Writer	**Steve Hayden**	Writer	**Billings Fuess**
Editor	**Steve Wystrach**	Director	**Linda Mevorach**
Director	**Adrian Lyne**	Client	**CBS**
Client	**Apple Computer**	Agency Producer	**John Massey/Ogilvy &**
Agency/Agency Producer	**Chiat/Day, Los Angeles/**		**Mather, New York**
	Richard O'Neill	Creative Director	**Malcolm End**
Prod'n Co Producer	**Paul Esposito**		

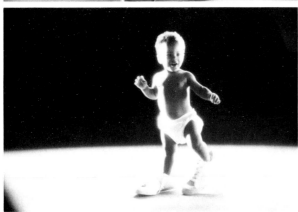

OLYMPIC NATIONAL/JOLLY JUMPER/BABY SHOES
60-second
SPORTS ANNCR: Representing the United States of America in the high jump . . .
(VO): There is no limit to how high a child can soar. But it takes talent, courage and lots of energy—energy devoted to years of practice and training. That's why, for 19 years, Atlantic Richfield has put its energy into children with the ARCO Jesse Owens Games—a track program for youngsters who just love to run, jump, dash . . . and a program that inspires those youngsters whose goal is to run, jump, and dash in the Olympics. That's why ARCO is an official sponsor of the 1984 Los Angeles Olympics Because ARCO is committed to using its energy to help our children soar higher than ever before.

LASER PRINTING/PHONE BOOTH/NURSERY
60-second
SFX Switch on.
That rotating mirrored ball might have been the inspiration for a remarkable breakthrough at Xerox.
See, by aiming a laser beam at rotating mirrors you can disperse it and use it to create the image of an entire page in a split second.
And that makes Electronic Printing possible.
The people at Xerox tell me Electronic Printing is growing as fast as copiers did in the 60's.
Isn't it nice to know Xerox invented them both.
I know, I know.
You're saying what kind of company is this Xerox.
Ideas in dance halls?

1193

Art Director	**Ralph Price**
Writer	**Michael Wagman**
Editor	**Jacques Dury**
Director	**David Stern**
Client	**Atlantic Richfield Company**
Agency	**FCB/LA/Len Levy**
Production Company	**Associates & Toback**
Creative Director	**Michael Wagman**

1194

Art Director	**Robert Cox**
Director	**Neil Tardio**
Client	**Xerox Corporation**
Agency	**Needham, Harper & Steers, New York**

FOOTBALL/THOR/CASA BLANCA
60-second
SFX: Crying
Coach: But, we *won* the game!
(VO): Oh, the disappointment when you find you're not booked on your favourite airline.
(VO): British Airways fly more people to more countries than any other airline. It's the world's favourite airline.

THE NEW PRELUDE/THE NEW CAR/NEW CIVICS
60-second
MUSIC
(VO): It began as a clean piece of paper. Designers sketched an aerodynamically superior shape. Once the shape was perfected, engineers made it into a car. With startling effect. The new Prelude from Honda.
Fasten your seatbelts.

	1195
Art Director	**Graham Cornthwaite**
Designers	**Jack Morrisey, Martin Johnson**
Writer	**Geoffrey Seymour**
Editor	**Terry Jones**
Director	**Barry Myers**
Client	**British Airways/Derek Dear**
Agency Producer	**Barbara Levett/Compton Advertising, New York**
Prod'n Co Producer	**Tim White**

	1196
Art Director	**Gary Yoshida**
Writer	**Bob Coburn**
Client	**American Honda Motor Company, Inc.**
Agency	**Needham, Harper & Steers, LA/Helmut Dorger, Gary Paticoff**

SIAM/MEXICO/SRI LANKA
60-second
ANNOUNCER:
It's early morning on the Chao Phraya (Chow Pie-Ya)
Siam's ancient river of the kings . . . A land of natural beauty.
It's mystical waters have created a fertile delta where some
of the world's most exotic fruit is grown . . . and today . . . Tim
Hansen . . . has come to this ancient floating market place . . .
to search for and buy some of this earth's sweetest tropical
fruit . . . lucious fruit for his Hansen tropical juices.
Tim travels the world for his friends who drink Hansen's
juices, buying only the finest natural ingredients . . . like
pineapple from Siam.

HUNCHBACK/MARIE ANTOINETTE/ DETECTIVE
60-second
BELLRINGER: Dahtahpember! Dahtahpember!
Crowd: Dahtahpember? What does he mean? What is he
saying?
BELLRINGER: Dahtahpember! Hey gimme a Dahtahpem-
ber! Dahtahpember! Dahtah!
BELLRINGER: Ah, thank you. Pooey! Watch my lips.
DR PEPPER. DR PEPPER.
MUSIC: Hold out for the out of the ordinary. Hold out for DR
PEPPER. Don't be sold out, it's a taste that's extraordinary . . .
GIRL: Shall we ring some bells?
MUSIC: There's no doubt, it's DR PEPPER. Hold out . . .

	1197
Art Directors/	**Richard C. Runyon,**
Designers	**Carol C. Clements**
Directors of Photography	**Brian Reynolds**
Writer	**John LaBrucherie**
Editors	**Brian Reynolds, Richard Runyon**
Director	**Richard C. Runyon**
Client	**Hansen Foods, Inc.**
Production Company	**Richard C. Runyon Design, Los Angeles/Howard Reekie, Tim Hansen**

	1198
Art Director	**Roy Tuck**
Writer	**Bill Appelman**
Editor	**Lanny Friedman**
Director	**Manny Perez**
Client	**Dr. Pepper/Regular/Sugar Free**
Agency Producer	**Roseanne Horn/Young & Rubicam, New York**
Production Company	**Film Fair**
Music Director	**Hunter Murtaugh/Young & Rubicam**

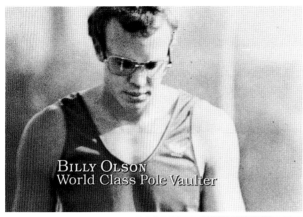

BILLY OLSON
World Class Pole Vaulter

THE DREAM BEGINS WITH FREEDOM.

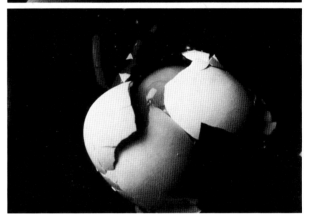

OLSON/OERTER/BIGGS
60-second
(MUSIC UNDER)
Billy Olson: The worst thing a vaulter can ever do is lose his nerve, because there are a lot of things in any sport that can get you down.
It's when you don't have the guts to get back up . . . that you're defeated.
ANNCR (VO): To train for the Olympics, an athlete devotes the part of his life called youth. To support that dedication, 7-Eleven is a major sponsor of the 1984 U.S. Olympic Team. We're proud to be giving great athletes like Billy Olson the freedom to become the best.
Billy Olson: I just keep one thought in my head. I'm going to go over that bar higher than anyone has ever gone over it.

SEAT BELTS
30-second
ANNCR. 1: If you drive a car or ride in one, this message is for you.
SFX: FLUTE-LIKE MUSIC.
ANNCR. 2: Volvo, from Gothenburg, Sweden, was the first car maker to install 3-point seat belts as standard equipment. The belts are incredibly strong . . . comfortable to wear;
SFX: ROLLING WHEELS.
ANNCR. 2: and some day, one of them could save your life. But only if you buckle it up.
SFX: BRAKES & CRASH OF CAR. SILENCE.
ANNCR: 2: Your metro New York New Jersey Volvo Dealers.

1199

Art Directors	**Jerry Roach, Clark Frankel**
Writers	**Joe Lovering, Jean Kondek**
Editor	**Michael Charles**
Director	**Michael Seresin**
Client	**The Southland Corporation-Seven/Eleven Olympics**
Agency Producer	**Mootsy Elliot/Young & Rubicam, New York**
Production Company	**Brooks, Fulford, Cramer, Seresin**
Y&R Music Director	**Hunter Murtaugh**

1200

Art Director	**Joe Schindelman**
Writer	**Ray Myers**
Client	**New York/New Jersey Volvo Dealers Assoc.**
Agency	**Scali, McCabe, Sloves, New York/Michael Moskowitz**

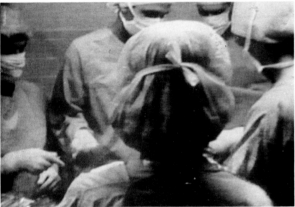

HEART ATTACK
60-second
ANNOUNCER: This man is 20 minutes away from a major heart attack. He's completely unprepared for it. But we've been preparing for this moment for over 20 years. In 1968 doctors at the Medical College of Virginia Hospitals performed America's second heart transplant.
(Restaurant Ambience)
In 1979 we learned how to clear blocked arteries without open heart surgery. Now we're teaching this procedure to other doctors at other hospitals.
(Restaurant Ambience)
Last year, Medical College of Virginia Hospitals was one of the first to use enzymes to limit the damage of heart attacks.
WOMAN: Are you O.K.?

DON'T BE A DOPE: "ROCK STARS"
30-second
Silent

	1201
Art Director	**Wayne Gibson**
Writers	**Kerry Feuerman, Bill Westbrook**
Client	**The Medical College of Virginia**
Agency	**Westbrook, Inc., Richmond, VA**

	1202
Art Director	**Barry Grimes**
Writers	**Steve Sohmer, Peter Ferrara**
Client	**NBC Entertainment, Burbank, CA**
Agency Producer	**Chuck Stepner**

COCKTAILS FOR TWO
30-second
SFX: Pop! Music up
SFX: Champagne pouring
ANNR: Do you suppose the people who litter make their homes as dirty as they make our city?
SFX: Bottle hits floor. Music changes
SFX: Dishes and silverware crash
SFX: Crash!
SFX: Table hits floor
ANNR: You don't dump garbage in your living room.
SFX: Grunting pig
ANNR: So don't dump it in our city.
ANNR: Pittsburgh is our home. Let's clean house.

1203

Art Directors	**Robert Griffing, Vann Jennings**
Writer	**Edward Fine**
Editor	**Jim McCartney**
Director	**Jim McCartney**
Client	**Pittsburgh Clean City Committee**
Agency	**Marc & Company, Inc., Pittsburgh**
Production Company	**Location Video/Warner Cable**

NELL CARTER - STATE
60-second
NELL CARTER: Hello Ladies—I'm Nell Carter. If you're a woman, black and *somewhere* between the age of 29 and 99—but still sweet, and sort of a . . . . . sassy—I'm talking to you. About Breast Cancer. How to *detect* it. Early—And protect yourself. Oh, wait, I know, I know, you don't want to hear this. And you think it's gonna hurt you. Well, honey, it's not the *exam* that hurts. A breast examination only takes one-half an hour, once a year. It's that fast. That easy. And ooh—it's free. And you can get it at the Breast Examination Center in the Harlem State Office Building. Ladies, wait . . . I am doing it for *my* health. You should do it for yours. 'Cause the truth is, early detection is the best protection—the *only* protection we have. So if you don't have your breasts examined,

---

1204

Art Director	**Cathy Edwards**
Writer	**Sherry Nemmers**
Director	**Neil Tardio**
Client	**Harlem Breast Exam Center**
Agency	**DFS, New York**
Production Company	**Lovinger, Tardio, Melsky, Inc.**

DRINKING AND DRIVING
CAN KILL A FRIENDSHIP

U.S. Dept. of Transp.   Ad Council

CRASHING GLASSES X 2/CHRISTMAS WREATH
30-second
When friends don't stop friends from drinking and driving
(SFX) friends die from drinking and driving (SFX)
friends die from drinking and
Drinking and driving can kill a friendship.

FLOATING INSTRUMENTS
30-second
(Music begins wih piano—transcends into other solo instruments and finally builds into entire orchestration with stereo
digitally mixed track).
ANNCR: (VO): Sound has a look all its own. But it never
looked like much on a home video cassette recorder, because it never sounded like much . . . until now.
Sony introduces the biggest breakthrough in Home Video
since we invented it: Sony Beta Hi-Fi.
At last, a VCR that, hooked up to your stereo system trans-
forms the home video experience into the home theater experience. And is fully compatible with all existing Beta tapes.
There's an incredible technological story behind it, but to
really appreciate Beta Hi-Fil, just sit back, relax, and open

GOLD AWARD

1205

Art Director	**Len Fink**
Director of Photography	**Phil Marco**
Writer	**Lou Linder**
Editor	**Larry Plastrick**
Director	**Phil Marco**
Client	**The Advertising Council National Highway Traffic Safety Administration**
Agency Producer	**Herbert A. Miller/Leber Katz Partners, New York**
Production Company	**Phil Marco Productions, Inc.**

1206

Art Director	**Dave Davis**
Tech. Coordinator	**Bruce Giuriceo**
Animators	**Robert Mrozowski & Kenneth Stytzer**
Cameraman	**B. David Green**
Writer	**John Sills**
Editor	**Larry Plastrik**
Director	**Randy Balsmeyer**
Client	**Sony Corp. of America**
Agency Producer	**Backer & Spielvogel, New York/Sally Smith**
Production Company	**R/Greenberg Associates, Inc./Robert M. Greenberg**

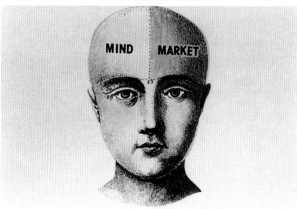

THE LOOK OF LEADERSHIP
60-second
For a company to become an industry leader, it should start with a leader at the helm. Francis Glidden was that kind of man. He, and those who followed him, had to surmount the challenges of technological change. And his small company grew throughout the next century, ultimately establishing a look of leadership for the evolving coatings industry.
(MUSIC START)
Glidden opened his shop in 1870 with two 150-gallon kettles, one helper and a horse and wagon. Within two years, he'd built a new factory for seven varnish-making fires and seven employees. Glidden even had a laboratory, which was one of the first in the industry.
At that time, chemical mixology was a mysterious art, with

NATIONAL SPORTS FILM
No Script-Just Music & FX

1207

Art Director	**Chris Dieck**
Artists	**David Bartholomew, Joe Busam, Susie Zimmerer**
Director of Photography	**Carle Anderson**
Editor	**David Kallaher**
Directors	**Chris Dieck, David Kallaher**
Client	**Glidden Coatings and Resins, Cleveland, Ohio**
Agency	**Meldrum and Fewsmith, Cleveland/Chris Dieck**
Production Company	**David Kallaher Inc.**
Creative Director	**Chris N. Perry**

1208

Art Director	**Chris Blum**
Client	**Levi Strauss**
Agency Producer	**Steve Neely/Foote, Cone & Belding, San Francisco**
Music	**Ken Nordine**
Computer Graphics	**One Pass Video**

LOOP PROMO
60-second
Video only with music under.

CALL OF THE WILD PROMO
90-second
Video only with music under.

<table>
<tr><td colspan="2" align="center">1209</td></tr>
<tr><td align="right">Art Directors</td><td>Doc Dochtermann, Jack Harvey</td></tr>
<tr><td align="right">Designer</td><td>Doc Dochtermann</td></tr>
<tr><td align="right">Director of Photography</td><td>Felix Alcala</td></tr>
<tr><td align="right">Writers</td><td>Don Ayers, Howard Epstein</td></tr>
<tr><td align="right">Editor</td><td>Gerald Weldon</td></tr>
<tr><td align="right">Director</td><td>David Farrow</td></tr>
<tr><td align="right">Client</td><td>Ford Division/Ford Motor Company</td></tr>
<tr><td align="right">Agency</td><td>J.W.T., Detroit/Don Ayers, Howard Epstein, Jon Ward</td></tr>
<tr><td align="right">Production Company</td><td>Paisley Productions/ Christine Kitch</td></tr>
</table>

<table>
<tr><td colspan="2" align="center">1210</td></tr>
<tr><td align="right">Art Directors</td><td>Doc Dochtermann, Carroll Raver</td></tr>
<tr><td align="right">Directors of Photography</td><td>Carroll Raver, David Shore</td></tr>
<tr><td align="right">Writer</td><td>Carroll Raver</td></tr>
<tr><td align="right">Editor</td><td>Gerald Weldon</td></tr>
<tr><td align="right">Director</td><td>Carroll Raver</td></tr>
<tr><td align="right">Client</td><td>Ford Division/Ford Motor Company</td></tr>
<tr><td align="right">Agency</td><td>J.W.T., Detroit/John Sands, Doc Dochtermann</td></tr>
<tr><td align="right">Production Company</td><td>Paisley Productions/Jon Ward</td></tr>
</table>

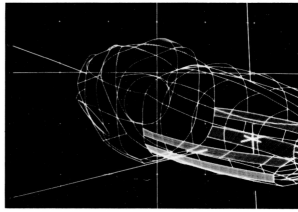

INSIDE JOUST
30-second
ANNCR: Long ago, in the distant future, where evil knights joust upon beasts of the air, you too must fly, joust and retrieve the enemy's egg before it hatches, and beware the lava below. You can experience this world, from the other side. It's called Joust, the arcade game, home now, only from Atari. A video game? Hardly. Joust. You don't play it. You live it.

EXCHANGING IDEAS
30-second
Anncr (VO): First someone gets an idea.
Then someone else may look at it differently.
Even add a thought or two.
technology from a company called TRW helps ideas get around.
Because getting an idea from one place to another is as important as getting an idea.
Tomorrow is taking shape at
A Company Called TRW.

1211

Art Director	**David Nathanson**
Designer	**David Nathanson**
Animator	**Kirk Henderson**
Writer	**Jeff Linder**
Director	**Drew Takahashi**
Client	**Atari**
Agency	**Doyle Dane Bernbach Inc., New York/Liza Leeds**
Production Company	**Colossal Pictures**
Music	**Elias Associates**

1212

Art Director	**Tom Smith**
Designers	**Tom Smith, Ken Mirman**
Artist	**Ken Mirman**
Writer	**Chuck Withrow**
Client	**TRW, Inc.**
Agency Producer	**Donna Baltas/Wyse Advertising, Cleveland**
Production Company	**Bob Abel & Assoc.**

CLUB NEWS

In this section in the Annual each year is the members' own story. Here is our annual report of past successes and future plans, of accomplishments and dreams. Chairmen have each written their reports summarizing the activities of their committees for the 1983-1984 season, one of the liveliest in the Club's history of diversity. While the Show is the main event, it is by no means the only one in town. There are members whose single concern is education and they give heart-and-soul to that activity. Others work on luncheon programs. Still others put in hours on bringing different sorts of smaller exhibitions into the Club's own galleries. We look backward to the year's record with pride and look ahead to a year of promise.

And, as the grand-daddy of all the art directors clubs of the world, we plan some surprises for next season. We will report to you same time, same place, next year.

Judging by Best Brings Out the Best

"**T**his is all going too good . . ." "Has anything gone wrong yet?"

Quite frankly, during a cold weekend in January, almost 18,000 entries were judged by more than 70 art directors and everything went very smoothly.

As chairman of the judging, I did exactly one thing right, I delegated most of the work to extremely competent people: Section chairman Harvey Gabor for T.V., Mark Shap for print advertising, Marty Pedersen for promotion and graphics, Sam Antupit for books and Will

Hopkins for editorial.

Most of all though, the judging works smoothly because of the club staff, headed by Paula Radding. There were several significant changes in the judging procedures beginning with the selection of judges. The final group of judges was truly a group of people actually doing some of the best work in their fields. They came from within and out of the club, from New York and across the country (this was the first year that the club invited and paid expenses for out-of-town judges). The judges' names were listed on the call for entries (also a first) . . . and almost all showed up for the full judging.

The judging took place at Parsons School of Design, which allowed ample space to spread out many entries at once, so that the judges could get a true sense of the calibre of entries. But they were also an extremely tough jury, accepting the lowest percentage of entries in memory. The result, they gave us a show of exceptionally high standards that reflects the state of our business in 1983.

A special note of thanks should go to Chris Hill for designing the call for entries and this Annual. Also, to the Lone Star Cafe for keeping the judges well fed, well beered and very content.

Bob Ciano *Chairman*

Louise Fili, Peter Bradford, Bascove, Al Grossman look at books

Andy Kner, Michael Chin, Wil Hopkins and Bob Ciano take a respite

Malcolm End, Tom Wolsey, Brian Harrod, Tony Gill at advertising judging

At the graphic design judging: Pete Turner, Neil Shakery, Rodney Wilson, Bill Cadge

Celebrate Winners at N.Y.'s Roseland

The Awards Presentation for the 63rd Annual was held in Roseland, the "world's most famous dancehall."

President Andy Kner started the evening by presenting the year's Management Award to Herman Miller, Inc. for its long-time leadership in contributing to a climate that makes a better world for designers and a better world, in general. Herman Miller is outstanding for its creative manufacturing and ideas for better living.

Art directors and their families and friends attended the show from California, Georgia, Illinois, Indiana, Massachusetts, Minnesota, Texas and Virginia as well as New York for the awarding of 39 Golds and 44 Silver Medals.

Presenters for the evening were Walter Kaprielian, chairman of this year's awards presentation and Harvey Gabor, television section chairman.

Then the guests took over for a fling on the famous Roseland dancehall floor.

Alan Friedlander and Billings Fuess, Ogilvy & Mather, accept silver medal. With Andy Kner and Walter Kaprielian

Milton Glaser accepts gold medal from Harvey Gabor, with president Andy Kner and awards coordinator, Dan Forte

Steve Snoey, v.p. International Operations, Herman Miller, accepts the ADC's Management Award

Ben Goldfarb, William Brockmeier and Roz Goldfarb celebrate

CLUB NEWS/ANNUAL SHOW

Month-Long Exhibit Seen by Record Crowds

The 63rd Annual Show went to the Lincoln Center area this year in the Harkness Pavilion Atrium on west 62nd Street. In this lively, open space, the 39 Gold, 44 Silver, 57 Distinctive Merit winners and all the pieces in this book were on view during June. The 1239 works were seen not only by members of the profession but by people from all walks of life, with special emphasis on music and theater goers on their way to and from Avery Fisher Hall and the Beaumont Theater.

The works were effectively displayed on panels with ample room for walking and stopping to examine the art at leisure. The high ceilings added an extra dimension giving the show impact and natural lighting seeped through during all hours of the viewing day

Scholarships and Ad Agency Programs Come from VCEF

Having gone on record with our intentions at the last Hall of Fame festivities, the Visual Communicators Education Fund has been gathering momentum in establishing several scholarship awards to outstanding art school students.

This year we expect to be giving at least one award to a top student of communication design (advertising or graphic) from Parsons, F.I.T., Pratt, Cooper, New York Tech, Pratt/Phoenix, School of Visual Arts and the High School of Art and Design.

At Pratt we will be establishing the award in memoriam to George Krikorian—as has been planned and directed by the ADC Board of Directors, and at Cooper a similar award will be established in memoriam to the late Herb Lubalin.

In addition, the Visual Communication Education Fund will be contributing to the newly formed "Herb Lubalin Study Center for Design and Typography" to be housed at Cooper Union's Foundation Building. This marvelous center will be open to all design students and professionals and is a worthy recipient of our time and efforts.

A change in eligibility for our awards activities in cooperation with the School Art League has been made this year. We have made this selection much more fair to participating students by limiting portfolios for the ADC/ School Art League Awards to only those students who are attending general academic schools and not primarily art schools.

We were successful in identifying several highly talented students, many of whom have already applied to some of the art schools mentioned above.

Our thanks go each year to those generous individuals past and present who through foundations or direct grants, help us identify and encourage these worthy students. But this year we are contacting our own members and their corporate managements to ask for continuing funding to establish joint ADC/ Corporate Scholarship awards. We are pleased to report that at this printing, Foote Cone & Belding and the Book-of-the-Month Club are co-sponsors with the VCEF and we are in conversation with several other companies.

We are also asking that a key aspect of these corporate grants, beyond the funding, should contain a provision for probationary employment for the winning student. After all, if the student is worth a prize for excellence, he or she is worth the chance to be a productive employee as well.

We've only just begun, and the beginning stages are the most difficult, but we are pleased that so many of our members have been so helpful and encouraging. The VCEF's activities give each of us another chance to give back a little of what we have enjoyed from this fascinating business.

Karl H. Steinbrenner
Chairman

Charles Dickenson
Dorothy Evans
Joanne Goldsmith
Len Sugarman
Zlata Paces
David Davidian
George Halpern
John Lucci

Students Get a Leg Up in Real Work World

Over 400 students participated in the Portfolio Review program this year. There were 12 separate sessions during April and May where some 80 professionals participated in reviewing the students' portfolios. This program has become a Club tradition and is one of the most important activities, members say, because they want to have a hand in directing young people about to enter the marketplace.

Every year, we give an overall opinion as to the quality and emphasis in the work we see. In our view, the student work showed education in design is improving steadily, but concepts were weaker. In this high-tech era we would prefer to have a well-rounded student that could handle all the different specialties in advertising and there were fewer young people trained to be all-around professionals this year. We feel also that there is a need for closer communications between the design schools and the Club on this program, and this will be one of our future goals.

We hope that, because of the excitement the program instills among members, it can be expanded to include even more graduate students and schools in the coming years.

This year the New Breed committee aided the students by providing them with tips on how to make it in today's job world. Since these younger members only recently graduated from schools themselves, this was an extremely beneficial idea for students.

**Jack Tauss and
Dick MacFarlane**
Co-chairmen

Jeff Babbitz, Herb Rosenthal and students

Judith Radice with new graduate

Chel Dong, Richard MacFarlane, Ethel Cutler look at books

A Very Good Year and Getting Better

It has been customary for the president of the Art Directors Club to write a few paragraphs for the Annual outlining the Club's activities during the previous year. But if there ever was an organization that could only be defined by the activities of its various parts, the Art Directors Club is it. On these pages are reports by all the committee chairmen, and it is their reports and the activities of their committees that define the Club. Reading them, I know you will be as proud of the Club as I am.

There are a few major points that I should bring to your attention. In looking through the 58th Annual—a book only six years old—I read in the President's report that the Club had a record number of submissions to the annual show—12,500 pieces. This past year we had 17,500 pieces submitted, and I think we'll pass that number next year. The reason for this phenomenal growth is that we have become not just a New York show but the one place where the best talent in the entire country comes to test itself. Ours is a national show, and the only place where the best in advertising *and* editorial *and* promotion design in the country can be seen is in the pages of this Annual.

Again while looking through old annuals I discovered that the club has been looking for new quarters for almost 10 years. Given the real estate situation in New York, that is not really surprising. But since our lease at 488 Madison is up in 1985, the search by this board, with the invaluable help of Bill Duffy, was understandably a bit more intense. Or maybe "desperate" is a better word. Since midtown prices are currently over $40 a square foot, (they were $20 when we last moved 15 years ago), we concentrated our search in the area south of midtown, an area where dozens of agencies and design studios have already relocated. I am happy to report that on June 18, 1984, we signed a lease for new quarters on Park Avenue South at 20th Street. The space is over 8,000 square feet—over twice what we now occupy at 488 Madison Avenue. This will permit us to dramatically increase our activities, including more evening programs, the mounting of major exhibitions, and the ability to have two programs going in different parts of our space at the same time. We hope to be in our new home before the end of 1984, and I will keep all informed of our progress as we move towards the occupancy of the new quarters.

There are two new activities I would particularly like to mention because they are innovative ideas that demonstrate the dynamic quality of Club activities. Bobbi Rosenthal's "New Breed" committee is aimed at all the young art directors in the Club, and is trying to answer both their professional and social needs with an incredible number of new activities. And, in conjunction with the New Breed Committee, Kurt Haiman has started a series of evening sessions where 15 of our greatest advertising art directors have agreed to make themselves available so that our younger members can meet and question those members of our profession who, by any standards, have reached the top. The thinking that went into the creation of these two activities shows that for our members innovation does not come only at the drawing board.

Another major breakthrough was the announcement that the long standing problems with the IRS concerning our tax-exempt status have finally been resolved in the Club's favor. This was welcome news, indeed, and should make the fund-raising we do for the Scholarship Fund easier next year, though this year's efforts, as reported by Karl Steinbrenner, are impressive enough as they are.

As you read the committee reports, you'll see what a good year it has been for all of us at the Art Directors Club. Membership is up, as is the involvement of those members in Club activities. And that, after all, is what we are all about.

Andy Kner

CLUB NEWS/BOARD OF DIRECTORS

OFFICERS

Andrew Kner
president

Ed Brodsky
first vice president

Lou Silverstein
second vice president

Jack G. Tauss
secretary

Blanche Fiorenza
assistant treasurer

Kurt Haiman
Treasurer

EXECUTIVE COMMITTEE

Bob Bruce

Bob Ciano

Lee Eptsein

Toby Moss

Jack Odette

Klaus Schmidt

CLUB NEWS/ADVISORY BOARD

Non-Retiring Past Presidents Take Active Role

Unlike the government of the United States, the Art Directors Club takes great advantage of the experience and knowledge of those who have served them as president.

In truth, no one is allowed to "Retire" once they have been president.

All past presidents of the Club belong to a special group composed only of men and women who enjoyed the honor and suffered the pain and problems associated with the job. This group is the Club's Advisory Board. The Advisory Board is traditionally chaired by the last retiring president.

This body, whose history ranges from last year back to 1929, is called upon to advise the Executive Board so that they may make their decisions with full knowledge of what had been done in the past, and what the ramifications of previous similar situations were. They do not have voting power, but participate in Board meetings on a regular basis.

This past year the Advisory Board has been active in the creation of the new Lecture Series by our advertising greats, encouraged the involvement of younger people which led to the Board's creation of "The New Breed" committee, and put together the Annual Awards Presentation held at Roseland on June 7th.

It plans to take a more active role in the judging of next year's show, the development of our new location and in any other area where the Executive Board feels it can use help.

To be sure, this group of men and women stand committed to the organization they served as president . . . and have no intention of sitting back on their laurels.

Walter Kaprielian
Chairman

Walter Grotz, Robert H. Blattner, Robert S. Smith, David Davidian, George Lois, Arthur Hawkins, William Brockmeier, Jack Jamison. Missing—William H. Buckley, Lou Dorfsman, Garrett P. Orr, John Peter, Eileen Hedy Schultz, William Taubin

Book Corporation Adds Team at the Top, Plans New Publishing Ventures

This 63rd Annual Book is produced by ADC Publications, Inc., an ADC subsidiary, with the invaluable assistance of the club staff. It is a coordinated effort that takes place over several months and this method of handling the book has proved to be highly successful.

The Publications division is run by members knowledgeable in all facets of publishing. Elections were held in the spring for the officers of the corporation and Ernest Scarfone, who has directed the operations of the subsidiary since its inception, was once again elected president. The other new officers are: Blanche Fiorenza, first vice president; Bob Ciano, second vice president; Steven Heller, secretary; and Jack Tauss, treasurer. These designers will be adding their skills and creative ideas as book professionals, and Scarfone reports that plans for the future include publishing some of the titles we have long hoped to produce.

As for this 63rd edition, Supermart Graphics, headed by Frank DeLuca, was the packager and Miriam L. Solomon was editor. This team handles every

Ernie Scarfone

aspect of the book from credit form typesetting through to printing and binding and have handled this assignment since 1979 when the ADC first started to publish its own book.

The ADC staff, under the direction of Diane Moore, coordinates the myriads of information, the credits, forms and photos, and the job would not be possible to handle without their Herculean efforts. The Hall of Fame section and the Club News were edited and written by Jo Yanow with associate Emmett Murphy.

The Annual was designed by Chris Hill of Houston who flew

from the Lone Star State to our offices, putting in many long hours. His concept was to unify all the graphic elements under the Statue of Liberty theme in the Call for Entries, Show Awards Program and the art in this book.

The AD Annual is available in major book stores and art material stores in the U.S. as well as overseas. Robert Silver & Associates handles trade book distribution for America and Canada and Feffer and Simons the foreign distribution. It is also distributed via direct mail and *Print Magazine.*

Membership Hits New Record for 64-Year Old Club

We broke our own record! The number of new members joining the club reached an all-time high of 89 for 1983. Last year we rejoiced because so many of our new members were young people showing enthusiasm, new ideas and an eagerness to be a part of the high professional level which is characteristic of our membership.

This year we rejoice because that spirit has multiplied in all directions. Famous names in our field who had never joined before are now members. Our out-of-town membership is up, attracting people from many nations, and now totals around 200.

How did we do it? It was easy. How could we miss? Our luncheons are not just interesting, they're up-to-the-minute learning experiences in our field. The food is gourmet. All the committees are busy, and as they work they are seen as important contributors to the art community. Attracting new members is a by-product of our many activities; our show, our annual, our involvement with the art colleges, our newsletter, our youthful members of all ages spreading vitality all add up to shared communication which is what our club is all about. Everyone wants to be where it's at, and it's here.

New members must qualify as functioning Art Directors for two years and require the sponsorship of two current members. Other categories of membership include: associate, non-resident, junior, corporate, institutional and professional. Details and applications are available at the ADC office.

We honor the year's new members at an annual reception. They receive a sterling silver pin bearing the club's logo, as well as a warm welcome, food and drink. This year we were treated to special entertainment from Sal Lazzarotti who serves on the membership committee. He's a professional singer as well as art director.

I have been asked if we are going to have a membership drive. We will as soon as we get a break from signing in new members.

Lorraine Allen *Chairman*

Joanne Coates
Charles Dickenson
Michael Fenga
Allan Philiba
Sal Lazzarotti
Dick MacFarlane
Toby Moss
Shinichiro Tora
Horst Winkler

New members Amy Goldman and Michele Kestin with Charles McDonald at annual reception

Ron Wickham and wife admire Lee Corey's sterling silver pin

Committee Scours City for Sites

The greatest task put before this committee is one of real estate. We are ever searching for new buildings and whether they will offer space for public use for display for the annual Art Directors Club Show.

We've been in touch with major names in the building and construction industry and touched base with just about every director of public affairs representing buildings in New York City.

Due to the determination and hard work of the committee members we've been able to come up with the answers . . . this year it's the Harkness Plaza Atrium near Lincoln Center.

Thanks to all of you!

Jacques Parker *Chairman*

ADC Aids Industry Through JEC

The Art Directors Club members Eileen Schultz, Bill Duffy, Garry Orr and Bob Bruce — plus Jack Jamison (one of the founders of and the Honorary Chairman of the Joint Ethics Committee) are the Club's permanently elected representatives to the JEC.

The Joint Ethics Committee was established in 1945 because its founders (The Art Directors Club, Society of Illustrators and Artists Guild) were concerned with the signs of growing misunderstandings, abuses and the disregard of uniform standards of ethical conduct and good business practices. Their response to these problems was to formulate a Code of Fair Practice for the graphic communications industry.

This Code has been updated several times over the years and expanded to meet the needs of a growing profession. And the number of sponsor organizations has grown in order to better represent all segments of the industry. Today, there are six responsible, respected member organizations involved: The American Institute of Graphic Arts; The Art Directors Club; The Graphic Artists Guild; The American Society of Magazine Photographers; The Society of Illustrators; and The Society of Photographer and Artist Representatives.

Selected representatives from these organizations serve as volunteers on the committee. The JEC's services, offered without charge, are available to anyone and everyone connected with the graphic communications industry, whether or not they are a member of any of the sponsoring organizations.

The committee provides a practical alternative to litigation in the clarification and settlement of ethical disputes through knowledgeable peer review methods — mainly through correspondence, and when necessary, and mutually agreed to, mediation and arbitration. In the arbitration process, additional experts, who are approved by both parties to the dispute, are called in to assist committee members in reaching a binding decision.

The JEC handles approximately forty cases each year and since its inception has settled over 1300 disputes between buyer and seller, without litigation.

While the committee primarily serves the needs of those in the Greater New York area, it offers assistance to those in other geographical areas where practical from a logistical standpoint. In addition, the JEC has formulated a functional guide for setting up regional or local committees in other cities. To date, there are five such groups — all following the JEC's established Code of Fair Practice.

The goal of the JEC continues to be to increase awareness of, and adherence to, sound ethical standards for the benefit of the professionals in the graphics industry.

For further information or to purchase the Code booklet for $3.00, please write to: Joint Ethics Committee, P.O. Box 179, Grand Central Station, New York, NY 10163.

Bill Duffy
Member for ADC

Success Ends Search for Club's New Home

This committee, because of the intricate, highly specialized nature of its function, has found it necessary to rely on the services of a number of outside consultants: a civil engineer; an architect; an interior designer; and an attorney specializing in real estate. This, in addition to the unceasing efforts of Diane Moore, as well as the participation of Andy Kner, Walter Kaprielian, the Executive Committee, the Advisory Board and our accounting firm. We have also had a great deal of valuable input from many Club members with leads to available space or to real estate agents.

The follow-up on all of these leads has been very time-consuming but essential, considering the difficult and expensive real estate situation in New York City. We have also tried to deal with city government, historical landmark and professional grant groups in the attempt to meet our special needs. Unfortunately, in every case, the properties offered either didn't fit our requirements or could not be successfully negotiated for.

We finally appointed a real estate agent on an exclusive basis in order to assure a greater degree of interest, time and effort in finding the right property at the right price.

Now we have found space which will meet all of our current, and future, needs. We believe we have a new home which will be not only functional and practical, but really exciting. It could be the showcase we have needed for years—one which will reflect the Club's standards and its standing in the graphic communications industry.

It should provide great exposure for the organization. This is the first time we have ever had a ground floor area. It is an environment for all sorts of newsworthy activities. Because of the ambience of our new surroundings, the *art* and *design* talents of the members should be apparent to the visitor. The decor, I might add, will be accomplished with a minimum of financial expenditure.

In this space in next year's Annual we will show—and tell—about the many programs in our new home.

Bill Duffy
Chairman

CLUB NEWS/LUNCHEONS

Every Year Luncheon Programs Attract More People

This season I think we scheduled 35 lunches and it seems to me that they averaged about 40 members and their guests attending. That means that about 1400 attended the Wednesday Lunches.

I think that's pretty good. I am delighted by the interest and enthusiasm. It gives the Lunch Committee encouragement to continue their hard work. They deserve a lot of credit, but in addition, the members of the Art Directors Club staff have to be thanked. There was Michele O'Brien who kept the invitations and schedules straight, Glenn Kubota who arranged for and set up the equipment every week, Casey Alexander who took reservations, Debra Woo our sensational chef, Debra Weathers who took our pictures and, of course, Diane Moore who was on top of everything that went on.

Once again, the major credit has to go to all the talented people who agreed to be the guest speakers at the ADC. They came with slides, films, equipment, assistants. Most of all, they brought a willingness to share their experiences and knowledge.

Ed Brodsky
Chairman

Cyd Kilby-Gorman
Roz Goldfarb
Carol Haley
Marie-Christine Lawrence
Bill McCaffery
Toby Moss
Dan Nelson
Jacques Parker
Judi Radice
Bobbi Rosenthal
Herb Rosenthal
Ellen Shapiro
Shinichiro Tora
Dorothy Wachtenheim
Jessica Weber

Syd Hap and her marionnettes charmed the audience

Ed Brodksy at the mike has been chairing innovative noon programs for three years

Hope Hanafin, costume designer, brought her colorful ideas

CLUB NEWS/HALL OF FAME

A Night of Stars at the Pierre

The talents and leadership of Aaron Burns, Seymour Chwast and Stephen O. Frankfurt were celebrated during the 1983 black-tie Hall of Fame dinner that brought together luminaries from advertising, art and design with family and friends. In addition, William Bernbach, benefactor to art directors, was given a special award.

Along with the presentations of beautiful work and speeches came a good deal of humor and surprises, too. William Buckley was head of management and planning and Arthur Hawkins chaired the diamond-polished Pierre Hotel festivities. There were no tickets to be had.

Inductee Seymour Chwast with Milton Glaser

Bill Buckley and Art Hawkins who orchestrated the event

George Lois and Jack Jamison

CLUB NEWS/HALL OF FAME

Inductee Aaron Burns with Kner

Everyone cheers

Andy Kner awards Steve Frankfurt

Bert Steinhauser

Scene from the glittering crowd

CLUB NEWS/SHOWS

Japanese Design Judged Here

It has been said that a country's fine arts may reveal its soul, but its graphics reveal more about the people and the way they live. This is certainly true of the Japanese Graphic Idea Exhibition 1984. The third such exhibition was held in New York from June 6 through July 31, 1984, at the Master Eagle Gallery under the joint sponsorship of the Nippon Graphic Design Committee in Tokyo and the Art Directors Club in New York. The exhibition is unique, not only because of the excellence of Japanese design, but also for the manner in which the prize-winning entries were determined.

In Tokyo, a total of 190 pieces were first selected by a panel of top Japanese art directors. These 190 pieces, including nominated winners, were shipped to New York where a panel of our leading art directors under Seymour Chwast, judging chairman, selected those to receive gold, silver, and distinctive merit awards! The exhibition's formal

Seymour Chwast catalogs entries

opening was held on June 7, 1984, at the Master Eagle Gallery with members of the Japanese designers group as well as many local art directors, illustrators and designers in attendance.

In January, 1985, the show will appear at the Parsons School of Design in New York City and then travel throughout the U.S.

The Committee: U.S.A.
Walter Kaprielian *President*
Shinichiro Tora *Chairman*
Meg Crane *Co-chairman*
Jessica Weber
Exhibition chairman
Seymour Chwast
Judging chairman
Ira F. Sturtevant *Treasurer and promotion director*

ADC Annuals Tour World Design Centers

Our 62nd Annual Exhibition traveled the U.S. from New York first to Denver, Colorado, appearing there from September 24 through October 5, 1983, at the Colorado Institute of Arts, then moved on to Houston, Texas, from October 12 to 20, 1983, where it was sponsored by Hill Design and Olivet Group. From October 26 through November 9, 1983, it was shown at Portfolio Center in Atlanta, Georgia. This year it moved to the Bixby Gallery in St. Louis, Missouri, from

April 8 to 23, and it is still traveling.

European travel exhibitions were arranged by Klaus Schmidt. It was exhibited during November, 1983, in Frankfurt, W. Germany. From there it went on to Vienna, Austria, during December and Zurich, Switzerland, for January, 1984.

Every year our annual show in Japan for Japanese graphic designers gets more recognition and creates ever higher expectations. The first exhibition was at Nagoya, from January 27 through February 2, 1984, at the Aichi Design Center and was sponsored by the Chubu Creaters Club. It then moved to Osaka from February 28 through March 3 and

appeared at the Osaka Design Center sponsored by Yao Design Institute. From April 10 to 14, 1984, it showed at Nippon Industrial Design Hall in Tokyo, also sponsored by Yao Design Institute. All exhibitions were supported by *Idea* magazine. Other Far East travel exhibitions included Hong Kong March 26 and 27, 1984, and travel to Sydney and Melbourne, Australia, as well as Taiwan.

The 63rd Annual started its schedule in Japan in the fall of '84 and, as in the past, was sponsored by our non-resident member in Tokyo, Yao Design Institute.

Shinichiro Tora *Chairman*

CLUB NEWS/SHOWS

Photos and Art in Galaxy of Gallery Shows

Gallery exhibits ranged from member Kurt Haiman's "Pen and Ink Drawings" to Margaret Cusack's "Christmas Carol Sampler" cloth art to the cartoons, type and design of brothers, Kenji and Minoru Morita. An attraction again this year was the "Japanese Calendar Art" show and auction, a splendid array coordinated by Meg Crane and Shinchiro Tora.

"Two in One" show in the gallery, Masakasu Tanabe, art, and Toshyuki, photos

Makato Nakamura exhibits his Shiseido Cosmetics posters

Onlooker admires Joseph Vento's fashion photography

The next generation of designers visits

Kurt Haiman at his show opening

CLUB NEWS/NEW BREED

Younger Members Do Their Own Thing Their Way

This is the first year the New Breed Committee is in action. The members of this committee are comprised of all ages; jr. members, regular members, and representatives from corporate memberships.

Our purpose is to bring new ideas into the arts community. To close the gaps between new and long-standing members. To make the Club more of a social gathering place for professionals. To help art students achieve their goals. As well as all this, we even lend a hand to our fellow committees.

Some of our projects: the Menu Design Exhibition, the Christmas and Easter-time parties, Shopping Bag Exhibition. We conduct rap sessions with art students (in conjunction with the annual portfolio review). We've implemented a classified employment bulletin board at the Club. We feature articles in the newsletter. There are many more ideas we have planned for the future. And we hope you'll be a part of them.

Many thanks to the Executive Board for having the belief in all of us and for their support. We have a lot of enthusiasm and energy and are committed to making the future brighter for all.

Bobbi Rosenthal, *Chairperson*
Judi Radice, *Co-chairperson*

Lee Corey
Gary DiLuca
Ann Dubiel
Amy Goldman
Michelle Kestin
Alma Phipps
Robin Poosikian
Robin Rappaport
Beverly Schraeger
Nancy Schulz
Brenda Suler
Amy Sussman
Amy Wolpert
Dorothy Wachtenheim

The New Breed committee and guests swing at their Creative Egg Design party

CLUB NEWS/ACTIVITIES

Something for Everyone in Club Programs

The S.R.O. event of the season was the "Evening with the Best" lectures with Lois, Federico, Epstein, Wolf, Goldberg, Sirowitz, Kaprielian, Frankfurt, et al. Intended for young people, everyone came. Many other activities included two boat rides, jazz at noon, special parties.

At a Hall of Fame meeting, Eileen Hedy Schultz, Diane Moore and Jack Jamison

There were two boat rides for the hale and hearty

Daniel Forte, Lynette Chun and Michael Chin display Club Spencerian script T-shirt

AN EVENING WITH ONE OF THE BEST

THE ART DIRECTOR'S CLUB PRESENTS:
THE MOVERS. THE SHAKERS. THE AD MAKERS.
MEET ONE THE THIRD THURSDAY OF EVERY MONTH. DETAILS TO FOLLOW.

"An Evening with the Best" lecture poster was shot by Carl Fischer

Ed Brodsky designed this year's newsletters

CLUB NEWS/ADC STAFF

Jacqueline Little, Office Manager; Deborah Weathers,
Publicity Coordinator, Editor, Staff Photographer; Casey
Alexander, Receptionist; Jose Arias, Kitchen Assistant;
Deborah Weitz, Administrative Assistant; Paula Radding,
Exhibition Supervisor; Debra Bock-Woo, Chef; Margaret
Busweiler, Hostess; Daniel Forte, Exhibition Assistant;
Diane Moore, Executive Administrator; Michael Chin, Asst.
Exhibition Supervisor; Glen Kubota, House/Exhibition
Assistant; S.J. Toy, Bartender

INDEX

MEMBERSHIP LIST 1984

Michael R. Abramson
Donald Adamec
Gaylord Adams
Patricia Addiss
Peter Adler
Charles Adorney
David Alcorn
Warren Aldoretta
Charles Allen
Lorraine Allen
Walter Allner
Carlo Ammirati
Gennaro Andreozzi
Ted Andresakes
Al Anthony
Robert Anthony
Tony Anthony
Masuteru Aoba
Andria L. Arnovitz
Herman Aronson
Tadashi Asano
Seymour Augenbraun
Avon Products Inc.
Gordon C. Aymar
Joel Azerrad

Jeff Babitz
Robert O. Bach
Jeffrey S. Bacon
Ronald Bacsa
Priscilla Baer
Frank Baker
Leslie Baker
Ronald W. Ballister
Don Barron
Robert J. Barthelmes
Gladys Barton
Matthew Basile
Mary K. Baumann
Allan Beaver
Peter Belliveau
Félix Beltrán
Ephram E. Benguiat
Edward J. Bennett
Howard Benson
Laurence Key Benson
David W. Bentley
John Berg
Sy Berkley
Park Berry
Peter J. Bertolami
Robert Best
Frank Biondo
Bruce Blair
Peter J. Blank
Robert Blattner
Robert Blend
Bruce Bloch
David S. Block
Robert Blue
Seth Blum
Arnold Blumberg
Robert Bode
Ronne Bonder
George Warren Booth
John Milne Boothroyd
William Bossert
Harold A. Bowman
Doug Boyd
Douglas C. Boyd
Deborah Bracken
Simeon Braguin

Joan Brandt
Pieter Brattinga
Fred J. Brauer
Al Braverman
Barry Braverman
Lynn Dreese Breslin
William P. Brockmeier
Ed Brodsky
Ruth Brody
John D. Brooke
Adrienne G. Brooks
Joe Brooks
Ilene Renee Brown
Cissy Bruce
Robert Bruce
Bruno E. Brugnatelli
Bernard Brussel-Smith
Lee Buchar
William H. Buckley
Bill Bundzak
Aaron Burns
Herman F. Burns
Cipe Pineles Burtin

William F. Cadge
Albert J. Calzetta
Arline Campbell
Jack D. Campbell
Stuart Campbell
Bryan Caniff
Tony Cappiello
Cardinal Type Service, Inc.
Thomas Carnase
David E. Carter
Ralph Casado
Salvatore Cascio
C. Edward Cerullo
Anthony Chaplinsky Jr.
Irene Charles
John V. Cherry
Alan Christie
Stanley Church
Seymour Chwast
Bob Ciano
Michelle R. Clay
Thomas F. Clemente
Mahlon A. Cline
Victor Closi
Joann C. Coates
Robert Adam Cohen
Charles Coiner
Michael Coll
Catherine Connors
David Corbett
Lee Corey
Sheldon Cotler
Ron Couture
Thomas Craddock
James Craig
Steven L. Craig
Meg Crane
Brian A. Cranner
Elaine Crawford
Robert Crozier
Robert Cullinane
Richard C. Cullom
Jerry Cummins
Charles Cutler
Ethel Cutler
Gregory F. Cutshaw

Royal Dadmun
Bilal Dallenbach
Derek Dalton
Wendy Seabrook Damico
Norman Dane
Mark Darlow

David Davidian
Julie Davidson
Clyde P. Davis
Herman Davis
Philip Davis
Haydee Verdia DeBlass
Robert Defrin
Vincent Del Mese
Joseph Del Sorbo
Donald C. Demaio
Mariusz Jan Demner
Jerry Demoney
Diane DePasque
David Deutsch
Frank M. DeVino
Francis DeVito
Peter J. Deweerdt
Charles Dickinson
Arthur Hill Diedrick
Carolyn Diehl
Edward P. Diehl
John F. Dignam
Gary DiLuca
Robert Dolobowsky
Louis Donato
Chel S. Dong
Louis Dorfsman
Marc Dorian
Kay Elizabeth Douglas
George Drance
Spencer Drate
Nick Driver
Ann Dubiel
Donald H. Duffy
William R. Duffy
Laura K. Duggan
Rosalyn C. Dunham
Randolph Dusek
Michael Dweck

Bernard Eckstein
Peter Edgar
Don Egensteiner
Antonie Eichenberg
Zeneth Eidel
Professor Benjamin Einhorn
Stanley Eisenman
Jane Eldershaw
Wallace W. Elton
Malcolm End
Maria Poythress Epes
David Epstein
Henry Epstein
Lee Epstein
Molly Epstein
Suren Ermoyan
Dorothy Evans

Titti Fabiani
Bob Farber
Abe Farrell
Leonard Favara
Gene Federico
Judy Fendelman
Michael Fenga
Lidia B. Ferrara
Denise B. Ficano
Michael Fidanzato
Lilly Filipow
William F. Finn
Blanche Fiorenza
Gonzalo Firpo
Carl Fischer
M. I. Fisher
John Flanagan
Donald P. Flock
Jan Foster

Robert Foster
John Fraioli
Richard Frankel
Stephen Frankfurt
Frederic B. Freyer
Oren Frost
Satoru Fujii
S. Neil Fujita
Takeshi Fukunaga
Terunobu Fukushima
Leonard Fury

Harvey Gabor
Leighton D. Gage
Robert Gage
Diana Garcia De Tolone
Gene Garlanda
David Gatti
Joseph T. Gauss
Alberto Gavasci
Charles Gennarelli
Gloria Gentile
Carl Georgi
Joseph Gering
Michael Germakian
Victor Gialleonardo
Edward Gibbs
Wayne A. Gibson
Richard B. Gillis
Frank C. Ginsberg
Sara Giovanitti
Akin Girav
George Giusti
Milton Glaser
Eric Gluckman
Seymour Goff
Bill Gold
Irwin Goldberg
Roz Goldfarb
Amy E. Goldman
Eli W. Goldowsky
Jean Goldsmith
Jo Ann Goldsmith
Phyllis Goldstein
Jean Govoni
Roy Grace
Albert Greenberg
Julie L. Greenfield
Jayne Greenstein
Robert L. Greenwell
Fred Greller
Richard Grider
Jack Griffin
Chris Grosse
Walter Grotz
Maurice Grunfeld
Nelson Gruppo
Dolores Gudzin
Lurelle Guild
Rollins S. Guild

J. Bruce Haag
Jane Haber
Hank Hachmann
Robert Hack
Kurt Haiman
George Halpern
Everett Halvorsen
Edward Hamilton
Frances M. Hamilton
Jerome A. Handman
Joan Hanley-Bendheim
Brian C. Hannigan
Harriett
Brian Harrod
Paul Hartelius Jr.
George Hartman

Lillian June Hartung
Alan Hartwell
Janet Hautau
Arthur Hawkins
Dorothy E. Hayes
Mark Hecker
Saul Heff
Shelley Heller
Steven Heller
Robert S. Herald
Beverly R. Herman
Louis F. Hernandez
Janice Hildebrand
Chris Hill
Jitsuo Hoashi
Ronald Hodes
Marilyn Hoffner
Leslie Hopkins
William Hopkins
Uwe Horstmann
Mitsutoshi Hosaka
W. David Houser
Jonathan M. Houston
Joseph Hovanec
Elizabeth Howard
Mark Howard
Paul Howard
Roy Alan Hughes
James Hunt
Jud Hurd
Morton Hyatt

Ana J. Inoa
Amir M. Iravani
Michael Israel
Michio Iwaki
Toshio Iwata

Robert T. Jackson
Harry M. Jacobs
Lee Ann Jaffee
Moritz S. Jaggi
Jack Jamison
John C. Jay
Patricia Jerina
Barbara John
D. Craig Johns
Susan Johnston
Robert M. Jones
Kristina M. Jorgensen
Roger Joslyn
Lenoard Jossel
Christian Julia
Barbara Junker

Asher Kalderon
Nita J. Kalish
Ron Kambourian
Kiyoshi Kanai
Eugenie Kapetan
Paulette J. Kaplan
Walter Kaprielian
Judy Katz
Rachel Katzen
M. Richard Kaufmann
Milton Kaye
Nancy Kent
Myron W. Kenzer
Michele Kestin
Cyd Kilbey-Gorman
Elizabeth Kim
Ran Hee Kim
Judith Klein
Hilda Stanger Klyde
Andrew Kner
Jean Knight
Henry Knoepfler

Ray Komai
Robert F. Kopelman
Yoshikatsu Kosakai
Oscar Krauss
Helmut Krone
Thaddeus B. Kubis
Gerard K. Kunkel
Anna Kurz

Roy La Grone
James E. Laird
Howard LaMarca
Abril Lamarque
Joseph O. Landi
John Larkin
Pearl Lau
Kenneth H. Lavey
Bonnie Lawrence
Marie-Christine Lawrence
Sal Lazzarotti
Jeffrey Leder
Daniel Lee
Lewis Barrett Lehrman
Norberto Leon
Dr. Robert L. Leslie
Olaf Leu
Leslie Leventman
David Levy
Robert Leydenfrost
Alexander Liberman
Victor Liebert
Beverly Littlewood
Leo Lobell
Ronald W. Longsdorf
H. Robert Loomis
Hans Looser
Rocco Lotito
George Gilbert Lott
Alfred Lowry
Ruth Lubell
John Lucci
John H. Luke
Thomas R. Lunde
Lisa Lurie
Larry Lurin
Robert W. Lyon Jr.
Michael Lyons

Charles MacDonald
Richard MacFarlane
David H. MacInnes
Frank Macri
Kazuki Maeda
Seiichi Maeda
Samuel Magdoff
Louis Magnani
Nancy Lou Makris
Anthony Mancino
Saul Mandel
Jean Marcellino
Joel J. Margulies
John S. Marmaras
Andrea Marquez
Al Marshall
William R. Martin
John Massey
Takao Matsumoto
Theodore Matyas
Marce Mayhew
William McCaffery
Constance McCaffrey
Robert McCallum
George McGinnis
Fernando Medina
Scott Mednick
William D. Meehan
Franz Merlicek

Mario G. Messina
Lyle Metzdorf
Emil T. Micha
Ann Fairlie Michelson
Eugene Milbauer
Jean Miller
Lawrence Miller
John Milligan
Isaac Millman
William Minko
Michael Miranda
Oswaldo Miranda
Leonard J. Mizerek
Michael Mohamad
Kenneth E. Morang
Burton A. Morgan
Margaret Morgan
Jeffrey Moriber
Minoru Morita
William R. Morrison
Thomas Morton
Roger Paul Mosconi
Geoffrey Moss
Tobias Moss
Dale Moyer
Marty Muller
Timothy Musios
Ralph J. Mutter

Yasuhara Nakahara
Makoto Nakamura
Daniel Nelson
Hilber Nelson
Technical College New York
  City
Stuart Nezin
Raymond Nichols
Susan Niles
Joseph Nissen
Ko Noda
Evelyn C. Noether
David November
C. Alexander Nuckols

Frank O'Blak
Edward O'Connor
Jack W. Odette
Toshiyuki Ohashi
Joseph O'Hehir
Takeshi Ohtaka
Shigeo Okamoto
Noriyuki Okazaki
John Okladek
Motoaki Okuizumi
John O'Neil
Tomoyuki Oho
Susan Alexis Orlie
Garrett P. Orr
Larry Ottino
Nina Ovryn
Bernard S. Owett

Onofrio Paccione
Zlata W. Paces
Maxine Paetro
Brad Pallas
Roxanne Panero
Nicholas Peter Pappas
Jacques Parker
Paul E. Parker Jr.
Grant Parrish
Parsons School of Design
Charles W. Pates
Leonard Pearl
Alan Peckolick
B. Martin Pedersen
Paul Pento

Vincent Pepi
Brendan C. Pereira
Victoria I. Peslak
John Pessolano
John Peter
Robert L. Peterson
Ken Petretti
Robert Petrocelli
Theodore D. Pettus
Stewart J. Phelps
Allan Philiba
Gerald M. Philips
Alma M. Phipps
George Pierson
Ernest Pioppo
Peter Pioppo
Melvin Platt
Robert Pliskin
Sherry Pollack
Joseph J. Pompeo Jr.
Robin Poosikian
Louis Portuesi
Anthony Pozsonyi
Brenda M. Preis
Benjamin Pride
Bob Procida

Robert Qually
Charles W. Queener
Elissa Querze
Anny Queyroy
Mario Quilles
Brigid Quinn
Kathleen Quinn
Mike Quon

Judith G. Radice
Uno Alexandre Ramat
Louis Efren Flores Ramirez
Paul Rand
Richard Randall
Robert C. Reed
Samuel Reed
Sheldon Reed
Patrick Reeves
Herbert O. Reinke
Dan Reisinger
Edwin C. Ricotta
Mitchell Rigie
Harry Rocker
Harlow Rockwell
Peter Rogers
Andy Romano
Louis C. Romita
Lester Rondell
Barbara Rosenthal
Herbert M. Rosenthal
Charles Rosner
Andrew Ross
James Francis Ross
Richard J. Ross
Richard Ross
Warren (Dusty) Rossell
Arnold Roston
Thomas Roth
Frank D. Rothmann
Iska Rothovius
Mort Rubenstein
Randee Rubin
Thomas P. Ruis
Robert Miles Runyan
Henry N. Russell
Albert Russo
John Russo
Don Ruther
Thomas Ruzicka

Stewart Sacklow
Martin Saint-Martin
Robert Saks
Robert Salpeter
George Samerjan
Barbara Sanders
Jim Sant'Andrea
John Sargeant
Betty B. Saronson
Vincent Sauchelli
Hans Sauer
Sam Scali
Peter Scannell
Ernest Scarfone
Timothy Schaible
Roland Schenk
Paula Scher
Klaus F. Schmidt
William H. Schneider
Annette Schonhaut
Beverly Faye Schrager
Carol Schulter
Eileen Hedy Schultz
Nancy K. Schultz
Victor Scocozza
Ruth Scott
William C. Seabrook III
Leslie Segal
Sheldon Seidler
John L. Sellers
Ellen Shapiro
Alexander Shear
William Sheldon
Mindee H. Shenkman
Brett D. Shevack
Takayuki Shirasu
Jerry Siano
Arthur Silver
Cary Silver
Louis Silverstein
Milt Simpson
Leonard Sirowitz
Jack Skolnick
O. Paul Slaughter
Pamela Smith
Paul Smith
Richard J. Smith
Robert S. Smith
Edward Sobel
Robert Sobel
Martin Solomon
Harold Sosnow
Nancy E. Spelbrink
Victor E. Spindler
Mindy Stanton
Karsten Stapelfeldt
Alexander Stauf
Irena Steckiv
Karl H. Steinbrenner
Vera Steiner
Charles M. Stern
Daniel E. Stewart
Richard Stewart
Linda Stillman
Leonard A. St. Louis
Ray Stollerman
Bernard Stone
Otto Storch
Celia Frances Stothard
William Strosahl
Ira F. Sturtevant
Edward Suchocki
Len Sugarman
Seiji Sugii
Brenda Suler
Amy Sussman
Yasuo Suzuki

Ken Sweeny
Leslie A. Sweet

Teruaki Takao
Robert Talarczyk
Nina Tallarico
Wendy Talvé
Masakazu Tanabe
Teruo Tanabe
Soji George Tanaka
Tricia Tanassy
Joseph Tarallo
Melissa K. Tardiff
Melcon Tashian
William Taubin
Jack George Tauss
Trudie E. ten Broeke
Giovanna Testani
Elizabeth Mifflin Thayer
Richard Thomas
Bradbury Thompson
Marion Thunberg
John Hepburn Tinker
Tisdell/Caspescha
Robert S. Todd
Harold Toledo
Yusaku Tomoeda
Toppan Printing Company,
    Ltd.
Shinichiro Tora
Peter Toth
Edward L. Towles
Victor Trasoff
Ronald Travisano
Susan B. Trowbridge
Joseph P. Tully
Michael Turek
Anne Twomey

Norio Uejo
Union Camp Corporation
John Urbain
Frank Urrutia

Michael Valli
Richard Vasquez
Daniel A. Verdino
Frank A. Vitale
Richard A. Voehl

Dorothy Wachtenheim
Walter Wagener
John Wagman
Charles W. Wagner
Allan Wahler
Ernest Waivada
Jurek Wajdowicz
Joseph O. Wallace
Charles Walsh
Mark Walton
Warner Amex Satellite
    Entertainment Company
Jim Warren
Jill Wasserman
Laurence S. Waxberg
Jessica Weber
William Weinberger
Art Weithas
Theo Welti
Ron Wetzel
Susan Whalen
Ken White
Ronald Wickham
Kosala Rohana
    Wickramanayake
Gail Wiggin
Richard Wilde

Rodney Williams
Jack Williamson
Horst Winkler
David Wiseltier
Rupert Witalis
Cynthia Wojdyla
David Wojdyla
Henry Wolf
Kjell Wollner
Amy Wolpert
Sam Woo
Elizabeth Woodson
Orest Woronewych
William K. Wurtzel

A. Hidehito Yamamoto
Yoji Yamamoto
Takeo Yao
Ira Yoffe
Zen Yonkovig

D. Bruce Zahor
Carmile S. Zaino
Faye Parsons Zasada
Paul H. Zasada
David Zeigerman
Perry C. Zompa
Alan Zwiebel

ADC INTERNATIONAL MEMBER LIST

ARGENTINA

Daniel Verdino

AUSTRALIA

Ron Kambourian

AUSTRIA

Mariusz Jan Demner
Franz Merlicck

BRAZIL

Leighton D. Gage
Oswaldo Miranda

CANADA

John D. Brooke
Brian Harrod
Ran Hee Kim
Mark Walton

ENGLAND

Janice Hildebrand
Roland Schenk

HOLLAND

Pieter Brattinga

INDIA

Brendan C. Pereira

ISRAEL

Asher Kalderon

ITALY

Titti Fabiani

JAPAN

Masuteru Aoba
Satoru Fujii
Terunobu Fukushima
Mitsutoshi Hosaka
Toshio Iwata
Yoshikatsu Kosakai
Kazuki Maeda
Seiichi Maeda
Takao Matsumoto
Yasuhara Nakahara
Makoto Nakamura
Toshiyuki Ohashi
Takeshi Ohtaka
Shigeo Okamoto
Motoaki Okuizumi
Tomoyuki Ono
Takayuki Shirasu
Seiji Sugii
Yasuo Suzuki
Teruaki Takao
Masakazu Tanabe
Soji George Tanaka
Yusaku Tomoeda
Norio Uejo
A. Hidehito Yamamoto
Yoji Yamamoto
Takeo Yao

MEXICO

Professor Felix Beltran
Diana Garcia De Tolone
Luis Efren Ramirez Flores

NORWAY

Kjell Wollner

SPAIN

Norberto Leon
Fernando Medina

SRI LANKA

Kosala Rohana
    Wickramanayake

SWITZERLAND

Bilal Dallenbach
Moritz S. Jaggi
Hans Looser

WEST GERMANY

Uwe Horstmann
Olaf Leu
Jan Michael

ADC AFFILIATE MEMBER LIST

AVON PRODUCTS INC.

Ronald Longsdorf
Timothy Musios
Perry Zompa

CARDINAL TYPE SERVICE

Michael Israel
Allan Wahler
David Zeigerman

NEW YORK CITY TECHNICAL COLLEGE

Benjamin Einhorn
George Halpern

PARSONS SCHOOL OF DESIGN

David Levy
John Russo

PETER ROGERS ASSOCIATES

Leonard Favara
Peter Rogers

UNION CAMP CORPORATION

Stewart J. Phelps
Robert S. Todd

WARNER AMEX SATELLITE ENTERTAINMENT COMPANY

Richard Frankel

TOPPAN PRINTING COMPANY LTD.

Takeo Hayano
Shinichi Soejima
Teruo Tanabe

INDEX

ART DIRECTORS

DESIGNERS

WRITERS

EDITORS

PRODUCERS

PHOTOGRAPHERS

CLIENTS

PUBLICATIONS